# THE AMERICAN HOME

# THE AMERICAN HOME

Architecture and Society, 1815~1915

## DAVID P. HANDLIN

Little, Brown and Company — Boston–Toronto

Library of Congress Catalog Card No. 79–14894

ISBN 0–316–342998

I  H  G  F  E  D  C  B  A

MV

*Published simultaneously in Canada
by Little, Brown & Company (Canada) Limited*

PRINTED IN THE UNITED STATES OF AMERICA

*To my father*
*and to the*
*memory of my mother*

I have written this book to illuminate a culture of domestic architecture that, although all-pervasive, has had little critical comment. I intend this book for everyone who participates in that culture and who is interested in how and where Americans lived. However, as an architect I also have a special message for practitioners: in thinking about how to build for the future it is important to become engaged with the culture, not to ignore it.

In writing this book I have received inspiration, encouragement, and help from many people. I owe a special debt to three teachers. Stephan Thernstrom taught me much of what I know about American society. From J. B. Jackson I learned that the American landscape is a rich source of study that, without making either more or less of it than actually exists, can be written about forthrightly. John Coolidge impressed upon me the importance of distinguishing between buildings and places that are culturally significant and those that have enduring aesthetic value. At an early point in my work he asked when the story I wanted to tell began. From the answer to this critical question, one which long haunted me, the entire book unfolded.

In the five years I spent at the University of Cambridge I was fortunate to have sympathetic colleagues with whom I could discuss the issues about which I was writing. With their knowledge about Germany and England Nicholas Bullock and Dean Hawkes helped sharpen my perception of what was unique in American domestic architecture, Robin Middleton made me aware of the importance of the major issues of architectural theory, and Lionel March and Richard MacCormac opened my eyes to the work of Frank Lloyd Wright. While in England I was also able to continue at close quarters my friendship with Henry Moss and through long discussions with him to shape my ideas about architecture.

My greatest debt is to my family. As parents and as students of American life, my father and mother have influenced me in ways that I would not dare even to begin to assess. My wife, Holly, encouraged me throughout; she was understanding when the book dominated our life; and she acted as my best critic. Finally, the arrival in 1977 of our son, Sam, and the experience of watching him grow helped me think more deeply about what the significance of "home" is.

# CONTENTS

*Introduction*    xi

Chapter 1: The Homes of the New World    3

Chapter 2: The Home Town    89

Chapter 3: The Home Grounds    167

Chapter 4: The House Beautiful    232

Chapter 5: House Plans for Everybody    330

Chapter 6: Good Housekeeping    386

Chapter 7: The Heart of the Home    452

The Home of the Future    487

*Notes*    491

*Index*    533

# INTRODUCTION

The first European settlers to arrive in the New World left few accounts of how they provided shelter for themselves. One reason for this reticence was that other matters like the establishment of a system of government and the conduct of religion were more important and, therefore, more noteworthy. But the settlers also did not write about their houses because they found little that was distinctive about them. The climate and materials of the new continent were different from those they had known in Europe, but in dealing with this context the settlers simply adapted as best they could the European precedents that had served them for generations.

This attitude toward houses prevailed until the end of the eighteenth century. By that time many of the inhabitants of the new nation were able to live in dwellings more comfortable than those of their ancestors, but still they rarely singled out their homes for special comment or analysis. They were content to follow the lessons of experience or to adapt building forms then customary in Europe.

In the first decades of the nineteenth century the assumptions that reinforced these long-standing habits were soon challenged. At that time a few Americans started to ask questions about the houses in which they lived and attempted to define the basis of a domestic architecture that was an improvement over what they had known in the past. This investigation was at first only remittently undertaken, but by the time of the First World War, the point at which I end this book, it had become a sustained and disciplined discussion to which many contributed.

*The American Home* is about what these questions were and what kinds of houses were built in response to them. In writing this book I have not tried to make a survey of American domestic architecture. Instead, I have been interested in the ideas that have formed the basis of American houses, and I have illustrated these concepts by focusing on important buildings, people, places, events, documents, and institutions.

# THE AMERICAN HOME

# 1

---

# THE HOMES OF THE NEW WORLD

WHEN THE SWEDISH AUTHOR Fredrika Bremer arrived in the United States in 1849, she had ambitious ideas about what she might learn during her visit. She came, she later wrote, "to observe the popular life, institutions, and circumstances of a new country; to become clearer . . . on certain questions connected with the development of nations and people." In the course of her travels from New England to Florida she met prominent politicians, businessmen, philanthropists, authors, publishers, and artists, and she avidly followed the important issues of the day.

Intriguing as these people, places, and events were, Bremer invariably found that another subject was far more fascinating. She believed that it was from the "threshold of the home" that one could obtain a "view of the future of humanity," so American homes became the primary focus of her attention. Because that subject then preoccupied many Americans, *The Homes of the New World*, the book in which she described her travels, was an immediate success when it was published in the United States in 1853.[1]

The American interest in the home grew during a period of unprecedented change. Between 1815 and 1865 the mechanization of both manufacturing and agriculture, the development of systems of rapid and reliable transportation, and the establishment of efficient business techniques all combined to set in motion forces that began to erode the foundations of a society Americans had assumed would remain stable. In 1815 the United States was still a nation of small, isolated settlements. A half century later, as Americans moved both to great cities and to the farthest reaches of what had previously been a largely unexplored continent, the different parts of the country were quickly becoming linked in a vast, interdependent system. This transition from a traditional to a modern society profoundly affected every aspect of American life.[2]

Many who lived through this period welcomed the transformed conditions and optimistically tried to define the basis of a new society; yet they also grieved for what they believed they had lost. How to preserve the best of traditional values and at the same time define new ones was a major preoccupation of the era.

Americans who wanted to direct the course of change tried to create a broad range of institutions to establish and maintain the evolving standards of behavior. But regardless of their particular interests, most of them recognized that the home was the most effective place in which to inculcate values and, therefore, to reconcile old and new.[3]

When Americans spoke of the home, they referred above all to a social institution. At the same time they also had in mind an idea about a proper physical setting, because they realized that domestic architecture was an important agent in the development of individual and, by extension, national character. Americans arrived at this appreciation of the significance of houses only gradually and by different routes. Nevertheless, by the time of the Civil War houses had become laden with meanings that they did not previously possess. Once they did, their design demanded a new degree of scrutiny and care.

✦✦✦

Americans first began to make a critical examination of their houses because of important changes that were taking place in the practice of Christianity. In the first half of the nineteenth century ministers of all denominations began to recognize that their congregations needed religious instruction that went beyond that given in the church. They generally agreed that the best location for this training was the home, and by 1860 "home religion" had become an accepted part of American Christianity. In the process of articulating what home religion was, ministers not only gave the institution of the home a new significance but also drew attention to its design.

This interest in home religion was the outcome of developments that had deep roots. For centuries most of Europe was united in one Church. But the Reformation fragmented Christendom. After the Peace of Westphalia in 1648 each state had its own religion and within its boundaries demanded uniformity of opinion among its citizens.

In the New World it was impossible to impose a strict allegiance to one doctrine. Each area had an established church, but the need to retain valuable citizens undermined its absolute authority. Generally under-populated by those with important skills, the colonies were forced to tolerate and grant land to dissenters or members of sects who performed services that were vital to the well-being of the community. Even where such toleration did not exist, those who disagreed with the established church could easily go where their talents were appreciated.

In the eighteenth century the established churches were further weak-ened by internal quarrels. Fearing that they were losing members, congre-gations were frequently divided between the revivalists, who felt that the only way to attract more converts was through direct religious experi-ence, and the traditionalists, who stressed correctness of belief and the proper observance of conventions. The revivalists were aided in their confrontation with the established church by small but increasingly vocal groups of people who held rationalist and deist beliefs and who defended the toleration of all religious differences.

By the American Revolution there was no effective distinction in status between established churches and sects. Americans recognized that uni-formity of religion could not be enforced by civil power, and their Constitution provided for freedom of worship. The result was denomi-nationalism, and until the beginning of the nineteenth century the state of religion in the new nation remained stable. At that time, however, the alliance between revivalists and rationalists was broken, since a belief in deism was interpreted as an attack on revealed Christianity itself. The resulting pact between traditionalists and revivalists posed a difficult prob-lem both within and between denominations. No group that wanted to augment its number could rely only on traditional techniques — either the accepted pattern of theological argument or the general day-to-day func-tions of the minister. Instead, each denomination had to depend on per-suasion and popular appeal for recruitment. As a way to achieve results, the revival eclipsed all other methods.[4]

Although many ministers were drawn to the revival, others felt that it had serious weaknesses. They argued that a momentary enthusiasm was not a sufficiently thorough religious experience, and they disapproved of the unproductive competition among denominations that the revival fostered. To rectify this situation, many ministers tried to establish the basis of a more effective religious training, one to which all denomina-tions could subscribe. They therefore began to emphasize the need for what came to be called home religion.

The case for this training was first articulated in the 1820s, but the clearest and most sustained statement of it was made in the following three decades by the Congregationalist minister Horace Bushnell. His analysis of the state of American society and religion not only indicated why he felt the need for home religion but also contained important implications for domestic architecture.[5]

The background of Bushnell's parents reflected the unsettled state of American Christianity at the end of the eighteenth century. His father was born a Methodist and his mother an Episcopalian, but while Horace was growing up in rural Connecticut, both were members of the Congregational church. Bushnell entered Yale in 1823, and his college years were filled with uncertainty about the Congregationalist doctrine upheld there by the imposing theologian Nathaniel W. Taylor. New England Congregationalists had always thought that religious truth was capable of intellectual demonstration through logical clarity, but Bushnell never wholly believed in this premise. While at Yale he frequently read Samuel Taylor Coleridge's *Aids to Reflection*, which claimed that Christianity was graspable primarily by intuition. Acquaintance with this volume did not resolve Bushnell's quandary, but it strengthened his conviction that religion appealed primarily to the heart, not to the intellect.[6]

When Bushnell graduated from Yale, he still entertained these doubts. He was first a teacher, then a journalist, in New York. Having decided that neither pursuit was his vocation, he returned to Yale in 1829 to study law. Two years later a great revival swept the university and profoundly affected Bushnell. No longer distressed by intellectual doubts, he resolved to embark on a life of Christian service. He enrolled at Yale Divinity School in 1831 and took up a pastorate at the North Congregational Church in Hartford in 1833.

Horace Bushnell's sense that Americans needed a new form of religious instruction came in part from his understanding of the profound changes that had taken place in the course of his lifetime. Like many of his contemporaries, Bushnell was struck by the fact that within one generation even the most basic aspects of daily life had been fundamentally and irretrievably altered. This transformation was his subject when he addressed an audience at the Litchfield County centennial celebration in 1851.

Bushnell's task was to summarize the significant developments of the preceding century. He called his speech "The Age of Homespun," because he believed that the making of clothes at home exemplified the spirit of an age already all but over. In the past the house had been a "factory on a farm," and the farm was a "grower and producer for the house."

The family was fed on homegrown products, and its clothir
duced in the home, spun from flax grown nearby. The hoi
been the setting for a special type of neighborly relationship.
did not make its own shoes, it purchased them from an itinerant cobbler
who fitted each person's feet individually, and periodically the school-
teacher "boarded round" in the house of each student.

By 1851 the term "domestic manufacture" had lost its meaning. Homespun had been replaced by "a dress of factory clothes, produced by
machinery and obtained by the exchanges of commerce." As the activities
of the home changed, so did the uses of the spaces that had formerly
been filled with the equipment for home production. The meat market
replaced the storage cellar, and other shops supplied items that formerly
either had been made in the home or had been available only from
itinerant peddlers or artisans.[7]

Bushnell believed that the Age of Homespun was being superseded
by "The Day of Roads." In a speech of that title he explained how the
isolation responsible for the backwardness of most of humanity was being
eliminated by new networks of communication. Roads, railroads, steam-
ships, and newspapers added up to a "Road for Thought," which would
become "a vast sensorium springing out its nerves of cognition and
feeling" and which would help to enlighten everyone who came into
contact with it.[8]

Bushnell was not sentimental about what was lost in this transition from
"mother and daughter power to water and steam power," from the Age
of Homespun to the Day of Roads. He explained to the members of his
audience, who undoubtedly understood from their own experience what
he meant, that everyday life was difficult in the Age of Homespun. The
daily diet was limited and the immediate environment had few comforts.
Every member of the household had to perform tasks that were vital in
providing for the bare necessities. The cycle of chores varied according
to the season, but it left few occasions for relaxation. Nevertheless,
Bushnell acknowledged that the former existence had an "old simplicity"
characterized by "severe virtues." Once the "rough necessities" of the
homespun age were removed, he hoped that these traits could be retained
as Americans benefited from the "new possibilities of culture" in the
Day of Roads.[9]

The importance of combining the best of the old with the new was
reinforced by Bushnell's knowledge that the progress of what he called
"civilization" was not guaranteed. A reversion to "barbarism" was always

possible. Bushnell advised his audiences to be ever watchful for signs of a retrogression to a primitive state. Those who lived in established areas, especially New England, ran the risk of barbarism if they lapsed into a "well nigh fatal" state of economic decline. The moment that the source of livelihood disappeared, Bushnell explained, "religion droops, good morals decline, hope, which is the nurse of character, yields to desperation, low and sordid passions grow rank in the mold of decay, one blames another, society rots into fragments, and every good interest is blasted."[10]

Barbarism was equally a danger in new communities. Transplantation sapped the vital force of the culture, not necessarily in the first generation, but in the second, third, or fourth. Such a decline had occurred when the Israelites went out of Egypt, when the first settlers came to New England, and it was still happening as Americans were moving west. If Bushnell was alarmed by the divisiveness of his native Hartford, he was equally shocked by what he saw when he traveled to California. In that new society he found few signs of a culture that might lift people out of barbarism.[11]

At the root of all Bushnell's suggestions about how to combine the old virtues with the new possibilities of culture and to prevent a reversion to barbarism was a belief in education. A tired city like Hartford could be revitalized only by an intelligent and lively population, and only thus could the new communities of the West shed the brutal habits that had given them the reputation of the "bowie-knife" civilization. Since "the best hopes of prosperity" lay in the unfolding of the "creative talent and genius" of the American people, Bushnell advised his audiences everywhere to "push your schools to the highest possible limit of perfection." He was a strong advocate of public education in Hartford, and when he went to California, he helped to choose the site for a university at Berkeley.[12]

Bushnell realized, however, that education began before children went to school, and he became interested in how the characters of young children developed. In doing so he ran counter to two concepts of childhood. Congregationalists had long accepted the principle of the theologian Jonathan Edwards that conversion after intense struggle was the normal method of entrance into the Kingdom of God.[13] According to this belief, until a child was old enough to make conscious decisions, he was an outsider, "a child of wrath," and there was nothing that anyone could do to affect his character. Even though Bushnell himself had undergone conversion in a revival, he could not accept this fundamental principle of

*1. "The Joy of the Dwelling." In family unity there was "domestic happiness thou only bliss of Paradise that had survived the fall."*

Congregational theology. If there was no trace of holiness in a child, he argued, he could not believe that there had been "no fault of piety" in the church or that the parents had "no lack of faithfulness . . . no indiscretion of manner or of temper . . . no mistake of duty."[14]

At the same time Bushnell had no tolerance for the then current idea that children were born free moral agents and that, therefore, any training was a "real oppression put upon their natural liberty." The notion that without restrictions a child would grow up "a genuine character, stunted by no cant or affectation — a large-minded, liberal, original, and beautiful soul" Bushnell aptly called "Ostrich Nurture."[15]

In place of both these ideas Bushnell posited a theory of "Christian Nurture." His answer to the all-important question: "What then is the true idea of Christian or divine nurture?" was that the "child is to grow up a Christian, and never know himself as being otherwise." Bushnell argued that a child should not spend his early years exposed to sin and then later be converted, nor should he be allowed simply to develop "in the freedom and beauty of the flowers." Instead, the child should learn to love what was good from the earliest age. He could do so, Bushnell believed, because a child's nature was neither good nor evil at birth. Instead, it was "plastic" or "ductile" and was gradually molded into shape.

Bushnell thought there were several distinct stages of childhood in each of which "impressions" could be imparted to an infant for better or worse. Even in the antenatal period, entire "rivers of disposition, good and bad," ran within the child. Then followed the early years, which were divided into the age of "impressions" and the age of "tuitional influences," the former defined by the will of the parents and the latter by the will and personal choice of the child.

It was especially in the age of impressions that the seeds of character could be sown. Impressions came from a variety of sources. Teaching children the lessons of scripture was important, but not in itself the essence of Christian Nurture. Bushnell had a more comprehensive idea of what constituted an education. He proposed that "the home, having a domestic spirit of grace dwelling in it, should become the church of childhood, the table and hearth a holy rite."

The "domestic spirit" affected the child in several ways. The parents were, of course, important. Bushnell argued that in the relationship of parent to child, there was "something like a law of organic connection. . . . The faith of one will be propagated in the other." The parents' will and character were, therefore, the "matrix of the child's will and character." This influence was inexorable: "The manners, personal views, prejudices, practical motives, and spirit of the house is an atmosphere which passes into all and pervades all as naturally as the air we breathe."

When Bushnell spoke of the "spirit of the house," he meant not only the powerful influence of the parents, but also the profound impact of inanimate objects on the growing child, particularly in the all-important early years. Bushnell, unlike theologians of an earlier generation, did not want to suppress an infant's instinct for play; instead, he advised members of his congregation to encourage these "pleasures of childhood." He therefore advised parents to create pleasant surroundings, to make "the house no mere prison, but a place of attraction." To do so would help to shape the child's character throughout the week, but especially on Sunday. Bushnell criticized those Congregationalist ministers who had prescribed an austere routine for the Sabbath. He was convinced that children would better appreciate the meaning of the day if they spent their time learning instructive lessons in sympathetic surroundings.[16]

Horace Bushnell set a theological framework for home religion; in his sermons he mentioned the need for a suitable home environment, but it was not his primary task to discuss what that environment should be.[17] The subject, however, interested many of his contemporaries. Some ministers discussed it in their sermons, which home missionary societies then published in magazines that were sent to remote hamlets across the nation.[18] The leaders of many denominations, however, realized that the teaching of home religion could be more effectively carried out in the less didactic form of popular literature. Ministers, therefore, often wrote wholesome stories and poems that illustrated the nature of the Christian home and published them in magazines started specifically to carry this message to the hearthside. These edifying tales were no different from much of the moral literature that appeared at the same time in secular

2.  *Cover*, The Happy Home and Parlor Magazine. *One of the period's many magazines that brought wholesome literature to American homes.*

journals like the *Mother's Magazine and Family Circle* and the *Happy Home and Parlor Magazine*.[19]

The stories and poems in these popular publications give a composite picture of what the religious home, as an institution and as architecture, was supposed to be. The most revealing single source that illustrates this concept is a short novel, *Home*, by Catharine Sedgwick, who, until Harriet Beecher Stowe published *Uncle Tom's Cabin* in 1852, was the period's most widely read female author. Born in 1789, Sedgwick lived near Stockbridge, Massachusetts. Her long literary career started with the publication in 1822 of *A New-England Tale*, a novel that was designed to "lend a helping hand to some of the humbler and unnoticed virtues." Thereafter, most of her writings dealt with the value of the home, as it had been in the colonial past and as she hoped it would emerge from the changing times in which she lived.[20]

*Home*, published in 1835, was about the life of William Barclay, a boy brought up by his mother and grandfather in a parsonage on the outskirts of Greenbrook, a village in a "picturesque district" in New England. William's childhood home was a simple wooden structure, adorned only with luxuriant flowers. When his grandfather died, he and his mother were forced to leave this idyllic dwelling, filled with so many pleasant memories, to live on the charity of friends and relatives in Greenbrook. During this difficult period William resolved someday to reacquire the house in which he had spent his early youth and which represented the virtues of order and domestic happiness he already so valued.

Having learned at an early age that life was full of vicissitudes, William Barclay studied hard and equipped himself with a skill. Like his model, Benjamin Franklin, he became a printer and established himself, not in Philadelphia but in New York. Believing that "home should be the sweetest of all words to the humblest member of a family," William and his wife did their best to create a home in the hostile environment of New York. Their house there bore little outward resemblance to the old parsonage for which they longed, yet they were able to endow it with the essential attributes of a true home. They acquired some carefully chosen furniture and what they could not afford Mrs. Barclay, a skillful housewife, managed to make. These objects "called forth delightful feelings" and helped to make the parlor a suitable place for the "domestic altar," the center of their Christian home.

Through patience and hard work Barclay prospered, but he did not squander his money by trying to be a member of "society," nor did he want to live in one of the fancy residences then being constructed in New York. These houses, which were decorated according to the latest fashions imported from Europe, could hardly be called homes. They acted much more as the setting for social and literary circles than for the family circle. The fate of Barclay's business partner served as a warning about life in such houses. In contrast to Barclay, he was a member of society. In the course of *Home* he was driven to financial ruin and finally to suicide by the profligacy of his son, who had been brought up to expect nothing but luxury. The members of Barclay's family did not turn their backs on the cultural opportunities that were offered only in a burgeoning and progressive city like New York, but their ultimate dream was to return someday to the old parsonage.

When Barclay was finally able to do so, he was all the more convinced that life in the country was far preferable to that in the city. Although the parsonage was a modest structure, it was located in a beautiful land-scape that the setting of not even the most opulent urban residence could rival. Nor did Barclay miss the city's social life. Despite distances between houses, there was a "social electric chain" that bound families in Greenbrook together and produced a "tie of human brotherhood" in the village.[21]

Since William Barclay was convinced of the value of home, he tried to communicate his belief to others. While living in New York, Barclay did everything he could to help the poor. He established a Sunday school in his home and tried to spread the idea of home religion to the children of Irish Catholic immigrants.[22] When the parents of one of these un-fortunates died, the Barclays did not allow the child to be sent to an orphanage, a poor substitute for a home, but instead adopted her.

Barclay's son carried the same message to the settlers of the western frontier, which was then in Ohio. When he migrated to that state, he brought with him mementos of the Greenbrook home to remind him of his background; he even planted slips of New England fruit trees around his Ohio log cabin. That two-room house did not yet have the important associations of the parsonage in Greenbrook, but Barclay's son hoped that as his new community became more settled and assumed the attributes of the admired New England village, his dwelling would become more of a home. To help make this prospect a reality, he established in one of the rooms of his cabin a library, which the young men of the community used as a reading room in the evenings and for prayers on Sunday.[23]

The idea that pervaded Catharine Sedgwick's novel, that the home

3. *The birthplace of John Howard Payne. This depiction ignored the fact that the East Hampton, Long Island, cottage was supposed to be "thatched."*

mirrored the moral and religious state of those who lived in it and consequently influenced the young who inevitably responded to it, was closely related to another theme often the subject of similar literature. The authors of many of the period's sermons, stories, poems, and songs claimed that the home not only was important in setting the character of a child in its early years but also had a vital role later on. When a child left home, he needed moral examples to guide him as he made his way in a world full of ruinous temptations. The lessons of a religious home helped serve this purpose, and so that these values could be easily remembered, especially in a moment of crisis, it was important to create a distinctive image of the home which could quickly summarize and communicate the meaning of the institution.

The theme of the home as a moral guide for those making their way in the storm of life frequently appeared in the popular literature of the time. It was succinctly summarized in "Home, Sweet Home," a song that John Howard Payne wrote in 1823. "Home, Sweet Home" soon became the most widely sung song of the day. It was not simply the "humble" home, the "lowly thatched cottage," with which Americans identified;

the image of the wanderer, the "exile" whom "splendor dazzled in vain," as he yearned for his childhood home, also had enormous attraction.[24]

The appeal of "Home, Sweet Home" was inseparable from myths about John Howard Payne's life. Born in 1791, he took an early interest in the stage and was forced to make his professional debut in 1809, soon after his father suffered bankruptcy. From that time till his death in 1852, Payne had an erratic sequence of successes and failures in the theatrical, literary, and publishing worlds of the United States and Europe. Editions of "Home, Sweet Home" were often accompanied by moving descriptions of the starving author in his garret and illustrations of his supposed birthplace at East Hampton, Long Island. In fact, when Payne wrote "Home, Sweet Home," he was living comfortably in the Palais Royal in Paris, and no one has ever been able to identify the house in which he was born. But accuracy meant little to nineteenth-century Americans, who were becoming more and more convinced that there was "no place like home."[25]

Authors like Catharine Sedgwick and John Howard Payne never specified the particular characteristics of an ideal home but claimed only that the quality they admired was a feeling, a spirit, or an atmosphere that was indefinable and indescribable. After all, the home was not the place either for the heartless analysis that ministers such as Horace Bushnell found so repellent in theological disputes or for the cold calculation that often made the business world seem so alien. One minister, writing about "home feeling," noted with alarm that the spirit of the "mechanical botanist," who looked at the outer world only as one "vast dissecting room," seemed to be gaining favor. A flower could be appreciated not as cut-up fragments but only as "the beautiful combinations" that existed when it was whole and living. Thus, the minister had no interest in analyzing what home feeling was. All he needed was "a picture," and he concluded: "If anyone should ask, what is the home feeling? we answer: it is as much to say — the home feeling."[26]

Such pictures were often drawn in the literature of the period. The admired houses or furnishings in works such as *Home* or "Home, Sweet Home" demonstrated either or both of two fundamental qualities. They were, first of all, beautiful. The beauty that the authors of home literature admired had little to do with definitions established by philosophers of aesthetics, another rational, heartless, and therefore misguided discipline. Instead, beauty was something that was felt by the individual and was best exemplified in nature. Nature, in turn, was seen as a reflection of

God. Since those who wrote about home feeling shunned rigorous analysis, they never systematically set out the basis of these relationships. They also were not eager to pursue the subject because the exaltation of the natural world sometimes seemed to lead to its worship, a dangerous heresy. Even so, they did frequently state that there was a connection between beauty, nature, and God. These relationships gave beauty a justification that it did not have simply as a matter of taste.

One implication of this concept of beauty was a predilection for simple, natural materials and an economical architecture. While those who wrote about beauty did not want to sanction anything mean or ungenerous, they believed that, as the fundamental patterns of nature mirrored and were examples of how God's universe was perfectly ordered with no waste and nothing out of place, so parallel patterns and principles of economy could serve man in designing his buildings and objects. If the use of simple means to achieve direct results did not precisely guarantee beauty, it was at least a vital guide to that end. Beauty's relationship to nature and God also meant that it could be perceived and created by anyone who had been inspired to do so. Special training or learning was not necessary; too much skill or knowledge might even inhibit a direct, personal perception of beauty.[27]

The second quality exemplified by houses and furnishings with home feeling was morality. Since beauty was connected to God, anything that was beautiful would manifest what was good. But moral values could also be expressed more didactically. Those who wrote about home feeling believed that because of their associations, certain types of houses and furnishings induced noble sentiments. To establish these values, it was important to live in dwellings and among possessions that encapsulated and transmitted them. In describing the power of the physical environment's associations, authors often underlined their arguments by drawing the connection between a virtuous family and its exemplary surroundings and, correspondingly, between base people and their sordid environment. But those of low character were not doomed to have their behavior constantly reinforced by the surroundings that reflected their failings. They could improve, and the first step toward that end often was the desire to possess some object — perhaps just a flower or a small picture of a biblical scene — that stood for what was good and, therefore, offered the promise of a better life.

The literature of the period frequently depicted the kind of house that embodied these principles of beauty and morality. Many poems and stories, especially those set in the past or those about the memory of a childhood scene, mentioned a humble home, located in a remote, rural district. This house was often described as "simple" in construction and decoration. It was usually made of wood from nearby forests or of stones from the surrounding soil. It had no gratuitous architectural ornament; its beauty came instead from a close tie with the natural setting. It often had a low, thatched roof, was covered with vines, and was framed by shade trees. Such a building hardly appeared man-made; it was a "type," an emblem either of the "better home in heaven" or of one in Eden.[28]

The inside of this cottage was imbued with "warmth" and "repose." It usually had one large room whose focus was the hearth, around which the family gathered for its meals and daily prayers. Ministers often argued that the first Christians erected their altar near the hearth: "It was their 'refuge in time of trouble' — their 'fortress' and 'strength,' 'the home of their salvation,' and their 'high tower.'" In fact, the fireplace was so important to the home that it was often virtually a member of the family. Many books of fireside stories, for instance Anna Bache's *Scenes at Home: Or the Adventures of a Fire Screen*, were narrated by a part of the fireplace — either the chimney, the fire, the screen, or the andirons — each personifying an elderly figure who possessed and dispensed the wisdom of long experience.

An essential part of all these home scenes, a fixture at the hearth, was the mother. She was commonly portrayed as blending in with the house itself. She did so by displaying in the style of her clothing and in her countenance those same timeless qualities that suffused the rest of the home. She could also bring about specific associations between herself and the home by wearing, for example, a scarf that she had made from the remnants of the material she had used to sew a tablecloth or pillow case. But the feature that she and the house shared most frequently was flowers. The mother cultivated the garden that surrounded the house, she trimmed the vines and creepers that embellished the porch, she tended house plants, and she herself wore flowers that came from all these places.[29]

The difficulty with this conception was that it was either an idealization of the home of a distant past or it represented a future resting place, the heavenly home. Some authors truly might have felt that nothing in the present could match such perfect homes. But most felt, however grudgingly, an obligation to the values of progress that were at the root of so many of the changes then taking place in all aspects of American life. The houses they described in stories and poems with a contemporary setting, therefore, were precariously balanced between the ideals symbolized by the humble home and those of modern civilization.

The authors often pointed out that old and new could be combined in any dwelling. In fact, in their sermons and stories they cited people, such as the Barclays in a crowded section of New York and their son in the wilderness of Ohio, who, against all odds, were able to make a true home out of the most unpromising surroundings. Nevertheless, there was a preferred contemporary context for home religion, and its outlines were frequently described.

Houses in many stories set in the present were not situated in a completely rural setting. They were, instead, located on land that was neither urban nor agricultural. They may once have been farmhouses, but they no longer served that purpose. The husband of the family that lived in such a house usually made his living elsewhere; he traveled daily to a nearby community and returned in the evening.

The humble home was usually isolated from other structures, but it contained its own community, a family of several generations. In the contemporary home grandparents still often lived with the family. Yet the house was also part of a broader community. Although it was a separate structure, one whose image would thus make a distinct impression on the memory, it was never so isolated as to preclude contacts with neighbors.

The exterior of the contemporary house also was poised between two worlds. The humble home receded into the landscape, often appearing about to become a ruin or to anticipate an Edenic state in which there was no need for shelter at all. The contemporary home was made with local, natural materials, but it was much more evidently the work of man than its country or heavenly counterpart. Nor was it supposed to give any hint that it had seen better days. When the Barclays went back to the parsonage at Greenbrook, they knocked down a rickety porch and made additions and alterations to the house. Even though they moved to the parsonage to retire, their home, which was customarily described as "well-kept" or "neat," indicated an active and ongoing interest in the affairs of the moment.

The same mixture of values was evident on the interior. The main living area was no longer one room. Cooking now had its own space, and the parlor became the family gathering place. That room was composed as a set of "scenes," each of which exuded a wholesome sentiment or lesson.

Such instructive scenes could be created by decorating walls with prints that depicted biblical stories or important historical events, or by placing plants and flowers around the windows, or by making a pleasant arrangement of treasured mementos on a table or shelf. Such gestures had to be tastefully done, but they did not need to cost much, because no matter how much times had changed, frugality was still one of life's most important virtues.

The most significant parlor scene was in the center of the room, where there was usually a small circular table on which the Bible was kept and around which the members of the family and their friends came together to converse and pray. Since "home was the first form of society," the round table was the focus of "social communion with the world," but it also symbolized the family circle, that invisible but always present force that joined all the members together, no matter where life's responsibilities had taken them.

Because the fireplace was not the focus of the parlor, it no longer had its previous significance. Nevertheless, even as efficient stoves and central heating systems became available, it was not removed completely. It was still valued for its associations. While the contemporary fireplace was not explicitly primitive in design, as it had been in the humble home, the essential features of the old-time hearth were still recognizable.[30]

Some authors hoped that the mother would be able to assume the additional responsibilities of educator without changing.

> In her own place the hearth beside
> The patriot's heart to cheer.
> The young unfolding mind to guide
> The future sage to rear . . .

To fulfill this role, however, she not only had to possess and express those matriarchal hearthside qualities of old but also had to be forward-looking, equally at home in the parlor and the kitchen.[31]

By 1860 no author had codified or translated into specific architectural terms the characteristics of the home that, as the contemporary context for home religion, combined both old and new. Yet these evocative images and terms of reference had become familiar to Americans and were already an inseparable part of their thought and culture.

Home scenes were frequently described in the biographies of prominent Americans. Their authors often emphasized how the example of the

4. *Daniel Webster's birthplace. Illustrations of the childhood home often had in the foreground a travel-weary figure approaching the structure. This picture appears to have a man who is showing his wife where he had grown up.*

5. *Marshfield, Daniel Webster's farm home in southern Massachusetts. In many ways this house is far different from Webster's birthplace, but at least it is a separate house in a rural setting.*

childhood home had guided a famous man or woman throughout life. In the process they also explained how the humble country home could be embodied in the contemporary house. They did so by citing two houses to summarize an illustrious career. The first, that in which a famous person was born and raised, usually was a modest one in a rural setting; the second, that in which the person lived after a rise to prominence, was more lavish and gave the impression of an increase in stature. Even so, although the second house evidently belonged to someone who was successful and often wealthy, it was never garish or in bad taste. The mere fact that the second home was usually still a country residence in itself established a basic affinity with the values embodied in the childhood home.

*Homes of American Authors*, published in 1852, was the first book entirely devoted to this theme. It contained chapters on Bryant, Cooper, Hawthorne, Irving, and other writers. Each account had illustrations of an author's homes and a text that underlined the importance of the birthplace in his development.[32] The success of *Homes of American Authors* encouraged its publishers to issue a companion volume, *Homes of American Statesmen*, which included accounts of the lives and houses of Washington, Jefferson, Jackson, Clay, Everett, Webster, and others.[33]

The idea that famous people came from humble homes was most successfully exploited by William Makepeace Thayer. In 1853 in *Life at the Fireside*, Thayer used the term "incidental education" to describe the invisible but important influence of the home environment on children. In two books that he wrote in 1857 — *The Poor Boy and Merchant Prince . . . The Life of Amos Lawrence* and *The Poor Girl and the True Woman . . . Life of Mary Lyon* — Thayer arrived at a form of biography that he later brought to perfection in *From Pioneer Home to White-House* (Abraham Lincoln), *From Farm House to White-House* (George Washington), and *From Log-Cabin to White-House* (James Garfield).[34]

Creating a home in which the future leaders of the nation might be nurtured was a great opportunity for nineteenth-century Americans. But with these dreams came new and sometimes onerous responsibilities. Because they understood how important they were as models for their children, nineteenth-century parents had to scrutinize every aspect of their own conduct to make sure that it was exemplary. Once mothers were relieved of the chores they always had to perform in the Age of Homespun, they then had to assume the harder to define role of homemaker. And when fathers no longer tilled the soil, they had to work in an often

6. *Title page*, From Log-Cabin to White-House: The Life of James A. Garfield. *Such books helped to popularize not only the idea that it was a virtue to have been born in a simple home but also the notion that the course of one's life could be charted by a sequence of houses.*

unpredictable and alien environment to provide support for this new kind of home.

Children also had to deal with unfamiliar pressures. Since they were brought up in a home designed for their nurture, they had to demonstrate that they were worthy of all the care taken on their behalf. Some of the problems that arose in doing so were illustrated in the life and literature of one notable absentee from *Homes of American Authors*. The omission of Edgar Allan Poe was probably deliberate. He was not a success, at least not in the way that the other authors included in the book were.

During his lifetime Poe had a dissolute reputation; that judgment was confirmed when he died after being found in a Baltimore street following a night of drinking. Shortly afterward, Nathaniel Parker Willis wrote that his friend had exemplified the ancient fable of "two antagonistic spirits imprisoned in one body." One aspect of Poe was docile and domestic. He lived quietly with his young wife in a little cottage in Fordham. But Willis also noted that when Poe drank a single glass of wine, "his whole nature was reversed, the demon became uppermost," and then his "*will* was palpably insane." Poe's contemporaries explained his behavior by the fact that he was an orphan. Although he had been adopted, he had never had the benefit of the stable home life that the Barclays, for instance, gave their Irish orphan. Without this background, Poe's dissipated side always tended to take over, and in the end it proved his undoing.[35]

This interpretation accorded well with contemporary ideas about the importance of the home, and many of Poe's stories — for instance, "The Imp of the Perverse" or "William Wilson" — can be read to confirm the view of the two antagonistic personalities. There is another meaning in Poe's literature, however, one that his contemporaries were less willing to acknowledge. The problem of many of the characters in Poe's stories was not that as they made their way in life, they were tempted to stray from the values that they had learned, perhaps inadequately, in their childhood homes. Instead, they found their childhood homes so appealing that they were incapable of leaving them to carve out a useful existence in the everyday world.

Many of Poe's stories and poems began in a remote rural setting, such as the Valley of the Many-Colored Grass in "Eleonora" or the "greenest of our valleys" in "The Haunted Palace." The "happy home" located there was so much a part of the green valley that it was hardly a physical structure at all. Poe's characters spent most of their time out-of-doors in their paradise.

This context was never permanent. Poe never said precisely why, but either his characters had to leave the green valley, or the idyllic setting was transformed by a catastrophic event. In either case, his characters did not fall victim to their new environment, nor like William Barclay in *Home* did they try to make the best of the situation. Instead, they withdrew from it, usually to a remote house, such as the one in "The Fall of the House of Usher." These structures were unlike anything either in the ordinary world or in the green valley. They usually had dim and winding staircases and passageways that led to an unconventionally shaped room. Its walls often were curved, and constantly shifting richly figured draperies further distorted its form.

These curious rooms were organized and decorated to stimulate dreams. In "The Assignation" Poe concluded that "properties of place, and especially of time, are the bugbears which terrify mankind from the contemplation of the magnificent." The goal of his characters was to be "Out of SPACE — out of TIME," and only in these other-worldly rooms might they separate their dreaming minds from their material selves. If they were able to do so, they might then catch a momentary glimpse of the idealized woman who appeared throughout Poe's stories and who symbolized the childhood paradise, the green valley, and the happy home.[36]

If old, retrospective values were not carefully balanced by new,

7. *"The Breaking of Home Ties." This scene was probably painted at the end of the nineteenth century, but its theme dates from the turbulent decades before the Civil War.*

HOME INFLUENCE
BY
GRACE AGUILAR

D. APPLETON. AND COMPANY.

8. *Title page*, Home Influence. *The works of Grace Aguilar, an English author who extolled the home virtues, were well and widely received in the United States. Such depictions of shipwrecks in the storms of life struck a responsive chord in American readers.*

forward-looking ones, home influence could make the domestic scene of childhood so sheltering and attractive that its young inhabitants could be completely prejudiced against, and therefore unable to deal with, the complex and often disagreeable affairs of the world outside. As nineteenth-century Americans came to value the home and the houses that were appropriate for it, it was easy for them to overlook the troubling aspects of the powerful culture they were creating.

+++

Since Americans who wrote about home feeling often claimed that it was unnecessary and even harmful to analyze what made an attractive house, they were usually hostile to those who formulated theories of aesthetics. Architects, however, have always needed theories to guide them in their practice. In the period in which Americans were becoming converted to home religion, architects had to do what on the surface seemed impossible: they had to formulate a theory of their discipline that was acceptable to those who distrusted theories. The extent to which at least one architect tried to accomplish this goal was a further indication of how much Americans had become interested in the home and in domestic architecture.

The central problem of architectural theory has always been whether and how architecture imitates nature. Since ancient times most philosophers have believed that the fine arts should be based in nature or at least in a principle that is derived from nature. Because architecture involves both the practical and the aesthetic, theoreticians have often been uncertain whether architecture is a fine art or merely a useful art. Even those writers who have included architecture among the fine arts have found the relationship between nature and building more difficult to establish than the connection between nature and the more directly imitative arts of painting and sculpture.[37]

The first systematic attempts since ancient times to codify a theory of architecture were made in Italy in the fifteenth and sixteenth centuries. At that time several writers tried to find systems of proportions or harmonies that they thought had a divine origin, and they then used those relationships to determine the dimensions of their buildings. They did so through the medium of the classical language of architecture, which they thought had been used in the greatest works of the past and which to them embodied ideals of learning and taste.[38]

In the following three centuries architects frequently disagreed about how buildings imitated nature and what version of the classical language was most appropriate for their age. But despite differences, from the middle of the fifteenth century through at least the beginning of the nineteenth, architects in Europe and America generally agreed not only that architecture imitated nature but also that it could best do so through a version of the classical language. The elements of classical architecture were attractive not only for their association with civilizations that had attained a high state of culture, but also for more mundane reasons. On the one hand the classical language contained a great subtlety that a skilled architect could manipulate with ingenuity and originality. On the other hand a builder could learn the basic details and rules of classical architecture from the many copybooks that had been published, and he could then use them in a straightforward, sensible, matter-of-fact manner.[39]

At the end of the eighteenth century the unanimity of assumptions that supported the long-standing adherence to classical architecture slowly started to crumble. One challenge came primarily from English philosophers of aesthetics who questioned whether beauty was the result of formal perfection or whether it came from the associations that an object or building raised in the mind of the beholder. According to this argument, a Greek temple was pleasing not only because of the excellence of its proportions but also because of the pleasant impressions about ancient civilization that the building evoked.[40]

This distinction had always been inherent in discussions about beauty and, therefore, about how architecture imitated nature. But since the use of the classical language was rarely challenged, the question of the relative value of formal properties and associations was hardly ever raised. Once this subject began to be discussed, architectural thought was irrevocably affected. Not only did some philosophers wonder how much weight to give to strictly formal properties and to associations, but also they began to think that from the associational point of view it was advantageous to use styles of architecture other than the classical. Many architects, especially those who lived in England and Germany, came to this conclusion when they started to search for a building style that had national associations. They then rejected classical precedents and looked for their heritage in the medieval world. The Gothic architecture they found there was based on principles that were very different from the classical language.[41]

In the United States this debate took a special course because the North

American continent did not have a native architecture to compare with that of the ancient or medieval world. Some architects, especially Thomas Jefferson, tried to rectify this deficiency by adopting Roman or Greek precedents, because they felt that there was an affinity between the cultural traits of the new nation and those they believed had existed in the Roman republic or the Greek democratic state. But although the architecture, for instance, of the University of Virginia and the Capitol in Washington, D.C., was classical, the reasons for the adoption of this style — its desirable associations — eventually proved the undoing of the classical tradition itself. A style of architecture appropriate to the United States could be and was interpreted in many ways, especially by a growing group of architects and patrons who were beginning to feel a cultural affinity to England.[42]

To a certain extent the acknowledgment of the importance of associations and the consequent multiplication of satisfactory styles of architecture could be accommodated by a modification of the traditional theory of architecture. Since the beauty of form and the beauty of associations both came from the perception of the external world, some writers on architecture tried to characterize and categorize all of these sensations. They attempted to classify types of buildings according to their appropriate styles — the regular, classical styles, for instance, were often said to be suitable for public architecture and the irregular derivatives of Gothic appropriate for domestic buildings. Within these broad categories, the argument went, specific choices of style and treatment depended on the program of the building and the structure's setting.

This line of reasoning not only satisfied the desire for a coherent set of principles but also had a great practical value. In the first decades of the nineteenth century many commentators were beginning to understand that a more versatile language of architecture was needed for the wide range of buildings that their society was demanding. As they often pointed out, it did not make sense to model both a bank and a house after a Greek temple.

Many Americans admired the buildings that were designed in response to these expanded categories of taste. Ever since European philosophers had expressed doubts about whether the arts could flourish in a country that did not have an established tradition of patronage, Americans had suffered from feelings of inferiority about their cultural output. Consequently, they were proud that individuals and institutions were commissioning buildings that had pretensions to taste, no matter how this

quality was defined, and they were keenly interested in any new structures of significance in their community.[43]

Others, however, found contemporary architecture unsatisfactory. In
principle it was possible to outline a theory of both forms and associations,
encompassing a number of architectural styles, but in practice it was
difficult to formulate firm guidelines for the use of such an expanded
language of architecture. Once architects departed from the solid, almost
indisputable substance of the classical tradition, their definitions of taste
seemed personal and ephemeral. When that happened, Americans became
skeptical. Many had considered the fine arts either effete or wasteful and
had never granted that architecture was more than a useful art. When
opinions about taste differed and changed, they had all the more reason
to doubt the authority of those who claimed to know how to distinguish
between good and bad.

Americans who shared this skepticism fell into several categories. The
members of one small group of philosophers, led by the sculptor and
critic Horatio Greenough, believed that no style of architecture was
pleasing in and of itself. Instead, they thought that beauty resulted from
a logical integration of the program into the building and an avoidance
of ornament not related to construction or structure. In effect, Greenough
argued that the more form followed function, the more beautiful a
building would be. Modern architects have found these ideas extremely
suggestive, but, except for a small group of transcendentalists, none of
Greenough's contemporaries paid any attention to what he wrote.[44]

Members of religious sects that advocated an austere life were also
dubious about principles of architectural aesthetics. In the first half of the
nineteenth century, the Shakers, for example, established communities
from Kentucky to Maine in which they built structures that were extremely simple in mass and devoid of almost all ornament. These straightforward buildings stood in stark contrast to the kind of architecture in
which other Americans lived. But although the architecture of the Shakers
and of other sects was frequently noted and often admired, it was not
seen to contain a message applicable outside the special communities in
which it was located.[45]

More telling criticisms of ideas of taste as applied to architecture were
made by two other groups. One was composed of the people who were
then urging the adoption of home religion. Like Horace Bushnell, so
deeply influenced by Coleridge's *Aids to Reflection*, they distrusted ob-
sessive theorizing and preferred what simply appealed to the heart. They

were doubly convinced they were right when they saw that confused ideas about architectural taste often were espoused both by pretentious aesthetes who were trying to emulate European models and by the ostentatious newly rich.[46] Although they were always quick to defend themselves against the charge that they had no standards, these exponents of the old values of thrift and sobriety always doubted the validity of a beauty that strayed too far from economy, and they liked associations that had a moral, not those that were simply for pleasure. If people had money to spare, it was once asked, "why should they not spend it in increasing the health, the knowledge, and the morality of the needy around them?" In this system of values an architecture based on refined theories of aesthetics was of a low priority.[47]

Builders also challenged those who were trying to articulate architectural principles. They had often questioned the special status of architecture, claiming that building was first and foremost a practical matter, a useful art. But in the first half of the nineteenth century they made this point more vociferously. With no special claim to expertise except tried and true know-how, builders often complained that architects alluded to higher principles simply to bolster their dubious superior status. Their argument was especially effective when architects, who had not yet formed any professional organizations, were not themselves clear about the principles of their discipline and also when the impracticalities or technical failings of their buildings were particularly glaring. Furthermore, in the first half of the nineteenth century there was a great increase in knowledge about methods of construction, properties of materials, and means to calculate the strength of a structure. These developments, often eclipsing traditional techniques of construction, befuddled builders as much as they did architects. Nevertheless, builders often used the growing importance of various types of engineering to further their claim that architecture was a useful art.[48]

The most successful efforts to bring order to this confusing tangle of potentially acrimonious issues were made by Andrew Jackson Downing. Born in 1815, Downing died in 1852 when the Hudson River steamboat on which he was traveling to New York caught fire and exploded. An excellent swimmer, Downing could easily have made his way to safety, but he was last seen trying to rescue fellow passengers. The notices of his untimely death expressed the nation's sense of loss. Downing was mourned in the prominent newspapers of the great cities, in monthly home journals, literary magazines, and the agricultural press.

The fact that Downing died at an early age and in a heroic manner may have added to what Americans felt for him, but by 1852 he had already come to represent an ideal that they considered of utmost importance. How Downing achieved his reputation is not at first apparent. He was born in Newburgh, New York, where his father, a gardener, had started a nursery. Downing and his brother took over the family business, but it ran into financial difficulty and finally failed in 1847. It was only then that Downing started a full-time career as landscape gardener and architect. In the following five years he completed little work. The design of only a few houses can definitely be attributed to him, and none of his landscapes is now recognizable. In 1851 Downing was invited to landscape the grounds of the national Capitol in Washington, D.C. He completed the plans for this commission, but approval of the project was held up by Congress, and when Downing died, what would have been his most significant project died with him.[49]

Although Downing did not design many buildings or landscapes, he was a prolific writer. In addition to his authoritative *The Fruits and Fruit Trees of America* (1845) and editorials for the *Horticulturalist*, Downing wrote three other books: *A Treatise on the Theory and Practice of Landscape Gardening* (1841), *Cottage Residences* (1842), and *The Architecture of Country Houses* (1850). All these books appeared in many editions and it was through them that Downing communicated his ideas to and established his reputation with the American public.

The difficulty in understanding what Downing had to say to Americans is that his books do not contain a consistent message. In the course of his career, important changes in Downing's ideas showed that at the same time that Americans were learning about architecture from Downing, Downing was also absorbing lessons from the criticisms of his countrymen.

Downing's books were not important for their originality. In outline and also in many details they resembled some of the works of the English landscape gardener and author John Claudius Loudon. Downing corresponded with Loudon, often quoted him, and edited an American edition of a gardening book by Loudon's wife.[50] Most important, Downing initially derived his theory of architecture from the concepts that Loudon elaborated in the last section of his monumental *Encyclopaedia of Cottage, Farm and Villa Architecture*. Yet even though this book was Downing's primary source, he did not follow Loudon's ideas completely. A comparison between the theories of the two is instructive, not only because it clarifies what Downing's architectural principles were, but also because it illuminates why and how he became so universally admired in the United States.[51]

In writing the *Encyclopaedia of Cottage, Farm and Villa Architecture* Loudon was not content simply to collect and order information. Although the work contained more than a thousand pages of facts, statistics, diagrams, references, designs, and bibliographies, Loudon intended it to be a text that would impart more than specific knowledge. At the beginning of the *Encyclopaedia* Loudon wrote that principles would emerge in the course of the book that he would summarize at the end. These principles were "fitness for the end in view," "expression of the end in view," and "expression of architectural style."

Fitness for the end in view encompassed certain practical matters, such as the arrangement of a building's spaces to suit its uses, the strength and durability of its construction, and the adjustment of the design to the financial resources of the client. Because fitness was so important, Loudon went to great lengths to advise the architect how properly to plan houses, what books to consult on the technical problems of construction, and how to estimate costs. Loudon's *Encyclopaedia*, in effect, was the essential source book for all these matters.

In order to satisfy Loudon's second principle, expression of the end in view, a building's external appearance had to express its use and its manner of construction. Loudon believed that each type of building had recognizable characteristics that had to be reflected in its design. A dwelling, for instance, could always be distinguished from another type of building by the nature of its windows, front door, and chimney. Loudon called such identifying qualities "general" features, but expression of the end in view was "particular" as well. A small cottage with a living room, a bedroom, and a closet would have windows of three sizes, all characteristically domestic. The largest would be understood to light the biggest space, the living room; the smallest would indicate the closet. A building could express its manner of construction in several ways. Loudon advised, for instance, that a brick structure had to be recognized as brick. It was not to be covered with stucco in patterns that made it look as if it were built with stone.

Loudon's first two principles were related. If a building was fit for and also expressed the end in view, then it possessed an "essential beauty." But Loudon acknowledged that architecture was also an "art of taste." The purpose of his third principle, expression of architectural style, was, therefore, to add to the essential beauty that combined use and truth. In discussing this matter Loudon distinguished between a "permanent" and a "temporary" beauty. The first, which Loudon called "universal and inherent," involved principles of architectural composition such as unity, variety, symmetry, and proportion — attributes often used to describe and assess the forms of buildings. Critics and philosophers of aesthetics had distilled these criteria from their perception of the external world and had codified them into ideals of formal perfection.

By the end of his discussion of "permanent" beauty Loudon had said nothing to indicate which historical style the architect was to use in his buildings or why it was necessary to use a style at all. He finally raised this subject when he dealt with "temporary" beauty. The only reason he could find to use styles was that people were familiar with them. He reasoned that everyone had "some crude idea of what is Grecian and what is Gothic, while comparatively few understand what constitutes a whole in mere combinations of forms." Loudon, in effect, acknowledged that because they were familiar, architectural styles summoned up convenient associations, so he finished his essay by describing the main styles and the building types to which they were best suited.[52]

Loudon's principles of architecture seem orderly and logical, but closer inspection reveals glaring discontinuities in them. At times Loudon seemed to indicate that architecture was first and foremost a useful art, that matters of architectural style were peripheral. But in the end Loudon did feel an obligation to architecture as "an art of taste," and thus he treated the three principles equally. In so doing he implied that it was possible to satisfy all of them in a building. Yet different requirements in buildings often conflict. Loudon's difficulty was that without priorities it was impossible for him to mediate among opposing interests and to decide what was most important.

In his discussion of the expression of the end in view, for example, Loudon acknowledged that a regular, cubical building was best for strength and economy. He explained that a structure in which openings in a wall occurred perpendicularly, one directly over the other, was stronger than one which was punctured indiscriminately. Similarly, a cube was more economical than other shapes (except a sphere) because it enclosed a greater volume of space for a given amount of envelope. But these requirements contradicted those demanded by the need to express the use of the building. It was unlikely that a cubical building with regular openings could accommodate the diverse uses of a dwelling and also satisfy "fitness of arrangement." Its even pattern of windows certainly would not have indicated to the "external spectator" what the different uses inside were.

There were also contradictions in Loudon's attitude toward beauty. He assumed that the "permanent" and the "temporary" beauty of architectural style could be reconciled, but he never explained how this "inessential" beauty was to be coordinated with the "essential" beauty of "expression of the end in view." Many of the buildings in the *Encyclopaedia* were illustrated in unarticulated diagrams that, because of their lack of detail, avoided this issue. But in the more fully illustrated structures, "architectural style," especially temporary beauty, seemed applied as an afterthought. Loudon sometimes even showed buildings with one plan and several elevations, each in a different style.[53]

Loudon's *Encyclopaedia* summarized many of the dilemmas that faced architects at a time when technical knowledge was increasing and theories of aesthetics were often muddled. The result of his approach was an architecture that satisfied to a degree the stated planning and technical requirements of a building but also one that was full of quirks.[54] Without an overriding principle, which had traditionally come from the conviction that architecture was a fine art and that it imitated nature, it was impossible to achieve the unity that had characterized the great works of the past.

Unlike Loudon, Andrew Jackson Downing never intended his books to be comprehensive texts. The goal of everything he wrote was to instruct his readers about the nature and value of beauty. In his first book, *A Treatise on the Theory and Practice of Landscape Gardening*, he described how this goal could be attained. Downing dealt primarily with issues like the arrangement of trees, the shaping of the terrain, the use of vines and climbing plants, and the treatment of water. But since no landscape could be created without taking into account the nature of the buildings that it surrounded, Downing, like others who had written about landscape gardening, included a section on domestic architecture.[55]

Downing's architectural principles in *Landscape Gardening* were the same, though not as succinctly and systematically stated, as those he outlined in *Cottage Residences*, which followed a year later. In both volumes Downing acknowledged that his discussion was guided by Loudon's *Encyclopaedia*. Like his mentor, Downing had three principles. He first discussed "fitness," which was primarily about questions of planning, construction, and the relationship of a building to the site. Like Loudon's, Downing's next category was "expression of purpose." He thought it was

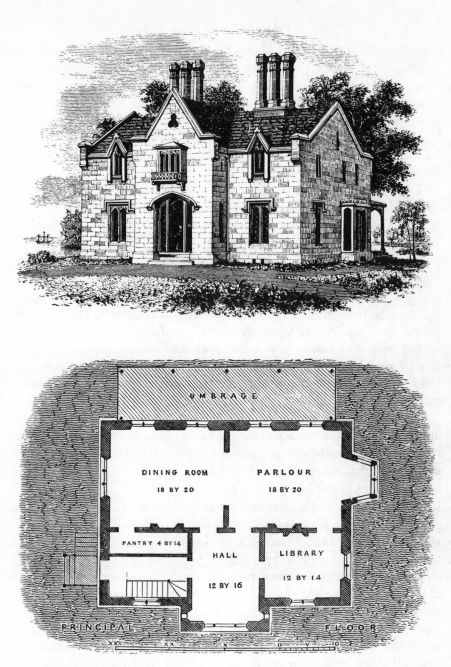

9. *Andrew Jackson Downing: "A Cottage in the Pointed or Tudor Style."* *As the treatment of the library and staircase shows, Downing was not rigorous about expressing different internal functions on the exterior of the house.*

important, for example, for houses to display features like chimneys and piazzas, by which they were customarily recognized. For the same reason, a barn, which was a utilitarian building, should have a "quiet, unobtrusive" color, while a cottage should be a "cheerful, mellow hue harmonizing with the verdure of the country." Downing also felt that it was desirable for windows to reflect the uses and characters of the rooms they lit, but he did not insist that the plan of a building be expressed as distinctly on the exterior as had Loudon.

Downing departed more decisively from Loudon in his discussion of the third principle, "expression of style." The difference was one of interpretation, not of definition. Downing did not waver in his conviction that architecture was a fine art. "The delight which the imagination receives from a building" was the primary purpose of architecture. It came from two sources, beauty of form and beauty of sentiment. The first encompassed certain rules that were used in the composition of buildings in any architectural style. Like other writers on aesthetics, Downing discussed qualities such as unity, symmetry, uniformity, and variety. The second source of beauty was a building's associations. Just as structures that possessed fine compositional qualities imparted delightful sensations to the observer, buildings in specific styles communicated pleasing associations, which by custom had come to be identified with them.

Downing, of course, did not believe that a style should be chosen indiscriminately for its associations. The choice had to be made with regard to the site, the climate, and the nature of the building to be constructed. In the North of the United States, for instance, colonnades and verandas were unsuitable for a large part of the year, and therefore the Italian and Greek styles were not advisable. Downing recommended that architects find the geographical context most closely approximating their own and use the style of building that had evolved out of it. At the same time Downing recognized that there would never be exact parallels. That fact gave the architect room for adaptation and innovation. Downing illustrated a cottage, for example, that he labeled "in the bracketed mode." Its front was symmetrical and was distinguished by a sharply overhanging roof, supported by large wooden brackets. This building was suitable for the southern states, because the roof made the upper story both cool and dry. Although he did not try to do so himself, Downing speculated that an architect who pursued these ideas might produce an American Cottage Style.

Downing's theory of architecture had distinct advantages over Loudon's.

Downing's interpretation of expression of purpose was primarily symbolic: porches, chimneys, and doors identified a building as a house, but the plan did not have to be expressed distinctly on the exterior. That gave Downing the freedom to compose his buildings more freely, and to manipulate the language of an architectural style to greater advantage. He planned one of his houses with two areas on either side of an entrance hall. To the right was a library; in the same position on the left was a staircase leading to a cellar below and to a floor of bedrooms above. The two functions were very different, but there was no hint of this distinction on the symmetrical elevation. Since Downing believed that expression of purpose was attained by characteristically domestic chimneys, doorways, and other features and, most important, since he believed that style was the primary consideration in architecture, he was able to resolve conflicts in design in a way that always eluded Loudon.[56]

*A Treatise on the Theory and Practice of Landscape Gardening* and *Cottage Residences* were both about the value and cultivation of taste. Downing wrote about European ideas, "adapted to North America," in the hope that he could inspire in his countrymen a perception of the beautiful and thereby elevate them. *Cottage Residences* contained such clear statements about the principles of domestic architecture that it is difficult to imagine why Downing had to write anything more on the subject. But in 1850 he published *The Architecture of Country Houses*. The reason he did so was that his ideas about beauty and the purpose of architecture had changed in the intervening years.

The nature of this transformation was evident in the first chapter, "The Real Meaning of Architecture." In this section, as in the corresponding discussions in his earlier books, Downing described three principles of architecture. In treating the "useful," he warned architects not to neglect utility for other ends, and throughout *The Architecture of Country Houses* Downing frequently discussed the details of construction, enumerated the costs of buildings, and gave hints about the proper planning of houses.

Although Downing's conception of the useful had not changed, his second category was completely different. Instead of expression of purpose or truthfulness, which even in *Cottage Residences* he did not construe as rigidly as Loudon, Downing followed the useful with "beauty." Downing's discussion of this subject explained why he altered his earlier sequence of architectural principles. In *The Architecture of Country Houses* Downing implied that his new conception of beauty was cut off from the traditions of what had previously been accepted as architectural taste. He stated that the beautiful was "something quite distinct from the Useful." It was not perceived by the ordinary senses. It appealed to a "wholly different part of our nature: it requires another portion of our being to receive and enjoy it." In short, the beautiful was "a worship by the heart, of a higher perfection manifested in material forms."

Beauty in this sense was not to be understood or judged by consulting the rigid and dry categories of taste, which were only abstract ideals. Instead, beauty could be perceived by experiencing nature, which was all but synonymous with God. Downing explained that "to see, or rather to feel how, in nature, matter is ennobled by being thus touched by a single thought of beauty, how it is almost deified by being made to shadow forth, even dimly, His attributes, constitutes the profound and thrilling satisfaction which we experience in contemplating the external works of art."

This belief in the value of the direct experience of nature had a profound impact on how Downing characterized beauty. As in his earlier books, in *The Architecture of Country Houses* Downing divided beauty into two categories, absolute and relative. But these categories were not the same as the earlier ones. Absolute beauty was the expression in material forms of "ideas of perfection which are universal in application." It did not entail, for instance, notions about unity, harmony, or symmetry that were defined by philosophers of taste, but instead referred to forms found universally in nature — "in the figures of the heavenly bodies, in the orbits of the planets, in drops of water, in animal forms, in the growth of trees, in the structure of crystals." These forms could be characterized by words such as proportion, symmetry, or harmony, but Downing, as if to draw a line between this discussion and that in his earlier books, emphasized the fact that no precise rules could be made. Each was something that an individual could only *feel*.

Relative beauty was as different from the beauty of sentiment as absolute beauty was from the beauty of form. Downing claimed that relative beauty expressed "peculiar moral, social, or intellectual ideas." He believed that "everything in architecture that [could] suggest or be made a symbol of social or domestic virtue add[ed] to its beauty and exalt[ed] its character." The sensations that were subsumed under relative beauty were, therefore, not simply pleasing notions about the civilizations that had nurtured particular styles of building but rather were associations with a moral content. The associations of styles of architecture that he dis-

10.   *Andrew Jackson Downing: "A House without Feeling."*

11.   *Andrew Jackson Downing: "A House with Feeling." The bay window, rustic trellises, bracketed canopy, and especially the vines expressed "feeling."*

cussed in his earlier books were still important; in concluding his discussion of relative beauty, Downing again mentioned them. But by the time he had written *The Architecture of Country Houses*, they had become secondary to those of domestic virtue.

Having placed beauty after the useful, Downing finally dealt with "truth," which encompassed many of the issues dealt with in his earlier books under the heading "expression of purpose." Downing's relegation of these subjects to this position in his system of architectural thought was a late reflection of modifications that he had earlier made to Loudon's theory. Unlike the English architect, Downing did not believe that the plan of a building had to be so rigorously expressed on the exterior, and, therefore, there was no need for the expression of purpose or truth to follow directly from utility. In *The Architecture of Country Houses* Downing stated that a house could be useful and beautiful but still not entirely satisfactory because "the intellect [had to] approve what the senses relish and the heart loves." As in his earlier books, therefore, he affirmed that each type of building had to contain the features with which it was readily identified; that it was important to build truthfully; "that the material should *appear* to be what it is"; but that these matters of the intellect had become secondary to those of the heart.[57]

Downing's change from his earlier idea of beauty to his notion of absolute beauty inspired by nature had a subtle effect on the design of the houses he illustrated in *The Architecture of Country Houses*. He depicted many of these structures with a more extreme perspective than he had used in his earlier books. This device emphasized the subjective impression of the house's form, not the objective relationships that one could obtain from an elevation or a more conventional perspective. Downing also emphasized the effect by placing his houses more definitely in a landscape and by casting deeper and darker shadows on his buildings.

Downing's illustration of relative beauty was more precise. He showed, for example, two views of the same cottage. One was well constructed and proportioned, but it was bare. The other displayed "*feeling.*" It had a bay window, which enhanced the cottage's "character." Little rustic arbors gave it an "impression of refinement and taste," and vines "express[ed] domesticity and the presence of heart." None of these elements was planted or designed by the architect or builder. Instead, they were the work of the inhabitants, especially the mother and daughters, and, therefore, they were "a labor of love offered up on the domestic altar." Such gestures made what was otherwise a drab building "truly a home."[58]

One factor that may have caused these important changes in Downing's thought was his reading of the works of John Ruskin. The English critic's first major writings on architecture were published in 1837–1838 under the pseudonym Kata Phusin, "according to nature." Although in these articles Ruskin at times questioned the assumptions of taste and aesthetic criticism that had become so widely accepted in England, his opinions on the whole amounted to little more than a reworking of traditional theories. But in the following decade, with the publication of *Modern Painters*, *The Stones of Venice*, and *The Seven Lamps of Architecture*, Ruskin drew away from the canons of taste and relied for his judgments much more on his own perceptions, which he had sharpened by directly observing the basic source of beauty, nature.

Between the publication of his two books on architecture Downing read Ruskin and mentioned the English critic several times in *The Architecture of Country Houses*. His distinction between relative and absolute beauty was reminiscent of one that Ruskin had drawn in *Modern Painters*.[59] But although Ruskin was important in Downing's development, other significant forces also had an impact on the American's views. In much of *The Architecture of Country Houses* Downing wrote as if responding to criticism of his earlier work. When Downing mentioned the "dry and barren" manner in which architects usually wrote about the "real meaning" of their discipline, he may have been offering a veiled acknowledgment of his earlier shortcomings. His first books had generally been well received. Americans were very proud that a fellow countryman had written such learned and readable works. Nevertheless, Downing did encounter a strong current of telling criticism that he could not ignore.[60]

The gist of this dissatisfaction was that Downing, as a person and in his interest in the arts of taste, was a snob and an aloof aesthete. Born the son of a laborer who had worked his way up in life, Downing did everything he could to deny his humble origins. When he was sixteen, he met the Austrian consul general to the United States, Baron de Liderer, who had a country house in Newburgh. Downing shared many interests with this man and learned about mineralogy and botany from him. But, more important, through Baron de Liderer Downing met other wealthy and cultured people who also lived in the area. These acquaintances included Raphael Hoyle, an English landscape painter, who instructed the young American about the theories of landscape design, and Charles Augustus Murray, another Englishman, who was a travel writer and a member "of the class that [Downing] never ceased to honor for their virtues and graces — the English gentleman." It was through this society that Downing met his wife, the granddaughter of John Quincy Adams.[61]

From these contacts Downing developed an admiration for the gentleman and a consequent disdain for anything that could be labeled "common." Unlike his namesake, Andrew Jackson, Downing was not a democrat. He once wrote of the "inextinguishable rights of superior organization in certain men and races of men which Nature everyday reaffirms, notwithstanding the socialistic and democratic theories of our politicians." Characterized as stiff, cold, proud, haughty, and reserved, Downing was so enamored of the life of the gentleman that he felt that any evidence of work was unpleasant. He even instructed that his lawns be mowed "by invisible hands" at night so that his family and guests would never have to see any trace of this distasteful activity.[62]

As Downing's reputation as a writer, landscape gardener, and architect grew, these personal traits and opinions also became known. Although they appreciated the fact that books such as *Landscape Gardening* and *Cottage Residences* had been written by a native, Americans, especially those solid members of the community who believed in simple home virtues, had little time for the aesthetic refinements of the gentleman. Downing could not have been insensible of this criticism. He may have taken it especially to heart in 1847 when his nursery business failed and he had to be helped out of bankruptcy by borrowing money from friends. Whether this crisis made Downing reassess his ideas of beauty or not, *The Architecture of Country Houses* restated what Americans had already long been feeling. They had criticized philosophers of aesthetics as materialists who appreciated and discussed beauty simply as a commodity. Once Downing aligned absolute beauty with nature and, by implication, with God, his theory had a higher justification.

Relative beauty, which existed when a part of a house was made a type or symbol of a moral virtue, was also a statement of what Americans had long been writing about. Throughout *The Architecture of Country Houses* Downing's language echoed that of American home literature. His statement that "the family whose religion lies away from its threshold, will show but slender results from the best teachings, compared with another where the family hearth is made a central point of the Beautiful and the Good" could have come from any of hundreds of contemporary books that discussed home religion, and so could his claim that "the mere sentiment of home, with its thousand associations, has, like a strong anchor, saved many a man from shipwreck in the storms of life."[63]

A second criticism of Downing came from builders, especially farmers, who often constructed their own houses. Some commentators in the agricultural press implied that in rigidly distinguishing among villas, cottages, and farmhouses — an aspect of "truthfulness" — Downing was making a judgment about the relative social worth of the inhabitants of each type of dwelling. That no house was too good for the American farmer was often the retort of their spokesmen.[64]

More important criticism took Downing to task for the opposite reason. The reviews of his books often claimed that Downing's designs for farmhouses were too elaborate. They revealed his ignorance about the condition of the American farmer and the facts of construction. Solon Robinson, the tireless advocate of the American farmer and the western immigrant, made these points in a review of *Cottage Residences*. He noted that "notwithstanding the high character and adaptability of Mr. Downing's works to the 'upper ten thousand,' the wants of the 'lower *ten hundred thousand*' [were] not satisfied."

For Robinson the primary virtue of a house was its cheapness, and he found that none of Downing's plans was designed on that basis. Robinson understood the farmer's hard life and knew from his own experience that the farmer had to devote all his efforts and resources to securing the crops. As examples of good designs, he sent to journals such as the *Albany Cultivator*, the *Prairie Farmer*, and the *Chicago Union Agriculturalist* plans of farmhouses, cattle sheds, and buildings for the storage of ice, all of which were economical to build.

Robinson also faulted Downing for not understanding what constituted "convenience" in a farmhouse. In a letter to the *Albany Cultivator* he included a plan of his own house, which did not have a "foot of waste space" and which also showed the location of the well, cistern, garden, cellar, and other "necessary parts of the 'fixings' about a farmer's house." In another plan Robinson explored a further dimension of convenience. He showed how a house could be built in separate stages to suit the emerging needs of a family as it settled a new farm. Robinson felt that these practical considerations would be useful to many farmers "who [would] never read *Cottage Residences*."[65]

In all of his discussions about farm architecture Robinson recognized that most western immigrants were not skilled carpenters, that they often did not have other people nearby to help them build their homes, and that they could not spend much money on materials. From the early 1840s on, Robinson, therefore, recommended that American farmers build

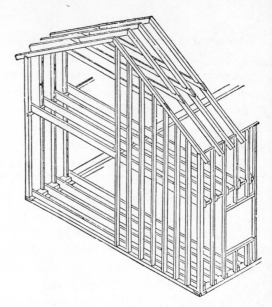

*12. Diagram of a balloon frame. The balloon frame was held together with nails and depended for its stiffness on sheathing and cladding, which usually completely covered the framing.*

their houses with the balloon frame system. This method of construction, which had been invented in Chicago in the 1830s, required only a fraction of the timber necessary in traditional construction.[66] Its stability depended on joints made with nails, not complicated mortises and tenons, and it could be constructed by just a few people. Robinson pointed out that booming cities such as Chicago and San Francisco could not have been built as quickly as they had been without the balloon frame and that this system was eminently practical for the farmer.[67]

Because of its many advantages, Robinson and other writers in agricultural journals criticized the authors of books on architecture for not adopting the balloon frame. Some of the skeptics doubted the stability of this method of construction; others regretted that it did not make use of the traditional skills of the carpenter. Andrew Jackson Downing also felt that the balloon frame was aesthetically unsatisfactory because, since it had to be clad on both sides, it did not give evidence of the building's structure. To make his construction "truthful," Downing clad the frames of his buildings with vertical boards and battens, a technique that at least reflected the underlying structure, even if it did not actually reveal the supporting members. Yet in the reckoning of practical men like Solon Robinson, this level of argument counted for very little.[68]

Downing insisted on such details in his buildings because he believed that the perception of beauty went hand in hand with an advance in

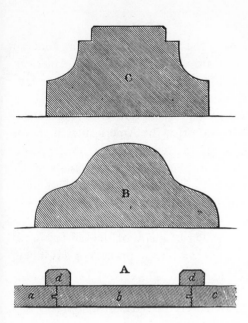

13. *Andrew Jackson Downing:
"Profiles of Battens." These
pieces of wood were to be placed
over the seams of the vertical
boarding that clad Downing's
houses (see illustration 11).*

civilization. Although some Americans associated the kinds of gestures
that constituted relative beauty with the humble architecture of a rural
past, Downing was too close to those structures to adopt such a point of
view. He never doubted that there were different grades of civilization
and that domestic architecture reflected them. As a "mere animal," he
explained, man's first necessity was to provide shelter. He usually did so
in a clumsy manner. Those on "the verge of civilization," for example,
the Croats of eastern Europe, lived in coarse houses that nonetheless were
strong and warm. The plain, rectangular, timber house found throughout
the rural United States indicated a higher state. It afforded perfect protection to the "physical nature of man." In short, it served utility. But
Downing's goal was a house that went beyond this basic level and had
the civilizing qualities that came with the perception of beauty.[69]

Downing's conviction about the power and importance of beauty grew
with the passage of years. In his earlier books he felt that an acquaintance
with the arts of taste was simply good for the development of the mind,
but in *The Architecture of Country Houses* he indicated that the perception of beauty contributed to a great moral crusade. Nevertheless, in
this, his last book, Downing did make a concession to the criticisms that
farmers had leveled at him. The section devoted to farm buildings in *The
Architecture of Country Houses* was much larger than that in *Cottage*

*Residences.* While he never lost sight of the fact that his primary concern was beauty, Downing was more realistic about the needs of American farmers. He included more detailed information, and most of his designs were more modest than those in *Cottage Residences.*

In turn, the agricultural press was not insensitive to Downing's arguments about the value of beauty. One sign that the American farmer was becoming concerned with more than utility was his interest in the farmhouses of an earlier day. In 1851 Solon Robinson wrote articles about "A Farmer's Kitchen of Old Times in New England" and "An Old-Fashioned New England Farmhouse," in which he explained how the everyday activities of a farm had been conducted in what already seemed like the distant past. Robinson regretted the passing of many of the old-fashioned ways but acknowledged that the farmer was in the process of advancing to a higher state of civilization.[70]

Once the American farmer began to examine his buildings in a new light, the need for beauty started to enter the agricultural press's discussions about farm architecture. "Farmer Slack" then was no longer just the man who did not do all his chores and who was content to live on a badly arranged farm; he was also the person who did not plant trees around his home and who neglected to keep his house freshly painted.[71]

When this change took place, the agricultural press could better appreciate the man who through his books had brought beauty to the American home. That was why, on learning of the terrible steamboat accident on the Hudson, the *Southern Cultivator* wrote that Downing's "sudden death may be regarded as a national calamity"; the *Michigan Farmer* stated that "there seems to be a void that no man can fill"; the *Prairie Farmer* of Chicago concluded that "his is a country's loss, and a country mourns him"; and the *New England Farmer* claimed that "the death of no man in the nation could be a greater loss." This outpouring of feeling was one further indication of how important Americans had come to consider houses.[72]

✦✦✦

One aspect of utility that Andrew Jackson Downing frequently discussed was health. He considered it important that architects and builders take precautions to protect the physical well-being of a house's inhabitants. Downing not only discussed the principles of heating and ventilating but also recommended several stoves and furnaces that were then commercially available. For the same reason Downing outlined the sanitary

14. *"Tumbledown Mansion — The House of Farmer Slack." Farmer Slack
had no feeling for beauty.*

15. *"The House of Farmer Snug." Farmer Snug recognized the importance
of beautiful surroundings.*

requirements of kitchens and bathrooms and gave many hints about how to plan these spaces.[73]

Ministers also wrote about the health of the home. They realized that the aesthetic and moral qualities of the everyday environment were not the only factors that affected the unfolding character of children; healthy surroundings were also important. Thus, when they spoke of the "atmosphere" of the home, they used the word literally as well as figuratively. Pure air was as important to the spirit of the house as any other influence.[74]

Before the nineteenth century the long-acknowledged relationship between health and the immediate environment was rarely the subject of a detailed investigation. But in the fifty years before the Civil War a few Americans tried to establish specific connections between health and buildings. They often focused on the home, where they thought this relationship was most critical. This interest reinforced the significance that ministers and architects for other reasons were then attributing to the home, and by 1860 Americans understood that their houses not only had to be religious and beautiful but also had to be healthy.

Architects and ministers did not take the lead in defining what made a healthy home. Nor did doctors. At the beginning of the nineteenth century their profession was in disarray. In an age that proclaimed the abilities of the common man, professional qualifications conferred by a select body were suspect. As a result, anyone could call himself a doctor, and the standards of practice suffered. Doctors also did not help their own reputation. After 1810 they challenged and rejected the theory of medicine articulated by the physicians of an earlier generation, but they could not quickly formulate a new set of principles to guide their day-to-day work. Even the most respected doctors did not agree about basic medical issues. Disputes were well-publicized, and Americans soon lost confidence in the profession.[75]

People then often turned for advice to popular writers on health. Some of these authors were well-intentioned and others were charlatans, but regardless of their motives, they had an important impact on Americans. Through the vast literature they produced, they promoted a general concern for health and in the process often drew attention to the quality of the immediate environment.

Many of the works of William Andrus Alcott illustrate how popular writers made this connection between health and everyday surroundings. Alcott was one of the period's most prolific and widely read authors.[76] He derived his interest in health from his broad view of history and from an understanding of the times in which he lived. Alcott believed in Adam's fall. From the beginning of time man had obscured his innate knowledge of God's laws by senseless habits of eating, dressing, and housing. The decrease in man's life span, which Alcott believed had greatly accelerated since the time of the American Revolution, was evidence of this decline. If Americans continued to water "the tree of licentiousness rather than that of liberty," the result would be disastrous. But, like other people who were profoundly worried by the conditions of the times, Alcott believed that progress, even the millennium, was still possible. The young country's newly discovered liberty, which had often led it astray, was the key. It gave Americans a unique opportunity to learn to live correctly.[77]

Alcott formulated his ideas as a means of personal salvation. As a youth he experienced a desire, kindled by reading Benjamin Franklin's *Autobiography*, to "do good." But into his twenties he had no firm ideas about how to accomplish this end. With his later more famous cousin, Bronson, he initially tried a career as a peddler. Then he became a teacher but soon was disillusioned by the slight effect he had on his students. Alcott's already delicate health deteriorated. He turned to medicine to learn about his condition, but he received no worthwhile guidance from that confused profession. Like thousands of other Americans, Alcott was victimized by indecisive doctors and became addicted to useless patent medicines.[78]

In a moment of crisis, Alcott realized that what he and many other Americans needed was an elucidation of God's physical laws. He decided that these laws of the body were as much a divine ordination as the ten commandments and were as essential to a true Christian life. For him they constituted a companion body of knowledge that would make Christian ethics meaningful on a day-to-day basis. Ultimately, Alcott arrived at a theory of medicine that shunned "the wilderness of powders and pills" and instead concentrated on the causes of health. He was then able to achieve his desire to do good by making available to his countrymen useful information about everyday concerns such as diet, dress, and housing; at the same time he improved his own debilitated condition.

Alcott's complex theory of physiology rested on a few simple principles. He thought that the body functioned best when it maintained a moderate and constant temperature. Alcott particularly feared the consumption of overstimulating substances and predicted ruin for those who indulged in alcohol, tea, coffee, sweets, condiments, and tobacco. Any of these produced a debilitating cycle of overheating followed by chills. Alcott's advice, therefore, was "Keep Cool."[79]

Body temperature was influenced externally as well as internally. Alcott advocated regular bathing, a practice virtually unknown in America before the 1830s. His purpose was not primarily to promote cleanliness, but to maintain a natural body temperature by keeping the pores open and allowing unhindered secretion so that perspiration could cool the skin. Alcott's advice on clothing and sleeping habits warned against over-heating. Hats made of heavy material, for instance, were dangerous because the head was naturally warmer than other parts of the body and needed cooling. Featherbeds caused an "unnatural degree of perspiration and thus induced weakness or debility." The air of the immediate environment was especially important because it influenced the body both externally and internally by regulating skin temperature and by affecting the circulation of the blood. Alcott particularly emphasized the need for adequate air in the home and frequently wrote about the dangers of bad ventilation.[80]

These ideas made Alcott critical of the construction of American buildings. He first addressed this matter in his *Essay on the Construction of School Houses*. He observed that communities often treated education as a "necessary evil" and provided their children only with "crowded, ill-looking, and sometimes disorderly and filthy huts . . . mis-called school houses." Alcott reasoned that it was a false economy to confine children to such buildings. Since he believed that the "arrangement and appearance of even inanimate things" had an extensive influence in forming character, in the *Essay* he discussed the complete design of the schoolhouse, from its location to details about the children's desks. Each topic was accompanied by drawings, precise dimensions, and specifications for materials.

In all these matters Alcott's criteria were based primarily on the health and comfort of the students. The school building had to be located on firm and elevated land to avoid the "unwholesome exhalations of stagnant water" that were feared to be a source of disease. A playground was necessary so that children could exercise properly. Alcott determined the size of windows by the amount of light they gave to every area of the room and recommended a type that would let impure air escape from the classroom.

Desks were especially important. Alcott had several motives for recommending a better type than the one then available. When students sat along benches, it was common to see several heads huddled together. "They may be engaged in study," Alcott noted, "but they may too be doing mischief." He therefore proposed a scheme for individual desks aligned in rows. This arrangement not only gave the schoolmaster easy access to each pupil for discipline or instruction but also assured that each child was surrounded by an adequate amount of air.

The most important aspect of this description of the ideal schoolhouse was not any particular detail but the general insight that a building was subject to deliberate design and that each decision could either add to or detract from the well-being of the inhabitants. Alcott believed that the burden was upon Americans to live in the right kinds of buildings. By making well-informed decisions, they opted for progress, but by failing to act or by acting in ignorance, they chose decline.

Although Alcott continued throughout his life to advocate these principles of construction for schools, he never achieved in education the dramatic results he hoped for. His faith in the public schools gradually waned, and he even came to sympathize with those critics who claimed that schools polluted the morals of good children by placing them in contact with bad ones. Alcott then turned to the family as a "hitherto undervalued . . . place of general instruction." As he succinctly put it, "the best school is the home school." The home was where individuals and the family could most directly control the immediate environment and thus improve their health. If they learned to do so — and it was to this end that Alcott wrote so many books intended for the hearthside — the home would become "the great and special school of Divine Providence."[82]

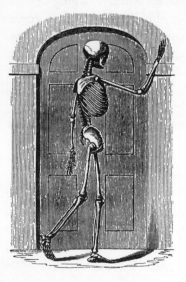

*16. William A. Alcott*: The House I Live In; *frontispiece, "I Am Fearfully and Wonderfully Made." In his concern for health Alcott reformulated the age-old connection between the body and architecture.*

In his books and pamphlets Alcott discussed various subjects that bore upon the health of family members at home. Many of these matters either touched upon or were directly concerned with domestic architecture. Alcott implicitly made the connection between health and the house in a children's physiology book entitled *The House I Live In*. In this volume Alcott described the functioning of the body through a grand analogy to domestic architecture. In a chapter called "Apartments and Furniture" he compared bodily organs to rooms, although he admitted that the analogy was not exact. The house was mainly based on straight lines and its rooms were only partially filled with furniture, whereas all the rooms of the body were curved and were completely filled with furniture, which, in Alcott's terms, meant air, blood, and other bodily fluids. Nevertheless, Alcott still thought the analogy appropriate enough to claim that the ears, nose, and mouth were the doors of the body. They were connected by "passages" to the "apartments" within.[83]

In other writings Alcott explored the more direct relationships between health and domestic architecture. When he was a teacher, he observed how fully formed were the characters of his students before they entered the classroom. In the home "silent influences . . . teachers that seem to teach not" had a far greater impact than the "direct" methods of formal schooling.[84] Since the home environment was so important to the health and character of children, how they were treated in their earliest years was critical. Alcott wrote extensively, therefore, about the nursery, a special area of the house to be set aside for the careful upbringing of children. His directions for the proper design of this important space reveal the full extent of his interest in the immediate environment of the home.

Alcott found that the nursery was often selected only because it was an extra room, and little attention was given to the purpose for which it was intended. The ideal nursery consisted of two connecting rooms: a child could be placed in one while the other was ventilated or cleaned. If the nursery was on the first floor, it was not to be shaded by trees or located where it received no sunlight. Its floor had to be of wood that would dry quickly when washed. Carpets, which attracted dust, dampness, or grease, had to be cleaned every week, yet they were useful because they were warm underfoot and protected children from falls. The windows of the nursery had to be tight. They also had to be equipped with shutters, so that the room could be completely darkened, and with bars, so that they could be opened without letting the children crawl out. For the same reason, the doors were not to open immediately onto staircases. Glaring colors on curtains were to be avoided because they injured the eyes of young children.

The nursery had to be warmed to the proper temperature. Alcott was concerned that the excessive heat of nurseries had caused "a great mortality," especially among very young children, not only because it overstimulated them, but also because it rendered them susceptible to cold later in life. He recommended that it was best to maintain a constant temperature in the nursery of 66 to 67 degrees. But in so doing, the safety of the children had to be kept in mind; Alcott advised that open wood fires be separated from the nursery by a high and substantial fender or screen.

Alcott did not want the nursery to be a place to which children were sent because they were being punished. Instead, he hoped that the nursery would be the room they would enjoy the most. It was to have as little furniture as possible, so that the children had the maximum amount of space in which to play. To make the nursery appealing, Alcott listed a number of games that would help to "exercise the memory, elicit ingenuity, excite a laudable emotion, and give the habit of patience and perseverance."

The only major piece of furniture Alcott recommended for the nursery was a bed, but he was particular about what kind was best. Feather mattresses were much too warm and also unhealthy because they discharged too much dust. For infants Alcott recommended a cradle that could be placed anywhere in the nursery to take advantage of either warmth or coolness, light or darkness. No matter what their ages, Alcott warned against children's sleeping together because they generated too much bodily heat and then threw off their blankets.[85]

The nursery was critical because small children spent most of their early years there. But the rest of the house also had an important bearing on health and character, especially on that of the mother and housewife. Alcott addressed most of his writing to her because he realized that it was she who would be most instrumental in the creation and care of the home. However, he believed that wives should not be subjected "to that round of duties amid pots and kettles, and a circle of objects, which as effectively stunts, dwarfs, diseases and gradually destroys the soul." He described equipment and techniques that would cut down the amount of housework and printed many recipes and hints that would replace old-fashioned methods.[86]

The housewife's special province was the kitchen, but Alcott also recommended that she spend time in the garden. That area was not just for growing useful plants and vegetables; it was also a place in which the housewife could exercise. The health of too many women that Alcott had known had been impaired because they were shut in all day. Alcott's intention in giving this advice was not to relieve the housewife of all her responsibilities but instead to establish for her the modern equivalent of a role she had lost in recent times. He wanted her to have more time to instruct her children, to improve herself, and to spend with her husband. Then she would again truly be his "help-meet."[87]

Alcott was less specific about the husband's role. He was to spend time tending the garden and preparing wood for fuel, but his primary responsibility was to make enough money to enable his family to live in the best possible house. By the 1830s Alcott already assumed that the modern husband would be securing this income away from his home.[88]

In deciding where to locate a house, Alcott found much to recommend in both city and country. The city had the advantage of a compact form, which enabled it to support institutions, especially those for health, such as bathing establishments. He also noted that "the busy appearance" of the town or city "quickens our pace" and "cheers our spirit." But if the city cheered the spirit, it could also excite the brain and nervous system. More important, the air was better in the country. Not only were most workers in the city confined during the day to insalubrious buildings, but they had no place to which to escape in the evenings and on the weekends. Alcott even found that the country was healthier than the city because it was green. "The health of the individual whose eye rests on the verdure of the country," he reasoned, "will be far more perfect, other things being equal, than that of the less fortunate individual whose eyes during the same season, are compelled to rest from morning till night, from day to day, and from month to month, on naked streets, and houses and walls."

All told, Alcott estimated that the advantages of the country were "a thousand times more numerous and more important." But he did not envisage a return to a rural society. Instead, the ideal was a town that would be settled as densely as possible "without interference with the purity of the air, the water, the habits or the morals." In such a scheme there would be a sufficient amount of land for agriculture and horticulture, but there would also be a suitable mix of mechanics, manufacturers, traders, and "literary people." The "purposes of education, improvement and religion" would then be best served, and the result would be "a heaven begun below."[89]

In his many writings on health Alcott touched upon a wide variety of subjects. But the wisdom of his advice on specific issues was less important than his telling his readers that the "material world was to be studied and improved." After the Civil War this directive was so generally accepted that it became possible to study more rigorously subjects that Alcott and other writers on popular health had been able only sketchily and idiosyncratically to touch upon. Even in the 1840s and 1850s, however, a few Americans were already undertaking this work. None of these early studies of aspects of the healthy home was definitive, but they were significant because they foreshadowed what was to come.

One subject that received more than a superficial treatment had traditionally been called "domestic economy." This phrase had for centuries referred to that body of knowledge needed to run and care for a household. Most often the rules of domestic economy were learned by example and were handed on orally from one generation to the next. Occasionally they were written down within the family. In time printed books transmitted useful information about the subject. These volumes were practical; they were filled with recipes, but not just for cooking. At a time when little could be bought that was ready-made, the housewife had to know how to concoct medicines, mix dyes, repair a hole in a pot, and perform many other tasks that involved complex formulas of ingredients and lengthy directions.[90]

In the few books on domestic economy, these topics were not set down in any systematic or even alphabetical order. The bits of useful information were related to each other only as they were haphazardly gathered over many years. The literature of domestic economy followed this format well into the nineteenth century. But by the early 1840s some writers understood that the old method was no longer satisfactory, and therefore they tried to outline an approach based on up-to-date information and ideas. In the process they focused the attention of their readers on, among other subjects, the state of the home's environment.

In his advice to mothers and housewives William Andrus Alcott was, in effect, rewriting traditional books on domestic economy. The person who undertook this task most effectively, however, was Catharine Beecher. Both her *Treatise on Domestic Economy* and the *Domestic Receipt Book* contained handy information and listed techniques and recipes for many household chores. They differed from earlier works in that they derived their information not from traditional sources but from what Catharine Beecher considered the latest scientific information.

Much of what Catharine Beecher wrote was about the proper care of the house. Central to this advice was an understanding of the "arrangement of rooms and the proper study of conveniences." In the *Treatise on Domestic Economy* Catharine Beecher pinpointed critical activities in the home and discussed the best arrangement of the furniture and utensils that were necessary for them. Many of her simple directions demonstrated a heightened level of concern for the interplay of all elements of the home environment. When she wrote that dining rooms should contain not only specific pieces of furniture but also a closet that communicated with the kitchen by a sliding window or door, she revealed an understanding about the interaction of activities, spaces, furniture, utensils, and sanitary requirements that had not appeared in earlier works on domestic economy.[91]

Another aspect of the healthy home that by the 1840s and 1850s started to receive a more rigorous analysis than a popularizer such as Alcott could make was the quality of air. In the first half of the nineteenth century many misleading and contradictory theories were articulated about what kind of air was healthy. The effusive claims about the numerous stoves and furnaces that were then invented, manufactured, and sold compounded the public's confusion. Independent and authoritative opinions were necessary, and it was in part by voicing their views on how best to heat and ventilate homes that some doctors slowly began to reestablish the credibility with the public that they had lost.

The leader in this work was Morrill Wyman, whose *Practical Treatise on Ventilation*, published in 1846, was the most authoritative American

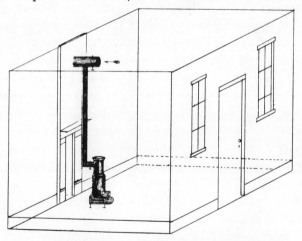

*17.   A Franklin stove. Although Benjamin Franklin first described the advantages of this method of heating in 1742, such stoves did not become popular in the United States until the 1830s.*

treatment of this subject. Wyman was a prominent doctor, a professor at the Harvard Medical School, and a pioneer in surgical techniques. The distinctive quality of his book was its clear and comprehensive nature. Wyman covered both general laws and specific applications and wrote for the layman. He described first the laws and properties of gases, especially the laws of their diffusion, which were so important for ventilation, and then the properties of air and the processes by which it might become "vitiated" through combustion and respiration. That subject led to the important question of how impurities could be removed from the air. To resolve that matter, Wyman first set forth the principles of the movements induced in the air by heat. He then analyzed the types of moving power best suited for ventilation and the quantity and quality of the air to be supplied.

At the end of *A Practical Treatise on Ventilation* Wyman explained how his analysis of the subject could be applied to specific building types. Although he described many useful devices and techniques for heating and ventilating, he recognized that no single treatment was best for all situations. He tried instead to itemize a set of suitable standards for each building. Wyman understood, for instance, that although it might be appropriate for other structures, a completely mechanized system of ventilation based on sealed double windows, as was then sometimes proposed, was inappropriate for domestic architecture.[92]

The significance of Wyman's description of how to ventilate a house

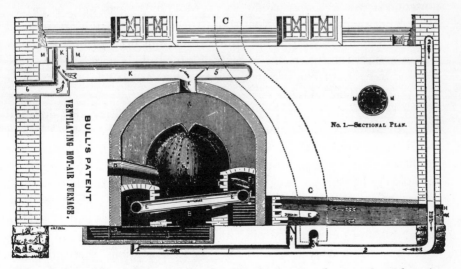

18.  *A central heating system. By the 1840s furnaces and networks of hot-air ducts were often installed in American homes.*

was not only that it entailed a sophisticated understanding of the functioning of the immediate environment throughout the seasons, but also that it gave those who did further work on house ventilation a standard they could accept, refute, or modify. By the 1850s several other American doctors had already written about this subject. They did not arrive at a consensus, but at least they had started a dialogue about an issue of great concern.[93]

Wyman's discussion of ventilation was also important because he tried to mediate between a mechanistic view and the frequently expressed opinion that nothing was a substitute for the old-time fireplace. A believer in progress, he was willing to use the knowledge that came from science and the equipment that was the product of invention. But he also recognized the significance of "old New England chimneys" for ventilation. In certain instances he was not averse to using traditional methods so long as the principles behind them were understood.[94]

Although their studies of domestic economy and heating and ventilation were far more detailed and reasoned than the comments that popular writers on health made about these subjects, Catharine Beecher and Morrill Wyman shared the concern for self-improvement and, therefore, the emphasis on the home that was so much a part of what motivated authors like William A. Alcott. Catharine Beecher wrote her books for a general audience in the hope that people would better themselves; in focusing on domestic economy she selected the home as the most important place where they could do so. Morrill Wyman did not restrict his writing on heating and ventilation to an audience of scientists and doctors. Rather, he addressed a broad readership because he thought it was important for Americans to be well informed about the general subject and to have correct information when they decided how best to heat and ventilate their houses.

The few people who before the Civil War tried to awaken local and state governments to the need for action to protect the public's health also, perhaps paradoxically, shared these beliefs in self-improvement and the home. In the seventeenth and eighteenth centuries the governors of the colonies had always been reluctant to take steps to protect the public against epidemics, in part because when one struck they did not know what to do about it. But they also believed that diseases and pestilence were a form of punishment from God. This attitude was inherent in their theology, and it undercut, with only a few exceptions, their efforts to take more than token action for the public's protection.

In the half century before the Civil War the context in which this long-standing attitude had been nurtured quickly changed. The size and number of cities increaséd drastically, and so did rates of morbidity and mortality. Many steps were taken to deal with these problems, but a few doctors and concerned citizens realized that it was necessary to make a more concerted effort to maintain the public's health than had been made in the past. They arrived at this point of view not only because of the sudden urgency of the problem, but also because they had begun to believe that the miserable conditions in the city were not part of God's impenetrable design, but instead were due to man's ignorance. Unlike their predecessors, they believed that through the application of science it would be possible to control the environment and to create an order that more closely approximated what God had intended.[95]

Public health reform was first most vigorously championed in Boston, where its primary advocate was Lemuel Shattuck. Born in 1793, Shattuck was deeply religious and, like William A. Alcott, believed that he could clarify God's plan. He did so, not by writing physiology textbooks but by collecting statistics, which, he believed, if properly codified and quantified, would reveal irrefutable laws. In 1841 he published an account of the vital statistics of Boston, showing that although longevity had increased up to 1820, it had then started to decline. Shattuck ascribed this disturbing fact to an increase in epidemic diseases.[96]

In 1845 Shattuck found further proof for the decrease in longevity when he compiled a city census of Boston, and in 1848 and 1850, when he conducted a sanitary survey of Massachusetts. In 1845 he believed that there would be no further increase in Boston's population. But in the following decade, with an influx of Irish immigrants, Boston's population increased by a third. Unlike other newcomers, the Irish tended to stay in the center of Boston near the wharves and the garment district where they were employed. They lived in old areas that had been abandoned by earlier inhabitants. As trade encroached upon these districts, real estate was allowed to deteriorate and elegant houses were soon turned into tenements. Once immigrants began to occupy these buildings, the spaces that used to surround the houses were filled with cheaply constructed shanties. The resulting warren of structures was crowded, ill-ventilated, badly lit, and improperly drained and had inadequate plumbing. By 1850, 586 basements in Boston were inhabited. Most of these sheltered from five to fifteen persons each, but at least one held thirty-nine people. In such environments outbreaks of cholera, tuberculosis, and other diseases became increasingly common.[97]

Although Shattuck pinpointed epidemic diseases as the immediate cause

of the high rate of morbidity and mortality, he recognized that underlying factors were also at work. In identifying them and in specifying a
remedy, he invariably determined that the individual was the ultimate
custodian of his health. Shattuck believed that filth was the medium in
which diseases were nurtured. Unlike other equally plausible etiologies,
this explanation implied that the home was the most likely breeding
ground of disease and, therefore, that the housekeeper had to be constantly on her guard. Shattuck, however, was reluctant to relate disease
to nonmedical forces, such as poverty or the real estate market that
caused the overcrowding. These explanations might also have taken the
burden off the individual and away from the home.[98]

Such predispositions affected Shattuck's attitude toward the function
of government in protecting the public's health. When he first studied
Boston's vital statistics, Shattuck prescribed a limited role for public bodies.
It was only when he later saw how out of hand conditions had become
and how incapable the immigrant population was of protecting itself that
he advocated a broader role for public institutions and the establishment
of organizations such as a state board of health. Even then, he continued
to argue that the adherence to strict codes of personal conduct, both
moral and physical, were vital to the maintenance of good health.[99]
"Municipal housekeeping," as public health reformers after the Civil
War sometimes called their work, still had to begin in the home.

+++

Horace Bushnell was often distressed by the constant bickering among
Protestant denominations. In 1847 he advised: "Let all such fences that
we may have raised up be broken down. We must have union or we cannot have strength, and union implies something more than we reside in
the same city." He then concluded that "there must be a fellow spirit, a
social worth, a living glow and a common aim."[100] Many ministers hoped
that a belief in the home would provide this unifying force, but not just
to resolve religious differences. They wanted the example of the home
to help repair the divisions that they thought were growing ever wider
in other aspects of American life.

The half century before the Civil War was a period in which, having
finally settled their differences with England in the War of 1812,
Americans had to decide what political values united them. At the same
time they had to come to terms with the fact that the great expansion
of agriculture, commerce, and industry was creating previously unimagin-

able extremes of both poverty and affluence. As they tried to cope with these political and economic issues, Americans became increasingly aware that they were an ethnically and culturally diverse people. Many citizens hoped that if everyone shared the values embodied in the Christian home, then specific political, economic, and social problems would resolve themselves. The inculcation of home religion was, therefore, often seen as the ultimate answer to matters in the public sphere.

But before Americans could arrive at this or any other solution to their many problems, they had to know the extent of the divisions among them. Failing a more accurate yardstick, the range of dwellings in a community, a city, or even the entire nation could be used to gauge distinctions between high and low, rich and poor, residents of the city and the country, or among different regions of the United States. Moreover, if houses were useful in summarizing distinctions and differences at a particular time, they also offered a comparison with the past. A new house could be contrasted with a familiar one from another period, and that comparison could be used to reflect on what progress, if any, there had been in the intervening years and, by extension, what there might be in the future. These comparisons were all the more compelling because houses were property. The ownership of property, its nature and extent, was one of the most important and divisive issues of the period, and no one could mention houses without revealing an opinion about this critical subject.

As Americans examined houses with these questions in mind, they began to read into their dwellings intricate meanings and symbolism. Once they did so, houses became all the more important to them; as well as asking what was a religious, a beautiful, and a healthy home, they also wondered what was an American home.

A discussion at the end of the eighteenth century formed the immediate background to this interest in the national home. At that time American colonists made frequent and pointed references to their houses to distinguish their society from that of Europe. The French-born American farmer J. Hector St. John de Crèvecoeur, for instance, wrote that a traveler in the New World did not see "the hostile castle, and the haughty mansion, contrasted with the clay-built hut and the miserable cabin, where cattle and men help to keep each other warm, and dwell in meanness, smoke and indigence." Instead, Crèvecoeur found a "pleasing uniformity of decent competence" in American houses and noted that even the meanest log cabin in the colonies was a comfortable habitation.

The simple farmhouse was an important symbol to Crèvecoeur. Not only did it encapsulate the lack of extremes that was characteristic of American social structure, but since it was customarily occupied by a freeholder, it also exemplified the virtues of that status.[101]

During and directly after the American Revolution political philosophers often wrote about houses in these terms, especially when they tried to define what the role and significance of property would be in the new nation. Thomas Jefferson articulated one point of view. He believed that all men shared certain fundamental, natural rights, those "of thinking, speaking, forming and giving opinions, and perhaps all those which can be fully exercised by the individual without the aid of exterior assistance." But men could not exist without society, which they formed to secure, not to abridge, their natural rights. Once men entered society, they established their civil rights, which were of "personal protection, of acquiring and possessing property."[102]

Jefferson did not include the right of property as one of the fundamental rights in the Declaration of Independence.[103] Nevertheless, he respected the importance of the right to possess property. Without property men could not exercise their natural abilities, either intellectually or economically. Jefferson advocated the breakdown of privileges that tended to create monopolies. He did so not to encourage communistic ownership but to permit all citizens to have a share in property. In the Virginia Constitution he stipulated that every citizen could receive fifty acres of land. Through that provision the individual would secure his independence and thus ensure his happiness. Only then would Americans attain Jefferson's ideal society of self-sufficient freeholders.[104]

Whereas Jefferson believed in man's innate morality, John Adams had little faith in human nature; he thought that self-interest and self-love were the mainsprings of human action. His reading of history confirmed his pessimistic vision. He concluded that man had a passion for distinction and that governments would be able to promote the public good only if they acknowledged this trait. He devised a system of government, therefore, based on elaborate checks and balances, that was designed to prevent a degeneration into conspiracy and faction. For its success this system required that as many people as possible have property and thus a stake in the society. Only with a wide sharing of property would Adams's vision of a stable but stratified social order, reflecting natural abilities, result.[105]

Even though Jefferson and Adams disagreed about the place of property in a system of political thought, both advocated extension of ownership because they believed that liberty was always threatened by the propertyless. Both were appalled by the contrast in Europe between the propertyless mobs, who, they noticed, lived in wretched hovels, and the wealthy, whose houses were unconscionably lavish. No matter how much they differed on other matters, Jefferson and Adams agreed that it would be disastrous if there ever was such a contrast in the new nation.

But when Jefferson and Adams both died on July 4, 1826, the context in which they had nurtured their ideas already seemed to be quickly receding into the past. The visions of the republic of self-sufficient farmers and of the well-ordered community both were giving way to a society in which no relationship was stable and all institutions were fragile. Americans then started to notice signs of the sharp divisions among citizens that Jefferson and Adams had earlier so abhorred in Europe. When they did so, they began to examine their houses all the more carefully.

Americans conducted this investigation from many points of view. Some Democrats wrote about houses to illustrate their suspicions of rich merchants and bankers. Neo-Federalists and Whigs examined houses not only because they were alarmed at what they thought was a growing propertyless class but also because they were worried about the increasing prominence in American life of newly wealthy merchants and businessmen. Those who lived in or had an allegiance to the country pointed to both the mansions and the tenements of the city and hoped that rural residents who were thinking of migrating to the nation's burgeoning urban centers would heed the warning implicit in this comparison. Foreign visitors inspected houses to compare the Old World and the New, as did Americans who traveled to Europe.

Such interpretations of American houses were made in several forms. They were often articulated in treatises on political economy, especially in those sections that dealt with property. The period's magazines, the lurid popular weeklies as well as the respectable monthlies, also contained many pointed references to houses. But houses were most thoroughly examined in literature. Authors of short stories and novels often elaborated upon and ascribed a symbolic significance to the houses in which their characters lived. In the first half of the nineteenth century virtually every work of fiction that offered an interpretation of American life did so at some level through a discussion of houses.

James Fenimore Cooper wrote about houses in all his novels. In *Home As Found*, published in 1838, the discussion of this subject occupied more than an incidental part of the story. When Mr. Effingham, the main character of the novel and a mouthpiece for Cooper's views, landed in New York after an extended trip to Europe, he was appalled by the houses and everything they represented, especially a level of meretricious wealth that had not previously existed. The city of quiet respectability that he remembered had changed into a "commercial town" in which real estate speculation was one of the chief occupations.

The countryside had also changed. As Effingham sailed up the Hudson to the town where his family home was located, he noticed dozens of garish villas along the riverbank. But the full implication of this new manifestation of wealth only became clear when he found that his own house, known as the Wigwam, had been changed in his absence. Its tasteful Palladian design had been altered to resemble a Greek temple. Aristabulus Bragg, a local entrepreneur and the archetypical man of the people, explained that the earlier design, no matter how excellent, had not met popular approval. In a democratic country it was necessary to consult "the whole neighborhood" before choosing a style of architecture.

Bragg had no independent standards of taste and no appreciation of local attachments. One of the novel's characters noted that in England people "loved to continue for generations on the same spot." They appreciated the trees that their "forefathers planted, the roof that they built, the fireside by which they sat." Bragg, who valued property only in financial terms, thought these words "very poetical" but a "great check" to business. He was proud to be a citizen of a nation that had "as few impediments as possible to outward impulses." The most pleasant tree he could remember was one that sawyers had turned into a thousand feet of lumber. Nor did he feel anything for the house in which he had been born. That structure had long since been torn down, and he advised Effingham to do the same with his home and to build anew.[106]

Cooper could come to terms with these attitudes only by postulating a three-stage theory of American civilization. When an area was first settled, people drew together despite differences in background, because they faced common hazards and deprivations. This period was followed by one in which the "ordinary passions" dominated. Although some of the original settlers still remained and, like Effingham, who continued to call his house the Wigwam, remembered the time of the "neutral ground," most of the inhabitants had no recollection of the earlier period. The result was the kind of flux described in *Home As Found*. Cooper hoped that this second phase was only transitional and would give way to one in which laws would regulate the passions that produced the attitudes toward houses and property characteristic of men like Bragg.[107]

As the years passed, Cooper wondered whether this phase would ever arrive. He then turned to another interpretation of American civilization, one which he had hinted at in *Home As Found*. On the day before Effingham left New York, a huge fire broke out near the Stock Exchange. The only way to stop it was to blow up all the buildings in the surrounding area. This destruction of property was horrifying, but Effingham could not help but think that it was a rebuke to "the rapacious longing for wealth." In 1838 Cooper still hoped that Americans would reform. But by 1848, when he wrote *The Crater*, he no longer had that faith. In that utopian novel he described a civilization that had started with high ideals but then became corrupt. At the end of *The Crater* the entire civilization was destroyed by a volcano.[108]

*Home As Found*, although interesting as social commentary, was not a great novel. One of the period's masterpieces of fiction, however, was specifically about a house. In *The House of the Seven Gables* Nathaniel Hawthorne not only identified his characters by their attitudes toward houses but also gave the house in which many of them lived a personality of its own. The house of the seven gables had an "aspect" and a "human countenance"; it was an important, if not the central, participant in the book.

It is possible to interpret *The House of the Seven Gables* in many ways. One of the novel's recurring themes is the divisiveness caused by disputes about property. Hawthorne set his romance in mid-nineteenth-century Salem, Massachusetts. In the course of the book he recounted the history of a curse that Matthew Maule had placed two hundred years earlier on a house built by Thomas Pyncheon. Maule felt that Pyncheon had cheated him out of the land on which the house was built. This grievance was maintained by generations of ne'er-do-well Maules, and the curse continued to haunt the prominent Pyncheons. The timeworn house thus not only embodied the history of the ancient quarrel but also remained the bone of contention between the descendants of the two families.

Another theme of *The House of the Seven Gables* was the conflict between tradition and change. The elderly Clifford felt this tension the most because he had been a victim of the long-standing dispute between the two families and as a result had spent most of his adult life in prison. This experience made him question the traditional importance of property. When he and his sister made a desperate attempt to leave their memory-laden house and to participate in the progress of the times by taking a railway ride, Clifford struck up a telling conversation with a fellow passenger, who commented that on a rainy day it was best to remain at home near a nice fire. Clifford disagreed; he believed that the railway was a symptom of the "vast and inevitable improvements" to come. However, he did not envisage that these manifestations of progress would result in the kind of higher state of civilization that Andrew Jackson Downing or James Fenimore Cooper anticipated. Instead, Clifford looked forward to these new developments, especially the increased mobility, because they would make possible a return to a more natural, nomadic state. He theorized that man first lived in temporary shelters, huts that could hardly be called buildings. "Such sweet homes . . . rather grew than were made with hands," Clifford told his listener. Why, he asked, should man "make himself a prisoner for life in brick, and stone, and old worm-eaten timber, when he can just as easily dwell . . . wherever the fit and beautiful shall offer him a home?"

At the conclusion of *The House of the Seven Gables* Hawthorne seemed to indicate with the marriage of Holgrave, a descendant of the Maules, and Phoebe, a Pyncheon, that divisions over property might be resolved and that there would be a satisfactory mediation between tradition, identified with Phoebe, and change, embodied in the radical Holgrave. But Hawthorne warned the reader against this optimistic conclusion in the book's preface. He acknowledged that he could not flatter himself with the slightest hope that his readers would learn anything from the book's message, "that the wrong-doing of one generation lives into the successive ones." To emphasize this point Hawthorne ended *The House of the Seven Gables* with Holgrave, who had always derided the wealthy and had wished that people would live only "in something as fragile and temporary as a bird's-nest," deciding to live with his new bride, not in the house of the seven gables, but in an even more sumptuous residence that belonged to the Pyncheon family.[109]

As novelists, Cooper and Hawthorne stood apart from the conditions about which they wrote. But other Americans were not so detached. They tried to do something about what they perceived to be the faults of society through a great variety of reform movements, some of which were concerned with the nature of property and also, therefore, with domestic architecture.

At the common level this interest was rhetorical. Since Americans of all political opinions frequently expressed the desire to maintain, attain, or regain a simple, rural life, a vision they often summarized in a description of an ideal country home, politicians found that they could more effectively put forward particular programs by associating their causes

*19. "William Henry Harrison The Farmer of North Bend" — a log cabin and hard cider. During the election campaign of 1840 the simple home and the virtues it represented were brought to national attention by the Whigs.*

with that appealing image. They therefore often evoked the example of the village, the farm, and the home of the early settler, all of which they associated with fundamental virtues. This rhetoric went back at least to the American Revolution. It was frequently used thereafter, but in 1840 the Whigs brought this theme to national attention with the phrase "a log cabin and hard cider," claiming that their candidates represented the qualities implicit in these symbols. In the 1840 campaign the Whigs often established their local headquarters in log cabins erected for the occasion, and they filled their election literature with references to the values embodied in this basic home. They sang:

> *I love the rough log cabin*
> *It tells of olden times,*
> *When a hardy and honest class*
> *Of freemen in their prime*
> *First left their fathers' peaceful home*
> *Where all was joy and rest*
> *With their axes on their shoulders,*
> *And sallied for the West.*

Through such songs the Whigs for the first time publicized on a national scale an image of the American home.[110]

Although many people identified at an emotional level with a rhetorical log cabin, few supported legislation to provide this simple home to every citizen who wanted one. That issue was one of the most complex and divisive of the period. After 1796, when the first law regulating the disposal of public lands was passed, many Americans pressed for legislation to provide settlers with land in the public domain. But free land was opposed by southerners who did not want to create more nonslave states and also by northerners who feared a drain on the labor force and on important government resources. A comprehensive Homestead Act, therefore, was not passed until 1862.[111] By then free land had been championed for a half century. In the process its supporters often discussed and publicized the importance of a particular type of home. The immediate focus of those who favored the passage of a Homestead Act was land, but in their rhetoric they often spoke of the simple farmer's home, an image that conveniently summed up the idea of self-sufficiency so important to them. "Home for the homeless and land for the landless" was their favorite slogan.[112]

While advocates of free land were pressing for farm homesteads, other Americans were beginning to discuss the related idea that it was in the national interest for the urban workingman to own his own home. As more Americans moved to towns and cities, rural self-sufficiency was transformed into a call for independence through the ownership of an urban home. Many journalists, including Walt Whitman, wrote about this subject. Like many other nineteenth-century Americans, Whitman's father had taken his family from its rural homestead, on Long Island, and moved to a nearby town, in this case Brooklyn, where for thirty years he was a carpenter and housebuilder. Whitman frequently expressed his fondness for his childhood home and transferred some of these feelings into his anonymous temperance novel of 1842, *Franklin Evans; Or, The Inebriate*. In that book he described the downfall of a young man who had left his country home on Long Island to make his fortune in New York. After a number of experiences in which Evans failed to live up to his namesake, Franklin, he seemed to be turning over a new leaf. He married and started to build a home. But in his haste for independence he overspent; his creditors then claimed his property. That blow led to the destruction of Evans's marriage and finally to his addiction to alcohol.[113]

At one level Walt Whitman simply followed in *Franklin Evans* the antiurban formulas of the popular literature of the time, but he also implied that the ownership of a home could be the means to a viable life in a city. Whitman repeated this theme in a less didactic manner in *Leaves of Grass*. In "Song of the Broad-Axe" he proclaimed:

> *A great city is that which has the greatest men and*
> *women,*
> *If it be a few ragged huts it is still the greatest*
> *city in the whole world.*

But the "shapes" were also important. When Whitman wrote:

> *The shape of the planks of the family home, the home of*
> *the friendly parents and children,*
> *The shape of the roof of the home of the happy young*
> *man and woman, the roof over the well-married young*
> *man and woman . . .*

he implied that there was a connection between the home and the prospering family.[114]

Whitman expanded upon this relationship in two articles, "Wicked Architecture," and "Decent Homes for Working-men." He claimed that after food and clothing a house was man's most vital necessity. But it was not sufficient simply to live in a house. "A man is not a whole and complete man," Whitman wrote, "unless he *owns* a house and the ground it stands on." He hoped that every American family would be able to own its own home, and he was outraged not only because so many residents of New York had to live in the many tenements that had recently sprung up, but also because they had to pay high rents for such miserable accommodation. Without the possibility of owning a home, couples deferred marriage. Those who did start families had to cope with rents that drained their income, and their marriages often did not survive the strain.[115]

If those who lived in tenements had little chance of owning a home, the opportunities open to the inhabitants of New York's boardinghouses were not much greater. Life in these institutions was a common topic in the literature of the period. Some writers were intrigued by the picturesque characters who lived in or ran boardinghouses and described and catalogued the endless variety of these establishments. But more often, authors and journalists condemned boardinghouse life. They told how young men were led astray by the disreputable people they met there and how family life was undermined by a context in which the mother could not fulfill her customary role in the kitchen.[116]

Walt Whitman spent many years in boardinghouses, and the people he met there probably provided him with material he used in his poetry and journalism. But Whitman never had a good thing to say about boardinghouses. Even a poet needed "a few clapboards around and shingles overhead on a lot of American soil owned," and he was relieved when he was able to settle in a modest home in Camden, New Jersey.[117]

To deal with New York's housing problem, Whitman called for the construction of "model lodging houses," which would contain sufficient space, light, ventilation, and sanitary facilities to provide a decent context for family life at reasonable rents. Middle-class families could use that type of accommodation, but the need was even more pressing for New York's working population. Although such buildings had been constructed in London in the 1840s, the idea was still novel in 1860. Farmers, merchants, and businessmen who lived in remote areas or small towns had often constructed housing for their workers because no other dwellings were available. The best-known examples of this kind of accommodation had been financed by mill owners in towns like Lowell, Massachusetts.[118] The construction of improved housing to be occupied by people not associated with a particular industry or business was a different proposition. In 1855, two years before Whitman wrote his articles, a group of New York's concerned citizens financed the first American model tenement. They hoped to provide improved accommodation at a reasonable rent, while making a modest profit. By the time of the Civil War it was still too early to tell whether this idea had any future.[119]

Although Whitman was an advocate of individualism, he recognized that where people congregated there needed to be rules. In addition to calling for the construction of model lodging houses, Whitman also favored the establishment of building regulations, of which New York then had few. Whitman was optimistic because in 1856 a Tenement House Commission had for the first time been appointed by the state legislature. Its report was brief and preliminary, but the existence of such a committee at least promised the passage of effective legislation.[120]

How many people lived in tenements, boardinghouses, or their own homes and what they thought about these choices is impossible to determine, but by 1860 spokesmen such as Walt Whitman had already formed their opinions about this subject. Model lodging houses and laws were important, but it was best for Americans to own their own homes. That was why Whitman considered Brooklyn, where men of moderate means could travel from their work to their houses, a more promising place than Manhattan.

One reason that home ownership was already popular by 1860 was that most Americans disapproved of other forms of tenure that were suggested as solutions to the nation's problems. These proposals attracted few followers, but they were important because they set into relief the inadequacies and inconsistencies of accepted institutions while providing an expanded range of examples that Americans could use to assess how and in what type of dwellings they could best live.

An extreme response to the changes taking place in American life was most forcefully outlined by Henry David Thoreau in *Walden*. Whereas others talked and wrote about wigwams, log cabins, birds' nests, and simple homes, Thoreau decided to build and live in one. By contrasting his house with the kind in which other Americans lived, he questioned the basic assumptions of a society dedicated to an ethic of material progress. From his solitary vantage point he was able to perceive a depth of meaning in houses that his contemporaries either overlooked or deliberately ignored.

Thoreau summarized his distaste for American society by pointing to two extremes of housing near Walden Pond. In his daily walks he saw shanties along the nearby railroad tracks where "human beings lived in sties." These hovels had no windows and afforded little protection from the cold for their Irish inhabitants. This extreme balanced another. Thoreau's prosperous neighbors in Concord had inherited property that not only had become millstones around their necks but also had prevented them from the appreciation of more important values. The "degraded poor" and the "degraded rich" were thus two sides of the same coin.

The alternative was a simple life that conformed to what was "necessary." Thoreau discussed several models for the house appropriate to this state. Neither repelled by nor sentimental about primitive dwellings, he thought there was much to learn from them. He found that the "naked savages" of Tierra del Fuego, the Laplanders, and the Penobscot Indians had minimal but satisfactory shelters. Besides, unlike nineteenth-century Americans, they all owned houses that were "as good as the best, and sufficient for [their] coarser and simpler wants."

Another suggestive model was the box, six feet long and three feet wide and high, in which railroad workmen locked their tools. Thoreau reasoned that everyone could buy such a box and use it for shelter at night and when it rained. A man could thus "love freedom in his box and in his soul be free." The person who did so would "sit up as late as [he] pleased, and, whenever [he] got up, go abroad without any landlord or houselord dogging [him] for rent."

But when Thoreau constructed his own house, he did not emulate the savage nor build himself a box. No matter how much he criticized nineteenth-century Americans, Thoreau still believed in progress. In *Walden* he outlined a theory of the evolution of the house. In the infancy of the human race "an enterprising mortal" crept into a hollow for shelter. From the cave, man advanced to "roofs of palm leaves, of bark and boughs, of linen woven and stretched, of grass and straw, of boards and shingles, of stones and tiles." Thoreau concluded that instead of following the primitive, it was necessary to combine the "hardiness" of the savage with the "intellectualness" of civilized man. He did not try to make a minimal shelter, nor was he rigorous about the simplicity or purity of his method of construction. His house was one room, but it had windows and a basement. Thoreau hewed his own timber and joined the lumber with mortise and tenon. But he also bought a shanty from a railroad worker and used its boards to clad his house.

Thoreau's point was that civilization had gone too far. The best house was that which was least self-conscious and which least distracted its inhabitants from the primary purpose of life. In explaining how to attain this state, Thoreau mentioned a sentimental reformer in architecture, probably Ruskin, who wanted to put "a core of truth in ornament." The trouble with that reformer was that he began at the cornice, not at the foundations. Thoreau concluded that "what of architectural beauty I now see, I know has gradually grown from within outward, out of the necessities and character of the indweller, who is the only builder — out of some unconscious truthfulness and nobleness, without even a thought for the appearance." The American house that best fulfilled these conditions was the simple log cabin. It reflected in a straightforward manner the lives of its inhabitants, and so would the "suburban box," Thoreau wrote, when the lives of its inhabitants could be "as simple and as agreeable to the imagination."

Thoreau equated self-sufficiency with ideas about a life beyond property. But at times he hinted that a detachment from material concerns could be achieved in a large community, a context that was the opposite of the solitude he had sought at Walden Pond. In one of *Walden*'s most enigmatic passages Thoreau described a house about which he often dreamed. This dwelling was not inhabited by one, isolated person. Instead, it was a "larger and more populous house" that had only one room, "a vast, rude, substantial, primitive hall, without ceiling or plastering, with bare rafters and purlins supporting a sort of lower heaven over one's head." Many people lived in this cavernous building, some "in the fireplaces, some in the recess of a window, and some on settles, some at one end of the hall, some at another, and some aloft on rafters with spiders."[121]

This dream house had many possible sources. Thoreau may have been thinking of the great halls of old English homes; parts of his description applied to the interiors of churches; and he may have known about the large dwellings of some American Indian tribes. But Thoreau's fantastic structure also bore certain similarities to the meeting halls of some of the communistic societies formed in the United States in the preceding half century. These communities were based on principles diametrically opposed to Thoreau's notion of self-sufficiency, but they too challenged contemporary assumptions about the proper function and nature of property. In so doing they also raised penetrating questions about domestic architecture.

The customary case for the individual ownership of property often followed the line of argument laid down by the popular political economist Francis Wayland. In *The Elements of Political Economy* Wayland argued that God had designed man to labor, but since man would not work without the promise of benefit, society had devised arrangements to allow every man to gain all that he could. Wayland's precondition for this state was the division of property, which was the "foundation of all accumulation of wealth, and of all progress in civilization." When property was divided, a motive existed for "regular and voluntary labor." Increased production and further exertion then ensued. But property held in common left everyone "at liberty to take what he will, and as much as he will, and to labor as much or as little as he pleases," a condition "prejudicial to the best interests of a society."[122]

Although most Americans accepted the basic outlines of this argument, several kinds of communitarian experiments offered alternatives to it. Sects such as the Shakers, the followers of George Rapp, and the Oneida Perfectionists settled in small communities under various forms of common ownership and living arrangements. The English industrialist Robert Owen started another type of community.[123] The housing built by the sects and the Owenites was of interest because it was a direct attempt to make a physical framework for a new social order. But the most note-worthy communistic experiments, at least from the point of view of domestic architecture, were those which put into practice the ideas of Charles Fourier. Born in 1772 in Besançon, France, Fourier inherited a large fortune that he lost within a year through faulty investment and the sacking of his warehouse by revolutionaries. His experiences as a dra-goon in the French army furthered his disaffection with the existing order, and in 1795 he started to study how a new society could be founded. He did not begin to publish on this subject until 1822, but when he died in 1837 he had attracted a small but devoted following.

Fourier wrote about a broad range of issues in a language that was often obscure, but his overriding aim was to increase society's wealth. He claimed that maximum productivity could be achieved, while suiting the talents of everyone concerned, by a unit of 1,600 people living on 5,000 acres of land. Under Fourier's scheme labor would prove both efficient and delightful, because every member of the community would have a varied routine. Each person would work at one task for at most two hours at a time. To enhance both the efficiency of work and the common social bond of the community, Fourier proposed that his society live in a large building, a "phalanstery," in which all domestic arrange-ments would be in common.[124]

The essential aspects of Fourier's ideas were first presented to the American public by his disciple Albert Brisbane in articles for the New York *Herald Tribune* in 1842. Fourier and Brisbane had their most noted impact on the small community founded a year earlier at Brook Farm, Massachusetts, by several prominent clergymen and intellectuals. The Brook Farm community began with intentions that differed sharply from those of Fourier. Its members were attracted to this "association," as the minister George Ripley called it, because they sought a way to achieve a modest level of subsistence by doing as little work as possible. In their daily arrangements, therefore, they emphasized qualities that were the opposite of efficiency and organization.

The first accounts of life in the association emphasized its idyllic aspects. The members of the community worked as they pleased and were unwilling to make rules. When George Ripley moved to Brook Farm, he had not yet arranged the terms for purchase of the land, nor had he even drawn up the plans and articles of association. When he finally produced such a document, he made no clear statement about what the members of the association had in common. There was a guarantee to support all members, but the society was not based on common property.

It was, instead, organized on joint-stock partnership — its capital divided into shares with a guaranteed interest of 5 percent a year.

The informal living arrangements of the community reflected this relaxed attitude. The original members moved into a farmhouse, called the "hive," that had two rooms on either side of a central entrance. One on the left was a parlor and the other served as a dining room, while the two on the right were occupied by a boarder. The rooms above were used for sleeping. When more people arrived, additions and alterations were made — the front and back rooms on the left were joined and a kitchen was added. This makeshift approach extended to other buildings. Farming sheds, some containing dormitory rooms on the second floor, were erected as needed. There was some correspondence between the purpose of the buildings and the avocations of the people who lived in them, but the Brook Farmers refused to apply any sort of organization to their community.

Although the terrain at Brook Farm was varied and included sites protected from the elements, George Ripley chose to forgo practicality and built his house on top of a large rock, where he would have a splendid view. Visitors to this building, called the Eyrie, had to ascend a long set of rickety stairs to arrive at the terrace on which the building was perched.[125]

Another house, the Cottage, was purchased from a neighboring farm. The spirit of the life in this dwelling was best captured in an anecdote about an attempt to build chimneys to warm it. The settlers did not do the work themselves, but hired local masons. Work proceeded "with apparent sweetness," and, one former inhabitant later recounted, everyone assumed that all was being done correctly, "until one day sitting in the parlor, I heard a strange noise, and looking up was horrified to see a yawning chasm where there ought to have been a fire place." The Cottage's inhabitants had failed to note that there was a cellar beneath the house and that there were no foundations to support the heavy masonry.[126]

This casual mood was satisfactory as long as the community was financially viable. Ralph Waldo Emerson, who did not join his many friends at Brook Farm, was always dubious about a scheme that did not have a leader and in which each person made his own hours. Nevertheless, the members hoped to support themselves through their farming and by running a boarding school. Neither venture proved as productive as anticipated. The farm was not on good soil, and few parents wanted to send their children to a school in such a community.

The first settlers in Brook Farm had known about Fourier and had considered his ideas interesting as a social experiment but antithetical to their views of moral freedom. Nevertheless, as the economic prospects of their noble experiment became bleaker, the Brook Farmers came to concede that Fourier's phalanstery, with its community kitchens, common living quarters, and cooperative buying, was much more economical.

Once the Brook Farmers adopted Fourier's system, the atmosphere of the community quickly changed. The society was incorporated by the state legislature, a new constitution was written, and a complex system of government and management according to Fourier's categories of work was instituted. The population increased and a large number of industries were added to the former farming community.

These changes were accompanied by the construction of a large building designed to house all the families of the community and to provide common rooms as well. The phalanstery was located on the brow of the hill, immediately in front of the Eyrie. As one inhabitant noted: "If it did not entirely obscure the Eyrie, it certainly spoiled the effect produced by that building when seen from a distance." Both the designer and the design of the phalanstery are unknown. As it was being constructed and as the outlines of the community were taking shape, a sudden fire of mysterious origin swept through the building.[127]

This conflagration effectively ended the Brook Farm experiment. Although other communities on Fourier's principles were started in the United States, Americans who followed the history of Brook Farm and other such communitarian experiments were skeptical about their value. No matter how difficult the daily life in the nation's homes at times seemed, the security of private ownership was still preferable to the extremes of anarchy and regimentation embodied in Brook Farm.

Communitarian experiments interested Americans, but they were not vitally important in the way that slavery was. Even if they did not consider it morally wrong, most contemporaries of Jefferson and Adams hoped that slavery would prove an economic liability and would soon die away. That expectation was not realized. By the 1820s it was evident that this troublesome institution would not simply come to a natural end. In the following years the contrast between a free and increasingly urban North and a slave and permanently rural South grew. Americans then had to decide what the two regions had in common. In doing so they often cited the houses of North and South to compare the two societies. The ideas about houses mentioned in this debate had been formulated in the discussion of other issues. But when used to measure the progress of North and South, they assumed some of their most powerful meanings.

American authors often pointed to typical houses to characterize the life of each region.[128] But Harriet Beecher Stowe's *Uncle Tom's Cabin* most directly connected a type of dwelling and a society. When that work began to appear in serialized form in June 1851, the discussion about slavery immediately intensified. In the process the debate about the nature of the American home also became more heated.

Harriet Beecher Stowe did not immediately explain the meaning of her title. Little of the story's action took place in Tom's home, and only the end of the book made the significance of his cabin clear. George Shelby, the chief character of the novel's last episode, as a young boy had befriended his father's slave, Uncle Tom. Mr. Shelby had been forced to sell Tom, but George resolved some day to buy him back and to set him free. Years later George traveled to Simon Legree's plantation to redeem his childhood friend, but he arrived too late. Tom had recently been savagely beaten and was about to die.

George Shelby returned to his plantation and vowed to work for "liberation." He freed his slaves and advised them to "think of your freedom, every time you see UNCLE TOM'S CABIN; and let it be a memorial to put you in mind to follow in his steps, and be as honest and faithful and Christian as he was." The cabin, therefore, was a symbol of the Christian life, patiently maintained in spite of the harsh cruelties of slavery. But Harriet Beecher Stowe's message was not just for slaves, or for southerners who lived in luxurious houses while their chattel eked out a miserable existence in rude huts. *Uncle Tom's Cabin* was also a criticism of northerners who ignored the Christian life in their quest for wealth, especially that which came from the cotton trade.

Harriet Beecher Stowe's message to both North and South was implicit in her descriptions of the houses in which her characters lived. Tom's cabin was simply a "small log building" and had few distinguishing features, other than the luxuriant flowers that grew around it. The one simple and neat room inside served as both parlor and bedroom. Both the room and its furniture were sparsely decorated, except for some "very brilliant scriptural prints" and a portrait of George Washington that adorned the wall over the fireplace. The structure and its contents reflected simplicity, repose, patriotism, and Christian virtue.

When Stowe introduced Miss Ophelia into her narrative, she described a New England farmhouse. Although more substantial than Uncle Tom's cabin, it embodied the same qualities. The author explained that a traveler in New England might encounter "in some cool village, the large farmhouse, with its clean-swept grassy yard, shaded by the dense and massy foliage of the sugar maple." He would later remember "the air of order and stillness, of perpetuity and unchanging repose, that seemed to breathe over the whole place." Inside the house the traveler would recall "the wide, clean rooms, where nothing ever seem[ed] to be doing or going to be done," where everything was "rigidly in place, and where all household arrangements move[d] with the punctual exactness of the old clock in the corner."[129]

"Perpetuity and unchanging repose" were not the characteristic qualities of the period. Although some southerners were sympathetic to the portrait of slavery in *Uncle Tom's Cabin* and some northerners may have understood the book's message about their region, few Americans could then sufficiently detach themselves from their immediate loyalties to be objective about this difficult issue. The events in Kansas in 1853 and 1854 and the Dred Scott decision in 1855 made the lines of discussion increasingly rigid. The example of the home was then frequently drawn upon to illustrate the virtues and defects of each system.

Several southerners chose to state the case for slavery by writing novels that reworked the plot of *Uncle Tom's Cabin*. In Mary Eastman's *Aunt Phillis's Cabin: Or, Southern Life As It Is* and Martha Haines Butt's *Antifanaticism: A Tale of the South*, the slaves lived in cabins described as "comfortable" — generally whitewashed, with neat gardens of "luxuriant" flowers, and often surrounded by well-kept picket fences. The interiors of the one-room houses were usually sparsely though "neatly" furnished. Mary Eastman concluded: "Yet are their cabins generally healthy and airy." The master's interests "as well as a wish for the comfort and happiness of the slave dictates an attention to his wants and feelings."[130]

These houses, ironically, were not dissimilar to Uncle Tom's cabin. But when Mary Eastman chose in a postscript to her novel to illustrate Harriet Beecher Stowe's biased use of evidence, she did not cite the description of Uncle Tom's cabin on the Shelby plantation. Instead, she focused upon an account of houses on another plantation that appeared elsewhere in *Uncle Tom's Cabin*. Stowe had described these dwellings as "rude shells destitute of any pieces of furniture, except a heap of straw fouled with dust, spread confusedly over the floor." According to Mary Eastman, this was a distorted picture, a typical example of northern exaggeration.[131]

In addition to correcting such images of slave life, southern writers were able to delineate other qualities of their society by elaborating upon the

20.  *"Negro Village on a Southern Plantation." Complex issues were raised by such images. These buildings resembled the simple log cabins in which many northerners lived. Such surroundings could be seen as a degraded environment that had to be improved, or they could be used to criticize the unconscionable wealth of northern merchants or southern planters.*

21.  *"Buckingham Hall." Adaptations of Palladian villas were built throughout the South during the antebellum period. Apologists for the South made no excuses for their opulence; magnificent houses suited the superior qualities of their owners.*

meanings of houses. The author of *Uncle Tom's Cabin Contrasted with Buckingham Hall* emphasized the fact that although black and white were inherently different, in the South each was treated according to his needs. The slaves in this novel lived in "white-washed cabins, surrounded by flowers and creeping plants." The neat rows of these houses looked like a well-ordered little town. In contrast, the master of the plantation, as suited his natural abilities and attainments, lived in Buckingham Hall, a kind of Palladian villa adapted to the southern climate. Every detail of this building showed "taste and elegance," evidence of the culture of the slave-owning class.[132]

By acknowledging that distinct strata of population existed in all societies, southern writers were able to make a pointed criticism of those who attacked slavery. They frequently cited the wide gulf between high and low in northern cities to show the cleanliness and neatness of their cabins, on the one hand, and the restraint and taste of their Buckingham Halls, on the other. Some of this criticism was also directed against England, where abolitionists had many supporters. Lucien B. Chase's *English Serfdom and American Slavery* was dedicated to those "aristocratic ladies of Great Britain" who looked with "graceful equanimity" on the horrible conditions of the "substratum of English society," while at the same time they discovered "fascinations in the sooty progeny of Ham." In this novel about working-class life in England, Chase contrasted the "wretched" cabins of rural weavers or the "damp" and "dimly lit" cellar tenements of London's laborers with the ostentatious houses of English aristocrats.[133]

More often, southern writers pointed to contrasts in the North, where houses also betrayed the inhumanity of an industrial society. *The North and South: Or, Slavery and Its Contrasts* explored one dimension of this theme by showing how the North made no provision for those who had once been wealthy but who, through adversity, had fallen into poverty. The novel traced the decline of a family that had once lived in a beautiful house, "furnished with all the adornments of wealth, all the luxurious comforts that make life pass like a 'golden holiday.'" This family was subsequently forced to live in a tiny tenement "in a little court up town known by the name of Quarry Street." The decline encapsulated in this change of habitation would not have occurred in the South, where there was no "unfeeling indifference," but was commonplace in the North, where acquisitive values dominated all others.[134]

Another telling contrast, of conditions under slavery with those in the North under freedom, was the gist of W. L. G. Smith's *Life at the South:*

*Or, Uncle Tom's Cabin As It Is.* The slave cabins in this novel had an "air of tidiness and gentility within." Tom, enticed by a northern teacher, left this benign setting and escaped to Buffalo, where he was exploited and could not make ends meet, even in a community established for runaway slaves. Finally, at the lowest ebb of his fortunes, hungry and almost frozen to death, Tom let his "memory carr[y] him back to that lowly but comfortable cabin, which never seemed half so dear before."[135]

The best-known of the works that drew this contrast in houses was William Grayson's *The Hireling and the Slave.* The slave's English counterpart, the hireling, lived: "In squalid hut — a kennel for the poor,/ Or noisome cellar, stretched out upon the floor. . . ." Compared with these conditions, "the cabin home, not comfortless, though rude," was a paradise. Grayson also chided the dreamers in the North who

> *. . . task their idle wits to find*
> *A short-hand method to enrich mankind.*
> *And Fourier's scheme or Owen's plans entice*
> *Expectant thousands with some deep device*
> *For raising wages, for aborting toil,*
> *And reaping crops from ill-attended soil.*[136]

Grayson could dismiss the communitarian experiments as foolish, but George Fitzhugh found a deeper significance for the South in the plans of Owen and Fourier. In *Sociology for the South and Cannibals All!* Fitzhugh rejected claims that government was based on the free association of equals. Instead, it had evolved to protect the weak from the strong. Blacks were manifestly unequal to whites, and thus southern society, which cared for and protected its slaves, was benevolent. Fitzhugh considered himself an advocate of socialism; he noted the decline of the peasantry in England and the sorry conditions of workers in Europe, and he looked forward to socialistic experiments there and in America. However, he considered that in many ways true socialism had already arrived in the South and that a plantation was "a form of communism" that Owen and Fourier might envy. The free laborer had none of the advantages of the slave. He had no place where he could "rightfully lay his head." He had "to inhale the close and putrid air of small rooms, damp cellars and crowded factories." But on the plantation all necessities were provided. Domestic affection thrived there, and it was, therefore, a true phalanstery.[137]

In the late 1850s, as positions in the sectional debate hardened, Americans feared that a permanent rift was all but inevitable. To demonstrate what North and South had in common they began desperately to search for symbols of national unity. One they found was Mount Vernon, George Washington's house on the banks of the Potomac.

The crusade to make Mount Vernon a national monument began in 1853 when Mrs. Louisa Cunningham, the wife of a wealthy South Carolina planter, was sailing from Philadelphia to Charleston. On that voyage she happened to catch a glimpse of Mount Vernon and was distressed by the estate's rundown condition. Since Washington's death in 1798, the house and farmland had passed through the hands of several descendants and in 1853 was the property of his great-nephew, who barely managed to keep the estate going. The house itself was in bad repair; some of the rooms had not been lived in for years, and many of the outbuildings had either been torn down or were unused.

Mrs. Cunningham's partially crippled daughter, Ann Pamela, heard about Mount Vernon's condition and was seized with the idea of purchasing the estate, restoring it, and presenting it to Virginia. In letters to newspapers she appealed for help to southern women. But with the aid of the actress and playwright Anna Cora Mowatt, she soon transformed this local appeal into a national movement, and in March 1856 the Mount

22.  *"Mount Vernon," the home of George Washington.*

Vernon Ladies' Association of the Union was chartered to raise money for the project.

The mission of Ann Pamela Cunningham and the ladies of the Mount Vernon Association went beyond the preservation of the estate. They believed that their actions had an important meaning for their times. Mount Vernon embodied the spirit of Washington, and Washington stood for national unity. Saving the estate through the combined activity of women in North and South would reflect what those involved hoped would happen in the realm of national politics. This nonprofit and totally disinterested cause was also an assertion of the values of the home over those of faction and competition that dominated the world of business and politics.[138]

Such sentiments were most forcefully expressed by the Mount Vernon Association's most important advocate, Edward Everett. Minister, man of letters, congressman, governor of Massachusetts, president of Harvard, secretary of state, and, in 1860, vice-presidential candidate of the Constitutional Union party, Everett was one of the few Americans in the late 1850s who tried to maintain the spirit of compromise Daniel Webster earlier had championed. Everett first spoke about George Washington as a symbol of national unity in a lecture in 1856 in Boston. He reminded his audience of what Jefferson had written to Washington in trying to dissuade the first President from declining a second nomination: "North and South will hang together while they have you to hang to." Everett wanted to make a national holiday of Washington's birthday, but shortly after the speech he heard about the association, and he decided to devote himself to that mission instead. On March 19, 1856, he delivered his speech again in Richmond, and when he met Miss Cunningham a few days later, he "consecrated" it to her. In the next three years Everett, whose nickname when a student at Harvard had been Ever-at-it, gave the speech 129 times, from Massachusetts to North Carolina and as far west as Detroit and St. Louis. Through these lectures Everett raised $70,000 for the cause, and on April 6, 1858, a contract to purchase Mount Vernon for $200,000 was finally signed.[139]

The crusade to save George Washington's home was, of course, only a partial success. The ladies of the Mount Vernon Association secured the estate for Americans to visit and enjoy, but their contemporaries were not impressed by the symbolic meaning that the women found in it. Even as the crusade was being carried out, some people noted that George Washington owned slaves, and they asked whether his house was, therefore, an appropriate national monument.

The ladies of the Mount Vernon Association hoped that Washington's home would be a symbol of national unity. But a more realistic appraisal of the nation's future, also in terms of homes, was made two months after the estate was purchased. On June 16, 1858, when a little-known Illinois lawyer accepted his party's nomination for a Senate seat, he summarized his message in one phrase: "A house divided against itself cannot stand." Abraham Lincoln's speech had an immediate and long-lasting impact. Within a few days the contents of the "House Divided" speech were discussed throughout the nation, Lincoln became a figure of national importance, and the debate about slavery took a direction that in two years led to a Civil War.[140]

While Lincoln probably would have conveyed the force of his message without the assistance of his metaphor, his choice of words was perceptive. "A house divided against itself cannot stand" was an encapsulation of a line from the Bible; the phrase had a long history of use. But in the half century before Lincoln's speech Americans had attached vital meanings and connotations to houses. By 1858 houses were charged with a significance that they did not previously have; any reference to them was sure to elicit an immediate response.

✦✦✦

The American interest in the home did not abate during the Civil War. In speeches and sermons politicians at home and ministers in the camps extended the meanings of houses developed in the period before the war. They spoke of the contrasted dwellings of North and South, not only to characterize the two civilizations, but also to remind citizens and soldiers of the cause at stake.

The home was most frequently referred to during the Civil War because no storm had ever shipwrecked more people than the years of fierce fighting. Americans both at home and in the camp needed to cling to an image of security and repose. When the Civil War started, most military experts believed that the conflict would be short. But the first Battle of Bull Run was not decisive, and then the fighting dragged on for months and years. The equipment and the techniques of combat rapidly improved, but there was no comparable development in medical and ambulance service. The resulting suffering and loss of life was without precedent.

Many of the new recruits had never before been far from home. Americans were deeply concerned, therefore, about the effect that fighting had

on the soldier's character. They also were worried about the evil influences to which he was susceptible in the camp. "Divorced from the
sympathies of home," the soldier became "the easy prey" of gambling,
drinking, prostitution, and other pernicious influences. New organizations
were formed to bolster the soldier's physical and spiritual health. In the
North the United States Sanitary Commission brought medical aid to
the soldiers. Its representatives raised money for supplies and set up hospitals to care for the wounded. A parallel organization, the United States
Christian Commission, took responsibility for spiritual needs, sending
volunteer ministers to visit camps and to tend to soldiers in distress.[141]

The representatives of these organizations often recognized that they
had a more general, but at the same time a more important, function.
They found that they could be most effective, not by bandaging wounds
or delivering sermons, but simply by acting as links between the home
and the camp. Walt Whitman, who served as a nurse to the Northern
troops, fully appreciated the importance of bringing home feeling to the
sick and wounded. In a letter to his mother he observed that the American
soldier was "full of affection and yearning for affection" and he was
grateful to have this yearning gratified when laid up with wounds, "far
away from home, among strangers." Whitman found that the presence
of a person who sent out "invisible, constant currents" of humanity and
love did the wounded more good than medicine.[142] Those who trained
and organized nurses often tried to minimize these qualities because they
wanted to establish badly needed standards of medical care. But nurses
frequently wrote about the good effects of simple human compassion, the
home feeling that the soldiers missed so much.[143]

Members of the Christian Commission found other ways to join the
home and the camp. They viewed the soldiers as "absent members of
Christian homes" and tried to act as "father, mother, brother, sister, wife
and friend, minister and church." They did so by emphasizing in their
sermons not the cold lessons of scripture, but themes that more easily
attracted the soldiers' sympathies.[144] Among them were the value and
example of the home. John F. W. Ware, a volunteer minister from
Boston, often spoke about this subject. In two sermons, *Home to the
Hospital* and *Home to the Camp*, which were printed in editions of
100,000 and distributed free, he called on soldiers to remember "the old
home love still about you, its invisible presence and influence enfolding,
upholding you" and to use this example to resist the temptations of the
camp.[145] Representatives of the Christian Commission also arranged

wholesome entertainment. One of the most popular activities they encouraged was baseball, the focus of which was "home." Baseball had only a gentlemanly reputation after it was first played in the 1830s, but its following greatly increased when it became a popular pastime in Northern camps during the Civil War.[146]

Auxiliaries of the commissions invented many methods to maintain "an electric chain between the hearth and the tent." Some of them achieved this end literally when they established a free telegraph service so that relatives could inquire about the well-being of brothers, husbands, and sons after a battle.[147] Other committees made or collected clothing and other needed goods for the soldiers. This handicraft was often exhibited or sold to raise funds at many "Sanitary Fairs" that women organized in cities throughout the country.[148]

No matter how effective these activities were, most Americans, especially women, understood that the best way to support the soldiers was simply to enhance the image of home. After the war Louisa May Alcott, who had been a nurse during the conflict, graphically described life at home during that difficult time in *Little Women*. Even while the war was being fought, there was a great outpouring of literature about the home virtues. The best examples were by Harriet Beecher Stowe and John F. W. Ware. At the beginning of the century these authors' famous fathers — Lyman Beecher and Henry Ware, the one a Congregationalist from Yale, the other a Unitarian president of Harvard — had been on opposite sides of an acrimonious theological dispute. By the time of the Civil War, however, their children had achieved a unanimity of outlook in their belief in the home. In *Home Life* Ware told how a child received "inevitable and indelible impressions from the house" in which he had been brought up, and then described some of the most important aspects of home religion.[149] In *House and Home Papers* and *The Chimney Corner* Harriet Beecher Stowe likewise emphasized the religious basis of home life, and since she also believed that "the influence of dwelling-houses for good or for evil . . . was one of those things that cannot be enough pondered," she gave her readers many hints about what made a good house.[150]

A direct way to project the image of home was suggested by the minister Samuel Osgood in "The Home and the Flag." Osgood explained that concepts such as "patriotism" and "country" were too abstract to inspire great emotions. It was important, therefore, to make "public interests a part of our private welfare." Unlike "country," "home" was "vivid

*23. The New England Kitchen at the Brooklyn and Long Island Fair, 1864. Northern women sponsored many fairs to raise funds for the Sanitary and Christian commissions. In producing goods for these fairs they began the first revival of interest in handicrafts and in the methods of production in the Age of Homespun.*

and stirring." Osgood noted that "with the sound of the word the eye rest[ed] upon or recall[ed] the cherished object itself." Because the home was "pictorial" and "graphic," allied with patriotism it would enable every American to "interpret his country by some such personal association." What sight could be more expressive, Osgood asked, than "the good mother seated at the window from which floats the household flag?" To transmit such associations, it became customary during the Civil War to display the flag near or on the home.[151]

Directly after the war a committee of doctors tried to assess its medical history. In addition to the many known diseases that were contracted during the Civil War, the authors noted the frequency of "nostalgia," an ailment that was hard to define. Throughout the Civil War doctors had often found soldiers paralyzed in their beds by "homesickness." Fixated by "images of home," those who suffered from this ailment were often so distracted that they were useless for action.[152]

The authors of this report did not reflect upon or draw conclusions about the origins or causes of nostalgia. Nor did most Americans. In the half century after the Civil War they rarely questioned the importance they attributed to the home. On the contrary, they became even more committed to that institution and were able to think about domestic architecture more thoroughly than before. The ensuing discussion proceeded at three levels. Some commentators were primarily interested in the context of the home. They tried to define in what kind of community the home could best be located and how to situate it among other houses. Other people were concerned about the house as property and as an architectural problem. They examined whether and how it should be owned and what it should look like. A third group was primarily interested in the interior of the home. They focused on what the proper purpose and relationship of rooms were, how to decorate and care for them, and how to connect them to mechanical servicing systems.

# 2

# THE HOME TOWN

IN 1820 THERE WERE 56 TOWNS in the United States with from 2,500 to 25,000 residents and 5 cities, ranging from New Orleans, with 27,000 inhabitants, to New York, where 152,000 people lived in what later would become the 5 boroughs. All told, these towns and cities contained only 7 percent of the nation's 9,618,000 inhabitants. In 1870 the percentage of people living in what had become 612 towns, 45 cities, and 6 metropolises with over 250,000 inhabitants had more than tripled: just under 25 percent of the 39,905,000 Americans lived in these communities. Urbanization continued in the following fifty years, so that by 1920 50 percent of the nation's 106,466,000 citizens lived in the 2,434 towns, 263 cities, and 25 metropolises.[1]

Although the rate of urban growth after the Civil War did not match that of the fifty years before the conflict, the increase in the number and size of communities in the postbellum period had a significance that the earlier development lacked. Before the Civil War, American communities, especially the larger cities, grew because of the expansion of those mercantile activities — trading, retailing, and warehousing — that had always been the basis of urban life. After the Civil War, the growth in the size and number of American communities was increasingly the result of manufacturing for nonlocal markets, an activity that existed at the beginning of the century only in small towns that were located near convenient sources of water power and that had little impact on large cities until steam power was available.[2]

This transformation of the American city from a mercantile to a manufacturing center was important because it set forces in motion that affected every aspect of urban life. It was also significant because the growth of cities at the beginning of the nineteenth century had occurred too suddenly, with too few precedents and with too much disruption for those who experienced it to think how these developments could best be directed. In the period from 1865 to 1915 Americans were often as bewildered by the changes they experienced as their ancestors had been, but at least by then they could see these developments from the perspective of a half century of urban growth. From that vantage point they were able to reflect constructively about what was happening. They then tried to formulate ideas both about what made a good community and about how to change their city or town to approximate that ideal. In the process they began to define such previously vague terms as neighborhood, village, town, suburb, and city. Once they did so, they could compare the merits of each type of settlement and assess which one was the best context for the home.

The ensuing discussion often centered around the distinction between town and city. Many Americans had lived in both and made the comparison on the basis of their own experience. William Dean Howells, for example, was born in 1837 in Martinsville, a hamlet on the Ohio side of Wheeling, West Virginia. When he was three, his parents settled in Hamilton, a town in southwestern Ohio. The family spent the next nine years there, but then changed homes frequently as Howells's father, a ne'er-do-well printer and journalist, sought employment in Ohio communities such as Eureka Mills, Ashtabula, and Jefferson.

In these wanderings the Howellses also stopped for periods in the growing urban centers of Cincinnati and Columbus. The future novelist and magazine editor realized that a literary career could best be nurtured in cities, and, after four years as American consul in Venice, he settled in Boston. He stayed there until 1885 when he moved to New York, where he remained until his death in 1910. But even while Howells lived in these two great East Coast centers, he continued to experience the contrasts between town and city. Howells tried to spend every summer in rural villages such as Townsend Harbor and Shirley, Massachusetts; Saratoga, New York; Kennebunkport, Maine; and Jaffrey, New Hampshire.

Although they found it convenient and telling to distinguish between town and city in discussing the nature of communities, Americans also drew another important level of contrast. They recognized that within both town and city there were many types of places in which to live. William Dean Howells knew that even the smallest villages in Ohio had different neighborhoods, and when he settled in Boston he and his wife found a wide choice of places in which to locate their home. They first settled in suburban Cambridge. Two and a half years later they moved to the newly built Back Bay area near the center of Boston. Within a year the Howellses went back to Cambridge, but they soon became dissatisfied with their house and decided to build a new one. Five years after they moved into this home they left it, this time to reside in Belmont, a small farming community then being settled by people who commuted to Cambridge and Boston. After three years of life in what was a distant suburb, the Howellses returned to the city, first to an apartment hotel in central Cambridge and then to a furnished apartment on Beacon Hill, the old section of Boston.

In addition to these choices of places in which to live, Howells frequently noticed that both town and city had areas in which he would never make his home, but in which those less fortunate had to reside. Every town had the "other side of the tracks," and so did cities. Boston's workingmen and its poor lived in their own neighborhoods, some in tenements in or close to fashionable districts in the downtown, others in pockets of suburban settlements. As Howells walked through the areas adjacent to Beacon Hill or in the Back Bay and as he traveled through unfamiliar districts in his horsecar rides from Cambridge to Boston, he could not help but reflect that the people in these places lived in the same city, and yet he knew little about them. As a novelist and concerned citizen, he set himself the task of finding out more.[3]

This multiplicity of places in which to live was made even more bewildering by the fact that both town and city were always changing. The boundaries and the areas within each contracted or expanded; at the same time the tone of the districts improved or declined. Like William Dean Howells, many Americans did not live in one place for very long, but even those who did could never take the context of their home for granted.

Confronted by these conditions, Americans frequently wondered not just in what kind of community they might best establish their home; they also asked what made a particular village, town, city, or neighborhood a community in the first place.

✦✦✦

Of all the places in which Howells lived, the one he remembered most fondly was Hamilton, Ohio, the small town in which he spent much of his boyhood and about which he wrote his autobiographical *A Boy's*

*Town.* In the half century after the Civil War most American writers shared Howells's appreciation of the small town. They found its local color an inexhaustible subject for their literature and implied that this setting had qualities that made it a far better place in which to live than either the isolated farm or the large city.[4]

Historians of the same period confirmed this judgment. Herbert Baxter Adams and John Fiske located the origins of democratic government in the institutions of the small town of Germanic Europe. They then traced how that seed had been transplanted to the New England towns of the colonial period and how the system of democratic government that was the mainstay of American society had eventually blossomed in those places. In carrying out these studies of the past, Adams and Fiske drew a lesson for their own times: if democratic institutions were to continue to flourish, they would have to do so in a context similar to that in which they had initially grown.[5]

Many Americans of widely divergent political beliefs agreed that the town provided the best context for the nation's economic life. Before the Civil War, Federalists and Whigs eulogized the hierarchical society of the small town as the ideal productive unit. In the following half century the inheritors of this tradition continued to emphasize the virtues of the town, whether its economic life was based in farming or manufacturing. Likewise, Jacksonians favored the town because it was the location of the freely operating, decentralized economy they admired. After the Civil War, many reformers championed a similar environment as they tried to adapt values of the earlier period to the conditions of their times.[6]

There were other reasons to support the town. Doctors and sanitarians claimed that the small, sparsely settled community was healthier than the city; ministers wrote and preached that Christian values could best be maintained in the intimate context of the town. But although many Americans admired the town, few such places actually possessed the order and stability attributed to them. Many suffered decline, some during periods of national depression, others when for local reasons their primary sources of livelihood suddenly dried up. No matter how it happened, the effects of decline were similar, and they were frequently described by the town's spokesmen. First, the enterprising inhabitants of the town left to seek better opportunities elsewhere. Their absence then affected the quality of life in the town. Little money was spent on "educating and civilizing forces," which sometimes completely disappeared. Once this process was set in motion, the slow "downward drag" soon accelerated.

In a short time the cultivated life of the town was replaced by "crude and low and gross" habits, and what had been a friendly community split into acrimonious factions. With these developments went a decline in the town's appearance. Houses were not painted; gardens and lawns went to seed.[7]

Other towns grew quickly, but the effects of economic prosperity could be as severe as decline. When a quiet town suddenly attracted an industry, when it became a stop on a railroad or canal, or when it became an important marketing center for agricultural produce or livestock, the social relationships that had earlier sustained it were easily destroyed. The qualities of intimacy that older inhabitants remembered soon disappeared when newcomers, especially those who did not speak English as their native language, arrived. As the distance between rich and poor and old and new increased, jealousies arose and disputes broke out among neighbors. A deterioration in the town's physical condition usually accompanied these difficulties. Ugly mills or railroad depots began to dominate the town's pastoral landscape, rivers became polluted, and increased traffic turned quiet pathways into noisy streets.[8]

Citizens who were concerned about these problems tried to deal with them through a wide variety of economic, social, religious, charitable, educational, and governmental reforms. But they also thought it was important to upgrade their physical surroundings. They made the case for these projects in three ways. Better roads or a more efficient railroad station enhanced the economic prospects of the community. An improved sewage system, clean streets, and the passage of legislation that dealt with other sanitation problems all helped to make a salubrious environment and thus contributed to the well-being of the town. Finally, citizens tried to make their town attractive, because they thought that a handsome setting would lure new residents to the community. But the creation of a beautiful town also had other, higher purposes that gave meaning to activities that might otherwise have seemed insignificant or ineffectual.

Those who wanted to improve their town's appearance thought that beauty had a strong moral and social value. They believed that beauty in the town, as in domestic architecture, exercised a beneficial influence on those who experienced it and that harmonious surroundings reflected and also helped to produce a harmonious community. The creation of a beautiful town was important also because, since it was work to which everyone could contribute, it served as a model of cooperation to be used in other aspects of the life of the often divided town. A campaign for beauty, a completely altruistic and nonmaterialistic goal, might, therefore, result in much more than an attractive town. It could start a general awakening of civic spirit and pride. Local households would then become "members of a larger family — the village family." When that happened, a "common interest and a common feeling would characterize the place and regulate the style and tone of life."[9]

Projects to improve a town's physical setting were initiated by village improvement societies. Antecedents of these organizations can be traced back to the seventeenth century. In the antebellum period they were frequently founded in rural districts to provide their members with a forum for entertainment and discussion. But they also began to carry out improvement projects or to try to convince the local government to do so. Horace Bushnell often urged the formation of such organizations so that people who lived in the country could share information about agriculture and could sponsor events that would be both entertaining and educational. At the same time he also discussed the importance of improvements to the local environment.[10] Andrew Jackson Downing frequently commented on the same theme. He believed that the power of beauty should be felt not only around the home but also in a much wider sphere, and so he urged his readers to initiate improvement projects in their towns.[11]

After the Civil War, village improvement societies continued to try to "quicken the intellectual life of the people" by supporting public education, helping to found libraries, organizing lyceum lectures, and establishing village reading rooms. They also promoted "good fellowship." Many improvement societies sponsored seasonal fairs and festivals and helped the town to celebrate national holidays by organizing parades. One of the year's most popular events in a small town was Old Home Day, which improvement organizations arranged for former inhabitants.[12]

Although the sponsoring and organizing of such activities and events was an important part of a village improvement society's work, after the Civil War these organizations were most widely known for their efforts to upgrade the physical setting of a town. The first society formed primarily to act as custodian of the local environment was the Laurel Hill Association, founded in 1853 in Stockbridge, Massachusetts. In subsequent years many other organizations with a similar purpose were started.[13]

The most important early supporter of village improvement was a friend of Horace Bushnell, a minister and teacher named Birdsey Grant

Northrop. Born in the farming community of Kent, Connecticut, in 1817, Northrop was called to the pastorate in Saxonville, Massachusetts, in 1845. During the ten years that he spent in this tiny hamlet, Northrop developed not only an appreciation of the problems of the small community, but also a broad conception of his function as a minister. In an attempt to enhance the welfare of Saxonville's residents, Northrop supplemented his duties in the church with educational work, and in 1857 he resigned his pastorate to devote himself to that cause. Although Northrop always believed in the power of the schools, by the late 1860s he was looking for an even more comprehensive way to influence Americans. He then realized that education would be effective only if communities subscribed to a more thorough "improvement" program. In 1869 he first wrote down his ideas about village improvement societies. But by then he had already lectured throughout New England on the subject. In the following decades he traveled throughout the United States and even to Hawaii to spread this idea.[14]

Village improvement societies were popular in farming communities where ministers, tradesmen, lawyers, other leading citizens, and especially local housewives often promoted the cause. These societies also flourished in manufacturing towns, particularly those dominated by an industry whose owner often acted as a benefactor of the community. Although village improvement began in New England and was always associated with that region, the concept was equally popular elsewhere, especially in new settlements. There were many societies in California, in the South, and throughout the Midwest.

Village improvement was attractive not only to residents, whose stake was clear, but also to those who had moved away yet wished to maintain ties with their home town. Some of the most noted improvement work was sponsored by wealthy people who, in effect, adopted towns. Another class of people took an interest in a town because they spent their vacations there. In the years after the Civil War many Americans who traveled in the summer to small villages by the sea or in the mountains were acutely conscious of the contrast between city and country and wanted to help preserve the best features of the communities they visited. Tracing this pattern of interest, one writer concluded that village improvement was "the offspring of the cities," and was often "paid for and engineered by those who have enjoyed city advantages."[15]

The work of village improvement societies varied. It depended on the nature of the town and the problems at hand, and in most communities it was entered into with no overall plan. Nevertheless, an underlying concept did guide the village improvement projects undertaken both in a particular place over a long period and in different towns across the nation. This fundamental goal was to make the town or village seem more town or villagelike. Such an end presupposed an image of an ideal community. The frequent use of the word "village" in itself was an expression of what the advocates of improvement had in mind. The vague image conjured up by this word was made more specific through references to two types of settlements.

One type was the New England town in its prime. Many of the people who started improvement societies had grown up in New England towns, and even if they later moved elsewhere they always admired that type of community. Others may never have been in New England, yet because their ancestors had come from that region, they maintained a loyalty to it. The other type was the foreign or folk community. Those who could not claim an allegiance to New England or who, having moved from that region, wanted to sever connections with it, often sought an alternative model in European sources. In the Southwest and in California, images of Indian or Spanish-American settlements sometimes came into play. These references were not based on any deep understanding of the forces that had shaped these towns and what they had actually been like. That knowledge might have challenged some of the most important preconceptions of the village improvement supporters and might have deterred them from pursuing their larger goals.

The first settlements in New England were made under special circumstances. The people who started them signed a covenant stipulating that the land of the township was to be held jointly. Home lots were granted to the head of each family and varied in size according to his wealth, the number of his dependents, and the services he performed for the community. Families were not allowed to settle anywhere they wanted in the township, which sometimes contained as much as a hundred square miles. Instead, the home lots of all members fronted on a street that served as the boundary for an area of common land. Farmland was located beyond this cluster of houses and was divided into small parcels that were distributed among the settlers to equalize variations in quality and location. No individual member of the community, therefore, possessed and lived on one large tract.[16]

This pattern of settlement did not last more than a few generations. It was considered a liability because farmers lost time walking from their homes to the dispersed parcels of land. It was also impractical because it did not provide for the growth of the community. As more settlers arrived, it soon became difficult to add to the cluster of houses. New and some-times competing villages were then started within the township. Dispersal increased when sons were given outer parcels on which to settle. Most important, with the passage of time the community lost the unity of purpose that had been the foundation of the original settlement. Children and grandchildren did not share their parents' commitment to the idea of the town, and recently arrived dissenters further weakened the bond of unanimity that had held the community together. Without this com-mon outlook, attitudes toward the land changed. By the beginning of the eighteenth century some towns even began to sell some of their land as a source of revenue.[17]

When the Marquis de Chastellux traveled in New England in the 1780s, he commented that "a *town* or *township*, is only a certain number of houses, dispersed over a great space, but which belong to the same incorporation." The center of this town, he observed, was a meetinghouse or church, but it usually either stood alone or had only four or five houses nearby. The village of houses clustered around a green had all but disappeared.[18]

The pattern of settlement in New England, therefore, had become similar to that in the mid-Atlantic states and the South, where huge tracts of land had been given by the British government to great proprietors. Since these men derived revenue from settlers, they often sold their land to promoters or speculators. Unable to develop large tracts of land them-selves, the new owners continually subdivided and sold the land as more colonists arrived.[19]

The shape of towns in the West was determined by the original pattern of land subdivision. In 1785, on the suggestion of Thomas Jefferson, Con-gress authorized a checkerboard grid for all territory north and west of the Ohio River. Government surveyors marked out twenty-four north and south lines, called the "principal meridians." The first was the dividing line between Ohio and Indiana; the last went through Oregon a little west of Portland. On each side of a principal meridian, subordinate meridians, called range lines, were marked off every six miles. Then a parallel of latitude, a base line, was drawn, and on each side of it township lines at six-mile intervals were marked off. Each township was further divided into thirty-six one-mile-square sections.[20]

This system had precedents that went back at least as far as ancient

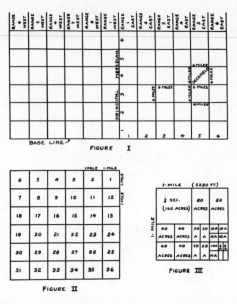

FIGURE I

FIGURE II

FIGURE III

24. *The American system of land subdivision. This pattern of land surveying was authorized by Congress in 1785 and was the basis of much of the land subdivision west of the Ohio River.*

Greece. It was sensible because it made possible the division of vast tracts of land quickly and efficiently. The laying out of this grid was more than a convenience, however. It had a profound impact on the subsequent development of the western territory. Although within each township a section was often reserved for a town, the rest of the land was sold off in large parcels, often either a quarter, a half, or a whole section. Because of the size of these farms, it was not practical for owners to live in a town and travel to their fields each day. Instead, they settled on their land, which was joined to the other farms of the township by country roads that were usually laid out along the section lines.[21]

Within towns the grid was usually retained for the pattern of local streets. One defect of such a grid was that since its lines converged only at right angles, it was difficult for a town to have a true focus. To compensate for this weakness, diagonal streets were occasionally superimposed on the grid. Not only did these streets make it easier to travel from one side of the town to the other, they also met at a central intersection.[22]

Since diagonal streets usually could be laid out only by cutting across the land of many property owners, most towns had to provide for a center in a simpler manner. Usually two streets, one north-south and the other east-west, were widened to indicate the town's main thoroughfares, and at the point where they intersected a block of land was designated as a public park or, following the New England analogy, a village green. Before the Civil War, a few towns planned on the surveying grid included spaces to serve as the focus of the community, but these towns were the exceptions to a monotonous rule.[23]

This varied history of land settlement was the background against which village improvement work was set. Many improvement projects were undertaken to rectify the mistakes of the past, whether consciously so or not. Supporters of improvement were especially disturbed by the lack of compactness in American towns. To enhance a community's appearance and increase opportunities for social intercourse, those interested in improvement often wrote about how to concentrate a community's buildings and prevent the helter-skelter spread of new development. Horace Bushnell stressed these issues before the Civil War. In a speech called "City Plans" he explained how to lay out a town for beauty and convenience. He stressed that cities in vast plains "extending in every direction" inflicted a "painful vacuity and an insupportable weariness." An inward-looking town not only was more practical because diverse facilities were closer at hand but also nurtured the "feeling of art and community." It was more attractive and enabled its inhabitants to communicate more readily with each other.[24]

After the Civil War, local improvement organizations often emphasized as their most important goal the creation of a suitable town center. When new towns were started, it was possible to designate a space for the green, common, or square from the beginning, but in older towns either a space had to be cleared or, if the semblance of one already existed, it had to be cleaned up and landscaped in a more attractive manner. The design of these village squares varied. A prominent building, a courthouse, a school, a library, or occasionally a church was sometimes set in the green. Of these structures the library was often considered the most important because it symbolized a commitment to knowledge and education that the members of improvement societies felt was the ultimate basis of the town's prosperity. After the Civil War, the idea spread rapidly, and a campaign for a public library often became the focus of improvement work.[25] The Village Improvement and Library Association of Pasadena, California, for instance, in the first years of its existence not only built a library but also made plans for the extension of the town. Because of the association's work, Pasadena was known as the "model town of Southern California."[26]

Although buildings were occasionally placed in the center of the green

*25. "Effect of Village Improvement Work at Charlotte, North Carolina."
The geometry of the planting was designed to override the effect of the
railroad siding, but the two form a telling contrast.*

*26. "School Gardens Combined with the Decoration of a Railroad Station
at Jamestown, North Dakota." Improvement societies often worked with
schools to beautify a town.*

or square, it was more common to locate them on the other sides of surrounding streets, leaving the space open, usually to be landscaped with
grass and shade trees. Often the planting scheme was arranged around a
Civil War monument. The erection of this memorial was only one of
several ways in which a town could make an overt demonstration of its
history. Village improvement societies frequently tried to save old buildings, often the home of the original settler, and sometimes converted these
structures into a local historical society.[27]

By coordinating the style of the buildings around the square or simply
by regulating their heights and their relationship to the adjacent street, it
was possible to create an effect of architectural uniformity, an outward
manifestation of the town's common purpose. In many towns merchants
tried to achieve the same effect along commercial streets. They often
started organizations, either chambers of commerce or fraternal societies,
that sponsored improvement programs to designate a specific area as a
business district and to set standards for its upkeep and appearance. Not
only did such work enhance local pride, but by identifying a business
district it gave the lethargic-looking town an appearance of activity.[28]

Another point of interest was the town's most prominent entrance, the
railroad station. Improvement associations encouraged railroad companies
to build more than utilitarian stations, to landscape them attractively, and
to control the all too frequent unruly sprawl of adjacent stables and
warehouses. An attractive station was particularly important in towns
that hoped to benefit from the trade of summer vacationers. One of the
most articulate advocates of village improvement, the author Donald G.
Mitchell, was especially adamant about the value of a pleasing station.
"Every little village," he reasoned, wanted "its little outlying green to
give character and dignity" to this important approach to the town. First
impressions counted a great deal, and a captivating village station would
attract vacationers who wanted to be "wooed to some summer home,"
where the trees "invite tranquility and promise enjoyment."[29]

Beyond the central square and the business district was the residential
sector of the town. The goal of village improvement activity in these
areas was to establish a uniformity of landscaping and architecture. The
owners of houses that were also business establishments were encouraged
to put evidence of nonresidential uses in the rear. Property owners helped
to establish the continuity of the street by deciding to build the same
fence or to have none at all, and the citizens of some towns chose a
common color for their houses. Sometimes they even volunteered to
move their houses to establish a uniform setback from the street. Some

village improvement societies also made available approved plans for domestic architecture.[30]

Public parks often linked residential areas both to the countryside beyond and to the central square of the business district. Horace Bushnell mounted a campaign in Hartford in 1854 for one of the earliest of these parks, and after the Civil War members of improvement associations often devoted much of their activity to convincing local governments to set aside land for this purpose. Some towns were given parks by benefactors. In Haddam, Connecticut, for instance, in 1878 a prominent local family donated two parks, which were designed by Frederick Law Olmsted. Such parks usually were only for recreation, but sometimes they contained important institutions. In the 1860s the Episcopal bishop Henry B. Whipple located the Seabury Divinity School, the Shattuck School for boys, and St. Mary's Hall for girls in a park of several hundred acres in Faribault, Minnesota. Cemeteries were also often used as parks. As early as 1831, when Mount Auburn Cemetery was laid out on the outskirts of Cambridge, Massachusetts, village burial grounds had been designed to serve this purpose.[31]

27. "A Street Fountain," erected by an improvement society in Calhoun, Georgia. The solidity of the fountain contrasts with the makeshift and unkempt houses nearby.

Because the different areas of the town were connected by its streets and roads, the village improvement society would make a special effort to improve the quality and appearance of its thoroughfares. It provided rustic seats under shady trees for the comfort of pedestrians, built sidewalks to make it possible to avoid muddy streets, and placed water troughs for horses at convenient spots. It also tried to have laws enacted to prevent the dropping of rubbish by the roadside and the painting of advertisements on prominent rocks. Connected with this work were efforts to make a better surface for roads, to construct proper sewage systems, and to designate a special place for the dumping of garbage.[32]

The most important feature of the street, and the element which contributed the most toward a continuity of greenery throughout a town, was its trees. In many places the primary activity of village improvement societies was the planting of trees. Settlers from Europe had early recognized the value of the abundant trees of North America. Trees gave shade that relieved the torrid summer heat, and it was thought that they acted as ventilators to improve the atmosphere and thus the health of the immediate environment. Throughout the colonial period and the first half of the nineteenth century, a few Americans continually urged the planting of trees. But the idea of focusing this activity in a tree-planting day was conceived in 1872 by J. Sterling Morton, formerly the governor of Nebraska. Morton, who was born in New York, regretted the barrenness of his adopted state and planted many trees around his home, Arbor Lodge. He started Arbor Day in Nebraska by offering rewards for the planting of the most trees. The contest was an immediate success and was repeated yearly. By the 1880s most states had followed Nebraska's lead and had designated a day, usually in April, for the planting of trees.[33]

For J. Sterling Morton trees had a great practical value, but their larger importance was symbolic. Trees did not simply embody beauty and the associated ideals of moral and social harmony; they had an even more profound meaning. In a speech at the University of Nebraska Morton explained that "as arboretums are developing the infant forests . . . so in the schools, the colleges, and universities are growing the mental timber" out of which would be made "those pillars and supports which are to bear up forever in America civil and religious liberty." He urged his audience "to plant wisely for years to come," and that was why, when Birdsey Grant Northrop suggested at a meeting of the National Education Association in 1884 that Arbor Day be recognized in the nation's schools, his resolution was adopted unanimously.[34]

28.  Jarvis Hunt: "A Village Street — Before and After"; Front Street,
Wheaton, Illinois, 1910. Hunt conceived the idea of giving Wheaton

In plans for an ideal farming community George Waring, the prominent sanitary engineer and authority on farming, illustrated how many of these elements of a town could be drawn together. Waring based his plan for a farm community on a standard township divided into settlements two miles square. Each of these had a central village, a quarter-mile square, surrounded by farms of varying sizes. The core of the village was a public park located at the intersection of two main streets. North and south of the square were sites for two churches, a schoolhouse, a store, and a tavern.

*"unity" and drew this scheme. His plan was to save the best of the old buildings but to give them new identities with stucco, brick, and half-timbering.*

Waring imagined these buildings as surrounded by trees, but the public park was to remain free of other landscaping. "Smooth, well-kept grass, and large trees planted in formal lines with an entire absence of fences, posts, chains, bushes, and all decorations" gave the area "a dignity and character which an excess of ornamentation would spoil."

On the streets leading east and west, Waring laid out sixteen lots, each 100 by 250 feet. On the streets leading north and south there were twelve lots, 50 by 650 feet, and eight lots, 100 by 650 feet. All the village lots were large enough for a kitchen-garden, barn, and barnyard, and all had

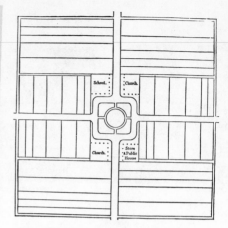

| 160 | 80 | 80 | 80 | 80 | 160 |
| 80 | 40 | 40 | 40 | 40 | 80 |
| 80 | 40 | 10 10 / 10 | 10 10 / 10 | 40 | 80 |
| 80 | 40 | 10 / 10 10 | 10 / 10 10 | 40 | 80 |
| 80 | 40 | 40 | 40 | 40 | 80 |
| 160 | 80 | 80 | 80 | 80 | 160 |

29. *George Waring: "Division of Four Square Miles with Central Village,"* a proposal for a farm village planned on the ordinance grid.

30. *George Waring: "Division of the Central Village."* Waring deflected the grid to create this central green space.

access from the rear so that their lawns could be kept clear. They could then be used for "ornamental purposes" and would enhance the village's appearance.

Waring speculated that the village population might be composed of two clergymen, two storekeepers, a doctor, a teacher, a baker, a shoe-maker, a tailor, a carpenter, a wheelwright, a blacksmith, a dressmaker, an innkeeper, and forty-four farmers. All told, there would be fifty-eight households with about three hundred fifty people. Waring acknowledged that the actual composition of the population would vary, but he thought that his allocation of occupations could be approximated in any agricultural village of this type.

Waring also devised a plan for a district that had already been settled and that was not based on a grid subdivision. He chose an area near Newport, Rhode Island, the same size as his farm example and with no semblance of a "neighborhood" at any point. Most of the sixty houses were occupied by farm families, but the area had few of the trades that were necessary to support this population. Waring's plan was to take land in the center of the district and set it aside for a compact village. He reasoned that the owners of large properties could create a suitable location for the village center by pooling odd parcels of their contiguous land. They would then donate the resulting area to the village and would agree to sell small building lots at a fixed low rate. Once a church, school-house, and store had been established as a "nucleus," other people might find it attractive to settle nearby.

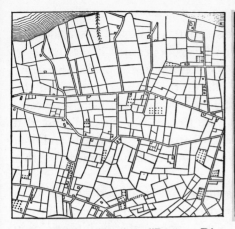 

31. *George Waring: "Present Division and Settlement of Tract in Rhode Island, Two Miles Square."*

32. *George Waring: "The Rhode Island Tract, with its Buildings Gathered into a Compact Village."*

The "characteristic feature" of Waring's town would be a single long strip, two hundred feet wide, mainly of grass, with either two or four rows of elms, leaving only a minimal width for a road and pathways. The church and the schoolhouse would be placed in broad recesses opposite the central point of the street. A line of simple fences would border the street front. Every part of the town would then "breathe homely influence and moral peacefulness."[35]

George Waring's plan of 1877, although smaller and for fewer people, was essentially the same as that adopted in 1908 by the Reclamation Service. This organization was started to restore wasteland in the West to fecundity. Those who conceived of the program did not envisage dispersed farms on this land. Instead, they planned towns for 1,000 to 5,000 people. All holdings of forty or eighty acres would be within three or four miles of these settlements. The town was based on a half-mile square, divided into eight sections by orthogonal and diagonal streets. Each of these sections was subdivided into house lots, which decreased in size toward the center. The nucleus of the town was a public square with a schoolhouse. Around the sides of this space were the town hall, post office, library, telegraph office, telephone exchange, and fire station.[36]

The plans of Waring and the Reclamation Service represent the continuity of an ideal of the village over almost half a century. But no matter how optimistic they were about their projects, the supporters of village improvement usually had to recognize that they had not achieved the results they had hoped for. One response to village improvement work was to acknowledge its ineffectiveness and to emphasize how much remained to be done. Supporters of improvement learned it was easier to state that there should be a "logical relationship and a perfect harmony between the different parts of the village" than it was to achieve this ideal. Buildings supposed to give prestige to a town often merely revealed how provincial the place actually was. Critics sometimes found that ambitious landscaping schemes were only partially executed, and that other gestures of beautification had been guided by sentimental rather than enduring aesthetic principles.

If these failings were apparent in farming communities, they were even more glaring in places with a mixed economy. It was never clear how to integrate factories and railroad yards into a concept that had its origins in a period before such facilities existed. Although supporters of improvement continually referred to the farm village, they were realistic enough to acknowledge that the livelihood of most small settlements depended in part on factors other than agriculture. In principle the pattern of settlement embodied in images of the New England or folk town was sufficiently flexible and general to accommodate new elements, but in reality efforts to make factories or railroad depots part of the whole were rarely successful. These new features were out of scale with the rest of the town and no matter where they were located and what was done to them, they always seemed to remain eyesores.[37]

Work places such as factories, railroad yards, and mills were not the only discordant elements in the town's landscape. The residents of the town ideally were supposed to live in different-sized houses on different-sized lots, as befitted their occupations and general stations in life. Despite these variations the houses were to be similar in that they were all situated on their own lots and were linked together by trees, fences, and universally adopted colors. Still, few improvement societies ever succeeded in instituting a full and effective set of these unifying measures.

More worrying was the presence of two kinds of houses that were completely outside the ideal pattern. Many towns had "exclusive" or "best" areas that were sharply demarcated from the rest of the community. They also often had, sometimes only a few yards from the center, blocks of tenements and areas with dense warrens of small wooden shacks. These buildings were sometimes considered positive elements because, in the case of the exclusive homes, they enhanced the town's reputation in the eyes of outsiders, or because, in the case of the closely clustered housing, they contributed to the compactness of the town's center. But this interpretation was not commonly accepted.[38]

Members of improvement societies found ready explanations for their lack of success in controlling the town's appearance. Those who took note of the poor quality of public buildings sometimes learned that the architect who designed these structures and the contractor who erected them had been chosen by local officials in an illegal or unethical manner. Others who wondered why and how a railroad had been granted a right of way through public land also found that something shady had taken place.

If there was so much disregard for the common interest in the disposition and use of public land, it was even harder to find evidence of a broader concern in what was done with private property. Thorstein Veblen, who knew as much about the country town as anyone, thought that real estate speculation was so central to the life of the town that he called it, and not some higher purpose, the "common bond of community interest." If land speculation was "the great American game . . . second only to poker," it was not hard to determine why there was so little interest in making improvements.[39]

The politics of many towns were scandalous by any standard, and individuals often outrageously abused their property rights. But by emphasizing extreme cases of corruption and avarice, members of improvement societies were able to avoid coming to terms with other explanations of what was happening in the town. It was possible to interpret what appeared to be disorder as a diversity that reflected the working out of the many varied and conflicting interests of the town. Improvement associations always believed that it was possible to define what the common or public interest was and that the town's physical appearance should be a reflection of that larger purpose. They wanted so complete a state of harmony that there would virtually be no need for politics at all. That was why most improvement organizations remained independent of political parties. They undertook their own projects and acted in an advisory capacity only.

Despite this stance and the higher purpose it was supposed to represent, village improvement often increased rather than relieved the friction within a town. When Andrew Jackson Downing tried to have the pigs removed from the streets of Newburgh, New York, where local residents had long let them roam, his efforts were vociferously opposed.[40] That scenario was often played out after the Civil War as improvement work was identified with the interests of a particular group, not with a common purpose. Farmers often wanted nothing to do with improvement work because they associated it with the town's genteel folk, some of whom were merchants with a monopoly on the trade from those

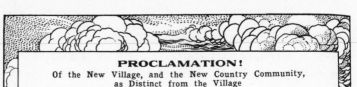

## PROCLAMATION!
### Of the New Village, and the New Country Community, as Distinct from the Village

THIS is a year of bumper crops, of harvest-home festivals. Through the mists of the happy waning year, a new village rises, and the new country community, in visions revealed to the rejoicing heart of faith.

And yet it needs no vision to see them. Walking across this land I have found them, little ganglions of life, promise of thousands more. The next generation will be that of the eminent village. The son of the farmer will be no longer dazzled and destroyed by the fires of the metropolis. He will travel, but only for what he can bring back. Just as his father sends half-way across the continent for good corn, or melon-seed, so he will make his village famous by transplanting and growing this idea or that. He will make it known for its pottery or its processions, its philosophy or its peacocks, its music or its swans, its golden roofs or its great union cathedral of all faiths. There are a thousand miscellaneous achievements within the scope of the great-hearted village. Our agricultural land to-day holds the plowboys who will bring these benefits. I have talked to these boys. I know them. I have seen their gleaming eyes.

And the lonely country neighborhood, as distinct from the village, shall make itself famous. There are river valleys that will be known all over the land for their tall men and milk-white maidens, as now for their well-bred horses. There are mountain lands that shall cultivate the tree of knowledge, as well as the apple-tree. There are sandy tracts that shall constantly ripen red and golden citrus fruit, but as well, philosophers comforting as the moon, and strength-giving as the sun.

These communities shall have their proud circles. They shall have families joined hand in hand for generations, to the end that new blood and new thoughts be constantly brought in, and no good force or leaven be lost. The country community shall awaken illustrious. This by faith, and a study of the signs, we proclaim!

NICHOLAS VACHEL LINDSAY.

(By courtesy of Farm and Fireside, Springfield, O.)

*33. Vachel Lindsay: "Proclamation! Of the New Village." Lindsay was one of many writers who hoped that the village would become a center for the enhancement of culture and that the United States would become a "new New England of ninety million people." Even so, as this proclamation indicates, he could not decide whether the village or the isolated farm was the ideal settlement.*

living in outlying districts. The farmers pointed out that better roads, rural free delivery of mail, telephones, mail-order catalogs, and, after the turn of the century, motor transportation all made the farm less isolated. They preferred to improve these services rather than to spend money on projects to make the town an attractive nucleus. This argument about the relative merits of centralization and dispersal often came to a head when a decision about school location had to be made. Supporters of village improvement claimed that one virtue of a compact town was that children could easily walk to a school, which, as a symbol of learning and improvement, was best located in the center near the green. Others argued that the real need was for better transportation or more schools, which, since they primarily served those in outlying areas, were best situated on the fringe of a town.[41]

Many improvement societies were not themselves happy families. Conflicting interests had to be worked out in them as well. Sometimes these differences were about matters of principle. The societies were always open to the criticism that in trying to create an attractive environment they were dealing only with what was on the surface. Some members argued that less visible but more urgent projects should be undertaken. Other disputes centered on more specific matters — whether, for instance, to spend scarce funds for a project in one part of a town or in another. Such arguments widened precisely those rifts that improvement was supposed to close.

Improvement was most successful in the few villages and towns that had one dominant group, but even in these special places the work was often met with, and was in part eroded by, an undercurrent of simmering resentment. This was sometimes expressed by older residents or those who remembered the town before it had been improved. Frederick Law Olmsted was well aware of some of the adverse consequences of improvement. He once recalled a town he had visited in his childhood. That rural community had a "consistent expression of character" in its architecture and its local landscape. It was "simple, unsophisticated, respectable"; it had a timeless beauty that Olmsted had never seen surpassed. This quality had been achieved with "no rural cemetery, no village improvement association, no branch of the Art Decorative, no reading club for the art periodicals, no park or parklet, no soldiers' monument, no fountains." And yet Olmsted imagined, with obvious bitterness, that all these features had since become part of the town. He speculated that what had been an unpretentious settlement probably now was connected

OLD HOME.

*34. "Residence of R. J. Allen, Section 12, Valley Centre Township,"
Kansas, ca. 1880. Such farms were sufficiently large to make daily contact
with the nearest town difficult. Although there must have been enough*

by railroad to a nearby city, that a large hotel had been constructed there, that several retired citizens had built "unretiring villas," that old houses had been "fixed up" and fences taken down, that tar walks had been laid, and that correspondents of the press were filling columns with "reports of improvement." The village probably had become so self-consciously quaint that it was really no longer a village at all.[42]

A similar pattern was sometimes evident in towns that were not vacation or suburban annexes of larger cities. The "frontier town" in which the novelist and literary critic French Strother lived did not suffer a decline or, as Horace Bushnell put it, a "reversion to barbarism" after the first years of settlement. The town had been transformed from one with "many traces of Mexican influence . . . to a civilized modern little city dominated intellectually by New England schoolma'ams." This change was summarized in the reshaping of the town's central "plaza" — a place

*trees on the site to erect the "old home," the trees that surround the house were probably planted by the owner, perhaps on Arbor Day.*

where hoboes formerly had rested in the shade — into a "courthouse park." Strother did not consider this process misguided or detrimental. It had great cultural and economic benefits. Nevertheless, the New Englanders' improvement projects had not created a more cohesive community. The settlement had first been populated by what Strother described as a diverse mixture of southerners, Scandinavians, Chinese, and Mexicans, none of whom were dominant in the town. As the New Englanders began to take over, social lines were drawn more closely and the whites dropped their custom of speaking Spanish as a second language.[43]

Many supporters of improvement acknowledged the shortcomings of their work only to press on all the more vigorously. After many years of effort on behalf of improvement, Harlan Paul Douglass, the secretary of the American Missionary Association, had no illusions about the small town. It was the "ugly accent in an endless panorama of interest and beauty." His picture of the midwestern town was hardly flattering. As one approached from the cultivated fields and pastures, Douglass wrote, unkempt barns, poultry yards, manure heaps, wood piles, and nondescript outbuildings were first evident. Towering over the town was the municipal water tank or standpipe. No beauty was attempted in the "drab and standardized orderliness" of the railroad sidings, lumberyard, and oil station. Main Street, with its pretentious "White Way" wasting electricity with expensive lights, was muddy and littered; elsewhere, there were few streetlights and no electricity in the homes. The public buildings consisted chiefly of small wooden churches located at random throughout the village, and a public school or two, usually dingy, with inadequate grounds. If the town was a county seat, it had "the inevitable court house, either utterly nondescript in architecture, or new and pretentious." Most small towns were bisected by a railroad, which frequently divided the town socially as well as geographically. On the other side of the tracks were "the poorer houses, the muddier and weedier streets, and the fewer sidewalks." On the town's farther edge were located its industrial plants, a flour mill or tile works, and also the inevitable baseball field with its rudimentary bleachers.

Nevertheless, Douglass continued to believe that improvement work could make the town "a nice place to live." He concluded that in the small towns greatness stood "humbly clad";

here patriotic labour is involved with charm; here deep social processes are bound up with intimate personal contacts; here especially the high fortunes of the open country are to be centered and inspired; here lies the pleasant middle-ground through which if one will have it so the Garden of Eden merges into the City of God.

As long as supporters of improvement believed that the town might have an awakening, even the smallest project could have great consequences. That possibility sustained many people against all adversity in their efforts at improvement.[44]

Many supporters of improvement could not maintain this faith. Yet they did not easily give up the ideal of a cohesive community and accept the fact that they belonged to interest groups that made known their points of view and affected the town's political process through voluntary organizations. No matter how active the participation in a community that functioned on this basis, the belief in an orderly environment had deep roots that were difficult to sever. This impulse was shared by more than the handful of people who, in joining improvement societies, made an overt demonstration of their desire to create and belong to a wider, "village family." It was fundamental, and anyone could feel it.

The disaffected could keep alive a belief in the well-ordered community by redefining the place to which they owed an allegiance. Some did so by moving to a town where the inhabitants were more sympathetic. In a few cases groups left one town to found a new community based on the principles that they could not sustain in the old one. Such people often had strong religious or ethnic bonds and because of these ties were able to achieve the coherence of outlook they did not find elsewhere.[45] Communities founded on this basis were often widely publicized, but less explicit redefinitions were more common. It was possible for citizens to change the community to which they owed a primary allegiance not by moving, but instead simply by identifying only with a neighborhood or part of the town. This reorientation was easier if the neighborhood was conveniently defined by a name or a distinctive geographical feature, but it did not depend on those factors. When a number of people felt it necessary to make the same change, they could formalize that decision. Some did so through property restrictions that prevented other people from intruding; others in extreme cases established separate local governments.

No matter how such communities were redefined, even these usually smaller and more protected places were not immune to change. If the common purpose again disappeared, Americans often came to rely on an even more limited unit — the home circle. No supporter of village improvement ever denied the importance of the home. Birdsey Grant Northrop, Nathaniel H. Egleston, J. Sterling Morton, and many others frequently spoke and wrote about the significance of the home for the shaping of character. Northrop claimed that the chief object of village improvement was to make the "environments of the home and the village healthful and beautiful." There was no conflict between the home and the town. The enhancement of one benefited the other and vice versa.[46]

Nevertheless, although it was possible to belong equally to the home family and the village family, many inhabitants of the small town felt that if they did not actually have to choose between the two, they at least had to emphasize one over the other. Given the relentless changes that engulfed many small towns, even those who wanted to be loyal to the place in which they lived invariably had to fall back upon the home as the basic unit of society. The fact that Nathaniel H. Egleston gave the second edition of *Village Improvement* the title *The Home and Its Surroundings* indicated a shift in vantage point that other Americans, even those who lived in the most harmonious towns, often had to make.

The home, of course, was not always a stable and sympathetic environment. Even though they craved its security, those who were dissatisfied with their homes often chose to escape all local confines, whether town, neighborhood, or family circle. Some lit out for the isolation of the wilderness, but as the continent became settled, more headed for the city, which was a wilderness in its own right.[47] Once they arrived, they had a different perspective on the community they had left. From a distance, it was easy not only to blur the distinction between home and town but also to overlook some of the more abrasive details of each. It was then possible to form a composite and more satisfying image of the two — the home town.

✦✦✦

Many supporters of the small town hoped that the growth of large cities would be halted, even reversed. They often claimed that the city was a culturally stultifying, economically deleterious, unhealthy, immoral, unchristian environment, and they developed theories about the rise and fall of civilizations to prove that a return to a society based on the small community was not only desirable, but also preordained.[48]

Most Americans probably shared this distaste for cities; at best they thought they were a necessary evil. But others were fascinated by them. If some authors and artists went to the countryside to seek the picturesque, others found equally captivating scenes in the streets of the nation's great cities. Through quick sketches, whether literary, artistic, or photographic, they captured the rapid pace and diversity of urban life and conveyed their enthusiasm for the city to the millions of Americans who were then reading well-illustrated daily, weekly, and monthly periodicals.[49]

A few historians and social scientists put this interest in the city into a broader context. They claimed that cities enhanced and were themselves an index of the advancement of civilization. They found that liberal thought flourished where people congregated. "The variety of occupation, interest and opinions in the city," the social scientist Adna Ferrin Weber claimed, produced an "intellectual friction" that led to "a broader and freer judgment and a great inclination to and appreciation of new thoughts, manners, and ideals." These lofty sentiments were balanced by rigorous arguments about the economic benefits that resulted from the growth of cities. In 1899, when Weber reviewed the urban development of the nineteenth century, he concluded that the city resident was better off than his country counterpart. Weber argued simply but persuasively that production increased with an increase in the concentration of population. In the city there was a greater opportunity for specialization; every person could be placed where he exerted his strength and skill to the best advantage. These economic facts had important political implications. Since a democracy depended for its survival on the independence of its citizens, the growth of cities and the consequent increase in wealth bolstered the American political system.[50]

The city's defenders even questioned whether it was healthier to live in the country. To those who said the city was inherently insalubrious,

35. *"Two Sides of the Way." "There is a chance of something better where the two sides of the way are in contrast — but how about the dark haunts of poverty or vice, where both sides . . . are alike? Fortunately, the modern Aladdin, whose name is Gotham, has a half-forgotten lamp, otherwise known as public spirit." The drawing was directed at New York, but its message could have applied to any American city.*

they pointed out that epidemics frequently occurred in the countryside, that it was difficult to obtain proper sanitary facilities in remote areas, and that many people in the rural parts of the nation lived in unheated homes.[51]

Many ministers also refused to write off America's burgeoning metropolises. They took the idea of the City of God literally, and they welcomed the challenge of creating one vast Christian community. Still, no matter what expectations people had for the city, it was difficult to ignore the fact that, as it existed, it had serious shortcomings. Authors and artists often found that parts of the city that at first seemed picturesque on closer examination turned out to be sordid. Those who championed the city as a cultural milieu had to recognize that many of the institutions they supported were only shallow imitations of the European ones they admired. Social scientists struggled to resolve the paradox that, despite a general increase in wealth, the city's population contained a growing number of hopelessly poor people. Although sanitarians wanted to believe that the city could be a healthy place in which to live, they were continually disturbed by its high rates of morbidity and mortality, and no matter how much they talked of the City of God, ministers were concerned that they had so little hold over their congregations.

Because they understood that the city was not self-regulating, those who believed in the benefits of urban life initiated a wide range of reforms. Although they were applied at a different scale, these measures were similar in purpose to those undertaken in small towns. The problems of the city were met by innumerable economic, social, educational, religious, cultural, and governmental reforms. In addition, many inhabitants of the city understood that the urban environment needed ordering. Like those with a similar outlook in small towns, the advocates of urban improvement argued that good harbors, markets, and transportation facilities enhanced the city's economy. They also connected the state of the physical environment to the health of the city's inhabitants.

A prosperous and salubrious city was, however, not necessarily a good one. Nineteenth-century reformers felt that to be a true community, the city had to be united by a common purpose transcending particular interests. They tried to induce a sense of higher principles in many ways, but the creation of a beautiful city was often the most important means to this elusive end. In the city, as in the small town, attractive surroundings would exercise a beneficial influence, their creation would serve as a model of cooperation, and efforts to attain them might even stimulate a general awakening that would help to resolve problems in other areas of daily life.

Americans who lived in small towns often felt that the changes taking place in their communities were proportionately as great as those in cities. However, in trying to create a coherent environment and thus a village family, they had pronounced advantages over those who wanted to achieve similar ends in cities. Towns may have seemed chaotic and full of divisions, but at least they were small enough to be comprehensible. In the nineteenth century American cities grew to an unprecedented size. Before 1800 a city contained 20,000 or, in the most extreme case, 100,000 inhabitants. The majority lived within walking distance of each other, usually within a mile or two. When the number of inhabitants reached not just 200,000 but even 1,000,000, the old limits had to expand, and the intimacy that had characterized even the most cosmopolitan city disappeared.

Problems created by city size were accentuated by the lack of precedents to inspire and guide those who tried to shape the urban community. No matter how much a village or town changed, the inhabitants could draw upon familiar images and examples in their efforts to transform their community. There were no parallel sources for the cities. The great capitals of Europe were sometimes mentioned as relevant to the American context, but they had been created by and symbolized an autocratic society with ideals markedly different from those of a democracy.

Because cities were so large and incomprehensible, it often seemed impossible, even a contradiction, to try to shape them with the sense of beauty and order that embodied the higher purpose essential to a true community. Some people, however, were not deterred. They mounted campaigns to build a beautiful city and to achieve everything that goal entailed. The most important work was done in Chicago. At the beginning of the nineteenth century New York was the nation's largest city, and it always remained so. But New York rarely was considered the archetypical American city. It was too old, and because Manhattan was an island, its pattern of building and land development was idiosyncratic. Chicago, on the other hand, did not have these liabilities. It was built entirely in the nineteenth century, it was in the middle of the United States, and it was located on flat prairie. Americans looked to Chicago for a glimpse of the future. That scrutiny put an additional responsibility on the inhabitants of Chicago who were trying to make their city a good place to live in.[52]

Because of its location between the Mississippi River and Lake Michigan, the land on which Chicago was eventually built had long been used by Indians. In 1673 Father Marquette and Louis Jolliet wintered there, and when the Indians ceded the land to the United States in 1795, a small settlement had already been on the site for several decades. The construction of Fort Dearborn in 1803 marked the official beginning of Chicago, but Chicago did not grow appreciably till the 1830s. When it opened in 1825, the Erie Canal created a new pathway for migration between the East, the Great Lakes, and Chicago. To connect this route to the Mississippi River, the Illinois legislature in 1829 appointed a commission to chart the course of a canal and dispose of the public lands along the way. The town was incorporated in 1833, and to prepare for the settlement that would inevitably grow near the canal, a pattern of streets was established. Like most western towns, Chicago was planned on a grid.[53]

Work on the canal did not begin until 1836 and was not finished until 1848. But in anticipation of its completion many people went to Chicago. Between 1830 and 1850 the city's population increased from 350 to 30,000. In that period steamboat traffic on Lake Michigan and overland trade expanded. As more people entered the city and new sites were needed for places of business, warehouses, stores, and homes, Chicago's street grid was extended.

Although Chicago had grown rapidly, in 1848 it was still not unlike other burgeoning midwestern cities. In the next seven years, however, it outstripped its competitors and became the communications center of the Midwest, if not of the nation. In 1848 the canal's completion brought to Chicago the Illinois River valley trade, which previously had been diverted to St. Louis, and in the same year Chicago's first telegraph line was installed. By 1850 two plank roads connecting Chicago to the northwestern and southeastern regions of Illinois had been constructed. These roads were joined to improved streets that ran from the outskirts of the city to the center.

These new lines of communication helped to increase the trade that came to Chicago, but they were important primarily because they gave the city a sufficient reason to attract the railroads. In 1848 Illinois had only a few railroads, and there was not even a single mile of track in Chicago. But in the next eight years, through a combination of private enterprise and government-sponsored internal improvements, a railroad system was completed that led to every part of the country. Chicago

*36. Henry R. Schoolcraft: Chicago in 1820. The settlement contained Fort Dearborn, a dozen log huts (characterized as "low, filthy and disgusting"), and about fifty inhabitants.*

*37. Currier and Ives: "The City of Chicago," 1892. At the time of the World's Columbian Exposition in 1893 the city covered almost two hundred square miles. Its 1,315,000 citizens increased to 2,448,000 by 1915.*

was the focus of this network; in 1856 it had ten trunk lines with close to 3,000 miles of track.[54]

The city suffered a severe setback during the depression of 1857 and at the outbreak of the Civil War. No one who lived through these difficult periods could ignore the possibility that similar recessions would occur in the future, but Chicago's economy seemed resilient enough to recover. Between 1856 and 1870 the number of communication lines to, from, and through Chicago continued to multiply. The amount of lumber and grain that poured into the city increased thirtyfold, and Chicago also became the center of the Midwest's wholesale trade in groceries, shoes, clothing, and hardware.

The most important aspect of Chicago's development in this period was the growth of manufacturing. Before the Civil War the city was primarily known as an exchange center, but by 1867 nearly everything of bulk used on railroads, in farming, or in the building and furnishing of houses was made there. The growth in manufacturing was reflected in the city's work force. Whereas only 2,000 of Chicago's 30,000 inhabitants were employed in manufacturing in 1850, 60,000 of its then nearly 300,000 citizens worked in industrial establishments in 1870.[55]

The transformation of Chicago from a commercial to a manufacturing center produced important changes in the city's physical environment. Before these developments most of Chicago's business was located in offices, warehouses, and craft shops near the harbor and the river front. Because there was no effective system of transportation within the city, the people who worked in these structures had to live within a few miles of them. Chicago always had fashionable areas where the merchants, bankers, and prominent citizens lived. Nearby, often just around the corner, resided some of the working population, either in small houses or in derelict buildings that had been constructed for another use. At the fringe of the city were suburban districts that contained a mixture of houses, small farms, and light manufacturing establishments that made goods for local consumption.

Although different areas of Chicago were always recognizable, they were never completely homogeneous. Even in fashionable districts houses often also served as business premises; many people lived above shops and craft industries near the edges of the lake and the river. These buildings varied in size and quality, but since the activities of the city were not highly specialized, in scale they were all part of a continuous urban landscape. The fact that Chicago grew and changed so quickly further discouraged a strict differentiation of the city.[56]

38.  *"Ashland Avenue," Chicago, 1874. Within a decade, many of the houses on this fashionable street were occupied by lodgers or were converted into furnished rooms.*

39.  *"Marshfield Avenue," Chicago, 1910. Such streets stretched over vast areas of the city.*

In the late 1850s and throughout the 1860s, however, several distinct areas of the city emerged. Chicago's commercial or business district had always lacked definition. But in 1867 Potter Palmer, a retail and wholesale merchant, bought three quarters of a mile along State Street and within two years gave the area an unmistakable identity. He persuaded other property owners and the City Council to widen the street, to tear down insubstantial structures, and to erect massive stores, offices, and hotels. By 1869 about forty stone-faced buildings had already been erected along State Street.

Much of the processing of the goods brought to Chicago had taken place along the banks of the Chicago River and its branches. In the 1860s even larger grain elevators and warehouses continued to be built at these locations, but the construction inland of vast, highly specialized manufacturing plants was the most important manifestation of Chicago's changing economy. On the West Side, a tract of 160 acres was given over entirely to steam-boiler factories and iron-processing plants. The most spectacular of these industrial areas was the Union Stockyard. Opened in 1865, this meat-processing plant occupied almost a square mile of land and was virtually a city in itself.

With the expansion and rationalization of the business and commercial district, Chicago's inhabitants had to change the pattern of where they lived. The wealthy began to build their houses along fashionable avenues far from the open sewer of the Chicago River. Streets along the lake on the North and South sides and on the West Side directly west of the main business district provided the context for separate and row houses of an opulence that had no precedent in Chicago.

In contrast to these elegant avenues were the streets on which the majority of Chicago's working population lived. These streets ringed the business district and sometimes came close to touching the prominent avenues. Their frontages were divided into small lots on which frame dwellings were constructed. Sometimes one house was built behind another on the same lot. Small manufacturing or service establishments in which many of the residents of the district worked were frequently interspersed among these dwellings. Although a high percentage of houses in such areas were still owned by those who occupied them, they did not receive the services that were so important to the residences on the fashionable avenues. Many of them were located on garbage-strewn alleys and unpaved streets in areas that already had a reputation for crime, vice, high mortality rates, and other problems.[57]

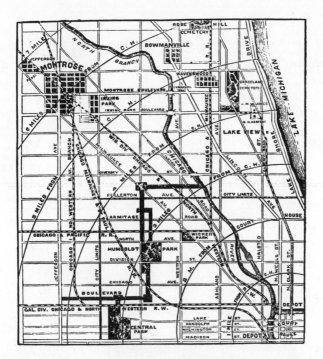

40. *Montrose, one of Chicago's suburbs, 1874. By the 1870s, as more people commuted to and from work, time as well as distance from the city center assumed a new importance.*

Beyond these areas and the large industrial districts were the suburbs of Chicago. In the late 1850s and throughout the 1860s dozens of small communities sprang up on the outskirts of the city as railroad, omnibus, and horsecar lines facilitated commuting to and from the center of the city. Chicago's suburbs were laid out and settled in different ways and quickly established their own reputations. Some communities grew up around small farming centers when the railroad that passed through them to bring agricultural produce to Chicago also began to serve as a commuter line. Other suburbs were started from scratch as real estate speculations. Individuals or companies bought tracts of land, usually along one of the transportation lines. They then subdivided it into house lots and added enough improvements to make the area attractive to potential homeowners. A few suburbs were begun by people with a common, often religious, bond. A group of wealthy Presbyterians bought land in Lake Forest in 1856 where they planned to focus their community around a university. Oak Park also had a religious basis when it was first settled,

*41. An advertisement for house lots in Humboldt, Chicago, 1871–1874.*

but it soon welcomed all denominations and prided itself on the number of its churches. Some suburbs, such as South Chicago, were started at important railroad crossings or river landings and attracted factories whose workers often purchased small house lots nearby. Occasionally a large company started its own community around a factory relocated from a downtown site.[58]

A few suburbs, especially those most distant from Chicago, were begun to attract vacationers as well as full-time residents. Wilmette, which dated back to 1829, was subdivided in 1869 and had as one of its attractions a large hotel. An elegant hotel that overlooked Lake Michigan was said to make Lake Forest as great a favorite of Chicago residents as Newport or Long Branch was of the "heated and worn out denizens" of New York and other eastern cities.[59]

The design of a suburb varied with and at the same time helped to establish the character of the area. Developers divided their land with an expectation of what kind of people might buy lots. Some laid out grids of streets with small parcels to attract the modest homeowner. Others thought a more varied plan would bring a wealthier population. The most famous suburb of this kind was Riverside, which was designed

42.  *Oak Park, Chicago, 1873. This suburb was laid out primarily on a grid. This view was drawn about fifteen years before Frank Lloyd Wright moved to Oak Park.*

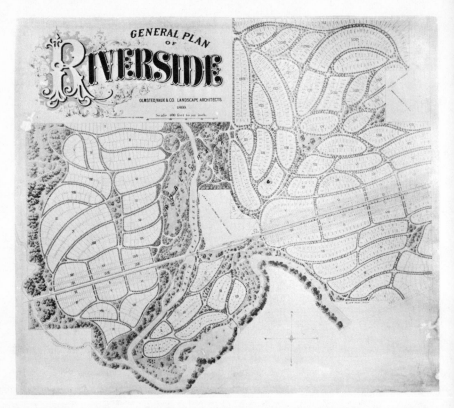

43. *"General Plan of Riverside," Chicago, 1869. In designing this suburb,
Frederick Law Olmsted tried to make the most of the varied landscape near
the Des Plaines River.*

by Frederick Law Olmsted. His plan, based not on a grid but on a system
of roadways curved to suit the contours of the land, included large areas
of public landscaping. Riverside's example was long important to American landscape architects, but it was not emulated in Chicago proper. The
development was hindered in its early years by financial difficulties and
the widely spread rumors that it was located on an unhealthy site.[60]

The final distinctive feature of Chicago in the 1860s was its vast tracts
of vacant land, not only located on the far perimeters of the suburbs but
also interspersed with settled land. Chicago's growth was so rapid that
land developers often bypassed vacant areas to build farther out, hoping
that the city would soon catch up to their settlements. Since prosperous
times were often punctuated by financial panics, substantial areas of land
would remain undeveloped because their owners did not have the capital

to make necessary improvements or because they were waiting for a more auspicious moment.

As Chicago took shape, no overall plan guided the many decisions about where to locate what types of buildings. Nevertheless, some of its citizens hoped to direct the development of the city for the common good. They realized that Chicago's economic future depended on the improvement of communication and transportation to and within the city. Despite squabbles between property owners, the City Council was able to pass ordinances to widen and improve streets. The raising of the street grade made it easier to travel through Chicago, and the straightening of the channel of the Chicago River was an important aid to the navigability of that vital route.

Chicago's continued growth and its future greatness also depended on the health of its citizens. Before 1870 the goal of projects to protect the public's health was primarily to ensure the removal of sewage and to provide fresh water. When the smell of the Chicago River became intolerable and epidemics of water-borne diseases became frequent, the City Council decided to provide for the disposal of wastes by reversing the flow of the then stagnant river. The city also tried to protect the purity of its water by building a new supply tunnel that started from a crib two miles off the shore of Lake Michigan. Such measures addressed only the most basic problems of public health, but they demonstrated what could be achieved by taking action for the common good.[61]

Some of Chicago's citizens also wanted to make their city beautiful. They pressed the City Council to keep the streets clean and to control the placement of billboards and advertisements. Bankers and businessmen often financed more than utilitarian buildings that their architects tried to position at prominent street intersections to give Chicago's downtown area the sense of presence that distinguished comparable districts in European cities. Some of this effort was often concentrated at the harbor and railroad stations, the entrances to the city. But no matter how much such improvement contributed to the creation of a beautiful city, none of these projects would have mattered if Chicago had not lived up to the motto *Urbs in Horto* — a City in a Garden — that it adopted early in its history.[62]

Americans who thought about what shape their cities should take invariably concluded that a great metropolis would be viable only if it was intimately related to a natural setting. Their arguments for this belief varied. Doctors and sanitarians thought that trees and open spaces ventilated the city and helped to bolster the health of the public. Other people argued that parks and promenades along streets and riverbanks were necessary for recreation.

These arguments were sufficient in themselves, but the case for a City in a Garden touched upon an even more fundamental nineteenth-century belief — that nature was a great source of inspiration, a medium through which one could almost perceive God. Those who were too far removed from nature ran the risk of losing their humanity. As cities grew, it was important to preserve this vital contact by interspersing the man-made environment with parks. Areas of landscape were also important because they aided the cause of social harmony. They provided a common ground on which the increasingly diverse and divisive population could mingle and meet, and they acted as the medium that tied together the disparate parts of a city. The landscape had made the village an Eden; on a completely different scale it could still help to create the community that so many migrants to the city believed they had lost.[63]

Anticipating that Manhattan would eventually be filled with people, New York's citizens made sure that a bit of landscape would be the focus of their daily lives by creating Central Park. The quest for a similar end resulted in a different conception in Chicago. The citizens who wanted to maintain Chicago's reputation as a City in a Garden envisioned a system of parks that would knit the entire city together. In the late 1860s land was procured for three parks on what were then the outer edges of the North, South, and West sides. Most of this terrain was flat and unwooded, but the park commissioners immediately hired prominent landscape architects to design ambitious and imaginative plans for each.

The original conception extended beyond the immediate boundaries of the three parks. The commissioners procured land for the Midway Plaisance, a 600-foot-wide strip that linked the upper and lower areas of the South Park, and by encouraging the laying out of broad, tree-lined boulevards, they tried to join the three parks with a continuous system of greenery. These prominent thoroughfares would be intersected by minor streets lined with trees. With this system as Chicago's matrix, it was possible to envisage a great metropolis that, despite its vast size, still had a basis in order.[64]

On October 8, 1871, a fire broke out on Chicago's West Side. When it was put out three days later, it had destroyed the whole of Chicago's commercial district and had made a third of the city's inhabitants homeless. In the following half century Chicago suffered other setbacks, but

the city always recovered. Between 1871 and 1910 the value of its manufacturing, trade, and produce increased tenfold. In the same period its
population grew from 325,000 to 2,185,283.[65]

A visitor to Chicago after the turn of the century would hardly have
recognized the city of before the fire. The distinctive areas that had
emerged in the 1860s still existed, but each had changed in scale, character, and location. In 1881 the Board of Trade decided to move to an
area left vacant after the fire. This change affected the location of Chicago's financial district, since offices and banks followed. Before 1880
only a few of Chicago's buildings exceeded six stories. But with the use
of the elevator and steel-frame construction, structures of twelve and
later twenty stories started to dominate Chicago's skyline.[66]

Large industrial complexes continued to be built throughout Chicago,
especially at important railway intersections. Philanthropic owners of
some of these factories built model housing nearby for their workers; the
best-known example was the town George Pullman built in the early
1880s. This community was organized around a square, the retail center
of the area. Nearby, Pullman built the Arcade, an elegant, glass-roofed
structure that contained not only shops, offices, and banks but also a
theater and a library. The housing in Pullman varied in quality, but it
was all located within easy walking distance of these facilities and the
factory.[67]

Chicago's fashionable streets also changed. On the South Side many
stockyard magnates chose to live on Michigan Avenue, which was turned
into a boulevard in 1880. When Potter Palmer built a new $250,000
home on the North Side in 1882, other businessmen and merchants soon
moved to what became Lake Shore Drive. The development of Washington Street on the West Side had a similar effect. None of these areas was
solely for separate or row houses. The reputation of these locations
attracted the construction of many apartment houses, a type of building
first erected in Chicago in the early 1870s. Some apartment houses were
sufficiently luxurious to add to the reputation of the neighborhood, but
others lowered the tone of the area and, as more were built, forced the
fashionable districts elsewhere.[68]

Beyond the sometimes derelict fringes of the downtown area and often
still close to the elegant boulevards were the seemingly endless miles of
workers' housing mixed in with small industries. Many of these dwellings
were occupied by the native and foreign immigrants who swelled the city's
population. Whereas before the fire Chicago's citizens had prided them-

selves that it was possible for every workingman to own a home, by the turn of the century no one could make such a claim. The zone in which most of the city's working population lived contained an uneven pattern of housing that reflected the successive stages of Chicago's development. As neighborhoods changed, elegant houses were turned into furnished rooms. Their spacious lawns came to be filled with small wooden structures or covered with a variety of multifamily tenements.[69]

The conversion of horsecar to cable lines in the early 1880s meant that more people could commute to work. A five-cent fare with one free transfer to any cross-line further stimulated suburban development. With the cable car the rate of travel increased from five to ten miles an hour, and with the elevated railways, which began to operate in 1892, traffic moved at an average of fifteen miles an hour. The expanded transit system was able to take more workers to the suburbs and helped to fill areas of undeveloped prairie with houses. As suburbs sprang up farther from the city, the characters of the older and closer settlements changed.[70]

As in the period before 1871, this transformation of Chicago was brought about by thousands of small, separate decisions made for circumscribed ends. Part of the change, however, was also determined by efforts to guide the city's growth. Large areas of Chicago were altered so that the city's economy would prosper; a concern for public health exercised an increasing but still restricted influence on the location and condition of buildings; and some citizens continued to try to make Chicago a beautiful city, a City in a Garden.

Projects to enhance Chicago's appearance were undertaken as soon as the fire was out. Even more important was the stimulus to civic improvement of the World's Columbian Exposition of 1893. The plan of the fair was coordinated by Daniel Burnham, the famous Chicago architect. Located in Jackson Park, facing Lake Michigan, the grounds were divided into two sections. The larger was designed by a group of the nation's foremost architects, landscape architects, and artists. It was sited on a series of lagoons and canals that provided a proper setting for the stark white classical buildings housing exhibits of the great accomplishments of the age. To the north, the second part of the exposition consisted of a diverse set of buildings, each with an exhibit from a state or a country. Joined to the fair on the nearby Midway Plaisance was another area containing a sequence of exotic displays that included a model of the Eiffel Tower, a German village, a street in Cairo, a Hungarian café, a Chinese theater, and a new invention, the Ferris wheel.[71]

*44. The World's Columbian Exposition, 1893, The Court of Honor, look-ing west. This was the first view that those arriving by boat had of the fair and also the image that probably lasted longest in their minds. Boats entered the basin through a peristyle (not shown) in the foreground. The Agricul-ture Building was on the right, Manufacture and Liberal Arts on the left, and Administration at the far end of the basin.*

Twenty-one million people visited this celebration of four hundred years of progress. Most were simply stunned into silence by what they saw, but others tried to find a meaning in the White City. When William Dean Howells visited Chicago, he was deeply troubled by the state of the nation. The labor difficulties that had culminated in the Haymarket Riot in Chicago in 1886 had not abated. In 1893 the country was in the midst of a depression, unemployment reached new peaks, and there were violent strikes in many cities, including Chicago. Howells felt that these events were only "the calm at the heart of the cyclone" and that a basic reorien-tation of American society was necessary to prevent a cataclysm.

In 1892 he had begun to describe what such a transformation would entail in *A Traveler from Altruria*, a utopian novel serialized in *Cosmo-politan* magazine, and which was followed a year later by a similar work, *Letters of an Altrurian Traveler*. By using the traveler as a mouthpiece,

Howells not only commented about what was wrong with the United States but also described his ideal civilization. For Howells the root of all evil was greed and competition. Nowhere was this curse felt more acutely than in American cities. A selfish individualism fragmented the population of a city into sharply defined classes and, except for a few places like Central Park, created a desert that reflected extreme affluence or poverty.

The American city stood in stark contrast to its Altrurian counterpart. Each region of Altruria and the nation itself had a capital. These centers were primarily for the administration of the state and for the arts. They contained office buildings, universities, theaters, museums, cathedrals, laboratories, and conservatories, all of which were separate structures, spread out in the landscape. The residents of the capitals, mainly administrators, artists, and intellectuals, lived in apartment houses located along spacious boulevards. The rest of Altruria's citizens lived in small villages joined to the capital by speedy railroads. These villages were based primarily in farming, but they also contained mills and factories that were well integrated with the landscape and looked like temples.

When the Altrurian traveler visited Chicago in 1893, he saw a version of the cities in his ideal country. Unlike the state exhibits and those on the Midway Plaisance, the main part of the World's Columbian Exposition was conceived in harmony. All parties had decided that profit would not be a motive. The result was a design that was the product of principle, "not the straggling and shapeless accretion of accident" that characterized American cities. Everything was perfectly ordered in the White City; the grounds were kept clean, and horses did not soil the premises because wheeled chairs pushed by high school and college boys were the primary means of transportation inside the fair. The spirit of the Columbian Exposition was best summarized by the white, classical architecture. This choice of style and the uniform coloring showed the dominance of "art over business."[72]

Many people thought that the fair was a one-time event, a dream city. But once it was closed, others looked for ways to perpetuate its message. William T. Stead, an English minister who visited Chicago in 1893, hoped that the fair would set "a great civic revival in motion." He discussed why the great metropolis of the Midwest needed an awakening in *If Christ Came to Chicago*, filling it with incidents and statistics that painted a grim picture of the city. The one ray of hope was Hull-House, the famous settlement house, which, like others in New York and Boston, was founded in the late 1880s on principles established at Toynbee Hall in

London. Stead thought that through settlement houses the "intelligent warm-hearted people" might establish "neighborly friendships with the crowded precincts" as unknown to them as Timbuctoo. He believed that "the healthy natural community" was that of "a small country town or village in which everyone knows his neighbor"; he wanted Chicago's citizens to create institutions that would help them achieve an atmosphere equivalent to the small-town spirit.

Stead hoped that the world's fair would provide the impetus to spread the message of Hull-House throughout the city. At the end of *If Christ Came to Chicago*, in a chapter called "In the Twentieth Century," he described how the fair inspired a band of "helpers" to dedicate themselves "to the redemption of the municipal and social system." These helpers had aroused the local citizenry to overthrow the corrupt political machine. With a clean government all the social, economic, political, and environmental problems that Stead had catalogued in his previous four hundred pages were resolved. Chicago became the greatest port in the world, the undisputed capital of the nation, and its most beautiful city.

Stead's vision of Chicago differed from Howells's Altrurian city. Instead of dispersal of the population from the administrative center to small villages, compactness characterized Stead's city. He envisaged one closely knit, well-ordered community in which private property was unnecessary. Everyone lived in apartment houses that gave easy access to all the cultural facilities only a great city like Chicago could support.[73]

Concerned citizens did not have to be specific about the vision of a great metropolis to call for improvement. If an awakening occurred, the details would take care of themselves. Throughout the 1890s many people worked toward the goal of a harmonious city by demanding political reform; others tried to make Chicago as beautiful as the world's fair. This effort focused on the extension of the park system throughout the city and was initiated mainly by Daniel Burnham. In the ten years after the fair Burnham worked on a series of plans to improve the lakefront from Jackson Park to Grant Park. He began to extend the park system through boulevards and an outer belt to encompass all of Chicago, but the more he examined the way Chicago functioned, the more he understood that planning parks was not enough. What was needed was a comprehensive plan for the entire city.[74]

Between 1902 and 1905 Burnham developed his ideas about how to plan on a comprehensive scale in projects for Washington, D.C., Cleveland, San Francisco, and Manila. Throughout these years Burnham made

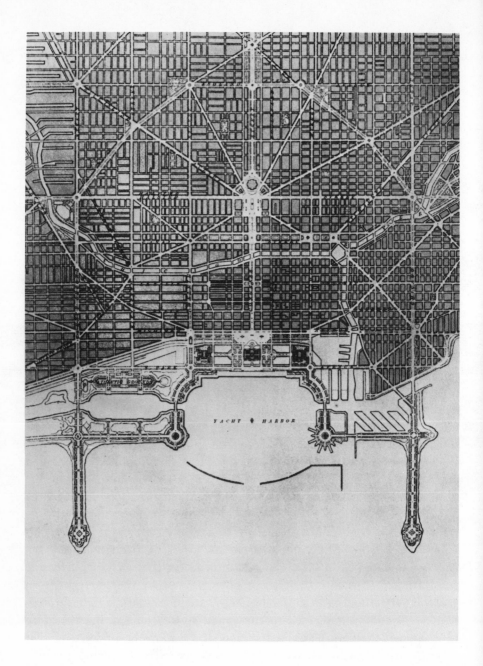

YACHT HARBOR

45. *The Heart of the City, Chicago, 1909. Daniel Burnham envisioned
Congress Street as a monumental axis that led from the Civic Center, past the
Railway Terminal, across Michigan Avenue, through the group of three
cultural buildings, and to the harbor. The result would be a "complete
organism in which all its functions are related one to another in such a
manner that it will become a unit."*

many overtures to prominent Chicago citizens about that city's need for a thorough plan, but the chance to make one came only in 1906 when a powerful business organization, the Commercial Club, commissioned him to do so.[75]

Burnham based his proposals not only on an assessment of how Chicago then functioned and what its future economic needs would be, but also on his vision of an ideal city and his understanding of the need "for the establishment of a beauty that shall be ever present to do its pure and noble work among us forever."[76] The area to which Burnham devoted the most care was the Heart of the City, the primary entrance to which would be a vast harbor, part of an improved Jackson Park, stretching southward along Lake Michigan. Immediately to the west of the harbor would be the city's cultural center, featuring the Field Museum, which gathered under one roof "the records of civilization culled from every portion of the globe, and representing man's struggle through the ages for advancement." To the north of this massive building would be a new structure for the Art Institute, which would help to make Chicago the most comprehensive art center in the country. To the south would be the new building for the Crerar Library, a gigantic repository of books for the students of the social, physical, natural, and applied sciences.

Parallel to this row of three buildings would be Michigan Avenue, which Burnham wanted to widen to 250 feet to contain the vast flow of the city's north-south traffic. He took great pains to design a two-level circulation route for Michigan Avenue, reserving the upper level for pedestrians and horse-drawn carriages and the lower one for service transportation. Through this careful zoning of different types of movement, Michigan Avenue would be free to become Chicago's ceremonial thoroughfare, adorned with sculpture and fountains in front of the three impressive buildings of the cultural center.

On axis with the harbor and the Field Museum and intersecting Michigan Avenue was another monumental boulevard, Congress Street, which led through Chicago's main business district of offices, hotels, stores, banks, theaters, and churches, all of which were restricted in height to create a uniform urban landscape. After Congress Street crossed the Chicago River, it intersected with Canal Street, which Burnham would transform into a unified complex of railway terminals. The street then would widen to 300 feet and culminate in a gigantic civic center featuring a huge city hall with a dome that dwarfed that of St. Peter's, Rome. This structure would be flanked by two other groups of monumental buildings, one to house the offices of the federal government, the other for Cook County administration.

If this sequence of boulevards and buildings was the heart of Chicago, the network of streets throughout the city was its arteries. Burnham managed to transform the grid of Chicago's streets into a comprehensive system that would serve the city's future growth. He widened many existing streets and divided them to accommodate different types of traffic. Burnham also planned diagonal streets that would lead to the Civic Center, so that it would be possible to move quickly from one corner of the city to another. The other major element in this transportation system was a series of ring roads around the city. The innermost one enclosed the Civic Center and the business district, the next was composed of the boulevards that from the 1860s had been laid out to connect Chicago's main parks, and the last was located on the far periphery of the city. A broad elliptical highway, this vast thoroughfare was designed to join the North, South, and West sides when Chicago had been extended in all directions by the automobile.

Chicago's transportation system was intimately linked to its parks, which ensured "good health and good order." Burnham's first priority was to join all the lakefront parks, thus reserving this area for public use. He connected this long strip by tree-lined boulevards to the city's major parks, to three new parks located on the outer ring road, and thence to a continuous system of nature reserves. By extending Chicago's parklands up to fifty miles from the center, the forward-looking Burnham made sure that the city's residents would always be close to this most valuable source of recreation and inspiration.[77]

In the *Plan of Chicago* Burnham often wrote about the Chicago Spirit and appealed to civic pride. "To love and render service to one's city," he exhorted, "to have a part in its advancement, to seek to better its conditions and to promote its highest interests — these are both the duty and the privilege of the patriot of peace." Just as political reformers were not satisfied with a city that was a community only insofar as it nurtured institutions and built facilities that allowed the members of its diverse groups to function with as little detriment as possible to one another, so Burnham did not want a city that merely worked. Instead, Chicago had to have a higher purpose. Burnham, like other reformers, felt that it was possible to determine what the public interest was and to create a city that not only reflected that purpose but also instilled it in its inhabitants.[78]

Once the plan was published, a campaign was mounted to publicize it.

In 1910 the plan was adopted by the City Council, and many of its recommendations were later fulfilled. The areas that have been affected by the plan, like those that were designed in response to earlier campaigns of improvement, still are some of the most distinguished in Chicago. However, the city was never to achieve the physical and social harmony that the formulators and sponsors of the plan wanted. The Chicago of the plan had no skyscrapers, a building type that in his more altruistic moments Burnham considered a manifestation of selfish and assertive individualism. He hoped that Chicago would restrict the height of buildings so that it would have an even skyline like that of Paris or Washington, D.C. Yet by 1909 many of the businessmen who belonged to the Commercial Club had already helped to punctuate Chicago's skyline with tall buildings. Despite their support of the plan, it was unlikely that they would cut profits from real estate ventures by stopping the construction of skyscrapers.

The plan's treatment of the housing of Chicago's citizens contained another glaring discrepancy between the ideal and the real. The authors said little about this subject, but their intention was made clear by Jules Guérin's breathtaking drawings, especially his bird's-eye perspectives, which showed the different parts of Chicago blending imperceptibly together. From the heart of the city to the most distant suburb few distinct boundaries or divisions were apparent. But in 1909, as ever since, the separation between groups was acute. When this gap was not marked by a great physical distance, there was, as sociologists later found, a social distance that was just as complete.[79]

Some citizens continued to believe that a Chicago Spirit would awaken the community. At the end of an article he wrote in 1913 praising the recently deceased Daniel Burnham, Hamlin Garland claimed that Chicago's civic awakening was proceeding "with accelerating momentum."[80] Other people could not sustain this faith. Still, they did not give up their desire for an orderly city. Instead, like the residents of the small town, they took several paths to find a more manageable community to which to belong. Some did so by moving to a more compatible city, but others redefined their community in less explicit ways. It was possible for people to live in a large city like Chicago, yet feel that another place was their real home town. When he tried to convince businessmen of "The Commercial Value of Beauty," Daniel Burnham berated those who made their money in Chicago but spent it in foreign travel or in the vacation communities where they had second homes and where they often started improvement associations.[81] Since vacationers lived in such communities for only a part of the year, they could overlook the untidy and unpleasant features of their surroundings. The village or small town then seemed a coherent entity, unlike the diverse and chaotic city.

The use of the village as a means to achieve the sense of community that the large city did not satisfy was not restricted to those who owned second homes or even to those who rented houses or stayed in hotels. The native village was important to European immigrants because it gave them an image of a secure and intimate community to which, especially in uncertain times, they could hope someday to return. The midwestern, southern, or New England farm village served the same purpose for the many native-born who flocked to large cities like Chicago.

The village did not have to be remote to be attractive. It was possible to think of a neighborhood or suburb, however defined, as inseparable from the city and, if necessary, to have pride both in the local and the larger community. But often one was emphasized over the other. The smaller entity, because of its size and comprehensibility, seemed to have advantages that the bigger one lacked. Many people were attracted to suburbs because they had once been farm communities, and many of the most exuberant improvement associations were started by newcomers to them. Once they were established there, it was possible to use the downtown district, as in William Dean Howells's Altrurian settlement pattern, only for business and culture.

When the primary allegiance was to the local community, it was easy to ignore the needs of the city at large. But even suburbs or small neighborhoods were not the secure communities their residents hoped them to be. Few were so well protected as to escape the ceaseless changes that throughout the nineteenth century transformed large cities. When that happened, Americans had all the more reason to reaffirm their belief that the home was the most important unit of society, the one on which they could most depend.

Authors who wrote about improvement work often described a city they admired as "A City of Homes."[82] A city's spirit, they tacitly argued, was best revealed in how well its homes were maintained. To care for one's home was not necessarily incompatible with broader improvement programs, but in the phrase, "A City of Homes," was the implication that if each family tended its own territory, it was fulfilling its primary obligation. Considering the state of the American city in the second half of the nineteenth century, this may have been the only feasible course of improvement action. Those who, however hesitantly, entertained visions of the great metropolis as a large cohesive village could not really complain about a concentration of effort on the home. But that emphasis had devastating consequences for broader ideas of what a city could be.

✦✦✦

Supporters of civic improvement tried to treat the city as if it were a large village. After the turn of the century, however, a few reformers began to emphasize that cities were not like small towns. With this premise as their starting point, they tried to determine how to treat the city in a manner that suited it, and between 1905 and 1915 they made a remarkable advance in the articulation of a theory of city planning. These ideas had profound implications not only for the purpose and shape of cities but also for the location and function of the home.

Reformers began their quest for a more substantial body of knowledge on which to base their work by questioning the lofty aims and hopes for awakenings that had motivated earlier village and civic improvement projects. One major impediment to improvement's success had been its ephemeral nature. The work undertaken on behalf of improvement usually came as a response to a specific event — a national celebration, an anniversary, or a crisis. Improvement societies were popular in the United States after 1865, when they erected memorials to the fallen heroes of the Civil War. They were active in the centennial year of 1876, on the four hundredth anniversary of Columbus's discovery of America, in 1900, and on anniversaries of a town's founding. Much improvement work also came after a disaster. When there was a depression, businessmen and politicians sometimes joined together to improve a road, harbor, or bridge to stimulate the economy of their city. Likewise, an epidemic, a riot, or a severe fire often drew attention to the city's physical environment and set in motion other improvement activities.

Although those who sponsored or worked for improvement hoped that specific actions would engender a civic spirit that would sustain the projects and inspire new ones in the future, the fervently hoped-for awakening rarely, if ever, occurred. Without it improvement work foundered. When the original enthusiasm or sense of urgency subsided, the improvement organization lost its effectiveness. Many associations were then disbanded and soon all traces of their work disappeared. In some cases the local government took over the responsibilities, but it was usually not able to maintain the original sense of purpose.

Before the turn of the century many people were interested in making their village, town, or city a better place in which to live. Ministers, doctors, architects, landscape architects, politicians, civic and business leaders, and journalists all pressed for improvements, but only a handful of them made this their central occupation. The practitioners of the primary professions were still struggling to establish the authority of their disciplines. Since it was hard enough in law, medicine, and architecture to codify rules and procedures and then to secure their acceptance by local and state governments, few people even contemplated the establishment of a new profession that focused on the condition of villages and cities.

Before 1894 supporters of improvement work did not even have a national organization through which they could share their experiences and discuss common problems. In the following decade several were founded, but although these organizations responded to a need that had long existed, none was sufficiently certain of its position in relation to the general subject of improvement to clarify a point of view. Some of these societies issued magazines or newsletters, but these publications contained mainly topical information or journalistic articles that did not add up to a sustained discussion about improvement.[83]

Because there was no authoritative journal devoted to the subject, important figures either did not write very much or published their articles in highly regarded monthlies like *Harper's* or the *Atlantic* or in professional and technical journals like the *American Architect and Building News*, the *Plumber and Sanitary Engineer*, and the *Journal of the Franklin Institute*. Many of these articles contained significant statements about various improvement issues, but because they appeared sporadically and in unpredictable sources, they never became the basis of a discipline about how to improve the American city.

The supporters of improvement had enthusiasm and energy, but since they did not have institutions to enhance the development of their ideas, their proposals were often shallow. Beneath idealistic images of the White City and optimistic hopes for an awakening, there was little understanding of the nature of the elements of the city and, more important, about how the elements were related. Between 1905 and 1915, however, there was a distinct change in the way American reformers thought about how the city functioned. In those years some people formerly associated with improvement emphasized that, if the growth of American cities was to be purposefully directed, projects had to have more substance and coordination. The need for both was particularly apparent in New York, the nation's most complex city, where prominent reformers increasingly insisted that the old way of carrying out improvement programs was no longer suitable. At the same time members of art leagues and improvement commissions in other places were arriving at a similar realization.

In March 1908 New York's Municipal Art Society and its Committee on Congestion of Population — two organizations in the improvement tradition, one emphasizing beauty and the other health — jointly mounted an extensive city planning exhibition that summarized both American and European work in this field. This exhibition prepared the way for the first National Conference on City Planning, convened in Washington, D.C., a year later. Dozens of reformers attended, and the conference started a tradition of annual meetings that for many years served as a focus for city planning activity.[84]

The proceedings of the National Conferences on City Planning were issued annually, and between 1905 and 1915 several journals devoted primarily to planning matters were started. These sources of information gave both laymen and experts an understanding of a subject that only a few years before had been all but inaccessible. It even became possible in this period to study city planning in a university; in 1909 the first American course in city planning was started at Harvard University.[85]

Municipal improvement involved many people but often depended on the support of a visible personality, either a benefactor or a prominent designer, for its success. City planning, on the other hand, was taken up by people who preferred to remain anonymous and to put their work on a more substantive footing. The development of city planning along these lines is amply illustrated by the career of Charles Mulford Robinson, who, if not a leader, was at least a representative figure. Robinson was born and brought up in Rochester, New York. When he graduated from college in 1891, he took a job as a newspaper reporter and for twenty-five years, until his untimely death in 1916, was one of the foremost exponents of city planning in the United States. Robinson made his views known primarily through his writing, but he also was an active planner. In his short career he prepared reports for cities and towns from Rochester to Honolulu.[86]

Robinson's interest in planning was formed in 1893 when he saw the World's Columbian Exposition in Chicago. He wrote that when a visitor passed from Lake Michigan into the fair's Court of Honor, "beauty surrounded him and was fairly shouted at him whichever way he turned." When Robinson left the fair, he claimed that "the Dream City that seemed so transitory is still to be seen by many eyes," and he spent the rest of his life trying to help Americans realize that vision.[87] In the five years after the fair Robinson wrote magazine articles about the improvements then being made in American cities and towns. These articles formed the basis of his first book, *The Improvement of Towns and Cities*. As the volume's title indicates, Robinson was writing within the tradition of improvement. He was not trying to elaborate a theory of the growth or functioning of towns. His primary concern was civic beauty, and so he dealt with such topics as advertising, how to make utilities beautiful, the importance of trees, the value of parks, and the need for sculpture at critical intersections of the city.[88]

Robinson extended this discussion in *Modern Civic Art*, but the best summary of the first phase of his career was a short volume, *The Call of the City*. This book was written in an ethereal, dreamlike tone and contained a spontaneous evocation of the charms of the city. Robinson saw every element of the city — the shops, museums, warehouses, even "the dust- and smoke-laden air," and the "wild, fantastic swirls of steam" — as part of a drama, one that was more appealing than nature. He concluded that the city had "romance, poetry, and tragedy," and he beckoned his readers to heed its call.[89]

By 1908, when *The Call of the City* was published, there already was a reaction against such forced attempts to stimulate civic spirit. The new direction of Robinson's career reflected this change of outlook. In 1910 he went for a year of study to Harvard's Department of Landscape Architecture, where he came into contact with other people who were trying to formulate a systematic approach to the study of cities. Robinson traveled in the same year to England, where he attended the second annual Town Planning Conference and met Raymond Unwin.

This important city planner had started his career as a protégé of Ebenezer Howard and a promoter of the ideas associated with the garden city movement. In *Tomorrow*, published in 1898, Howard had suggested an alternative to city and country that had the advantages of both and none of the liabilities. He proposed the construction of cities with a maximum of about 30,000 people. Each would be surrounded by an inviolable greenbelt of agricultural land on which food would be grown for the community. Howard's conception of the garden city was more than a proposal for new towns. It was a utopian vision of a new society, one that was brought about, as the subtitle of *Tomorrow*'s third edition indicated, through a "peaceful path to reform." Raymond Unwin participated in the design of Letchworth, a garden city that was planned in

1903, but then he turned from the idealistic vision of a complete reworking of society to the articulation of concrete principles of city planning
that could be applied to the rebuilding of old cities and to the development of new suburbs. Unwin summarized his ideas on these subjects in
*Town Planning in Practice*, which, when it was published in 1909,
quickly became the accepted manual of planning thought both in England and the United States.[90]

The influence of the quest for a "scientific" approach to city planning
and of Raymond Unwin was evident in Robinson's next book, *The Width
and Arrangement of Streets* (1911). Republished in 1916 as *City Planning*, this volume had a down-to-earth tone that was in marked contrast
to the evocative exhortations of *The Improvement of Towns and Cities*,
*Modern Civic Art*, and *The Call of the City*. In *City Planning* Robinson
did not deny the importance of beauty or cease to call for a civic awakening. The change was one of emphasis. He departed from his earlier writings in insisting that lofty aims had to be realized in the context of an
efficient city. Supporters of improvement had always acknowledged the
need for projects that enhanced the health and economic life of the city,
but at the same time they argued that these pragmatic ends were not
sufficient. The arrangement and appearance of the city, and hence the
life of its inhabitants, had to be governed by a higher purpose, and that
was why beauty was so important. By 1915, however, Robinson and
others who previously had pressed for civic improvement thought that
this emphasis had to be reversed. In *City Planning* Robinson thus was
not as interested in what a city looked like as in how it worked.

The desire to understand the functioning of the city as one complex
network of cause and effect put a new importance on the street system.
At the National Conference on City Planning in 1910, John Nolen had
outlined the basic context of urban development. Streets, he claimed,
were the "framework of a city." They controlled and regulated all land
development. No other feature was so permanent; no other so difficult
to change. Streets had "the most direct and intimate influence upon the
economic, sanitary, and aesthetic development of city life." Every decision about streets — their location and width, the division into roadway
and sidewalk, the planning of utilities underneath — was vital. Those who
attended the conference acknowledged that they knew little about these
issues, so in the following years planners like Nolen and Robinson tried
to formulate a science of street design in order to establish the appropriate context for urban development.[91]

In *City Planning* Robinson proposed a classification of roads. The ideal city had a distinct focus. From it emanated the main arteries, which, because of their size and location, attracted the bulk of the traffic. Within this pattern of primary thoroughfares was a secondary network of local roads and within that a tertiary system of residential streets. This hierarchy was similar to a system of rivers, streams, and brooks, a classification differing sharply from that which usually resulted from the conventional grid pattern.

Robinson recognized that the rectilinear method of land subdivision had many virtues. It was easily extendable and it defined economically sized lots. A grid of streets could be simply and cheaply laid out by amateur surveyors, and with regular streets it was easy to compute distances. But Robinson believed that the advantages of the grid were outweighed by its defects. Supporters of improvement had often criticized the grid system because it did not provide a focus for a town and also because it was incompatible with a rolling or hilly landscape. Robinson reiterated these points, but he went beyond this level of criticism to more fundamental issues.

Robinson acknowledged that it was possible to establish a grid with varying dimensions between streets, but this was rarely done. The grid was usually uniformly applied and the result was a standard layout: one size of block was repeated throughout the city. Robinson felt that this practice contradicted common sense. Different activities of the city had different needs and, therefore, had to be accommodated in different areas. Robinson urged the planner to follow the architect who designed each room of a house for its own function and who then arranged all the spaces so that the house worked properly as an entity. Thus, a city should have distinct commercial, manufacturing, and residential districts, each of which would be based on a street system that defined areas of land suited to its needs and which would also be properly located in relation to the others.[92]

Robinson showed how unduly narrow streets that carried primary traffic impeded the flow of goods and decreased the value of commercial property. He cited a report demonstrating that it cost as much to deliver supplies within Chicago as it did to transport them a hundred miles across Lake Michigan. In *City Planning*, however, Robinson did not analyze in depth the needs of the commercial and industrial sectors of the city. Instead, he focused on housing.

Robinson chose this emphasis because he thought there had been an unprecedented amount of land subdivision and laying out of streets since the custom of selling house lots on a small down payment had begun. He illustrated this phenomenon by describing a study which showed that in Omaha, Nebraska, between 1903 and 1913, an average of 535 acres per year had been subdivided. Thus, at five lots to the acre, 2,675 lots were annually laid out in Omaha. The increase in population from 1900 to 1910 had been approximately 2,200 people per year. Robinson assumed that more than an average of about one person lived on the new lots, and therefore that there was a new demand for suburban housing, not only from newcomers but also from old residents who wished to move. From this not very rigorous report, Robinson had learned the purpose of "the

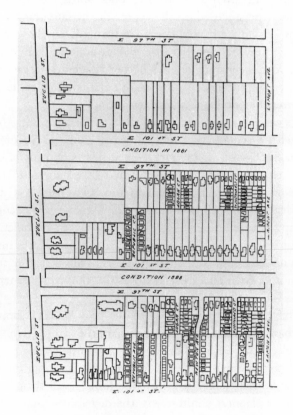

46. *"A Block in Cleveland, Ohio," in 1881, 1898, and 1912. To prevent the deterioration of such areas, city planners urged the passage of zoning laws.*

continuous outward growth of cities." It was "the new hope, of a real home," one with light and air on all sides, privacy, and a garden. This new hope was not a fad; its roots went deep into human nature and were "bound up with the love of home and the yearning for it." So important was the promise of this demand for homes on the outskirts of cities that no claim was higher on the city planner than to try to satisfy it.[93]

This argument justified an emphasis on housing, but Robinson's concern was not due simply to the new demand for homes. That demand had existed before the turn of the century and before it was possible to buy lots on a small down payment. Instead, Robinson's emphasis reflected a desire to correct a bias of earlier improvement work. Supporters of improvement, in their attempt to awaken civic spirit and to unify villages and cities, had often focused on the center of the community as the place that was most visible and most needed reform. Even those who thought of the city as a City of Homes had not done housing full justice because they tended to concentrate on the better residential areas, where they emphasized the importance of attractive surroundings rather than more practical matters like drainage and street paving.

Robinson's earlier books had shared these predispositions. *Modern Civic Art* began with a section that proclaimed a "New Day for Cities" and moved on to discussions of the city's focal points and of its business district. Only then did Robinson explain how to treat the residential sectors. His chapters on this subject proceeded from "On Great Avenues" to "On Minor Residential Streets" and finally to "Among the Tenements." In that last chapter he acknowledged that steps had to be taken to prevent overcrowding and mentioned what a few of these measures might be. But the creation of the "new Jerusalem" was primarily a matter for civic art, and so Robinson focused on ways to make the city's tenements more beautiful.[94]

Planners have never fully agreed about how to treat housing in the scope of urban problems, but for many of the people who first called themselves city planners the discovery of housing was extremely important. Having subdued their calls for a civic awakening, planners found another cause in their desire to help Americans fulfill their "new hope."

One way that planners could satisfy the demand for new homes was to determine how to make them more accessible. Robinson described how major arteries had to be designed to accommodate rapid streetcar transportation, but the more important task was to coordinate a city's entire transportation system. The significance of low, flat fares for the accessibility of inexpensive suburban homes had long been understood. But as planners began to refine their discipline, they started to perceive how complex these relationships were. They saw that the construction of a transit line often raised the value of land, and therefore the cost of the housing that was built on it. Then two- or three-story structures with several apartments were built instead of the single-family homes that were the new hope. To be effective, therefore, a transit system not only had to be inexpensive but also had to extend simultaneously to competing areas. How to make it do so entailed a degree of expertise that advocates of improvement had never understood it was necessary to acquire.[95]

As planners tried to analyze the complex relationship of transportation and housing, they had to take into consideration not only various forms of mass transit but also the automobile. After 1910 the usefulness of the automobile, not just for sporting and pleasure, but also for commuting, was increasingly emphasized. An article in 1913, entitled "The Automobile and Its Mission," summarized the change that had taken place in the previous few years. At the turn of the century the automobile was a novelty; by 1908 it was still a "transcendent play thing — thrilling, seductive, desperately expensive." In the following five years production increased fivefold, and by 1913 the automobile was already making possible a new pattern of residential settlement by opening up large areas of urban land that the less versatile streetcar and railroad could not reach.[96]

Better accessibility was important for housing, but Robinson and other planners also tried to illuminate other issues that were related to the nature and quality of homes. They attached great importance to the widths of the streets on which houses were located. This dimension was critical in establishing the cost of nearby buildings. Robinson explained that a developer or landlord had to pay interest on his capital outlay for the site, the roads, and the buildings. He also had expenses for repairs, management, taxes, and insurance. Of these factors, site development costs, the expenditure on roads, the taxes, and the insurance payments all depended on the street arrangement. The scale of rents was, therefore, largely determined by the street planner.

Evidence of this relationship came from France, where it had been discussed in a report at the Congrès International des Habitations à Bon Marché, and from England where Raymond Unwin had worked out the costs of different arrangements of roads. In America the Topographical Survey Commission of Baltimore challenged the traditional practice of making all streets 66 feet wide with 50 feet of paved roadway. The commission showed that when the pavement of a minor street could be reduced to 24 feet, there would be a substantial saving on paving alone. Frederick Law Olmsted, Jr., extended the argument beyond this simple level of calculation. He related the cost of land subdivision not only to the width of the street, but also to the length and depth of lots along it, thus showing how a developer could reduce expenses and at the same time define pieces of land on which well-planned houses could be constructed.[97]

The economic implications of the width of streets were matched in importance by social consequences. Planning experts in Europe had often noticed the relationship between street widths and the prevalence of slums. The great cost of a broad street made it necessary to squeeze large rents from the frontage, either by building tall tenements, as in Paris or Berlin, or by erecting houses one behind another deep into a block, as was the practice in some English cities. American planners recognized that both phenomena were common in the United States. Large tenements were bad, but the cheap houses constructed in back yards or along alleys were worse. These structures were not controllable by ordinary police inspection and were not open to public observation and criticism. Although it had long been alleged that these places were breeding grounds for disease and vice, in the years before the First World War public health officials and social scientists gathered rigorous data about this subject and pooled their expertise to establish the specific nature of the relationship.[98]

Medical research further underlined the relationship of street width to health by showing that dust caused or aggravated several diseases, the most serious of which was tuberculosis. According to this argument, wide, uninterrupted streets were bad because they easily collected dust that was then blown into adjacent buildings. A road system laid out on the four quadrants was also harmful because one side of all houses on east-west streets had to face north. Rooms with that orientation received no sunlight and, therefore, violated a first principle of public health. Some of these relationships had been discussed at least since the middle of the nineteenth century. But after 1900 the subject received a degree of scrutiny it had not previously attracted.[99]

The precise nature of the streets to be defined by these economic, social, and sanitary considerations depended on the type of houses on them. Robinson argued that just as residential districts had to be distinguishable from business, commercial, industrial, and other areas, so it was necessary to separate one type of housing from another. In American cities planned on a uniform grid there had been a misfit between the quality of a house and the size of a lot. That was why, when inexpensive houses were constructed on large lots, back yards and unoccupied spaces had often been sold off to provide sites for ramshackle buildings.

Robinson reasoned that those who lived in a populous community were never all of "like conditions and circumstances." The street plan had to reflect that fact, and so he distinguished between two types of residential streets, "minor high-class streets" and "minor streets for humble homes." No sharp line could be drawn between the two, but the first had substantial houses on large lots and was laid out to take advantage of the local topography. Precedents for such streets went back to Roland Park, a suburb built in Baltimore in the 1890s, to Riverside in Chicago in the late 1860s, and ultimately to the first suburban community, Llewellyn Park, which had been laid out in Orange, New Jersey, in the 1850s. The desirability of the informal pattern of residential streets within the boundaries defined by main traffic thoroughfares was also being emphasized by European plannners like Raymond Unwin and Bernard Kampffmeyer, the chairman of the German Garden City Association. By 1915 American planners were as aware of these precedents as they were of those in their own tradition of suburban design.[100]

For reasons of economy the second type of street had to be laid out more rigidly than the first. House lots on it were smaller, but Robinson believed that with proper planning it would be possible not only to make attractive streets but also to provide workingmen with their own homes. These streets could be located in two types of districts. One was nearer the center of town than the "high-class" areas. From that location workmen could easily travel to their jobs. Robinson did caution that streets near downtown areas had to be carefully designed to counteract the attractions of the cheap entertainment that inevitably gathered on nearby main thoroughfares. He recognized that these streets had a vitality that was important to the lives of those "craving distraction from the narrow round of oppressive duty." Nevertheless, it was not a "correct social or civic ideal" to plan housing on these avenues. The planner's job instead was "to provide the individual home on a more livable street" nearby.[101]

The second area in which "humble homes" could be located was in industrial suburbs. From the middle of the nineteenth century on, a few philanthropic factory owners had tried to locate their businesses on the outskirts of the city and to build housing nearby for their employees.

The town of Pullman on the edge of Chicago was the best known of these industrial suburbs. But after the turn of the century planners inspired by Ebenezer Howard increasingly discussed the possibility for decentralizing both industry and housing. An American Garden City Association was founded in 1905 to build the completely self-sufficient communities that Howard had outlined. Because of the depression of 1907, the organization never had a chance to put its ideals into practice.[102]

Many diluted versions of the garden city were built. The most widely discussed and perhaps the least successful was in Gary, Indiana, where the United States Steel Corporation built a city for 12,000 on what had been marshland and sand dunes. To save expenses the corporation did not hire a planner and left the construction of the housing to real estate developers. The result was an ill-considered grid of streets and a lakefront that was not preserved for recreation. The Goodyear Tire and Rubber Company hired the talented landscape architect Warren Manning, who built a more successful community on a hundred-acre tract near Akron, Ohio. The architect Grosvenor Atterbury planned a similar development for the Norton Grinding Company in Worcester, Massachusetts. Several other companies built garden suburbs in such places as Billerica, Massachusetts; Kistler, Pennsylvania; Duluth, Minnesota; and Beloit, Wisconsin. These satellites of larger cities were not numerous, but they were important because in coordinating industry, housing, and other facilities they showed the advantages of planning.[103]

Planners differed about how to draw distinctions between types of streets and the houses on them, but they were unanimous that the desired pattern of streets had to be set down in a comprehensive plan by a local planning commission. In 1907 Hartford, Connecticut, became the first American city to make such an organization part of its government, and in the following five years New York, New Jersey, Ohio, California, and Pennsylvania passed laws enabling their cities and towns to establish planning organizations. But Massachusetts set the standard in 1913 by requiring all cities and towns with more than 10,000 people to create planning boards that in addition to other duties were specifically charged to make plans for the "proper housing" of their residents.[104]

Laws were necessary to put the plans into practice. One type of legislation that was frequently discussed dealt with taxation. Ever since Henry George wrote *Our Land and Land Policy* in 1871, many Americans had claimed that it was more equitable to tax land rather than, as was customary in the United States, the buildings on it. George believed that every man had a natural right to apply his labor to land. When he had to pay rent for the privilege of working the land, he was robbed of some of his labor. A single tax on land would not only prevent the ownership of large tracts by a few people; it would also relieve industry and commerce of the tax burden they then had to shoulder.[105]

George's ideas were primarily popular among farmers, but they also applied to cities. Advocates of the single tax argued that if land on the outskirts of cities was freed, then the cost of housing would be reduced and more Americans could own their own homes. After the turn of the century some planners were attracted to these ideas. No legislation seemed more important to them than laws to shift the burden of taxes. Some of them linked this reform to other measures. They suggested Americans follow the example of German municipalities that, to prevent speculation in land, had acquired large tracts within the city limits and had built inexpensive homes for their citizens.[106]

Other city planners disagreed with these proposals. They reasoned that if the owners of skyscrapers in Manhattan, to cite the extreme case, were relieved of taxes, then the great mass of home owners would have to pay more. Besides, if land was taxed instead of buildings, it would be wise to use it intensively; more tenements and fewer individual homes would then be built.[107]

These were complicated issues that, because they touched on the very nature and function of property, often led to acrimony. Most planners were interested in taxation but preferred not to take a stand on it. They believed, or at least hoped, that efficient planning would itself solve the problems that the advocates of the taxation of land were addressing.[108]

The legislation planners considered most important for the implementation of their procedures dealt with the zoning of land to establish and fix the character of an area. Zoning laws not only created a differentiated city but also prevented the great inefficiency of continuously changing neighborhoods. American planners recommended two types of legislation: one, a law to fix the bulk of building allowable on a lot of land by establishing the maximum percentage of coverage, the height of the structure, and the setback from the street and property lines; the other, a law to distinguish among different uses of land. Planners and housing experts assumed that a particular type of building was most satisfactory when it was surrounded by others of its own kind. To create this condition, they designated areas of a city for residential, commercial, industrial, or other uses, but they also differentiated among types of housing. How they defined the distinctions varied. Some planners thought it was primarily necessary to separate multifamily houses from those for one family; others distinguished between individual houses on large and small lots.

Zoning legislation in the United States was an extension of long-standing laws to prevent nuisances. Many communities have always had regulations that, in effect, declared that it was illegal to use one's rights to infringe on those of another. But the designation of a district for a specific use was first made only in the early 1880s. Legislation similar to later zoning laws was at that time passed in California to restrict the location of Chinese laundries that were mixed in with houses. The basic motive was discriminatory, but the ordinances were couched in arguments about sanitation and public welfare and set a precedent for later restrictions on the use of land.

The powers inherent in these laws were not widely used until after the turn of the century. The first major ordinance was passed in Los Angeles in 1909, and by 1915 every part of that city was covered by zoning laws. These regulations divided Los Angeles into a large residential district in which only the lightest manufacturing was allowed, twenty-seven industrial districts in which all kinds of factories were permitted, and about a hundred areas in which all but the heaviest and most objectionable industries could be located.[109]

Robinson understood the need for and supported such legislation, but he was not altogether happy with the divisions it created. On the one hand he argued that "both rich and poor are probably happier in their own environment, among their own kind, where each can lead his own life, in his own way, without covetousness or odious comparison." On the other hand he acknowledged that there was much to say for mixing classes as a "sociological ideal." Other planners shared Robinson's quandary. Some hoped to resolve it by designating only small areas for specific types of housing, making it possible for a variety of people to live close together. For Robinson this procedure was the "saving clause" of his dilemma.[110]

Robinson assumed that with good planning separate districts would not be vast, undifferentiated areas. He did not specify the best size for a residential district or the ideal distribution of people within it, but the type of community he favored was a version of the village. He explored his ideal in *Third Ward Traits*, a pamphlet he wrote about the district in which he had grown up in Rochester. The Third Ward was near the center of the city, but it was not "far fetched to liken it to a village." It had the atmosphere of one in its "homesteads in their ample gardens along the tree-arched streets" and in "the simple customs, the pride of locality and pride of family, the petty leaders, whose pretensions are thoroughly understood, the little stores on the borders — some of them very village-like." The ward had its own history, churches, schools, a public library, and "just enough poor to keep its sympathies alive."[111]

Many of the period's reformers were born and raised in small towns, and similar descriptions appear in their autobiographical writings. This background informed their thought about the best context for the home in the city. The way they adapted their idea of the village to the city was to define the outlines of an area, a "neighborhood unit," that provided a focus for the lives of its residents. The concept of the neighborhood unit initially grew out of an innovation in the use of schools. Educational theorists who noticed that schools were used only a few hours of the day and not at all on weekends and in the summer started to call for their "wider use." In many cities they started evening classes. Some were remedial; teaching English to immigrants was especially popular. Others were for people with general interests. Advocates of wider use also wanted school playgrounds to be opened during vacations. Newark, New Jersey, put this idea into practice with an ambitious program of "directed play" in its school yards.[112]

While the wider-use movement was originally concerned only with extending specific educational programs to people who needed them, some educators hoped to fulfill a broader purpose. The school might be a community or social center that would serve as a public forum where important issues could be discussed and disparate members of the community could meet. The best example of use of a school system as a network of community centers was in Rochester, New York. One of the leaders there was Edward J. Ward, a Presbyterian minister who had a broad definition of his religious duties. An organizer of youth activities and a community leader, Ward hoped that the extended use of the school buildings in large cities might engender a neighborly spirit that would be equivalent to that which he believed had existed in towns. Gatherings in the social center would be similar to the old town meetings held in little red schoolhouses in New England.[113]

Architects and planners quickly learned that the neighborhood and the social center had important implications for their work. The wider use of the school meant that the building itself had to change, and for a neighborhood to be effective it was important to know how large such a place should be and how to define it in the context of other urban functions. Planners pointed out that a community's public facilities usually were not planned in a coordinated manner. A few shops were often grouped together, but they had no ostensible relationship to places for recreation, libraries, post offices, schools, or churches. To bring these facilities together, they urged that the nucleus of an urban neighborhood be formed by joining school and playground and then by grouping other public buildings nearby.[114]

Landscape architects and city planners realized that the size of the neighborhood depended on the density of settlement within it, but they came to consider the maximum walking distance to a school a critical dimension. Studies showed that this distance was between a quarter and a half mile and therefore the maximum size of a neighborhood unit

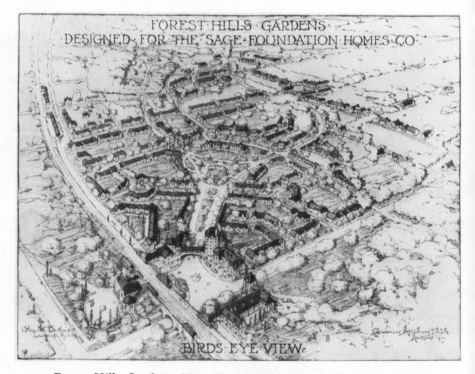

*47. Forest Hills Gardens, New York. The purpose of this development, which was begun in 1909, was to create a "harmonious neighborhood." Grosvenor Atterbury was the architect; Frederick Law Olmsted, Jr., the landscape architect. Station Square is at the bottom of this perspective. It extends into the Village Green.*

was about one hundred sixty acres. Henry Hubbard polled a number of experts and found that they agreed on these figures, George Ford surveyed children who used playgrounds in Newark and learned that all lived within a quarter-mile radius, and in a plan for suburban communities in Detroit Arthur Comey also arrived at the same measure.[115]

In 1909 the Russell Sage Foundation sponsored the first explicitly designed neighborhood unit, Forest Hills Gardens, Long Island. Frederick Law Olmsted, Jr., Grosvenor Atterbury, and Clarence Perry brought together the talents of landscape architect, architect, and educator to create a garden suburb with Long Island Railroad connections to Manhattan. The community of 174 acres was intended for about five thousand people or roughly thirty people per acre.

For the community to be a distinct entity it was important to separate Forest Hills Gardens from other areas. The land was cut off on two sides by a highway and a railroad; the other sides were unimproved land. With such distinct boundaries, the area would be used primarily by its own residents. The nature of the internal road system reinforced the sense of neighborhood. Only two roads were through streets; the rest were entirely local, thereby keeping external traffic away. The focal point of the street system was Station Square, where commuters took trains to Manhattan and housewives did their shopping. Two curving thoroughfares fed into this center. All the other streets were narrower and frequently curved. Where the two main streets converged, there was a triangular green of about an acre and a half, broken into two sections of lawn and shrubbery. The green had a flagpole and later a monument to residents who served during the First World War.[116]

With their emphasis on rigorous methods of analysis, on the need for a city plan based on a rational transportation system, on the role of housing, on the importance of zoning legislation, and on the proper definition of a neighborhood unit, American plannners had made significant advances over the techniques and ideas of their predecessors. Yet there was still much they did not know. Their estimates, for example, of the volume and impact of transportation, especially by automobile, were rudimentary; they had little conception of the uses to which zoning could be put; and their idea of efficiency was naive and self-defeating. Nevertheless, in a few years they had prepared the foundation for most of the city planning of the following half century.

But with this achievement there were losses. In their best moments supporters of improvement were motivated by the often incoherently formulated belief that, no matter what its size, the village or city could be one vast community. As improvement became planning and as the concerned citizen was replaced by the expert and the bureaucrat, this vision of the all-encompassing community faded. In the years that followed there were periods in which the idea flickered back to life. Indeed, it probably has never been completely extinguished. But planners have generally not gauged the success of a city by the amount of spirit it engenders. For them the city has been meaningful primarily insofar as it efficiently delivers services, goods, information, education, entertainment, and jobs to its homes.

+++

A competition for the development of a quarter section of land on the outskirts of Chicago best summarized American thought about the nature of a neighborhood just before the First World War. This competition was sponsored in 1913 by the City Club, a civic organization with a broader membership than the exclusive Commercial Club. The purpose of the City Club was to stimulate discussion about the political, social, and economic conditions of the community and to make proposals for improvements to the local government. Each member belonged to committees that studied Chicago's problems.[117]

The man most directly identified with the City Club was its civic secretary, George E. Hooker. Born in 1861, Hooker had been a lawyer and a minister before he became a writer for Chicago newspapers and then civic secretary of the City Club. Hooker coordinated the City Club's work, but his role was not solely administrative. A man of great energy and humor, Hooker transmitted his interests and enthusiasms to many of the club's members.[118]

Hooker had long been concerned about urban problems. He was secretary of the special street railway committee of the City Council of Chicago in 1897 and 1898, and he often spoke about transportation problems to the City Club.[119] He was also interested in the city's appearance. Hooker was one of the first Americans to become acquainted with the work of the Viennese architect Camillo Sitte, who, saddened by the deterioration of European cities, wrote *Der Stadtebau*, in which he described how to design cities while preserving and taking advantage of the buildings and spaces that gave them character. Much impressed, Hooker wrote several articles about how Sitte's principles could be used in the United States.[120]

*48. Rudolf Schindler: A neighborhood center for
a suburb of Chicago. Schindler came to Chicago
from Austria in 1914. Shortly thereafter, he made
this plan of a neighborhood center for a competition sponsored by the Chicago Architectural Club
and the City Club.*

Although other Americans shared these interests, Hooker explained later that much early improvement work had been unsatisfactory. Until after the turn of the century, those who were attacking the housing problem, struggling with transportation issues, trying to do something about the lack of recreational facilities, or "bewailing the architectural ugliness" were "separately seeing only unsatisfactory conditions" and hardly anyone was finding anything promising. Then the situation changed; "there came into the air the phrase 'city planning,' and it seemed like the clearing of a clouded sky."[121]

The City Club reflected this new interest. After 1910 the city planning committee was among the club's most active groups, and in 1911 it began a comprehensive survey of the physical condition of Chicago. To assist this work Hooker and another member attended that year's National Conference on City Planning. The housing committee was also popular and energetic. In 1912 it prepared a report on the laws and regulations of Illinois and Chicago that affected housing, and of the one hundred fifty people who attended that year's National Conference on Housing eleven came from the City Club.[122]

In March 1913 the housing committee organized an exhibition and in conjunction with that event sponsored the competition for the development of a quarter section of land that was connected by streetcar lines to Chicago's business district, about eight miles away. The square tract had not yet been subdivided and was without trees or buildings, but the surrounding area was laid out with the prevailing grid of streets and had on it a typical array of scattered frame houses. Large factories were located a half mile to four miles from the site. The competition's rules stipulated only that a maximum of 1,280 families be accommodated on the quarter section. There were no further directions about what kind of housing was required or what additional facilities were necessary.

This open-ended brief gave the contestants the freedom to show "the essentials of good housing in its broadest sense." However, the City Club's predisposition was reflected in the pamphlets it put on sale as a convenience to the competitors. These works described "the progress of the garden city and the garden suburb movement." The entries were extremely varied. One was submitted by a sanitarian whose primary concern was the orientation of buildings to sunlight. Other contestants wanted to create a neighborhood with an impressive center. They ran main, diagonal streets from the corners of the site to an imposing focal complex of buildings that contained a neighborhood center, shops, a post office, banks, and other facilities for the public.

The schemes that took the first two prizes also tried to deflect the grid
as it entered the site but did so with curved streets that avoided "deadly
monotony" and added "character" to the suburban development. As at
Forest Hills Gardens and European garden suburbs, the winning schemes
distinguished among several grades of streets that were laid out so that
through traffic routes did not intersect with quiet, residential areas. The
housing was sited according to well-defined rules, but within this context
it was deliberately varied to add to the picturesqueness of the street. As
the focus of the site, each scheme had a neighborhood center near a
public park.[123]

Each of the first two prize schemes, like many of the other entries, had
positive qualities. But two other designs stood out from the rest because

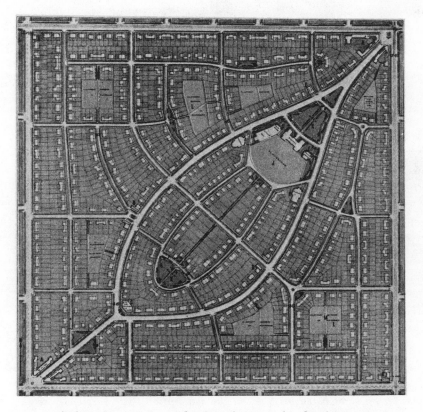

*49. Arthur Comey: Second-prize plan for the development of a
quarter section of Chicago, 1913. Like Comey, most entrants to this
competition used curved streets to vary their design and to give the
site a central focus.*

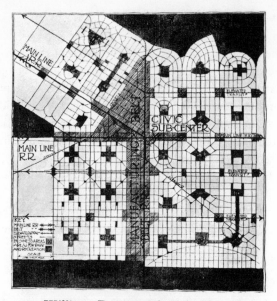

50. *William Drummond: "A City Area
Developed on the 'Neighborhood Unit'
Plan," 1913. Drummond was the only en-
trant to place the quarter section in the
larger context of Chicago and to exploit the
important connection between land use and
transportation.*

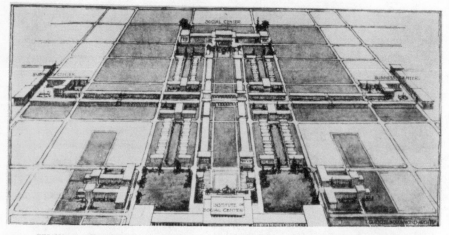

51. *William Drummond: "Bird's-eye View of Two Adjoining Units,"
1913. Drummond based his plan on the assumption that the quarter section
would be developed over a long period. He tried to create an initial nucleus
that would be self-sufficient but that would also serve as the basis for future
developments.*

they were endowed with a special perception about the possibilities of urban development in the Midwest. William Drummond, the progressive Chicago architect, was the author of one of these entries. He was an ardent believer in garden suburbs. At the National Conference on Housing in 1913 he announced that "city society is sick" and outlined a vision not only of a city settled in garden suburbs but also of a society that acknowledged that "human life is the most precious thing we know."[124]

Drummond believed that a tax on the unearned increment of land would provide the funds to finance the building of the communities that would be the context of his benevolent society. His ideal settlement was a version of the "neighborhood unit." Drummond divided the entire city into areas approximately a quarter section in size that were linked together by Chicago's transportation routes. Each would be a social and political unit with an "institute" that would serve as the nucleus of the community's intellectual, recreational, and civic life.

Drummond's plan stands out from other schemes based on neighborhood centers not only because of the intensity of his idealistic vision of what a community could be but also because he made a unique interpretation of its physical form. Instead of creating an introverted community by laying out curved streets, Drummond tried to find a system of streets and landscaping compatible with the flat prairie. Since Chicago's "greatest claim to the eye" was the "long-sweeping distances everywhere evident," Drummond created vistas "so disposed as to emphasize the freedom of involvement and the breadth of space which are the chief characteristics of the great western prairie."

He achieved this effect in a plan designed to accommodate the growth of the community. Apartment buildings, low-cost housing, the institute, and the business center would be constructed first to provide "a nucleus or frame in the articulation of the plan." This group of buildings would establish the basis for the pattern of development that was to follow as outlying areas would later be filled in with other structures. In the interim, vacant areas could be used for agriculture. However, no matter how many buildings were later added, once the nucleus was constructed, the basis of the community was established.

In the brief competition entry Drummond did not describe in detail how his plan would be put into practice; nevertheless, his drawings and his notion of the nucleus of future development suggest ideas that were far ahead of their time. When everyone else was trying to find ways to minimize the effects of urban growth and change, Drummond seemed to intimate that these forces could be used as the basis not only of a new type of community but also of a new urban aesthetic.[125]

The other significant scheme, a noncompetitive entry, was by Frank Lloyd Wright. He prefaced the remarks that accompanied his drawings with Thomas Carlyle's statement: "Fool! The Ideal is within thyself. The condition is but the stuff thou shalt use to shape that same Ideal out of." Unlike William Drummond, Wright did not base his plan on a vision of an ideal society, nor was he interested in applying European ideas to the American context. In city planning, he wrote, "we are obsessed by the old world thing, in the old world way with the result that, in this grim workshop, our finer possibilities are usually handed over to fashion and sham. Confusing art with manners and aristocracy, we ape the academic Gaston or steal from 'My Lord' his admirable traditions when our problems need, not fashioning from *without*, but development from *within*." Wright accepted the "characteristic agglomeration" of business buildings, apartments, and houses that existed in every suburban part of Chicago. He also extended the grid of streets through the site. These elements provided a more than adequate base for a satisfactory community. To them Wright added only "minor modifications in harmony with the nature of the aggregation."

Wright's zoning of the site put larger buildings on the band of blocks at the north and south, where the transportation lines led to Chicago's business district. The southern band of blocks, which was bordered by a less traveled street than that on the north, contained groups of several kinds of multiple residences. These "background" buildings protected the rest of the quarter section from noisy city traffic. The north and south parts of the site were connected by a meandering greenbelt, which provided a walkway for children and contained all the educational facilities of the community, as well as a lagoon for ice-skating and swimming. The greater part of the quarter section was, therefore, left "quiet and clear" for houses. Wright covered this area with his "quadruple blocks," a system of land subdivision that gave each house a corner lot and left each home owner automatically protected from all others. "His windows," Wright explained, "all look upon open vistas and upon no one's unsightly necessities. His building is in unconscious but necessary grouping with three of his neighbors', looking out upon harmonious groups of other neighbors."

Although Wright acknowledged different categories of residents, everyone had easy access to the public facilities. The quarter section

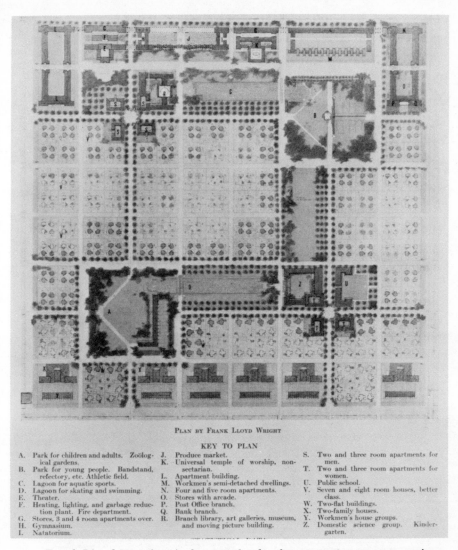

PLAN BY FRANK LLOYD WRIGHT

### KEY TO PLAN

A.  Park for children and adults. Zoölog-
    ical gardens.
B.  Park for young people. Bandstand,
    refectory, etc. Athletic field.
C.  Lagoon for aquatic sports.
D.  Lagoon for skating and swimming.
E.  Theater.
F.  Heating, lighting, and garbage reduc-
    tion plant. Fire department.
G.  Stores, 3 and 4 room apartments over.
H.  Gymnasium.
I.  Natatorium.

J.  Produce market.
K.  Universal temple of worship, non-
    sectarian.
L.  Apartment building.
M.  Workmen's semi-detached dwellings.
N.  Four and five room apartments.
O.  Stores with arcade.
P.  Post Office branch.
Q.  Bank branch.
R.  Branch library, art galleries, museum,
    and moving picture building.

S.  Two and three room apartments for
    men.
T.  Two and three room apartments for
    women.
U.  Public school.
V.  Seven and eight room houses, better
    class.
W.  Two-flat buildings.
X.  Two-family houses.
Y.  Workmen's house groups.
Z.  Domestic science group. Kinder-
    garten.

*52. Frank Lloyd Wright: A plan for the development of a quarter section
of Chicago, 1913. Wright used elements of the landscape and the grid of
streets to structure his quarter section.*

would be a neighborhood insofar as the residents used and supported
these institutions, but Wright understood that in a modern society a
sense of community could exist in many spatial realms. He saw no reason
to emphasize the identity or insularity of the quarter section. The relationship with the surrounding areas was equally important. To make this

point, Wright extended the grid of streets through the site and used it as the basis of his plan.

Unlike other architects who despised the grid, Wright attributed a great significance and subtlety to it. The grid extended out from the quarter section to other parts of Chicago, to roads laid out on the ordinance survey lines, and ultimately to the most remote corners of the United States. Within the quarter section, when properly inflected, the grid organized the buildings and landscape and continued into the pattern of sidewalks and the planning modules of the houses.

The grid had an important meaning in time as well as in space. It had its origins early in American history, and its use extended back to ancient civilizations. In 1913 the grid was still useful, and Wright could then only assume that it would guide future development. The grid of streets, in summary, joined neighbors, Americans from coast to coast, and people throughout the world, past, present, and future. Instead of fragmenting a neighborhood, it could be the basis of a community that was much richer and more complex than a version of the self-contained village of the past.[126]

# 3

## THE HOME GROUNDS

By the First World War, American reformers were trying to define the characteristics and boundaries of a neighborhood. This discussion proceeded in part on its own terms, but it could not be divorced from another long-standing debate. Since the middle of the nineteenth century there had been many conflicting opinions about how to situate a house in relationship to its immediate neighbors. One important part of this discussion centered around the country or suburban house. Separateness was essential to the identity of such a house, but there was no consensus about how the land between houses should be divided or about how it should be used.

An extreme statement of one point of view was the quadruple block plan that Frank Lloyd Wright first designed in 1906 and later used for the quarter section on the outskirts of Chicago. Wright tried to give each house as spacious and prominent a piece of land as possible: a corner lot. He huddled the outbuildings, kitchen gardens, and service yards of the four houses in the back, so that there would be broad lawns in the front. In his landscaping of the areas that faced the street Wright differentiated the boundaries of each house's property only by a small strip of planting. The lawn, sidewalk, and street were all one continuous public landscape.[1]

The lack of a distinct definition of private property was the very feature that irritated Vernon L. Parrington, the scholar of American intellectual history. In an article written in 1904 Parrington found that in the conventional suburban layout Americans were more interested in courting the approval of neighbors and strangers than in securing their own comfort and privacy. As an example he recalled a block in Seattle

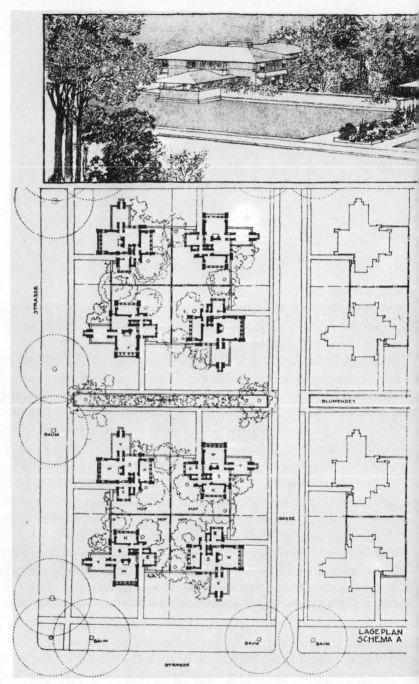

53. *Frank Lloyd Wright: Quadruple block plan for the prairie. Wright
based this plan not only on the pattern of streets*

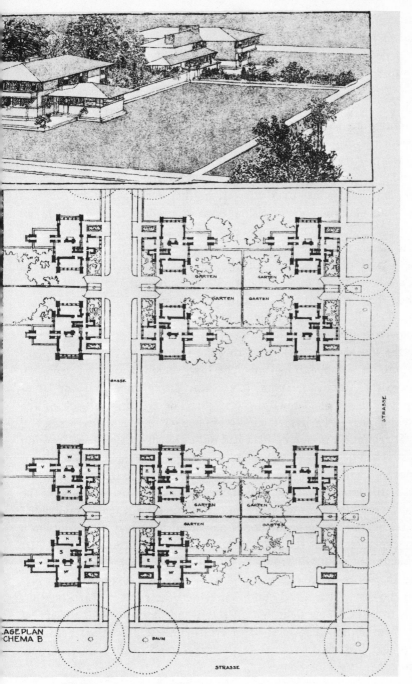

that stemmed from the ordinance survey grid but also on the assumption that corner lots were most desirable.

that had expensive and tasteful houses on four corners but no alleys or fences to demarcate individual property lines. The four houses were set in a continuous greensward interrupted only by an occasional clump of shrubs or flowers. Parrington acknowledged that this openness was public-spirited, but he did not think that it made a good place in which to live. In attempting to formulate an alternative arrangement Parrington tried to discover the origins of this "curious love of publicity." He speculated that it was a survival from a frontier period when new settlers were undergoing deprivation and loneliness. In such circumstances it was natural to seek companionship. Moreover, in that early state, since it was impossible to undertake every task at once, the public front of the house was generally finished first. Improvements at the rear had to wait until later and often were never made.

Writing just after the turn of the century, Parrington argued that Americans were living in a fundamentally new period and should, therefore, shed the vestiges of frontier attitudes that still were preserved in the suburbs. City life afforded enough contact with the crowd; when the suburban resident returned home in the evening, it was entirely proper to shut the world out. Parrington, therefore, drew two contrasting plans for a house on a conventional lot. The first, which was a representation of the typical American layout, gave great prominence to front lawns and a porch that looked out on the street. The area in the back of the house was haphazardly divided among kitchen gardens, laundry yards, and stables. Parrington's preferred plan had only a small area of grass fronting on the street. The focus of the house was toward the back, where a generous porch opened onto a large, hedge-enclosed garden. In this plan the laundry yard, kitchen garden, and stables were not near the back of the house but were located as far away on the perimeter of the lot as possible.[2]

The tradition Parrington deplored may well have had deep roots in a frontier experience, but the suburbs laid out shortly after the Civil War were themselves a kind of frontier. The homes there were not as isolated as those in the country, but they were also not as crowded together as those in the city. That novel condition caused the residents of these subdivisions to make a new definition of the proper disposition of the spaces around their homes. The method of treating these areas then became a standard that was used to measure the nature and quality of the spaces between other types of houses.

✦✦✦

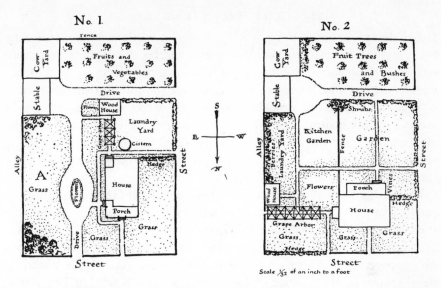

No. 1.    No. 2

*54. V. L. Parrington: "On The Lack of Privacy in American Village Homes," 1903. Frank J. Scott called the practice of growing a high hedge in front of one's house not only "unneighborly" but also "heathen."*

Between 1865 and 1915 there was a great increase in writing about all matters that touched upon the care and use of the home grounds. Some of this output took the form of learned studies of horticulture, floriculture, and arboriculture. Much of what was written, however, was intended for general readers who wanted to learn how best to treat the spaces around their homes. Many books on gardening and magazines such as *Country Life in America, Suburban Life, House and Garden,* and the *American Garden* put the discussion before a broad audience, while newspapers tried to increase their circulations by hiring experts to write about the cultivation of flowers, the care of the lawn, and related topics.[3]

Of all this literature *The Art of Beautifying the Home Grounds,* the first book devoted entirely to the subject of suburban gardening, is the best introduction to the issues involved in the design and use of the spaces around American houses. Writing in 1870, Frank J. Scott, the entertaining author of this handsomely illustrated volume, readily acknowledged his debt to Andrew Jackson Downing. Scott intended his book to do for the suburban home of the 1870s what Downing's books had done for the country villas, cottages, and farmhouses of the 1840s and 1850s.[4]

In addition to Downing, Scott had another significant predecessor, his father, Jesup W. Scott. Born in Ridgefield, Connecticut, in 1799, the elder Scott moved in 1830 to the Maumee River region of Ohio and then settled in Toledo, where he acquired substantial tracts of land. Once established in Ohio, Scott began to elaborate the theory that the greatest city in the nation and probably also in the world would eventually be located on the central plain of the United States. He predicted that this city would be at the west end of Lake Erie, an area with outstanding natural advantages, and he frequently promoted Toledo as his choice for the great metropolis of the future.[5]

In the 1840s and 1850s Scott continued to marshal facts and statistics to prove that the era of great midwestern cities was about to dawn, but the task of making a reality of this vision belonged to the succeeding generation. Jesup Scott's son, Frank, also tried to promote a federal system of improvements and other measures that would further the economic development of the interior of the United States.[6] In writing *The Art of Beautifying the Home Grounds*, however, he was primarily interested

55. *"Landscape View of Madisonville," Ohio, 1874. Access to this suburban village near Cincinnati was enhanced when the Marietta and Cincinnati Railroad was extended to it in the early 1870s. This view gives some sense of how the railroad and the suburban village were both seen as compatible with the countryside.*

in setting standards to guide the design and layout of these burgeoning settlements.

Scott applauded recent examples of public landscaping like Central Park in New York, but he thought that such parks could have only a minor impact on a city, especially compared with those that could be created around beautiful private homes. Scott's perfect community was not a version of the great metropolis but instead an idealization of the suburban village to which many American families were first attracted in the 1860s. It was a "township of land, with streets and roads and streams, dotted with a thousand suburban homes peeping from their groves." This settlement had a "broader, more generous and cosmopolitan character than old-fashioned villages." It had shops, a post office, and other useful facilities, but most of its buildings were houses, knit together by generous landscaping that gave the community the appearance of a continuous suburban park.

*The Art of Beautifying the Home Grounds* was, therefore, a commuter's manual, and its readers were those who appreciated "more than the very rich, or the poor, all the heart's cheer, the refined pleasures, and the beauty that should attach to a suburban home." Scott disdained those who wanted to own elaborate country houses, "young Chatsworths." Although he drew on English sources for specific information, Scott realized that British precedents did not apply to the American situation. In the United States it was impossible to find the labor to maintain expensive estates, and in any case, since Americans had become so mobile, there was little chance that family homes would pass from one generation to the next.

If Scott did not intend to address those who wanted an ancestral estate, neither did he write for those who had grown up on farms and who dreamed of "broad pastures, sweet meadows, and fine cattle and horses." Scott's audience was more urbane. In fact, his directions for laying out the home grounds discouraged any vestige of the farm. He disapproved of attempts to grow fruit and vegetables on the suburban lot, except for those fruits that took little care and were brought to perfection only when they ripened where they were to be eaten. A productive garden was not only too time-consuming and expensive, but also atavistic. In Scott's view the suburban house was supposed to be the context of higher pleasures. He reminded his readers that "the eye is a constant feeder, that never sates with beauty, and is ever refining the mind by the influence of its hunger." Even luscious fruits, however, gave only "momentary pleasure."

56. *Frank J. Scott: "The Home Grounds and the Suburban Street."*

In landscaping the grounds around the homes in this suburban park, the object was not to obscure individual dwellings from view by building walls, grading hills, or planting groves of trees. Instead, it was to make the houses a sequence of "pictures" that could be seen when walking or driving through the community. For Scott decorative planting was, therefore, "the art of picture making and picture framing, by means of the varied forms of vegetable growth."

It was difficult to achieve this ideal landscape because suburban homes had to be relatively close together. Lot size was partially determined by a new consideration — the need of suburban women for neighborly companionship. Scott explained that during his daily absence the husband was constantly in contact with his acquaintances, but the members of the family at home also needed "the enlivening influences of easy intercourse with their equals." It was, therefore, undesirable to live in an isolated house. Yet Scott did not want women to be attracted by the other extreme: city life. A "happy medium" could be attained by making sure that each house had both natural surroundings and the proximity of neighbors. To satisfy this condition, Scott recommended a house lot of

57.   Frank J. Scott: "Laying out the Home Grounds." In the 1870s, as ever since, the opportunity to have and care for a garden was a major attraction of the suburbs. Scott always insisted that the design of the suburban lot be conceived as a whole.

*58. Frank J. Scott: Views from the street and sidewalk across the lawn to the porch. Maintaining these sight lines was the most important issue in laying out the suburban home grounds. Having urnlike planters in front of the home was a convention that Frank Lloyd Wright maintained and modified (see illustrations 119 and 123).*

from a half to four or five acres. This range was broad enough to include many types of houses and approaches to landscaping, but most of the homes Scott illustrated were located on smaller lots. He frequently identified the family of moderate income with a half acre. Scott calculated that in towns with from 5,000 to 50,000 inhabitants there were enough moderately priced sites within easy walking distance of the business center. In larger cities horsecars and steam railways could easily transport "tired workers" to homes in "cheerful villages."

The central issue in *The Art of Beautifying the Home Grounds* was how owners of such house lots could lay out their land to satisfy their own needs and at the same time preserve the continuity of the suburban park. To solve this problem, it was first necessary to have the right degree of contact between the home grounds and the street. If the house was higher than the street, for instance, it was important to grade the lawn gradually up to the dwelling, so that a passerby's view would not be cut off. To achieve this effect, the type of separation, if any, between the home ground and sidewalk was crucial. Scott thought that the practice of hedging one's grounds so that a passerby could not enjoy its beauty "was one of the barbarisms of old gardening." The most suitable barrier was one that was "least seen, and best seen through" and would "least conceal the lawn and other beauties beyond it."

Scott's book had many diagrams illustrating specific types of fences that encouraged this subtle relationship between the passerby and the home. He recommended iron fences made of ornate repeated elements. These were readily available and easily assembled. The picket fence was a less expensive, but still dignified, solution to the same problem. Its only drawback was that when seen from an angle it tended to shut out the view of the grounds. So Scott recommended an unusual type that accentuated the horizontal members more than the vertical.

When Scott considered divisions between two adjoining lots, he also favored a minimal barrier. The correct device depended on the distance between the houses, but in general Scott concluded that people would "deprive themselves of what costs them nothing and profits them much," if they insisted on dividing their improved grounds from that of their neighbors. Like shutting out the passerby, this practice was unchristian and

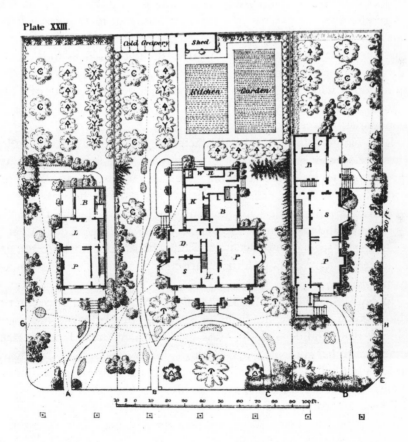

*59.  Frank J. Scott: Three houses at the end of a block 200 feet wide and on lots 200 feet deep. This density of settlement makes a telling contrast with that of New York City blocks, which also were 200 feet wide (see illustrations 69 and 70).*

unneighborly. Scott did concede that if a man believed that he and his family were bad neighbors, they certainly ought to fence themselves in. Or if for some reason they thought their neighbors were of the same sort, they would be advised to make sure of the "height and strength of the devices between them." But Scott preferred to imagine "that our neighbors are kindly gentlemen and women, with well-bred families, who can enjoy the views across others' grounds without trespassing upon them."

Scott recognized that problems might ensue from this policy of openness. One frequent source of friction was the invasion of a family's grounds by a neighbor's boisterous children. High fences were useless against enterprising youngsters. Scott advised, therefore, that it was far more effective for parents to train their offspring to respect their neighbor's property. Although children might be disciplined to acknowledge these limits, it was much harder to train domestic animals to do so. Scott, always drawing a distinction between higher and lower levels of civilization, coped with this problem by designing a devious system of disguised ditches that would invisibly but effectively deter dogs from traversing boundaries between neighbors.

Like his guidelines for the perimeter of the grounds, Scott's rules for the development of the interior of a house lot were largely determined by an attempt to make the dwelling "the central interest of a picture." In order to do so it was necessary to treat lawns, trees, flowers, and shrubs in a manner compatible with the climate, the size of the lot, the nature of the terrain, and many other factors. Scott showed how to design yards for a number of special circumstances — odd-shaped lots, sloping sites, prominent trees. But overriding all these particular considerations were important principles.

In explaining the rules for landscaping, Scott remained uncommitted in the ongoing controversy about the aesthetics of gardening. He was convinced that landscape design was an important art. Man, he claimed, should not be content with "nature's lower levels; for that spark of divinity within us — Imagination — suggests to us progress and improvement." The arts that added beauty to life were those that grafted upon the wildness of nature the "refinements and harmonies which the Deity through the Imagination" was ever suggesting. Still, in taking this view of man's ability to make improvements, Scott did not conclude that one method of landscaping was better than another. That landscape which emphasized the wildness of rude nature and that which softened it to create "polished beauty" were equal. Topiary gardens and "natural" landscapes each represented a type of beauty and illustrated the diversity of human taste.

Although *The Art of Beautifying the Home Grounds* had long sections on different types of plants, flowers, and trees, Scott, unlike most other landscape designers, did not encourage suburban residents to become absorbed in these gardening details. Such highly cultivated interests often consumed too much time and money, commodities that the new suburban resident could not afford to squander. Rather, Scott's book was intended for the "busy men and women who desire the greatest amount of beauty which their means will enable them to maintain, and the minimum expense and care that will secure it."

Scott did not dwell for long on specific elements of the home grounds because he thought gardening was essentially an "art of arrangement." For him the central feature of any well-arranged planting scheme was a lawn. He felt that it was always necessary to preserve a large expanse of uninterrupted grass. To achieve this effect, trees, shrubs, and flowers were not to be scattered about the grounds but instead had to be confined in clumps between lines that radiated from the house to the outside of the lot. Within these clumps larger trees and shrubs were to be placed so

60. *"Rustic Furniture" for the porch. The vines that intertwined with the members supporting the porch roof furnished the material for this furniture.*

that the residents could see the smaller ones in front of them. That arrangement would create vistas from the principal windows and porches across the lawn to the sidewalk and street or to adjoining property, thus connecting the house to the community at large.

Having created this context, Scott recommended that the house should be drawn into the picture by making it appear to grow out of the landscape. This effect could be achieved in a number of ways. Instead of allowing the house to meet the ground abruptly, it was important to ease this transition by planting shrubs around the foundation. Bushes were much more useful than ornamental flower gardens. Vines and creepers served to make the building a part of the landscape, and a sense of unity could also be furthered by painting the house a compatible color, instead of the habitual white.

Scott emphasized gardening as an art of arrangement and the lawn as the focus of that art because he believed that the suburban home was supposed to be a "haven of repose" and that the suburba family would be better off using the home grounds for new forms oi relaxation and entertainment than worrying about a gardener's bill. One of these leisurely pursuits was the care of the lawn itself. "The velvety lawn, flecked with sunlight and the shadows of common trees," Scott claimed, was a very

61. Equipment for planting and cutting the lawn. By the 1870s such machinery was readily available.

"inexpensive, and may be a very elegant refreshment for the business-wearied eye." The tired commuter was not expected to exhaust himself when he returned home, nor was it important for his wife to master the abstruse principles of horticulture. Instead, Scott recommended the pleasures of a less intellectually rigorous activity — lawn mowing. Before the invention of the lawn mower it was difficult and tiring to cut a lawn. Not only was a scythe hard to wield, but in order to keep its blade sharp it was necessary first to even out the ground by rolling it. When inexpensive lawn mowers became available in the 1860s, people could maintain lawns without hired help. So enthusiastic was Scott about the lawn mower that he told his readers: "Whoever spends the early hours of one summer while the dew spangles in the grass, in pushing these grass cutters over a velvety lawn, breathing the fresh sweetness of the morning air and the perfume of the new mown hay, will never rest contented in the city."[7]

Suburban residents not only came to appreciate the relaxation of lawn mowing as an end in itself but also valued the greensward as the context for the numerous lawn games that became popular throughout the United States in the years after the Civil War. The first of these pastimes was croquet. Imported from England in the late 1860s, croquet was originally played in clubs but soon became a "social, family, home game," increasing in popularity as it spread from cities to small towns, when summer vacationers introduced it to the countryside. Croquet could be played by both sexes and by all ages. It was appealing not just because it was good fun but also because of its effect on the players. One commentator observed: "A half hour on the croquet ground, under adversity, will better display the real disposition of a person than any other acquaintance of years' duration." As the price of a croquet set dropped, the fascination for the game "increased in violence and became epidemic."[8]

Croquet never lost its popularity, but it soon had competitors. For a time baseball was thought to be a home sport, but Americans soon realized that baseball needed more space than an ordinary lawn, and also that it was not suitable for both sexes. Archery was croquet's first real competitor. Like croquet, archery was imported from England, but it became popular in the United States for new reasons. The stretching of the bow, it was argued, aided the development of the female figure. Women who were aware of this claim wore specially tailored suits when they played at archery and thus introduced fashion into sport. Other games were also played on the lawn. Tennis, for those with a large enough yard, became popular in the United States in the late 1870s, and many other

*62. Croquet. Of all the games for which the lawn was the setting, croquet was the most popular.*

games were invented for people to play on suburban and village home grounds.[9]

Although people of all ages could play these outdoor games and were encouraged to do so, the home grounds were the special domain of children. In the 1860s and 1870s children's magazines such as *Work and Play* and *St. Nicholas* started to describe games that often presupposed a lawn as the appropriate setting. The areas in the back of the house — stable, laundry yard, kitchen garden, perhaps an alley — were also attractive to children, particularly because the animals were kept there. Scott made every effort to draw domestic animals and their dwellings into the home picture. "What more pleasing sight," he noted, "than to glance over a smooth lawn, under trees or through vistas of shrubbery, to the sunlit open spaces around the carriage-house doors where the horse in the brightly colored 'buggy' stands neighing at you. . . . Ah, the children are at home there! One has not learned the art of enjoying home till he knows how much of beauty and delight there may be in the domestic workplaces set apart for the animals that serve us." Thus the children remained safely under the influence of the home spirit even while playing in the areas separate from the house itself.[10]

Many authors who wrote about gardening after the publication of *The Art of Beautifying the Home Grounds* disagreed with Frank J. Scott on particular subjects. They did not share his uncommitted position on the theory of landscaping. Some disdained topiary gardening and the cultivation of freak plants, trees, and shrubs; others encouraged Americans to use only those plants native to a region; still others argued that it was in the spirit of modern civilization to absorb foreign influences and that plants incompatible with a new landscape would be weeded out by natural selection. Similarly, some authorities on gardening argued for a contemporary approach to landscaping, but others studied and used aspects of the gardens of the past. They published books about the gardens of colonial America; an equally avid interest in French, English, Italian, and Japanese gardening developed. Unlike Scott, some writers urged their readers to take more than an amateur interest in floriculture. Even Scott's view that the home grounds should not be treated as a source of produce was often challenged. Many authors claimed that home cultivation could be a paying activity, and they cited this argument as one of the primary reasons for moving to the suburbs.[11]

In principle, no matter how substantial these differences of opinion and taste were, the concept of the home grounds as a family refuge in a community park was flexible enough to accommodate all of them. As long as the basic relationships among home, street, and neighbors were maintained, what was done on a particular lot could vary. In practice, however, the line between individual and community interests could not always be so precisely drawn. When that happened, many other issues became entangled with the seemingly self-contained subject of landscaping the home grounds.

+++

Frank J. Scott suggested that the best way to settle a suburb was for a group of people to buy a tract of land, divide it, and lay out their grounds according to agreed-upon principles. Through such an arrangement they could control the degree of separation between houses and undertake a comprehensive scheme of planting that would benefit everyone.

Some of the first and best-known suburban communities were settled in this manner. Shortly after Andrew Jackson Downing's death, his partner, Alexander Jackson Davis, planned Llewellyn Park, a community in Orange, New Jersey, which set a standard of cooperation among neighbors. This settlement was started by Llewellyn S. Haskell, a wealthy New York businessman who believed that through "right living" it was possible to attain a standard of absolute perfection while on earth. He derived an

**63.** *The entrance to Llewellyn Park. To emphasize that they were entities detached from other parts of a city or town, many suburbs or small developments had distinct entries that were often identified by a gate or gatehouse.*

intense satisfaction from a constant association with trees, hills, fields, streams, and fresh air, and, although an active businessman, he always tried to live as far away from cities as possible. In 1853 he bought twenty-one acres of land on the side of the Orange Mountains in New Jersey and persuaded friends to purchase adjoining property. The group soon controlled four hundred acres and placed the property under what was called the "Park Covenant."

This document set out rules for the maintenance of Llewellyn Park. Since Haskell wanted the settlement to be a retreat where each resident could exercise to the utmost his own rights without inconveniencing his neighbors, it was agreed that on the one hand there should be no fences in the community, but on the other hand no house was to be erected upon less than one acre of ground. Those provisions defined the community park; to perpetuate it each resident had to pay a yearly rate for the maintenance of the landscape. Three trustees were appointed for life to ensure that the basic features of Llewellyn Park were preserved. They oversaw the settlement's common land, primarily a wide strip that encompassed two parallel roadways extending from the entrance of the community up the mountains to an area called The Ramble. The trustees also encouraged the residents to maintain the original rugged state of the landscape. They wanted to keep underbrush in its primitive tangle and as many tall trees as possible.[12]

In the following half century the first settlers of many communities adopted regulations similar to those of Llewellyn Park. After 1900 they were encouraged to do so by city planners who conceived of these rules as an important way to define what Charles M. Robinson called "high-class" streets. Brentmoor Park in St. Louis was laid out along these lines in 1911. Fifteen families bought a tract of land and asked a landscape architect to subdivide it into house lots, each with a desirable building site, that together would make the most beautiful community. The property included a valley retained as a private park around which the fifteen building lots were located. The landscape architect provided access to each house by a road system that consisted of an interior driveway for residents and guests and an exterior service road. To preserve the scheme, the first inhabitants formulated careful restrictions about how individual building lots should be landscaped and used.[13]

Although communities like Llewellyn Park and Brentmoor Park were started by people with a common outlook, it was often difficult to maintain or enforce the regulations, no matter how liberal, that set the standards of landscaping around the houses built there. Llewellyn Park, for example, was originally conceived as a haven for individualists. Some of its first residents, like Llewellyn S. Haskell, were Perfectionists; others were said to be atheists; a few of those who lived there simply were recluses. These people could tolerate such peculiar activities as a marriage ceremony at sunrise under a great tree and the burial of a young woman with only a shroud between her body and Mother Earth, but there was a limit to their tolerance. The demand for the construction of a community clubhouse indicated that at least some residents thought individual interests had gone too far. The problem was exacerbated by second- and third-generation inhabitants who, even though they had agreed to the covenant when they decided to live in Llewellyn Park, were not in complete accord with all its provisions. On a more practical level, the maintenance of a standard of landscaping often entailed expenses that drastically increased as years passed and that the inhabitants felt they could no longer sustain, especially since they also had to pay taxes to the town in which the community was located.[14]

If it was difficult to achieve the atmosphere of a community park in suburban settlements started by a group of residents, it was even harder to do so in communities promoted by land speculators. There were always a few enlightened developers. Frederick Law Olmsted was hired by one to design Riverside in Chicago, and in the 1890s he was commissioned by Edward H. Bouton, another public-spirited real estate developer, to lay out Roland Park, a Baltimore suburb with carefully elaborated restrictions about how each lot was to be used.[15] City planners and landscape architects later cited Roland Park to show how designers and developers could cooperate. Bouton also wanted to promote this relationship; that was why he attended city planning conferences and acted as an adviser for the City Club of Chicago's competition for the development of a quarter section in 1913.[16]

But although places like Riverside and Roland Park set a standard, few communities, especially large ones that contained a greater cross section of people, were so carefully planned and regulated. It was far more common for a land developer to lay out a subdivision and to sell lots to residents with no restrictions on its use at all. In such case the cities or towns in which the new subdivisions were located had to make rules for the proper and orderly development of residential land.

Most communities have always had some rules that touch upon issues such as the minimum setback of buildings from streets and the height of fences that divide property. But at the turn of the century a few progressive towns took a more active role in trying to create a parklike atmosphere. The first step was usually to establish the town's jurisdiction over sidewalks and the planting along them. No matter where the legal property boundary was, before 1900 a tradition had developed throughout the United States that trees along the sidewalk belonged to the owner of the property before which they stood. This custom gave each house owner a degree of responsibility in maintaining the appearance of the community, but it often led to the neglect of the trees. Village improvement societies tried to encourage local citizens to take care of the trees in front of their houses; where that did not prove effective, they campaigned to establish municipal jurisdiction over the sidewalks. Only at the turn of the century did cities and then states pass laws to establish their control over the sidewalks, thereby asserting the value of trees to the community as a whole. Massachusetts led the way by passing a law in 1899 that made it mandatory for each town to have a tree warden.[17]

There was no consensus about the ideal landscaping of streets and sidewalks. One theory advocated placing one species of tree at equal intervals along the street. Another favored a varied planting, especially in

*64. Trees on Midland Avenue, East Orange, New Jersey, 1910. The use of one variety of tree created a uniform appearance, but a disease could then destroy all the trees.*

areas with winding roads. In both cases it was necessary to define how much area would be cut out of the sidewalk where the trunk met the ground. Many towns solved this problem by planting the trees on grass strips between the sidewalk and the street, and they established regulations about how property owners could interrupt this area with driveways. It was customary to have identical landscaping on both sides of the street, but when the terrain varied, some landscape architects tried to differentiate the two sides. When, for example, because of the slope of the ground, the houses on one side of the street were higher than those on the other, the lower sidewalk could be placed closer to the road with only a narrow, intervening planting strip or none at all. In contrast the upper sidewalk could be separated from the street by a generous, sloping terrace.[18]

By asserting this level of control over the landscaping of the street, a town could start to establish a parklike environment. No matter how zoning laws fixed the uses of buildings along streets, however, towns changed. Roads frequently had to be widened, and rows of mature trees then had to be removed. In laying out new residential areas, it was always possible to anticipate this problem by making wide streets. But too much paved area was undesirable. A more sophisticated approach was the "elastic street," the most elaborate version of which was used in Phila-

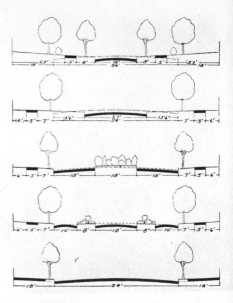

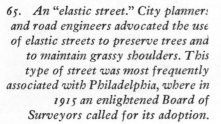

65.  *An "elastic street." City planners and road engineers advocated the use of elastic streets to preserve trees and to maintain grassy shoulders. This type of street was most frequently associated with Philadelphia, where in 1915 an enlightened Board of Surveyors called for its adoption.*

delphia. The elastic street was planned to accommodate, with the minimum inconvenience, successive widenings. Initially, the paved area was narrow and was flanked on either side by broad, grassy spaces with two rows of trees, located so that neither would have to be removed at the first widening and only one at the second. Catch basins and drains were placed well back in the grassy area to avoid the expense of relocation.[19]

Electric and telephone wires were a further threat to trees. When these services were first installed in towns, there were no regulations about how they were to be disposed. Utility companies erected poles along the street and strung wires between them. Often there was such a tangle of wires that the view across the lawn and out into the street was severely obstructed. More important, to put up the wires, it was sometimes necessary to cut down nearby trees or at least to remove impeding branches. This surgery was often performed without consulting the town or nearby residents and with little consideration for the health of the trees or the quality of the local environment. Outraged by these depredations, members of improvement associations pressed for regulations to control the indiscriminate stringing of wires.[20]

In addition to the placement and care of trees the quality of the street surface itself was also important to the community park. By 1915, with the increase in automobile traffic, dirt roads were no longer feasible for residential areas. Unlike slow-moving horse-drawn vehicles, the speeding cars raised clouds of dust that settled on adjoining property. This transfer of dirt not only was harmful to the health of residents but also damaged the road. It was always necessary to have sand or dust on broken stone roads as a check against excessive wear. When a surface was free from dirt, there was nothing to prevent the exposed stone fragments from "raveling," or losing their hold. Because automobiles raised so much dust, dirt roads deteriorated quickly as cars became more common. Initially, attempts were made to retain the dust by pouring oil or even just water over the streets. But when it became evident that a more permanent surface was necessary, towns started to build asphalt roads.[21]

By exercising control over sidewalks, trees, wires, and street surfaces, cities, towns, and suburbs maintained some of the atmosphere of a community park. But the ultimate success of this vision depended on the public's acknowledgment that a common attitude toward the treatment of private home grounds was a desirable goal. In areas settled by people of similar outlook, it was easier to establish this consensus; in places with a diverse population, special efforts had to be taken to inculcate a sense of the home grounds' wider meaning.

By 1915 hundreds of American cities and towns had community organizations that promoted the improvement of yards and gardens. These societies were outgrowths of the larger village improvement movement that flourished throughout the United States after the Civil War. The model for an organization that dealt specifically with the state of a community's home grounds was established in Northampton, Massachusetts, in 1887 by the novelist George Washington Cable. Until the early 1880s Cable lived in his native Louisiana. The local culture of that state had furnished him with the material for *The Grandissimes*, *Old Creole Days*, and other successful books. Once established as a writer, however, Cable became increasingly outspoken about social issues. With the publication of *The Silent South*, a collection of articles on the state of the Negro and the convict lease system, Cable became *persona non grata* in his native region. He then looked for a new home, settling first in Simsbury, Connecticut, and finally in Northampton, Massachusetts.

Cable had always connected the achievement of social equality with the dispersal of culture. Both were lacking in the South. Once settled in Northampton, the transplanted southerner was eager to become involved in the affairs of his new community and to demonstrate the progress that was possible in a liberal environment. When Cable arrived, Northampton, like other New England towns, was no longer the quiet village that older citizens remembered. Instead, it was a prosperous manufacturing center whose population had been swelled in recent years by a large influx of immigrants.[22]

These foreign, uneducated workers offered Cable a great challenge. He first attempted to "elevate the masses," as he put it, by establishing in Northampton a network of Home Culture Clubs, organizations that were not dissimilar to the many home-study programs in which people met on a regular basis to read aloud and discuss books. The purpose of these home-study evenings had always been divided between self-improvement and entertainment and fellowship. In Northampton Cable put the emphasis on uplift. He hoped that through his organizations the wealthy and cultured members of the community would meet the poor and uneducated. If these encounters took place in the homes of each group, real understanding would follow.[23]

By 1889 eighteen groups had been started in Northampton, but it soon became evident that the masses were not eager to hold home-study meetings in their houses. Cable did not give up his broad plan but decided to turn what had been a small administrative office into a cultural center for the town. An entire building was soon procured, and, with the aid of Smith College faculty and students, a broad range of adult education programs was set up. The shift of focus from the fireside to the community center was a disappointment for Cable, but the Home Culture Club soon made up for this letdown with the zeal of its activity.[24]

Cable had always been fascinated by gardening and frequently wrote essays about what the cultivation of his home grounds meant to him. These articles, which were collected in a volume entitled *The Amateur Garden*, are illuminating not only for what they reveal about the genesis of yard improvement programs but also because they provide an excellent description of what the home grounds meant to a person who, in describing his own experience, was also probably speaking for many other Americans.

In his Northampton years Cable continued to write and often traveled great distances to lecture and read from his novels. Wearied by this strenuous activity, Cable looked to his home grounds as a refuge and source of relaxation. Each aspect of his garden — the types of plants and trees, the methods of making drains and small water dams, or the cutting of paths through rough terrain — became a subject of great fascination. In the essays of *The Amateur Garden* Cable described these matters in the most minute detail. Captivated by the intricacies of garden tools, soils, the weather, and flower beds, he expected that his readers would be equally absorbed.

Cable's garden came close to being the central concern of his life. From it he derived much more than relaxation. He claimed that his garden taught him lessons about his writing. He likened it to a story, one that "actually and naturally occurs, yet occurs under its master's guidance and control and with artistic effect." A well-designed garden was not only a "true story happening artistically" but also one that passed through a new revision every year and, therefore, was superior to what any writer could create. In effect, Cable's garden helped him establish standards of excellence for literature.

Cable's home grounds also took him outside of his own concerns and provided a basis for social intercourse. Through his interest in gardening Cable met many of his most valuable friends. He knew some of these "acquaintances" only through their gardening books; for instance, Liberty Hyde Bailey through his *Cyclopaedia of American Horticulture* was a constant companion. Others were local farmers who gave the amateur gardener valuable bits of advice or more famous practitioners like George Waring, who lived nearby in Lenox and who advised Cable about how to divert a brook through his garden.[25]

Although his garden and all that it entailed represented an ideal universe in miniature, Cable found that other people did not derive such value from their home grounds. Good gardening was "not democratically general with us." The result was an unfriendly atmosphere: American cities and towns were filled with "home-dwellers each privately puzzled to know why every one of his neighbors' houses, however respectable in architecture, stares at him and after him with a vacant, deaf-mute air of having just landed in this country, without friends."

In Northampton Cable hoped to change this inhospitable situation by establishing a garden improvement contest in which the whole community would participate. Of all the home culture programs this contest took the most effort to organize and attracted the largest number of Northampton's citizens. Early in the spring a committee of ladies, "volunteer garden visitors," called on residents to enroll them in the contest. This first phase was followed by periodic "visits of observation, inquiry and counsel," and once a month the ladies met with Cable to report the progress made. Cable emphasized that the importance of these house calls was not confined to the advancement of good gardening. He explained that they promoted "fellowship among neighbours and kind feelings between widely parted elements of society."

Strict guidelines about what made a good garden were laid down during these visits. The residents of Northampton were told to mow their lawns as often as the mower would cut the grass. An unweeded lawn would almost certainly result in failure to win any of the garden contest prizes. In laying out the planting, straight lines and hard angles were to be avoided. "The double curve, or wavy line," the committee decreed, was "the clue of grace." The number of flowers in the home grounds did not matter, as long as shrubs behind them gave a strong and lasting effect even when the flowers were not in bloom. Residents were also supposed to plant against the foundations of their houses. If all these rules were followed, the result would "make the whole place one single picture of a *home*, with the house the chief element and the boundary lines of the lot the frame."

The entire contest was supervised by volunteers and usually cost only a minimal sum to run. In 1907 Andrew Carnegie, a gardening enthusiast, a friend of Cable, and a frequent visitor to Northampton, donated $8,500 to the contest. This sum paid for the construction of plant houses, where in the following years the Home Culture Club raised flowers that it sold at moderate prices to residents of Northampton.[26]

At one prize-giving ceremony Cable noted with pride that a large majority of those present were "men and women who earn their daily bread with their hands." The contest was as valuable for the individual as it was for the community. One report described the effect of the Home Culture Club's campaign on Michael Burke, a dyer in the local silk mill. When the volunteer garden visitor first saw his front yard, it was completely bare except for seven geraniums. Burke's shopmates said that he "couldn't grow cabbages," but he entered the contest nevertheless. The report noted that Burke had become an avid gardener: "Mr. Burke now rises nearly every morning at 4 o'clock and works on his place until it is time to go to the mill." Through this activity both his health and his character improved. Such a result was gratifying. In summing up the meaning of the contest, Cable claimed that the residents of Northampton "had made the matter a public, concerted movement, and were interested in its results and rewards as spiritual proprietors in a common possession much wider than personal ownership under law." The final meaning of the garden contest was that it had furthered a "wider sentiment of community."[27]

From 1890 to 1915 garden contests rapidly gained popularity in the United States. They were initiated by a variety of organizations with many different motives. During this period of labor unrest, strikes, and lockouts, large factories often sponsored them for their workers. The garden contest was one of many programs of "welfare work" undertaken to strengthen the faltering dialogue between labor and management.

The National Cash Register Company at Dayton, Ohio, started one of the most active welfare work schemes. The company's president, John H. Patterson, was primarily responsible for these projects, which involved "labor and capital working together for the benefit of both." Within ten years Patterson converted National Cash Register from a company of thirteen employees to one of America's largest businesses. Patterson's welfare work was indispensable to his firm's success. He noted of the program, "it pays." His projects were both hygienic and recreational. The walls of the new National Cash Register factory were almost entirely glass to give the workers better light and ventilation, and noontime lunches were served in the Welfare Hall, which seated 2,500. Classes in calisthenics and a gymnasium were available to the workers, as well as a library, a training school, and educational trips.[28]

The promotion of gardening was one of the most important of National Cash Register's welfare work projects. The company's program of landscaping improvements began in 1896. At that time both the factory's grounds and the areas around its workers' houses were in deplorable condition. Weather-stained cottages, "built for shelter, not for beauty," straggled along ill-kept streets. The new factory, despite its substantial architecture, lost much of its pleasing character because of this unsightly setting. Since Patterson felt that top-quality work could not be done in such surroundings, he asked John C. Olmsted to assist the company in formulating beautification plans. The choice of landscape architect had a significance that the company frequently mentioned in the pamphlets describing the improvements at National Cash Register. Olmsted's father's firm had designed not only the grounds of the world's fair in Chicago but also William Rockefeller's enormous country estate in the Adirondacks and George Washington Vanderbilt's Biltmore in Asheville, North Carolina. Thus through the agency of National Cash Register, the company's workers were the patrons of the most eminent landscaping firm in the country.[29]

Part of Olmsted's work was to design a planting scheme for the factory. The judicious placement of trees, bushes, flowers, and vines made the abrupt architecture of the huge factory part of a continuous natural setting. Patterson also wanted to improve the home grounds of his workers. As a first step in a grand campaign to promote the idea, he asked Olmsted to design a planting scheme for a city lot that would serve as a model for the workers to follow. Liberty Hyde Bailey came to Dayton to formulate this educational program. Under his direction National Cash Register published booklets that explained the rudiments of landscape gardening and collected thousands of lantern slides to illustrate aspects of the subject in lectures given throughout Dayton. Practical examples of planting supplemented lessons; the vines and plants the company recommended were shown planted in the factory's grounds, and the company brought trainloads of them to Dayton and sold them at cost. Any purchaser could consult a professional gardener, hired by National Cash Register, about how best to plant and care for this greenery.[30] Not content with "preaching the gospel of outdoor art," the company offered rewards for yard improvement. Prizes were established for the best-kept premises, the most beautiful effects, and the most decorative window boxes. Like those in the contest at Northampton, these awards were presented at a mass meeting that was an important event in promoting enthusiasm for the project.[31]

National Cash Register claimed that the effect of its garden improvement campaign was "widespread and immediate." The district around the factory, known as "Slidertown," grew to be "like a park"; fences were first hidden under vines and finally removed; rickety sheds were torn down. "Slidertown" was forgotten and "South Park" became one of the "show neighborhoods" of the city. The cost in effort for everyone concerned was great, but the consensus was that it was worth it: "The factory owner or the householder who is eager to make his property something besides a smudge on the face of Nature, who enjoys beautiful surroundings and hates the dreary, who would rather be an influence for good than for evil, who seeks opportunity to develop the finer instincts in himself and in those about him rather than let the coarser gain power — to such a man or woman the cost lies mostly in the enthusiasm with which the work is prosecuted."[32]

Other companies soon followed National Cash Register's lead and started garden contests and yard improvement campaigns. Newspapers also initiated such programs. At the time of the Democratic National Convention of 1900 in Kansas City, for instance, a local newspaper offered a prize for the best-kept lawn. Public-spirited citizens took up this idea and established twenty-six prizes totaling $1,200 for lawns, floral displays, and the neatest vacant lot.[33] Rotary Clubs, with the aid of the agricultural extension departments of state universities, also sponsored yard improvement campaigns. A contest in Davenport, Iowa, where the local Rotary

Club was helped by the Iowa State College of Agriculture and Mechanic Arts, was particularly successful.[34]

Most of the sponsors of yard improvement contests had straightforward or even simplistic views of what made a good garden. In fact, in the pamphlets issued by the agricultural experiment stations and the local chambers of commerce the quality of the home grounds often seemed less important than the civic pride the gardening activity was supposed to boost. But among this pedestrian literature there is one document that is remarkable for its bold vision and poetic language. It explains what, at its best, this community concern for the home grounds meant.

Entitled *The Prairie Spirit in Landscape Gardening*, this pamphlet was issued by the Illinois Agricultural Experiment Station in conjunction with the University of Illinois College of Agriculture, and was written by Wilhelm Miller, a prominent landscape architect and editor of *Garden* magazine. Miller traced the notion of a prairie style of landscape gardening to O. C. Simonds, who in 1880 had started to transplant the common Illinois trees from the wilds of the prairie to the parks and home grounds of Chicago. Simonds was the first to conduct extensive landscape restoration projects in the Midwest. Jens Jensen and Walter Burley Griffin were his most notable followers. Jensen collected hundreds of flowers from the banks of the Des Plaines River and planted them around the homes of his clients. Griffin also used as high a percentage of native plants as possible in his designs for commissions in towns and suburbs like De Kalb, Decatur, Oak Park, Hubbard's Woods, and Edwardsville. These "prairie style" landscape architects did not share a specific set of design principles, but they all used native plants and tried to emphasize in their landscaping the flatness of the prairie.[35]

In *The Prairie Spirit in Landscape Gardening* Miller's goal was to perpetuate the essence of a landscape that was quickly disappearing. He pressed for a three-part program that would "conserve" typical western scenery where it still existed; re-create this landscape as much as possible through "restoration"; and where the true variety of the prairie scenery could not be re-created, suggest what an earlier state might have been like through the "repetition" of a particular tree or flower.

Large conservation, restoration, and repetition projects — for instance, the development of municipal parklands — were important, but Miller was adamant in his view that every citizen had something to contribute. A farmer could "idealize" the prairie by framing a view of its vast expanse with haws, crabtrees, or honey locusts. The city dweller could

66. *Wilhelm Miller: Good and bad taste in landscape gardening, 1915. The back yard was the place for the expression of individual taste; the front yard was for neighborly cooperation.*

"conventionalize" the prairie in his garden by planting flat-topped flowers that suggested the wider, horizontal landscape. And finally, even in tenements, a single brown-eyed daisy in a window box could keep alive the hopes of "freedom, prosperity and a life amid more beautiful surroundings" by "symbolizing" the prairie. Every home in Illinois could, therefore, be connected "with the greatest source of inspiration in middlewestern society."

Miller's pamphlet explained how to undertake each aspect of this program by citing dozens of instances in which the prairie had been idealized, conventionalized, or symbolized. In his fervent appeal to preserve the landscape it was clear that Miller wanted to re-create not only the prairie's scenery but also the broader prairie spirit that he thought the first Illinois settlers shared. How the two went hand in hand was expressed in the credo of the Prairie Spirit at the end of the pamphlet:

I believe that one of the greatest races of men in the world will be developed in the region of the prairies. I will help to prove that vast plains need not level down humanity to a dead monotony in appearance, conduct, and ideals.

I feel the uplifting influence of the rich, rolling prairie and will bring its spirit into my daily life. If my home surroundings are monotonous and ugly, I will make them varied and beautiful. I will emulate the independence and progressiveness of the pioneer.[36]

Like other advocates of yard improvement, Miller hoped that the citizens of his state would develop a consistent attitude toward the landscape. To do so would be a public-spirited gesture, a symbolic recognition of all the forces that bound the members of the community together. Much more worrying than an aberrant opinion or taste, however, was indifference. Miller and those Americans who believed in the power of beauty thought that people who showed no interest in their home grounds not only snubbed the community, but also in cutting themselves off from nature removed themselves from the greatest source of inspiration. That act was tantamount to denying their own humanity. It was unthinkable to have a true home on this basis.

✦✦✦

There were many ways that residents of cities who did not live in separate houses could be brought into contact with nature. The great public parks were designed for this purpose. Still, many reformers who believed in the importance of nature felt that huge areas of greenery, even if extended by planting trees along boulevards and local streets, were not sufficient. They wanted to put the city dweller into a more intimate, day-to-day contact with the natural environment.

Before the Civil War a few educators argued that every school should have a playground. By the 1880s many reformers supported this idea, and

67. *A rooftop kindergarten, 1914. Schools without playgrounds often utilized their rooftops, especially when the prevention of tuberculosis was identified with open-air play.*

in the 1890s they started a national playground movement to convince local school committees not only to locate schools on suitable sites but also to equip and maintain them properly.[37] In densely settled areas, especially in New York, where vacant land was extremely scarce, the supporters of playgrounds urged school boards to provide rooftop play spaces. A concern about tuberculosis lent an urgency to their cause, and the "open air" school became an important part of a large program to prevent that disease. Nature study, which was first introduced to the school as a part of kindergarten education and which later was recommended for older children, also made outdoor areas necessary to the school.[38]

Another way to put the city resident in touch with nature was to provide him with an allotment garden. A program to make land available on which to grow vegetables was first begun on a broad scale in Detroit during the severe economic depression that started in 1893. In the spring of 1894 it occurred to Mayor Hazen Pingree that people on relief could at least procure food for their families by growing their own vegetables. Pingree wanted to show critics of the relief program that those without jobs were willing to work. He found several thousand acres of vacant land in Detroit and appealed to the owners of these sites to let people on relief use them. In the first year the value of the crops exceeded the money spent in establishing the program. "Pingree's Potato Patches" attracted attention throughout the nation, and in the following three years allotment programs were established in most major cities.[39]

The most direct way to put city inhabitants, especially those who lived in tenements, in contact with nature was simply to give them flowers. Members of charity organizations started this practice, and "flower missions" were later run by improvement associations. Of all the work undertaken by these organizations, the distribution of flowers to slum dwellers often proved the most popular. This practice was continued in many cities well into this century.[40]

All of these programs brought the city resident closer to nature. No matter how much they campaigned for public parks, allotment gardens, playgrounds, or flower missions, however, most reformers agreed that these measures would be ineffective without the proper regulation of the spaces in and around multiple dwellings. As soon as the inhabitants of cities began to crowd into houses, these dangerous spaces were vividly described. When Charles Dickens came to the United States in 1841, he visited the Five Points district of New York and in *American Notes*

*68. Lewis Hine: "Louse Alley," Washington, D.C. To dramatize the need for regulation of such alleys, Hine emphasized their proximity to the Capitol.*

beckoned his readers to come with him: "Ascend these pitch-dark stairs, heedful of a false footing on the trembling boards, and grope your way with me into this wolfish den, where neither ray of light nor breath of air, appears to come."[41] In the following decades journalists, social workers, and concerned citizens used similar language to describe the condition of the slums to other Americans. They augmented their written accounts with illustrations — first skillful line drawings, then startling photographs of dark alleys, courtyards, squalid halls, and stairwells.[42]

Although they never established a precise connection between the nature of these spaces and social or physical ills, housing reformers frequently singled them out as the breeding grounds of crime, juvenile delinquency, prostitution, and disease.[43] They assumed that these areas would never be suitable for social intercourse or relaxation. At best they could provide light and air to the rooms of tenements, safe access in case of fire, and clean surroundings immediately outside the home. Housing reformers, therefore, worked for legislation that would make landlords supervise and maintain the public spaces in and around multiple dwellings, and for building regulations that specified minimum dimensions for these areas.[44]

The success of the first objective usually depended on how much of a debt the local or state government owed to the interests of the owners of real estate. Reformers often worked for many years before they convinced politicians that a housing law was necessary.[45] The establishment of minimum dimensions was largely a problem of determining the best layout for a given building density. Because New York had the highest concentration of people in the country, the planning of tenements there took place under especially stringent conditions and resulted in unique buildings.

In 1876 Frederick Law Olmsted described the problem that faced anyone who tried to erect a successful multiple dwelling in New York. The difficulty stemmed not only from the density of the population to be housed, but also from the layout of streets that had been established in Manhattan in 1807: a pattern of repeating blocks 200 feet deep and 800 feet long from Houston Street north. Each block was divided into building lots of 25 by 100 feet. As Manhattan was settled, few exceptions to this simple pattern were made. Nevertheless, Olmsted thought that the grid of streets had significant defects. A uniform system of blocks limited the placement of all buildings to only one orientation. No matter how different were the requirements of a church, a blast furnace, an opera house, or a toy shop, there was only one way that all of these facilities could be located. In addition, because the grid plan had no diagonal streets leading to focal sites, New York could not construct the monumental buildings that added distinction to European cities.

But for Olmsted the most important fault of the grid was the effect it had on the design of housing. The dimensions of New York's grid worked against a suitable arrangement of houses, first of all because they prevented adequate access to back yards. The plan was laid down when the city had no gas, water, or sewage system. Privies were built over cesspools as far away from houses as possible, at the back of the hundred-foot lots. Because the individual home was usually part of an entire block of row houses, when the cesspool was cleaned its contents had to be taken in baskets through the house to the street. The daily garbage and trash traveled the same route.

A second defect of the New York lot dimensions was that they made difficult the provision of decent, separate houses for the city's working population. A building lot 100 feet deep was too large for one inexpensive home, so by the middle of the century it had become customary to construct either one large building on most of the lot or a series of small houses, one behind the other. Structures of the first type often contained windowless rooms. Those of the second kind were separated from one another only by a network of narrow, dark alleys and courtyards, which also permitted only a small proportion of well-lit and ventilated rooms.[46]

Two choices were open to those who wanted to correct this condition. They could either accept the limitations of New York's grid and try to make the best of it, or they could seek alternative ordering systems. The first was adopted by the *Plumber and Sanitary Engineer* in 1878 when it announced a competition for an improved tenement. Prominent civic and religious leaders sponsored the contest, but the role of the *Plumber and Sanitary Engineer* was important. This magazine discussed a broader range of issues than its title suggested. Not only did it help to establish standards of performance and safety for the new plumbing and heating systems then being installed in American buildings, but, largely through the initiative of its editor, Charles F. Wingate, it published articles about and took positions on many social issues connected with building.[47]

The magazine's competition had two basic conditions. Entrants had to produce a plan for a simple 25- by 100-foot lot that would not only benefit tenement dwellers but also return a moderate profit. Each building, it was calculated, had to house at least twenty rent-paying families. The winning solution took the shape of what came to be known as the "dumbbell" plan. Extending far back into the lot, the building had fourteen rooms on a floor, seven on either side of a central dividing wall. Four families occupied each of five or six floors. Those in the front had four rooms; those in the back, three. The largest room contained approximately 140 square feet, the smallest had 65. Ten of the fourteen rooms on each floor were lit only by a narrow air shaft, an indentation about twenty-eight inches wide on either side of the building.[48]

The *Plumber and Sanitary Engineer*'s competition was widely publicized in New York and the layout of the dumbbell was incorporated into a Tenement House Law of 1879. Until that law was superseded in 1901, thousands of dumbbell tenements were constructed. Generations of New Yorkers thus grew up with an air shaft that communicated noise and smells and was a fire hazard as a prominent feature of their daily environment.[49]

Although the requirement by law of a well to light and ventilate every room was an improvement, the narrow scope of the competition was noted even before the results were announced. George Waring acknowledged the pernicious effects of overcrowding, filthy conditions, and the

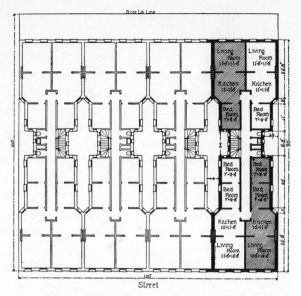

70.  *Ernest Flagg: Plan for a 200-foot by 200-foot building lot in New York. By creating a large courtyard, Flagg gave every room more light and ventilation than did the dumbbell arrangement.*

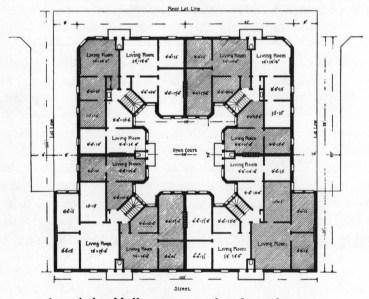

69.  *A dumbbell apartment plan. In such structures, there were four apartments per floor on each building lot. Except at the ends of blocks, ten of fourteen rooms looked out only on a light well.*

lack of sunlight and fresh air — all of which the prize design would aim to eliminate. But he claimed that suitable plumbing could do just as much for the prevention of disease as this futile exercise in tenement house planning. More important, George William Curtis questioned the wisdom of planning for only one building lot. He suggested that with a bigger site architects would have more room for invention and could do more to shape the spaces around the home.[50]

Because there was little agitation for an improved tenement house law in the 1880s, Curtis's idea was not tested until 1894, when Ernest Flagg demonstrated the advantages of planning houses on lots bigger than 25 by 100 feet. Flagg was then becoming one of the nation's most prominent architects. During his career he designed dozens of monumental buildings that were the archetypical products of an education at the Ecole des Beaux Arts in Paris. Flagg claimed, however, that the most important skill he learned as a student was not the facile manipulation of architectural styles but the ability to produce a logical and "scientific" plan. It was precisely this ability that Flagg used in designing a tenement to supersede the dumbbell flat.[51]

Flagg showed how it was possible on large lots to design housing that furnished light, air, health, and comfort at the same rent that the great majority of New York's tenement dwellers then paid, if not at a lower one. Flagg's proposal for large lots was not irrelevant to the way New York's housing was built. Many small builders owned only a single lot and erected a dumbbell tenement on it, but even though others had bigger pieces of property, they persisted in erecting this type of building in repeated units.

Flagg's scheme was based on the fact that the square was the most economical shape for the enclosure of space. A square building 20 feet on a side would enclose 400 square feet of space with 80 feet of wall. By comparison, an elongated building 10 by 40 feet would enclose the same amount of space with 100 feet of wall. Moreover, the four rooms in the corners of the first plan could all be reached by a small entrance hall, but in the elongated plan a wasteful corridor was needed to give access to four strung-out rooms. The first plan was best suited to the country where there was sufficient open space to have free-standing buildings, the second, more appropriate to the city, where deep lots made a narrow plan necessary. Flagg thought, however, that if large lots were available, it would be possible to have most of the advantages of the square plan in the city.

Flagg designed a building to occupy four New York City lots. These

10,000 square feet included 5,600 square feet of rentable space, the same as four dumbbell tenements; 350 square feet for brick partitions as against 515 in the dumbbell plan; 290 square feet for stairs and corridors as against 800; 50 square feet for water closets as against 175; and 3,060 square feet for light and air as against 2,060. In Flagg's plan light was provided by a 28-foot-square central court that gave better illlumination to the adjacent rooms than the narrow light well of the dumbbell. The fact that the dividing walls in the square plan were true fire walls, unpierced by windows, was a further advantage. The only drawback to Flagg's solution was that the square plan had three apartments on each floor for each lot occupied, instead of the four in the dumbbell unit. Flagg reasoned that crowding four families onto a floor was "not right or decent," nor was it proper to have a bedroom 7 by 9 feet that might be occupied by several people. In total, Flagg figured that the space in his plan not only was more desirable but also could be rented for 15 percent less. Yet the fact that his plan had fewer apartments was probably the reason it was not adopted by New York builders.[52]

Flagg's chance to test his square plan came in a competition sponsored in 1896 by the Improved Dwelling Council, an organization that tried to build better tenement houses which still returned a profit. Contestants were to design a building, not for a single lot but for an entire city block. The buildings submitted had to be as economical in built area as structures based on the dumbbell plan, no light wells or shafts were to be used, and interior courts had to have at least 900 square feet. In addition, every apartment facing the long avenues had to be entered from the side streets so that none of the frontage would be lost to stores on the ground floor. Apartments had to be planned so that it was possible to enter the living room from the public corridor or staircase without passing through another room, and no bedroom could be entered from another bedroom. Minimal areas were given for the living room and bedrooms, and every apartment had to have its own bathroom, which vented directly to the outside.

With only a few variations Flagg's square plan fit these conditions perfectly and won the competition. His scheme was built by the City and Suburban Homes Company, a philanthropic housing organization, in 1897. In 1901 Flagg demonstrated how a similar arrangement could be used for a building on a 50-foot frontage, and in 1911 he produced a variant of his 1894 design, planned for a 50-foot lot and adapted to improved fireproof construction. This scheme had twenty-eight rooms per

71. *Henry Atterbury Smith: East River Homes, New York City, 1910.
These buildings had triple-hung windows to bring plenty of fresh air into
each room.*

floor, seven more than his original plan, but had smaller rooms and toilets
that were entered from the living rooms or kitchens.[53]

No better plan was ever devised for a similar program. In a competition
sponsored by the Tenement House Committee of the Charity Organization Society in 1900 most of the designs submitted were variations of
Flagg's 1894 plan. The one innovation was a scheme in the square format
that used "open stairs." Its architect, Henry Atterbury Smith, claimed
that "in the anatomy of a tenement no part is more subject to horrors,
physical and moral, than the halls and stairs." In his design open staircases
in the four corners gave direct entrance to each apartment, thus securing
greater privacy and quiet in the building and eliminating the "dark, ill
ventilated, disease-breeding interior hall and staircase."

Smith later developed his ideas about a direct orientation to the outdoors in buildings he designed to protect residents against tuberculosis.
His scheme was based on principles learned from European sanatoria,
where doctors had demonstrated that the right environment could help
improve health. But this knowledge was of little benefit to the poor, who
could not afford to leave their jobs and families for a stay in an open-air
sanatorium. Smith's chance to build suitable housing for tuberculosis

72. *Henry Atterbury Smith: Open-air stairways of the East River Homes, New York, 1910. These stairways not only allowed fresh air to reach the front door of every apartment but also gave residents a protected place in which to sit.*

patients came when Mrs. William K. Vanderbilt provided the land adjoining John Jay Park. Called East River Homes, these courtyard buildings occupied a site of 200 by 200 feet. There was access to each building from ground-level passageways that extended through the structures from street to street, ensuring a free circulation of air in all the courts. The corner stairs were provided with safety treads set in concrete, had an easy pitch, and were protected from rain and snow by louvers of wire glass. At each turn of the stair was a seat, a resting place for children and invalids.

The roofs of these buildings were used for outdoor activities and fresh-air treatment. They were provided with vine-covered loggias, comfortable seating areas, and spaces for drying clothes. But, most important, the roof was used for an open-air school. The facades of the building facing the park and streets also were directly connected to the outdoors. Balconies were entered from bedrooms and living rooms by triple-hung windows that extended from floor to ceiling, making possible outdoor sleeping and dining.[54]

The East River Homes design was the definitive statement of one line of thinking about how best to cluster dwellings. Working within tight financial constraints, Flagg and Smith used the requirements of sanitation as their primary guide and produced an integral block of housing around a courtyard. But it was possible to think about housing in other terms and to arrive at a different organization of the spaces in and around a building. In the course of five decades the architect Edward Tuckerman Potter produced a remarkable series of diagrams that showed the advantages of creating what he called a "system of concentrated residence," based not on one massive block of apartments but instead on multiples of the small individual house.

The son of an Episcopal bishop, Potter began his career by working for Richard Upjohn, a famous ecclesiastical architect of the pre-Civil War years. Potter and his brother then started their own architectural practice, designing mainly churches and college buildings. An intensely religious man, Potter was a follower of John Ruskin and tried to instill his architecture with the essence of Gothic. The harmony he perceived in the great cathedrals corresponded to that in his other passion, music. In the 1870s he moved from New York City to Newport, Rhode Island, where his independently wealthy wife had a house. He gradually withdrew from architectural practice so that he could think about more fundamental matters. Potter wrote about how the harnessing of solar power would enhance the lot of mankind by making the deserts bloom. Believing that rapid communications would bring people of all nations closer together, he tried to define an ideal system of transportation. Toward the end of his life he was designing a modular system of housing that could be erected in any climate throughout the world.[55]

Most of these projects were speculative, but records do exist of Potter's thoughts on the system of concentrated residence. He began this lifelong interest in 1854 when he helped design some model tenements sponsored by the Association for Improving the Condition of the Poor. In the following years he became more familiar with the living conditions of New York's working population through his work as a district visitor for a charity. Potter concluded that although landlords were frequently greedy and tenants were often indifferent, many of the worst evils of New York's tenement houses were due to their planning. He believed that although crowding could not be prevented, the evils from overcrowding could be. Like other architects interested in improved tenements, Potter thought that the precondition of decent housing was adequate ventilation. It was only with the frequent passage of air through dwellings that diseases could be prevented. But Potter also recognized that successful housing had to satisfy the social needs of the tenants. It was through his desire to balance these two objectives that he arrived at his system.

Potter's first model for a satisfactory alternative to the common New York tenement house came from an improbable source, a Long Branch, New Jersey, resort hotel in which each suite of two rooms was entered from an external gallery. Because that arrangement made through ventilation possible, it was far better than one with rooms on either side of a central corridor. Potter's first scheme for an improved tenement was based on this plan. Instead of working with the 25-foot by 100-foot lot, on which he considered it impossible to arrange buildings successfully, Potter ran a secondary street north and south between New York's east-west streets. Fronting on this access way was a 200-foot-long, two-room-deep tenement. Stairs at the ends of this building were connected by galleries in the open air that led to apartments on each level.

This system of spaces had many sanitary advantages. Every room had sunlight at some part of the day, and each apartment was adequately ventilated by breezes that swept through the secondary streets. Potter's housing also had no dark and dangerous interior corridors and stairs. Because the galleries were open, "in plain sight of everybody," they were also "less likely to be neglected and subject to nuisances." Potter avoided the always troublesome yard by placing toilets inside the tenement and by providing space on the sunny roof for drying clothes. Instead of leaving each housewife to cope as best she could with the difficult problem of washing the family's clothing, Potter included common laundries on each floor at the ends of the gallery. Every story also had running water, a dumbwaiter, and a chute for garbage.

This system of housing not only met sanitary requirements but also was designed to be a context for community life. Potter imagined that his housing would have the friendliness and intimacy of a village. Children would play on the secondary streets and also on the roofs, which would be "resorts for all the tenants on summer evenings." People would also congregate on the galleries, but Potter thought that the apartments would have as much privacy as dwellings "situated on a village street."

Potter realized the fallacy of the analogy with the village when a journeyman barber who had examined the plan remarked of the common laundries: "What! is my wife expected to carry a pail of water along those galleries, up in the air, with all the neighbors a-looking at her? How would a rich man's wife like that, if she was in her place?" Potter then understood that in his eagerness to create a village atmosphere he had neglected "the human factor"; he had not provided enough privacy "to avoid any wound to the self-respect of the occupants." This incident

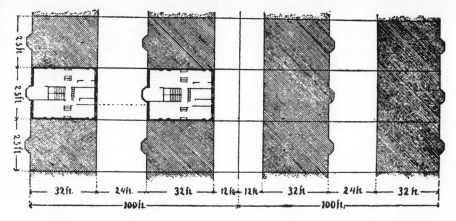

73. *E. T. Potter: A compact arrangement of small houses. Potter preferred separate row houses as in Philadelphia. But to handle the prevailing density of population in New York, he planned this scheme with two apartments on each floor.*

marked a turning point in Potter's thinking about concentrated residences. He decided that self-respect and privacy could best be maintained in separate homes. In his subsequent housing schemes he eliminated shared facilities — the gallery, common lavatories, laundries, and garbage chutes — and tried to plan within the rigid context of New York's blocks the most compact arrangement of separate houses.[56]

In starting this investigation Potter was attracted by the pattern of housing that had been built in Philadelphia. Like New York, Philadelphia was laid out on a uniform grid of streets, but each block in Philadelphia was subdivided by alleys. These secondary streets made it possible to divide land into large and small lots for a variety of house sizes; that was why a broad range of Philadelphia's population had always been able to own homes.[57]

Potter thought that he could emulate Philadelphia's example by again placing secondary streets, running north-south, on the New York blocks. The resulting pattern would be two rows of 40-foot-deep lots alternating with 20-foot-wide secondary streets. Potter figured that each house would be a little over 14 feet wide and 30 feet deep, leaving a 10-foot yard or altogether 20 feet between the backs of the two rows of houses. Given Potter's requirements for privacy and light and air, this pattern of housing was the most compact possible arrangement. Since the houses would only be two stories high, the volume of building did not match that which could be constructed with New York's typical tenements. But

Potter showed that he could adapt his basic plan to apartment buildings that would equal the great density of New York City's dumbbell structures and still provide a better social and sanitary environment. He planned these 200-foot-long buildings not with a gallery system but instead with a series of separate entrances and staircases, each of which gave access only to two through apartments on a floor. These dwellings had good ventilation and more privacy than those in tenements planned with four or more apartments on each level.[58]

Ernest Flagg and Henry Atterbury Smith thought about tenement house design in narrow terms. They were primarily interested in planning buildings that were economical and that embodied their ideas about the relationship of built form to health. Edward Tuckerman Potter took a broader view. Although concerned about economy and health, as a district visitor among New York's poor he had had direct experience of crowded living conditions that made him take into account "the human factor." Those who did not have this background rarely appreciated the importance of trying to avoid "any wound to the self-respect of the occupants."

This gap in understanding was particularly apparent in the way that after the turn of the century city planners and those who called themselves "housing experts" discussed how best to organize the public spaces in and around multiple dwellings. Their attitudes were summarized in Lawrence Veiller's "Buildings in Relation to Street and Site," a paper he delivered at the Third National Conference on City Planning in 1911. In order to examine the way blocks were divided, Veiller sent a questionnaire to all cities in the United States with over 100,000 people. He found that there was no standard way to divide blocks, but he concluded that one constant seemed to be the deep lot, which existed for two reasons. When cities were comparatively small and when there was no great population pressure, economy-minded city officials laid out as few streets as far apart as was compatible with the needs of the community. The deep lot was also common because people wanted to have not only an ample back garden, but also a spacious front yard, thus creating the attractive appearance of American cities.[59]

The problem, as all observers of American cities then understood, was that areas of "high class fashionable residences" usually deteriorated. Like other reformers, Veiller therefore proposed a form of zoning to fix the character of different areas by determining what kinds of houses could be built in each one. In extreme cases, such as New York, it was necessary to construct large multiple dwellings. Veiller thought that in planning such buildings there was little room for innovation or the kind of creative examination of the problem that Edward Tuckerman Potter was undertaking.[60] Instead, he wanted gradually to improve tenements through the passage of better housing laws that would specify how such buildings should be located on their sites and how the interior corridors, lobbies, and staircases should be designed. Veiller had been instrumental in writing the sections of the 1901 New York Tenement House Law that dealt with these matters, and in *A Model Tenement House Law* he had set out dimensions, terms, and conditions that could be used by any city or state in formulating the parts of a housing law about public spaces in and around multiple dwellings.[61]

Veiller hoped, however, that it would not often be necessary to construct such densely occupied buildings. He favored as an ideal a three-class system of 125-, 50-, and 25-foot-deep lots. Architects and planners well understood how to lay out houses on parcels of the first size. At the time that Veiller delivered his paper there were already many examples of sensitive arrangements that took advantage of the character of the landscape and avoided the ruthless rigidity of a grid of streets and property lines.

On house lots of a minimum of 50 feet deep Veiller thought it was still possible to produce the effect of the first type of house, but on a reduced scale. To ensure that separate houses would still appear to be dotted on the landscape, it was necessary to zone the area for single-family dwellings and to specify satisfactory minimum dimensions for the lot frontage, for the setback of the house from the street, and for the position of the house in relation to adjoining property. The issue that most concerned professionals in laying out this type of housing was whether there should be alleys at the back of the lots. The advantages and disadvantages were readily apparent. Alleys were desirable because they served as exits for garbage and other types of waste; they were also entrance points for coal, ice, and other deliveries. Utilities could be brought to the house through the alleys; that meant that ugly telephone and electric wires did not have to disfigure the street. The main drawback of the alley was that it was hard to patrol and keep clean. It was a breeding ground for disease, and because "the human waste" of cities always seemed to gather there, it was "the side entrance to the juvenile court or reformatory."[62]

In high-class neighborhoods alleys or service driveways were usually considered satisfactory because residents who could afford the luxury of keeping the street clear of tradesmen's vehicles and of requiring back-door deliveries could also pay to maintain an alley. Housing reformers also felt that blocks of row houses or tenements needed alleys, because without them it would be necessary to carry wastes through the adjacent buildings. To protect these spaces, they insisted that alleys be publicly owned, well lit and paved, and frequently cleaned and patrolled. Alleys in blocks with intermediate-sized lots were more problematical. With separate houses on small parcels of land it was still possible to make deliveries along the sides of the house and thus avoid the development and maintenance expenses of the alley. A frequent compromise was to make deliveries from the front, but to reserve an easement in the back of the abutting lots for the placement of utilities.[63]

Before the First World War those who thought about the best way to place houses on lots had little understanding of what the automobile would mean for the delicate relationship of front to back. On large residential lots, no matter whether there was an alley in the rear, there was every reason to think that the automobile would follow its predecessor, the horse and carriage, and enter by a grand driveway that would eventually lead to a garage somewhere near the back. It was assumed that the owners of separate houses on small lots would want to park their cars near their homes, not in public garages. But some people reasoned that it would be better for automobiles to drive down alleys and park at the back of the home rather than enter by the street. A driveway for each house was wasteful. It was undesirable for cars frequently to cross the curb, and, besides, because automobiles were considered fire hazards, their garages had to be located as far back in the lot as possible anyway. These arguments were sensible, but architects and planners obviously could not yet comprehend the effect that pride of ownership had on automobile drivers, nor did they understand the nature of the intimate connection automobiles would come to have to the comings and goings of the household.[64]

The most controversial part of Veiller's classification of types of house lots was his third level of housing. He called for shallow blocks 25 feet deep. That dimension permitted a house with only a front and back room per floor, but each would have adequate light and ventilation. The buildings would be like the small Philadelphia row houses that Potter had earlier admired, but with one exception. Since one side faced one street and the other another, they would have no back yard at all. Veiller later recognized the waste in this multiplicity of streets, and suggested that the areas between the rows of houses be covered in grass and be in the public domain.[65]

Veiller's formulation of this type of housing was prompted by his assessment of how the families of workingmen used their gardens. He thought the notion of a garden in the back of the house and a front lawn was a "beautiful ideal," but it was utopian. The ordinary laborer, especially the "foreign population" that was "coming to predominate in our American cities," did not have time after a ten-hour working day to cultivate a garden, nor did his wife if she gave her children the attention they required. Gardens for such people would be only the "gathering place for the waste material of family existence."[66]

When Raymond Unwin, who had traveled to the United States to attend the city planning conference, heard Veiller's paper he was astonished. He was "more hopeful" than Veiller. Although England was more densely populated than the United States, planners and architects there still kept a wide space between the backs of houses. Unwin distinguished between two types of housing, the cottage and the multiple dwelling. The first was far better than the second, which was "the most difficult with which to assimilate any sense of home, and absolutely the most miserable type of place in which children can be raised." But Unwin did not differentiate between types of cottages, and no matter how small the cottage, the garden was essential.[67]

Grosvenor Atterbury explained to Unwin that he came from a country in which people were "more docile, not to say more orderly and of better aesthetic instinct" than in the United States. The back yard was so abused among the "poorest class" that even though there were some people who could maintain it, it was better to deny the privilege to everyone who lived in certain grades of housing than to run the risk of having these spaces become derelict. In brief, Atterbury asserted, Unwin did not understand "what bad bedfellows Liberty, Equality and Fraternity are."[68]

Veiller's specification foreshadowed the subsequent decades' bleak blocks of public housing isolated in areas of paving or grass. But more important than the form of housing was the attitude that shaped it. Veiller, Atterbury, and many housing reformers since the First World War felt that it was part of their task to protect urban inhabitants not only from many external evils but also "from themselves." How they arrived at this conclusion varied, but too often this presumptuous attitude led to great misunderstandings and ultimately to new housing that was as bad as, if not worse than, that which it replaced.[69]

In addition to the houses that Lawrence Veiller described, reformers occasionally touched on other types. Between the single-family home and the tenement there were several kinds of houses, each of which had a special relationship to its home grounds. The Philadelphia row house was joined on two sides and therefore was not really a separate house. The semidetached house, which at the turn of the century was frequently constructed in Philadelphia and elsewhere, was more separate, but still not quite an individual home. The Philadelphia quadruple block, a group of four houses clustered around a cruciform party wall, was in the same category. So to a lesser extent were the many types of two- and three-story detached structures that had a family on each level and that began to proliferate in American cities at the end of the nineteenth century.[70]

Reformers sometimes thought that these houses served a useful purpose. In making a survey of Newark, New Jersey, George Ford came to understand the virtue of the structure with a family on each floor. He found that these buildings were often built and owned by a workingman who lived on the ground floor and rented the other apartments for enough money to pay his mortgage, taxes, and other overhead charges. He lived rent-free; he was "a good citizen . . . free and independent in every way." But if reformers did not think of these structures as outright menaces, they rarely considered them valid in themselves. At best their importance came from the fact that they were stepping-stones to separate houses, which was the ideal to which everyone should aspire.[71]

While the subject of two- and three-story structures was being discussed at a housing conference in Philadelphia in 1912, George Hooker suggested that it was advisable not to make such compromises. The spaces around a house were valuable not only because they could be used as a garden and for growing vegetables but also because they served an important perceptual purpose. Hooker felt that a home that had to be recognized by the street number did not have a "proper individuality." Children could not identify with it; therefore they could not use it to develop "poetry and imagination."[72]

Hooker was only reiterating what had become a commonplace even before the Civil War. It was important for a home to have an "image." At the most basic level this image came from separateness. No matter what its specific uses were, the ultimate function of the home grounds was to give the house this identity.

✦✦✦

Many people who promoted apartment houses did so because they believed that a compact type of residence was necessary if American cities

**FIRST FLOOR PLAN**

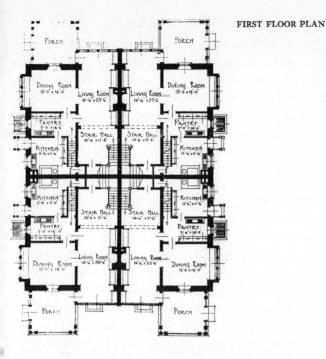

**SECOND FLOOR PLAN**

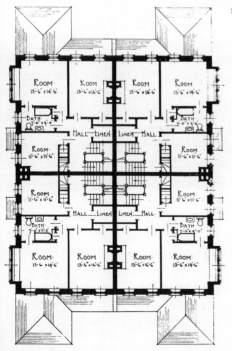

74. *Duhring, Okie and Ziegler:
A quadruple house in
Philadelphia, 1911. Except for an
indirect route from the front
door to the kitchen, these houses
were well planned. But they
were not emulated in
Philadelphia or elsewhere very
frequently.*

were to become great centers of commerce and culture. O. B. Bunce, the editor of *Appleton's Monthly*, wrote about the importance of apartment houses because he disliked the inconvenience of travel to and from suburbs. He thought that the pleasures of a city had to be "spontaneous and immediate," and he argued that a city's important commercial and cultural facilities would not flourish unless a large number of people lived nearby.[73]

In a period in which no one was certain what shape the American city would take, many arguments were marshaled in favor of the great, compact metropolis. No matter how they were justified, these visions usually included vast public parks around or in which apartment houses were located. These tracts of landscape were vital to the well-being of the city; without them the apartment house was incomplete. Moreover, for this type of building to be successful, its home grounds — the courtyards, roof gardens, lobbies, corridors, staircases, and elevators — also had to be properly ordered. These spaces were shaped by many of the same concerns that figured in the design of the dwellings of the city's poor and working population. The architect of even the most lavish apartment houses could rarely ignore the rules of efficient spatial organization; more important, he had to decide whether to base his building on the individual home or on a more comprehensive structure.

Some apartment houses were planned on the assumption that a large number of people living under one roof constituted a community. These buildings contained more than a group of isolated apartments; they had common spaces — courtyard gardens, generous lobbies, roof terraces — which all the residents could use. This kind of dwelling was attractive to many people. It appealed to the Boston architect John Pickering Putnam because he believed it was appropriate to Nationalism, the program of reform Edward Bellamy outlined in *Looking Backward*. In that utopian novel Bellamy contrived to have his hero, Julian West, wake up a century in the future. The device gave Bellamy the opportunity to contrast America of the late 1880s with his ideal civilization. The details of Nationalism were explained by Dr. Leete, who characterized the earlier "age of individualism" by the fact that in nineteenth-century cities like Boston people put up three hundred thousand separate umbrellas when it rained. But in the "age of concert," when the first drops fell, a "continuous waterproof covering" descended over the sidewalks of the city and made a well-lit and perfectly dry corridor, even at corners. Nationalism, therefore, demonstrated to each citizen the full value of his fellow

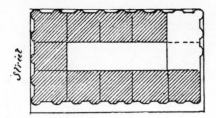

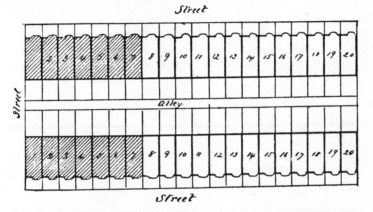

76. J. P. Putnam: Ground area occupied by individual and apartment houses. Because there was so much "unavailable space" in row houses, a given amount of "available space" could be more efficiently accommodated in the apartment house.

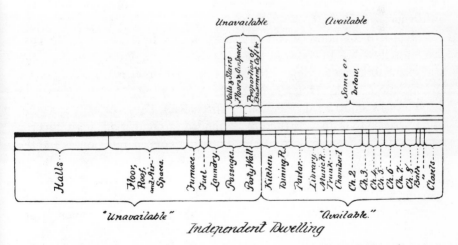

75. J. P. Putnam: Available and unavailable space in individual and apartment houses. Putnam, an early American advocate of the metric system, believed in efficiency. On that account, this diagram shows a telling contrast between apartment and row houses.

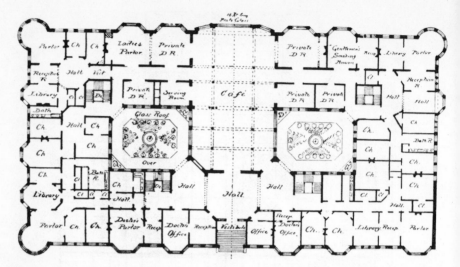

77. *J. P. Putnam: The apartment house. This plan represented Putnam's ideal housing accommodation. In addition to the apartments, the building contained two glass-covered courtyards, a "café," and other common facilities for the use of the residents.*

men. Universal education with equal opportunities and material advantages produced the highest qualities of mind. Individuals were then able to understand that they were "necessary to each other through their very differences of character."[74]

The apartment house was important not only because it was the context of fellowship but also because it was efficient. Putnam outlined his arguments first in an article in the *American Architect and Building News* and later in a book, *Architecture under Nationalism*. To demonstrate his principles he contrasted a section of forty Back Bay row houses with a hypothetical five-story structure, arranged around two glass-covered courtyards, in the same Boston area. The group of separate houses and the apartment house each accommodated the same number of people. But in the first, which Putnam called "towers," in contrast to the "flats" of the apartment house, the amount of "unavailable space," that which was devoted to halls, corridors, staircases, and storage areas, was much larger than in the second. In one large structure it was possible to group all these wasted spaces economically. The result, according to Putnam's argument, was that "available space," the useful rooms of an apartment, was much cheaper in the apartment building.

Because of this economy it was possible to provide extra areas in the apartment building that everyone living there could use. Putnam's apartment house had a large, comfortable lobby at the entrance and a spacious café between the two glass-covered courts. Equally important, all the residents could share the space around the apartment house. Putnam demonstrated that his building was far more compact than the Back Bay row houses and therefore occupied less land. He envisioned that apartment houses similar to the one he designed would be set in a verdant landscape and would be sufficiently separated so that they would not cast shadows on one another. In the process the "natural beauties of the landscape" would be preserved.[75]

Those who designed or commissioned apartment buildings did not have to have progressive ideas to include some of the features that appealed to Putnam in their structures. From the time that apartment buildings were first constructed, those who saw them as the appropriate type of housing for a great city imagined that the spaces in, around, and especially on top

*78. Harry Fenn: "The City of the Future," 1872. In commenting on this drawing, the editor of* Appleton's Journal *exclaimed: "How picturesque roofgardens would make our town streets, what charming pictures they would supply to every prospect, what a grace they would add to our domestic architecture." Residents of these apartment houses would use the flags to send messages to their friends.*

of them would be used by all the residents. O. B. Bunce was particularly enthusiastic about the potential of the tops of apartment houses for roof gardens. Writing in 1870, Bunce already recognized the importance of the steam elevator. It would provide quick access to the roof and would allow structures to be much higher than those based on staircases. "Far up under the unobstructed heavens," Bunce argued, "flowers may blossom and fruits ripen." He imagined that water tanks placed on the roofs of these buildings could be turned into decorative fountains that would service the roof gardens. As vines from rooftop planting trailed down the building, the apartment house would be encompassed by nature. A city filled with such structures would be truly picturesque.[76]

From the 1860s on, when apartment houses were first widely constructed in New York, it was not uncommon to have roof gardens. They did not add up to the urban landscape of Bunce's imagination, but some were spacious and well-planted and afforded the residents marvelous views of the surrounding city. The most luxurious apartment house of the period, the Apthorp, between Seventy-eighth and Seventy-ninth streets and Broadway and West End Avenue, had on its roof a shaded promenade from which it was possible to look out across the Hudson River to New Jersey on the west and back toward the city in the other directions. The roof also contained a large playroom for the building's children.

When apartment buildings were planned around a courtyard, that space could also be used by the tenants. The Apthorp, which occupied a square block, had a central courtyard entered through an archway so that residents had to leave their vehicles only when they were away from the street. Immediately below the courtyard there was a service driveway with an entrance on Seventy-ninth Street. Wagons proceeded directly into the basement, stopped opposite one of the four service elevators, and left the building by driving around the center of the floor. But the Apthorp's courtyard was not just for access. It had a display of flowers that one critic said would "grace a botanical garden," two fountains, and benches on which residents could relax.[77]

Another part of the home grounds of such buildings was the sequence of spaces from the entrance to the front door of each apartment. This progression followed in a reduced manner the format of a hotel. The most lavish of these structures began with a porte cochere that instead of protruding from the apartment house over the sidewalk was part of the ground floor of the building. Lesser structures had a canopy leading up to the entrance. A doorman also distinguished various grades of buildings.

79. *Clinton and Russell: Graham Court, 1900. The courtyard of this prominent New York apartment house was large enough to be more than a transitional space from the arched gateway to the entrance areas at the four corners.*

In the better apartment houses the lobby was often a large space because it gave access to a bank of elevators and a "grand staircase," which, as the primary point of vertical circulation, had to be near the center of the building. Off the lobby many apartment houses had public rooms. Most of these spaces were simply for waiting and were furnished accordingly, but some had more precise functions. They could be used by the residents to hold large dinners; occasionally a room was reserved specifically for the women who lived in the building. On floors with apartments, the elevators opened onto a network of corridors. In the best buildings entrances to apartments along the two sides of the corridor were staggered so that residents would not have to confront each other if they opened their doors at the same time.[78]

When Americans started to build and live in such buildings, they looked to Europe for precedents. They usually found the most useful examples in Paris, where there was a long tradition of apartment house living.

However, the interpretation of the French apartment house could vary. Lewis Leeds, the well-known writer on sanitation and plumbing, found that the Parisian courtyard was a catalyst for a particular type of social intercourse. He noted that in principle Americans deplored the existence of classes, but in practice in the United States there was a danger of dividing society into classes "more decisively and more objectionably than obtained in any of the old countries." The American pattern was for "every man to look out for himself, and let his neighbor do the same." This meant that the "rich and the strong" secured the best locations for their fine houses, while the poorer and laboring classes were either crowded into unhealthy areas or had to travel several hours each day to and from work.

In Paris the special configuration of the apartment house made possible the mixing of classes. Leeds described the premises of one of the most successful plumbing establishments in Europe. The ground floor of the building contained workshops, stables, a carriage house, storage areas, and showrooms. The elegant apartments of the proprietors were located on the next level. Above that were the rooms of the company's working-men, and servants occupied the top of the building. Although the three classes of inhabitants were distinctly maintained in the organization of the structure, the fact that all the apartments fronted on the same street and all were entered from the same central courtyard brought about a certain level of equality.[79]

Americans who were concerned about the ever-expanding divisions among city dwellers often hoped that the apartment house would be a meeting ground for disparate people. In William Stead's vision of the twentieth-century city, the apartment house was the characteristic form of residence, as it was in the regional centers of William Dean Howells's Altruria.[80] Given the exigencies of the moment, plans for such classless buildings had to be deferred. Nevertheless, the sense of a community, which Leeds had found in the Parisian apartment building, could still be nurtured among those of similar background.

Leeds's interpretation may have appealed to some Americans, but others read into the same kind of building an antithetical meaning, and they used that analysis to define a different type of apartment building. Sarah Gilman Young, a literary critic, had lived for five years in Paris and seven in other European cities. She used that experience to study different ways of building apartment houses. She was convinced that as cities became more crowded, Americans would have to adopt that form of dwelling.

To do so was in accordance with the "theory of evolution applied to architecture." The United States was in a "transition state from the simple to the more elaborate and complex" and would soon need a form of housing that went beyond the rudimentary individual home.

She recommended to Americans buildings similar to and in some instances actually taken from those that César Daly illustrated in *L'Architecture Privée au XIX^me Siècle*. Like other Americans who traveled to Paris, Young noticed that the chief feature of such apartment houses was the courtyard. She specified minimal dimensions to ensure that adequate sunlight and fresh air entered the courtyard, but the more important characteristic of the space was how it functioned as an entrance to the apartment house.

Young's notion of apartment house living was based on exclusivity. Her ideal was not to mix with neighbors but to be able to have in this compact context a private existence with as little contact, interference, and oversight as possible. From this point of view the courtyard had several important advantages. Once you entered it, you were quickly shut off from the noisy, public street. Unlike the apartment building with a main doorway, a large lobby, and a major staircase and elevators that at each level led to a network of corridors, the kind of apartment house about which Young wrote had small entrances and staircases that led to landings on which only a few apartments were located. These entrances were usually situated in the corners of the courtyard, which was not intended for the gathering of residents or for relaxation but only for quick and convenient access to the apartment entrances. Since the goal of this kind of building was privacy, the one drawback was the concierge, a "domestic spy" who patrolled the entrance to the courtyard and was a source of gossip, but who, Young granted, performed some important services.[81]

The architects of some of the earliest apartment buildings in the United States tried to follow this format. In New York the best-known structure was the Dakota. Designed in 1884 by Henry J. Hardenbergh, the Dakota was massive for its time. A nine-story structure, it was 200 feet square, had a central courtyard, the largest dimension of which was 95 feet, and was entered by a two-story-high porte cochere. Each corner of the Dakota's courtyard had a staircase and elevator, an arrangement permitting only one or two apartments to be located on each landing.[82]

The architect who probably was most familiar with the Parisian apartment house and who best understood its nature was Philip Hubert. Born in Paris in 1830, he came to the United States in 1849 and settled in

Cincinnati, where he made a living teaching French. In 1853 he took a position at Girard College in Philadelphia and went to Boston in 1859. Before he came to the United States, Hubert had studied architecture with his father, but it was only in 1865 that he moved to New York and started a practice.[83]

For Hubert the essence of the French system of housing was that people actually did not live in apartments but instead in "small private dwelling houses" built one over the other. Although there was often a courtyard at the center of the building, that space and the staircases leading to the apartments served no communal purpose. No money was spent on them; they were maintained only for cleanliness. Isolation was further secured by the sturdy masonry construction. No flimsy stud partition walls were used, and the spaces between floor joists were filled to ensure acoustical privacy. Nor did sound travel through the holes that were usually made in the fabric of a building to accommodate pipes and conduits, because the plumbing in these buildings was primitive or nonexistent. Water closets were usually located in an isolated tower, connected by a short walkway to each level. Water for daily use had to be carried up to each apartment.[84]

Hubert tried to transfer this quality of separate houses in a large building to the American context. His best-known building was the Central Park, or Navarro, on Seventh Avenue and Fifty-eighth and Fifty-ninth streets facing Central Park. Although this structure appeared to be one massive block, it was actually eight separate buildings organized around

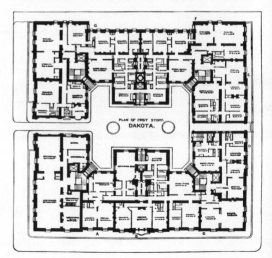

*80.  Henry J. Hardenbergh: The Dakota apartment house, 1884. The courtyard provided light and air and access to the entrances at the corners, but it was not designed for any other uses.*

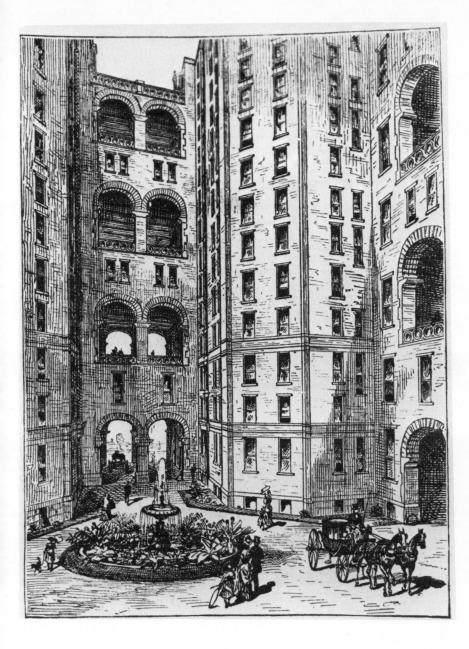

*81. Philip G. Hubert: The courtyard of the Navarro apartment house,
1883. This picturesque space served mainly as access to the Navarro's duplex
apartments.*

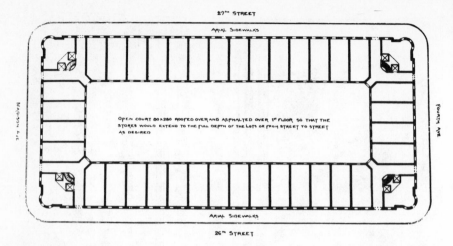

82. *Philip G. Hubert: An apartment building based on "aerial sidewalks,"*
*1890. Staircases and elevators at the four corners were connected by elevated*
*sidewalks that gave access to two-story "houses." This thirteen-story struc-*
*ture would have been the most ambitious building of its kind, but it was not*
*constructed.*

a sequence of spaces that formed an interior street in the center of the complex.[85]

Hubert's concept of housing would have been most magnificently demonstrated in a huge building that he planned for the site of Madison Square. This structure was to be a thirteen-story courtyard building. Two elevators located at each of the external corners stopped at every other floor because the building was composed of two-story apartments. From the elevator landings, 14-foot-wide "aerial sidewalks" led directly to each dwelling. Hubert designed his access system so that the "public hall and the stairs" would be a "mere continuation of the public street." Each apartment, therefore, would be "in all essentials a separate home."[86]

A law limiting building height prevented Hubert from constructing this extraordinary scheme. Hubert wanted to reconcile vast, rationally planned structures with the individual home. But the future of the apartment house that emphasized privacy did not lie in large buildings. Structures like the Dakota and the Navarro were not common because it was difficult to acquire large sites and to finance such ambitious projects. These big buildings were also not favored because there were other ways to design discreet and private apartments.

One method was to make the apartment building resemble as much as possible the individual city home, which in New York was a four-, five-, or six-story row house, entered directly from the street, sometimes up a short flight of steps. Another model was the college dormitory, a three-

or four-story building organized in a courtyard or U-shaped configuration, with several separate entrances. In either case the lobby and nearby staircase were not modeled after the corresponding parts in a hotel but instead were domestic in scale. Each level of the building usually only had one or two apartments.[87]

As these structures were being built, architects worked out rules for the design of the public spaces in them. The Chicago architect Irving Pond advised that the entrance to each apartment had to be "a separate and distinct feature," and that the doors of two apartments should never be adjacent to each other. These guidelines were, he explained, a response to the natural and proper demand on the part of "refined and sensitive householders to have their homes in outward expression, as in absolute fact, places of refuge and retirement." If the building had a service elevator, privacy could be achieved by preventing it from opening off the public hall, as it did in many apartment houses. Once that happened, the public hall, which should have been for the residents and their guests, became "the runway of the butcher, the baker, the grocer, and the servants in the garrets of the kitchen and the scullery," and where then, Pond asked, was "self-respect"?[88]

Although apartment buildings were of two distinct types, the one emphasizing community, the other, privacy, it was not uncommon for architects to try to combine elements of both. The Apthorp, for example, was organized around a courtyard with entrances and small landings at the corners, and yet it also had extensive gardens on the roof and in the court itself. Usually these attempts to create an environment of what one author called "promiscuous exclusivity" were compromises.[89] There was one architect, however, who tried to combine the two types into a comprehensive vision of what urban living could be.

Edward Tuckerman Potter not only wanted to design an apartment house that would unite the best features of the individual home with the advantages that came from many people living close together, but he also tried to make a building for everyone. After many years of attempting to design a suitable system of houses for New York's working population, Potter shifted the focus of his attention when a lady who had inspected one of his plans remarked that the dwellings were "too good for the poor." Like his conversation with the journeyman barber, that comment marked another turning point in Potter's thought. Potter decided to plan for no one class: "what was not good enough for one, was good enough for none." Instead, he tried to determine what constituted the fundamental requirements of housing, not just for New York but for anywhere in the

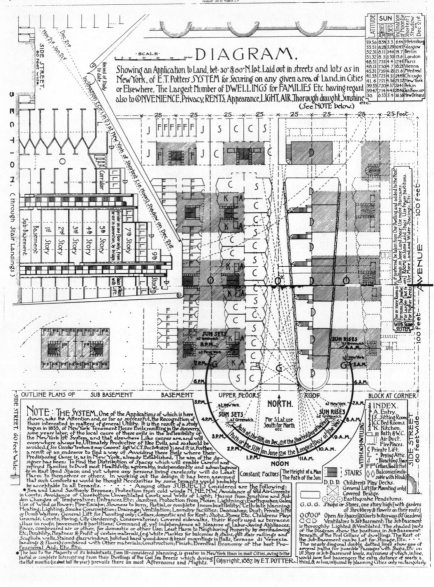

*83.   E. T. Potter: Diagram for a system of concentrated residence, 1887. In this diagram and an accompanying chart Potter attempted to make a system of housing that was equally applicable to everyone everywhere.*

world. The result of this investigation was a design that was the period's summary statement about apartment houses.[90]

Potter's building was a series of parallel structures, oriented north and south. Each of these fingers stepped up from four to nine stories as it approached the northern side of the site, where it was joined to the others by a connecting structure running east and west. The basic organization of this system of concentrated residence was derived from the need to give through ventilation and sunlight to each apartment. Potter did not design a courtyard building because with that configuration it was impossible to avoid sunless rooms. All of his apartments had through ventilation, and because of the orientation and sloping configuration of the building, they all had at least some sunlight every day.

Potter also shaped the spaces around the apartment so that they could be useful to the inhabitants. He did so by avoiding corridors, which he found detrimental to quiet and privacy and which usually were impediments to the planning of apartments with through ventilation. He gave each apartment a private balcony and oriented the windows so that there would be no direct overlooking. In addition, Potter allocated specific activities to the outdoor areas. The ground level of the structure was devoted to shops. The roof spaces above these shops and between the parallel buildings were planted with shrubbery and flowers. On the roofs of the buildings there were play decks for children and glass-enclosed conservatories.

Potter represented his building in one comprehensive drawing and an equally detailed explanatory chart, both of which were published in the *American Architect and Building News*. Potter's conception and the diagrams that he produced to represent it had a quality of both precision and imagination that was unmatched in its time. He based his building on an idea of fundamental individual and communal needs, and he tried to realize his design by taking maximum advantage, through natural and artificial means, of the surrounding environment.[91]

The result reflected Potter's personal concerns, but it also summarized and gave form to the hesitantly articulated aspirations that Americans in the last half of the nineteenth century occasionally had for the great metropolis. For most of these people the distance between vision and reality was too vast. Except on rare occasions, they could not generate the commitment to bridge it. They could not ignore a visionary like Potter. His articles and diagrams were published in professional and general magazines, and he received a medal from the American Institute of

Architects.[92] But despite such recognition, he was never really listened to. It is no wonder that he withdrew from New York to travel in Europe and finally to live in comparative isolation in Newport, Rhode Island, where he worked out his visionary designs and composed his music.

Most apartment houses were not shaped to fulfill part of a vision of a great metropolis. These buildings were usually not occupied out of choice; their residents were attracted to them because they needed temporary accommodation or because they could not afford their own homes. Philip Hubert illustrated what could happen in such buildings by relating the experiences that some friends of his had with the spaces in and around their apartment house. This structure was five stories high with an apartment on each floor. Since the building was 20 feet wide and 80 feet deep, each unit was arranged around a well in the center of the plan. The difference between this building and a tenement was in the space allotted to each apartment and the quality of the entrance and the stairway, not in the size of the light well.

When Hubert's friends moved into this building, everything was "*couleur de rose.*" But when other tenants arrived, their enthusiasm started to diminish. They could hear every step above them, and the residents on the top floor had two ill-bred boys who did not rub their feet on the front doormat and left prints from their dirty boots all the way upstairs. In May and June Hubert's friends observed another objectionable feature of the building. The street on which it and many similar structures were located was not like one with single-family houses. The total population of the street was enormous, and in warm weather people, especially the "Little Lord Fauntleroy and other juvenile types," congregated outside the buildings. They made parlors of and held receptions on the stoops that led to the front entrances. At the same time Hubert's friends noticed many "apartment to let" signs. Most of the tenants were too genteel to spend their summers in town, but not sufficiently wealthy to pay rent for apartments they did not occupy. When Hubert's friends returned in the fall from their vacation, they found that half the building's residents had changed.

They took all of this in stride. But their first serious disenchantment with apartment house living came when an aunt arrived for a visit and was given the center room in back of the parlor. Until then this room had only been used for storage. Once the aunt settled there, its inadequacies were soon realized. It was evident that a space 10 by 12 feet with a window on an enclosed well and overlooked by the corresponding window of the apartment in the adjoining building hardly complied with the notion that the first requirement of a bedroom was privacy. Fortunately, the tenants across the way were quiet and respectable, but they soon moved and were replaced by people "whose conduct, especially at night, made the center room unfit for a lady's occupancy."

By that time the building had lost much of its original attraction. The showy but somewhat cheap carpeting in the landings and stairs was already worn, and, worst of all, a "certain atmosphere," well known to the occupants of such apartment houses, had begun to establish its presence. New tenants, but of "a lower grade," arrived. They smoked on the stairs and landings "which they used as a regular part of their holdings, and where they appeared with a painful disregard as to their toilet." Conditions worsened and finally Hubert's friends moved away, "pronouncing the house a worthless, ill-planned, ill-built sham, unfit for human habitation."[93]

It was partly because of such experiences that Hubert wanted to accentuate the separateness of each unit in the design of apartment houses. After twenty-five years of trying, he finally gave up and settled in Southern California.[94] Most families did not have to make such an abrupt choice. They balanced efficient housekeeping and the convenience of a flat against the qualities of a separate house in a nearby suburban village. Such houses had many advantages, but how to build and own one was not a clear-cut matter.

# 4

## THE HOUSE BEAUTIFUL

WHEN AMERICANS WANTED TO SUMMON UP AN IMAGE of the building that was the ideal context for domestic values, they often used the phrase, The House Beautiful.[1] That was Mark Twain's title for the chapter of *Life on the Mississippi* in which he described the house that in his youth had been "the finest dwelling" in every town from Baton Rouge to St. Louis. Between the sidewalk and the house beautiful there invariably had been a "large grassy yard with paling fence painted white — in fair repair; brick walk from gate to door." The house itself was "big, like a Grecian temple." Inside, there usually was an uncarpeted hall with planed boards and opening out of it a parlor. This most important room had an "ingrain carpet; mahogany center-table; lamp on it, with green-paper shade — standing on a gridiron, so to speak, made of high-colored yarns, by the young ladies of the house, and called a lamp-mat." Twain then satirically itemized the rest of the parlor's sentimental objects — the mementos of trips taken to New Orleans, the pressed flowers, the daguerreotype of husband and wife, the window shade stenciled with milkmaids and ruined castles.[2]

Like the imposing fluted Corinthian columns that actually were made of white pine, everything about the house beautiful was a "pathetic sham." But no matter how savagely Twain attacked it, the house beautiful was a difficult edifice to pull down. When he returned in 1867 from the trip to Europe that furnished him with the material for *The Innocents Abroad*, Twain was anxious to find just such a house. Shortly after disembarking, Twain visited Hartford, Connecticut, a city of gentility and traditional values that might have repelled the western man. But for all his idiosyncrasies, Twain was not unlike other wandering Americans. Wanting to stabilize his unsettled life, he was attracted by the fact that Hartford was a "sterling old Puritan community" and by the houses that did so much to establish the character of the city. Hartford, Twain wrote, was "composed almost entirely of dwelling houses — not shingle-shaped affairs, stood on end and packed together like a 'deck' of cards." Instead, they were "massive private hotels, scattered along the broad straight streets, from fifty all the way up to two hundred yards apart." Each house sat in the midst of "about an acre of green grass, or flower beds, or ornamental shrubbery." Everywhere the eye turned it was "blessed with a vision of refreshing green." Twain concluded: "You do not know what beauty is if you have not been here."

Twain continued to lead a peripatetic life, but in 1869 he bought an interest in the Buffalo *Express* and in the following year settled in nearby Elmira with his new bride. During this time Twain visited Hartford on several occasions. Having soon become disgruntled with his work for the *Express*, he took his wife to live permanently in the "sterling old Puritan community," which then seemed even more attractive than it had on his first visit.[3]

In Hartford Twain decided to live at Nook Farm, a tract of land where in the early 1860s Charles Dudley Warner, Harriet Beecher Stowe, and other members of Hartford's literary and intellectual circle had built homes. While living in a rented house, the Twains commissioned Edward Tuckerman Potter, the architect of the system of concentrated residence, to design them a home. The Twain residence differed in style and detail from the finest dwellings in the towns along the Mississippi River in the antebellum period, but it was still a house beautiful. Instead of Corinthian columns, Potter, who was a disciple of John Ruskin, used intricate patterns of brick, wooden railings, and colored roof tiles to give character to the house and to create what the Hartford *Times* called "one of the oddest looking buildings in the State ever designed for a dwelling, if not in the whole country."

The elaborate forms that resulted from the conglomeration of turrets, balconies, porches, jutting roofs, and projecting porte cochere were matched on the interior. The generous entrance hall led to a spacious staircase that joined the house's nineteen rooms. Each space was decorated with different woods and wallpapers. The tops of the chest-high built-in bookcases of the library were covered with knickknacks that Twain collected in his travels. The bedrooms were filled with carved

*84. E. T. Potter: Mark Twain's house, Hartford, Connecticut, 1874. Potter was the architect who designed the system of concentrated residence. This house was made primarily of brick. During his first visit to Hartford Twain had written disparagingly of "shingle-shaped" houses. He wanted something more solid and permanent.*

furniture bought in Europe, and a huge conservatory was supplied with exotic plants from a greenhouse elsewhere on the Twain property. By 1874 the previously rootless but already successful writer had put $21,000 of furniture into a $70,000 house on five acres of land worth $31,000.[4]

Just after he moved into his new house, Twain described himself as "thoroughly and uniformly and unceasingly happy." In many ways his was a truly happy home. In the decade after they moved to Hartford his wife gave birth to three girls. Since Twain worked at home, he could often take time off to tell his children stories, play charades, and act in family theatricals. The activities of the home circle often intersected with those of the other families that lived at Nook Farm. Twain valued the company of his neighbors, and members of the small community often wandered over to the peculiar-looking house, where in warm weather they sat on the large covered porch, the "ombra." The house also welcomed a constant stream of famous guests who sometimes arrived with little notice and stayed a long time.

Although Twain often exulted in his happiness, his home was also a setting for tension and sadness. Several bad business investments put him in a precarious financial position and intensified the always heavy burden of running an elaborate household. In 1891, bankrupt, he and his wife closed the house to travel to Europe, where they thought they could live more cheaply. He always intended to go back permanently to Hartford. But when his favorite daughter died in 1896, Twain could hardly bear the thought of returning to a scene that was so redolent with memories. The house, as Twain wrote in 1897, "was not unsentient matter — it had a heart, and a soul, and eyes to see us with; and approvals, and solicitudes and deep sympathies; it was of us, and we were in its confidence, and lived in its grace and in the peace of its benediction. . . . We could not enter it unmoved." In the late 1890s he visited Hartford several times and often talked about again living there, but Twain, who was then growing more disillusioned with American life, never went back to his home and finally offered it for sale in 1902.[5]

Family histories like that of the Twains were familiar to Americans who lived through the period. No one who thought about such cases could delude himself that to live in a house beautiful in itself guaranteed happiness. But as long as Americans believed in the power of beauty, it was plausible to think that an attractive house might at least further the attainment of happiness; in any case, it certainly did not hinder that end. A house might put a financial burden on those who owned it, but it was not the house's fault that the family was living beyond its means.

Since Americans generally thought it desirable to live in a house beautiful, they had to resolve two issues. One was primarily the concern of architects. They had to define what a beautiful home was. That was the task that Andrew Jackson Downing had set himself. Influenced by the powerful ethos of home religion and all it entailed, he had made important revisions to his theory of architecture just before his tragic death. In the following half century, tastes changed, and few, if any, architects acknowledged Downing as a predecessor. Nevertheless, many of the problems that he tried to solve were perennial ones, and architects could not avoid addressing them.

The other crucial issue was how to provide as many people as possible with beautiful homes. When Fredrika Bremer came to the United States, she visited Downing and frequently took walks with him along the banks of the Hudson. On one excursion Downing pointed out what Bremer later described as "a beautiful little house, a frame-house, with green verandah and garden." It belonged, Downing explained, to a man who drove a cart that carried stones for road-making, and it emphasized a difference between the old and new worlds. Unlike his counterpart in Europe, the workingman in the United States "by the hard labor of his hands" could obtain one of "the more refined pleasures of life, a beautiful home."[6]

Before the Civil War the American workingman was often depicted "hastening home to enjoy repose" in a cottage along a country lane.[7] At that time it might have been satisfactory to think that he could attain this ideal simply by "the hard labor of his hands," but after the Civil War many philanthropists and reformers realized that institutions had to be established to assist him. How to enhance home ownership then became one of the period's important issues.

Downing often linked beauty and possession. "With the perception of proportion, symmetry, order and beauty," he wrote, "awakens the desire for possession, and with them comes that refinement of manners which distinguishes a civilized from a coarse and brutal people."[8] After the Civil War Americans rarely made this connection so explicitly. Those who were concerned about beauty and possession usually focused their efforts on one or the other. Even so, they continued to assume, if only tacitly, that the two went hand in hand.

✦✦✦

In the postbellum period several kinds of measures were taken to enhance home ownership. The cost of a home, especially a separate home, depended in part on the availability of cheap land. By the middle of the nineteenth century building sites near the center of a large city were too expensive for all but the most lavish houses. But there was abundant, cheaper land in the suburbs, and many of the entrepreneurs who financed the construction of transit lines used the seemingly universal desire for homes to justify their ventures. The cost of commuting to work offset some of the advantages of the cheap housing in the suburbs, but the operators of omnibus, streetcar, and railroad lines tried to minimize this penalty by instituting flat fares. The construction of transportation lines, especially those with flat fares, could be seen as part of a larger program that included measures to bring down the price of home sites by taxing underutilized land. Others argued, however, that if transportation was efficient, then the taxes proposed by the followers of Henry George would not be necessary.[9]

The cost of a house also depended on the price of construction. In a period in which houses and the equipment they were expected to contain both became more complex, there were two main ways to keep construction costs down. One was to use cheap labor. Since building was a seasonal industry that took place on sites scattered throughout a city, not at a few factory locations, it was difficult for those employed in construction to organize and to make a unified demand for higher wages. Workers with special skills sometimes were able to make an exception to this rule, but the houses built in the last half of the nineteenth century were constructed primarily by poorly paid laborers, many of whom were newly arrived immigrants who had to take whatever jobs they could get.

The other way to reduce the costs of construction was to use efficient building techniques. In the decades before the Civil War countless machines were invented to mass-produce and shape building products. The number and efficiency of these inventions continued to grow after the war and helped to turn what had been a craft into an activity appropriate for an industrial society. A few architects tried to take mechanization a step further. Instead of rationalizing the elements of a building, they argued that the cost of housing could be radically reduced by mass-producing large parts or even entire houses. By the First World War this proposition had not been sufficiently tested to know whether it was valid, but at least then it was already being widely discussed.[10]

Rapid transit and efficient building techniques, especially when assisted by expensive labor, helped to make more and cheaper homes available. But since home ownership involved a financial transaction, many people contended that before Americans could live in places that were their own, it was necessary to regularize the method of purchasing houses. To do so, they often urged the formation of building and loan associations.

The first of these institutions, the Oxford Provident, was started in Frankford, Pennsylvania, in 1831. The next was founded five years later, and in the 1840s and 1850s others were started, mainly in and near Philadelphia and New York. The great period of expansion for building and loan associations came after the Civil War. When the Department of Labor conducted a survey in 1893, it found that only nine of the 5,838 building and loan organizations then in operation had existed before 1863. In the twenty years after the Civil War this type of bank became a national institution as it spread from large eastern cities to small western towns where credit was always in demand. By 1890 every state had at least one association, and in 1915 there were more than sixty-eight hundred, with a membership of over three million and total assets of almost a billion and a half dollars.

Building and loan associations financed a significant number of houses. In 1893 approximately 30 percent of the close to 1,750,000 members had mortgages. The number of homes financed through building and loan associations then increased rapidly. In 1901 new mortgages were granted for 50,000 homes, in 1910 for 87,000, and in 1915 for 114,000.[11]

The significance of building and loan associations did not lie only in the number of its members or the amount of houses financed. The early history of these organizations was also important because it was against this background that the home financing practices of subsequent decades were set. One of the most important precedents established before the First World War was the preferential tax treatment for home owners. This subsidy was largely the result of lobbying efforts of the United States League, a national organization that represented the interests of building and loan associations. In 1894, the year after it was founded, the league pressured the Finance Committee of the United States Senate to exempt building and loan associations from the 2 percent levy on the net incomes of corporations that had been proposed in the Wilson Tariff Act. Al-

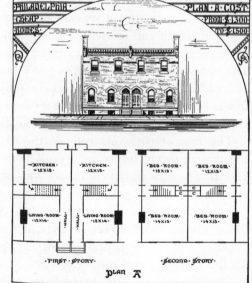

85. Houses financed by a building and loan association in Philadelphia, 1876. The housing for artisans that made Philadelphia known as the "City of Homes" was generally much starker than these elevations.

though this act was later declared unconstitutional for other reasons, the principle of exemption had been established and it was upheld, often against considerable opposition, in subsequent acts that taxed both corporations and individuals.[12]

Building and loan associations first became popular because they responded to deficiencies in the American banking system. During most of the nineteenth century commercial banks made loans that could only be paid back in one lump sum at a fixed date, usually within three to five years. These were daunting terms for a person who was saving to pay for a home he had already purchased. The uncertainty of meeting the final payment was compounded by the dubious reputation of banks. Throughout the nineteenth century, especially during depressions, banks often failed and many people lost their savings. Moreover, the occasional unmasking of unscrupulous directors did not encourage Americans to trust banks.

Building and loan associations overcame these problems because they were corporations in which every member was a stockholder who assumed unlimited liability and participated in the election of directors. The main difference between building and loan associations and other corporations was that instead of paying for stock when it was bought, the member or shareholder subscribed for a number of shares on which he had to pay a stipulated sum each week or month until the shares matured. The payments ("dues"), their frequency, and their par value varied, but generally one dollar was paid on every share once a month until a par value of two hundred dollars was reached. When the share matured, the member was paid its value. To ensure that members met their dues, small fines were levied against those who were delinquent.

The amount brought in by dues and fines increased because it was lent at interest to borrowers. Those who wanted a loan told the association's directors on what property they intended to build or what house they wanted to buy. An appraiser's report was made, and the directors decided whether the investment was sound. Which members should have a loan was determined at auctions held when enough money had been paid into the association. Bidding began at a minimum interest rate fixed by the bylaws. The security for a loan usually was a mortgage on real estate and an assignation to the association of the borrower's stock. The par value of a member's shares was usually the maximum value for which he could bid.

The advantages of building and loan associations to the saver were obvious. Whereas the return on bank accounts was frequently only 2 percent and rarely over 5, a member of a building and loan association received at least the minimum lending rate, usually 6 percent. The amount above that figure was the difference between extra income (from the interest charged to borrowers, the penalties for late payment of dues, and the portion of profits sacrificed by those who withdrew their money before their shares matured) and overheads, which associations always tried to keep to a minimum.

Savers had more assurance that their money was safer in a building and loan association than in a bank. Shareholders elected the directors of the organization, most of whom received no pay. To differentiate building and loan associations even more sharply from banks, the bylaws usually stated that directors were elected for a limited period, not for life, and that they could not serve consecutive terms. Most of the literature that publicized these organizations stressed the measures taken to guard against swindling and embezzlement.

It was often argued that if building and loan associations were advantageous for savers, they could not be so for borrowers, especially since banks usually offered money at 6 percent interest, whereas members of building and loan associations had to bid beyond that figure for a loan. However, loans were not always available at banks. Without one the only way to purchase a home was the time- and money-consuming process of saving the whole sum while paying rent. Even if a bank loan was available, its 6 percent interest was deceptive. A loan was usually obtained through a broker who charged a commission of 1 or 2 percent. Those who could not pay the short-term bank loan when it was due had to try to renew it, but they had to pay an additional commission for doing so. Building and loan associations also charged less for legal work than the going rate.[13]

Most of the early building and loan associations operated under charters that terminated as soon as every member had received and repaid a loan. These terminating societies had distinct disadvantages. Members who subscribed to stock after the first date of issue had to pay all back dues, a sum that became prohibitively large as the society grew older. The more important deficiency of the terminating society was that toward the end of its life it became difficult to lend the influx of savings and thus to produce income. Some societies coped with this problem by stipulating that the directors could dictate when shareholders had to take out loans. Others gave their directors the authority to retire the shares of nonborrowing members before maturity; they then lost a special premium for keeping their money in the society until the stock matured.

Despite these measures, a more flexible system was necessary. Serial societies, which put out new issues of stock at stated intervals, met many of the deficiencies of the terminating organization. New members were able to join the society without paying back dues, and since the money taken in and lent out in different series of stocks was pooled, it was less common to have an excess of savings. Although the structure and rules of the society still assumed that every saver would eventually be a borrower, this correlation was not as crucial in a serial society as it had been in a terminating association.

The first building and loan societies were begun by a group of people who met at stated intervals and who joined together in the running of the association. The change to serial societies put the organization on an ongoing basis, but the members of each series were still bound together because they all attended meetings and paid their dues on regular occasions. The founding of permanent associations transferred whatever emphasis the serial society had put on the group to the individual. Through advanced bookkeeping techniques, permanent societies were able to treat the account of each member as a separate series. He deposited his money at stated intervals and withdrew the full value when his series matured, provided that payments on a loan were not still outstanding.

The tendency to cater to the individual was also furthered by an attempt to differentiate between savers and borrowers. Since many building and loan associations were founded in areas where credit was short, it was advantageous to attract funds from people who intended to be savers only. But to do so, the building and loan association had to offer terms that were competitive with those of mutual savings banks, which had been founded to return a high but safe interest on a depositor's money. Some building and loan societies, therefore, established limited liability for each shareholder and devised a system of operation and a method of electing officers that did not require participation.[14]

Other developments further changed the original basis of the building and loan association. The fact that these organizations served a small geographical area ensured that members at least came from the same place, even if they had nothing else in common. Seymour Dexter, an upstate New York judge who was the first president of the United States League, was always adamant about the importance of the building and loan association's basis in the immediate community. Without this relationship the broader purposes of the society would not be served and, at a more practical level, directors would not be familiar with the property that members proposed to buy or build upon. However, organizations that drew members from wider areas had the great advantage that they could transfer funds from one place to another. Individuals then did not have to depend on other people nearby to start a building and loan society. To take advantage of this deficiency in the local association, several large national organizations were started in the 1880s and 1890s.[15]

By 1915 most building and loan associations were still small and local, but they had lost the group basis that was so important to their original supporters. In their operation and management they were then not unlike commercial banks, some of which had begun to offer many of the building and loan association's services. These changes can be seen simply as the inevitable working out of the most convenient banking rules and procedures, but in the transformation other forces were at work.

The first building and loan associations were started for the sole purpose of financing the buying of homes. But the idea soon attracted the support of people who did not need the assistance of these institutions. Robert Treat Paine, a Boston financier and philanthropist, often proclaimed the value of home ownership. He believed that the glory of New England was that every citizen was a freeholder. Since "no American had the right to be poor," he advised that no one should be content until

THE OCCUPANT OF THIS HOUSE    THE OCCUPANT OF THIS HOUSE

IS PAYING FOR IT THROUGH THE    HAS NOT YET HEARD OF THE

CO-OPERATIVE BANK.    CO-OPERATIVE BANK.

*86.  Robert Treat Paine: "Own Your Own Home," 1881. This contrast was the basis of the appeal of building and loan associations.*

reaching "the grand position of our American ancestors, who all struggled and succeeded: sturdy freeholders who made the strength and glory of this country." Paine supported building and loan associations because he felt that home ownership was the modern equivalent of having a freehold.[16]

Paine also thought that the importance of building and loan associations extended beyond the immediate fact of owning one's own home. These institutions fostered other virtues. One of the most important was thrift — the basis of all prosperity, a guard against sickness, and a means of avoiding poverty in old age. Ten dollars a month for thirty years invested at compound interest resulted in not only a plot of land and a house but also $20,000. Given this emphasis on thrift, the great hero of building and loan associations, especially those in Pennsylvania where these organizations were first founded, was Benjamin Franklin. Through industry and frugality, "the guiding rule of life," he had become "rich in purse, and eminent in knowledge." That was "the working man's way to wealth."[17]

Another purpose of building and loan associations was educational. Each one was the equivalent of a business school. At the monthly meetings members discussed how to save money, invest safely, manage a piece of property, and evaluate the merits of houses. They also learned other lessons; for instance, "how to keep out of and hate liquor shops and all the other costly and deadly allurements of the devil." Building and loan associations, in short, taught how to build up a "wise plan of life" that led to "the grand result of home and independence and competence and character." That was the building and loan association's "diploma."

The values of thrift and education were important, but the one often most emphasized by spokesmen like Paine was "cooperation." Building and loan associations showed how the interests of capital and labor were united. They gave to the poor the advantages of the rich; they made the worker a capitalist. The laborer who deposited his money in a building and loan association and who eventually bought a piece of land on which to build a home would in so doing "join the other party, and, belonging to both, he the more readily sees that it is for the interest of both to work together."[18]

In trying to create this relationship between capital and labor, the building and loan association was only one of the period's many cooperative ventures. Beginning in the 1860s a few forward-looking factory owners and businessmen advocated the formation of member-owned institutions not only for the saving of money and the building of houses but also for the distribution of goods. Cooperative stores gave those who belonged to and used them a stake in the organization's success, and they reduced the cost of goods by eliminating unnecessary middlemen. Cooperation was also possible in the production of goods. Some factory owners established schemes to encourage their employees to buy stock in the company and to share in profits.[19]

Factory owners, businessmen, and reformers who tried to foster cooperation often did so as a partial means of realizing their ideas, however tacitly stated, of an ideal community. In trying to achieve this goal, however, they first had to come to terms with the reputations of the many mill and factory towns that were built throughout the United States from the beginning of the nineteenth century on. The relationship of worker to employer in these communities varied. It was often brought out most forcefully in the way the workers were housed.

In 1888 the owner of the Howland Mill in New Bedford, Massachusetts, built fifty houses for which his workers paid only about 15 percent of their monthly income. The tenants were free to use these buildings as they wanted as long as they maintained them. When many workers had to be laid off in the depression of 1893, the mill owner lowered the rent and in some cases did not collect it at all. That generosity was one of the reasons he lost financial control of the mill.[20]

Such cases were the exception rather than the rule. Other factory owners made demands on the conduct of their tenants and collected rents no matter whether the times were good or bad. George Pullman, who in the early 1880s built a community for his workers on the South Side of Chicago, did not invent these policies, but he became the most notorious executor of them. When Richard Ely wrote about the town of Pullman in 1885, he was impressed by its cleanliness, the excellence of its architecture, and the fact that rents were low compared with those elsewhere in Chicago. Even so, Ely found an "all-pervading feeling of insecurity at Pullman." The community had no newspaper in which its citizens could voice their views. In the local government of the town of Hyde Park, which encompassed Pullman, the managers of the factory, but not the workers, were represented. Religion was neglected; only an eighth of Pullman's inhabitants attended church. Wages in Pullman were no higher than elsewhere, and unskilled workers had to struggle to make ends meet. Many lived in cheap flats sited on the periphery of the community where they would not attract attention. Ely found that even the efforts to beautify Pullman were, on closer inspection, a sham. He summarized his impression of Pullman by quoting a worker who complained that "the company cares nothing for our souls. They only want to get as much work as possible out of our bodies."

Much of this attitude was attributable to the fact that workers could not buy the houses that Pullman had erected. Their leases could be terminated at ten days' notice with no reason or hearing. Ely recognized that "the desire of the American to acquire a home is justly considered commendable and hopeful." It promoted thrift, and "the habits acquired in the effort to pay for it are often the foundation of a future career." Pullman discouraged individual initiative; the town was "un-American, benevolent, well-wishing feudalism."[21]

Ely predicted that a large number of home owners was a safeguard against "violent movements of social discontent." The events of the next decade seemed to prove him right. A small strike in 1886 tarnished Pullman's reputation as a model factory town. Whatever illusions remained about the community were finally destroyed during a strike in 1894. When Pullman had to reduce wages because the number of orders had fallen at the factory, his employees demanded that he reduce rents in factory-owned houses as well. Pullman answered that he had not raised rents during prosperous times and that he expected to receive a constant 4 percent profit on his investment. The strike was long and bitter. When it threatened to spread throughout Chicago and paralyze the city, federal troops were brought in. Despite public opinion in their favor, the strikers finally had to give up their cause.[22]

Jane Addams best summarized the tragedy at Pullman by likening it to *King Lear*. Pullman built his town with the honest desire to give his employees the best surroundings, but this benevolence was also a form of self-aggrandizement. He demanded unquestioning admiration and gratitude from his dependents. Similarly, Lear honestly intended to benefit his daughters by dividing his kingdom, but instead of giving the land freely, he demanded the price of outlandish avowals of filial devotion — a price that Cordelia refused to pay. When the strike started, Pullman was shocked because he could not understand the changes that had taken place in the American labor movement in the period after he constructed his town. He would not accept that his employees had needs different from those he thought were good for them — that they were no longer his children (Pullman referred to them as such). Correspondingly, Lear could not understand that Cordelia could be moved by ideas and feelings, such as a love for truth, that were outside of him. As events overtook them and people refused to act as they should, these two once powerful figures became pathetic. Addams, however, also pointed out that some of the responsibility for the tragedies rested with the child figures, the workers and Cordelia. Instead of attempting to empathize with their fathers, the children rigidly maintained their positions and, because of the bitter past, could express no pity.[23]

Most factory owners probably would not have considered it their duty to build housing for their workers in the first place, but if put in George Pullman's position, they would have acted as he did. Even so, a few enlightened factory owners, financiers, and philanthropists wanted to avoid situations like that at Pullman. Instead of erecting company-owned houses, they supported building and loan associations or equivalent schemes to help workers become independent.

Ostensibly, there was no need for businessmen or financiers in an organization that was run by its own members. Building and loan associations often prided themselves on the fact that they were not banks and that they did not have self-perpetuating directors. But Robert Treat Paine thought that it was important for prominent members of the community to serve in an advisory capacity. Those who freely gave their time and effort to the building and loan society not only demonstrated their interest in the association's welfare and the values it stood for but also offered "a new testimony of the strong human sympathy between those who have got on in the world and those who are trying to do so . . . a new bond of our common brotherhood which makes our towns and our country pre-eminently great."[24] The danger in this relationship was that instead of enhancing the bond of common brotherhood, the interest of prominent members of the community would be interpreted as another example of paternalism.

The communities that supporters of building and loan associations thought successful illustrate not only some of the characteristics of what they considered an ideal society but also the role these people envisaged for themselves in the building of such utopias. Edward Everett Hale, one of the most vocal supporters of building and loan societies, often discussed the kind of community they could create. A nephew of Edward Everett, Hale was one of the postbellum period's most famous ministers and the author of many works of didactic fiction, including the popular story "The Man without a Country." In "How They Live in Boston, and How They Die There" Hale described the effects of bad housing in a large city. A husband who was aware of the conditions in the center of Boston told his wife why the rate of infant mortality was so high. Accompanied by a city health official, he took his wife to one of Boston's worst districts. Hale described in great detail the crowded and insanitary conditions they saw. He concluded that it was not enough for a minister to serve the spiritual needs of his parishioners. Charities were also necessary, but Hale understood that even the work of these organizations was ineffective when people lived in decrepit tenements.[25]

Unlike other ministers who in the same period were arriving at a similar conception of their duties, Hale did not consider the great metropolis worthy of improvement. His ideal was a small community. In *Old and New* he occasionally described towns that deserved emulation. He praised Saltaire, the town constructed by the English industrialist Titus Salt, where workers lived in cottages for less than a London artisan paid for a crowded garret and also had the advantage of reading rooms, a bath house, and other facilities.[26]

Hale also admired Riverside in Chicago. Its generous landscaping "encouraged domesticity" and "promoted sociability, intercommunication, exercise, and the enjoyment of the pure air."[27] But not many people could afford to live in such a place. Hale considered that the most relevant example for building and loan associations was Vineland, New Jersey. This town was founded in 1861 by Charles K. Landis, a man of extraordinary energy and vision, on a tract of 30,000 acres in a sparsely settled part of New Jersey near Cape May. The land itself had no obvious advantages. All its timber had been cut down long before, and it contained no easily extractable minerals. However, Landis hoped to take advantage of the good soil to start fruit and vegetable farms that would supply the nearby markets of New York and Philadelphia. A recently completed railroad provided the necessary transportation to these centers.

Landis's immediate problem was labor. Near his land lived a few people who had been "kept down by the great landlords and manufacturers in the vicinity." None was literate, and they had no schools. They lived in log cabins with dirt floors. Most were employed as woodcutters and were paid only in coupons to be exchanged at a store owned by those who kept them in a state of "degradation and brutal ignorance."

Landis hired some of these men, doubled their wages, paid them in gold, and proceeded to lay out a town. Its mile-square center eventually contained factories, schools, shops, recreation halls, churches, and private residences. Around this area were farms, gardens, orchards, and vineyards. The plan was a "practical and convenient" grid of streets. Landis tried to compensate for "the want of the picturesque" in this layout by providing for the planting of shade trees along Vineland's roads.

Since the success of Vineland depended on the satisfaction of those involved, Landis offered his workmen ten acres of land at twenty-five dollars an acre and furnished them with timber and a carpenter to help them erect their houses. Subsequent settlers were sold house lots at reasonable rates. The only stipulation in the sale was that they had to sign a contract that contained Landis's "system," presented under two headings, Material and Moral. The first had to do with the physical state of Vineland. Purchasers of land were not to build houses less than 20 feet from the street within the town and 75 in outlying districts. Each home owner had to plant shade trees along the street and seed the grass near the roadside. As his contribution to the appearance of the town, Landis laid out squares for "public ornament," donated a 45-acre park, drained swamps to create agricultural land, and, to avoid unsightly outbuildings, gave each householder an earth closet. All the sewage was collected and turned into fertilizer.

The chief "moral" problem concerned the sale of liquor. Landis noted that those who were "sober in their habits" were usually successful. He was not a strict temperance man and simply tried to persuade Vineland's residents not to allow the sale of liquor within the town's limits. Licenses were always voted down in local elections, and the results were reflected in the small amount of money spent on police and poor relief.

To enhance the quality of life in the community, Landis persuaded the New Jersey legislature to make Vineland a separate township governed by an annually elected five-man committee. He also gave land to religious denominations and set up agricultural, horticultural, and literary societies. In his account of Vineland's progress Hale filled almost four pages with a list of business, reform, agricultural, educational, learned, benevolent, and religious associations.

No problem was too difficult to overcome. Landis hired an agent to market the produce raised by newcomers who had not yet learned how to run their businesses. When freight rates seemed exorbitant, Landis set up a competing railroad. The presence of the new line forced the original one to lower its rates, added to the total trackage of the town, increased the value of property, and opened new markets for Vineland's produce. Since Landis did not want Vineland to be dominated by agriculture, he tried to encourage manufacturing. He erected a large building equipped with a steam engine and rented space for a minimal fee. In a few years boots, shoes, buttons, straw hats, pocket books, and several wood products were being made in Vineland. Landis also tried to protect the town's residents from commercial monopolies. When merchants in Philadelphia charged too much for flour and seed, Landis started his own mill in which he resolved to make only the best products at prices that met costs. Soon his only problem was to supply the ever-increasing demand. By 1875 Vineland ranked fourth among New Jersey townships in agricultural production and had fifteen factories. Its 10,500 inhabitants were prosperous, and the great majority of them lived in their own homes.[28]

Many factors made Vineland special; not the least of them was Landis's capital, which financed the venture in the first difficult years. Other people who wanted to start a community were rarely so well endowed, but Edward Everett Hale hoped that building and loan associations could help to make up this deficiency. In "How They Lived at Naguadavick" he described how the associations could be the catalyst for the development of a new community. Naguadavick was a typical thriving New England town of 30,000 that badly needed housing. Hale thought it was too difficult for individuals to purchase land and to supervise the construction of their own houses. Moreover, that method of growth would only duplicate Naguadavick's haphazard development. The alternative was a "combined enterprise, which seeks everybody's good." Hale wanted a group of people to join together and to start a building and loan association. The organization would then find a farm outside the center of the city and persuade the owner to divide it into lots to be sold at a fixed price. Because of the power of numbers, the building and loan association would also be able to convince a railroad to set up commuter trains and to keep the rates fixed for a preestablished period. Everyone would, therefore, make a modest profit. The farmer, assured of a list of subscribers in advance, would not have to juggle the costs of his lots, the railroad would have no competition, and the prospective home owners would know exactly what they were buying. In his story Hale told how, with the assistance and encouragement of a local minister, residents of Naguadavick put this plan into practice and founded a new community, Rosedale.[29]

Hale twice assisted attempts to turn fiction into fact. With Josiah Quincy, a prominent Boston businessman and philanthropist, he arranged in the early 1870s to start a community in the Wollaston section of suburban Quincy.[30] The more interesting settlement, however, was in the Oakdale section of Dedham. It was begun by a group of Lutheran immi-

87. *Edmund Quincy, Jr., and Ware and Van Brunt: "Model Houses at East Dedham for the Quincy German Homestead Association," 1871. About a dozen of these houses were built.*

grants from Germany who had first lived in East Boston, a district that was becoming increasingly crowded in the 1860s. The Lutherans had been familiar with workingmen's credit banks in Germany and with Quincy's assistance tried to finance their home building along similar lines. They purchased a 60-acre farm near a railway station in Dedham and conveyed the land to Quincy as a trustee. They then organized the equivalent of a building and loan association and contracted to build ten houses. The first subscribers paid six dollars a week for a house that was designed in the office of the famous architects Ware and Van Brunt.

Once enough Lutherans had settled in Dedham, they persuaded a pastor to join them. An old Congregational church was purchased and renovated. The community constructed buildings for two clubs, the Fidelia and the Liederkranz. The premises of both were used for a variety of community purposes, including meetings about cooperative banking and insurance societies. Many of the settlers worked in the area at a piano factory owned by one of the families. The Lutheran children went to public schools, but their classes were taught in German until the First World War, when, as a patriotic gesture, they began to be conducted in English.[31]

Friedrich Engels would have said that the desire of prominent factory owners, financiers, ministers, or reformers to play an overt role in enhancing home ownership and in founding new communities like Oakdale was the clinching bit of evidence for the argument he made in 1874 in *The Housing Question.* In that pamphlet he pointed to the abysmal living conditions of workers as proof of the injustices of a capitalist society, but he had little respect for home ownership or the efforts of reformers to enable laborers to purchase their houses. By making "little capitalists" out of workers, financiers and philanthropists were diffusing, at least temporarily, the conflict between capital and labor. The desire to own a home was a handicap that for centuries had restrained peasants. Engels thought that once workers migrated to cities, freedom of movement would be the "first condition of their existence." If they owned their own homes, they would again be chained to the soil and would lose their power to strike because they would be afraid that they would not meet the payments on their houses.

Engels even claimed that owning a home produced a reduction in a worker's wage. In his theory of economics capital was command over the unpaid labor of others. A worker's house could become capital only if it was rented to another person, part of whose labor product was, therefore, appropriated in the form of rent. If a worker lived in his own home, it was not capital. Equally important, once workers owned their

88. *Seymour Dexter: "The American Home, the Safeguard of American Liberties." Seymour Dexter was the founder and first president of the United States League of Building and Loan Associations. This picture was adopted by the league at its first convention in 1893.*

houses, capitalists no longer felt obliged to pay them high wages because the amount for shelter no longer had to be included in their calculation of a minimum sum for subsistence.[32]

In the United States the alternative to the meddling of those who "had got on in the world" was not the revolution that Engels hoped would soon take place. Because Americans were wary of the role of benefactors, they tended to shun any broader involvement whatsoever and to stress the autonomy and thus the security of their own homes. This condition was one reason why building and loan associations eventually catered more to the individual than to the group and became more a service than a community organization.

✦✦✦

When supporters of building and loan associations discussed who would benefit from these organizations, they often used terms like workers, the working classes, laborers, and the poor. This imprecision masked the difficult fact that not everyone could afford a home, no matter how effective the building and loan association was. The kind of house in which a person lived depended to a large extent on his earning power, and there was a great difference between a skilled artisan, an unskilled laborer with a steady job, the un- and underemployed, and those who, for whatever reason, were incapable of making a living.

Few users of building and loan associations probably were members of that vaguely defined group, the working class. Even fewer were poor, no matter how that word was defined. They were, instead, primarily skilled workers with steady employment who could make regular monthly mortgage payments. If it was difficult for them to purchase houses, it was even more so for people with an irregular earning pattern. How to provide decent housing for those without skills and without steady employment was one of the period's most perplexing issues. Many concerned people thought that the most that could be done was to try to raise housing standards by instituting stricter building codes. Others disagreed, maintaining that although a rise in standards led to improvements, it also made housing more expensive. For them the real problem was the real estate market, which determined the supply and rental levels of housing. The only way to provide better housing for those on the margin was, therefore, to develop an alternative to this system.

Beginning in the late 1860s a few people tried to achieve this end by starting organizations to build cheaper and better housing than that available on the open market. These organizations were not charities; they were companies created to make a profit, which, although limited by law, would be sufficient to encourage others to start similar ventures and thus eventually to solve the housing problem.

The profitability of housing did not depend only on how buildings were constructed, financed, and managed; the conduct of the residents was also important. Excellent housing, shaped by the most up-to-date theories of health and sanitation, could be undermined by tenants who failed to pay rent or who did not take care of the premises. The investors who started limited-dividend housing companies were well aware that many of the tenants they wanted to attract were not reliable. But they considered this an opportunity, not a liability. In addition to building sound housing, philanthropists and the stockholders of limited-dividend housing companies had an educational mission. They wanted to nurture in their tenants an appreciation of orderly habits and the value of good home surroundings. Once the residents had learned these lessons, they would be able to lead responsible lives, secure regular employment, and ultimately become home owners.

These were ambitious goals. When they were first articulated, no one had had much experience with this kind of housing, so it seemed reasonable to think that limited-dividend housing companies could accomplish what their founders intended. The history of one of the first of these organizations amply illustrates the problems of putting this financial and educational plan into practice.

The Boston Cooperative Building Company was formed by a group of prominent Massachusetts citizens in 1871. It was largely the idea of Henry Ingersoll Bowditch, an eminent doctor and professor at the Harvard Medical School. Before the Civil War Bowditch took a lively interest in social problems. He gave free medical treatment to patients who otherwise could not afford it, was an ardent abolitionist, and taught children of the poor at Boston's Warren Street Chapel. In 1846 he attended a meeting to discuss Lemuel Shattuck's report to the City Council on the perilous density of Boston's population, and as a result of the ensuing discussion he co-authored a report that recommended that dwellings for Boston's laboring population be constructed by a cooperative building company.[33]

Nothing came of this idea for twenty years. Throughout the 1850s Bowditch was occupied with his medical practice and pioneered in research about the causes of tuberculosis. Before Bowditch published

DIAGRAM showing position of a house, in Massachusetts, in which Consumption has been Very previlent.

*89. Henry I. Bowditch:* "DIAGRAM *showing position of a house, in Massachusetts, in which Consumption has been Very previlent," 1862. Through such analyses, Bowditch came to appreciate more than the connection between dampness and consumption; he began to understand that there was a deep relationship between the local environment and all aspects of health.*

*Consumption in New England* in 1862, most doctors thought that tuberculosis was endemic to large regions. By carefully compiling statistics, Bowditch tried to show that the disease was bred in specific, usually damp, locations. This conclusion gave him an appreciation of the profound effect of the immediate environment on health.[34]

In the late 1860s Bowditch helped to establish a State Board of Health in Massachusetts, and at that time he resumed his earlier interest in better housing. In 1869 Bowditch traveled to England, saw some of London's worst slums, and met the noted housing reformers Sidney Waterlow and Octavia Hill. Not only had they been able to build or recondition with a modest profit good housing for London's laboring population but in the process they had brought about an improvement in the characters of the residents. Instead of immediately giving tenants new and spacious quarters that they might not appreciate or know how to care for, Octavia Hill had devised a scheme in which good tenants were gradually rewarded for proper behavior by the opportunity to live in progressively larger and more commodious dwellings.[35]

Conscious of the fact that conditions similar to London's existed in Boston, Bowditch was determined to do something about them when he returned. He described to the State Board of Health a building derisively called the Crystal Palace, reputedly the worst tenement in Boston.

Bowditch concluded that housing and social improvement were intimately connected. "Take away a man's or woman's self respect and you tend to drive them to low habits of body and thence come disease and death," he argued. But, "place the same person in clean, well-appointed apartments, where they can live in comfort with their families, and can attend to the decencies and proprieties of life, and they will be lifted up morally."[36] Bowditch soon tried to test this proposition. The Boston Cooperative Building Company was set up by an act of the Massachusetts legislature to build and improve houses for workingmen. By the nature of its incorporation, the company was not a charitable organization. Octavia Hill had shown that charities neither uplifted the tenants nor provided an example that others would emulate.[37]

Since there was no clear precedent for this kind of housing in the United States, it was hard to know exactly how best to proceed.[38] The project of the Boston Cooperative Building Company that initially attracted the most attention was an attempt to rehabilitate the Crystal Palace. The company took a five-year lease on the renamed Lincoln Building, removed tenants from cellars, built ventilating shafts to give light and air to every room, and made repairs throughout the approximately sixty apartments.

In addition, some stockholders of the Boston Cooperative Building Company tried to establish a close relationship with the tenants. The company's first annual report noted that members of a visiting committee "have counseled, they have comforted, have procured work for those who need it, have, in short, stood in relation of friend to every tenant who desired such a relation." A liquor store in the building was closed, and a coffee shop was started in its place. A sewing school was established for girls, "singing meetings" were arranged, and to encourage thrift, bank books were issued to every boy and girl. At the end of the first year the company was highly satisfied with its efforts and announced that in the future it intended "to introduce some comforts into the house, as our funds should warrant, and the needs of the tenants rise above those of animals, upon which plane many of them may properly be said to have been, when we took the house in charge."

The next two annual reports were more cautious. "Efforts at humanizing the tenants" went well, but there were problems. Some of the tenants had to be evicted when the initial repairs were made. Others were asked to leave for failure to pay rent and for disorderly conduct. In the first three years a total of fifty-three families were evicted. Nor was the venture yet profitable. Repairs were costly, and the company's income was hurt by families that did not pay rent.

In the fourth annual report the cautious tone became more sober. A nationwide depression in 1873 had hurt both the earnings of the tenants and the profits of the company. Many tenants had moved, and ten apartments were vacant. In the same year taxes on the building rose, and there was a costly fire. A year later the depression was worse; many families could not pay the rent, and the company lost hundreds of dollars. As the five-year period ended, the Boston Cooperative Building Company announced that the lease on the Lincoln Building would not be renewed.

In a short time great expectations had been completely deflated. One of the first annual reports noted that Octavia Hill had been able to maintain a "firm relation between landlord and tenant." The stockholders wanted to prove that a "soulless corporation" could do the same. But neither they nor their agents, who collected the rents and made the repairs, had had any success in establishing such a productive rapport. The characters of the residents had not improved, and the venture still did not make a profit.

These facts were clear, but the lesson to be learned from them was not. From the failure of the Lincoln Building experiment the stockholders could have concluded that the tenants needed more intensive and also different kinds of services. It was also possible to acknowledge that all services, no matter of what kind, were ineffectual in such depressed and disorienting times. Either of these conclusions might have led the company to reassess its original expectations and would have allowed it to seek more modest but still important results from the better living conditions it made available.

Instead, the directors pointed to external circumstances that, if different, might have produced another outcome. They mentioned that police protection for the building had not been sufficient and that outsiders had disrupted the tenants. More important, they blamed the type of building for the failure. "A building of so great size and constructed as the Lincoln Building is, with passages, stairways, and water conveniences in common," they wrote, "was totally unfit for the proper lodging of those human beings who need the oversight of others to keep them."

The demise of the experiment confirmed what many of the stockholders felt they knew all along: instead of repairing an old tenement, it was better to build detached houses in the suburbs. In the fourth annual report, when it was already evident that the Lincoln Building would be a failure, the directors announced that they had bought ten acres of land in Dorchester, a suburb of Boston, on which they planned to build forty to fifty separate houses.

Henry Bowditch did not agree with the new direction. When the lease of the Lincoln Building was not renewed, he ceased to be active in the Boston Cooperative Building Company. Yet in some ways suburban houses had always been attractive to Bowditch. In his 1846 report he had concluded that on the outskirts of Boston the families of workingmen might "have more room and better air, and the women and children might cultivate a small garden." In 1873, while making a survey of housing conditions for the Board of Health, Bowditch visited a dozen towns in Massachusetts and found decrepit living conditions in all of them except Lynn. There the shoe industry had attracted a class of thrifty laborers whose well-kept houses had a significant impact on the appearance of the town. Bowditch noted with approval the "great number of neat and comfortable, although small, dwellings, the homes of the working class." And he concluded "that it is impossible not to draw the inference that there is some intimate relation between the wise policy of separate homes . . . and the condition of public health."[39]

Nevertheless, Bowditch always resisted the idea of workers living in the suburbs. He had practical reasons for this position. The 1846 report noted that railroads were reluctant to have workingmen on their trains because "it might prove annoying to the passengers to have numbers of laborers assembled at the depots." Such people would also depress the value of land and "discourage the settlement of a richer class." Besides, railroads would not lower their rates to make commuting economical for laborers. Even if these problems could be solved, Bowditch wondered whether suburban homes would be popular because the "workingman had a strong prejudice in favor of a *home* near his work." The laborer could not be "induced to remove so far from his work, his friends, and his church." He would "have to bring his dinner with him, or buy it in town and would be put to many inconveniences, connected with the Rail Road hours."[40]

Practical considerations and the "disinclinations of the worker" to live away from the center of town reinforced Bowditch's ideas of housing reform, which had been shaped by those of Octavia Hill. Bowditch thought that the Boston Cooperative Building Company should provide housing for people not yet ready to move to their own houses. The guidance given by representatives of the company would help the residents of such housing acquire habits that would enable them to attain steady employment and eventually their own homes: "the average worker must grow up tediously to an appreciation of what is possible to him in his home." The necessary "oversight of others" could best be rendered to those who were concentrated in one place. The dilemma arising from the Lincoln Building experience was that the oversight of the company had had no discernable impact. Whether another approach could have produced different results is debatable, but in financing the Dorchester homes, the company seemed not to be interested in finding out. Even if these suburban houses had been intended for the kind of person who lived in the Lincoln Building, the dispersed character of the settlement would have made close supervision impractical.

In 1875 Sidney and Waterlow streets, named after the English housing philanthropist, were laid out on the company's land in Dorchester. The site was near horsecar and railroad commuting lines. Thirteen detached houses were initially built. Each purchaser paid the company $200 down and $25 a month.[41] At the end of each half year, taxes, interest, and insurance were deducted from the $150 paid, and the remaining sum was subtracted from the purchase price. Under these terms it took an average of ten years to buy the house outright.

From the beginning the company was unclear about for whom the Dorchester homes were intended. Members of the "country-house committee" of the company had written that they wanted to make houses available to those who earned a "moderate salary." They soon found out what kind of a house a moderate salary would afford. By 1876 only five of the thirteen houses had been contracted for. A year later the depression reached its worst point, and the company noted that the Dorchester scheme had been seriously affected. The following year only three more houses were sold, and one tenant was not meeting the payments. The next annual report announced that most families had reneged on their agreement. By 1882 only two houses were under full contract. In 1886 a decision was made to sell the land in Dorchester, but the company could not divest itself of the last bit of property there until 1897.

As with the demise of the Lincoln Building, many explanations were possible for the failure of the Dorchester homes. If the depression had been completely to blame for the erratic histories of the tenants, neighboring properties would have had similar problems, and once the worst times were over, the houses would have been more successful. But the venture did not survive the depression, and others in Dorchester did not have the same problems.[42] The primary reason that the Dorchester homes were not successful was probably that the company's terms of purchase were not competitive with those of other housing developers. In 1884 the directors were instructed by the stockholders to find out whether cheaper homes could be built. The directors examined houses constructed in Providence, Rhode Island, for only $600, but they reported that the low price was due to bad workmanship. This judgment may have had some substance, but small builders were also probably able to build cheaply because they had a greater grasp of local conditions and therefore more flexibility with their ventures, especially in depressed times, than an organization like the Boston Cooperative Building Company, which was run by part-time directors.

Admitting this fact would have cast doubts on the validity of the Boston Cooperative Building Company. When the directors announced the decision to sell the rest of the Dorchester land, they did not acknowledge that the houses had not been cheap enough even for those with moderate incomes. Instead, they reasoned that they had somehow concentrated on the wrong population group all along and explained that the company could best fulfill its purpose by providing housing for the "poorest classes."

When the Dorchester homes were doing badly, the company's directors and stockholders never questioned whether they were really suited to "moral and physical health," as the members of the country-house committee claimed. This proposition could easily have been tested by compiling statistics about the residents, as had been done for the inhabitants of the Lincoln Building. But no such study was ever made. The new direction taken in 1886 did not negate the belief that the individual suburban home was the best type of residence. Instead, the company reverted to the kind of argument that Henry Bowditch had made to justify the Lincoln Building. It was necessary to provide families with decent housing until they were able to move to better accommodation. However, the wisdom that came from experience told the company to attract tenants who were not quite as down and out as those who had lived in the Lincoln Building; who, in fact, were not really of the "poorest classes" but who had "the smallest regular income." After 1886, therefore, the company constructed housing of a quality somewhere between that of the Lincoln Building and the Dorchester houses.

From its beginning the company had built houses like that, but they did not receive the attention given to either the Lincoln Building or the

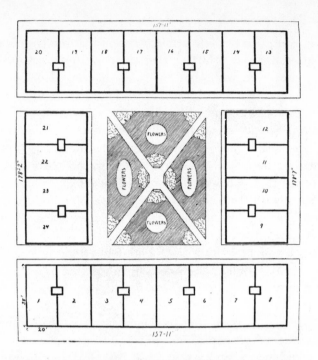

90. *W. P. P. Longfellow: Harrison Avenue Estate of the Boston Cooperative Building Company, Boston, Massachusetts, 1893. The space in the middle of the four blocks was used mainly as a playground for the building's children.*

Dorchester homes. In the early 1870s the company bought land on East Canton Street in Boston's South End, a large and fashionable development of a few decades earlier that had already seen better days. The stockholders resolved not to build tenements but instead to construct row houses with apartments on each floor. At the same time the company purchased nine small wooden houses in the North End, the oldest part of Boston. One of these, the company noted, perhaps with anticipation for its future tenants, was the place in which Edward Everett had been born. In the late 1880s, when the company decided on the best course of action to follow, more buildings in the North End were purchased, and in 1892 the company constructed a large complex of houses on Harrison Avenue, near the buildings it had already built on East Canton Street. These were also row houses, but they were grouped around a small park that, as a public amenity, was exempted from taxation by a special act of the Massachusetts legislature.

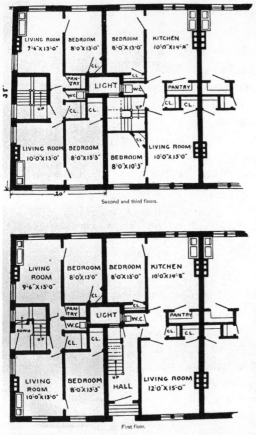

Second and third floors.

First floor.

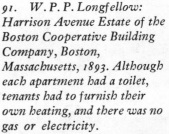

*91. W. P. P. Longfellow: Harrison Avenue Estate of the Boston Cooperative Building Company, Boston, Massachusetts, 1893. Although each apartment had a toilet, tenants had to furnish their own heating, and there was no gas or electricity.*

Such structures were more successful than either the Lincoln Building or the Dorchester homes, but they were not free from trouble. During the depression of the 1870s many tenants in the East Canton Street property did not meet their rents, and in 1874 there were many vacancies in these newly built houses. In the following year the company had to reduce rents, and it reported that of the 129 tenants in the East Canton Street buildings only 31 had never been in arrears. Not until the early 1880s were the rents regularly paid in these buildings.

Upkeep and maintenance were also always difficult and expensive. The Boston Cooperative Building Company found that it was not enough to make initial renovations to old buildings or to expect new houses to be repair-free for a long time. When the East Canton Street Buildings were eight years old, they needed extensive repairs. In 1882 the roofs were rebuilt, outside woodwork was repainted, and the chimneys were refurbished. In 1887 several pipes burst during the winter and caused extensive damage. From the time of their opening the Harrison Avenue houses had similar problems. Even though the company hired a prominent architect to design the buildings, the construction was faulty. The walls were not properly protected against moisture penetration, and the first-floor apartments often flooded. Within a few years this condition had to be corrected by expensive alterations.

All the Boston Cooperative Building Company's houses were constructed in a period of rapid technological improvement and continually had to be updated. New requirements in the Massachusetts plumbing laws in 1885 meant extensive work on pipes and drains, and electricity and central heating later had to be added. All buildings incurred these expenses, but the burden fell especially hard on an institution like the Boston Cooperative Building Company, which had only limited resources for these additional outlays.

The company also had problems with its tenants. Despite its stated goal to admit only applicants of good character to the Harrison Avenue houses, the tenants there were often drunk and disorderly, and failure to pay rent continued to be a problem. From this experience the agents of the company learned how to screen applicants more carefully. Those who stayed the longest tended to be the best tenants. Those who had a history of changing their lodgings caused "much care and labor."

To acknowledge that the permanent tenant was the most desirable complicated the already muddled goals of the company. After a decade of experience the company understood that if it wanted both to realize a profit and to supply housing to those who could better themselves, it could not serve "the poorest classes." Those with that level of means were "doomed to live in a wretched class of wooden buildings." City laws forbade the construction of such cheap tenements, but they did permit the indefinite repair of existing ones. The company noted that its houses were carefully planned and soundly built. But since they had to be constructed of brick, they were expensive in comparison with wooden structures and therefore had to be rented for more than most people could afford.

If the acknowledgment that the Boston Cooperative Building Company could hardly serve even those with "the smallest regular income" disappointed stockholders who wanted to house the "poorest classes," then the understanding that the best tenants were those who remained the longest undercut their aspirations for uplift. Those who remained in the East Canton Street or Harrison Avenue houses for a decade or two

*92.   Alfred T. White: "Improved Dwellings for the Laboring Classes,"
Brooklyn, New York, 1878. This was the first of three successful groups of
buildings that the philanthropist Alfred T. White built in Brooklyn. Although he founded the Improved Dwellings Company to carry out this
work, White and members of his family were the only investors for at least
the first twenty years of this organization's existence.*

probably were not upwardly mobile people who saved for their own
homes in the suburbs. Instead, the houses of the Boston Cooperative Building Company attracted a static population, neither poor nor ambitious.

In its first years the company had lofty aspirations for what it might
accomplish. The stockholders looked forward to a time when there would
be a permanent solution to the housing problem. They noted the interest
in their scheme in other cities and anticipated the growth of their company. The author of one of the first annual reports asked: "Will not our
successors, twenty years hence, find this question thoroughly answered,
and be free to turn their energies in some new direction?" The stockholders did not have to wait quite twenty years to find out. In the sixteenth annual report the directors admitted that "it is true that at present, on account of the limited field of our operations, our influence counts
for little."

In 1910 Lawrence Veiller showed that the model tenements built in
the previous forty years in Manhattan had housed only 3,588 families, or
17,940 people. In the same period speculative builders had erected tenements for 253,510 families, or over a million people. There is no record

of how much model housing was built in other cities, but the total for the rest of the country probably did not exceed what was constructed in New York. The organizations that built housing varied in their aims and techniques. They may have been more successful than the Boston Cooperative Building Company, but so little accommodation suggested that the Boston Company's disappointing experience was not exceptional.[43]

Just as there were many ways to explain each of the Boston Cooperative Building Company's setbacks, reformers had various responses to the general failure of limited-dividend housing. Some said that the meager results showed that housing could be produced only by speculative builders, and therefore better legislation to regulate what was constructed was necessary. Others pointed out that the real estate market had not solved the housing problem in the past, so they had no confidence that every American would be provided with decent accommodation through that means in the future. Those who made this criticism often claimed that limited-dividend housing companies had not built more because they had so little capital. They argued that if larger organizations invested their money in housing it would be possible to build a significant number of better and cheaper homes.

In the 1890s schemes to insure workingmen against sickness, accident, and old age were instituted in Germany and Belgium. The funds collected for this insurance were lent to public-service corporations, some of which built housing. Reformers who knew of the European precedents occasionally suggested that American insurance companies take similar action, but the type of investment they could make was often limited by law. Insurance companies also had many safer investment opportunities. However, the officers of a few companies did feel an obligation to housing, and after the turn of the century some of them undertook to promote it. The Metropolitan Life Insurance Company was the first to do so on more than a token scale. In 1910 it began the first of its many housing ventures by lending $650,000 to a developer to build houses in Brooklyn. Metropolitan Life supervised the planning, construction, and pricing of these houses so that prospective buyers would be assured of sound homes at a cost that included only what the builder had agreed was a fair profit.[44]

If insurance companies could finance housing, so could the local, state, or national government. This argument was occasionally made in the 1890s, and after the turn of the century housing reformers were increasingly attracted to it. But so strong was the belief in private enterprise that Massachusetts was the only state before the First World War to try to put this principle into practice, and then only on a small scale. In 1915 a constitutional amendment permitting the state to engage in housing activities was ratified by the voters, and in 1917 an appropriation was made for the construction of fifty houses in Lowell. Because of rising costs, only twelve were built.[45]

Reformers who wanted large corporations or the state to finance housing were often as imprecise as the supporters of limited-dividend companies about for whom this action should be taken. The Metropolitan Life Insurance Company described the people who bought their houses as "workingmen," but each home cost $5,500. The houses in Lowell, Massachusetts, ranged from $2,400 to $3,100 to build, but that was still more than an unskilled worker could afford. The implications of these figures were disappointing, but since the financing of housing by large corporations and the state was still in its infancy, many reformers believed that with more experience it would be possible to bring the price of a home within the range of more Americans.[46]

Only a few people questioned this assumption or thought about what should be done if it did not turn out to be valid. Since all housing proposals depended on tenants' making a decent, regular income, a handful of reformers claimed that the housing problem was really a wage problem. They argued that insurance against accident, sickness, and old age and the establishment of a minimum wage and unemployment compensation were the most important ingredients of a housing policy. Without these measures a large sector of Americans would never afford their own homes. This line of argument was common in European discussions about housing, but since the proposals were still novel in the United States, it did not influence American thinking. So strong was the tendency to compartmentalize issues that it would be several decades before the formulators of social policy would accept the fact that wages and housing were so intimately related.[47]

An even smaller number of reformers questioned whether it was necessary for people to pay for their own home in the first place. At the National Conference on Housing in 1913 George Hooker claimed that it was more important to live in proper housing than to pay for it. After all, Americans were not barred from public-school education because they could not shoulder their share of the expenses. This argument went unheard. Americans considered the home vitally important, but much of its value came from the fact that it had been bought through the efforts of the occupants and thus represented independence. By the First World

War this ethic had become so ingrained that virtually no one challenged it.[48]

✦✦✦

Many people who discussed home ownership distinguished between two strikingly different contexts: New York and the rest of the nation. Manhattan's special circumstances had nurtured a peculiar system of financing buildings that raised costs, made an intensive use of the land necessary, and forced all but the very wealthy to live in multiple dwellings. The building process usually involved three people, an Operator, a Builder, and an Investor. The Operator bought the piece of property, which he sold to a Builder, agreeing at the same time to lend the Builder a mortgage equivalent to the purchase value of the property on the condition that he erect a particular type of building. In addition, the Operator advanced the Builder money as the construction progressed. The amount of this second mortgage varied, but it usually totaled up to 50 percent of the construction cost. The Builder paid for the rest.

When the construction was complete, the Builder obtained a permanent loan to pay off his two mortgages. At this point the Operator had concluded his part of the transaction. He had made a profit on the sale of the land and from the interest he had received on the money he had loaned. The Builder owned an apartment house with a large mortgage and some of his own funds tied up in it. So that he did not have to shoulder the extra burden of being a landlord, the Builder's task was to rent the apartment house and then to find an Investor who would consider the building's revenue sufficiently attractive to purchase it.

This process was filled with pitfalls. The Operator had to have a shrewd sense of property values so that he would not end up with land that he could not sell. Sometimes he bought large, unimproved lots, hoping initially to sell a few and thus to increase the value of the others. Another approach was to secure lots in a developed neighborhood that a Builder would find attractive. The most advantageous method was to purchase a property after the Builder had agreed to repurchase it. If the Operator had to hold land, he lost money from interest charges and taxes. He was also at risk if the Builder failed to receive a permanent mortgage. He either had to advance more money on the second mortgage, hoping that the Builder would eventually receive financing, or he had to let him fail. If that happened, the Operator had to foreclose his mortgage, buy the property back with perhaps a half-finished building on it, and either finish it himself or sell it to someone else. Labor unions often prevented the expeditious completion of a building that had been foreclosed. If a plumber had not been paid for his work and his lien had been removed through the foreclosure proceedings, another plumber would not finish the job without being paid a fee large enough to cover the amount owed to the first plumber.

Because of these circumstances the Builder was under great pressure to finish the construction. Since he was usually strapped for funds, he tried to do so cheaply, but only in ways that would not be evident to the bank granting him the permanent mortgage and to the Investor who eventually purchased the building. The apartment house, therefore, was built to remain in top condition for only a few years. After that period it could deteriorate rapidly, and the Investor had to be an astute judge of his building's construction and fittings. The Builder also tried to deceive the Investor by inflating the amount of income the apartment house appeared to bring in. One of the many ruses was to give the first tenants leases with several months of free rent to make the monthly figures seem higher than they actually were.[49]

The tenants who lived in buildings constructed under such conditions had to pay rents that were sufficient to make the investment attractive to a buyer. Most people who wanted to live in New York were at the mercy of the system. They could only hope that the real estate market would fluctuate and that Builders or Investors would be eager to attract tenants. But in 1880 Philip Hubert, the pioneer in apartment house design, tried to establish an alternative method of financing. He thought that cooperation was as applicable to apartment houses as Robert Treat Paine said it was to separate homes. Hubert urged that prospective tenants group together to finance and build their own apartment house.

What soon came to be called the Hubert Home Club was essentially a corporation formed by a number of people each of whom contributed a sum; the total collected was used as a down payment to secure a mortgage to meet the cost of a building. The corporation owned the entire property, but the subscribers received certificates of stock as well as a lease in perpetuity of an apartment. Each subscriber could occupy, sublet, or even sell his apartment, depending on the regulations of the association. The only monthly payment, therefore, was a sum to defer the running costs. To reduce these expenses, many Home Club buildings contained, in addition to those of the members, a few apartments for rent. The revenue from these was used to pay the carrying charges and cost of operation. Any that was left was either paid as dividends or used to reduce the mortgage.[50]

The cooperative method was a plausible way to build an apartment house, but in the 1880s few were constructed along these lines. Hubert's plan had many problems. To make the system work, it was necessary either to have a substantial amount of capital for the equity or to attract more subscribers. Few people had cash ready to invest in such a venture, and it was difficult to coordinate many people in a Home Club. Hubert and other supporters of this scheme were aware that prospective tenants might be put off by some of the connotations of cooperation (hence the name "Home Club") and always emphasized that it was not necessary for members to know each other. But without the bond of familiarity, it was difficult to attract people to such a new venture.[51]

Cooperatives also were not foolproof. When running costs rose or it was difficult to rent apartments, the cost to each subscriber could soar. Most members of Home Clubs had little experience in financing and managing real estate. When it turned out that one Home Club had not adequately secured title to its land, the principle itself went into disrepute. After the early 1880s no more cooperative apartment houses were built in New York until 1897, when the idea was revived by a group of artists who built studios for themselves. Cooperative apartments then became more popular, but they never constituted a significant percentage of the total amount of residential construction in New York. From the initial failure of his idea, Philip Hubert concluded that the only way to secure good housing in New York was to have a different method of taxing land. He became a supporter of Henry George's principles and hoped that a levy on land would help to open up more home sites in the areas that surrounded Manhattan.[52]

The method of financing an apartment house was often reflected on its exterior. The investors in a cooperative building wanted to cut costs as much as possible and often emphasized that they did not waste money on needless ornament. The cooperative apartment house's public side — the facade, lobby, and entrance — tended, therefore, to be restrained in its architecture.[53] The speculative builder also wanted to reduce costs. Sometimes he constructed buildings with a severe appearance, not out of any conviction that a straightforward elevation was correct but simply because he did not want to waste a penny more than was necessary to satisfy the building regulations. But since the speculative builder's success depended on attracting renters after the apartment house had been constructed, he often took the opposite approach. He regarded the building's exterior as a kind of advertisement and instructed his architect or designer to give the structure, as one critic put it, "the appearance of more appearance." The speculative apartment house, therefore, was often distinguished by exaggerated and sometimes grotesque architectural ornament.[54]

In some European cities a sense of architectural unity was created by municipal regulations that dictated the heights of cornice lines, roof setbacks, and other critical dimensions. Before the First World War no American city had such regulations. Continuity from one structure to the next could result, therefore, only from an agreement between adjacent property owners, and that rarely happened. When an apartment house was built over an entire block, it was bound to have some sense of uniformity, since it was one design. But because of the nature of the method of financing, few builders could afford such large structures. Their apartment houses usually occupied only small parcels and were designed to be as distinct from their neighbors as possible.[55]

Compared with the tightly constrained context of the city, the suburb and the small town afforded the architect much more compatible conditions for the design of houses. As long as one house was visible from the next, the architect was always under some pressure to pay attention to conventions, no matter how tacitly they were stated. But, on the whole, the separate site gave him the best opportunity to work out his conception of the house beautiful.

✦✦✦

Although they rarely proclaimed its moral value as overtly as had Andrew Jackson Downing, most American architects in the half century after the Civil War believed that beauty was the primary consideration in domestic architecture and that it did not simply result from coming to terms with utility. But the fact that this assumption was widely held did not produce a uniform architecture. The houses of the postbellum period bore little outward resemblance to their predecessors, and they differed greatly among themselves.

This diversity was not surprising. The appearance of buildings was bound to vary as long as excellence ultimately depended on difficult to define matters of taste or of the heart. Discussions of these issues did not abate after the Civil War. Few architects disagreed that formal values as well as associations contributed to the attractiveness of a building, but there was no unanimity about what these qualities were, how they should be combined, and what relationship they should have to the planning, construction, and structure of a building.

Differences of opinion about these matters often were evident in discussions about the purpose of architectural ornament. Few architects thought that buildings were satisfactory without any ornament, but decoration unrelated to some aspect of structure or construction was not generally sanctioned either. However, having rejected the two extremes, they found it difficult to decide the correct position in between — to what degree, for example, was it proper to embellish a bracket that supported a balcony?

Architects differed as much about the meaning of ornament as they did about its functional purpose. In the discussion of this issue the role of historical precedent was of special importance. Some architects acknowledged that their culture was different from that which had nurtured the great styles of the past, and they tried to formulate the basis of an American architecture. Since there was no native architecture to speak of, instead of historical precedents they drew upon motifs from nature, which in any case, it was often argued, had been the ultimate source of all great architecture. But as much as Americans were unique, they were also descended from people in other countries, and to that extent their heritage extended beyond the nation's borders. Architects, therefore, had an obligation to the buildings of the past and especially to those in Europe.

This debate about tradition did not depend only on nationalistic arguments. Architects living in both Europe and America wondered what meaning the past had in an age of such rapid change. When they examined how thoroughly every aspect of their culture had been transformed in so short a period, they could conclude either that a new architecture was necessary or that traditions were all the more important.

Thus, how to be innovative while preserving traditions was the great architectural question of the day. The spectrum of opinions about this matter ranged from the espousal of abrupt change to a call for a slow evolution of tried and true precedents. But in certain periods the need to rely on history weighed more heavily than in others. In the 1870s and 1880s American architects were still able to take, as one of them put it, a "go-as-you-please" attitude in their work.[56] They drew upon the history of architecture, adapting precedents to their needs with no great concern for correctness. A few architects had the training, intelligence, and sensitivity to use this freedom to articulate in their buildings a language that was both original and coherent. Most, however, did not have this ability, and the language of their buildings, as John Wellborn Root commented in 1887, was as bizarre as that of a "chattering chimpanzee."[57] When architects began to worry about the resulting babble, they became increasingly self-conscious about what innovation entailed. By 1890 they were examining historical precedents more carefully than before in the hope that the correct use of these sources would result in a more satisfactory architecture.

In deciding how to design a house, architects recognized that even though beauty transcended questions of utility, the materials of construction, like the arrangement of the plans, still had a bearing on the structure's appearance. They disagreed about what weight to give this aspect of utility and how to manifest it in a building. Materials were important nonetheless, and in their domestic work many architects favored wood. Timber was inexpensive, light, and easily transportable, and since it was usually precut at a mill to standard or prescribed sizes, it came to a building site in a convenient form. Once it was there, workmen needed only simple tools to transform timber either into the rough framework of a house or into finely crafted elements such as doors, windows, and built-in furnishings.

Architects also found that wood was an expressive material. Native

*93. McKim, Mead and White: Robert Goelet House, Newport, Rhode Island, 1882–1883. In their early work McKim, Mead and White freely drew upon a variety of historical sources in designing summer houses that were irregularly massed and were made mainly of wood.*

*94. McKim, Mead and White: H. A. C. Taylor Residence, Newport, Rhode Island, 1886. In the second phase of their work McKim, Mead and White adapted forms from American colonial architecture.*

*95. McKim, Mead and White: F. W. Vanderbilt House, Hyde Park, New York, 1896. By 1890 McKim, Mead and White had become more scholarly in their approach to design. They were trying to follow Renaissance precedents, and in the process they favored masonry over wood, which had rustic or primitive connotations.*

forests had a vast number of trees with different grains, colors, and hardnesses, all of which could be used to design new forms and details. Also, the history of domestic architecture offered a broad range of choice in how to use wood on both the exterior and interior of a house. When American architects looked for precedents for their designs, they found that most European countries, especially the northern ones, had rich traditions of using timber in domestic architecture. Once they began to learn about and travel to Japan, they found another method of building timber houses. They also discovered suggestive traditions of wood construction in their own past. Throughout the half century after the Civil War they continually studied and admired the timber houses of the colonial period.[58]

Because of all these admirable qualities, wood was frequently used in the construction of American domestic architecture, and some of the finest houses of the period were made of it. They included the shingled houses that Henry Hobson Richardson started to build in New England in the 1870s, McKim, Mead and White's neocolonial houses of the late 1880s and the 1890s, the exotic buildings of Bernard Maybeck, the Japanese-inspired bungalows that the Greene brothers designed in Southern California after the turn of the century, and the stylistically eclectic work of countless other architects and builders across the United States.[59]

Many architects considered wood nature's true material, the uniquely American building product, and they anticipated that a native style of architecture would emerge from its proper use.[60] Other architects, however, thought that wood had serious liabilities and were thus attracted to solid construction of stone, brick, or concrete. Their choice was based in part on economic grounds. When the price of wood soared, as it occasionally did, they questioned the financial advantages of timber and predicted that it would be even more expensive as American forests became depleted. They also argued that even though the initial cost of a timber house was less than that of one in brick, stone, or concrete (and they often disputed this point), the long-term expense was greater. They pointed out that unlike the materials used in solid construction, timber deteriorated quickly, needed constant upkeep, and attracted harmful insects and rodents. More important, timber was combustible. At a time when major areas of American cities were frequently destroyed by fires and when new suburbs did not have efficient fire-fighting systems, the fact that masonry was fireproof was a compelling argument in favor of solid construction.[61]

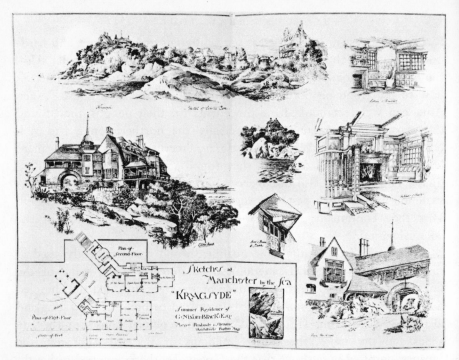

96. *Peabody and Stearns (drawn by Eldon Dean): Kragsyde, Manchester-by-the-Sea, Massachusetts, 1882. The evocative qualities of wood, the material often associated with the dawn of architecture, were manipulated to best advantage in vacation houses, a building type in which residents were freed from the conventions of life in cities and even suburbs. Kragsyde appears to take its irregular form from the landscape; it is an outgrowth of the rugged rocks and trees.*

The ephemeral nature of wood was more than an economic liability; it also had serious aesthetic disadvantages. In *The Architecture of Country Houses* Downing argued that the idea of eternal duration added incalculably to the effect of any work of art, including a building. Masonry gave the impression of permanence, whereas wood always looked temporary.[62] The evolution of architecture was often cited to confirm this judgment. Historians had long noted how the Greek temple originally had been constructed of timber. They reasoned that in the course of many centuries its elements had been formalized in stone, and that a similar process in domestic architecture marked and was itself the sign of an advance in civilization.[63]

These arguments were reinforced by the fact that masonry could be considered just as natural as wood. After all, stones came from the ground, and bricks and concrete were made from earth products. There were also many fruitful historical precedents for the use of these materials, not only in the domestic architecture of Europe but also in early American architecture. At the same time that some architects were studying the wood houses of New England, others were examining the brick and stone structures of the Middle Atlantic states.[64]

Some architects tried to resolve this argument about the relative merits of wood and masonry by distinguishing where and for what kinds of buildings each was appropriate. Those who were especially concerned about fire wanted to restrict the use of wood to rural or suburban areas. Others argued that wood was appropriate for houses and masonry for civic buildings. Still others claimed that it was appropriate to build vacation houses of wood, whereas permanent residences demanded more durable materials.

No matter how such distinctions were made, many architects thought it advisable to build houses out of materials other than wood. Of the different types of solid construction, concrete best illustrates the many

*97.   Abbé Laugier: "The Primitive Hut." This drawing not only illustrates that columns (not walls) are the fundamental structural elements of architecture; it also shows that masonry forms had their origin in wood. Whether or not American architects read Laugier's Treatise, most of them accepted the fact that ideas of progress were involved in the choice of material.*

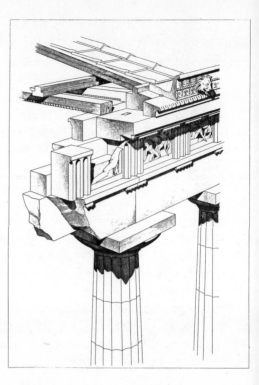

*98. Eugène Viollet-le-Duc: Construction of a Greek temple. For Viollet-le-Duc the elements of Greek architecture were direct manifestations of principles of construction.*

approaches to the design of houses taken after the Civil War. Concrete's interest lies in part in its versatility. Since it is used as a block, as a semi-fluid substance that solidifies in formwork, and as a rendering placed on other materials, it can be shaped to embody many different values. But the significance of concrete also stems from the legacy of its peculiar history in Western architecture. The Romans discovered that lime and stone aggregate, when mixed together, produce a strong compound, and they used concrete extensively in their buildings, usually as a core material that was clad with brick or stone. But after the Roman era concrete was largely neglected because it was considered an inferior imitation of stone and also because it was associated with traditional methods of making cheap structures of compacted earth or burnt clay.[65]

An interest in concrete in Europe was rekindled only at the end of the eighteenth century. From the beginning of its use in the United States, probably in the 1840s, concrete retained its age-old reputation as an inexpensive and inferior material. A few architects welcomed this association, but most considered it a burden. When they used concrete, they had to find ways to divest it of its inevitable associations. It was, therefore, even more important for architects who designed houses in concrete to transcend utility than for those who used other materials.

The use of earth as a building material extends far back into American history. The simplest type of dirt structure was made of piled-up pieces of sod. The first settlers of the prairies often used this technique, not only because they did not have other materials with which to build their houses but also because they could use their farming tools to assist the process of construction. They found that a plow could cut a continuous row of sod to a depth of about four inches. They then reduced the strip to pieces of uniform length. With these sod building blocks they erected houses around wooden window and door frames. Since it was impossible to span distances with sod, the roofs of these structures generally had to be framed with timber.[66]

Other settlers made houses out of unburnt brick. They learned that a compound of clay and straw left in the open air for a few days made a serviceable building material. Sometimes they molded the substance in a crude formwork to produce a clay unit. This method of construction was obviously of most value in a sunny, dry climate. It was used at the beginning of the nineteenth century in South Carolina. When pioneers arrived in the Southwest, they found that sun-dried clay or adobe was especially suited to that region's climate and had been used since the seventeenth century by Spanish settlers.[67]

99.   A sod house. The battered wall and small windows were characteristic
of the loosely constructed sod house.

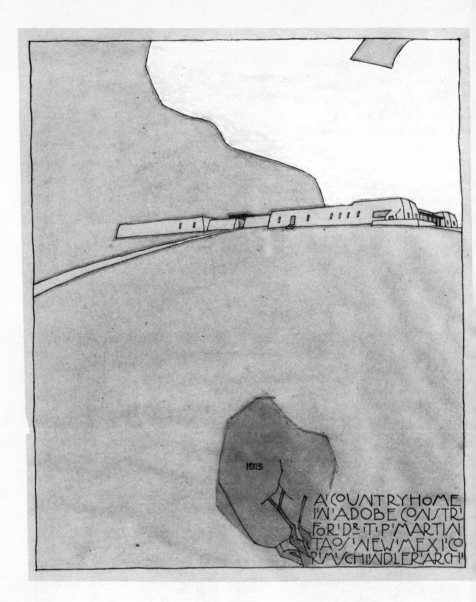

Inside the drawing:

1915

A COUNTRY HOME
IN ADOBE CONSTR
FOR DR T P MARTIN
TAOS NEW MEXICO
R M SCHINDLER ARCH

*100.   Rudolf Schindler: A country home in "adobe construction," 1915. On a visit to the Southwest, Schindler was impressed by adobe architecture. He transformed the characteristic features of that type of construction in this striking design.*

It was also possible to make houses out of compacted earth. In this method of construction, known in Europe as pisé, movable formwork consisting of two parallel boards held rigidly apart was first erected. Dirt was then rammed into it. When the earth was sufficiently compact, the boards were moved either horizontally to extend the wall or vertically to make it higher. In wet climates the resulting structure was stuccoed on the outside to make it durable.[68]

Each of these methods of construction had a definite impact on the appearance of the resulting building. Since sod or adobe units were usually not fixed together with mortar, houses made of them often had walls that grew progressively thicker toward the ground. Tamped-earth houses usually did not have tapered walls because each course was made with the same formwork, but their distinctive feature was the horizontal lines that marked the courses.

The people who built houses with these methods generally were not content with the bare form. Some thought of these structures only as temporary shelter, to be replaced as soon as possible by houses that not only were physically more enduring but also would embody the lasting values associated with a home designed to transcend utility. Others accepted their earth-built house as permanent but tried to make it truly a home. Sometimes, by planting flowers or adding decorative door and window frames, they did so without disguising the distinctive features of the method of construction. But often the owners of earth houses deliberately tried to mask all evidence of the house's humble origins to show that civilizing tendencies were dominant. The fact that earth structures often had to be protected with a coat of stucco supplied the functional excuse to make the house appear not as its construction indicated but instead as the owners wanted it to be.

These early methods of earth construction raised issues about the treatment of materials that later reappeared in discussions about concrete. They also anticipated some of the techniques used to shape concrete products. The earliest concrete blocks were made by shoveling a dry mixture of concrete into a mold and tamping it as the formwork was filled. By the beginning of this century automatic tampers replaced hand labor. Other concrete blocks were made by a related process in which the mold was first completely filled and then the concrete mechanically compressed. This method was considered an improvement over tamping because it ensured a block with a more uniform density. Blocks made by pouring a liquid solution of concrete into a mold to harden were still

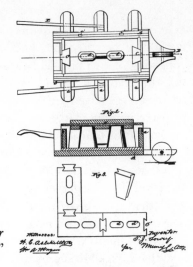

*101.  T. J. Lowry: "Patent Mold for*
*Building Blocks, 1850."*

further advanced. When concrete was fluid, the aggregates of gravel became thoroughly coated, a better crystallization took place, and a stronger block was produced. By 1905 manufacturers of wet blocks were beginning to outstrip those who used tamping and compression.[69]

No matter how blocks were made, the aim of the first manufacturers was to produce an inexpensive material that was cheaper than bricks and more durable than traditional earth construction. Concrete blocks were, therefore, first used in buildings that were considered utilitarian. Housing for agricultural laborers, factories, and, after the turn of the century, automobile garages were made out of them. The use of concrete blocks in some of the first garages was especially revealing about the reputation of this material. Since the early owners of cars often worried that the gasoline in their vehicles would ignite, they thought it was necessary to house their automobiles in fireproof structures. But the reason they used concrete blocks instead of, for example, bricks, which did not have such overt cheap and temporary connotations, probably stemmed from some deep-rooted uncertainty about whether the automobile truly belonged near the home.[70]

Manufacturers of concrete blocks, not content to relegate their products to this class of building, found they could transform a structure's appearance by covering blocks with stucco. The impulse to do so was enhanced by the fact that concrete blocks were not good insulants, nor did they effectively prevent the passage of water from the outside to the interior. Some manufacturers tried to correct these defects by separating the two faces of a concrete block wall. The first patent for a hollow

The Trellis on This Concrete Garage Is Eventually to Be Covered with Grape-vines

Concrete and Plaster Were Used in the Construction of This Garage for E. C. Martin, of Oak Park, Ill.

This Two-story Solid Concrete Garage at Oak Park, Ill., Is Distinctly Modern in Its Architecture

The Clock and the Bell Are Unusual Features of This Garage, Belonging to John Farson, in a Chicago Suburb

An Interesting Concrete Garage at Denver, Col., the Property of Edward George Reinert

An Inexpensive Stucco Garage Designed to House a Single Machine

*102. "Small Garages Built of Cement," 1911. The fortuitous inclusion of one of Frank Lloyd Wright's garages on this page provides an opportunity to compare his architectural language with that of some of his contemporaries.*

concrete block was taken out in 1866. In the following half century there were numerous modifications and improvements of this principle, and many machines were invented to produce blocks with partitions that only tenuously connected the outer and inner faces. Other manufacturers tried to reduce moisture penetration with waterproofing solutions they either mixed in the concrete or applied to the wall after it was built. But even with hollow blocks and waterproofing, it could always be argued that a coat of stucco was an additional protection.[71]

Many decisions were involved in the application of stucco. Since it was difficult to cover an entire wall evenly at one time, architects looked for ways to break up the surfaces of a house. They experimented with different textures, sometimes alternating rough and smooth areas on the same wall. By applying the stucco with special tools, it was also possible to make a repeated pattern over a surface. Other architects impressed geometrical or natural shapes into the stucco after it had been applied and before it set. Colored tiles could also enliven a wall. The relationship of the house to the landscape had a further bearing on the nature of its stucco coating. Shadows cast by trees on plain surfaces were themselves a decorative element, ivy created a similar effect, and trellises contrasted patterns from nature with a geometrical grid. Architects even used the fact that stucco changed with age and the weather in determining how best to treat a surface in this material.[72]

Although the application of stucco to concrete blocks may have seemed untruthful to the underlying material, its use was often sanctioned for moral reasons. Ever since John Ruskin had written in "The Nature of Gothic" about how important it was for those who constructed a building to identify the work they had done, he and his followers, especially William Morris, had emphasized the need for the craftsman's contribution. Unlike some other materials that were applied or manipulated only in a repetitive and anonymous way, stucco gave both the architect and the workman a chance for self-expression. The architect determined the basic design of a stucco wall, but no two people ever applied the material in the same way. Each workman had his own stucco handwriting.[73]

Stucco, of course, could be used with materials other than masonry. When it covered a wood frame and disguised the fact that there was light construction underneath, some architects drew the line. They revealed part of the frame, in the tradition of English half-timbering.[74] But many other architects did not consider putting stucco over a frame inappropriate. The extreme case came not with a wood frame but with lightweight metal constructions. At the turn of the century a few builders and architects tried to use small steel sections, metal lath, and stucco to produce a new fireproof building system for houses. They framed the walls, floors, and roofs with steel sections that were riveted or bolted together. The result, as the name of the system, "metal lumber," indicated, was little more than an imitation of wood-frame construction. These houses were entirely covered with stucco, and there was no exterior evidence of the light frame.[75]

A more adventurous approach to metal-frame constructon was to put pipes together and to fill them for rigidity with concrete. The resulting frame was then tightly wrapped with wire wherever floors and walls were needed. Expanded metal was fixed to the wire to receive concrete for floors (in which case the wire acted as reinforcement) and stucco and plaster for the outside and inside of walls. The chief virtue of this method of construction was speed. But the product did not reflect the process. Like metal lumber, the frame of thin pipes wrapped in wire could be given almost any appearance with the application of stucco. The result could be indistinguishable from a conventionally built house to all but the most discerning observer.[76]

Manufacturers and architects who thought that concrete blocks were

*103. M. J. Morehouse: Dresser House, Glencoe, Illinois, 1908. The structure of this "skeleton house" was made of pipes around which wires were wrapped as reinforcement for the walls and floors. Since the house was covered with stucco, nothing of this substructure was visible.*

*104. Lord and Hewlett: E. S. Harkness Residence, New London, Connecticut, 1910. This house was made principally of concrete blocks, but the architects were able to adapt that material to conform to precedents from Italian Renaissance architecture.*

presentable without a coating of stucco still had to make decisions about what they should look like. The block did not simply result from the manufacturing process. Within certain limits the proportions of the block were variable, and the sides of the mold in which it was made could be designed with almost any pattern. By the turn of the century dozens of concrete blocks with surfaces textured or mottled to imitate stone were on the market. Although such blocks were widely used, most respected architects disapproved of such overt artifice. But the alternative was not a plain block or even one with an abstract geometrical pattern. Instead, most architects called for a subtle adaptation of masonry precedents. In the E. S. Harkness House in New London, Connecticut, the architects, Lord and Hewlett, chose the dimensions of their concrete blocks to suit the proportions of the building. The blocks were surfaced with a carefully selected aggregate of coarse gravel pressed into a wet mixture. After the blocks had initially set, the face of each was scrubbed to expose the aggregate and to produce a textured quality. This effect was heightened by projecting the face of the block from the joint, thus creating a pattern of shadows on the wall. What the blocks, even in this carefully controlled state, lacked in architectural interest was compensated for by the addition of classical details that were cast in concrete. Other architects who designed with concrete blocks did not adhere so strictly to precedents, but their aim in using this new masonry unit was usually to articulate a wall, not to create a stark surface.[77]

By carefully controlling every aspect of its design, the concrete block did not have to "pretend to be what it was not." But there were many other ways to use concrete in buildings. A few architects argued that instead of making a small unit to compete with the brick, builders would be better advised to produce larger components. Real economies would result from precasting walls, roofs, and floor slabs and erecting them on site. Grosvenor Atterbury, the architect for Forest Hills Gardens, was the most prominent exponent of this approach to the use of concrete. He traced his interest in efficient building techniques to his belief in garden suburbs. Like other architects and reformers, Atterbury was convinced that a low-density context was the best place for the home. Unfortunately, the cost of commuting added appreciably to the price of a house in a garden suburb, and so did the fact that the standard of accommodation was higher in a separate house than in a tenement apartment. Atterbury concluded, therefore, that the only way to save money in building houses away from the center of the city was through efficient construction.[78]

He outlined three ways to achieve this end. An honest and effective municipal government was necessary to protect the public against corrupt contractors and building inspectors. Scientific building regulations and a national building code based on standard engineering practices would also help to reduce construction costs. Finally, organized research was important in determining the most efficient methods of construction. In his own work Atterbury was most interested in the third objective. He was convinced that with sufficient study and experience he could do for housing "what Ford had done for the automobile."

The analogy with the automobile led Atterbury to several conclusions. He believed that economies would inevitably ensue from mass production; "co-operation against disjointed individual effort" was necessary. Mechanization and the elimination of hand labor furthered this end, but there was no use changing the processes of production without altering the conditions under which they took place. Atterbury thought that for efficiency it was best to make the components of a house in a factory, ship them to the site, and then erect them with as little hand labor as possible. To fulfill these conditions the building units had to be bigger,

105. *Grosvenor Atterbury: Houses at Forest Hills Gardens under construction, 1916. Atterbury began building with this precast system in 1910. He called his method "child's blocks raised to the Nth power."*

106. *Grosvenor Atterbury: Houses at Forest Hills Gardens completed, 1916. The addition of dormers, entrance porches, and vines was reminiscent of Downing (see illustration 11), except that these elements were provided by the architect and landscape architect, not the residents.*

and there had to be fewer of them, their maximum size determined only by the constraints of the production and handling processes.

Atterbury was attracted to concrete because it was durable and, since it could be poured into a reusable mold, lent itself to mass production. His approach was to precast one- to three-ton panels that formed the walls, floors, and roof of a house. After these panels had hardened, they were transported to the site by truck and lifted into place by a crane. By traveling along a track the crane could work on an indefinite number of houses in a row. The panels were fixed together in place by tongue-and-groove joints bedded in mortar. The sloping roof panels had an overlapping waterproof joint. Once this monolithic shell had been made, it was necessary only to fix door and window frames to enclose the building. On the inside all that had to be done to finish the house was to install plumbing and electricity and to attach wood floors, picture rails, and skirtings to the concrete. Atterbury assisted in the first task by casting electrical conduits into the concrete panels and by leaving holes for plumbing fixtures in predetermined places. So that wood could be attached to the precast surfaces, Atterbury invented "Nailcrete," a substance that was almost as strong as concrete, had the same coefficient of expansion, did not corrode metal nails, did not swell when exposed to dampness, and was as nailable as white pine.

Although Atterbury wanted standardization, he still recognized that the end result had to be compatible with "aesthetic standards." He did not simply leave the exteriors with the smooth finish that came out of the molds. Instead, most of each panel was worked with a wire brush to expose the texture of the gravel aggregate. This area was surrounded by a border of the smooth surface. Atterbury emphasized this picturesque quality in several ways. He did not arrange the houses at Forest Hills Gardens all in a rigid row. Some were set back and others were joined together in a varied pattern, the eccentricity of which was emphasized by the sloping roofs. Frederick Law Olmsted, Jr., the project's landscape architect, planted trees and bushes around the houses and vines by the walls. The result was hardly recognizable as a mass-produced concrete house. The structures looked like those in an English garden suburb, if not in a traditional village.[79]

Atterbury's method of producing concrete houses entailed a radical reorganization of the American construction industry. Before the First World War few builders were ready even to contemplate such a change. But many were erecting houses by building on-site formwork into which concrete was poured until it hardened. This method entailed lots of site labor, which Atterbury thought was wasteful. From the time that it was rediscovered as a building material, however, poured concrete had been associated with cheap ways of building houses, and many architects and builders thought that its use could help solve the housing problem. Poured concrete, like sod, adobe, and pisé, was made of relatively inexpensive, readily available earth materials, and its manufacture, although labor-intensive, did not require expensive skilled workers.

Orson Squire Fowler was one of the first Americans to understand the advantages of concrete. Fowler derived his interest in concrete from an improbable source, phrenology. The advocates of this popular pseudoscience of the 1840s and 1850s believed that by studying the bumps on people's heads it was possible to analyze their characters. As it was practiced in the United States, phrenology was more than a way merely to measure intelligence or personality traits. It was also linked to a belief in self-improvement. It stood to reason that if a person knew his strong points and defects, he could take steps to emphasize or correct them. Like William Andrus Alcott, who was an ardent advocate of this theory, phrenologists often wrote about the need for a vegetarian diet, daily exercise, fresh air, and good housing.[80]

Fowler addressed the issue of the importance of the physical environment most fully in *A Home for All*, first published in 1848 and reprinted many times in the following decade. Fowler believed, on the one hand, that the quality of a person's house reflected his character and station in life, but, on the other hand, since these traits were not fixed, one way to improve was to try to live in a decent house. Since many Americans could not afford a suitable home, Fowler wrote *A Home for All* to help them obtain one, but his interest in efficient methods of construction went beyond this simple objective. Since one of the prime phrenological faculties was "inhabitiveness," Fowler believed that people had a "building faculty" and that to erect one's own home was a pleasure in itself. "No labour of my life," he claimed, "has given me more lively delight than the planning and building of my own home, and to all it can likewise be rendered almost intoxicating."

Fowler believed that his home for all should be octagonal because that shape, which approximated a circle, was economical. It circumscribed more area per length of wall than any other plan form. Fowler also used concrete as the primary material of the house. He believed that concrete was appropriate, not just because, since it was mainly gravel and sand, it

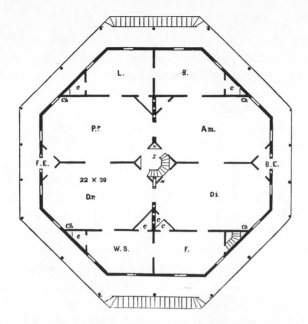

107. First-floor plan of Fowler's Octagon
House. Fowler favored the octagon house because it circumscribed a great area per length
of wall. But some of the economy of the
octagon was lost in the odd shapes that resulted when it was divided into rooms.

108. The Octagon House of Orson Squire Fowler, Fishkill, New York.
Fowler built the house himself out of concrete, which he called "nature's
own material."

was cheap, but also because he was convinced that the supply of wood was running out. As the earth became more populated, he reasoned, more land would have to be used for the cultivation of food and less for forests. Concrete was, therefore, not only "nature's building material," it was also the material of the future.

Fowler discussed two ways to construct the octagonal house. The builders of concrete houses he had seen in Wisconsin in 1850 erected their walls by using a method similar to pisé construction. They built movable formwork that, after one pouring of concrete had hardened, could be used to extend the wall horizontally or vertically. Fowler first tried this technique, but since he found that it took too long, he built the formwork for an entire wall before pouring. With either method Fowler's goal was economy. He shared with many of his contemporaries a suspicion of the fine arts as wasteful and with the American farmer a belief in simple know-how. Thus he came close to saying that beauty resulted from economy, but he did not go quite that far. Nature "never puts on anything *exclusively* for ornament AS SUCH," Fowler claimed. "She appends only what is useful and even absolutely *necessary*, yet so appends it as that all necessary appendages add to the beauty." Fowler's octagon reflected these values. Although it was starkly detailed, a few "necessary" parts, such as the brackets to hold up a porch, the capitals of the columns, and the window frames, were embellished. It is difficult to determine whether these details, for instance the vestiges of a simplified Doric capital, served an underlying functional purpose, but it certainly would have been possible to have even simpler forms. Other builders of octagons did not draw as fine a line as Fowler. The octagonal shape recalled precedents from the Renaissance and classical worlds, and many of these curious structures had explicit classical details.[81]

The impulse to build one's own home has lasted well beyond Fowler's day. As Americans moved to cities, they often tried to satisfy this propensity by building vacation houses. Many magazines published articles that explained to the urban resident how to reattain the constructional skills he had lost when he moved to the city. The *Craftsman* specialized in such information. Between 1901 and 1916, the years in which this fascinating magazine was published, it often contained plans and details for houses that could have been used by homesteaders, but that were no doubt of most value to summer vacationers. Many of the *Craftsman*'s designs were in wood, but houses to be made of concrete were also included. As if to emphasize the humble or folk nature of these struc-

*109. Gustave Stickley: A Craftsman concrete bungalow, 1913. This house was to be built with movable formwork, reminiscent of pisé construction. Although designed for simplicity and economy, it was far removed from the pioneer's home of tamped earth or sod (see illustration 99).*

tures, the directions often specified the use of movable formwork, a carryover from pisé construction.

The difference between a homesteader's and a vacationer's house was reflected in the appearance of the structures illustrated in the *Craftsman*. Whereas sod, adobe, and pisé houses, at least when they were first built, had rough and makeshift doors, windows, and roofs, the same elements in the *Craftsman*'s self-built concrete bungalows were consciously picturesque. The windows had diamond-leaded panes, the front door was carved and stouter than necessary, and the area under the eaves was covered with shingles.[82]

Movable formwork not only was used in buildings intended to recapture the spirit of earlier times but also could be part of an advanced system of mass production. Whereas Grosvenor Atterbury thought that the best way to systematize concrete construction was to make prefabricated panels, other architects tried to achieve the same end by rationalizing the techniques of on-site pouring. Milton Dana Morrill invented a system of

*110. Milton Dana Morrill: "Industrial Houses, The Concrete City, Nanticoke, Pa.," 1912. The fact that these houses were built by the Delaware, Lackawanna and Western Railroad Company suited the method of construction, but Morrill thought that using a railroad to assist mass production had a broader applicability.*

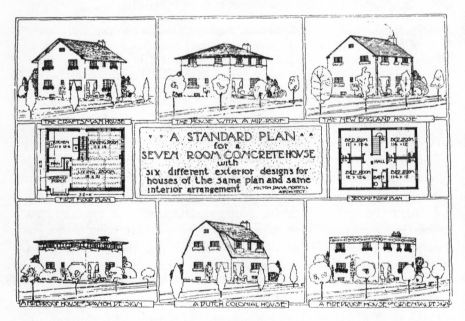

*111. Milton Dana Morrill: A standard plan for a seven-room house with six exterior designs. Diagrams of different styles for the same plan were common. This drawing can be compared with Frank Lloyd Wright's three houses for Edward C. Waller (see illustration 122). Wright knew that as the roof changes, so the plan has to adjust.*

adaptable steel molds that were erected in two rows to make a troughlike box to be filled with concrete. After the concrete had set for a few hours in one tier, the plates were disconnected and swung up on hinges to form another trough on top.

Morrill used his system in many places but best carried out his ideas about the rationalization of the construction process at Nanticoke, Pennsylvania, where he built some houses for the employees of the Delaware, Lackawanna and Western Railroad. The houses were arranged in a rectangle, a track was laid around the group, and a mixing plant was mounted on a flatcar that was followed by cars with sand, cement, and cinders. The concrete produced in this moving plant was hoisted from the mixer to an elevated hopper, from which it was poured into the steel forms. After a section of one house was completed, the mixing train moved to the next and proceeded around the circuit of houses each time the adaptable formwork was ready to be filled.[83]

Although the opportunity to use a train so integrally in the construction process rarely arose, many companies adopted variations of Morrill's system of molds. With them they built large tracts of concrete houses in places like Youngstown, Ohio; Gary, Indiana; and Rochester, New York. The purpose of this process was to cut costs; the builders and architects who used it had no illusions that the rough casting created an intrinsically beautiful product. To improve the appearance of these rapidly built houses, they stuccoed or stained the concrete to produce a more even finish. Builders also recommended the planting of vines and creepers to soften the harsh forms.[84] Morrill, who thought that his process could be used for all grades of housing, often showed how concrete houses could be modified to emulate traditional styles. By taking a standard plan and altering only the roof, doors, and windows, he produced houses in the Spanish, Dutch Colonial, Oriental, New England, and Craftsman styles.[85]

The ultimate extension of Grosvenor Atterbury's and Milton Morrill's ideas was to erect formwork for an entire house, fill it with concrete in one pour, and then reuse the molds to produce an endless number of similar structures. This improbable approach to construction was adopted by Thomas Edison when in 1906 he became interested in the housing problem and began to search for a spectacular way to solve it. Unlike some of his other inventions, this one did not work.[86]

One reason that Edison's poured concrete houses failed was economic. He thought he could do away with the expense of erecting formwork for each house, but he found that the initial costs of what turned out to be highly complicated molds were great, and, since the molds were so heavy, they were also expensive to move and maneuver into place. Furthermore, there were great practical problems in pouring concrete simultaneously in both horizontal and vertical cavities. Edison's more telling difficulty, however, was aesthetic. His plans for these instant houses received much publicity in the press. Americans were impressed by the concept's efficiency but repelled by the prospect of one mold turning out an endless number of similar houses. Anticipating this criticism, Edison first tried to compensate for the monotony of repetition by elaborately decorating the basic house. But since it would have been difficult for concrete to flow into all the tiny nooks and crannies of the intricate details, Edison had to jettison this design. He later suggested that a level of ornament might be added to the initial concrete structure once it had been poured, but since only a few of his houses were ever built, Edison never really had to face up to the problem of repetition.[87]

Architects who designed houses in poured concrete for a particular site and client did not have to worry about repetition. Their designs reflected every type of taste. One of the first concrete houses in the United States overlooked the Hudson River and had crenellated balustrades on its roof to emphasize its castlelike appearance. Dutch Colonial houses, which originally had been made of stone, were particularly popular with architects who designed in concrete, as were adobe mission-style structures.[88]

In fact, architects often thought that the aesthetic possibilities of concrete were unlimited. In the concluding chapter of his book on concrete and stucco houses Oswald Hering predicted "The Dawn of American Architecture." To describe the characteristics of this new aesthetic, he outlined the basic properties of concrete construction. Especially when reinforced with steel, concrete could span great distances without intervening walls or columns. It was, therefore, false to imitate stone in concrete because a load-bearing stone wall could only have relatively small openings. Reinforced concrete was also sufficiently strong to bear a heavy snow load, so the new material made the pitched roof obsolete. A flat roof could be used for a garden, and Hering envisaged that when every house had a solarium on the roof, traditional living and sleeping rooms would be abandoned and most of everyday life, at least in temperate climates, would be oriented toward the sky. The aesthetic effect of using concrete to its limits would be staggering; concrete promised "far greater possibilities in construction and beauty" than had ever been recorded "even in the architecture of the Greeks or the Goths."

Hering believed that these possibilities would be realized only when what was "crude and utilitarian" acquired "refinement." He did not admire concrete in its rough state, which to him symbolized "retarded social development." Instead, he thought that concrete had to have special finishes, textures, and colors. These qualifications did not necessarily prevent the formulation of an architectural language that departed from precedent, but despite his predictions about the Dawn of American Architecture, the buildings Hering admired and illustrated in his book were traditional. They were imitations and adaptations of Dutch Colonial and Renaissance houses.

Hering did not try to break away from these precedents because of his idea of progress. Like other critics, he believed that the architectural styles of the past had portrayed the characteristics of civilizations at a high stage of development. Americans had had no consistent architectural style since colonial days because their civilization had been changing so rapidly that new ideas were superseded before they could be used. Hering concluded that when Americans settled down, they would again have a consistent architecture. Then the potential of concrete could be fully realized. In the meantime, Hering advised architects not to follow any of the fads that in the visual arts had started with Impressionism. He ridiculed in particular certain architects in the Midwest who were calling for an indigenous style. This cult of individualism illustrated "the folly of the revolutionist's single-handed attempt to achieve victory with the bomb." Instead of this "architectural socialism," it was much better to adhere "to scientific truths" and gradually to modify "existing customs to suit new conditions." The way to hasten the Dawn was to be precise in construction and to adapt slowly but surely the precedents of history.[89]

One architect who came under these midwestern influences and who evolved a unique architectural language in concrete and stucco was Irving Gill. The son of a building contractor in Syracuse, New York, Gill left his home town in 1890 at the age of twenty to work for the firm of Adler and Sullivan in Chicago. Although he had never met Louis Sullivan or read anything the Chicago architect had written, Gill had heard about Sullivan and was convinced that his office was the only place in which to learn about architecture.[90] For reasons of health, Gill left Chicago in 1893 and settled in San Diego, California. Like other easterners who migrated to the Golden State, Gill was impressed not only by the lush and varied landscape but also by the fact that it was still largely unspoiled. "In California," he later wrote, "we have great wide plains, arched by blue skies that are fresh chapters as yet unwritten. We have noble mountains, lovely little hills and canyons waiting to hold the record of this generation's history, ideals, imagination, sense of romance and honesty."

Gill always tried to live up to the challenge that the landscape of Southern California presented, but it took him many years to articulate architectural principles that were appropriate to it. His early work was well received and had many original qualities, but it was still within accepted architectural conventions. His houses varied in appearance: some were shingle-clad adaptations of buildings on the East Coast, others were half-timbered. Gill also designed brick houses that were reminiscent of the progressive architecture of Chicago and imitations of the local adobe architecture — simple, white-stuccoed structures with pitched roofs of colored tiles.

In 1906 Gill's work started to assume a clarity that it had not previously possessed. Thereafter, his houses were all of concrete or stucco. Gill experimented with methods for making thin, stucco-covered walls, and he also built houses with walls cast in formwork on the ground and then

# THE HOME OF THE FUTURE: THE NEW ARCHITECTURE OF THE WEST: SMALL HOMES FOR A GREAT COUNTRY: BY IRVING J. GILL: NUMBER FOUR
"An artist is known rather by what he omits."

*112. Irving Gill: Residence of Marion Olmsted, San Diego, California, 1911. Gill set simple white buildings composed of basic geometrical shapes against the lush California landscape.*

*113. Irving Gill: The entrance to Bella Vista Terrace, Sierra Madre, California, 1910. This entrance led to a development of twelve houses, all of which were on the perimeter of a communal garden. The site sloped and afforded spectacular views of the surrounding mountains against which Gill's buildings were set.*

tilted into place when dry. With either method the result was a building of simple, cubical volumes without pitched roofs. The window and door openings in Gill's white walls were all either basic rectangles or arches, and the only ornamentation came from nature. All of Gill's houses were carefully landscaped with lush planting. Summarizing his feelings about this architecture in an article in the *Craftsman*, Gill wrote: "There is something very restful and satisfying in the simple cube house with creamy walls, sheer and plain, rising boldly into the sky, unrelieved by cornices or overhang of roof, unornamented save for the vines that soften a line or creepers that wreathe a pillar or flowers that inlay color more sentiently than any tile could do."

These buildings did not herald a new machine-age aesthetic, nor was the impulse behind them anarchic. Instead, Gill wanted to create a timeless architecture. He was not satisfied with forms that had particular associations. He wanted to identify the "source of all architectural strength" and found it in simple geometrical and structural shapes — the straight line, the arch, the square, and the circle. For him each of these "units of architectural language" had a basis in nature and was endowed with a higher significance. The straight line was associated with the horizon and was a "symbol of greatness, grandeur, and nobility." The arch recalled the dome of the sky and represented "exultation, reverence, aspiration." The circle was the sign of "completeness, motion, and progression," and the square was the symbol of "power, justice, honesty, and firmness."

Gill tried to articulate this timeless language of architecture because he wanted to use it to reflect and thus to preserve or even to re-create a type of society that he thought had existed in California's early days. His architecture was fundamental not only because it was based in a deeply personal interpretation of nature but also because it permitted that consistency of treatment which most American architects believed to have disappeared with the advance of civilization to a more complex but not necessarily more desirable state. Unlike other architects who, to satisfy their ideas of fitness or truthfulness, used different forms for different types of buildings, Gill adapted his basic language to whatever he designed — community centers, schools, and, most important, different types of houses. The forms, materials, and colors of the Dodge House, a 6,500-square-foot structure in West Hollywood for the man whose fortune came from the product Tiz, "for tired feet," were essentially the same as those of Lewis Court, a group of low-cost houses in Sierra Madre.[91]

This correspondence and the social affinity that it symbolized were vitally important to Gill. In 1916 he still believed that the West had an "opportunity unparalleled in the history of the world." It was "the newest white page turned for registration." He hoped that what would be written on that white page would be both an architectural and social ideal, and for the rest of his life he refused to be deterred from his dream. Other California architects, however, did not share Gill's ideals. By 1910 some of them were designing buildings that had original qualities, but they soon turned to a highly ornamented architecture, one often indistinguishable from what was then being built elsewhere in the United States. In the last twenty years of his life Gill received few commissions. When he died in 1936 he and his work had been all but forgotten.[92]

✦✦✦

When Irving Gill moved to California in 1893, he took with him ideas about architecture that had been nurtured in the previous decade in Chicago. Until the mid-1890s and especially after John W. Root's death in 1891, Louis Sullivan was the most outspoken advocate of a point of view about architecture that was already identified with Chicago. Then, as Sullivan's practice declined and his personal problems increased, Frank Lloyd Wright assumed the position of leadership that his former employer had occupied.

Wright's authority was especially pronounced in domestic architecture. Sullivan was an architect primarily of commercial buildings; he received few commissions for houses, and those that he did he handed to apprentices like Wright and Gill. Wright's practice was the opposite of Sullivan's. Although he was always willing to design public buildings, houses constituted the bulk of his work. He was fascinated, even possessed, by them. In the twenty years after he left Sullivan's office, he built over one hundred houses and produced designs for many others.[93]

Wright used concrete in many of these houses. He best expressed his vision of cast-in-place concrete for domestic architecture in a design for a Fireproof House that was published in the *Ladies' Home Journal* in 1907. In the accompanying article Wright noted the increase in the price of wood and concluded that a concrete house was then within the reach of the "average home-maker." The entire structure of the Fireproof House was cast in concrete; the overhanging roof slab and the first floor of the square house were supported in the center by a large fireplace. Wright did not say how he planned to cast this building, but by the time he published the design he had already had considerable experi-

*114, 115. Advertisements of the Atlas Portland Cement Company. Frank
Lloyd Wright was known for his work in concrete, and he was not
above lending his name to support cement manufacturers. In addition*

ence with concrete, and he was then about to begin the construction of
Unity Temple, a Unitarian church in Oak Park that was one of the
largest reinforced concrete structures of the period.[94]

The walls of many of Wright's houses were covered with stucco on
expanded metal or wood lathing. In some of these dwellings stucco was
only one of several surface materials; in others the major part of the
building was covered with the cement coating. Wright treated stucco in
many ways. Since he recognized that it was possible to put only a limited
amount of wet stucco on a wall at once, Wright often divided the planes
of his buildings with wooden bands. The precise colors of the stucco are

*to this affiliation with the Atlas Portland Cement Company, Wright
designed an exhibition for the Universal Portland Cement Company.*

now difficult to determine because many of the owners of the houses
subsequently painted them white, but contemporary renderings and
Wright's own comments indicate that he probably dyed the stucco with
soft, pastel colors. Wright also placed tiles in stucco: the most striking
example is on the Avery Coonley house in Riverside, Illinois. Wright
imbedded the walls of that building with a marvelously intricate geometrical pattern of yellow and red tiles interwoven with repetitive marks
pressed into the stucco. On the upper part of the walls of other houses
Wright placed stucco-cast moldings or friezes. He covered the area above
the sill lines of the second-story windows in the Winslow House with a

pattern that was inspired by his studies of nature. Elsewhere, Wright used geometrical compositions and patterns composed of human figures designed by artist and sculptor friends.[95]

Since the structure of so many of Wright's early houses is covered in stucco, it is difficult to tell whether any are made of concrete blocks. Nevertheless, he was certainly thinking about the implications of this material, and in 1916 he announced the results of that speculation. Wright did not consider the concrete block as simply a larger brick; he thought of it as the primary part of an integral method of construction that he called the "American Ready Cut System of House Building" and tried to market through a company in Milwaukee.[96]

Wright's concrete houses stand out from the rest of the period's buildings in that material, but his superiority was not limited to houses made of concrete. Whatever the material, the buildings he designed after he left Louis Sullivan's office have a quality that is lacking in the work of his contemporaries, both those in Chicago and those elsewhere. Wright's buildings have style. All of them are easily identifiable as the work of Frank Lloyd Wright and of no one else, but they also have style in a sense that transcends personal authorship. They have an immediately recognizable quality that all great works of architecture possess.

*116. Frank Lloyd Wright: The Curtis Publishing Company Fireproof House, 1907. Wright used poured-in-place concrete for this design because it was fireproof and inexpensive.*

To discuss Frank Lloyd Wright's houses in terms of style is not inappropriate. Like earlier discussions about beauty, defining and coming to terms with the meaning of style was a key issue for the most important European architectural theorists of the second half of the nineteenth century, and style was very much on the minds of many architects in Chicago during Frank Lloyd Wright's formative years.

One way to understand style was simply to define its attributes. John W. Root took this approach in a speech on "Style" that he delivered in 1887. Although he thought this elusive quality was inherent, " a thing of the heart, not of the epidermis," he chose to focus on those qualities that were most immediately apparent. Since the use of no particular forms in themselves guaranteed style, Root sought a definition that transcended the historical styles. His characterization stemmed from his belief that architecture was a "polite" art. A building with style was one that was "not to be avoided by its neighbors"; its distinguishing qualities, like those of a gentleman, were repose, refinement, self-containment, sympathy, discretion, knowledge, urbanity, and modesty. Root explained the relevance of each of these attributes to architecture and concluded that the sum total of these qualities made "a perfect building."[97]

Although other architects often attempted similar definitions, a few tried to find a deeper principle by penetrating beneath the surface of buildings and relating architecture to nature. In a series of lectures on the history of architecture William Le Baron Jenney frequently quoted Eugène Viollet-le-Duc, the eminent French architect and writer, to explain what gave the outstanding buildings of each period their enduring qualities. A work of architecture, like any organism, Jenney explained, had style when it expressed the necessities that called it into existence. Nature always had style, because it always "submitted to laws and invariable principles." Every part of a flower had a distinct function, and so did every part of a building with style.[98] Jenney reflected his interest in the function of building elements in his studies of and innovations in structure and construction. It was, therefore, not inconsistent that one issue of the *Inland Architect* contained not only one of his lectures on architectural history but also a speech to the Chicago Academy of Science on "Building-Stone."[99]

The argument about the relationship of style to purpose was often mentioned, but one of its weaknesses was that it did not fully account for the persistence of ornament or decoration. In fact, embellishment was often considered proof of a society's ability to transcend simple material needs. To resolve this contradiction, those who emphasized the importance of the expression of a building's construction and its purpose often drew a line between ornament which reflected or was an outgrowth of what was necessary and that which was extrinsic to functional requirements. N. Clifford Ricker, a professor in the University of Illinois's Department of Architecture who introduced Midwest architects to the writings of many European historians and theorists, offered one explanation of this distinction. He felt that the masterpieces of architecture had what was tantamount to "an organic life." Construction and structure were the bones of the building; decorative forms constituted its flesh. However, it was not sufficient simply to have these two aspects in the relationship which this analogy implied. The "genius" of a building, "that divine harmony of construction and decoration which unites both, and endows the structure with immortal life," was also vital. An architectural grammar encompassed all three qualities.[100]

To elucidate this theory and to clarify what constituted an architectural grammar Ricker often discussed each prominent style of architecture, starting with the Egyptian. His method was first to set out a brief history of a civilization, then to analyze its government, religion, climate, and landscape, and finally to explain the characteristic building forms that had emerged from this political, cultural, and geographical context. Ricker never pinpointed precisely how a style of architecture was related to or evolved from the larger milieu that he described; nor did he say how the style of one period was transformed into that of another. Nevertheless, he thought that the signs for the development of a "new and national style of architecture" in the United States were promising:

We have an abundance of all kinds of constructive materials, many suggesting and requiring new methods of artistic treatment, unknown to the past; a system of popular government permitting the most complete freedom of the individual, compatible with the general welfare of the community; a mixed race, descended from the most enterprising individuals of the various European races; wealth sufficient to provide for the cost of structures of almost any desired magnitude; an appreciation of good art, which is still youthful, but which is growing with a rapidity unknown in the past history of the world, and whose results in some of our great cities are even now scarcely inferior to those to be found in any time or any style; and we also find a strong and united feeling among the members of our profession, impelling them to unite and to labor for the common good.[101]

With such favorable conditions American architects only had to make a thorough study of the architectural grammars of the past before they would soon learn by analogy and extrapolation how to produce a great style of their own. But if architecture in the last analysis was derived from nature, it could be argued that the best way to articulate an architectural grammar appropriate to late nineteenth-century America was not to study the historical styles, but instead to delve directly into the ultimate source of inspiration. This was the point Louis Sullivan made when he discussed "Style" at the Chicago Architectural Sketch Club in 1888. He did not refer to buildings of the past, nor did he define style's attributes. That kind of analysis could at best "but discourse of [style's] grosser material envelopings, or formulate abstractions concerning its rythms [sic]." Sullivan, therefore, advised his audience to forget about "the word style." He wanted them instead to note "the thing style" and to open their hearts to "the essence style."[102] A year before, Sullivan read an "Essay on Inspiration" to the annual convention of the Western Association of Architects. More a poem than an essay, Sullivan's work described the endless variety and wonder of nature, themes to which he returned throughout his life. Only when architects immersed themselves in nature, Sullivan maintained, would they be able to find and tap the true source of creativity and only then would they produce a suitably American architecture.[103]

In his early years Frank Lloyd Wright was well aware of the significance of style. In 1908 he claimed that in formulating the principles of his work the question uppermost in his mind had been "not 'what style' but 'what is style?' "[104] How Wright answered this question is difficult to trace because less is known about his early life than might be expected of someone who lived until 1959. Wright's father was trained as a lawyer and like many New Englanders settled in the Midwest. In 1859 he arrived in Wisconsin, where he practiced law and dabbled in local politics. In 1863 he gave up those careers and was ordained a Baptist minister. His first wife died in 1864, and in 1866 he married Anna Lloyd-Jones, a member of a prominent Welsh family that had immigrated to Wisconsin in 1845. On June 8, 1867, Frank Lloyd Wright was born.

The future architect's childhood was dominated by his father's restlessness and inability to find a suitable position as Baptist minister. In the late 1860s he was pastor to several churches in Wisconsin. In 1871 the Wrights moved to Pawtucket, Rhode Island; in 1874, to Weymouth, Massachusetts; and finally, in 1878, back to Madison, Wisconsin. Wright's parents' marriage then became increasingly strained, and they werę divorced in 1885.[105]

This background had an immediate impact on Frank Lloyd Wright's career. Because of his family's financial problems, Wright left high school in 1885 and started to work for a professor of civil engineering at the University of Wisconsin. His employer convinced him to enroll at the university as a special student in 1886, but Wright stayed there for only two semesters. During that year Wright helped to supervise the construction of a church designed by Joseph Lyman Silsbee for his uncle, the eminent Unitarian minister Jenkin Lloyd-Jones. Early in 1887 Wright left Madison to work in Chicago for Silsbee. Shortly thereafter he joined the firm of Adler and Sullivan. Wright worked there until the beginning of 1893, when he started his own practice. A dispute with Sullivan about some houses Wright had designed away from the office precipitated the break, but by 1893 Wright had established his own direction in architecture and no doubt would have left his master even without the quarrel.[106]

During the following fifteen years Wright's reputation grew rapidly. He lived in suburban Oak Park and designed houses there for many of his prosperous neighbors. He was also attracting notice elsewhere. Prior to his article on the Fireproof House, two of his other designs were published in the *Ladies' Home Journal*. A friend, the architect Robert Spencer, wrote a long article about Wright in the Boston magazine *Architectural Review*, and the eminent critic Montgomery Schuyler hailed Wright as an outstanding new talent.

The upward trajectory of Wright's career did not continue uninterrupted. In 1889 Wright married the daughter of a prosperous businessman. She bore him six children and was instrumental in helping him adjust to life in suburban Chicago, a milieu of which he had had little experience. But as his reputation increased, Wright outgrew both his relationship with his wife and with the society that centered around Oak Park. He was attracted to Mamah Cheney, the wife of a neighbor, and in 1909, scandalizing everyone, the two traveled together to Europe. When Wright returned to Chicago, he attempted a reconciliation with his wife, but soon moved with his "soul mate" to Taliesin, a summer house Wright had built in Wisconsin. They lived there until August 14, 1914, when the cook at Taliesin locked the residents, including Mrs. Cheney, in the building and set fire to it. When Wright, who was in Chicago at the time, rushed back to Wisconsin by train, he found that the few who escaped the fire had been murdered by the crazed cook. This horrendous event marked the end of Wright's early period. He was then forty-seven; he had already designed more buildings than most architects did in a lifetime, and yet his life was only half over.[107]

During this period Wright met and conversed with prominent architects, artists, and authors, bought and read many books, and was an avid collector of works of art. These contacts and sources should form a rich background against which to chart Wright's development, but few records of them exist. Parts of Wright's autobiographical writings are revealing, but others are notoriously unreliable. Nor do accounts of his contemporaries and members of his family elucidate these early years. Few letters remain, and if Wright kept diaries or notes, they were probably all burned in the fire at Taliesin. The two primary sources for studying the development of Wright's architectural style are, therefore, his buildings and a handful of articles he wrote.[108]

These sources make it clear that the foundation of all of Wright's thought and architecture was a belief in democracy. Like other architects of the second half of the nineteenth century, he assumed that architecture was intimately connected to the society that built it. He followed Louis Sullivan in dividing history into two periods. The founding of the United States marked a sharp break with the past. Until then man's abilities had been shackled by a repressive system, which Sullivan called Feudalism. Democracy was a "man-search." America, Wright wrote, placed "a life premium upon individuality — the highest possible development of the individual consistent with a harmonious whole." This orientation toward the individual had a profound significance for architecture. Under democracy, architecture would not be dominated by one style, but instead each architect would be able to create a personal architecture that was commensurate with his abilities. Wright did not doubt that man would rise to the challenge. "The average of human intelligence rises steadily," he claimed in 1908, "and as the individual unit grows more and more to be trusted we will have an architecture with richer variety in unity than has ever arisen before." Wright, therefore, was never interested in a national style of architecture, except insofar as the full expression of individual abilities would in itself constitute a style appropriate to democratic America.[109]

Later in his life Wright developed a comprehensive theory about democratic institutions and the relationship of the individual to them, but in his early years he focused on the family. Perhaps because his childhood had been so unsettled, Wright came to believe in a state of family harmony in which one could live in "simplicity and repose," guided by "togetherness." For the creation and maintenance of this felicitous state, the quality of the immediate environment was all-important. Wright often discussed these ideas, but his most lucid early statement of them was *The House Beautiful*, a hand-printed book that he illustrated and the Unitarian minister William Channing Gannett wrote. The contents, however, were as much Wright's as Gannett's. The book, as Wright explained, was "an interlinear web," a phrase that also summarized the integral relationship of family life to God, nature, and the beautiful.[110]

Wright began the design of the buildings that acted as the framework for family life by analyzing the needs of particular clients. He believed that "there should be as many kinds (styles) of houses as there are kinds (styles) of people." But he usually found that houses needed only three main rooms — living room, dining room, and kitchen — on the first floor, and he located the bedrooms on the levels above. Within this format Wright emphasized the individuality of each house plan, but he readily acknowledged that there were rules governing the planning of space. He used a "simple axial law" and an "ordered spacing upon a system of certain structural units." The result was "more articulate" — the parts of the plan were more differentiated — than the designs produced by students at the Ecole des Beaux Arts, but his method of planning with grids was akin to that taught there.

Although house plans were important to Wright, he considered them "merely the actual projection of a carefully considered whole." He did not design an elevation from a preconceived ground plan. Nor did he first fashion a perspective image of the house and then try to "fudge the plan to suit." Instead, Wright conceived his houses in three dimensions as "organic entities." But just as Wright needed rules to help him arrange the spaces of his houses in plan, he also had to have guidelines to establish the building's organization in three dimensions.[111]

There are several possible interpretations of what these rules were. In the early part of his career Wright undoubtedly drew on his childhood experience of the Froebel kindergarten method to generate some of the basic volumes of his houses. The Swiss educator Friedrich Froebel wanted to create a system that would help children appreciate natural forms and their laws of combination. To do so he devised a series of "gifts," blocks of different shapes and colors. A child had to master a number of games associated with each gift before he could receive the next one. Frank Lloyd Wright's mother, who had been convinced, even

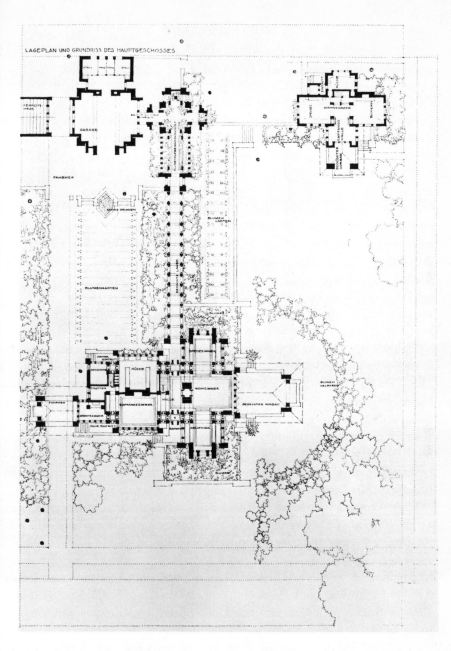

*117. Frank Lloyd Wright: First-floor plan of the D. D. Martin House, Buffalo, New York, 1904. Wright's use of grids and axes as a planning technique was probably most brilliantly demonstrated both in the main part of the Martin House and in the way that he joined the main house to the garage, conservatory, and guest house.*

before he was born, that her son would be an architect, saw the Froebel gifts when she visited the Centennial Exhibition in Philadelphia. She purchased a set and soon began to give them to her son. Wright vividly remembered the impact these games had on him: "That early kindergarten experience with the straight line; the flat plane; the square; the triangle; the circle . . . these primary forms and figures were the secret of all effects . . . which were ever got into the architecture of the world."[112]

When the Froebel combinations are compared with some of Wright's buildings, it is possible to perceive a debt to his childhood experience. Many of Wright's works have a unique, volumetric quality. The direct power of these forms, as well as the intricate way in which they are interwoven, was, and remains, so fresh that it probably could have resulted only from an encounter with a device or body of knowledge, like the Froebel gifts, that was extrinsic to the sources architects traditionally drew upon. However, what makes Wright's buildings all the more intriguing is that they are not merely pure volumes. Their form, as in any work of architecture, is defined as different spaces and parts are shaped and joined together to fit the program, as the structure meets the ground, as openings are made in walls, and as the roof shelters the rooms below. Wright's building masses are also highly differentiated; they are articulated with textures, colors, and superimposed materials. In effect, although they may sometimes appear novel and seem only to recall the abstract shapes of the kindergarten gifts, Wright's forms, at least in part, resulted from resolving age-old architectural problems. To endow his buildings with a presence or physiognomy, Wright needed, as for his plans, rules of organization that were generic to buildings.

How Wright arrived at this ordering system in three dimensions can be understood as a response to problems that he encountered in the houses he designed while still working for Louis Sullivan. Some of these structures were little more than well-executed bits of pastiche, but the more telling houses were good examples of a type of suburban wood-frame dwelling that was built throughout the United States in the 1870s and 1880s and on which Wright probably worked when he was a draftsman in Silsbee's office.

A few of these residences were located on Chicago Avenue in Oak Park, just a few yards from the house Wright designed for himself. These Chicago houses raised, but did not resolve, four issues that Wright addressed in the houses he designed after 1893. First of all, the structures met the ground in a clumsy way. Because each had a cellar, the first

*118. Frank Lloyd Wright: The Thomas H. Gale House, Oak Park, 1892. This is one of the houses of the period just before Wright left Sullivan's office. Of these structures Wright later said, "I couldn't invent the terms of my own overnight."*

floor was several feet above the ground. To enter the house, therefore, it was necessary to walk up a staircase that, as was then the custom, led to a porch. On the sides of the house, the foundation wall came directly out of the ground to a height sufficient for cellar windows. Above that level the house was covered with clapboard.

The configuration of the roofs of these houses was as uncertain as the relation of the building to the ground. One way to cap such a house was to raise from a constant level a simple pitched roof that contained an attic, perhaps with gable windows or dormers. The other method was to take the roof down to different levels at different places in the house. By doing so it was possible to encompass full rooms under the roof and to create varied forms. In the Chicago Avenue houses Wright could not choose one or the other. He seemed to want to draw a straight line across the elevation, thus demarcating where the house ended and the roof began. But the line actually was not continuous, and the roof was too high to be only an attic. In his own house Wright produced a partial solution to the problem. Across the main elevation he drew a distinct line, forming the bottom of a tall triangular roof that contained an additional story. Although this method of capping the house was less equivocal than the one he used on the others nearby, the roof still was too high to make a convincing resolution of the elevation.

The relationship of the house to the ground and the connection of the body of the building to its roof both bore upon another question, how to organize windows within the elevation. Wright adopted a functional approach in dealing with this issue. Each window revealed its special purpose. Those in the living room were large and looked out upon the front lawn and street, secondary rooms had smaller openings, and the type of windows in the front door appeared nowhere else in the building. But even with the identity of each window determined, it was difficult to relate them in elevation. Wright may have had some sense of a balance or harmony between the solid wall and the voids of the openings. Beyond that, he could only coordinate the elevation with implied horizontal lines that were halfhearted accentuations of the clapboard siding. This unresolved quality was especially apparent on the sides where the sill and head heights seemed simply to be determined by the requirements of the rooms.

If these elevations had little coherence in themselves, they had even less together. The Chicago Avenue lots did not have a wide frontage. Like other architects of suburban houses, Wright dealt with this condition by making the front of the house the primary elevation, distinctly differentiating it from the sides of the house. Because of the narrowness of the lot, only the front of the building would be seen, especially as one approached the street-facing entrance, so there was little incentive to carry an architectural theme around the building.

Only a few years after he designed the Chicago Avenue houses, Wright was producing a fluent architecture that had none of the awkward qualities of the earlier work, that was distinctly his own, that, in short, had style. This remarkable transformation cannot simply be due to the fact that, once on his own, he no longer had to stifle his innate talent. If he had had that talent all along, it would have shown through in his work, but there were few indications in his early houses of what was to follow.

Although Wright may have been groping for his own approach to architecture for a long time, the development of his work from pastiche to style happened in a short period in the early 1890s. With plans then being made for the world's fair and with the emergence of a historicist classicism, those were years of intense introspection for many American architects, including Frank Lloyd Wright.

One source Wright drew upon to find an ordering system for his buildings was nature. In his first major statement about architecture, he declared his faith in nature, which "furnished the materials for architectural motifs out of which the architectural forms" had developed. Many times thereafter Wright extolled nature, or, as he called it, the organic, as the basic source of all architecture.

Many architects had felt the need to relate architecture to nature; what distinguished them were the principles they derived from nature and the way they used them in their buildings. Wright consulted nature for reasons that differed from those of his mentor Louis Sullivan. The man whom Wright called "The Genius" looked to nature primarily for inspiration. That was the lesson Sullivan taught in the "Essay on Inspiration," *Kindergarten Chats*, and many other writings. But in his *Autobiography*, Wright recalled that when Sullivan read him the "Essay on Inspiration" it seemed like "a kind of baying at the moon." As much as he admired Sullivan, Wright could not submit himself so completely to nature. Although inspiration was important, he wanted to derive something more specific from nature.[113]

Wright understood that in its most immediate form, in its "external, obvious aspect," nature was not a fruitful source for the architect. "As Nature is never right for a picture so is she never right for the architect — that is, not ready made," Wright asserted. Nevertheless, with "inherent vision" it was possible to see beneath the external surface and to gain a "comprehension of natural law." Having done so, the architect could then develop "that sense of reality that . . . will lift him far above the realistic in his art." In nature he would find "sentiment that will never degenerate to sentimentality," and he would learn to draw "with a sure hand the ever-perplexing line between the curious and the beautiful."[114]

In a note to one of the drawings in the portfolio that he published in Germany in 1910, Wright provided a clue about what law he derived from nature and how it applied to his architecture. Wright always acknowledged the Winslow House, constructed in 1893 shortly after he began his own practice, to be the first of his own work. He noted that a beautiful elm nearby had given him the idea for the mass of the building. The tree had a three-part division of roots, trunk, and branches, and the Winslow House's front elevation was similarly organized. At the ground it had a solid plinth that projected from the walls and indicated a basement. The next zone of the elevation ended with a continuous horizontal molding at the second-story sill line; above that was another

*119. Frank Lloyd Wright: The William H. Winslow House, River Forest, 1893. Wright later claimed this to be the first of his own houses. The tree in front, now long since gone, may have been the beautiful elm that "gave the suggestion for the mass of the building."*

area that culminated at the wide-spreading eaves of the low-hipped roof. The Winslow House was, therefore, akin to a tree not in the "ready made" sense, but in terms that were appropriate to an architect's work.

In the early 1890s the three-part division had been used in Sullivan's office, but the elm tree had enabled Wright to understand this organizing principle in a fresh way and helped him solve many of the problems that were so evident in his early houses. In the Winslow House the plinth was a forceful and effective means of bringing the building to the ground, the crisp horizontal line of the low eaves clearly demarcated the roof and attic from the rest of the building, and the zoning of the elevation above and below the second-story sill line gave him a strong context in which to organize the front elevation. The Winslow House was a simple, blocklike building, and although Wright carried his system around the sides, he was still unable to use it to encompass the untidy elements at the back. Nevertheless, this building marked a great breakthrough.[115]

Nature was not the only source of what Wright termed his grammar. He derived the same rules from the history of architecture. Wright sometimes denied all debt to the past, but his buildings and writings are full of the evidence of his knowledge of precedents. In the beginning of his first "In the Cause of Architecture" article, Wright not only indicated his interest in the past but also hinted at what type of architecture was most important to him. He acknowledged that although his work was radical, it was also "dedicated to a cause conservative in the best sense of the word." His buildings did not deny the "elemental law and order inherent in all great architecture." They were a "declaration of love for the spirit of that law and order, and a reverential recognition of the elements that made its ancient letter in its time vital and beautiful."[116]

These opaque phrases, especially the references to "the elements" and "the ancient letter," suggest an interest in classical architecture. Wright was not unlike other architects who in the late 1880s and early 1890s were becoming increasingly fascinated by the buildings of antiquity and of the Renaissance. In many of the houses he designed before he left Louis Sullivan's office Wright freely used classical detailing, but he was also capable of producing designs that drew literally on particular precedents. His entry for the Milwaukee Public Library competition was a knowing adaptation of Claude Perrault's facade of the Louvre.[117]

Wright soon lost whatever attraction this architecture had had for him. When Daniel Burnham offered to send him to the newly founded American Academy in Rome, Wright did not accept, and in the following years his antipathy to the kind of architecture championed at that institution grew.[118] In 1908, for instance, Wright ridiculed the method of design that then fascinated so many American architects. Nature, he wrote, did not sanction "establishing an 'order,' a colonnade, then building walls between the columns of the order reducing them to pilasters, thereafter cutting holes in the wall and pasting on cornices with more pilasters around them." The result of this procedure, which Wright knew all too well, was that every form was outraged, and the whole was "an abominable mutilation."[119] In 1909 Wright traveled to Italy, saw some of the monuments of Renaissance architecture, and was even more convinced of their evil influence. "From these Italian flames," he concluded, "were lighted myriad of French, German, and English lights that flourished, flickered feebly for a time, and soon smouldered in the sensuality and extravagance of later periods, until they were extinguished in the banal architecture like Rococo or in nondescript structures such as the Louvre," the very building that had inspired his design for the Milwaukee Public Library.[120]

Wright's dismissal of the sensuality and extravagance of the architecture that had its roots in the Italian Renaissance was reminiscent of the critique of the same buildings that John Ruskin had made in *The Stones of Venice*. Ruskin preferred Gothic architecture and hoped that there would be a revival of the spirit that had brought the great monuments of the medieval world into being. Wright also wrote approvingly of the same structures. He admired them because they had been the summary cultural expression of their time; they had provided a physical framework for all the other arts. At a smaller scale Wright often tried to achieve the same effect in his buildings, but he never used Gothic's most characteristic feature, the pointed arch, and in no other sense can his work be said to be Gothic.[121]

Criticisms of Renaissance architecture have not only been made to demonstrate the virtues of Gothic. During the eighteenth and nineteenth centuries architectural historians and theorists often wrote disparagingly of Renaissance buildings and their derivatives to underline the need for a return to principles embodied in a pure classical language, one based not on compromised Roman and Renaissance precedents but instead on Greek sources. In the middle of the eighteenth century Marc Antoine Laugier criticized the architecture of his period by deriving lessons from the fundamental characteristics of the Greek temple. A century later, for different ends, Viollet-le-Duc also contrasted Greek with Roman architecture and its derivatives. The Greeks had a "refined sensibility," but the Romans were "pirates, who, with barbarous and tasteless pride, adorn[ed] themselves with foreign and incongruous spoils."[122]

Beginning in the 1820s many American architects became interested in Greek buildings. Some did so only because they perceived connections between the Greek state and the young democracy in which they lived, but others thought the Greeks designed their buildings according to fundamental principles that they hoped to rediscover and to use as the basis of their architecture. Thus Horatio Greenough wrote: "I contend for Greek principles, not Greek things." No American architect ever really penetrated beneath the Greek "things," but a few at least understood that there was an elusive ideal in Greek architecture that was worth aspiring to.[123]

Once architects were attracted to styles outside the classical tradition, fascination with Greek architecture waned in most parts of the United States. In the Midwest, however, admiration for the achievement of the Greeks never disappeared. The continuation of this interest was not due to an intellectual time lag between the Midwest and the East Coast. Rather, many architects in cities like Chicago, Cincinnati, Detroit, Milwaukee, and St. Louis admired the Greek achievement because the orientation of their education, like much of the rest of their culture, was more toward Germany, where an interest in Greek architecture had persisted throughout the nineteenth century, than toward France, where Renaissance architecture, at least as many American students perceived the situation, was favored at the Ecole des Beaux Arts.[124]

Some of Chicago's most articulate architects were born in Germany, and at a time when there was only a handful of architecture schools in the United States, a few students from the Midwest went to Berlin for their training. Even those educated in France either found little of interest in the Ecole des Beaux Arts or instead attended courses in engineering at the Ecole Centrale.[125] Through whatever channel, many architects in Chicago had a deep interest in German culture and, by extension, in Greek architecture. N. Clifford Ricker, for example, thought that there was something to be gained by examining every period of architectural history, but he singled out the Parthenon as the outstanding building of all time.[126] William Le Baron Jenney considered Greek architecture "the finest ever known." In his course of lectures he asked why Americans should not simply copy these marvelous precedents. The answer was that the requirements of nineteenth-century institutions were different from those in ancient Greece. It was necessary, therefore, to work as the Greeks did, not by copying, but by studying "each feature and each detail, accepting what suits our purposes and arranging all with fitness and good taste."[127] The German-born engineer Frederick Baumann, who was best known for his important work on foundations, also spoke of the significance of the Greeks and urged American architects to become acquainted with "the lofty secrets of Greek architecture" so that they could become "elevated far enough above the common level to enable them to impart life to their designs, and thus give them a character of a higher nobility."[128]

Frank Lloyd Wright may have derived an interest in the Greek achievement from reading Viollet-le-Duc's *Discourses on Architecture* or from the general milieu of architectural discussion in Chicago, but no matter what the source, many aspects of his work manifest evidence of it.[129] At the most basic level, the artifacts of Greek civilization represented an ideal of beauty and provided a source of inspiration. In an early speech, criticizing "Colonial and Renaissance, the château and the chalet," Wright asked, "And the classic? How the beauty-sophisticated Greek would shudder with impotent disgust if he could see the chaste proportions of his work mummified in your whitewashed imitations of his legitimately beautiful creations." Wright admired Greek sculpture and had copies of several well-known works in his studio and home. The Winged Victory of Samothrace was his favorite. A facsimile of it was strategically placed, as if to indicate a connection between the architecture and the source that inspired it, in several early photographs of Wright's buildings.[130]

An ideal of beauty and a source of inspiration were crucial, but Wright also needed something more specific. He had to have principles with which to coordinate the parts of his building. In the first "In the Cause of Architecture" article, Wright described in Greek terms the elements he had defined in the Winslow House. The base was "what the stylobate was to the ancient Greek temple," the area above the second-story sill was a "frieze," the line at the eaves was a "cornice," and his low roofs often ended with a simple "pediment." Greek architecture — that which was most fundamental and therefore closest in its origins to nature — taught the same lesson as the tree near the Winslow House. That this was the basis of Wright's principles and that he was searching through history to discover these concepts were understood by at least one perceptive critic. In 1908, in commenting on the base of Wright's Larkin Building in Buffalo, Russell Sturgis noted: "it is the Attic base reduced to its simplest form, the familiar old Attic base, with its rounded mouldings turned back into the square-edged bands which those mouldings were in their origins."[131]

The works that most explicitly resemble Greek buildings are two of Wright's public structures. He characterized the auditorium of Unity Temple as a "frank revival of the old temple form." With its bold stylobate, its undifferentiated surface to the sill line, then a row of columnar elements and finally its cornice, it echoed the basic format of the porch of the Erechtheum and other Greek buildings. The design for the *Brickbuilder*'s "Village Bank" series was also a temple, "a temple to the God of Money," and had the same templelike elements.[132]

Wright, however, did not restrict the use of his principles to these buildings. Everything he designed before 1915 was shaped by the ordering devices he derived from both nature and history. Wright's public buildings — from tennis clubs to large office structures — and his residential architecture — model dwellings for factory workers, urban apartment houses, vacation cottages on heavily wooded, hilly sites, suburban homes on both large and small flat prairie lots, and vast lakeside estates for Chicago millionaires — all were based on the same concepts. Wright's principles thus were strong and supple enough to encompass the ever

*120. Frank Lloyd Wright: Unity Temple, Oak Park, 1906.
Wright described this building as "a frank revival of the old
temple form."*

*121. Frank Lloyd Wright and Richard Bock: Scoville Park Fountain, Oak
Park, 1911. This fountain is composed of the distilled elements of Wright's
grammar.*

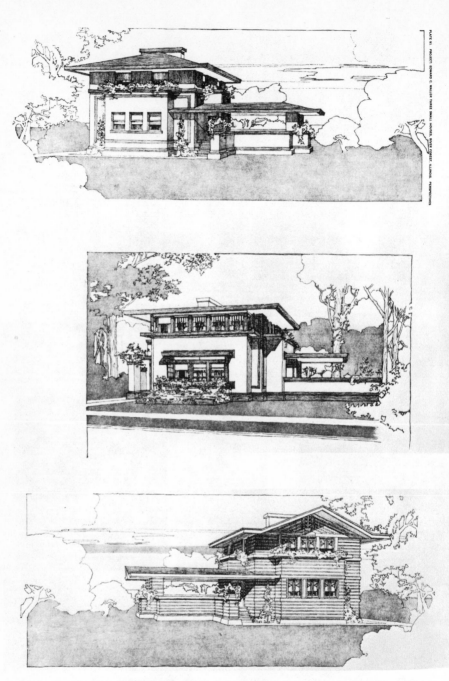

*122.  Frank Lloyd Wright: Three small houses for E. C. Waller, River Forest. These houses demonstrate the three types of roofs that Wright used in his early period.*

more varied institutions of his time, just as the classical language
had served a traditional society. To achieve this quality in his work was
one more reason why Wright "deliberately chose to break with traditions
in order to be more true to Tradition than current conventions and
ideals" then permitted.[133]

Wright established his architectural grammar in the Winslow House,
but in subsequent structures he varied and transformed it. He revealed
how he approached each new design in a comment about Louis Sullivan
in his *Autobiography*. He had found that Sullivan had been interested in
finding "the rule so broad as to admit of no exception," a quest usually
entailing a promethean struggle to resolve opposites. Most of Sullivan's
designs were based on a dialogue between straight lines and curves, between squares and circles. The result was rarely conclusive. Sullivan's
buildings, both in general outline and in detail, had a restless quality that
was the product of a tortured spirit seeking an essence always just out of
reach. Frank Lloyd Wright could not understand this fascination with the
rule. "For the life of me," he wrote, "I could not help, then or now, being
more interested in the exception proving the rule useful or useless." Having established his principles in the Winslow House, he used the horizontal divisions as a point of departure from which to formulate an
almost endless set of permutations in his subsequent buildings.[134]

Wright divided his houses into three types, which he classified by their
roofs. He designed houses with low-pitched hip roofs, either "heaped
together in pyramidal fashion," or "presenting quiet unbroken sky lines";
other houses had low roofs "with simple pediments countering on long
ridges"; and some were capped with simple flat roofs. The three types
are most easily compared in the 1909 project for the three small houses
for Edward C. Waller. Like Wright's other houses, these dwellings did
not resemble the temple format as clearly as, for example, Unity Temple
did, because they had to have windows on the ground floor. Wright
claimed that he used "to gloat over the beautiful buildings I could build
if only it were unnecessary to cut holes in them." At first, as in the
Winslow House, he accomplished this task awkwardly by punching
holes in the wall. Soon he learned to place windows between structural
mullions, and that device gave him a method of fenestration that not only
made sense with his horizontal divisions but also enhanced them.[135]

In small compact houses like those for Edward C. Waller, Wright used
his grammar explicitly. But in larger houses with highly articulate plans
and hip roofs "heaped together in pyramidal fashion," he not only inter-

*123. Frank Lloyd Wright: The Robie House, Chicago, 1908. A comparison between this house and the Winslow House indicates the extent of Wright's development in fifteen years. The horizontal bands no longer simply wrap around a rectangular solid. They interweave in different planes to produce a set of dynamic forms. The planters are abstracted into pure shapes and are placed at pivotal positions to assist this result.*

preted his levels more freely but also added other parallel lines, usually the copings of balustrades or the lintels above windows, to create an intricate pattern of exceptions countering the basic rule that governed the mass of the building. Using this format as a point of departure, Wright created in his masterpieces — the Darwin D. Martin House in Buffalo, the Robie House in Chicago, the Ward Willets House in Highland Park, and the Avery Coonley House in Riverside — a complex network of interwoven horizontal planes. The result, an architecture that was both organic and "classic," was vastly different from the static symmetry of the front of the Winslow House. Through careful experimentation from design to design, Wright eventually achieved an architecture in which the forms appear almost to escape their inert nature and to become a living organism. It was this dynamic quality that, especially after the publication of his work in Berlin in 1910, excited European practitioners and eventually had a profound impact on the development of modern architecture.[136]

Wright acknowledged that with the manipulation of the basic levels, the forms of his buildings were essentially complete. He once wrote about the attraction of a totally undecorated architecture, but he recognized that there was an "ingrained human love of ornament," so his buildings needed, in addition to the underlying grammar of levels, what he called "efflorescence."

Ornament for Wright was "an emphasis of structure, a realization in graceful terms of the nature of that which is ornamented." Since Wright believed that true beauty resulted "from that repose which the mind feels when the eye, the intellect, the affections, are satisfied from the absence of any want — in other words, when we take joy in the thing," he always tried to relate ornament to constituent parts of the building and never let it be "purposely constructed."[137]

Wright most frequently used nature to make his houses blossom forth. Since most of them were located on unwooded prairie, he encouraged the planting of trees on the level lawns that led directly up to the base of the house. Wright usually did not interrupt these areas of grass with bushes or low vegetation, especially in his suburban houses. His buildings are thus seen through a screen of trees. From this perspective the roots, trunk, and boughs mirror the house's three basic horizontal bands, which, in turn, reflect the flatness of the prairie.

Although Wright's lawns are not interrupted by clumps of planting, most of the houses have areas for flowers that are integral to the architecture. He often used rectilinear planters located at the edges of balconies or under windows. When their plants are in bloom, they both accentuate and soften the horizontal lines of the buildings. Wright also used abstract urns. Those in the Winslow House have lips that directly recall classical predecessors and are placed symmetrically at the entrance. In his subsequent work Wright constantly altered the location and design of these urns. He integrated them more completely into the form of the house so that, as in the Robie House, they occupy pivotal positions in the architecture. Wright achieved this effect by abstracting the urns; they eventually became bold variations on spheres and rectangular solids. The thick edge of the urn is another horizontal line that reinforces or counteracts the house's basic levels.

Although Wright achieved efflorescence most directly through the relationship of the house to the surrounding landscape and through integral planting, he also tried to make the building itself blossom forth through a careful use of materials. He manipulated brick, stone, and wood as inventively as concrete and stucco. No matter what the material, he always altered its conventional color, shape, or disposition. Without being assertive or awkward, the material then called attention to itself.

Wright's brickwork was a case in point. He rarely used ordinary bricks; his houses most often were made of attenuated Roman bricks more red, yellow, brown, or orange than those commonly available. Wright set these bricks in novel patterns. He accentuated the linearity of the bricks by raking the horizontal mortar joints and by coloring the vertical ones to match the brick. Often he set alternating courses in different planes to create a distinct pattern of shadows. Wright manipulated wood siding in a similar manner. The area between the stylobate and the second-story sill line of his country houses was often clad in wood, but never in conventional clapboard. Wright instead designed many patterns of wide and narrow boarding to wrap around the base of his buildings.

Even Wright's windows effloresce. The leaded panes in many of his houses resemble conventionalized trees. Wright designed new patterns for each house, some recalling specific motifs from nature, others being more abstract. From the inside of a house this patterned glass acts as an intermediate screen of nature through which to observe the landscape beyond. Because the window is made of many pieces that are all slightly out of plane, from the outside the glass picks up the sunlight in an uneven pattern that creates the effect of a faceted surface. Wright also included in his windows pieces of Favrile glass that when struck by sunlight glisten with rich and constantly changing colors.

Such effects could also be created by manipulating forms and elements that were familiar from the history of architecture. Efflorescence through classical, if not specifically Greek, architecture is evident in Wright's buildings at several levels. In his mature work he always used a trabeated, post-and-beam structure. He created windows by juxtaposing strong structural mullions with horizontal lintels. This device gave to sections of Wright's houses a columnar rhythm that he did not copy from any specific building of the past but that certainly was an adaptation of a classical theme.[138]

The three-part, classically derived organization that informed the overall building also found its way into many parts. The garden walls of Wright's houses are usually variations on a theme of stylobate, shaft, and capital coping, and the same organization is evident in the design of many of his columns. Sometimes Wright's columns are unarticulated, but often they are free adaptations of geometrical Doric or florid Corinthian orders. Wright designed variations on these general themes to suit each building. Occasionally they figure prominently in the overall design; elsewhere they are less obtrusive. Wright supported the roof of the loggia of the Frank

*124. Frank Lloyd Wright, A page from* The House Beautiful, *1897. The combination of curves from nature and geometrical grids not only was the basis of much that Wright designed but was also a metaphor for a state of familial togetherness that he desired but could not always achieve.*

Thomas House in Oak Park, for example, with a sequence of wood columns, some freestanding, others abutting walls in different configurations. To embellish these columns, Wright not only designed a subtle decorative scheme that could be executed with simple carpentry but also modified it logically to suit each columnar condition. Although they play only a minor role in the overall design, these columns add the tiny bit of efflorescence that is necessary to relieve the stark wall below.

*125. Frank Lloyd Wright: The Frank Thomas House, Oak Park, 1901. This corner demonstrates Wright's grammar at two scales. The overall structure is divided up into distinct layers; the posts that define the "frieze" level and hold up the "pediment" are similarly organized.*

A few of Wright's houses had a decorative frieze of human figures that directly recalled Greek precedents, but at this level of detail he also drew upon other sources. In some of the capitals of his columns and in decorative stucco work, Mayan or pre-Columbian influences are evident.[139] Wright had an avid interest in Japanese culture; he was impressed by the Japanese building at the Chicago world's fair in 1893 and traveled to Japan in 1905. The impact of these contacts was evident in Wright's reverence for nature, in the way he drew, and in the rectilinear patterns of timber that articulated the stucco surfaces of some of his houses.[140] Even motifs from English domestic architecture came into play in Wright's buildings, as the use of diamond-paned windows in the Isabel Roberts House suggests.[141]

One reason Wright could be so inventive with materials was that he did not have sentimental ideas about craftsmanship. Many followers of John Ruskin and William Morris shared an antipathy toward the machine and were adamant about the moral necessity of maintaining handicraft traditions. In "The Art and Craft of the Machine," a speech he gave in 1901 at Hull-House in Chicago, Wright acknowledged a debt to Ruskin and Morris, but he also indicated that it was then neither possible nor desirable to deny the machine. "In the Machine," he declared, lay the "only future of art and craft." The machine was capable of "carrying to fruition high ideals in art — higher than the world has yet seen."

If Wright was not sentimental about the handicraft way of building, neither did he express his faith in the machine by making the forms of his buildings machinelike, as European architects later did. Nor did he think that the machine when applied to houses necessarily meant systems of mass assembly or prefabrication. Instead, Wright simply learned what machines could do and used them to help execute the overall intention of his architecture.[142]

These views helped to set Wright apart from other architects. His buildings not only were rooted deep in the past — where history merged with nature — but also utilized and were an expression of the full capacities of a modern society. When he wrote the first "In the Cause of Architecture" article in 1908, Wright was justifiably proud of his achievement. He looked forward to a time in the not too distant future when other architects would forgo the "Frenchite" traditions and would design buildings commensurate with their abilities. Just as he had emerged from the influence of Louis Sullivan to establish his own architecture, he expected that the apprentices who worked for him would make their own mark.

By 1914, however, Wright no longer was optimistic. In the second "In the Cause of Architecture" article, he directed his criticism not against the retrogressive architects of the East Coast, but against former employees, who, instead of formulating their own language, had made a "movement" of the so-called Midwest architecture and had, in effect, turned Wright's forms into yet another style. In a few years "a promising garden" had become "rapidly overgrown with weeds."

Wright no longer believed that architecture's downward course, which started when "the Men of Florence patched together fragments of the art of Greece and Rome and in vain endeavour to re-establish its eminence manufactured the Renaissance," was about to be interrupted. His contemporaries had forsaken the ideal of the "heavenly Goddess of Antiquity" and had accepted as a standard "the thrifty cow of the present day." The society was as much to blame as the architect. Whereas in 1908 Wright still believed that democracy had created a state in which "the average of human intelligence rises steadily," in 1914 he complained that to the man in the street democracy was no more than the gospel of mediocrity.

*126. Frank Lloyd Wright, Browne's Bookstore, Chicago, 1908. The fact that "the heavenly goddess of antiquity" was set against the phrase "a life-long friend" was not accidental. Wright was an avid photographer and would have been very careful about how his buildings were represented.*

Everybody was out for success; principles and ideals mattered only if they did not stand in the way.[143]

Wright undoubtedly was disillusioned by the intolerant reaction to his domestic affairs, and many of his former employees probably did capitalize on his reputation.[144] But Wright's bitterness was not engendered entirely by external forces. Having worked in one vein for twenty years, he may have felt, especially after returning from Europe, that he had exhausted the possibilities of his architecture and that he did not know how to revitalize it. Wright did not remain in this state for long. The tragic events at Taliesin a few months after the second "In the Cause of Architecture" article was published forced him to reassess his life and work. He then began to look even deeper into nature and history, and he embarked on the second phase of his career.

If after August 1914 the future was uncertain for Wright, there was nothing equivocal about the record of the past. From the time he had left Louis Sullivan's office, he had produced a body of work that included houses which not only summarized and epitomized a century of American thought about the home but which were, and still remain, the most outstanding contribution to domestic architecture since Palladio built his villas in the Veneto at the end of the sixteenth century.

# 5

# HOUSE PLANS FOR EVERYBODY

IN FRANK LLOYD WRIGHT'S HOUSES the interior space was just as important as the external forms. In a truly organic architecture, the two were inseparable. Wright's appreciation of the significance of the interior was enhanced by his knowledge that the house's inhabitants, both young and old, received profound impressions from their surroundings. He thought of his own house, which was built in Oak Park in 1889, as a source of inspiration both for himself as an architect and for his family. Wright often changed and added to his house and thus used it to test ideas for the buildings he was designing. The alterations also served to accommodate his growing family, but Wright did not think of his children's needs only in terms of more space; his aim was always to create a beautiful home for their proper upbringing.[1]

The rooms in Wright's houses did not have definite boundaries but instead often seemed to merge into each other. Wright developed his own way to achieve this quality of interior space, but the general effect had long been present in American homes. It was precisely what disturbed Henry James about American domestic architecture. When he returned to the United States in 1905 from his long exile in Europe, he noticed a "diffused vagueness of separation between apartments, between hall and room, between one room and another, between the one you are in and the one you are not in, between the place of passage and place of privacy." James went on:

Thus we see systematized the indefinite extension of all spaces and the definite merging of all functions; the enlargement of every opening, the exaggeration of every passage, the substitution of gaping arches and far perspectives and resounding voids for enclosing walls, for practicable doors, for controllable windows, for all the rest of the essence of the room-character, that room-suggestion which is so indispensable not only to occupation and concentration, but to conversation itself, to the play of the social relation at any other pitch than the pitch of a shriek or a shout.

James reminded his readers that it took "an endless amount of history to make even a little tradition, and an endless amount of tradition to make even a little taste, and an endless amount of taste, by the same token, to make even a little tranquillity." Until Americans developed a sense of history, they would never have tranquillity. They would continue to be beguiled by the superficial, and their houses would remain a "combination of the hall of echoes and the toy 'transparency' held against the light."[2]

Having decided to live permanently in Europe, James could see aspects of American life that those who lived in the houses he visited may have missed. But because of his perspective, James did not have the advantage of familiarity, and there was much that he did not understand. The nature

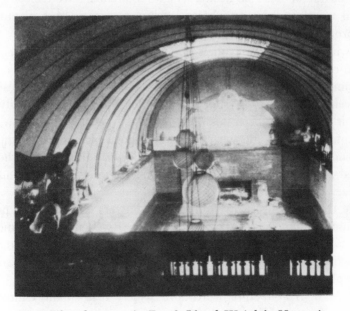

*127. The playroom in Frank Lloyd Wright's House in Oak Park, 1895. Wright's family often played music together in this room. Wright played the piano, which was located on the balcony in the foreground. "The heavenly goddess of antiquity" presided over the activities below.*

of the spaces in the American homes was more complex than James perceived. The open and seemingly indeterminate spaces that he abhorred were the ones that Americans identified with tradition. On the other hand those finite rooms that James admired represented progress to Americans. The problem, as they saw it, was not how to make one dominate the other but instead how to combine the best of the two.

✦✦✦

Architects who designed with the classical language usually used symmetry and strong axes to organize their plans, but once they began to put a high priority on the relationship of a house to character, they had to invent different ordering principles. Andrew Jackson Downing was one of the first architects to state that the plan of a house should reflect the tastes and characters of the inhabitants, and in his books he often showed how a plan had been shaped to accommodate the needs of a particular person. Requirements often conflicted and, no matter how flexible it was, architectural space usually could not take into account every character trait. To decide which requirements were most important and to translate them into space, architects had to have planning rules and procedures.

Downing was never explicit about what these rules were and what, therefore, separated good plans from bad. He used phrases like "ample accommodation," "a fine suite of rooms," "advantageously placed," or "agreeable size and proportion." By reading his books and analyzing his plans, it might have been possible to obtain a general impression of what these phrases meant and what constituted good planning. But impressions were not principles, and without rules it was difficult for those who wanted to use Downing as a source to know how to put his ideas into practice.[3]

Like Downing, his many immediate followers illustrated the principles of house planning only by citing examples of well-arranged homes. After the Civil War, architects often discussed the need to fill this void. Many of them consulted two English works that were virtually textbooks of house planning. Robert Kerr's *The Gentleman's House* and J. J. Stevenson's *House Architecture* were both widely read in the United States, and plans for parts, if not entire floors, of many American houses designed after the 1860s were taken from these two volumes. The authors of both books analyzed each space of the house and tried to define the best use and treatment of that area. They then indicated how to orient rooms to take advantage of the site and how to combine groups of rooms. These guidelines supplied at least the basis of a good house plan.[4]

American architects continued to take English advice on house planning, but they also wrote their own books.[5] *Notes on the Art of House Planning*, published in 1888 by Charles Francis Osborne, a professor at Cornell, was slimmer than the works of Kerr and Stevenson but in some ways more advanced. Osborne was interested in "principles"; to proceed systematically, he began with a definition. Planning was "the art of so shaping and disposing the various divisions of a building that it shall best serve the uses of the occupants for whom it is designed." To satisfy this definition, it was first necessary to know what these uses were. But since all requirements could never be completely met, planning then involved "weighing the claims of various *conflicting* interests" and skillfully adjusting and arranging rooms "to produce for all concerned the best average results."

Osborne called for a "science of domology," a study of the "ethnological and political history" of the builders and users of houses. Without such a study architects would not have the basic background for properly planning a house. The kind of study that Osborne had in mind was the first volume of Stevenson's *House Architecture*, an extended interpretation of the evolution of the house throughout history. This work was only one of the many on the same subject that appeared in the second half of the nineteenth century. The best-known was Viollet-le-Duc's *The Habitation of Man in All Ages*, which was published in translation in the United States in 1876. But Osborne's reference to ethnology and his call for a science of domology indicated that he also knew about native works on the early history of houses. In 1885 Lewis Henry Morgan had written *Houses and Home Life of the American Aborigine*, which departed from other works on Indian culture by trying to correlate the plan and arrangement of houses and the kinship patterns and customs of the occupants. Osborne implied that it might be possible to make a similar correlation between contemporary mores and houses.

Unfortunately, he did not pursue this matter. In *Notes on the Art of House Planning* he was primarily concerned with houses for special clients, not Americans in general. He felt it was enough for an architect to try to understand his clients' "special wants and natures." Osborne gave no guidance about how to do so, except to advise that the architect might have to "stand for the time being in the relation of father confessor to his clients." No matter how the architect obtained the appropriate

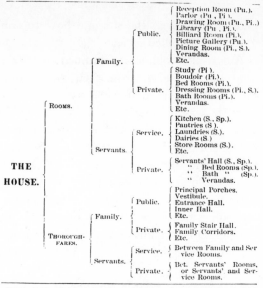

| | | | | Reception Room (Pu.). |
|---|---|---|---|---|

THE
HOUSE.

Rooms.
- Family.
  - Public.
    - Reception Room (Pu.).
    - Parlor (Pu , Pi ).
    - Drawing Room (Pu., Pi..)
    - Library (Pu , Pi ).
    - Billiard Room (Pi.).
    - Picture Gallery (Pu.).
    - Dining Room (Pi., S.).
    - Verandas.
    - Etc.
  - Private.
    - Study (Pi ).
    - Boudoir (Pi.).
    - Bed Rooms (Pi.).
    - Dressing Rooms (Pi., S.).
    - Bath Rooms (Pi.).
    - Verandas.
    - Etc.
- Servants.
  - Service.
    - Kitchen (S., Sp.).
    - Pantries (S ).
    - Laundries (S.).
    - Dairies (S )
    - Store Rooms (S.).
    - Etc.
  - Private.
    - Servants' Hall (S., Sp.).
    - " Bed Rooms (Sp.).
    - " Bath " (Sp.).
    - " Verandas.

Thorough-fares.
- Family.
  - Public.
    - Principal Porches.
    - Vestibule.
    - Entrance Hall.
    - Inner Hall.
    - Etc.
  - Private.
    - Family Stair Hall.
    - Family Corridors.
    - Etc.
- Servants.
  - Service.
    - Between Family and Service Rooms.
  - Private.
    - Bet. Servants' Rooms, or Servants' and Service Rooms.

*128. Charles F. Osborne: "Analysis of the House Plan," 1888. This classification system indicates how complex the spaces in the home had become by the end of the nineteenth century.*

NOTE.—Letters in brackets indicate the proper thoroughfares upon which the room should be found ; where two thoroughfares are indicated the room may or should be upon both ; Pu., public family ; Pi., private family ; S., service ; Sp , servants' private thoroughfares.

information or substance for house planning, Osborne still believed that making a proper plan could be an "exact science," and in *Notes on the Art of House Planning* he set forth rules and procedures to be used to shape the information.

To clarify the nature and relation of spaces in a house, Osborne invented a system of diagrams. One was a hierarchical chart that arranged the spaces of a house, first into distinct branches of rooms and circulation and then, within these primary categories, into public and private zones. Another diagram charted the movement of different types of people from space to space and thus located the points of circulation conflict in a home. A third type of plan showed the relationship of furniture, closets, doors, windows, and fireplaces within a room. Through these diagrams the architect could clarify the internal functioning of the house and organize the information that, as domologist or father confessor, he had elicited from his client. The diagrams would help him sort out his information and tell him where the critical points of conflict were. In the process a good house plan would emerge.[6]

As informative as his diagrams were, Osborne never showed how they could be used to interpret the needs of a real person or family or how a building could emerge from their application. That was precisely the task that Eugene C. Gardner often set himself when he wrote about

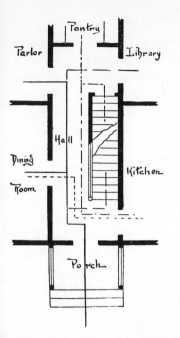

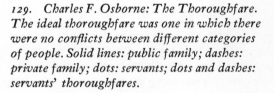

129. *Charles F. Osborne: The Thoroughfare.
The ideal thoroughfare was one in which there
were no conflicts between different categories
of people. Solid lines: public family; dashes:
private family; dots: servants; dots and dashes:
servants' thoroughfares.*

houses. Gardner's work is notable not only because it illustrates in depth
how one architect dealt with house planning, but also because it illuminates
some aspects of this subject that were general to American domestic
architecture.

Gardner spent most of his life in Massachusetts, where until his death
in 1915 he conducted an active architectural practice. Although illustrations and descriptions of Gardner's buildings were frequently published,
he achieved more than a local reputation through his writings about
domestic architecture. Gardner's appeal lay not only in his commonsense
advice about how to plan, construct, and decorate homes but also in his
folksy writing style, which he probably learned from his friend the author
Donald G. Mitchell.[7]

Gardner touched on many topics in his works on domestic architecture,
but he firmly believed that the design of a house had to spring from
utility. In *Homes and How to Make Them* Gardner advised a prospective
client: "Whatever building is nobly and enduringly useful, thoroughly
adapted to its uses, cannot be uncomely." Gardner thus began the design
process by analyzing the functions of a building and then by formulating
a plan, a diagram that he specifically shaped to indicate how those
functions were disposed and related.[8]

Gardner's ideas about house planning were related to those of the phrenologist Orson Squire Fowler, who believed that "men's habitations [should] correspond with their characteristics." Just as the depth of a person's character was revealed in the number of phrenological categories he fulfilled, so also it was reflected in the number of rooms in his house. Since Fowler thought that each household activity should be confined to its own space, the octagonal house with its subdivisions resembled the phrenological chart, a diagram of the human head where the faculties were located in closely packed compartments. Although Fowler acknowledged that the size of a house depended on the resources available, he urged his readers always to anticipate better days and to build houses that were slightly larger than they could afford. Their efforts to attain and maintain that house would be an exercise in self-improvement. Fowler followed his own argument; his octagon was four stories high and had thirty-one rooms.[9]

Fowler's peculiar logic did not prevent him from influencing the way Americans thought about houses. By the middle of the nineteenth century they were accustomed to examining house plans to find out more than the size and location of rooms. Evidence of the impact of these ideas is found in much of what Eugene C. Gardner wrote about domestic architecture. In *The House that Jill Built, after Jack's Had Proved a Failure*, for example, Gardner drew an "architectural phrenology" of roofs, showing how different profiles of roofs conformed to the characters of different people as represented by their hats.[10]

If character was revealed in the appearance of buildings, it was also evident in house plans. Gardner's most explicit use of this connection was in *Illustrated Homes*, a series of essays that described, as the book's subtitle indicated, *Real Homes and Real People*. Each essay contained a conversation with a person who was identified by his occupation or profession. Gardner used the facts that emerged from the portrait as the substance for a house plan illustrated at the end of the essay.[11]

In other books and articles Gardner approached the subject more directly. He asked his fictional client first to define the desired rooms, then he estimated the size of the rooms by finding out what furniture each space would contain, and finally he proposed a suitable arrangement for this "bill of particulars." Gardner followed this method in a series of articles in *Good Housekeeping*. He began by describing the family of a prosperous businessman in a medium-sized town. The housewife, the person primarily responsible for dealing with the architect and seeing that the family obtained a suitable dwelling, started her list of spaces with a sitting room that had to be central and sunny. She also wanted another room of similar character for special occasions. This space was to serve as a library, but it was also supposed to be where young people, as they grew older, could entertain company with some privacy. A separate dining room was necessary because, as Gardner reasoned, although eating ordinarily occupied only a small part of each day, the machinery of housekeeping ran far more smoothly when the table and its complicated accessories were set apart from other uses. An entrance hall was also indispensable to a home, and so were a kitchen, a dining-room pantry, a kitchen pantry, and a general storeroom. In addition, the housewife wanted a small conservatory and a toilet room. On the second floor there had to be four sleeping rooms, a sewing room, a bathroom and at least one closet for each bedroom. In the attic Gardner's client required at least one or two finished rooms for servants or emergencies, and the basement had to have space for a laundry.

The next step was to determine the size of each room. Gardner helped the housewife in this task by making her think about furniture. After some deliberation the housewife decided that the sitting room had to be large enough to hold an upright piano, a lounge, a table in the center with chairs around it, and one or two easy chairs. Fifteen feet was the minimum width that would give space convenient enough to move around in when occupied by several, if not all, members of the family, not to mention neighbors and relatives. To accommodate the piano, however, Gardner calculated that the room had to be at least 20 feet wide. He made similar estimates for the other rooms. The library, which included a bookcase and window seat, had to be 15 feet wide. The dining room had to be larger than most people would have estimated. Gardner reckoned that a small dining room meant "narrow hospitality," and that a generous room cost little more than a small one, except for heating in cold weather. Even so, it was much easier to keep warm in a large room than to keep cool in one that was small and crowded. Heating could be dealt with easily, but there was no cure for too much warmth at the table "except total abstinence from food and drink and speedy withdrawal."

Once he defined the qualities and requirements of the kitchen, bedrooms, entrance halls, and other rooms, Gardner had the makings of a typical home for a prosperous American family. His task then was to arrange the elements in a coherent building. This work was the special province of the architect. Gardner often discussed how he proceeded in vague and mysterious terms and made this level of house planning seem like a secret and inscrutable act. Gardner had a system, however, one which can easily be extracted from his plans.[12]

Gardner's method was first to zone rooms according to level. He often expressed a preference for low, single-story houses. He could not guarantee that it would cost no more to build a house with rooms all on one level than one with rooms piled up on two or three, but he thought a family that spread itself out would be better off than one in a compact house because an "ample hospitality emanates unceasingly from the wide, low, genial roofs that are never built by men of narrow soul." However, Gardner rarely designed houses on one level. Convention was too strong, so he used steep, pitched roofs to make his houses appear as low as possible.

His houses usually had three floors. The public rooms — the living room, kitchen, dining room, library, and children's room — were on the first floor, except sometimes in houses on a sloping site. In that case it was possible to enter the house on one level and to have the kitchen and dining room on a lower level, especially if the view was pleasant. The second floor was the domain of the bedrooms, and the third floor was for an attic. The area under the high roofs of old houses had a "wonderful fascination" for Gardner. "The rain upon the shingles, the mingled fragrance of seeds and drying herbs, the surprising bigness of the chimney, the mysteries hidden in the worm-eaten chests, the almost saintly charm of the long-unused spinning wheels, crumbling mementoes of the patient industry of former generations, or the shine of the stars through the chinks in the shrunken boards" all made the old garret a vital part of what a home was really all about. Despite his belief in "modern conveniences" and everything that went with them, Gardner doubted that there was any contemporary equivalent to "this happiest of playrooms, this storehouse of heirlooms, this silent but potent tie, that binds us to the life, the labor, and the love of the past."[13]

Having determined these three levels of zoning, Gardner began by organizing the first floor. In *Illustrated Homes* the most revealing example of how he accomplished this task appeared in an essay entitled "The Poet's Abiding Place." Like the other chapters of the book, this sketch contained a conversation between the architect and his client. The poet had recently bought a farm and was full of theories about what a house should be. He started with the idea that a house's plan should be round, but for practical reasons he rejected both that shape and Fowler's octagon and instead settled upon a square. The reason he wanted this shape was

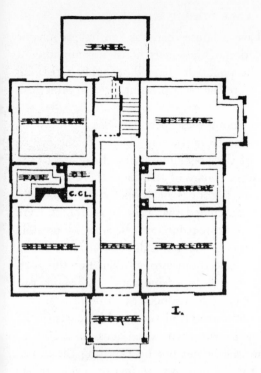

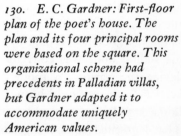

130. *E. C. Gardner: First-floor plan of the poet's house. The plan and its four principal rooms were based on the square. This organizational scheme had precedents in Palladian villas, but Gardner adapted it to accommodate uniquely American values.*

*131. E. C. Gardner: "The Poet's Abiding Place," front elevation. The house was as high as it was broad and deep.*

that he felt it was his duty to have a house that was "an irreproachable model." The economy and perfection of the square house was tantamount to a plan for reform, because the poet felt that "thoroughly satisfying houses for the common people" were the most pressing need in American society.

Gardner at first was skeptical about these peculiar ideas, but as the poet's philanthropic motives became clear, the two began to see eye to eye. Not only the overall shape of the poet's house but also that of each room was a square. To fill the larger square of the house there had to be either one, four, or nine rooms on a floor. One room was not enough; nine was too many. So the poet concluded that four equal rooms were most suitable and economical for human habitation. Because of possible furniture arrangements, 13 feet was the minimum dimension for a room. Wide doors could be used to open one room into another. For the poet, the sliding door was convenient as well as "democratic." Through this device the parlor, "a room dear to the instincts of American house-keepers," was not only brought within reach of the humbler parts of the home but also was placed "on a level with them when occasion requires." That happened not by degrading the higher but by elevating the lower.

The house Gardner designed for the poet was 36 feet on a side. It had a dining room, kitchen, sitting room, and parlor in the four corners. These four rooms were separated by a cruciform servicing area. A hall ran down the center of the house from an external porch to a stair between the kitchen and the sitting room. Between the kitchen and the dining room there were a pantry, fireplace, and coat closet. The sitting room was separated from the parlor by a small library. Generous sliding doors opened up the sitting room, library, and parlor into one area. Both the dining room and the parlor opened to the hall. The plan of the second floor followed a similar pattern. There were four bedrooms in the corners; the hall was over the corresponding space below, and between the rooms on left and right were closets, chimney flues, a bathroom, and a staircase to the attic.

In designing this house based on squares, Gardner did not arbitrarily place the building on its site. Every main room received generous sunlight, and the areas between rooms had exposures suitable to their uses. The entrance hall faced south, the library east, the stairway north, and the pantry west. The only exceptions to the square plan were a bay window in the sitting room, a two-story porch, and an unfinished room for fuel, empty barrels, and tools.

The poet's house was not only a square but also a cube, since the pyramidal roof culminated in a point 36 feet above the ground. At the end of the essay Gardner concluded that "mathematical" houses had been vindicated. They had many advantages. The rooms of the square plan were separate, but, except for the kitchen and pantry, they could all join together. The square plan made structural sense and also permitted a uniformity of detailing that was cheap and pleasing. Partitions on the second floor fell with no difficulty directly over those on the first.

Most of the houses in *Illustrated Homes* were variants of this square planning. Gardner distorted the dimensions of the square to suit particular requirements, but the basic square relationship was still evident in the final plan. In addition to the rooms of a normal home, a professor, for instance, needed a substantial library to house his books and to serve as a sitting room. This professor also wanted a nursery or children's room, but not in the attic or the basement. A further requirement was that the children's bedrooms communicate with both the hall and the parents' room. The resulting plan was square, although not as distinctly so as the house for the poet. To accentuate its importance, the library had a large bay window and a fireplace at the end. A hall bisected the plan and a staircase and closets divided the four rooms in the other direction. Because the family needed four main rooms — dining, children's, parlor, and library — on the first floor, the kitchen and pantry areas were appended to the back of the house with servants' quarters above.

Gardner used the same principles for a southern planter's house. For shade and protection from the climate the structure needed "piazzas *ad infinitum*." The architect placed the building on a pedestal, six feet off the ground. There was a two-story-high piazza on four sides. On the first floor a hall ran from east to west through the building, and "modern conveniences" occupied the corresponding spaces on the other axis. The four corner rooms were a bedroom, dining room, family room, and parlor. The kitchen, as was customary in the South, was separate from the house. On the second floor two bedrooms were located under a sloping double roof, well insulated to protect the inhabitants from a blistering sun.

The square pattern was also suitable for modest homes. In *Illustrated Homes* Gardner included plans for workers' cottages to be built in a village in the Berkshires by King Kole. In undertaking this project this "landowner and practical philanthropist" announced: "On the building-lots of which I hold the deeds, homes for the multitude shall rise, better and cheaper than any ever built before." His reason was that the workers

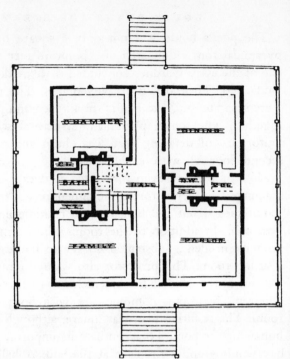

*132. E. C. Gardner: "The Planter's First Floor." Like that of the poet's house, this plan was based on the square but adapted to a warm climate.*

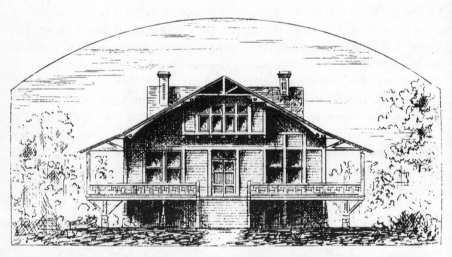

*133. E. C. Gardner: "The Planter's House," front elevation. Gardner always tried to make the appearance of his houses seem a logical result of the way they were structured and built.*

were the foundation of society: "Raise the foundation, and the super-structure rises safe and sound. Attempt to lift it by the roof, and it crashes into ruin. The marble palace of the merchant prince is less a blessing to humanity than a simple cottage that shows by its own economy and loveliness how sweet a home is possible for every honest man." Gardner and King Kole selected a sloping site to give shape to these senti-ments. Instead of leveling the land, they decided to follow the direction of the fall. The houses were based on a square plan but a more compact one than that used for substantial residences. The land fell from east to west, so on the first floor Gardner planned a kitchen and dining room, looking down the hill, and stairs and storage in the back. The second main floor had a sitting room, parlor, bedroom, and porch and staircase in the four corners. The third floor had three bedrooms with the staircase and a large storage area occupying the other corner.[14]

Eugene C. Gardner was able to manipulate the square to accommodate a wide variety of requirements, but the square had its limits. It was not suited to larger houses. Although some clients required more than four rooms on a floor, few needed as many as nine, so Gardner had to find systems to plan houses of an intermediate size. Other architects used dif-ferent organizing techniques. Instead of the square, many preferred less deterministic geometries. They based their plans on symmetry or on a theme of repetitive modules that usually was related to structural bays or window openings. In reaction to these principles, still other architects avoided geometry as much as possible so that their plans could be what they considered a more accurate reflection of the needs of the inhabitants. Such plans also tended to result in irregular exteriors, an effect that archi-tects often wanted to cultivate.[15]

Although planning methods and clients' needs varied, the spaces of the houses designed for the type of person that Gardner served — a broad clientele ranging from those who had just enough money to contemplate owning a home to those who were comfortably well off — invariably had common characteristics. An analysis of these qualities is tantamount to the domology of American homes that Charles F. Osborne mentioned but never formulated.

The spaces of American houses constructed in the second half of the nineteenth century were usually characterized by three levels of am-biguity. One paradox of Gardner's houses and of the period's residences in general concerned the identity of rooms. Like other architects of the period, Gardner was more careful than his predecessors to give precise names to each of the rooms of his houses and to shape each space to accommodate the use for which it was intended. But he also recognized that rooms had to be the context for other, often contradictory uses. The library, a place for the husband's solitude and concentration, sometimes served as a room for entertainment or for children's play. The living or sitting room, ostensibly a formal area in which guests could be received, might also be used for intimate family activities. The identity of bedrooms was similarly ambiguous. Primarily for sleeping and dressing, a bedroom could also serve as a study and playroom for the children or a sewing room for the housewife. This equivocation about the true uses of spaces had an effect on the size of rooms in American houses. Architects like Gardner established dimensions of particular areas to contain the furniture that set the context for the intended activities, but since the rooms had to serve other, sometimes undefined purposes, architects tended to make them larger than perhaps they needed to be. Visitors from Europe, especially from England, frequently noted how large American rooms were.

A second level of ambiguity in American houses was evident in attempts to separate one room, and the functions for which it supposedly acted as a framework, from another. On the one hand spaces were parceled out more than ever before into designated rooms. Elaborate networks of corridors, hallways, staircases, and service rooms ensured that it was possible

*134. E. C. Gardner: "Where Shall the Pictures Be?" — doors in the home. This drawing illustrates a degree of enclosure that Americans found repugnant.*

to go from one part of the house to another without invading intervening rooms. On the other hand the same houses were usually planned to achieve the opposite result. By opening sliding doors, removing screens, or pushing back portieres, most of the rooms, especially those on the first floor, could be thrown together to become one interconnected space.

Gardner was emphatic about the need for opening up a house. He criticized the multiplicity of doors that often monopolized a room. Doors were inconvenient because they took up too much space and crowded the placement of furniture. They also often were discordant elements in an otherwise fine interior of paintings and wall decorations. But most of all Gardner did not like doors because they were antisocial. It was impossible for two people to enter a room together through a door, and, as the poet observed, a wider opening equalized the importance of different rooms.

Gardner suggested several alternatives. The spaces of the poet's home were linked by sliding doors, but elsewhere Gardner criticized this device. He thought there was something "barny" about sliding doors but mounted more substantial objections as well. It was hard to coordinate the walls of a room with them. Three surfaces might be handsomely decorated, but the fourth was "one huge barricade of panel-work." There was also something unsubtle about the way sliding doors opened. There was an "ever present fear" that the doors would suddenly fly open with an "impetuous recoil." Usually, however, the sliding doors could be moved only with much pushing and pulling, especially when they had become warped, as was often the case because of different levels of heating on the two sides.

Heavy curtains were better than sliding doors. Although they were usually kept open, curtains retained as much heat in the room as other space dividers. They could be drawn back gracefully, and they could fit within the pattern of the room's decoration. In discussing how to enter a room, Gardner wondered what woman could "walk like a goddess while forcing an entrance between two siding-doors maybe wedging fast halfway through?" How different it was to pass "in great dignity beneath the rich folds of overhanging drapery." A screen was also convenient for separating space, either within or between rooms. This simple device was pleasant to look at, it was easy to walk past, and it provided the proper degree of visual privacy.[16]

In many American houses not only were distinctions between supposedly separate rooms ignored, but the line between rooms and circu-

*135. A spindle transom and portiere, 1888. These were two of the many devices that were used to create a balance between the separateness of and connection between rooms.*

*136. H. Hudson Holly: Staircase hall, 1878. In such houses the hall was more than a space that gave access to adjacent rooms. Here the large windows lit the hall as well as the staircase landing.*

FIFTEEN GOOD HALLS AND STAIRWAYS

Selected from Photographs Taken in All Parts of the Country

A pretty hallway in Wilkesbarre, Pennsylvania. The fine coloring, unfortunately, cannot be reproduced.

An old pictorial wall paper has here been retained to preserve the character of this hall in Portsmouth, New Hampshire.

A cozy nook and fireplace in this hallway in Chestnut Hill, Brookline, Massachusetts, have been ingeniously contrived.

The arrangement of this hall in Hartford, Connecticut, as well as the newel posts and stair rail, is worth noticing.

A pretty door and window, with well-designed glass, are found in this hallway in Wellesley Hills, Massachusetts.

One of the few examples of a double staircase, to be found in a New England house. The scheme is most effective.

A pretty and ingenious arrangement of a staircase, with some excellent furniture, is found in this hall.

A spacious apartment, designed as both living-room and hall, is seen in this summer home in Kennebunkport, Maine.

A combination living-room and hallway in Glen Cove, Long Island, with white woodwork and mahogany furniture.

A hall in Boston, Massachusetts, with excellent wall covering and paneling. The furnishing is in good taste.

This hall in a Providence, Rhode Island, house has been divided by an arch without encroaching upon the floor space.

A leather-upholstered hall settle and screen in a hallway in Danvers, Massachusetts. The leaded glass is effective.

A simple front door, with fanlight above, has been made for this Colonial hall. The entire scheme is consistent.

An inexpensively finished hall in Kennebunkport, Maine. The red brick fireplace is exceptionally good.

This spacious stairway is found at St. David's Station, Pennsylvania. The rugs make the interior warm and cozy.

137.  "Fifteen Good Halls and Stairways," 1899. The halls of American houses were invariably shaped to be open and welcoming, no matter in what style they were designed.

*138. E. C. Gardner: Views outside. No house of the period had a window as large as the one in this illustration. But this exaggeration expressed an intention that was realized in other ways.*

"LOOK OUT, NOT IN."

lation spaces was also often blurred. It was common for the hallways, staircases, and corridors to occupy more space than their immediate functions demanded. Stairways often had bay windows and built-in seats on half landings; halls, especially on the ground floor, were fitted with furniture around a fireplace, a scene that was not in accord with the transitional nature of the space. Halls thus furnished were by no means humble parts of the house; wide entranceways from them to a living room, dining room, or library further established the equality of all spaces.[17]

The separation between the inside and outside of American houses was often as tenuous as the function of rooms and the demarcation of separate spaces. Architects and home owners had many ways of joining the inside and outside to create this third level of ambiguity. They adorned the interior of the house with plants and made special floral arrangements in front of windows that sometimes had colored panes to recall the foliage outside. Flower-patterned wallpaper and carpets also added to the impression of a garden within the home.[18]

One effective way to bring the outdoors inside was to pay special attention to the shape and position of windows. Gardner was typical of a group of architects who in the years right after the Civil War began to put a high priority on the orientation of their houses to sunlight. They did so in part because they connected sunlight to health, but they also felt that sunshine in a room was aesthetically pleasing. Gardner therefore always tried to arrange his rooms so that they would face the sun when they were most used.[19]

Bay windows let light into rooms from several directions, but Gardner did not like the way they jutted out from the house. He preferred to extend the whole wall of the room in the form of a half hexagon or three sides of an octagon. Even better was a simple, large window that in country and suburban houses acted as a picture frame for the landscape.

Gardner placed these windows where they would most likely afford views from within a room. But the views through the house, from one room to another and then out into the landscape, were equally important. He found that when the openings from room to room were unobstructed, it was possible to feel oneself in the midst of "an all-surrounding beauty," which was far superior to a view from one point only.[20]

The provision of "outdoor rooms" in American houses was the most explicit way in which a distinct demarcation between outside and inside was blurred. The custom of adding porches, piazzas, porticoes, and verandas to houses to serve as outdoor living rooms probably extended back to the early eighteenth century. By the middle of the nineteenth century this practice had become more deliberate. Architects then began to differentiate what previously had been a general covered outdoor space so that it could serve specific functions. They planned separate dining areas, either for breakfast or dinner, on the side of the house that not only was convenient to the kitchen but also had the appropriate orientation to the sun. The distinction between the outdoor living and dining areas was also made through furnishings. A wide range of comfortable native and Oriental wicker and willow furniture found its way onto American porches. Dining demanded harder, more upright chairs: white-painted, plain wooden furniture from Holland suited that purpose.[21]

The most specialized outdoor area usually was the sleeping porch.

*139. Window decoration. Through such floral arrangements it was possible to soften the distinction between inside and out.*

Vacation houses built after the Civil War often included spaces for outdoor sleeping, and by 1900 it was certainly no longer a fad for suburban houses to have areas for this purpose. Since sleeping porches were to be used year-round, not just in warm weather, they had to be equipped with special beds and bedding and had to be oriented toward the rising sun. For those who slept outdoors in cool weather, easy access from the porch to an indoor dressing room was essential.[22]

To control the penetration of the outdoors into these partially enclosed spaces, architects and home owners used a wide variety of semipermanent surfaces to fend off the sun, wind, and rain. The porches of many houses were equipped with blinds or awnings to protect against the sun; others were fitted with windows that could be removed or installed as the season demanded. The wire screen protected the porch against insects and flies. A house that used many of these devices had, in effect, a shell of transitional spaces surrounding a permanent indoor core. In most instances porches with these different coverings were added after the initial structure had been built. But when they were conceived as part of the house from the outset, these elements could be used to great architectural advantage by creating a contrast between permanent and temporary, solid and transparent forms.[23]

The ambiguous nature of domestic interiors resulted from and was an expression of the mixed feelings many Americans had about the type of life they wanted to lead in their houses. On the one hand they were attracted to a routine based on rules of etiquette and manners. They considered this life an advance or improvement over a coarser pattern of daily existence. On the other hand they wanted a simple life that they imagined had existed in the past and they regretted had been lost.

Americans who had grown up in rural areas or crowded city tenements were ill-prepared for the life of refined social rituals to which they aspired. To learn what was proper, they consulted the vast literature on the subject. The period's fiction implicitly instructed readers about the distinction between coarse and refined habits; books and magazines on etiquette offered more specific advice. They told an audience that feared it might appear socially inept how to organize a tea party, what to wear, what subjects were appropriate for polite conversation, and how to cope with dozens of other daily problems.[24]

People who were eager to understand the rules of etiquette also wanted to live in the appropriate type of house. To guide them about what was correct in domestic architecture, the etiquette literature often included

This Swing Couch Consists of a Spring Bed, to Which Chains Have Been Attached by Means of Eyes Riveted to the Iron Frame

An Awning Is Used To Afford Protection on This Open Porch. There Is Also a Canvas Curtain Which Can Be Dropped

A Regulation Iron-bed Is Used on This Porch, a Sliding Curtain Being Hung about It on a Light Wire

A Simple Arrangement of Fly Netting To Protect the Sleeper from Mosquitos Is Shown in This Picture

*140.   Outdoor sleeping rooms. There was a great variation in the degree of enclosure for sleeping porches.*

sections about how to arrange and decorate a home. Some writers discussed only obliquely what made a good house. The author of "All about the House," a column in *Good Housekeeping*, listed a set of precepts that were to be followed in each room. The reader was told that in the drawing room, for instance, "true politeness" created "perfect ease and freedom." A person who was "constrained, uneasy and ungraceful" could spoil everyone's happiness. A guest had to strive not to be embarrassed, because "embarrassment [was] so embarrassing." A hostess had to display "punctilious devotion, propriety and self-respect."[25]

It was possible to infer from this advice how to arrange and decorate a drawing room that would be appropriate for the manners and rituals implicit in these precepts. Other authors discussed more directly what made good rooms. They either described the general atmosphere that each room of the house was supposed to have or gave a detailed account, sometimes accompanied by pictures, of a praiseworthy room that the reader could use as a model. But no matter how the rooms of these descriptions differed in scope or detail, spaces that were appropriate for a period of "advance and improvement" usually had many features in common. They were shaped for specific purposes, each was clearly distinguished from the next, and there was always a definite boundary between indoors and outdoors.

A room's specificity was important because the establishment of distinctions and differentiations was considered one of the most significant characteristics of a society devoted to progress. Just as the division of labor separated the contemporary economy from its predecessor, so the identification and parceling out of specific household functions distinguished the modern from the primitive home. The most compelling justification for houses so organized was that the needs of each member of the family could best be accommodated thereby. The division of labor affected small units of society as well as large ones. In the modern family father, mother, children, and servants had distinct roles, and the spaces of the home were designed and shaped specifically to accommodate them. Even in the living and dining rooms — areas for the whole family — places were set aside for each member according to his or her importance.

Americans welcomed the possibility of living in houses that embodied the values of an advanced state of society, but only a very thin line sometimes separated those who tried to better themselves from those who turned the same impulse into social climbing and a fascination with the world of fashion. When this all-important boundary was transgressed, Americans often lamented the passing of older ways and called for the reinstatement of daily customs not dominated by formalities and manners. At the same time that some writers explained the intricacies of etiquette to an audience that wanted to leave behind the vestiges of a coarser existence, other authors showed what life had been like before it was necessary to keep up with the neighbors and to consult a book about what to do on the simplest everyday occasions.

The period these authors admired varied; it was usually far enough in the past so as not to be simply an extension of the present but not so far as to be completely beyond memory. The colonial period satisfied these criteria and was the one most often studied. Descriptions of daily life in those enviable days did not contain a systematic analysis of old houses and what went on in them. Nineteenth-century views of the past were deeply colored by a concern for the problems of the time. Thus, the spatial quality that authors found most characteristic of the old home was a lack of rigid boundaries within the house and between indoors and out. According to this interpretation, the family spent most of its indoor working hours in one room around the hearth; there was no rigid distinction between spaces for cooking, dining, and relaxation. Children were not separated from adults; guests were welcomed into the household without undue ceremony and did not have to sit in a proper but uncomfortable parlor. Since the family's livelihood depended on a close relationship with the outdoors, evidence of work on the surrounding land pervaded every space of the home.[26]

This sense of openness and the lack of boundaries between spaces was important to nineteenth-century Americans because, although they approved in principle of the quest for self-improvement and the desire to learn what was proper, they worried that these impulses fragmented human relationships, especially those that joined the family circle together. The husband who hid himself "behind the daily paper immediately on entering the house" and the mother who devoted "every spare moment to some busy occupation in household affairs or to making or receiving calls" became familiar figures in the period's literature. Unlike their counterparts in the past, these parents spent little time with their children. Preoccupied by the world of business or fashion, the modern father and

*141. Balcony and living room, 1912. A sleeping loft or a lounge on a balcony that overlooked a living room was one device used in suburban and vacation houses to minimize the boundaries between activities and thus to emulate the informal pattern of everyday life that supposedly characterized the openness of the "old home."*

mother abandoned their offspring to nurses and servants, saw their children only at prearranged times, and were so separated from them by the network of spaces in their modern houses that they often could not even hear them playing.

The forces that took the members of the family either to different parts of the house or away from the home altogether were so strong that the family had to make special and seemingly contrived efforts to achieve its ideal of togetherness. Those who wrote about this problem wanted to re-create the scene of the family grouped around the hearth, where they read from the Bible and told stories while doing small but vital household chores. But since such activities either no longer held the family's interest or were not integral to its daily routine, it was necessary to invent other pastimes. Americans who wanted to fill this void often found that the family could most effectively reestablish its unity in the evening by playing games.

In some houses a special room was set aside for this activity, but it was also important for the games to take place in the parlor, living room, or library — rooms that had specific functions and that except on prescribed occasions were out of bounds to the younger members of the family. Playing games in these spaces was an overt demonstration that the rooms were not cold and formal. After all, games were not just for fun and entertainment. They also, it was often claimed, sharpened children's verbal and mathematical skills. Thus, the central round table, which should have held the family's Bible, was used as the focus for the parlor games that Americans avidly played. If these pastimes did not hold the family's attention, the table made an excellent surface for the many board games that became popular in the period.[27]

Every American home built in the half century after the Civil War inevitably embodied in its plan both old and new values. The proportions of the mix depended in part on the generation of the residents. People who had grown up in a traditional home sometimes eagerly clutched at the opportunity to shed every vestige of that former existence and to live in a house that suggested culture and refinement. But just as often, even when they had the means to escape from a context that was shaped by the stringent pressures of economy, they felt it was important to resist these opportunities and to insist that the old home was still good enough. Members of the succeeding generation retained some of these values, but they often made it a point to live in precisely the type of house that their parents were reluctant to accept. Having grown up accustomed to these advanced surroundings, grandchildren then sometimes wanted to reinstate some aspects of their grandparents' home, a context they may have known only from early memories or from stories told by their parents.

The combination of old and new values depended as much on where the house was located as on the progression of generations. City houses on small plots usually could not be open to the outdoors, and because space was at a premium, they had to have compact rooms. But precisely because of these conditions, urban residents sometimes went out of their way to achieve the sense of openness that seemed to be denied to them. Vacation houses did not suffer from the same constraints; their siting and holiday atmosphere allowed them to have a degree of openness that was not possible in the city. Often, however, the owners of vacation houses felt the need to counteract these conditions and to assert the primacy of civilizing values in the layout of their rooms.

Climate triggered a similar pattern of complex motivations in the arrangement of domestic interiors. Houses in warm regions could be more open to the outdoors than those in places with severe winters. They also needed through ventilation, which provided a pretext for joining one room with the next. But as much as they wanted an architecture that responded to the environment, Americans also felt it was important to assert their independence of the elements, an overt statement about the distinction between higher and lower states of civilization. Many houses in the South and West thus had rooms that were all but indistinguishable from those in the most refined houses in the East. With the aid of central heating, houses in places with subzero winter temperatures could have windows that were as large as those where it was never necessary to treat the internal environment.

The location of a house within a city also influenced how its spaces were shaped. People sometimes moved to new suburban communities to be liberated from the stifling manners that characterized domestic life in the city's established areas, and they expressed this impulse in the plans of their houses. On the other hand settlers of a new community sometimes considered it their personal mission to establish a culture of refinement and manners.

What was true within a city or town was also valid at the national level. Those who moved to new states often were pleased that they did not have to put up with the stilted routines they associated with the East Coast or New England. But because they also did not want to appear uncultured, they sometimes organized their houses more rigidly than the people who supposedly represented propriety and tradition.

Since most houses were shaped by conflicting impulses, their interiors often lacked a coherence that distinguished the houses of a more settled society, and they were easy targets for critics. Some, like Henry James, claimed that awkward interiors proved Americans would have a satisfactory architecture only when they had a strong sense of history. Others drew from the same spaces a lesson about the effects of too much civilization. Still, it was not inherently impossible to make a satisfactory architecture that embodied the values of both old and new. A few skillful architects were able to manipulate the identity of rooms, the distinctions between spaces, and the separation of indoors and out to create houses that were lucid statements about the complex life they contained. These structures could have been built whenever and wherever clients were willing to accept the conflicting forces that played upon the home and architects were able to interpret them. But the best examples were designed at the turn of the century in the suburbs of Chicago. This was fitting: houses there had to be designed to cope with extremes of summer and winter; they also had to come to terms with contradictory pressures of the cultural climate. By the turn of the century many Chicagoans were sufficiently accustomed to the new values to feel the loss of the old; suburbs were located between the city and the country; and the Midwest was then positioned between the area that was first settled and the region that contained the last vestiges of the frontier.

✦✦✦

The idea that a house should reflect not the current state of its occupants but instead what they might expect to be like in the not-too-distant future was expressed in many American books on architecture written in the 1870s and 1880s. The title of Samuel B. Reed's *House-Plans for Everybody* was similar to Orson Fowler's *A Home for All*, and Fowler's basic message about the relationship of a house's plan to the character of its inhabitants was an integral part of Reed's book. "To a certain extent," Reed wrote, "one's dwelling is an index of his character. Any effort at building expresses the owner's ability, taste and purpose." Reed also believed that character was not fixed. "Every industrious man, starting in life," Reed assured his readers, "has a right, and should be encouraged, to anticipate prosperity, as the sure reward of honest worth; and he may, with propriety, give emphasis to such anticipations in every step, and with every blow struck." These "anticipations" had an important bearing on the layout and design of a house. According to Reed, it was proper to "express the progressive character, rather than the conclusive result."

Therefore, not only was the anticipated state as much a part of a person's character as the current one, but it stood to reason that the act of building and living in a "progressive" house somehow impelled the inhabitant to further achievements.[28]

A family could build a home with only a room or two, live in it for a while, and then complete the design when it could afford to do so. Some of the plans in *House-Plans for Everybody* were designed for this transformation over time. The first stage was a simple rectangular structure divided into a living room, a pantry, and a bedroom. This building provided only shelter and minimal conveniences; a fireplace in the middle of the house served for both heating and cooking. Nevertheless, a newly married couple could construct such a house in a few weeks and add to it as its needs and resources dictated. When the second stage was built, the first could be converted into the kitchen of the expanded house.[29]

In this example Reed expected that the builder would have in mind from the outset a final design and would work toward that end over a period of years. But it was not always possible to tell what would be necessary in the future, and additions often had to be made in an improvised fashion. Most houses, especially those made of wood, were easy to adapt, but an ad hoc process of addition and conversion usually left quirks in the plan. Houses built in stages often had what looked like more than one front door. Spaces that had originally served a different purpose appeared larger or smaller than they needed to be and had eccentric shapes. Some architects criticized this additive approach because it resulted in contorted plans and misshapen house forms. But others admired houses built over an extended period because they were picturesque. They traced the long building histories of old farmhouses and claimed that by continually adapting a house to new needs it would be possible to produce equally satisfying architecture.[30]

Adding onto a house was one way to express a progressive character, but there was another, more important way to do so. As its title indicated, Reed's book was intended for "everybody"; it contained plans of houses that cost from $250 to $8,000. The implication of this range of plans was that, as a person's fortune increased, he would be able to live in progressively more sumptuous houses. This idea was embodied in the plans themselves. Placed side by side, the cheapest and the most expensive seem to have little connection. But when they are seen as two ends of a series, the expensive house gradually emerges from the cheapest. Although each house was complete in itself, by widening a hall, enlarging a kitchen, or

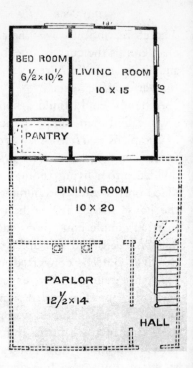

BED ROOM
6½ x 10½

LIVING ROOM
10 X 15

PANTRY

DINING ROOM
10 X 20

PARLOR
12½ x 14

HALL

*142. Samuel B. Reed: Plan of a cottage costing $250. The area within dotted lines was to be added to the basic house. The original structure would then be converted into a kitchen.*

DESIGN I.

*143. Samuel B. Reed: "A Cottage, Costing $250." To anticipate the conversion of this house into a larger one, it was necessary from the outset to build high foundations that eventually would add to "the prominence and good appearance of the building."*

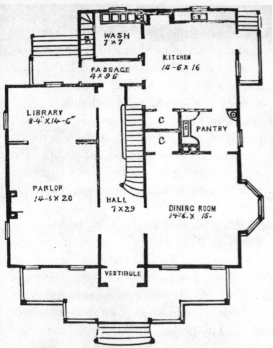

WASH
7 × 7

KITCHEN
14-6 × 16

PASSAGE
4 × 9 6

LIBRARY
8·4 × 14-6"

C

S

PANTRY

C

PARLOR
14-6 × 2.0

HALL
7 × 2.9

DINING ROOM
14-6 × 15·

VESTIBULE

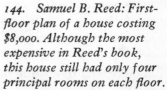

*144. Samuel B. Reed: First-floor plan of a house costing $8,000. Although the most expensive in Reed's book, this house still had only four principal rooms on each floor.*

*145. Samuel B. Reed: "A House Costing $8,000." Unlike E. C. Gardner, the architect of this house saw no need to make ornament relate to structure and construction (see illustrations 131 and 133).*

adding a bedroom, a gradual expansion of the plan occurred. Unlike the typical sequence of European house plans, which usually were progressively diminished versions of an expensive and imposing model, the plans in Reed's book, arranged in sequence from cheapest to most expensive, were progressively expanded versions of the simple, basic home.

Despite its broad range, Reed's book did not really encompass houses for "everybody." By the late 1870s, when Reed wrote, some Americans, especially those who had recently amassed huge fortunes in industry and transportation, were commissioning architects to design houses that bore no relationship to even the most expensive house in *House-Plans for Everybody*.

For several decades the Vanderbilts set the standard for lavishness in American houses. In the early 1880s William Henry Vanderbilt and two of his sons each built conspicuous houses on Fifth Avenue in New York. In the following decade members of the family commissioned even more impressive country houses in Newport, Rhode Island, and Asheville, North Carolina. These buildings were distinguished from those in which even quite well-to-do Americans lived by lavish detailing, use of expensive materials, and blatant associations with French châteaux and Renaissance palaces.

But Americans found more telling ways to rank houses. They began to describe houses by how much they cost. The phrase "a one-hundred-thousand-dollar house" had an immediate impact that other descriptive terms could not match. Size was another important index. As the range of houses seemed to widen, Americans began to attach a great significance to the number of rooms or bedrooms. The fact that George Washington Vanderbilt's Biltmore was known to have forty bedrooms probably made a deeper impression than the architecture's magisterial references to the château at Blois.[31]

Reactions to big houses varied. Some economists pointed out that the expenditure of vast sums of money on such structures gave employment to dozens of workmen.[32] But the more cogent argument in favor of houses like Biltmore was that they provided architects with the chance to design significant buildings. This point was often made, but Herbert Croly, who was the editor of *Architectural Record* from 1899 to 1906, turned it into what amounted to a theory of American culture.

When he published *The Promise of American Life* in 1909, Croly became a major figure in American political thought. His early interest in architecture, however, was not separate from the ideas of his important book. When Croly later explained the sources of inspiration for *The Promise of American Life*, he singled out *Unleavened Bread*, a novel by Robert Grant that he had read in 1900. Grant's book was about a dedicated architect, a man of genuine ability whose talents never matured because of the cutthroat ethics of the American business world. The moral that Croly drew from Grant's story was that American life was based too much on an empty individualism and that the artist suffered from the lack of a "well-domesticated tradition" that could provide a context for his creativity.[33]

This deficiency had not always existed. In the decades before the American Revolution, colonial architecture showed great promise, not because architects and builders were especially talented, but because the wealthy citizens were "people of taste, in whom the ideal of respectability was still fortunately allied with some notion of good form." These merchants and planters did not constitute a leisure class, but in setting

*146. Richard Morris Hunt: Biltmore, Asheville, North Carolina, 1892. George W. Vanderbilt's country home had 250 rooms and was located on a 146,000-acre estate.*

standards for others to emulate they achieved the same result as a European elite.

With the signing of the Declaration of Independence, a "period of reconstruction" was begun. Privileges were abolished, and the typical American became "a shrewd, good-natured, easy-mannered, hustling fellow, who could and did turn his hand to many things." The rise of the common man was politically salutary, but it had disastrous cultural consequences. The classical forms of colonial architecture were abandoned because craftsmen and architects as well as their newly rich clients were interested only in novelty.

Fortunately, from Croly's point of view, by the turn of the century this "transitional" phase was coming to a conclusion. More American architects were then being trained either at the Ecole des Beaux Arts or at schools modeled on it. These architects learned to negate individualism. In a "disinterested" way they copied the models of the past, gradually modifying them to make buildings that suited the American landscape and way of life.

Equally important, a new type of client then seemed willing to employ these architects. Men who had made fortunes from railroads or manufacturing not only were like the people who sponsored the architecture of the mid-eighteenth century, but also resembled another group of "self-made men," the princes of the Italian Renaissance. Croly characterized that period as "a rough democracy, in which any man, who had the necessary luck, brains, and will might struggle to the top and fight for the privilege of staying there." He acknowledged that W. J. Ghent had argued in *Our Benevolent Feudalism* that American millionaires were becoming a baronial caste, but Croly was not convinced. Industrial leaders did not have political ambitions. What was important was that they might sponsor a flowering of the arts and a revival of domestic architecture that would be similar in impact to that which had taken place in the Renaissance.[34]

During Croly's editorship the *Architectural Record* frequently published articles about the houses not just of American millionaires but also of a new class, the billionaires. The architects who designed these houses took the claims of critics like Croly to heart and modeled their work on French châteaux, English country houses, and Renaissance palaces. Nevertheless, these buildings rarely were as lavish or large as their precedents. There were many reasons for this discrepancy. Some people felt that it was important to make a kind of self-effacing gesture in their houses.

Those who were sensitive about being labeled nouveau riche did not go so far as to live in an ordinary home, but they learned not to flaunt their wealth. Other captains of industry, while desiring homes commensurate with their status, felt uncomfortable in lavish ones. Many of them had grown up in simple homes and never really felt at home anywhere else. They expressed their ambivalence not so much in their city houses, where it was necessary to maintain appearances, as in their country homes, which often were deliberately austere. The same fondness for the old times later led a few industrialists to finance the reconstruction of colonial towns in Williamsburg, Virginia, and Dearborn, Michigan.[35]

Another reason why *House-Plans for Everybody* did not encompass "everybody" was that as more Americans moved to large cities, fewer people could afford even Reed's simplest house. Many architects tried to devise plans for the simple cheap home, but no matter how basic it was, the single-family house needed land on which to be built, and by the late nineteenth century such lots were economically available only on the outskirts of big cities.[36] The last section of *House-Plans for Everybody* contained, almost as an appendix, plans for multiple residences. In the final

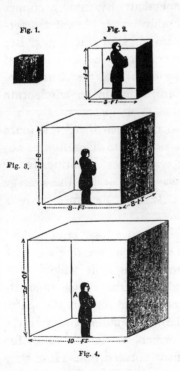

Fig. 1.    Fig. 2.

Fig. 3.

Fig. 4.

*147. Breathing space, 1865. A graphic representation of the difference between 125, 512, and 1,000 cubic feet of space per person. The box at the upper left is 14 cubic feet, the amount of air breathed in an hour. This quantity, when exhaled, supposedly "vitiated" (made noxious) an additional 100 cubic feet of air.*

article in his series in *Good Housekeeping*, Eugene Gardner explained the design of a similar building. Reed and Gardner included these structures because no matter how much they believed that the individual family should express its character in the plan of an individual house, they recognized that, if only as a temporary expedient, many people had to live in tenements and that it was important to plan these buildings properly.

Much of the effort to design suitable homes for the bulk of the American working population centered on an attempt to define the properties of a minimal housing unit within a multiple dwelling. Some housing reformers tried to address this issue by establishing a measure of overcrowding. In their investigation of the slums they often emphasized the degree of overcrowding by calculating the cubic feet of air per occupant and by comparing that figure with estimates of the minimum volume of air that a person breathed during a night of sleep. Doctors began to make these calculations before the Civil War and continued to refine their figures at least until the turn of the century.[37] In the 1880s and 1890s they often cited as a model of what they might achieve in their work the experiments about dietary standards performed by W. O. Atwater, a professor at Wesleyan University in Connecticut. By using a copper chamber especially designed for measuring bodily wastes, Atwater determined the amount of food required to maintain physical efficiency.[38] But a space standard based on the amount of air consumed in a given period was much more difficult to establish. Housing reformers, therefore, were usually forced to express the requirement for space in an unscientific term, a ratio of people to the number of rooms in an apartment. By 1915 overcrowding was generally considered to occur when there was more than an average of one and a half persons per room. This figure was adopted not because it represented what was either scientifically or ideally a minimum, but instead because it was more or less the average that had been found in tenement surveys. It was, therefore, only a convenient yardstick.[39]

A more fruitful way to establish the properties of a basic housing unit was to define the minimal sizes of its spaces and the nature of their relationship. Although a philanthropist like Gardner's King Kole could finance housing that embodied "model" or "improved" ideas about what an apartment in a multiple dwelling should be, the best way to regulate the spaces within such structures was to establish standards in building codes. In the last half of the nineteenth century many reformers continually called for the upgrading of the quality of new tenement construction. How they wrote space requirements into building codes varied from city to city.

The best summary of this work was Lawrence Veiller's *A Model Tenement House Law*. Veiller wrote this book to give reformers who were inexperienced in framing housing legislation guidelines about standards and advice about how to anticipate legal loopholes. In defining the minimum standards for tenement houses, Veiller first established requirements for lighting and ventilation. Public health officials had long tried to rid apartments of unlit and unventilated rooms. Veiller thought it was essential, therefore, that every room have a window opening directly to the outdoors, which, in the worst case, could be a court of established minimum dimensions. To ensure that there would be enough light and ventilation, he also defined the minimum size of the windows as a fraction of the area of the room.

Rooms not only had to be well lit and ventilated, they also had to be of a minimum size. To prevent the construction of small rooms, Veiller stipulated that every apartment had to have one room of not less than 150 square feet; every other room, except water closets and bathrooms, had to have at least 90 square feet. By including a special clause on alcoves, Veiller tried to stop unscrupulous builders from circumventing these requirements. Veiller also included separate dimensions for water closets and bathrooms, which were to be included in every apartment, not shared.

Under the heading "Privacy," Veiller defined the relationship of rooms. He thought that there had to be access to every living room and bedroom and to at least one bathroom without passing through any bedroom. Veiller recognized that although it was desirable to include a hall in every apartment, it was not economically feasible to do so. But his requirement ensured that there would be a minimum level of privacy in every apartment, a provision that was especially important when a family took in lodgers.[40]

With these simple requirements Veiller was able to define the size and quality of the spaces in a minimal apartment in a multiple dwelling. Like definitions of overcrowding, his figures were not based on scientific data; they were simply the product of his extensive experience in housing. Nor did they embody an ideal. They represented a compromise between what was desirable and what was possible, given the pressures of the real estate market. Because they were framed in this way, Veiller's guidelines could be criticized in detail or in principle. Although he mentioned the need for light, he said nothing about the orientation of rooms. The requirement of a 9-foot ceiling height made little sense, even at a time when spaces were generally taller than they were later. Owners of real estate thought his requirements, especially the one for a water closet in every apartment, too stringent; reformers, who knew how many people might eventually live in an apartment built even along these improved guidelines, claimed that he was too lax. Nevertheless, Veiller's law was an important landmark in the history of American housing. It was not only a summary of a half century of legislation about housing conditions but also the initial document in what became an ongoing attempt to establish improved space requirements for housing.[41]

If it was difficult to regulate how new housing was to be built, then it often seemed next to impossible to control changes that were made to old buildings. Every type of structure — hotels, factories, and even churches — could be converted to multiple-occupancy housing.[42] But two types of buildings posed especially severe problems. One was the shanty housing that sprang up in every American city on otherwise unused parcels of land. Sometimes this housing was located on the outskirts of the city; just as often it was near the center. In either case, little is known about it. Some authors wrote about shantytowns because they thought they were picturesque, but the view from this perspective was at best superficial. Reformers thought they detected a familiar pattern in this type of seemingly spontaneous housing. The settlement may have started with a few modest cottages, but with the passage of years additions were built and the spaces between houses were filled with other structures. The result was a network of haphazardly constructed buildings in which the incidence of indigence, disease, prostitution, crime, and other ills was high. However, since these communities were constantly changing and in many cases ephemeral, solid statistics and reliable accounts to measure and describe them are rare. Those available convey only a shallow impression of the configuration of household space and the life for which it acted as a framework.[43]

More is known about another type of housing, one that was exactly the opposite of progressive. Reformers and social workers often found that once-elegant mansions contained the worst housing conditions. As cities grew, vast suburban areas often changed rapidly. Old houses were not systematically swept away once they were abandoned by the people who first lived in them. Instead, they were either converted to other uses — as stables, small factories, or warehouses — or they were altered to accommodate several families.[44]

Observers of city life had long noticed this pattern, but it was systematically studied only after the turn of the century. In their examination of family life in furnished rooms in Chicago, Sophonisba P. Breckinridge and

AN OLD LANE, BOULEVARD NEAR 94TH STREET.

BOULEVARD NEAR 95TH STREET.

IN SHANTYTOWN.

*148. Shantytown, 1892. Such settlements existed in every American city. Authors and artists often thought they were picturesque, but no one knew much about them.*

Edith Abbott found that, paradoxically, the worst conditions were in once-elegant houses. They continually commented on the contrast that time had created. The old Shuettler residence, a large rambling brick house, was still surrounded by a wide lawn. It had once been converted into furnished rooms, but since it was expensive to heat the high-ceilinged spaces, it was being made ready for a third life as a stable. A few blocks away, a house that had once belonged to the prominent Crane family was

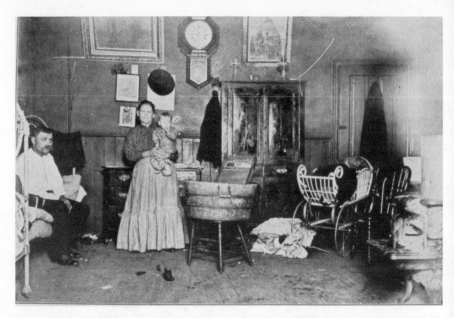

*149. Lewis Hine: A family in a one-room apartment in Homestead, Pennsylvania, 1910.*

full of tenants. Another house nearby was the one in which Abraham Lincoln's widow was said to have made her home.

In these houses the high ceilings, walnut staircases, hardwood floors, marble fireplaces, and large rooms connected by double doors were all evidence of a luxurious past. But in front of the marble fireplace there was usually an airtight cooking stove. The double doors were permanently closed, and since the reception rooms to which they led had no closets, clothes were hung against them.

The very grandeur of these houses made it difficult to convert them into apartments. The adaptation was usually undertaken only to create a maximum of rentable space. It followed one of two patterns. Since the rooms, especially those on the first floor, had been so large, either each one was divided into tiny cubicles, all of which might be inhabited by one family, or they were simply left as they were. In the first case, many of these cubicles, because of the depth of the original rooms, had no light or ventilation. In the second, families were forced to live, eat, entertain themselves, and sleep within one room.

Reflecting the period's crude ideas about the consumption of air, the

Chicago building code stipulated that no room in a tenement house could be occupied that did not have at least 400 cubic feet of space for each person over twelve years old, and 200 for those under that age. But Breckinridge and Abbott found that this minimum legal requirement was violated in at least 15 percent of the sleeping rooms they visited and perhaps many more. Old houses did have light. Because the reception rooms of these buildings often had floor-to-ceiling glass doors that opened out onto a lawn and the bedrooms had bay windows, the building-code requirement of window space equal to 10 percent of the room's floor area was rarely violated. But an excess of windows often made the rooms hard to heat in the winter.

The provision of plumbing was the most inadequate aspect of these furnished rooms. Some of the old houses had been constructed before flushing toilets were common; even when they were single-family, they had never been updated. Those that had suitable facilities for one family had to be extensively revised to accommodate many tenants. The Chicago ordinance governing tenements required one toilet for every new apartment of more than two rooms and one for every two apartments of one or two rooms. The only requirement for old houses was that sanitary facilities be "adequate," an indefinite and unenforceable stipulation. In practice, Breckinridge and Abbott found, there was usually only one toilet for the entire house, however great the number of families. These rooms invariably were filthy and in bad repair. The limited toilet accommodation was matched by the inadequacy of the water supply. All of the tenants of an entire house were often dependent upon a single sink for the water used for cooking, washing, and all other household purposes.

The hallways and staircases had once been generous spaces, but since they were often at the core of the building, they were usually lit from the outside only by the windows of the surrounding large rooms with double doors. Once the house was broken up into apartments or furnished rooms, these apertures had to be closed. Then the hallways became so dark that Breckinridge and Abbott found that they could make their way through them only by groping. Of the twenty-eight houses they visited, only four had artificial illumination in the hallways. Without light, these spaces formed the context of "well-known moral dangers," were hard to keep clean, and were fire hazards.

As bad as overcrowding, filthy sanitary facilities, dark halls, and danger from fire were, the greatest evil of the furnished apartment was the degradation that came from living with someone else's dilapidated possessions. The furniture provided in such accommodation was usually cheap and badly maintained. When a landlord, often a woman, first went into business, she made her own furniture, sometimes bought long ago, go as far as possible. She added secondhand pieces purchased from the used-furniture stores that abounded in the neighborhood, but she rarely acquired anything new. The apartments Breckinridge and Abbott visited usually had a stove, a bed, a table, two chairs, a bureau, several dishes, and a few cooking utensils. Carpets were rare. The bedding, which was handed on from tenant to tenant, was one of the most "repulsive features" of these houses. Clean towels and pillowcases were supposed to be furnished weekly to each tenant, but too often they were as dirty as the bedding.

Without responsibility or sense of ownership, even if only for small possessions, the residents of these rooms found it impossible to have hope for the future. The investigators discovered that the families who lived in furnished accommodation followed a pattern interwoven with their housing. Many had once had their own apartment or home but because of some misfortune had been obliged to give it up. When they did so, they stored their furniture and rented a furnished room equipped for "light housekeeping." Once this decision was made, it was easier for the family to go on paying the weekly sum than it was to save enough to get its goods out of storage and to pay a monthly rent in advance for an apartment. In many cases the amount paid for the storage was soon greater than the value of the furniture, which was then abandoned. The family thus had no way to escape from the furnished apartment, except by saving enough to make a first payment on some new furniture. Without the self-esteem that came from "handling their own property or embodying their earnings and taste" in the objects with which these people were surrounded, a downward spiral was all but inevitable. Like other investigators of the furnished room, Breckinridge and Abbott noticed that tuberculosis tended to breed in this type of accommodation, vice and prostitution were common, and a striking number of its inhabitants were alcoholics. Under these conditions it was hard for the family to survive.

Little could be done to help the residents of furnished rooms once they were caught in this demoralizing syndrome. Breckinridge and Abbott called for municipal regulation. They advised that building codes had to be stricter and more systematically enforced. But no matter how effective these measures might be, the investigators understood that only greater social services could help the people who lived in furnished rooms. Any charitable agency, however, would be attempting the impossible without first removing families from these surroundings. Having surveyed life in a furnished room, Breckinridge and Abbott were all the more convinced that to secure the family relationship, it was first necessary to establish an independent household.[45]

Social workers who wanted to help families were often discouraged when they found a boarder in the household. Lodgers seemed to be an intrusion on privacy and indicated that the family accepting them had no concern for healthy domestic relationships. Although housing reformers made this criticism of families of all backgrounds, they were especially quick to condemn immigrants for the practice. They wondered whether those who shared the space in their home with outsiders would ever achieve a true sense of home life and, therefore, whether they ever could or should become American citizens.[46]

A few people with more confidence in the immigrant took a closer look at the relationship between lodger and family and tried to understand how this arrangement affected the houses and home life of a struggling working population. They found that by the end of the nineteenth century the boardinghouse, which had been so common in large cities fifty years earlier, was quickly disappearing. Writers like Walt Whitman may have criticized that institution, but by 1900 housing reformers were already nostalgic for what they thought had been its friendly atmosphere. Single people who previously might have lived in a boardinghouse, which at least had a common dining room, then had even less palatable choices. Rooming houses, as distinct from lodging houses, were for "the great army of mercantile employees and skilled mechanics — the clerks, salesmen, bookkeepers, stenographers, dressmakers, milliners, bankers, restaurant keepers, policemen, nurses and unmarried journeymen, carpenters, painters, machinists, electricians. . . ." These were single men and women with a skill. In Boston between 25,000 and 70,000 of them lived in the South End. From 1855 to 1870 streetcar lines opened up this area, and many streets of bow-fronted brick row houses were built there. The South End was then an attractive district; it had many small parks and for a quarter of a century it was a choice area of private homes. But with the laying out of suburbs farther from the center of Boston, the South End soon declined. By 1900 it was a wilderness of factories, tenements, and rooming houses, which then made up five sixths of the old houses. Each inhabitant of these establishments customarily lived in his own room. He paid rent by the week or month but did not board there. Instead, he either cooked as best he could or more frequently ate at one of the many cheap restaurants in the area.[47]

Lodging houses were mainly for unskilled laborers, most of whom were immigrants. They were either single or, if married, had come to the United States alone to get settled before they sent for their families. In either case, they could not afford their own room. In Chicago, as elsewhere, they lived in several kinds of accommodation. Many stayed in large anonymous dormitories where they paid by the night. The terms occasionally included meals, but usually the men obtained their own food. Other immigrants organized themselves. They chose a "boss" who was responsible for the cooking, the washing, and the care of the rooms. Sometimes the boss hired a cook or sent out the washing; married couples, therefore, often shared the chores of the boss.[48]

Lodging houses of all types occurred in a variety of buildings. Some of them were located in old houses in the furnished-room district; others were found in small cottages behind more imposing buildings. Rooms and floors in large tenement houses were also used for this purpose. But no matter what kind of building the lodging house was in, it usually was the most crowded of any type of housing. Only 281 of 939 people surveyed in Chicago lodging houses lived in rooms that had over the minimum 400 cubic feet per person. Many rooms were crowded with bunk beds, some of which were slept on by several shifts of men during the course of a day.[49]

Although immigrants from different countries often preferred one type of lodging house over another, they all considered the chance to live as a boarder with a family a step above the sordid dormitory conditions.[50] The question that concerned social workers and housing reformers, however, was not the benefit of this arrangement for the boarder but the welfare of the family.[51] The key issue was whether the wage-earning family truly needed the added income from the lodger. Until systematic studies of household budgets and living conditions were made, people who took in boarders could always be accused of jeopardizing family relationships by trying to earn a few extra dollars.

Between 1900 and 1915 several studies shed light on the relationship of the lodger to family income, rent, and apartment size. The most extensive and reliable was Robert Coit Chapin's *The Standard of Living among Workingmen's Families in New York City*. Chapin interviewed 391 families with annual incomes between $400 and $1,100. He arranged his data according to family size, sources of income, size of apartment, amount

*150. R. R. Earle: A Bulgarian lodging group in South Chicago, 1910. The apartment housed eighteen men, the "boarding boss," and her husband and children. Six men slept in this room.*

spent for rent, and several other categories. By rigorous analysis he was able to make a substantive evaluation of issues about which other people only had opinions.

Chapin found that the opportunities open to the families he interviewed were severely limited by their incomes. The father's earnings usually were the main source of income. A family could make more than $700 or $800 a year only if the mother or children worked or if it took in lodgers. Chapin concluded, therefore, that lodgers, rather than disrupting the family, aided the security of the home. They allowed the mother and children to stay at home and brought the family additional income it could use to provide a fuller life for its members.

One reason families wanted a higher income was to secure better housing. Chapin found that the amount paid for rent increased with an increase in income, but, as a percentage of all expenditures, the money paid for rent diminished with an increase in income. The families he studied uniformly used additional income for better housing. The number of rooms increased with an increase in income and they were also better rooms; those who paid less had fewer rooms with no access to outside light or air.

Ironically, since higher incomes and therefore better housing often could only be attained by taking in lodgers, larger and better accommodation did not reduce the amount of overcrowding. Chapin, using one and a half persons per room as a standard, found that roughly half the families he interviewed lived in overcrowded accommodation. Although overcrowding generally diminished with an increase in income, in any income category families with lodgers had more overcrowding than those without. Chapin explained this condition by the fact that families usually considered taking in a lodger a temporary measure. Once they could truly afford their more spacious housing, they would no longer have to have extra people in their home.[52]

Others interested in the lodger problem reached the same conclusions. No group was more impugned for betraying the family to gain a few extra dollars than immigrants from eastern Europe. It was partly because these newcomers had this reputation that Emily Balch, a professor at Wellesley College, decided to follow their path from Europe to America.[53] She did not assume that in deciding to live in the United States these immigrants were automatically ascending from a lower to a higher state of civilization. The houses in which they lived in eastern Europe were generally hovels, but they had certain virtues, especially when compared with those they would probably occupy in the United States. The Croatians, for instance, slept huddled together in featherbeds, but at least their air did not come from an airshaft, and in the summer everyone spent most of the day out-of-doors in the fields. Most observers would have thought the lack of a chimney in the Croatian house a sure sign of a primitive state. In books that charted the development of domestic architecture and thus of civilization, the ability to build a chimney was always considered a sign of progress.[54] Emily Balch did not romanticize the fact that Croatians cooked over an open fire on a stone hearth in the center of their main room and vented the smoke through a trapdoor in the ceiling. But at least she understood how this habit was an integral part of the pattern of daily life and how the Croatians had accommodated it in the way they built their houses.

Balch found that when the Polish, Bulgarian, Serbian, Croatian, or Montenegrin immigrant arrived in the United States, it made sense for him to lodge with a family. Usually the only other type of dwelling available was the dirty and impersonal lodging house. A family, on the other hand, could give him valuable advice, assist him with the new language, and help him retain a sense of home life until he was able to send for his own family or to start one. Couples took in lodgers as much because they wanted to help their fellow countrymen as because they needed extra money. The burden inevitably fell on the housewife, but Balch knew that wages for women as servants and factory laborers were low.[55] Thus, instead of criticizing the "boarding boss" for neglecting her duties, Balch marveled at her skill in managing such a complex household.

Like Robert Coit Chapin, Emily Balch considered the lodger a temporary phenomenon. As much as she understood the reasons why this arrangement was necessary, she felt that in the long run the family should be a self-contained unit. The Slavic families she knew in the United States were eager to assert their independence in their own homes and tended to abandon lodging as a source of income when they were able to do so. This step was not a sign of assimilation to an American way of life. Balch was convinced that the family was the basis of all societies, and that in understanding what family life was all about, Americans had as much to learn from immigrants as immigrants had from Americans. She hoped that the result of this interchange between "fellow citizens" would be a culture of previously unequaled richness and variety.[56]

A sure sign that families of workingmen were beginning to establish a sense of home life was the setting aside of a room specifically for family entertainment. In her study of steelworkers in Homestead, Pennsylvania, Margaret Byington found that, as in New York, the lowest-paid workers spent a higher percentage of their income for rent. These families lived in overcrowded conditions and had only a narrow range of housing choices. But with an increase in income, families tended to purchase more spacious and better housing. Even though they may have had many children, families often did not use this extra space for sleeping. Byington noted that "the first evidence of the growth of the social instinct in any family is the desire to have a parlor," and she found that many families in Homestead tried, often to the inconvenience of other activities, to have the "semblance of a room devoted to sociability."

The folding bed thus became an important piece of furniture in the households of workingmen's families. Byington found that a family with seven children had in one of its three rooms a folding bed, a wardrobe, a carriage in which a baby slept, and a sewing machine. Although the furniture was diverse in its functions, each piece displayed a sense of taste, and there were portraits, colored lithographs, and a mirror over the mantelpiece. The family tried to make this room the focus of activity in the evening. The mother sewed there while the children sang and

*151. Lewis Hine: A "front room" in one of the better houses in Homestead, Pennsylvania, 1910.*

danced. The family thus referred to this room as the "front room," a phrase with a significance "quite beyond its suggestion of locality."

In Homestead the use of the rooms changed with the size of the house. In the four-room houses, the family ate in the kitchen. In the five-room houses, there was a room known as a dining room. Although sometimes there was a full set of furniture there, the dining room was rarely used for meals. The family ate in the kitchen and used the dining room for other activities, especially sewing and ironing. Byington speculated that eating in the kitchen may have persisted because, without a servant, it was easier for the housewife to serve meals there. That explanation made sense, but other forces may also have been at work. By the time a family was able to afford a five-room house, it may already have begun to sense the loss of a feeling it thought it had when it was compelled to live in a home that had fewer and less differentiated rooms and thus seemed more unified. The home most often associated with this feeling was the one in the old village, whether in Europe or in a rural part of the United States. But as they grew more prosperous and adopted new customs, it was also possible for the members of a family to miss or simply to look back fondly upon the crowded tenements in which they had lived when they first came to the city. No matter how disorienting those buildings had been at the time, in retrospect even they could be seen, especially by children and grandchildren who barely remembered them, to have served as the context for a kind of unified family life that was later sorely missed.[57]

+++

The problems of creating a real home in an apartment house were different from those that the inhabitants of tiny tenement flats faced, but they sometimes seemed equally complex to those who had to solve them. Just as one approach to the planning of the spaces outside an apartment was to treat each unit as if it were a house, so some architects tried to arrange the interior spaces to achieve the same end. Those who wanted to imbue an apartment with the atmosphere of a house generally did so by planning a unit on two levels. Philip Hubert pioneered the development of the duplex apartment in New York. In some of his earliest buildings the living room, library, dining room, kitchen, and related pantries were grouped on one floor that had a high ceiling. This level was connected by an internal stair to another floor that had a lower ceiling height and contained bedrooms and bathrooms.

The difficulty with this arrangement was that while it made sense to have magnificent 15-foot-high living rooms, libraries, and dining rooms, it was a waste to have kitchens and pantries that tall. If two stories were squeezed into the 15 feet, the resulting 7-foot-high spaces would be too low for kitchen, pantries, bedrooms, and bathrooms. In the Navarro Hubert resolved this dilemma. That building was organized by intertwining two apartments. For every two stories of living rooms, which Hubert placed in the front of the building, there were three stories in the rear. Each apartment, therefore, had a high level of living rooms and one and a half levels of service spaces and bedrooms.[58]

Hubert built several of these duplex apartment houses in the early 1880s, but they soon went out of fashion. Imaginative in layout, they were too lavish for the average real estate developer. From the mid-1880s to the mid-1890s the only duplex apartment building constructed in New York was designed by McKim, Mead and White for Louis C. Tiffany. The building covered a lot 75 by 100 feet. It had three apartments, each two stories high. One author, writing in 1912, commented that the extravagance of space in this building seemed like a crime. The central feature of each apartment was a vast two-story dining room, one wall of which was entirely devoted to three interconnected fireplaces. The levels of each apartment were joined by a private stair that was generous enough to be called monumental.[59]

152. *McKim, Mead and White: The studio in the Louis C. Tiffany House, New York, 1886. The architectural details and furnishings of this vast space were all drawn from exotic sources. The room's ambiance of cultivated informality has never been surpassed.*

Interest in duplex apartments was rekindled in the late 1890s. A group of artists started the fad. Artists had always had a difficult time finding well-planned studio space in New York, because it did not pay speculative builders to construct such special buildings. To obtain the space they wanted, the landscape painter Henry W. Ranger and several other artists decided to build their own studio apartments with a cooperative financing plan. The group bought a lot on the north side of Sixty-seventh Street, between Central Park West and Columbus Avenue, for which an architect designed a fourteen-story building that contained two-story apartments, all of which were oriented toward the back of the lot to benefit from the north light. To ensure that this orientation would not be cut off in the future, the artists also bought the land on the corresponding plot on the south side of Sixty-eighth Street and leased it with the stipulation that only a low building could be constructed there.

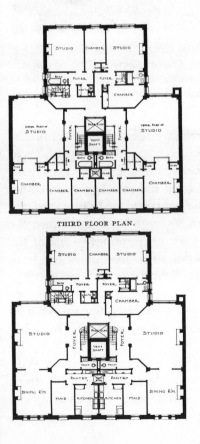

THIRD FLOOR PLAN.

*153.  Sturgis and Simonson: Plans of a studio apartment house in New York, 1910. Through a system of half-landings it was possible to plan this building so that there were seven studios in front and ten of the smaller ones in back. All faced north.*

*154. The studio of Henry W. Ranger, 1901. Except for the detail on the columns and the balcony, this space was unornamented. The generous dimensions of the space and the artist's possessions established the atmosphere of the room.*

The arrangement inside, although previously used in New York and Paris, was ingenious. The building had fourteen studio apartments, seven on either side of a stair and elevator core. Each of the studio apartments had an 18-foot-high space that faced the back and two lower levels that looked toward the street. The mezzanine contained bedrooms, and the area under it had a dining room, a kitchen, and a living room. When the artist invited guests to the apartment to show his paintings — one of the chief functions of the studio — the gathering of course spilled out from the living room into the vast studio space. Behind the stair and elevator were additional apartments that provided a rental income for the co-operative. All of these apartments were one level high, but since ten of them occupied the building's fourteen stories, their ceilings were higher than was customary.[60]

A larger building on the same principle was soon constructed on West Fifty-seventh Street. Since this building was on the south side of the street, the architect was able to place the studios in the front of the building and the smaller rooms to the rear. The rear apartments did not have high ceilings, although the living rooms had unusually large windows. To compensate for this lack of tall space, the architect placed a studio between the two primary apartments in the front of the building. Access to it was through the public hall, and it could be rented by those in a smaller apartment or by people who did not live in the building at all.[61]

By the turn of the century many buildings with studio apartments had been or were being constructed in New York City. People other than artists found this accommodation attractive. One critic succinctly described how the studio apartment found a wider audience:

Mrs. Apartment Seeker has been to a tea or reception at Mr. Artist's studio apartment and has seen his magnificent studio as a part of an apartment, to him a necessity. Such an attractive place for his "soirée" and so appropriate for the display of his pictures and work. How lovely it would be for her to give such teas and musicals, how effective. She immediately starts looking for one, and that room will be the main consideration in the renting of the apartment; only those will be looked at which have a studio.

Thus most studio apartment buildings were never intended for artists. In many cases the two-story-high space did not even face north, and the apartment plan was uneconomical and inefficient.[62]

Elisha Harris Janes, an architect who designed many apartment buildings, showed precisely how much a duplex apartment with a studio cost by replanning one on a single level. He lowered the studio to one story and omitted the stairs, thus creating an apartment with a living room of over nine hundred square feet of space instead of a studio half that size. With intelligent planning he reduced circulation space and by installing double doors made possible just as much privacy between the public and bedroom areas on one level as there had been on two. There was also no need to climb stairs and no additional cost for an internal servants' elevator. Janes calculated that the studio apartment cost over a thousand dollars a year more in rent than equivalent accommodation on one level.[63]

The chance to have soirées and to ape the life of the artist may have been sufficient compensation for those who paid this premium, but the studio apartment was also attractive because people thought they could create a more homelike atmosphere in it. The fact that it was on two levels and had a staircase made the studio apartment more like a house, but there were other connections between the two types of residence.

The first studio apartment building was deliberately austere. Because of the cooperative nature of the financing, no money was wasted on tawdry architectural advertising. The entrance was plain and the hallway on the ground floor was narrower and much less ornate than was customary in apartment houses. The interior of the apartments was equally simple. The wood trim was "machine-made," in other words inexpensive. Ceilings consisted of the beams of the fireproof floor immediately above; plaster and a neutral coat of paint were the standard finishes.

The artists who financed and lived in this building, however, did not leave their apartments in this bare state. They wanted a basic shell that they could adapt to their needs and tastes. Each studio was arranged to permit a variety of spatial organizations. Some artists used the room leading off the large studio as a dining room; for others it was a library. Usually partitions were erected to separate this area from the studio, but a few artists preferred to create the effect of a continuous space. Photographs of the interiors revealed a cultivated informality. The walls of the public spaces under the mezzanine often were finished in elegant paneling and were matched by well-chosen furniture, but these features were offset by the clutter of the artist's life in the studio. Batches of paintings were propped up against the walls, animal skins were used for rugs, and there was bric-a-brac everywhere. In one apartment a piano was haphazardly pushed into a corner with half-finished paintings on top, drapes and sets for still lifes hung over the balcony, and carpets were strewn irregularly across the floor.[64]

People who lived in studio apartments did not copy this bohemian informality directly. Instead, they tried to transpose their perception of the spirit of these studios to suit their own needs. The double-height space ceased to be a studio, but it was decorated to exude a warm, convivial feeling. In the apartment that Elisha Harris Janes hypothetically replanned, the studio was called the "salon," but with its balconies, inglenooks, and adjoining library and dining room it more closely resembled a medieval hall.

This was one of the favorite images of the interior designers who helped clients decorate their studio apartments. In an attempt to conjure up a vague association with an ancestral home, they were not rigorous about what style of furnishing they used. But no matter how freely they worked, they knew that the most association-laden furniture — that of the French Renaissance and Elizabethan England — had been conceived with little consideration for spatial economy. The chairs made in those periods were heavy and elaborate. Antique chests, highboys, and court cupboards also tended to dwarf conventional rooms. The advantage of

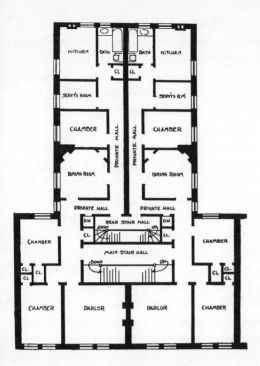

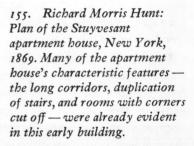

155. *Richard Morris Hunt: Plan of the Stuyvesant apartment house, New York, 1869. Many of the apartment house's characteristic features — the long corridors, duplication of stairs, and rooms with corners cut off — were already evident in this early building.*

the studio apartment, therefore, was that it offered "every chance to gather pieces of various periods, no matter of what size, together with great old *torchères* and candlesticks and pottery, so that one achieves finally a warm, mellow, dignified interior, full of significance and suggestion."[65]

Architects and interior decorators who designed these spaces understood that in manipulating objects and furnishings to create a desired effect, "no architectural proprieties" had to be deferred to, "no canons of consistency between outside and inside" had to be observed. The exterior of most studio apartment buildings was conceived, however awkwardly, as a compositional whole. There was little attempt to manifest the outlines of each apartment on the facade. The only elements that were common to both interior and exterior were the windows. Since they were usually placed neutrally in the elevation, the interior decorator could easily work around them. He was then free to infuse the interior of the apartment not so much with the qualities of a particular time, place, or architecture, but simply with decorative gestures that added up to something difficult to define called "atmosphere."[66]

For all its attractions, the studio apartment was not everyone's ideal.

Many housewives, especially those who found maintaining a house difficult or a waste of time, favored the single-floor "flat," which was designed more for convenience than for atmosphere. Such apartments were first built in New York in the late 1860s and quickly became the standard form of accommodation in multiple-occupancy dwellings.[67] The lack of an internal staircase in a flat saved footsteps and energy, but many planning problems ensued from the fact that all the rooms of this type of apartment were on one level. The layout of flats was determined, first of all, by the shape and size of the lot on which the building was located. Building codes dictated how much of the lot could be covered, what dimensions for light wells were permissible, and whether it was necessary to have more than one exit from the flat. Within these constraints, the architect had to satisfy certain conventions about the zoning of space within a flat. There had to be a distinct separation between living and sleeping areas, so that when guests passed from a parlor to a dining room, they did not have to walk past bedrooms, bathrooms, and kitchens. In the better grade of flats, it was also necessary to separate the areas that servants occupied, primarily the kitchen, from those used by the family. This requirement was often difficult to meet. Since servants had to walk from the kitchen to the dining room, there was often no choice but for them to pass the family's bedrooms. Also, to avoid awkward confrontations on the staircase that led to the apartment, it was necessary to have a separate entrance for servants, but to do so entailed further planning problems as well as added expense.[68]

The plans that resulted from these requirements had a distinct character. Since it was necessary to arrange the flat in a volume that used the dimensions of the lot to the utmost, the rules of axial planning and symmetry did not hold. From the entrance hall most flats were organized around a frequently contorted corridor that bypassed some rooms to get to others. To make way for this corridor, to get light from an internal well, or to let an adjacent space have an outside window, the corners of the rooms in flats often were cut off. Some architects were able to resolve these spaces into regular shapes by inserting built-in closets, small bathrooms, or pipe chases. But in most buildings, especially those in which space was at a premium, economical planning simply dictated the shape of the spaces. In such flats it often appeared that "the corners of every room were in some other room."[69]

Within each room, it was important to have uninterrupted lengths of wall to allow for the proper placement of the anticipated furniture. The location of doors and windows was important, and even the lighting had to be arranged with reference to the other elements of the room. Special care had to be taken so that outlets for gas lamps and electricity were not placed in the walls at positions that would inhibit the use of the space. The swing of doors, the placement of the telephone, and other seemingly small requirements all had to be carefully examined. Architects who designed flats found that inches counted in planning, and this consideration extended even to the details of construction. To gain two inches, they omitted to fir the external walls and used waterproofing preparations instead. They also frequently designed built-in furnishings to save space. Extra bits of space along the corridors were filled with closets, and the kitchen, bathrooms, and bedrooms were also fitted out with convenient storage systems.[70]

A particular type of furniture suited these conditions. Since a seven-foot sofa was normally the largest that could fit the rooms of a flat, the caned daybed and the chaise longue were frequently used instead. The center table was effective only in a room of a certain size and therefore was out of place in a flat. The alternative was to have a proliferation of little tables — magazine tables, smoking tables, lamp tables, tea tables. Each had its own place, function, and character, but they were all sometimes equipped with extra leaves or flaps so that they could be extended. Even the style of furniture had to adapt to the context of the flat. Whereas studio apartments were conceived to accommodate large, even self-consciously cumbersome pieces of furniture, in the flat compactness and lightness were at a premium. After the turn of the century Chippendale furniture was especially popular in flats because it was delicate in outline, took up little space, and did not dominate the room.[71]

The efficiency of flats depended as much on the facilities for convenient housekeeping as on the compact arrangement of rooms. Closets, built-in furnishings, and the most up-to-date kitchen and bathroom equipment were often cited in advertisements that tried to lure families to flats. Because it was her job to care for the home, the housewife had a special stake in deciding what made a particular type of accommodation the best in which to live. Many issues were involved in housekeeping, however, and the efficient flat was not the only challenge to the larger and more difficult to maintain separate home.

# 6

# GOOD HOUSEKEEPING

THE AMERICAN HOME was the special domain of the housewife. This point was often made before the Civil War and was reiterated in the following decades in dozens of books and magazines about housekeeping. Many women were at ease in this refuge, but others found it a trap. In *Beauty for Ashes*, a remarkable autobiography, the housing reformer Albion Fellows Bacon explained how disquieting forces often pervaded the otherwise serene homes of the period. Like many other Americans, Bacon had been brought up in a small rural town. Her memories of childhood in McCutchanville, Indiana, began just after the Civil War, a time when, she recalled, the graves of soldiers were cared for by school children. The church pervaded every aspect of McCutchanville's life. Bacon's mother spent her days "in a passion of self-sacrifice, ministering to all who were in trouble"; she imbued her children with the religion of the age: "personal righteousness."

While growing up, Bacon never thought about a career, but she did sometimes sense a "deep chord" within her. Looking across the great sweep of the valley to the hills beyond, she wondered about "the cities — the poets who lived there — the beauty one could learn to know and to create." But these "voices of the future" were faint, until she was suddenly seized by a desire to go to art school.

To prepare for that goal she went to a town high school. What happened next is vague. "On and on I went," Bacon recounted, "till the wonderland of childhood was left behind. After a while the hills grew steeper, but there were green fields all along, on both sides. Then, all of a sudden the road forked." There was a lonely path that led to the city of the art university; there was a "charming lane" and a charming man in the other direction. Bacon decided not to study art. Instead, she soon married and moved to the edge of town, "where the houses were far apart, and everyone had his own individual air to breathe." The duties of housekeeping occupied her. "My husband, my housekeeping, flowers, music, reading, my friends and a pleasant social round filled up the hours." Two children were born; Bacon took cooking lessons and attended art classes.

Then something went wrong with this idyllic life. Bacon referred to these events only in veiled terms:

There was one long while that I could not hold [the children] in my arms. The house was hushed and darkened, and the servants went about with noiseless steps. For months I was very ill. Then, for nearly a year, I dragged about, white and thin as "snaw wreathes in the thaw," weary, listless, indifferent, with no special interest in anything but my family. . . .

Nervous prostration does that. It was two years before I took an interest in people, two more before the shadow of the eclipse had wholly moved off my world. It was eight years at least before all my energies and enthusiasm and joy of living returned.

Bacon's "awakening" occurred only gradually, but the real turning point came when she visited her children's school. She found that many of their classmates were ragged and the school had no place for the children to play. Indignant, she discussed the matter with the local civic improvement association, organized a group of mothers, and went to the city authorities to demand that a tract of land near the school be turned into a playground. This experience was "like a plunge through ice into freezing water." She had been initiated into civic work. Her campaign for the playground led first to a concern about the spread of scarlet fever, then to an interest in sanitation and social work, and finally to housing reform. Between 1910 and 1913 Bacon lobbied for the passage of a law to regulate housing conditions in Indiana. When she first undertook this work, almost no one else was interested in it. In writing the housing law she received assistance from Lawrence Veiller, but on a day-to-day basis she often had to fight alone for her cause.[1]

In order to relieve her nervous prostration and to respond to the deep chord within her, Bacon had to undertake work outside the home. But she was an ardent defender of the home and often felt guilty about spending time away from her family and her housework. Bacon may have been drawn to housing reform instead of to a career as an artist because that work provided her with a way to resolve her dilemma. She could justify her absence from her home by thinking that, in making better homes available to those less fortunate, she was fortifying the home. This logic may have been satisfactory for Bacon, but it did not work for other women. They had to make a clearer choice between housework and a career. The resulting tension was reflected throughout the home.

✦✦✦

In the half century after the Civil War, Americans accepted that profound changes were happening to the household, but they disagreed about the direction these changes were taking. Some people thought that even though mother and daughter power was being replaced by water and steam power, the family would remain the unit of society and the housewife would maintain a transformed version of the position she always had occupied. Others thought that progress entailed a tendency toward the grouping of people into larger units and argued that housekeeping could best be done cooperatively by a number of families. This theory had significant implications for the housewife, the organization of family activities, and the architecture of the home.

Cooperative housekeeping was not an offshoot of the utopian reform movements of the antebellum period. It was conceived after the Civil War in response to problems particular to that time. The case for cooperative housekeeping was first outlined in 1869 by Melusina Fay Peirce, a Cambridge, Massachusetts, housewife. Mrs. Peirce's desire to remove cooking, sewing, and laundering from the home to a central building, where these chores would be executed by trained servants, came from her understanding of the problems then shared by "intelligent and ambitious young matrons of moderate means." As a child, Peirce had known women who had accomplished all their household tasks "with no more effort than a glittering engine," which seemed to run easily but which in reality was "driving with mighty energy a hundred wheels, and employing ceaselessly a hundred hands." These matriarchs used to walk "in cool quiet," their whole lives "stretching behind and before [them] in fair order and freshness, milestoned with gracious duties remembered afar off and beautifully finished with love and care, each in its own time and for its own sake."

Peirce envied these women, but at the same time she recognized that they were already a part of the past. Her contemporaries were "rushing in feverish haste, overtaxed, inaccurate, anxious." They wanted to be good housekeepers, but because they had received an education, they had higher aspirations. The chores of the household always competed with the "varied culture of books, travel and society." Torn between these two ideals, the American woman grew "thin, nervous, even prematurely old." She hurried along "in the general rush, though neither as cook, seamstress, musician, student, or fine lady, but a catch-work apology for them all."

Peirce's resolution of this dilemma came from her interpretation of John Stuart Mill's theory of political economy. In describing the organization of society, Mill distinguished between consumers and producers. He then divided producers into three types — agricultural, manufacturing, and distributing. Manufacturing had always been the "true feminine sphere." Women had traditionally made the family's food and clothing and so had earned their living by virtue of their "indispensable labor." In "all those twilight generations," Peirce argued, women had, therefore, lived a life of "beneficent activity."

But by the middle of the nineteenth century this condition had changed. Sewing machines had taken from women their most important productive activity. They were no longer the manufacturers but instead had been degraded into the position of "unproductive consumers." Their new vocation was "to please, not to act." As a result, they had lost their independence, and since men frowned on their attempts to be self-supporting, women had no way to reciprocate for the expensive residences, the costly furniture, the rich jewels, and the elaborate clothing that were then often lavished upon them.

The situation presented two clear alternatives. Melusina Fay Peirce asked:

Shall we float blindly down the current of unearned luxury and busy idleness, as our Asiatic and European sisters have done, until we find ourselves, like them, valued principally for our bodies? or shall we determine by earnest effort to keep at least the relative position with which the sexes started in the American wilderness — to catch up quickly with our winged-footed brother, and render ourselves so dear, so indispensable to him, that he not only cannot, but would not, leave us behind?

If women accepted this challenge, they had to find an unexploited opportunity in John Stuart Mill's scheme of political economy. Women could not maintain their position by competing in agricultural and manufacturing production because they were not sufficiently strong. But Peirce thought there was an opportunity in the distributive sphere. The retail trade seemed particularly feminine and was then squandering the talents of men. It took them from their natural vocations, herding them together in towns and cities where they lived unmarried and on small incomes. In these effeminate surroundings they tended to "shrink physically and mentally" and to "degenerate morally through the lying and cheating" they unblushingly practiced.

Peirce's plan was to set up women-owned and -run cooperative stores similar to those that had been started by the Pioneers in Rochdale, England. If this enterprise succeeded, women would then be self-supporting. First, however, three immediate stumbling blocks had to be overcome. Women had no capital, there was social pressure against such employment, and the need to spend time on daily housekeeping created an unnatural division of labor that would inevitably impede the success of the business. The answer to all of these problems was cooperative housekeeping. Melusina Fay Peirce proposed to establish an organization that would furnish the households of its members with clean laundry, food, and clothing. The cooperative's laundry would be a copy of establishments that already existed. Restaurants, hotels, and bakeries offered models for the cooperative's kitchen, and in Europe methods had been devised for transporting warm food from cookshops to houses. Peirce's sewing establishment had no immediate prototype. She envisaged a business in a three-story building. The first would contain a counting room, consulting room, and fitting room; the second would have the working area; and on the third there would be a dining room, a gymnasium, and a reading room to be used by the cooperative's staff.

Peirce predicted that the benefits of the cooperative would be enormous. By doing away with cooking, washing, and sewing, the housewife would be saved all the expenses, and "all the waste of ignorant and unprincipled servants and sewing women, all the dust, steam, and smell from the kitchen, and all the fatigue and worry of mind occasioned by the thousand details of our modern housekeeping." Not only would cooperative housekeeping be cheaper and more efficient but also a subscribing member would share in the profits of the cooperative. Women could use these savings as security to support themselves in old age. But, most important, women, "if liberated from the fetters of the needle, the broom, and the receipt-book," would be able to participate in the professions on an equal footing with men. Law, charity, education, journalism, and, above all, the arts would all benefit from women's undivided efforts.

Peirce also anticipated that many women would be interested in running the cooperative facilities themselves. They would, of course, be paid a salary for the work. Peirce did not expect the members of the cooperative to do manual labor. The true function of educated women was the superintendence of others. The girls who then were house servants were the obvious source of labor for the cooperative. This arrangement had great advantages for those who ran the organization because one of the most difficult aspects of housekeeping in the moderately well-to-do family was the superintendence of servants. Under cooperative housekeeping "those outrageous little kingdoms of insubordination, ignorance, lying, waste, sloth, carelessness, and dirt" would all be merged "into a thoroughly organized, well-balanced central despotism." Everything then would be arranged "with the most scrupulous exactness," and "lynx-eyed masters and officers" would have "nothing else to do but to note that each servant does exactly the right thing at the right moment, and sees the place for everything and puts everything in its place."

Peirce did not indicate what benefits the servants would derive from cooperative housekeeping, except that if the mistress worked, the servants "would no longer have before their eyes that demoralizing ideal of indolent and luxurious fine-ladyism which has ruined so many pleasure-loving unfortunates." But she did say what the gains for men would be. They would be released from the retail trades and could then bolster the sagging agricultural economy by starting cooperative farm communities, the basic outline of which Peirce also described.[2]

Melusina Fay Peirce was not simply a theoretician. She was also the founding member of the Cambridge Cooperative Housekeeping Society, incorporated in 1869. The experiment was widely publicized but it collapsed after about a year.[3] In retrospect it appeared to Peirce that tactical mistakes had been made. The basic problem was that the members of the Cambridge Cooperative Housekeeping Society had forgotten that all modern housekeepers were buyers. The cooperative should initially have started a store. That enterprise would have put the whole organization on a sound financial basis. Then other departments could have been established. Unfortunately, once the Cambridge women had found a suitable building, they first opened a laundry. That service, however, was already available, and the cooperative failed to attract the clientele that was necessary to support such an operation in its early and difficult stages.

In addition to this tactical error, the attitude of many of the members impeded the organization's progress. Since they were people of means, they considered cooperative housekeeping only a convenience. They did not think it their duty to make the effort succeed. Most of them, Peirce explained, "subscribed their money as a charity, and there, for them, the matter ended." Nevertheless, she continued to believe that a properly run cooperative could succeed, and the fact that one such experiment failed did not deter other people from trying to put into practice some of the Cambridge Cooperative Housekeeping Society's principles.[4]

From the late 1860s to the time of the First World War cooperative housekeeping associations were continually founded in the United States. Many of the members of these organizations were probably like Melusina Fay Peirce; they were educated, well-to-do women who wanted an alternative to the frustrating task of running a complex household. But cooperative housekeeping would not have had such a continuous appeal if it had drawn its advocates only from this select group. Women who lived in small suburban houses and whose budget did not allow for servants also were attracted to cooperative housekeeping. Such people wanted to maintain an image of respectability, but they had to watch every penny and work hard to do so. Cooperative housekeeping seemed to offer them a way to save money and effort, and it also gave those who wanted to work in the organization a kind of neighborly contact that they otherwise might have lacked.[5]

None of the housekeeping schemes was as ambitious as Peirce's, nor did their members set out their aims with such entertaining fervor. Most had short lives; nevertheless, they suggested one version of what the future might hold and thus they always represented an alternative to the existing, imperfect way of running a household.

To understand their impact on domestic architecture, these experiments can be divided into distinct groups. The advocates of one approach followed the path of the Cambridge Cooperative Housekeeping Society and tried to remove activities from the household. The basis of this version was the argument that as society developed, everyday tasks would be done more efficiently in the public sphere. Edward Bellamy made this point in an article on the future of the household. He saw an irreversible trend "from variety, complexity and isolation, toward uniformity, simplicity and outside dependence." He advised housewives not to resist what was inevitable.[6]

The impact on the home of removing an activity depended on what the nature of the activity, its equipment, and its spatial requirements had been. For instance, discussions of cooperative housekeeping often cited the Parisian women who did the sewing and mending for a group of families. If several families could guarantee a seamstress enough work to make a decent wage, then neither the housewife nor her servants would have to perform these tedious tasks. The success of this exercise in cooperation depended primarily on how well the participating families coordinated their demands upon the seamstress's time. But no matter whether the scheme worked or not, it could never have significant consequences, either for the life of the home or for the shape of the premises, because, although they were important, sewing and mending generally were not critical activities in the routine of the household.[7]

However, it was often argued that more substantial changes could be made if cleaning and cooking could be contracted out in a similar way. Bellamy suggested that if one or two hundred women agreed to give their cleaning work to a cooperative agency, which they established and managed on a cooperative basis, the "cleaning question" would be solved.[8] In the 1880s and 1890s there were several attempts to set up such a system. In New York the New Century Guild of Working Women was started to train women to do a variety of cleaning chores, including caring for silver and washing windows. The history of this cooperative enterprise and others like it is hard to reconstruct. The guild probably did not last long, in part because the idea of a cleaning agency was soon adopted, if it had not already been, by private companies whose managers were more efficient and reliable than the idealistic women who participated in the "guilds." In any case, few families probably dispensed with all their cleaning chores in the home. If they had decided, for instance, to have all their clothes washed outside the home, the absence of that activity would have had a tangible impact on the organization of domestic space because an entire room and several other subsidiary areas would have been freed. But if a family used the cooperative agency only as a convenience for special tasks and occasions, then no such reorientation could take place.[9]

Sewing and cleaning companies were not nearly as controversial nor were they as suggestive about the future of the household as organizations that delivered prepared meals to the home. The French Fourneau Economique and the German Volks Küche had both demonstrated, American proponents argued, that it was possible to prepare nutritious food more cheaply in the mass than at home. This idea was potentially attractive to working women of poor families. In several American cities, kitchens that supplied inexpensive meals to poor families were started to lighten the load at home of working women and also to improve what was presumed to be the limited diet of the recipients. The New England Kitchen, which was founded by the Boston Cooking School, was the most famous of these organizations. Started in 1885, it delivered meals to Boston's laboring population throughout a long and successful history.[10]

Such organizations were not created to supplant housekeeping permanently. Many poor families had inadequate cooking facilities or none at all, and the attainment of an adequate kitchen, like a parlor, was regarded as an advance. The food-supply companies that were seen as an alternative to home cooking catered to a population that valued convenience of service and variety of cuisine more than economy. A number of these companies were formed in the 1880s and 1890s. Much of their success depended on the equipment they used to transport hot meals. One of the most elaborate delivery systems was developed by a company started in New York in 1890.[11]

In 1900 a similar enterprise, the Twentieth Century Food Company, was started in New Haven, Connecticut, as an answer to the apparent waste in the production of food. The principle of the organization was that food, bought at wholesale prices and prepared for a hundred families with only a few fires and cooks, could be furnished at less cost than that which was bought by individuals and prepared in many separate homes. The Twentieth Century Food Company, like its predecessor in New York, developed new equipment for the delivery of hot meals. A special pail, much less cumbersome than all previous containers, was the key to the company's delivery system. Because of the pail's insulating properties, the company could deliver a meal several hours in advance. The blue container was so attractive that subscribers often served the food directly from it, instead of transferring the meal to cold china.

Despite this clever equipment, however, the Twentieth Century Food Company survived for only several months. Its problems were typical of other meal-supplying ventures. The company's system demanded that meals be ordered the day before delivery; this rule was often neglected, and poor service resulted. To encourage business, the company had started by offering lavish meals, but then its clients came to expect too much and soon became disgruntled. The organization also suffered from a chef's extravagance, and the manager had difficulty in gauging how much variety in the menu was desirable. Most important, the company's starting capital was too small to sustain the operation in the initial months, especially in such a "conservative, home-loving town" as New Haven.[12]

Cooperative food-supply companies varied greatly in the population they intended to serve. Those who started organizations like the Twentieth Century Food Company thought that they could serve almost an unlimited clientele. But most had to limit their operations. A company in Evanston, Illinois, served fifty families and was often mentioned as an ideal example of cooperation, but it failed after "a painfully short time."[13]

The more successful companies catered to fewer families, usually not many more than ten. A small cooperative was advantageous because it could be directed by one strong-willed person who usually stressed the practical over the idealistic aspects of the work. One such person lived in Mansfield, Ohio. There, Bertha Grimes established a successful branch of the Twentieth Century Food Company. She devised a systematic method of cooking food, keeping it warm, and transporting it in enameled containers. Grimes felt that the key to the scheme was the container. She was convinced that with this device, a central kitchen, one woman in charge, two delivery boys, and ten or twelve participating families, everything previously made in the home could be delivered there more cheaply. She was sure that the central kitchen would soon be a part of daily life. "It will be a necessity to the happiness of American homes," she declared. "There are advancements in every other line, why not in this?"[14]

One practical answer to the question was that few companies, especially the larger ones, could cope with a widely dispersed clientele. No matter how well-insulated the containers were, the means of transportation available made it difficult, if not impossible, to deliver these goods and services efficiently. But cooperative housekeeping could be practiced in other ways, and many of the attempts to carry it out were based on efforts to diminish the problem of dispersal. As far as meals were concerned, some advocates of cooperative housekeeping argued that it was more efficient for families to eat in a central building than for meals to be brought from a main kitchen to individual homes.

Edward Bellamy articulated one version of this approach to cooperative housekeeping in *Looking Backward*. Under Nationalism everyone had an equal income, but each person could dispose of it as he liked and in so doing could live in a variety of houses. The family with whom Bellamy's hero lived usually had two minor meals at home, but the third was taken at a large central building. The advantage of eating at this "dining-house" was excellent service and food, the results of a system based on "concert." Bellamy, however, did not envisage a huge, open dining room. Each family had its own small, private room, but these looked out onto a great courtyard where a fountain "played to a great height and music made the air electric." This building was not just for dining but was also a "great pleasure-house and social rendezvous of the quarter and no appliance of entertainment or recreation seemed lacking."[15]

After the publication of *Looking Backward* many Nationalist Clubs were started throughout the United States, especially in the Far West. The members of some of these clubs established central dining halls, and in the period from 1865 to 1915 similar facilities were set up for a variety of other reasons. Community clubhouses, many types of social centers, and country clubs all often offered this service. But no matter why they were established, such dining rooms were rarely seen as a complete substitute for the one at home. This was no doubt due to feelings about the importance of the home, but even for those who wanted an alternative to the home, the central refectory was impractical because it was necessary to travel inconvenient distances to it.

Nevertheless, there were other spatial patterns in which it was thought that cooperative housekeeping could operate more successfully. Homes already grouped close together formed a natural community, and if the number was not too great, the difficulties either of dispersal or of traveling to a central place could be overcome. An article in the *Atlantic Monthly* in 1882 suggested under what circumstances this might be possible. Noting that the "centripetal force which draws men together in united action" was one of the "most potent and far-reaching influences now at work in society," the author considered the separateness of families a contradiction. Instead, he advocated the construction of a "central depot" in which all the work of the home would be carried out. He envisaged a city block bounded on three sides with houses. The fourth side would be occupied by the central depot building, which perhaps could extend into the central area. In any case, that space would be owned in common, not divided up into separate gardens.

The working appliances of the central depot would be a steam generator, a steam engine, a blowing engine that would furnish compressed air for a pneumatic dispatcher and for ventilation, an electric-light apparatus run on batteries that would power the wires connecting the depot with the houses, a hotel range for heavy cooking, a brick oven, and a laundry with machinery that would make it possible to do washing and ironing in any

*156. Leonard E. Ladd: Improvements in dwelling houses, Philadelphia, 1890. The kitchen and laundry work of all the houses in this group was to be handled in the building at the center of the block, where there would also be rooms for servants. The pavilionlike structures behind each house contained a dining room with a tent-covered upper floor for summer eating. The passageway to the central building served as a runway for the delivery of food and as a large conduit for heating ducts, electric wires, and speaking tubes.*

weather. The "missing link" until 1882 had been a system to serve the houses from the domestic depot. But the telephone and pneumatic tube supplied the answer. Wires would connect the two points to deliver messages, and a pneumatic system would enable packages of considerable size to be sent from the depot to the home.[16]

The author of this article described his plans in visionary terms, citing the latest technological developments. In some respects, however, his ideas were not outside their times. By the 1880s large institutions like hospitals, prisons, and universities had central buildings from which a variety of services were delivered. On the basis of these models, it was perhaps reasonable to think that a similar principle could be applied to a group of family houses. After *Looking Backward* was published, followers of Bellamy occasionally proposed this pattern of housing as appropriate to Nationalism.[17] But several schemes along these lines had by then already been constructed in the United States. They varied in the functions to be

carried out at the central depot, which was either located in the center
of the block or on a fourth side. Sometimes, as in a housing development
in Brooklyn, New York, steam heating and power were the only services
that linked all the participating homes.

In 1882 a system similar to the one described in the *Atlantic Monthly*
was put into operation in a section of Brookline, Massachusetts. A group
of row houses surrounded a six-acre park, which not only contained space
for tennis courts, a playground, and a shaded walk but also a "casino."
This building had bowling alleys, billiard rooms, and space that residents
could hire for large parties and theatricals. Although meals were not supplied from a central source, all the houses in the group were served with
heat, electricity, and gas. In addition, by pressing an electric button, an
experience that was like having "Aladdin's wonderful lamp in the house,"
a servant could be summoned to clear the steps of snow, to take a horse
to the stable, to shine the family's shoes, or to wash the windows.[18]

These schemes all tried to maintain a balance between the separate home
and the central, cooperating depot. To some this combination was ideal,
but to others it was a contradiction. For them the logical framework for
cooperative housekeeping was one building. Some of the first apartment
houses were designed on the principles of cooperative housekeeping, and
from the 1860s on, there was always at least a vocal minority of Ameri-

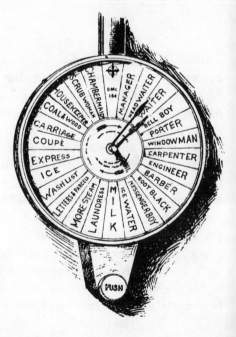

*157. An electrical call device, 1890.
This communication system was
central to the appeal of large hotels
and apartment buildings.*

cans who thought that some form of this building would eventually be the dominant type of residence in American cities.

The first examples of such buildings were designed for people of modest means, but the idea soon became fashionable among those who could have afforded other accommodation. An enthusiastic account of a visit to one of these early apartment houses explains what made this form of housing distinctive and why it was considered an innovation. The building had an "imposing entrance" with gas lights, plate-glass windows, and handsome stone steps. The guest was ushered into the building by a doorman and then into the office of a manager, who, as if by magic, touched an electric button, whispered the guest's name into a speaking tube, and applied his ear to the receiver. He then motioned to the doorman to take the visitor upstairs. As the author waited to proceed, he noticed a marvelous phenomenon: "A small fraction of the upper story . . . gleaming with gas lights, plate glass and upholstery" slid down into the hall. The author entered what must have been a steam-powered elevator and noted: "Smoothly and softly we slide upward, catching sight of two or three rosy children's faces gazing in from the halls as we pass." The inside of his friends' apartment was in good taste. The rooms were well-proportioned and the fittings were handsome, if not luxurious. His hosts had been able to give the rooms "a warm and home-like tone by the manifold pretty ornaments and nameless trinkets which speak of settled habitation and personal taste."

Even so, the building had the atmosphere of a hotel. When the coal fire was low and the scuttle empty, the author's friends pressed a knob, and a servant brought up more fuel. In the same way one could obtain a bucket of ice water or mail a letter without going out into the street. The doorman and other security measures made locked doors unnecessary. When the author and his hosts descended to the dining room, they felt the friendly atmosphere of the building as they passed open doors that allowed "cheerful glimpses of blazing fires, and children, and pretty family interiors," while in one suite they saw "a jolly dinner party." This convivial atmosphere was maintained even in the elevator. As they descended, the author's friends chatted with a neighbor and took the opportunity to make an appointment for that evening.[19]

This apartment house was obviously for wealthy people who were willing to pay for convenience. Those who joined Hubert Home Clubs to finance the construction of cooperative apartment houses, while certainly not poor, had less money to spend on housing. This method of

*158. J. Pickering Putnam: The Commonwealth Hotel,
Boston, 1895. This building, containing hotel rooms and*

financing was attractive because they wanted to have the equivalent of
their own home in the city. Thus many of the advertisements for Home
Clubs explicitly stated that the cooperative nature of the enterprise was
purely a legal and financial convenience. Nevertheless, the residents of
some cooperative apartment houses did try to capitalize on the advantage
that proximity seemed to offer. Some buildings had dining rooms, reading
lobbies, and roof gardens to which all residents had access, and many of
them had common services. All the apartments were steam-heated and
there was a central refrigeration plant. In addition, the residents of some
of these buildings pooled their servants, who did housekeeping chores
like baking and laundering for all the tenants.[20]

Although Edward Bellamy did not cite the apartment house as the
appropriate context for a Nationalist society, J. Pickering Putnam did.
Cooperative living was a logical part of the "congeniality" that he hoped

*apartments for light housekeeping, would have been the
most sumptuous of its kind, but it was never built.*

to achieve in his version of the apartment house. The structure he illustrated in *American Architect and Building News* had common dining
rooms and laundry facilities. His plan was an idealized version of what
should have been built in Boston's Back Bay, but Putnam never approached this goal. He designed one large apartment house that overlooked the Fenway, but there is no indication that it contained common
dining facilities.[21] In 1895 Putnam published an article in the *Brickbuilder*
about his intentions for the Commonwealth Hotel, a building that probably would have been the largest and best-appointed cooperative apartment house. But by the mid-1890s the fervor for Nationalism was waning,
and the drastic depression probably put an end to this ambitious scheme.[22]

Even so, cooperative housekeeping continued to attract new advocates. At the turn of the century Charlotte Perkins Gilman, a forceful
champion of equal rights for women, extended the ideas that had been

articulated several decades earlier by Melusina Fay Peirce, and like her predecessor pointed to the necessity of cooperative housekeeping for the modern woman. The home had to be based on something more substantial than the "stomach as a family tie." Gilman imagined a building in which apartments would not have kitchens. All the cooking would be done in a central facility. Meals could be served in the apartments or in common dining rooms. "Efficient women" would do the cleaning for all the families, and well-trained professional nurses and teachers would take care of and instruct the building's children in a kindergarten. Charlotte Perkins Gilman spent the last years of her life in a New York building that matched this description.[23]

Ironically, after the turn of the century cooperative housekeeping in an apartment building did not gain its reputation as much from an association with advanced ideas, whether Nationalist, feminist, or other, as from sources that the followers of people like Bellamy and Gilman would no doubt have found repellent. Cooperative housekeeping was often identified with the apartment hotel. This institution in some ways was similar to a boardinghouse, but its facilities usually were much more luxurious and its residents lived there out of choice, not necessity.

By 1900 apartment hotels were being constructed in all American cities, but they were especially popular in New York. In the first years of this century not only did the number of such structures there increase rapidly, but they seemed to observers of this new way of living to be ever more lavish.[24] The Ansonia, on Broadway between Seventy-third and Seventy-fourth streets, was probably the most complete apartment hotel ever constructed. It was seventeen stories high and contained over twenty-five hundred rooms. The plan was simple: on each floor two wide corridors, connected by a cross corridor at the center, gave access to all the apartments. The cross corridor was approached by six public elevators and a wide staircase. The apartments varied from bachelor accommodations with only one room and bath up to housekeeping suites of fourteen rooms.

The basement of the Ansonia contained a swimming pool, Turkish baths, storage facilities, a repair area for automobiles, a grocery store, barbershop, manicuring parlor, safe-deposit vaults, cold-storage room for furs, laundry, kitchens, and electric lighting and refrigerating plants. The seventeenth floor had a conservatory dining room served by express food lifts from the basement. The whole building was tied together by a system of pneumatic tubes that was controlled from the manager's office.[25]

An article in *Architectural Record* described this type of building as a "big bold twentieth century boarding house." It was patronized by "business bohemians" who, since they spent money freely on restaurants and theaters, needed a central location. Other residents of the apartment hotel spent most of the year on country estates and then a few months in a rented suite. For both types the apartment hotel was "the consummate flower of domestic cooperation," but in the opinion of *Architectural Record* it was also "the consummate flower of domestic irresponsibility." It meant the sacrifice of "everything implied by 'home.' " That word, the magazine claimed, stood for a place in which the joint life of a married couple had some chance of individual expression. Home was the center around which the interests and activities of a woman's life were focused. But a woman who resided in an apartment hotel had nothing to do. "She resign[ed] in favor of the manager." Her personal preferences were completely swallowed up in the general standards of the institution. Unable to run her own household and to create "an atmosphere of manners and things around her own personality," she could not bring up her children as she liked. The apartment hotel was thus "the most dangerous enemy American domesticity has had to encounter."[26]

A more balanced view of how the American household might evolve was that of Robert and Martha Bruère, two students of Simon Patten. From the late 1880s on, this distinguished economist tried to determine the implications of what he perceived to be a fundamental change in civilization. Until the nineteenth century, Patten argued, every society had to cope with an economy of scarcity. But industrialization had made a surplus possible. Society's task was, therefore, no longer how to make do with less, as it always had been, but instead how to learn to live with abundance. This change was so fundamental that Patten thought it would entail a complete transformation of values.[27]

Patten spent much of his life writing about what the new basis of civilization would be, but Robert and Martha Bruère drew out the implications of his economics for the household. The Bruères wanted to find how to maximize a family's potential. They believed that this goal could no longer be achieved by the traditional methods of saving and frugality. Instead, the family had to make judicious expenditures for equipment or services so that its members, particularly the housewife, could save time to devote to activities of self-improvement.

The Bruères found that one way the modern family could help itself was to give up the illusion of separateness. They thought it was important for people to understand that gas mains, electric wires, telephone lines, the post office, and many other services tied them to the world at large and that they would be better off when they learned to take advantage of this context. Because of these services, the type of house in which one lived did not matter so much anymore. The Bruères recognized that many people would still prefer the individual home, but they saw nothing wrong with the apartment house. Cooperative housekeeping had some advantages, but on the whole the Bruères thought that arrangement too restricting. Since the essence of the modern city was its multiplicity of opportunities, the family was better advised to use an ordinary apartment building as the base from which it could partake of the services — whether cultural or for the immediate running of the household — that were available in the community at large.[28]

Other people were not so dispassionate. They considered apartment houses and cooperative housekeeping a threat to the family, and they believed that there was only one suitable context for the home — the separate house. Because of this conviction, they had to take deliberate steps to make the home more attractive to the housewife.

✦✦✦

Many forms of cooperative housekeeping were available to single women living in cities. For those who did not live with a family and wanted to avoid the uncertainties of the boardinghouse and lodging house, philanthropists and charitable organizations built "women's hotels." In Europe large companies, especially department stores, often built housing for their female employees. This example was not often followed in the United States, but the women's hotel offered similar conditions and terms: room, board, the use of public rooms, and access to lectures and entertainment.[29]

Those who found these institutions too restrictive were attracted to living arrangements which they themselves helped to manage. By the turn of the century there were several cooperatively run homes in New York for working girls on small salaries. Jane Addams helped to organize a similar home in Chicago. The Jane Club consisted of thirty girls who lived in their own hired house at a weekly expense of $3 each. The club was self-governing and self-supporting. A steward and a managing committee were chosen at regular elections. The girls did the lighter housework, but servants were hired for cooking and heavy tasks.[30]

Another type of cooperative housekeeping was for several girls to rent an apartment. At the turn of the century this practice was still considered novel. In 1902 the *Ladies' Home Journal* wrote with interest about five female art students who rented an apartment in New York and who shared the housekeeping. In 1912 another author still thought the fact that women occupied "bachelor apartments" was a new development.[31]

No matter what success women's hotels, cooperatively run clubs, or apartments had, when their residents eventually married, they rarely challenged the belief that the best place for family life was the separate home. Some Americans may have thought that housekeeping in the future should be done cooperatively, but most emphasized the need for continuity with the independent household of the past. They did not make their case simply by praising old habits. They wanted instead to adapt to this traditional context the products of an advanced society. Their attempts to do so contributed to a profound change in the function of the housewife and in the architecture of the home.

Catharine Beecher and Harriet Beecher Stowe both often wrote about the importance of maintaining the essence of the traditional home. They were as awed by the women of an earlier generation as was Melusina Fay Peirce, but they drew entirely different conclusions from their admiration of these impressive matriarchs. For them the inability of contemporary women to cope with household chores did not indicate a need to define the outlines of a new civilization. Instead, the Beecher sisters tried to reaffirm the values of the old.

Their attitude about the past, as well as their sense of what was necessary in the future, was forcefully summarized in an article Harriet Beecher Stowe wrote about the women of Hartford, Connecticut. She recalled that dust and mud were two of Hartford's most pervasive characteristics, and she had special reasons for singling out such a mundane matter for discussion. The presence of dust and mud had helped to produce "a tribe of housekeepers whose fame ought to be celebrated." The housewife of Hartford took "pleasure in her dust and favored the sores thereof." She had learned, in short, "to suffer and be strong." These old housekeepers had eyes that "ran to and fro in their houses, and were as flames to fire to detect a flaw in duty anywhere." They ruled their households diligently and brought up their daughters "to walk in their steps." The Beecher sisters wanted to follow this tradition; their aim was to create a Christian home in which the housewife, through her self-sacrificing labor, was the "chief minister."[32]

*The American Woman's Home*, which the Beecher sisters co-authored in 1869, explained how to perpetuate this tradition in a modern context.[33]

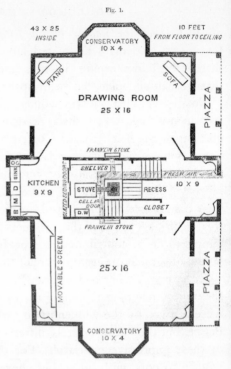

*159. Catharine E. Beecher and Harriet Beecher Stowe: First-floor plan of the American woman's home, 1869. The plan is a rationalized central-entrance colonial house. The piazzas, conservatories, and entrance have been added on. The kitchen, which used to be around a fireplace in one of the main rooms, has become systematized in its own space.*

The beginning of this book on housekeeping contained plans and details of a home that served as the basis for much of the rest of the discussion. This home's progressive and traditional qualities were evident in its external appearance. The Gothic trim, bay windows, and conservatories made it very much a house of the 1860s, but if these accretions had been stripped off, the result would have been a traditional New England home. Inside, the plan reinforced the ambiguous nature of the house. The main rooms were shaped for contemporary uses, but the basic layout — rooms on both sides of a central core that contained entrance hall, staircase, and some form of services — had been constructed in New England throughout the seventeenth and eighteenth centuries.

The Beecher sisters' genius in designing a house that preserved the essential framework of traditional values and added enough adjustments to cope with modern conditions was most evident in the interior details. The house was designed to achieve a perennial goal, the economizing of "time, labor, and expense," but the means toward this end had a new rigor. As in many older New England houses, the main rooms served several functions. Catharine Beecher and Harriet Beecher Stowe achieved this versatility with a new device, a storage cupboard on rollers. One

160.  *Catharine E. Beecher and Harriet Beecher Stowe: The kitchen in the American woman's home, 1869. The kitchen most fulfilled the adage: "a place for everything and everything in its place."*

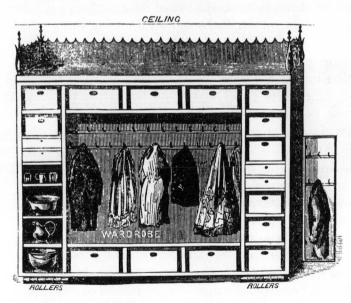

161.  *Catharine E. Beecher and Harriet Beecher Stowe: A movable "screen." This device was used to make a room serve several purposes (see illustration 159). The authors assumed the housewife would make this piece of furniture herself.*

side of this piece of furniture, which was also a partition, served the needs of a bedroom. It had a wardrobe and shelves with boxes for clothing and personal accessories. This side of the storage cupboard faced two beds that telescoped together like a traditional trundle bed. The other side of the device was supposed to face a sitting room and had a decorated canvas screen. Thus during the day this storage system–partition could be pushed to one end of the room to create a generous sitting area; at night it was rolled in the other direction to make space for a bedroom.

Economy could also be achieved through "the close-packing of conveniences." The Beecher sisters accomplished this goal most ingeniously in the kitchen, which consisted of two rooms, one for preparation and the other for cooking. The two were separated by a glazed sliding door that shut out the heat and smells. Their inspiration for the cooking area was a steamship galley, in which every item used in cooking for up to two hundred people was virtually within arm's reach. Their equivalent of this convenient arrangement was a system of well-organized shelves near the stove. The height and depth of each shelf was determined by the dimensions of the objects that were to be placed on it.

The sink and preparation area was just as orderly. Each space and niche had a prescribed function. On the left of the area there was a flour barrel with a lower door for admission and a lid on top that could be raised when flour was needed. Beside this lid was the working counter. One side was used for preparing vegetables and meat, and the other for making bread. Next to that was a dish-drying area, which was hinged so that it could be turned over either to rest on the preparation counter or to cover a sink. Below the sink and the drying and preparation counters were shelves for the storage of provisions and dishwashing materials. The walls above the work top were lined with shelves for additional storage.[34]

The advanced nature of these designs can be understood by comparing them with the proposals for a kitchen made by Joseph B. and Laura Lyman in *The Philosophy of Housekeeping*, published in 1867. The Lymans, like Catharine Beecher and Harriet Beecher Stowe, were well aware of what was at stake in the arrangement of a house and the organization within a room. Something "apparently so slight as the awkward allocation of the stove, the pantry, closet, and sink" could cause, the Lymans calculated, "an enormous difference in the amount of leisure and strength that the housewife might bestow on something better than mere household drudgery." Yet the Lymans were unable to embody this concern in a well-organized kitchen. The plan in *The Philosophy of Housekeeping* had few details and revealed little understanding about how to anticipate and coordinate activities, objects, and furniture within a space. The Lymans' main innovation was a pass-through from the fuel shed to the kitchen, an extremely rudimentary device when compared with the kitchen arrangements in *The American Woman's Home*.[35]

After the 1860s the task of preserving the traditional home while adjusting it to modern conditions was taken up by advocates of home economics. When this difficult-to-define subject was first taught and studied is impossible to pinpoint, but lectures on the care of the home were given at agricultural societies before the Civil War. In 1866 the National Grange in its first "declaration of purposes" stated that its primary object was "to establish a better manhood and womanhood and enhance the comforts and attractions of our homes," and in the following years there usually was a place on grange programs for the discussion of home subjects. Some of the land-grant colleges established under the Morrill Act taught home economics. During the 1870s the Iowa State Agricultural College offered lectures to women on housekeeping, the Kansas State Agricultural College taught sewing and the chemistry of cooking, and the Illinois Industrial University established a School of Domestic Economy. Other universities soon followed.[36]

Home economics was also taught in eastern cities. Before the Civil War a few women's colleges offered instruction in the subject. As higher education for women became more popular after the Civil War, more courses were given, and home economics gradually became a part of the high school curriculum. The subject was also then taught in special schools. In 1876 Juliet Corson helped to organize the New York Cooking School, and Maria Parloa and Sarah T. Rorer soon established similar institutions in Boston and Philadelphia. These women wrote extensively about home economics, their articles appearing in popular magazines. They also helped to start journals such as the *Boston Cooking School Magazine* and the *American Kitchen Magazine*, which led the way in making information on home economics available to a broad audience.[37]

This interest in home economics was consolidated at the World's Columbian Exposition in 1893, where several states had housekeeping exhibitions. New York included a Workingman's Model Home, a three-bedroom wood-frame house designed to cost $1,000 and furnished to suit the means of a family of five. Experiments in feeding such a family were conducted in this house while the fair was in progress. Other cookery experiments were carried out by Sarah T. Rorer as part of the Illinois exhibit, and by Maria Daniell and Ellen Richards in the Rumford Kitchen, which was housed in the Massachusetts building.[38]

The Women's Congress at the fair founded the National Household Economics Association, which was later sponsored by the American Federation of Women's Clubs. The N.H.E.A.'s aim was to promote the knowledge of food, fuels, and sanitation as well as to organize schools of home economics. By 1900 over thirty universities had departments of home economics, and many other institutions had training courses on the subject. Because the home economics movement had expanded so much, several of its leaders felt there was a need for an organization that was independent of the American Federation of Women's Clubs. In 1899 the first of ten Lake Placid conferences on home economics was held to coordinate home economics activities throughout the nation and to act as a forum for the discussion of important aspects of that subject. By 1909 an annual conference was no longer sufficient, and the American Home Economics Association was founded.[39]

The name was important. "Home economics" was more satisfying than "domestic science" or Ellen Richards's word "euthenics," because it both confirmed the continuity with the traditional concept of "economy" and associated the subject with a progressive discipline. Recognizing that the home had changed, the association's founders believed that women could best deal with this transformation by consolidating their traditional positions.[40]

One way to achieve this end was to master the science of housekeeping. Throughout the half century after the Civil War, but especially after 1890, there was a remarkable increase in information about nutrition, sanitation, and other related subjects. Some of this research was sponsored by the United States government; other studies were undertaken at universities. No matter where it came from, such work took the discussion to a higher plane than the one it had been on when it was treated only by dedicated but limited authors like William Andrus Alcott and the Beecher sisters. From the home economics point of view, the problem with this outpouring of information was that it came from diverse sources in an uneven form, and it was, therefore, difficult to distinguish the important from the trivial. But even when it was possible to make such judgments, interpretations often differed.

Sanitation was a case in point. No subject was more important to the care of the household, and yet experts disagreed fundamentally about how diseases spread. Charles V. Chapin, a prominent public health reformer, believed that germs did not live long outside the body. While a strong advocate of personal cleanliness, he understood that attempts to disinfect the immediate environment to prevent the spread of disease through contact with inanimate objects were largely useless. Yet well into this century many respected doctors and sanitarians voiced the opposite opinion.[41]

The American Home Economics Association was founded in part to sort out such issues and to present authoritative opinions and information to the housewife. But since it was difficult to know whom to trust, the woman who was willing to discard habits that she had learned from her mother was often confused about what "science" actually entailed. The result of these quandaries was a heightened awareness of the problem but no solution. Housekeeping, therefore, became an even more complex and baffling subject.

Cleaning the house, for example, demanded a new level of care. Programs of "municipal housekeeping" were not enough to protect the home. The housewife always had to be on her guard. Once she was aware of all the possible consequences of dust and dirt, it was no longer sufficient to dust pictures, walls, bric-a-brac, and books, to beat upholstered furniture, to wipe wood and metal surfaces, or to clean floors, carpets, and rugs. If no less an authority than Ellen Richards, who was the first female professor at the Massachusetts Institute of Technology, claimed that "to shake rugs and dusters out of the window in a closely settled sector should be a statute offence as also should be the sweeping of house and porch dirt onto the sidewalk or into the street," then the Hartford women who took pleasure in their dust had to reconsider how to clean their homes.[42]

The scientific program of housecleaning began with the construction of the house itself. It was necessary to seal the house with screens against disease-carrying flies and to prevent the penetration of dirt and germ-bearing rodents and vermin. Internal surfaces had to be chosen that did not attract dust and were easy to clean. Carpets were especially suspect, and materials like linoleum were favored for floors, particularly in areas where food was prepared. Walls also had to have smooth surfaces; textured wallpaper, for example, was hard to clean.

Measures were also taken to isolate objects, especially those that touched the body, so that they would not attract dust. The desire to keep clothing, linen, crockery, and kitchen utensils clean added a new incentive to establish a context in which the traditional goal of "a place for every-

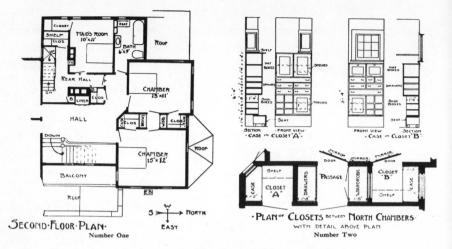

*162. Convenient closets, 1908. The organization of built-in storage space was frequently examined by architects, housewives, and students of home economics.*

thing and everything in its place" could be achieved. Students of home economics devised innumerable closets, cupboards, shelving systems, and other useful containers. They examined each activity of the family's daily routine, anticipated the storage required for the things necessary to that activity, and then devised a suitable place for those goods. As the categorization of types of objects reached an unprecedented complexity, highly differentiated storage systems were built throughout the house.[43]

The bewilderment created by interpreting what science prescribed for the household was compounded by the argument that insistence on rigorous methods of cleaning, cooking, and caring for clothing killed the human atmosphere of the home — the very quality that advocates of home economics supposedly wanted to preserve. Thus at the same time that science became important in the household, an enormous volume of literature described what home life and housekeeping had been in the past. The implication of this literature was that the essence, if not the particular details and methods of these traditions, had to be maintained.

This literature on old-time housekeeping had a form of its own. It was often written as a dialogue between an old woman and an eager young one. The matriarch, whether grandmother, aunt, or friend of the family, passed down the traditional knowledge to the well-intentioned but bumbling modern housewife. In Harriet Beecher Stowe's *House and Home Papers* and *The Chimney Corner* Christopher Crowfield, a masculine version of the matriarch, was one of the first of these characters. Sarah Josepha Hale used a similar character and format in *Manners: Or, Happy Homes or Good Society All the Year Round.* Laura Lyman contributed housekeeping columns to *Hearth and Home* as "Aunt Hunnibee." In one of the most popular books of this genre, *The Complete Home* by Julia McNair Wright, the aged Aunt Sophronia explained how best to execute each household chore by recalling old cooking recipes and long-forgotten ways to remove stains from different types of clothing.[44]

The most popular of these authors was Mary Virginia Terhune, whose pen name was Marion Harland. In addition to over twenty novels, she wrote about twenty-five books on housekeeping and etiquette and a dozen other volumes on travel, biography, and colonial history, including one about George Washington's mother and two on "colonial homesteads." Terhune also edited two women's magazines, *The Homemaker* and *The Housekeeper*, and contributed syndicated columns on household subjects to the Philadelphia *North American* and the Chicago *Tribune*. This diverse output had in common a saccharine eulogizing of the old-time home, more fiction than fact, and the implication that this setting had a crucial meaning for the home of the late nineteenth and early twentieth centuries.

Mary Virginia Terhune continued to write until she was eighty-nine years old; she died three years later. But that was not the end of her influence. Three of her children became authors and helped, directly or indirectly, to popularize the values of the traditional home. Albert Payson Terhune wrote dog stories for children, and Christine Terhune Herrick and Virginia Terhune Van der Water wrote about household matters and etiquette.[45]

In teaching home economics, science and tradition often came into conflict. Discussions about the appropriateness of handwork sometimes focused the dilemma. Many teachers argued that manual skills were no longer necessary, and that it was most important to learn principles derived from chemistry and biology. Others thought that it was important to master handwork skills, for two reasons. They argued that learning by doing, which was so well exemplified in the old techniques, aided the educational process by directly connecting a child to the subject being taught. They also argued that it was necessary to link future housewives to old housekeeping traditions. A resolution of the dilemma was made at the first Lake Placid conference. It was decided that the home economics curriculum should first stress handwork, but as children progressed through the school, the emphasis would gradually shift to scientific and scholarly studies.[46]

This resolution accorded well with contemporary ideas about progress, but it did not completely satisfy the advocates of either science or tradition, and there was no easy, parallel way for the housewife to divide her loyalties between traditional techniques and science. The result often was anguish, confusion, and an extraordinary amount of work. It is difficult to estimate how much time was spent in housekeeping, but books on the subject indicate what was expected of the housewife. In *Home Economics* Maria Parloa gave a schedule of the tasks that a good housewife had to perform each day. She itemized ten essential jobs:

1) Make the fires, and air the dining room and hall.
2) Prepare the breakfast and set the table.
3) Put the bedroom to air while the family is at breakfast.
4) Remove the breakfast dishes; put away the food. Sort the dishes and put to soak all dishes and utensils that have food in them which would be likely to stick.
5) Put dining-room and sitting room in order, arrange them well.
6) Wash the dishes, and put the kitchen and pantries in order. Prepare dishes that require slow cooking, and put them to cook.
7) Make the beds and put sleeping rooms and bath-room in order.
8) Trim the lamps.
9) Dust the halls and stairs; sweep piazzas and sidewalks.
10) Do the special work of the day.

The "special work of the day" varied. On some days it was necessary to do the washing; on others cleaning or long-term cooking demanded attention. In each case, the directions were rigorous. Parloa's ideas about how to clean a room typified the level of work she expected. She began with the ominous warning that "a house may be made to look clean and orderly when in fact it is quite the reverse." It was necessary, therefore, to take everything out of a carpeted room, first brushing and dusting each piece thoroughly. Heavy furniture that could not be moved had to be covered with cloths. Then the pictures on the walls were to be dusted with a soft feather duster for the frames and a coarse brush for the backs. After the pictures had been covered with a piece of coarse unbleached cotton, the doors were closed and the windows opened. Then it was time to proceed with the real cleaning tasks: beating the carpet and scrubbing the walls, floors, ceiling, and woodwork.[47]

In 1908 Ellen Richards calculated how long it took to clean a house. To remove dust and tracked-in dirt, an eight-room house required eighteen hours a week. If the house had a furnace as well as open fire-places, it needed four special cleanings of twenty hours each during the course of the year. Washing the windows took ten hours a month. The blinds and porch coverings demanded an additional eight hours. The washing of walls and painted woodwork took fifteen hours six times a year. Finally, the laundering of curtains and drapes was an eight-hour-a-month job. All told, these tasks took about fourteen hundred hours a year or twenty-seven hours per week. These figures, of course, were for cleaning only. They did not include time for cooking, making beds, mending and washing clothing, and dozens of other chores.[48]

Servants provided one way to reduce this drudgery. The pros and cons of hiring domestic help were constantly discussed by housewives. Servants had always been considered anomalous in the United States. The relationship of servant to master was reminiscent of the European class system and, therefore, inappropriate in a democratic country. Mothers also wondered whether it was wise to trust their household to uneducated girls, especially since children inevitably came under a servant's influence. It also often seemed that it took the housewife as much time to instruct the servant as to do the work herself. Nevertheless, it was usually argued that even if the benefits were not clear-cut for the household, the system was good for the servants. It was better to let girls live in a comfortable home than to relinquish them to the other source of employment, the mills of Lowell and Pittsburgh. By observing and participating in the household, servant girls would learn how to be good mothers and housewives.

Uneasy compromises were worked out to resolve these conflicting argu-ments. Servants often were not required to wear uniforms, the outward sign of rank, and the family sometimes tried to treat "Bridget" as one of its own. But despite these gestures of equality, the relationship was always full of friction, and most housewives would have welcomed an alternative.[49]

One way to do without servants and to lighten the burden of house-work was to use machines. From the beginning of the nineteenth century on, there was a deluge of inventions that purported to reduce the time and energy spent in accomplishing household tasks. The United States Patent Office recorded a never-ending stream of inventions from apple corers to washing machines.[50] Although these devices were the products of science and progress, they were not welcomed with open arms. Many of them merely did indirectly what more easily could be achieved by hand — an argument often made by those who had an even more fundamental reason for disliking machines. They contended that these devices were antithetical to the human element and that the housewife who used them betrayed her true role in the home.

Uncertainty about what the housewife would do with the time supposedly saved by machines reinforced these arguments. Since machines cost money, some women tried to use their extra time to produce salable goods and thus to justify their purchase of machines. This commercial activity could be seen as the continuation of the production function of the old-time housewife. But more often it was considered incompatible with the true nature of the home, especially if the housewife was successful in selling what she produced and seemed to be making a career of her hobby.

To justify machines, it was argued that the housewife could use extra time for her children. The answer to this point was that the mother could best exercise her influence not by rushing through her work but by carrying it out calmly and systematically. With order there would be time for everything; that was the best of all possible lessons that could be taught to children. Like the Beechers, many writers on the care of the home, therefore, emphasized the importance of habits of neatness, system, and order and never mentioned many of the available household conveniences.[51]

American industry, however, depended on the housewife to buy not only machinery and gadgets for the household but also products like soap, prepared food, baking powder, and linens, all of which formerly had been made in the home. The housewife had to be a consumer as well as — or, some manufacturers argued, instead of — a producer. But if she purchased these goods, then she would lose her traditional function in the home and would be tempted by careers other than that of housewife.

Mary Pattison, a New Jersey housewife and the author of *Principles of Domestic Engineering*, found a way to resolve this dilemma. Pattison believed that her problems were similar to those of many other women of the period. She realized that much of the cost of living as well as the "dissatisfaction in the kitchen" came from the passing of the "old ideals" and the need for new ones. But she had no use for cooperative housekeeping. She granted that it might be cheaper to live in "hotels, or blocks, with one source of supply, one management, one method," but the preservation of the family was vastly more important than saving money, and she had no doubt where that goal could best be attained. On the title page of *Principles of Domestic Engineering* Pattison quoted Ralph Waldo Emerson:

> *Thou shalt make thy house*
> *The temple of a nation's vows.*

Her book was dedicated to the "Conservation of the Individual Home."[52]

Instead of encouraging women to enter the professions and thus to weaken the home, Pattison wanted to find a way to "professionalize" housework and homemaking. But homemaking had too many "variables" to be "unified," and Pattison at one point concluded that "no general system could possibly apply because each home was a law unto itself, with human nature as the controlling factor." Then one day, while picking up the evening mail, Pattison noticed a book, *The Principles of Scientific Management*, by Frederick Winslow Taylor, who was systematizing procedures for analyzing, measuring, and redesigning factory processes and equipment. She started to read Taylor's book, and "verily it seemed like an answer from above." Before the evening was over, she had read the book twice and concluded that Taylor's was "a system devised by man for man's pursuits, but equally applicable to women, and prophetic of a new unity of purpose." It was the "return-home call to Nature's own."

Pattison must have contacted Taylor, because he wrote an introduction to *Principles of Domestic Engineering* in which he left no doubt about the importance of Pattison's undertaking: "In a smaller way perhaps she is doing pioneer work similar to that of Leonardo da Vinci in his *Il Codice Atlantico*, Newton in his *Principia*, and Darwin in his *Origin of Species*." A few months after she had read Taylor's book, Pattison started an agricultural experiment station in Colonia, New Jersey, where she began to carry out her momentous undertaking: the application of time and motion studies to the activities of the home.[53]

The key concept of her book was "System in Housekeeping," the application to the household of the "twelve principles of scientific management" that Taylor's colleague Harrington Emerson had codified for the organization of industrial processes. The housewife was to analyze the "work tasks" in the home and then calculate the best way to do each job. She had to "standardize" movements while doing dishes, perform "motion studies" to save energy while cleaning, prepare the family budget, learn to "plan and dispatch" tasks to other members of the household, keep "records" of bills, checks, and receipts, maintain "indexes" and "scorecards" of catalogs and addresses, give "efficiency rewards" to industrious children, and "coordinate" the equipment and utensils of the household. The bulk of Pattison's book explained how and why these methods could make housekeeping more efficient.

Mrs. Pattison's ideal was an "Auto-Operative" home in which the housewife was the manager and businessman. The first step in achieving this end was to do away with the "servant class." This decision did not come from sympathy for the servant. Since the demand was greater than the supply, standards of work were low. Besides, educated women understood that it was unwise to leave the critical work of the home to ignorant and careless servants, "the lowest class of human beings claiming respectability."

The next step in achieving the "Auto-Operative" home was to give the housewife the equipment and premises commensurate with her new status as the "executive of the home." She needed a typewriter, dictating machine, and file cabinet in an office where she could conduct the "business and clerical work of the establishment." But, more important, Pattison took an unequivocal stand on household utensils and machinery:

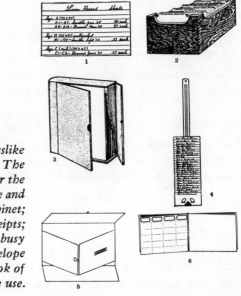

*163. Christine Frederick: "Businesslike Equipment for the Home." The housewife needed ( 1 ) cards for the home record cabinet; ( 2 ) a "time and worry saving" home record cabinet; ( 3 ) a vertical letter file for receipts; ( 4 ) a "tickler" that reminded the busy housewife; ( 5 ) a vertical file envelope for saving large clippings; ( 6 ) a book of handy labels for home use.*

Any and all machinery that can be made to best further this end [the welfare of the home], is not only worth desiring, but it becomes the duty of the individual and society to see to it that such desires be encouraged to the point of properly incorporating every device known to us, that can be made to advance the standard of the household.[54]

In the back of *Principles of Domestic Engineering* Pattison had a list of the best household utensils, devices, and machines then available, although her book had no illustrations. However, the need for this equipment was then being emphasized by other people with a similar outlook. Christine Frederick was the most important contributor to the cause. In articles in the *Ladies' Home Journal*, which were later collected in a book, she illustrated the most up-to-date improvements in all domestic appliances. In her opinion vacuum cleaners, floor polishers, washing machines, "dustless dusters," as well as the favorite time, energy, and material saver, the pressure cooker, were all necessities. But Frederick's most important message was that electricity could be the household's "modern servant."[55]

The early history of electricity in the home was uneven. At the beginning of the nineteenth century doorbells and annunciators of various kinds were operated by electricity. By mid-century fire-alarm systems,

*164. Christine Frederick: "Stepsavers." (1) The "Lazy Susan" or "Silent Waitress"; (2) a wheel tray; (3) a kitchen cabinet "Which is a Pantry and Table in One"; (4) a disappearing icebox. The icebox is a curious transitional device between cold storage in the cellar and an electrically operated refrigerator in the kitchen.*

*165. An electric sewing machine, 1890. For the housewife, the sewing machine, whether hand or electrically powered, was an ambiguous invention. It replaced age-old methods of sewing, but it also allowed those who bought and used these machines to think that they could reassert the tradition of home production and in the process avoid buying factory-made goods.*

thermostats, and clocks were also electrified. As more houses were connected to the mains and with the invention of the telephone and the incandescent light bulb, such devices became more common, but in 1890 they were still considered novelties. Even more rare at that time were appliances run by electric motors. Fans, sewing machines, carpet sweepers, shoe polishers, lawn mowers, cigar lighters, and many other household machines and gadgets had already been run by electric motors.[56] Some of these were displayed at the World's Columbian Exposition in 1893. Still, they were all considered playthings that would only be generally available, if at all, in an undefined future.[57] Even by 1910 the electric clothes washer, refrigerator, stove, iron, vacuum cleaner, and dishwasher were still in their infancy.[58]

The reason for this pace of development was partly cost. Electric motors were expensive to produce, and only the wealthy (those who had servants and who, therefore, least needed time-saving equipment) could afford appliances with them. Also, like other machines and gadgets, electrical appliances were shunned because they challenged traditional ideas about the housewife's work. The very fact that they required virtually no effort to use made them all the more suspect.

The breakthrough that Pattison and Frederick made was to give the

166. *The Thor electric washing machine, 1915. The popularization of the electric washing machine was due primarily to Neil C. Hurley. After manufacturing the first Thor in 1907, he spent the next four years trying to create a market for them by visiting electric companies and "preaching the gospel of domestic efficiency."*

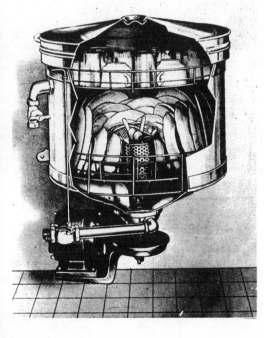

167. *The Walker dishwasher, 1916. As early as 1896, Willard R. and Forrest A. Walker began to make machines for washing dishes in the home. They did not produce their first electric model until 1909, and they had to wait until the end of the First World War to produce dishwashers in volume at their factory in Syracuse, New York.*

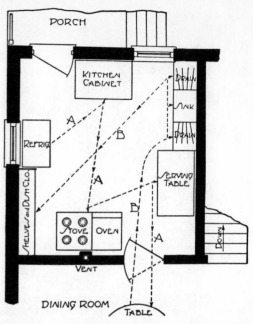

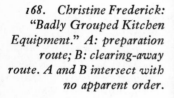

*168. Christine Frederick: "Badly Grouped Kitchen Equipment." A: preparation route; B: clearing-away route. A and B intersect with no apparent order.*

housewife machinery — but not the extra time that had often been associated with it. With a gadget it was possible to do a particular task more quickly than with hand labor. Pattison and Frederick thought that this gained time was to be spent in the home. It could be used for tending the children and making the house more attractive, tasks that sometimes had been neglected in the past. Primarily, however, any extra time was to be spent in the efficient management of the home. That was how the housewife would become the "executive of the home."[59]

This ambivalence between old and new values was reflected throughout Christine Frederick's house, especially in the allocation and arrangement of space. The essence of the time and motion procedure was to define a task, break it down into its component parts, and then determine the best method for carrying out each activity. Using motion pictures, Frank Gilbreth pioneered this method of analysis in a study of bricklaying.[60] The same method could be applied to the activities of the home. First, each activity was defined, then it was analyzed, and finally all the necessary furnishings and objects were designed and arranged so that the stated goals could be achieved.

In the plans of Christine Frederick's home, each room was a separate space with its own designated activity, but sometimes the living room, dining room, and hall could all join together when sliding doors were

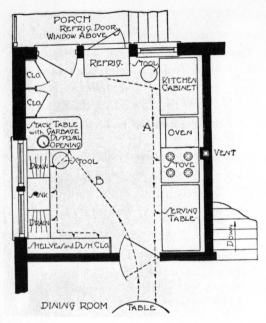

PORCH
REFRIG. DOOR,
WINDOW ABOVE

REFRIG.   STOOL

CLO.

KITCHEN CABINET

CLO.

STACK TABLE with GARBAGE DISPOSAL OPENING

A

OVEN

DRAIN   STOOL

VENT

B

STOVE

SINK

DRAIN

SERVING TABLE

SHELVES and DISH CLO.

DOWN

DINING ROOM   TABLE

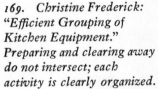

*169. Christine Frederick: "Efficient Grouping of Kitchen Equipment." Preparing and clearing away do not intersect; each activity is clearly organized.*

opened. To achieve a compact arrangement, rooms were generally clustered symmetrically around a hall that to save steps was kept at a minimum size. Within each space, much of the furniture was built in. Frank Gilbreth frequently wrote that in any task it was possible to determine what he called "the one best way." So in planning a house the best arrangement of all the spaces could be decided in advance. Shelves and counters were built into the kitchen, closets were rearranged, storage spaces were properly allocated to each room, dining nooks were designated, and in the bedroom there was an obvious best place for the bed. But although the plan and many of the details of this house were determined systematically, the structure did not have a mechanical or clinical appearance. Like the house in the Beecher sisters' *The American Woman's Home*, Christine Frederick's residence was unmistakably contemporary. Yet, through its wood details and rustic appearance, it also suggested an architecture of the past.[61]

Just how confused the values of domestic production and consumption could be was evident in the editorials of the *Ladies' Home Journal* at the time that Frederick's articles were appearing. In 1914 there was a national recession. With the outbreak of war in Europe, the American economy was affected, and thousands of American workers were laid off. Edward Bok, the editor of the *Ladies' Home Journal*, told his readers that for the first time the present generation was being taught economy. Americans had forgotten humanity's first lesson, "that of learning with how little we can do." Since the American housewife had to practice ever more diligently the old arts of economy, the *Ladies' Home Journal* published articles that described the preparation of inexpensive meals, the fashioning of new dresses out of old ones, and many other ways to make do with what was already at hand.

A few months later, however, another theme emerged in the *Ladies' Home Journal*. Bok recognized that the recession was partly due to the closing of European ports. American exports had been cut, and, more important, the import of foreign goods was restricted. Bok told his readers:

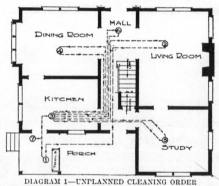

DIAGRAM 1—UNPLANNED CLEANING ORDER

*Method.*—Worker gets tools from tool closet (1), and walks down hall and begins on living room (2) ; returns with trash to kitchen (3), and walks to dining room (4) ; after cleaning it, again returns to kitchen with trash, and proceeds to clean the study (5) ; she walks back to kitchen again, and last cleans hall (6), ending by bringing back tools and last refuse to kitchen again, before taking the final walk back to tool closet (1). This is not an exaggeration, but the method used by a so-called "good worker."

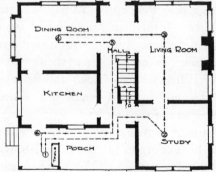

DIAGRAM 2—PLANNED CLEANING ORDER

*170. Christine Frederick:*
*Unplanned and planned*
*cleaning order.*

*Method.*—Worker gets tools from tool closet (1), and proceeds direct to study (2) ; from study through door to parlor (3) ; across parlor hallway to dining room (4) ; she then begins at upper end of hallway (5), and cleans its length back to the door opening on rear porch, carrying all waste and tools back directly to service porch (6). Note that this method eliminates *all tracking to kitchen* and results in about two-thirds less unnecessary steps and walking.

"The dressmakers of Paris have laid down the scissors for the sword." This act was a challenge: "America has today the opportunity to show what she can do — to manufacture herself what heretofore she has bought from others." The American manufacturer was willing and ready; the only difficulty was that the American housewife did not "encourage him by buying his goods." She had an "unparalleled chance to show her duty to American industries." She could start up the wheels and the looms that were still, and she could put millions of men back to work. To further this end, Bok suggested a slogan to be placed on all goods produced in the United States: "Made in America."

A few months later Mrs. Percy Pennybacker, the president of the American Federation of Women's Clubs, reiterated Bok's challenge and in so doing showed how complex these issues were. She also wanted American women to patronize American industries. But "industry" meant something entirely different to her. "This is a time," she claimed, "when we can do much to forward the revival of the old hand industries."[62]

✦✦✦

In every aspect of the care of the home the modern housewife had to determine how much of the home industries to maintain. Evidence of an approach to the resolution of this problem was often most tellingly apparent in how the home was decorated. The furniture and furnishings of a home revealed how much the housewife thought she had to make herself and how much she could buy in a store. Deciding between the two had an important bearing not only on what the interiors of American homes looked like but also on the role the housewife defined for herself.

Catharine Beecher's and Harriet Beecher Stowe's opinions typified one approach to the decoration of the home. Their ideas about this subject, as about other household issues, were shaped by their experience of the old New England home. In *Educational Reminiscences*, a short autobiography written in 1874, Catharine Beecher recalled how her mother had made a carpet from a bale of cotton her father had bought on an impulse from a traveling peddler. Mrs. Beecher first carded the cotton and then spun it into yarn. Since she did not own a loom, she contracted with a neighbor to weave the material. Once the cotton had been transformed into a continuous piece of fabric, Mrs. Beecher cut it to fit the parlor and sewed a border on its edges. To put a design on the plain carpet, first she stretched the material by nailing it to the attic floor. Then she brushed it with paste so that the surface could receive an even application of color. Since no paint was available in Litchfield, she sent to New York for materials with which to make oil paints. When they arrived, she learned how to prepare them from accounts in her book of household information. She was then finally ready to decorate the carpet with a pattern of flowers, "imitating those in her small yard and garden."[63]

The world in which Mrs. Beecher lived, at least as seen through the eyes of her daughter, was largely governed by economy. When resources were scarce, efficiency and frugality were necessary. Even when there was an opportunity to make something, like a carpet, that was not strictly useful, careful calculation was important. Under these conditions any manifestation of economy was good, and, therefore, was beautiful. The beauty of economy was sufficient in itself, but it could be enhanced by the addition or superimposition of patterns or ornament, like the floral decorations on Mrs. Beecher's carpet, provided they had explicit moral connotations.

In magazine articles she wrote in the 1860s, Harriet Beecher Stowe left little doubt that she thought her mother's age had qualities that had to be perpetuated in her own day. In *House and Home Papers'* first episode, "The Ravages of a Carpet," she described a household that had been furnished "in the old-fashioned jog-trot days" when everything was made to last from generation to generation. Nothing the family owned was too good for them. The parlor announced to friends that the members of the family were "wide-spread, easy-going, and jolly folk." Daily life revolved around the household altar, the blazing wood fire, with its "wholesome, hearty crackle." This fire was especially attractive to the children. A room "all warmed, lighted, and ventilated and abounding in every proper resource of amusement to the rising race" had been set aside for them, but the fire always drew the pattering feet to it.

This scene was disrupted when a daughter complained that the parlor was not "fit to be seen in." It had always been "a sort of log-cabin — library, study, nursery, greenhouse, all combined." Her parents acknowledged her complaint by consenting to replace an old carpet, but they soon found it necessary to put blinds on the windows to keep the sun from spoiling the new acquisition. Then the house plants and a canary were banished from the parlor for fear that they might soil the carpet, and finally the dust- and soot-producing fireplace had to go. Succumbing to fashion and buying a carpet, therefore, turned out to be like "Adam taking the apple."[64]

Stowe extended this discussion in a short essay with the significant title, "The Cheapness of Beauty." She compared how $80 that might be spent on a carpet could be more effectively used for materials for home-made furnishings. Stowe argued that a floor could be covered with matting that cost only a few dollars. Some of the rest of the money could be spent on wallpaper and on a satin border, both of which the housewife could apply herself. A couch, an easy chair, a table, mattresses, pillows, and curtains could all be made from raw materials bought with the extra money. Stowe gave precise directions about how to make each of these things. Since the materials for the matting, wallpaper, and furniture amounted only to $61.75, Stowe recommended that the rest could be used for reproductions of works of art. She suggested well-known paintings of the period: Miss Oakey's *The Little Snap-Book Maker*, Eastman Johnson's *Barefoot Boy*, and Bierstadt's *Sunset in the Yosemite Valley*. The presence of these paintings would enhance the beauty of economy that suffused the furnishings of the room.[65]

At the time that Catharine Beecher's mother made her carpet, no one else in Litchfield had one. Housewives in the area usually covered their floors with lumps of wet sand that they stroked with a broom into even zigzag lines.[66] Until 1820 almost all of what little carpeting was made in the United States was used in the homes where it had been produced. The only exception was in the Philadelphia area, where hand looms were operated by independent craftsmen in small workshops. But this system did not appreciably increase the supply of woven goods much beyond the boundaries of Philadelphia.

Carpets were made for broad consumption only when three large weaving companies, one in Connecticut and two in Massachusetts, were started in the 1820s. These companies employed over a hundred people each and soon acquired a large capital. Their example was quickly followed. In 1845 an industrial census reported that there were fifty-six mills in the United States. At least half primarily manufactured carpeting.[67]

Carpets, of course, were not the only goods that were produced in factories after the 1820s. Dozens of products that either had been made in the home or had been completely inaccessible became available in the course of the nineteenth century. These goods made their presence felt as they were distributed to stores across the nation. But housewives did not have to venture outside the home to see what was available. Catharine Beecher's mother ordered her paints from a New York store that some-how she knew sold them. By the 1860s it was no longer necessary to rely on such tenuous contacts. Housewives in even the most remote areas could learn what was available from mail-order catalogs that revealed to them a world of goods they hardly knew existed. Advertisements in local newspapers and national magazines had a similar effect.

Some people, like Harriet Beecher Stowe, made a virtue of resisting ready-made goods. Sometimes they argued that it was unnecessary even to buy raw materials for furnishings and decoration. With real frugality materials could be salvaged from other sources or saved in the course of housework. Many magazines, especially farm journals, had "Household Hints" columns well into this century. But it was difficult to be as steadfast as Harriet Beecher Stowe wanted. The goods offered in stores were hard to resist, especially since growing industries depended on selling them.

One way to accept store-bought goods while not acknowledging their origin was to transfer the arts of economy to the act of consumption. Since it was often difficult to tell how or of what store-bought goods were made, housewives tried to extend their home-oriented knowledge of materials and processes to become astute purchasers. They were also careful to find out which stores were reliable, and who gave testimonials for what products. Above all, they were especially attentive to "bargains." As Stowe lamented in *House and Home Papers*, being able to say "it's so cheap" justified any acquisition.[68]

Many ready-made goods, especially those for home furnishings and decorating, were made acceptable to the reluctant buyer because they were embellished with a pattern that conveyed a moral message and thus mimicked home-produced goods. Moreover, those who thought that such touches had to be personal could put their own imprint on ready-made objects. Stores sold half-finished goods to which the buyer could add her own decorative pattern. Another way to make a purchase look as if it had been produced in the home was to mask it with something homemade. A handmade bedspread and pillowcase rendered a store-bought bed suitable to the values of economy. A display of flowers from the garden justified a table or even a piano.

Purchasing ready-made goods on this basis avoided the issues raised by products from outside the home. By seeking out goods that had a home-made look or by transforming them for the same end, the housewife shut out a world of culture foreign to the humble home, where beauty was judged primarily by cheapness. Many goods sold in stores, especially furniture and furnishings, were produced by means of skills not common in the home circle. Their beauty was judged according to aesthetic values, those of taste, which were different from traditional ones. These values, of course, often deteriorated into or were confused with fashion, but by not acknowledging store-bought goods for what they were, the housewife did not allow herself the chance to learn to distinguish between the two. The housewife also denied herself opportunities by spending an unnecessary amount of time in purchasing manufactured products and in adapting them to the aesthetic of economy. Part of the value of ready-made goods came from the fact that they obviated the need to make things at home. Freed from that burden, the housewife could pursue other interests. But if she used store-bought goods only to make work for herself, then she did not give herself the opportunity to find out about subjects beyond the home.

The beauty of economy probably remained the dominant aesthetic in American homes at least until the time of the First World War. But some women tried to seize the opportunities that ready-made products offered. Buying goods on this basis was not a simple matter. Women who had been trained to have rigorous ideas about economy and to judge what they bought by what they could transform it into found it difficult to learn principles of home decoration based on independent values. In turn, their confusion often indicated how difficult it was to make the transition from the old to the new home.

Before the Civil War it was assumed that the cultured and wealthy understood what constituted taste in home furnishing. That subject was part of their upbringing and education. If they needed advice, they had the connections and resources to obtain it. They consulted architects or skilled craftsmen who designed their homes and advised them about where to buy or who could make what furniture. Those who did not have these advantages, but who were willing and able to furnish and decorate their home, had to consult other sources. Yet by the 1850s there were no American books on this subject, and magazines rarely had articles about it. This lack of information on taste in home furnishing was one reason why Andrew Jackson Downing's books were popular. They were the first widely available American works that contained sections on how to furnish the home, not through the products of home manufacture (although in *The Architecture of Country Houses* Downing had second thoughts about that subject) but instead by applying principles to guide the purchase of goods from stores, some of which he mentioned by name.[69]

By the late 1860s discussions about good and bad taste were more common. The problem then was not how to find information but how to choose among conflicting opinions. Taste to many designers and critics was largely synonymous with ornament. They pointed out the significant features of different styles of furniture and told what principles to use to coordinate the colors and materials of the walls, floors, and ceilings of a room. Different styles had different connotations and were chosen accordingly. But what distinguished all of them was that they did not appear homemade. Through their detailing, materials, and ornament such furniture and furnishings were overtly produced by skilled workers and appeared to be worth what they cost.

The same was true of the overall arrangement of the rooms. The desired effect was to show that each room had been designed not through a process of accretion but instead in a coordinated manner. Furniture had to match and be arranged in suites. One piece generally balanced another, and there was a correspondence in design between objects and the surfaces of the room.

When people who knew little about the models they were trying to emulate bought goods, abuses inevitably crept into the process of design and production. Much of the furniture and furnishings produced for this clientele lacked the craftsmanship and materials of the originals. At best, it had a kind of naiveté; at worst, it appealed simply because it was gaudy. When taste became fashion, some designers and critics not only decried that which offered only "the most glare and glitter" for the money but also wanted to reinterpret the very nature and function of ornament. The alternative they offered to the historical styles of furniture and furnishings and to the latest innovations from fashion-conscious France was "the beauty of simplicity." The precedents that interested them were not those associated with stylish or luxurious periods but instead those which had "old-fashioned austerity."[70]

In producing furniture and fabrics that had this quality, American designers were originally inspired by English artists, architects, and craftsmen like William Morris and Edwin Godwin, who, having been repelled by the quality of goods at the Great Exhibition in 1851, tried to reorient the values of design. By the 1870s, and especially after the Centennial Exhibition, which was an important stimulus to the discussion of matters of taste in interior design, enough Americans were attracted to simplicity and old-fashioned austerity to form a native movement.[71]

The work they produced was first most effectively brought to the public's attention in a series of articles that the art critic Clarence Cook wrote for *Scribner's Monthly* and later published in a book, *The House*

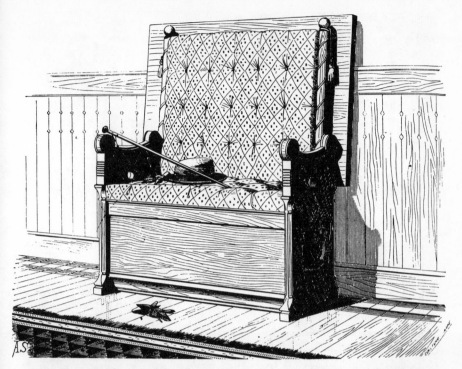

*171. G. F. Babb: A settle, 1875. This piece of furniture was illustrated in the first of Clarence Cook's articles on home decoration. Designers who admired "old-fashioned austerity" often tried to transform traditional furniture, especially that which was associated with a humble setting, to suit the needs of their times.*

*Beautiful.* With the aid of attractive drawings, Cook discussed not only the latest English furniture, Chinese cabinets, Japanese tables, Italian screens, but also old New England furniture and recent American designs modeled after it. These goods had in common an aesthetic of simplicity that was diametrically opposed to the overstuffed, ornate furnishings then considered fashionable. The objects that appealed to Cook's taste had little, if any, ornament and were made of bare, everyday materials like pine, oak, rattan, rush, and cane. But although these goods were conceived as a response to fashionable furniture, there was nothing crude or sentimental about them. For all their references to the early furniture of New England and other places, the designers of these goods did not emulate the imprecision of home-produced goods, nor did they emphasize moral messages in their ornament. Their concept of simplicity had a degree of refinement that had never been a part of economy.

These values were as evident when the furniture was grouped together

*172. Clarence Cook: A corner in the House Beautiful, 1876. Although austerity may have been a virtue in the design of the individual object, the total impression a room was supposed to convey was that of a rich variety that capitalized on "much in little space." These rooms were not organized symmetrically and were not supposed to be seen on axis. Several pieces of furniture were crowded into a corner, plants were juxtaposed with statues, bric-a-brac was displayed on hanging shelves, and a painting was contrasted with a plate taken out of context and mounted on a wall.*

*173. The dining room of John V. C. Pruyn, Albany, New York, 1876. This room is very much in transition. Its symmetrical arrangement and the moldings on the ceiling embody principles of advancement and good taste. But the Eastlake sideboard and the bric-a-brac on the mantel indicate that by 1876 the owner may have had enough of the formal life for which the dining room had been a setting and felt the need to assert some aspect of the "old home."*

as in the individual piece. Cook thought there was no reason to have "symmetry" in home furnishings. All the objects in a room did not have to match or be of one style. Instead, he favored a controlled disorder that in a carefully calculated way often set one object against another. Thus instead of the customary axial views of rooms and groups of furniture, the point of perspective of the drawings that accompanied Cook's articles was taken at an oblique angle. But as much as this cultivated informality was set against the stiff orderliness that made living rooms become cold parlors, it did not go to the other extreme, the pattern that characterized a house in which the tools for home production were intermixed with the family's furniture.

Cook's attitude toward carpets summarized many of his ideas. He recognized that large carpets covering all or most of the floor in a room were associated with comfort and thus were eagerly sought after. Whether Catharine Beecher understood it, that must have been one of the reasons her mother went to such lengths to make one. But Cook thought that carpets had liabilities. It seemed wasteful to cover parts of them with furniture, and they also attracted dust. He did not reject carpets because of economy or cleanliness, however. His main objection was that he did not like their effect on the appearance of rooms. Bare floors with the occasional small rug were more appealing because that combination produced a background compatible with the simple furniture and the asymmetrical arrangement that he liked.

Over the two years during which his articles appeared, Cook received many letters about them, and on several occasions he mentioned his readers' comments. He was not disturbed by those who criticized him for rejecting the self-consciously sophisticated furniture that was associated with good taste. The more problematical letters were from those who, although enthusiastic, were dismayed because the goods he discussed were not cheap. When they priced these simple chairs, tables, and fabrics, they found that they cost more than goods that were supposed to be expensive. Even chairs "as ostentatiously bare and matter-of-fact" as the bentwood furniture of Vienna and those made by the Shakers were as expensive as some in fashionable shops that tried to make "a good deal of show."

The same was true of the work associated with the English designer Charles Eastlake. In *Hints on Household Taste*, a book that was published in England in 1868 and went through six editions in the United States by 1881, Eastlake invoked Viollet-le-Duc's principles of structural and constructional integrity to expose the deceits of contemporary furniture design. Eastlake overtly displayed the way his chairs, tables, sideboards, and other pieces of furniture were made. He did not attempt to cover up joints with ornament or to conceal hinges and other pieces of hardware. In fact, he made features out of the pegs that held the furniture together and the handles that opened cupboards and drawers. His furniture thus looked as if it had been "on the dissecting table and flayed alive." Americans were attracted to it because they felt they were getting a lot for their money. But they soon found out that they had to pay more for Eastlake furniture than they expected.

Cook thought it was a virtue that "wherever the money goes, it does not go to carving, and flourish, and display for display's sake." He assumed that his readers would appreciate this refinement in taste and would prefer it to the historical styles of furniture or to the latest fashions from Europe. Evidently, however, they were not yet that advanced. Cook acknowledged that his readers were mainly the grandchildren of people who had lived

*174.   Charles L. Eastlake: Dining room sideboard, 1869. Eastlake's furniture designs were based on an explicit demonstration of the manner in which each piece was put together. Purchasers thought that such "honest" construction would be cheap, but they found out that it usually was more expensive to make a frank but neat expression of joints than to cover them up.*

amidst goods that were "perfectly fitted" for their uses. Either because they were suspicious of the world of taste or because they were nostalgic for the old values, Cook's readers were eager to recapture some aspect of the traditional home in their surroundings. Even so, having had at least a glimmer of the values of taste, they could not accept that a refined simplicity cost more than what was ornate.[72]

Antique furniture brought out this dilemma even more poignantly than bentwood chairs and Eastlake cupboards. In the 1870s, especially after the Centennial Exhibition, antique American furniture came into fashion, and the countryside was scoured by people looking for old sideboards and brass andirons. Because of this interest, it was not uncommon to see "the drawing-room of modern indolence furnished with the spinning-wheels of an industrious ancestry, the wood-work shining in coats of fresh varnish." The housewife who "chose to loll on cushions and contemplate the uncomfortable chair in which her great-grandmother used to sit as bolt upright as if she had swallowed the ramrod of Bunker Hill" may have had genuine feelings about the need to accommodate those tokens of the old days in the modern home. But in making old furniture desirable, she raised its price; then those who had bought it in the past as an economy measure could no longer afford it.[73]

If trying to understand what constituted good taste was confusing, then women who bought ready-made goods had equally large problems in deciding how to use their spare time. Melusina Fay Peirce thought that women could enter a wide range of professions, but she and many others singled out the arts, especially the decorative arts, as most suited for women. After the Civil War many more women than in previous generations contemplated a career in art. The problems they had in pursuing this interest and the effect these difficulties ultimately had on the decoration of the home is well illustrated by Candace Wheeler's career in the decorative arts, a field that she called (as distinct from the applied arts, which pertained to the design of small objects) "all art which enriches or beautifies architecture."[74]

Wheeler was born in 1827 in Delhi, a small settlement in central New York. She grew up amidst household industries. Throughout her childhood she wore clothes made of material that had been grown on her family's farm and spun in her house. From an early age she helped to make butter and cheese, dip candles, and smoke meats. When Wheeler married in 1844, she moved to New York, already a very different milieu from the small rural settlement of her childhood. During the following decade she became acquainted with many painters, and in 1854 she and her husband, like other members of New York's literary and artistic circle, built a cottage, Nestledown, on Long Island near the old village of Jamaica. Artists from New York's Tenth Street Studio frequently visited the Wheelers, and it was at Nestledown that Eastman Johnson and Sanford Gifford did some of their best paintings.

Although Wheeler was surrounded by these influences for many years, until her early fifties her primary occupation was wife and mother. A turning point came in 1876 when she visited the Centennial Exposition, where she was attracted to the work of the Kensington School in a pavilion of the Royal School of Art and Needlework. One aim of the founders of the Kensington School, an offshoot of the Pre-Raphaelite movement, was to revive the old skills of needlework. This rekindled interest also had a practical purpose; it provided employment and an income for "decayed gentlewomen" who had lost their means of support. Such women were pathetic figures, and the Kensington School offered them an honorable way of making a living.

Candace Wheeler recognized that there were many women in the United States who had to cope with the "necessity of remunerative work." Inspired by the Kensington School's example, she enlisted the aid of Mrs. David Lane, who during the Civil War had organized fairs for the Sanitary Commission in New York, and started the Society of Decorative Art. Although the Kensington School was its model, the Society of Decorative Art did not restrict the work of its members to embroidery and needlework, and it tried to avoid the genteel reputation of its English counterpart. The organizers emphasized that the society was a business venture. It had rooms in which women could exhibit and sell what they made, and it established useful connections for its members with dealers. The Society of Decorative Art departed from the Kensington School in even more fundamental ways. In addition to helping decayed gentlewomen, it tried to provide an outlet for "the ability of educated women." By making art education and the possibility of a profitable career available to women, Candace Wheeler and the founders of the society hoped to enhance their position.

The immediate response to this organization was "astonishing." It seemed, Wheeler later recalled, that all the early members had storehouses of articles already prepared for sale before the society was started. As gratifying as this enthusiasm was, Candace Wheeler was disturbed by the poor quality of the goods. In the weeks after the society was founded, the abysmal standard of most of the objects submitted for display became more and more embarrassing. It was also apparent that classes would not quickly help to produce better results. Most of the women who enrolled either were too impatient to learn the proper techniques or did not have enough time to master them.[75]

The Society's membership expanded in the year after its beginning, and auxiliary organizations were started in other cities. But Candace Wheeler felt the organization had to compromise itself because it was compelled to accept things that "were good in their own way" but that did not belong to the "category of art." She resolved this dilemma by helping to found another society, the Women's Exchange. Through that organization women could make and sell anything they wanted, with no distinctions as to quality. A few organizations similar to the Women's Exchange had been started earlier. They offered for sale goods produced by women "who had seen better days," but their primary purpose was to solicit donations for their members. Most of the over one hundred Women's Exchanges that were started after 1879 tried to reverse this emphasis, but few were able to do so. Because of the way the Women's

*175. Dora Wheeler Keith: The ceiling of the Library of the Woman's Building at the World's Columbian Exposition, 1893. Dora Wheeler Keith was Candace Wheeler's daughter.*

Exchange was run, buyers could never count on the availability of goods. The Women's Exchange, therefore, never competed effectively with local businesses, and most of its revenue came from private contributions and from charity balls and benefits.

Most Women's Exchanges probably would never have succeeded on any other basis, no matter who contributed to them, but many did not help their own cause by limiting their contributors to women who really needed the income. This policy stemmed in part from a desire to screen older and more needy women from the competition of younger and perhaps more capable housewives, but it was also in accord with the prevalent view that if housewives wanted to work in their spare time, they should do so for a charitable cause, not to make money. One unfortunate effect of this policy was to make housewives who wanted to earn money sell their goods through commercial organizations that paid them only a pittance for their work.[76]

Once the Women's Exchange was founded, the Society of Decorative Art could concentrate on furthering the cause of art education. Candace Wheeler intended this training for two types of women. Previously, an unmarried woman, "the superfluous female," had always been an embarrassment. But Wheeler thought that times had changed. "The old maid" had become the "New Woman." The work she did was as valuable and as necessary as the work of men, and Wheeler was confident that the New Woman would be respected for what she accomplished. At the same time Wheeler believed that every woman had a "natural capacity . . . for family direction and family life." Even so, since a woman usually still had one third of her life to live after her children had grown up, she had to prepare herself for another career. Having mastered a subject, she would be "ten times more a woman" while still a housewife and mother, and later she would not have to become one of those pathetic ladies forced to seek remunerative work.[77]

Wheeler was always ready to encourage women to become artists. In 1897, in summarizing the previous twenty years in art education, she mentioned with pride the increase in female artists. Notwithstanding these achievements, however, she thought women were especially suited for the decorative arts, having an "apparently instinctive knowledge" of subjects like textiles. But "natural ability" was not enough. Women needed training, and that was why organizations like the Society of Decorative Art were important.[78]

The other, broader field to which women were especially suited was interior decoration, and Wheeler predicted that there would be an ever-increasing demand for people who could make "a perfect mosaic of excellence" within a building. Women who wanted to be interior decorators needed training as much as those who wanted to concentrate in textiles. Being able to "make the most of it" and having "an eye for color" were not enough. To be an interior decorator, an art education was essential, but Wheeler thought that experience in an architect's office was also necessary.[79]

Although Candace Wheeler thought it was important to put the Society for Decorative Art on a solid footing, she found the work so taxing that she did not have the time to pursue her own interests in textile design. The opportunity to do so came in 1879 when Louis C. Tiffany, who already was known for his artistic glass work, proposed that she join him in forming a company to carry out projects in the decorative arts. Lockwood de Forest, an expert on wood carving and Oriental design, and the painter Samuel Colman added other skills to the Associated Artists, a name chosen by Candace Wheeler.

A drop curtain for the new Madison Square Theater was the Associated Artists' first important commission. Other work soon followed. During the summer of 1881 Wheeler contributed some designs to Mark Twain's home in Hartford, but the Associated Artists' most important commission was the redecoration of the Blue, East, and Red Rooms of the White House. With their tools, brushes, and needles, the Associated Artists were able to intertwine woods, metals, glass, mother-of-pearl, canvas, silk, serge, and other materials to produce brilliantly colored designs with imagery from exotic cultures, motifs from nature, and themes from the American past. One critic called this work "the first fruits of the American Renaissance."[80]

After three years of cooperative work, the tapestry and embroidery side of the Associated Artists had developed so rapidly that Candace Wheeler decided to split from Tiffany, de Forest, and Colman and to form her own business, which she continued to call the Associated Artists. The Associated Artists still accepted individual commissions, through which Candace Wheeler was able to further her earlier innovations in tapestry design, but she also wanted to cater to a wider clientele. The Associated Artists, therefore, supplied designs to the prominent silk manufacturers, the Cheney Brothers of Connecticut. Moreover, in her desire to upgrade the general quality of American design, Wheeler experimented with cheap fabrics — chintz, cotton, Kentucky jean, and denim. The imagery she used in these designs came from many sources, but she was particularly eager to adapt American flowers to these American products.[81]

The Associated Artists did not restrict its activities to textiles. By the late 1880s the organization had branched out into interior decoration.[82] Candace Wheeler had specific ideas about the decoration of the home. She believed that the decorator was subordinate to the architect and was not to treat a building as "a theater for the display of his talents." Decorators could help to enhance the qualities of rooms mainly by understanding the nature of walls. Wheeler believed that walls were one of the first necessities of civilization, but because they confined, they were not altogether agreeable. The task of the decorator was to disguise this limit and make the occupant forget that a wall is a barrier. There were many ways to do so, but the two essential qualities were color and nature, for both of which people had an "instinctive love." How she applied natural patterns and color to the wall depended on the size, location, and function of the room. Each space had its own character, but Wheeler usually placed darker finishes between the baseboard and the dado, a lighter one on the main part of the wall up to a rail that was at or above the height of windows, and finally a cream or white surface above the rail and onto the ceiling. Although Wheeler liked wallpapers with flowers, she always thought walls had to be the background for the objects in the rooms.[83]

Some women did make their mark in the decorative arts, but others, like Albion Fellows Bacon, who wanted to study in an art school or work in an atelier of the decorative arts, could never adequately accommodate that interest to their responsibilities in the home. Their problem was not simply that they did not have time to learn. Since many of them were uncertain about what they should do, they were also probably afraid that if they did learn, they would be drawn away from the home, where their true duties lay.

In the 1890s an important change in the approach to the decorative and applied arts affected the increasing number of women who found themselves in this complex position. Those who had become interested in the decorative arts in the 1870s and 1880s were repelled by the quality of goods available in stores, but they had no fundamental misgivings about the economic system of which those stores were a part. As a practitioner of the decorative arts, Candace Wheeler, for example, felt no inconsistency in designing and personally making a unique tapestry for a special client, in setting a pattern that other women in the Associated Artists repeated with inevitable small variations, or in making a design for cloth that would be mass-produced by a machine operated by unskilled or semi-skilled workers. She believed that there was a need for all types of work, and her design principles were not specific to any one of these techniques. Wheeler was ardently interested in the handwork of the past. She collected and wrote about samplers, embroidery, quilts, crewelwork, and lace that women had made in the days of the home industries. But she believed that when society's full capabilities — both those of women and of machines — were used, even better work could be produced.[84]

This point of view was similar to the one that Frank Lloyd Wright articulated in 1901 in his Hull-House speech, "The Art and Craft of the Machine." Wright did not despise machines; he considered them advanced tools that, if used properly, could help to produce higher standards of design. However, when he delivered his speech, he found that "several brilliant disciples of Ruskin and Morris" swept his propositions aside "in a flood of sentimental eloquence."[85] Many people at this time found Wright's position difficult to maintain. They believed that a radical change in the scale of American industry was then taking place. The small factory was being replaced by gigantic industries in which workmen were no more than cogs. The violent strikes of the late 1880s, the ensuing labor difficulties, and then the severe depression of 1893 had begun to focus attention on these conditions.

Proof of the degrading nature of the industrial system lay not only in the appalling factory conditions, the low wages, and the tenements of large cities but also in the quality of what was produced. Machines turned out goods that revealed no imprint of the workman's hand. The objects labeled "art" were no more satisfactory. They were destined primarily for the modern equivalent of an aristocracy. Their sterile and artificial forms showed how barren the whole field of art, whether pure, applied, or decorative, had become.[86] In view of the scope of the problem, it was no longer sufficient to focus on design principles. Instead, a fundamental reorientation of the system of production was necessary.

Different approaches to John Ruskin and William Morris summarized this change of outlook. Before 1890 Ruskin and Morris were primarily of interest to architects, artists, and decorators in the United States because of the designs they produced or fostered, not for their ideas about society.[87] But by the early 1890s many people who were perplexed by the changes taking place in American life began to turn to the political and economic writings not only of Ruskin and Morris but also of Carlyle, Kropotkin, Tolstoy, and many others who wanted to turn back the course of industrial development. All of these authors implicitly or explicitly argued that first it was important to create a humane society; only then could satisfactory products be made. Versions of this society varied, but in most of them the division of labor was minimal, wealth came directly from the land, and craftsmen, not artists or machines, made the everyday goods. The model of the ideal citizen in this felicitous state was the medieval artisan. He was a member of a society of equals, and he was free to work as he wanted, unencumbered by abstruse ideas about what "art" was.[88]

Several communities were founded in the United States to put these ideas into practice. Their histories and ideologies are difficult to trace, but because it published a magazine, the *Artsman*, and because its founder often explained his philosophy, the Rose Valley Association's ideas are easily accessible. This community was started in 1901 by William L. Price, a Philadelphia architect who was an innovator in concrete construction.[89] Located fourteen miles from Philadelphia, the Rose Valley Association was modeled after C. R. Ashbee's Guild of Handicraft in Chipping Campden, England.[90] It had workshops for making pottery and furniture, which it sold through a salesroom in Philadelphia until the community went bankrupt in 1909.

The Rose Valley Association was based on a disdain for industrial society and on a desire to return to a "natural" existence. This entailed a regimen of unadulterated food, fresh air and exercise, and as few restrictions on personal behavior as possible. Although the *Artsman* equivocated about what types of machines were allowable and when, hand labor was the basis of everything made in the community. The importance of hand labor was so emphasized that it often seemed the process of production was more important that the quality of the goods produced. Thus the members of Rose Valley were not artists; they were "artsmen" who emphasized that they made "practical" things.[91]

Their ideal was summarized in an article by Price that contrasted "a chair that is built and any other chair." A chair that was "not built" could be just as beautiful in design as one that was; it could have tighter joints and a better finish. But those qualities did not make it a good chair. What separated the two was, first of all, the material. In the old days,

176.  *Will Price: An Artsman chair, 1904. Unlike other advocates of arts and crafts, Will Price did not draw a strict line between ornament related to structure and construction and that which was not.*

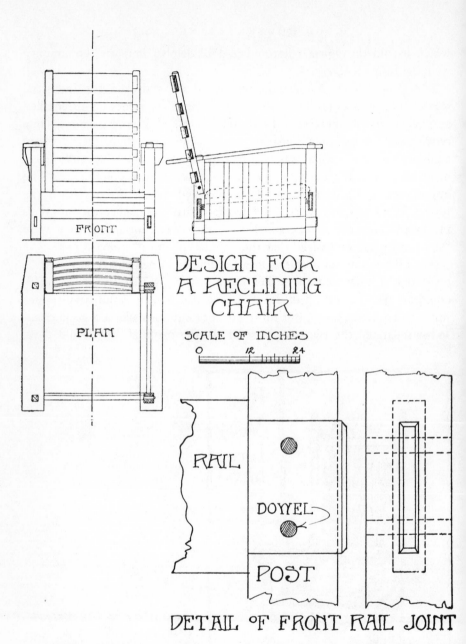

FRONT

PLAN

DESIGN FOR
A RECLINING
CHAIR

SCALE OF INCHES

0    12    24

RAIL

DOWEL

POST

DETAIL OF FRONT RAIL JOINT

*177. Gustave Stickley: A Craftsman chair. Stickley offered this version of the Morris chair for sale at his store in New York and through mail-order catalogs. But he also encouraged readers of the* Craftsman *to make the chair themselves. The lack of more precise details in the magazine may have been a way of influencing those who were undecided about whether to buy or build.*

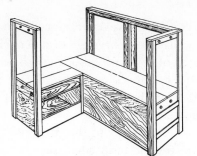

Corner Seat Made From Two Packing-Boxes

The Corner Bookcase was Made in Two Sections

From Baked-Beans Boxes        Writing and Manuscript Desk        Another View of the Desk

*178. Louise Brigham: Box furniture, 1911. Of all the furniture designers of the period, Louise Brigham was the one who came closest to realizing the ideal of simplicity. She studied with Josef Hoffman and Charles Rennie McIntosh in Europe. When she returned to the United States, she ran programs to teach children from the Lower East Side of New York City to make simple furniture from discarded boxes and packing crates.*

Price wrote, the woodsman swung his ax against the tree best fitted for its future use. The great trunk was cut into logs in winter when it was least full of sap. It was then floated down the river, purified of any sap, cut to size, and air-dried. The true artsman then shaped this wood, taking into account "the accidental beauty spot or curl or knot" which he "so lovingly fondle[d] and subdue[d] to his purpose." The second superior quality of the "built" chair was its "honest" construction. While most chairs were held together with nothing but dowels and glue, and sometimes even nails, the joints of the chair that was "built" used a mortise or, even better, a wedge and tenon construction. Nothing was disguised, and the chair lasted as long as the wood.[92]

The founders of the Rose Valley Association hoped that other such communities would be started. It was difficult, however, for people, no matter how sympathetic they were, to make the break. Oscar Lovell Triggs, one of the most ardent advocates of a return to a crafts-based society, realized that it was impossible to call for a general strike or a cessation of industrial work. Since there could be no radical break with existing conditions, he founded the Industrial Arts League in Chicago in 1896. This organization ran night courses for workers so that they could sharpen their craft skills and thus prepare for the unspecified time when there would somehow be a conversion to a state in which it would again be possible to do meaningful work.[93]

In the same period, arts and crafts courses were started in schools. Whereas some educational theorists thought that this activity was important only for children, others thought that it also was relevant for grown-ups.[94] By the turn of the century many arts and crafts societies, primarily for housewives, had been founded, and arts and crafts, coupled with courses in folklore, were taught at summer schools. Those who did not have access to these associations or programs could learn about the subject from articles in magazines like the *Craftsman* and *House and Garden*.[95]

The general message to the women who were attracted to arts and crafts was very different from that expressed by those who earlier had been interested in the decorative and applied arts. Unlike factory workers, women did not have to wait for a great change in society. As housewives they had always been adept at arts and crafts. Thus, by joining associations to relearn these skills, they were reestablishing their true role. Whereas Candace Wheeler had emphasized the need for special training and the distinction between art and lower levels of creative activity, many of the supporters of the arts and crafts did not demand and even demeaned that expertise. Some women who became devotees of arts and crafts undoubtedly brought the highest levels of judgment to bear on what they made, and they produced exemplary goods.[96] But once craft was emphasized more than art, it was easy for others to be content with knitting according to a pattern cut out from a magazine or attending the weekly pottery class. Those women probably rarely worried about a career outside the home, but, considering the eight years that Albion Fellows Bacon spent in "eclipse," perhaps that was wise.

By doing arts and crafts the housewife could claim to have a form of self-expression that did not clash with, but instead enhanced, her role as homemaker. The things she made could also help her justify the ready-

# Good Taste and Bad Taste in Chairs

*179. "Good Taste and Bad Taste in Chairs," 1903. This comparison from the* Ladies' Home Journal *conveys a general idea about the virtue of simplicity, although it was often difficult to draw the line between simplicity and a cold austerity.*

made goods that she bought. One conflict she may have felt as a consumer, however, was whether to buy the products of an organization like the Rose Valley Association. In an article in the *Artsman* Will Price acknowledged that only the well-to-do could afford Rose Valley products. For the community to survive, its goods had to be expensive. This situation was regrettable, but it was necessary "until our new world is born." Horace Traubel, who had been a protégé of Walt Whitman and was a supporter of Rose Valley, was not satisfied with this excuse. He asked:

Has the artsman a message for palaces and no message for houses? Has the artsman no means by which to influence the main stream? Is he only to play in the eddies and with the side-currents? Is a Rose Valley chair to be a special privilege or a common benefaction? Is Rose Valley to cover the books of the poor? Can no way be devised by which the average man may participate in the blessings that accrue to a revival of the crafts? Are we to admit that ten dollars means honesty and one dollar means fraud?[97]

The *Artsman* had no answer. Earlier, when readers complained to Clarence Cook that the furniture he wrote about was expensive, he could claim that it was, no matter how simple and austere, in a higher creative category than were not only those products that were passed off as fashionable, but also those that made cheapness a virtue. To be told that a "practical chair" was expensive made no sense, except insofar as one accepted that this was the price to be paid until the new world was born.

Thorstein Veblen was one of the few Americans who was able to put these complex issues into perspective. Veblen was a friend of Oscar Triggs, and he wrote a review of Triggs's *Chapters in the History of the Arts and Crafts Movement*. As much as he tried to be kind to his friend and to the Industrial Arts League, he thought that arts and crafts were largely futile.[98] In *The Theory of the Leisure Class* he explained why.

Veblen's work contains an interpretation of the broad development of civilization. It ranges over thousands of years and cites examples — Bushmen, Eskimos, North American Indians, Chinese, Polynesian islanders — from all over the world. The book is written in an objective and analytical manner, but beneath Veblen's long words and ponderous phrases, there is an incisive, ironic humor. Written in 1898, *The Theory of the Leisure Class* can be read as an interpretation not just of the broad development of civilization but also of the preceding half century in the United States.

*The Theory of the Leisure Class* is based on a distinction between two successive stages of civilization. The first was the "savage" state in which people lived in small settlements. They were poor, sedentary, classless, and peaceful; individual ownership was not a part of their economic system. In the savage stage some differentiation of function existed between men and women, but these distinctions were not so pronounced as to be invidious.

When the sedentary community adopted a predatory way of life, the savage state gave way to a "barbarian" state. Some members of the society then could easily obtain a subsistence. They were exempted from steady labor and formed a leisure class. The tribe thus became differentiated. The men and women of the barbarian civilization were separated by occupations. Men did the jobs that were classed as "exploit," those tasks considered worthy, honorable, and noble. To women fell the "drudgery," work that was debasing, unworthy, and ignoble. In a later stage of barbarism the distinctions that first separated men and women appeared among different groups of men. The further the stage of barbarism, the more differentiation there was in the society.

Once this differentiation occurred and a leisure class was formed, it was important to manifest evidence of status. One way to do so was to exhibit "conspicuous leisure" by abstaining from labor — in other words, to adopt habits directly opposite to those of thrift and industry. A similar activity was "conspicuous consumption." Just as it was necessary for the members of the leisure class to exhibit their leisure as a "mark of superior pecuniary achievement," so it was important not just to accumulate property, but to waste it through a consumption that went beyond what was necessary for subsistence.

Thus, the ownership of property was an important attribute of the leisure class. According to Veblen, the earliest objects of private ownership were women. They were seized in the first stages of barbarism as trophies for the demonstration of prowess. In later stages this custom developed into the institution of marriage, but Veblen claimed that the relationship of husband and wife still remained essentially that of master and servant. The husband, therefore, could enhance his conspicuous leisure by having a wife who worked for him or, in a later stage of barbarism, who revealed his prominence by remaining idle and unproductive. A wife who made an occupation of conspicuously consuming inessential goods was a manifestation of an even more advanced state.

So strong were the impulses of emulation among men that even those who could not afford to indulge in conspicuous leisure or consumption needed a kind of "vicarious experience," which they gained through their wives. Veblen noted that "it is by no means an uncommon spectacle to find a man applying himself to work with the utmost assiduity, in order that his wife may in due form render for him that degree of vicarious leisure which the common sense of the time demands."

In the later stages of barbarism Veblen found that women in this leisured and therefore incapacitated state did not remain indolent or idle. That habit was then looked down upon. The wife of advanced barbarism did not "disown her hands and feet." Instead, she applied herself "assiduously to household cares." But these activities were still a form of conspicuous leisure and consumption because they served "little or no ulterior end beyond showing that she does not occupy herself with anything that is gainful or that is of substantial use."

Veblen believed that everyone had an "instinct for workmanship," a "taste for effective work, and a distaste for futile effort." In the production of goods or in the execution or any task, "serviceability" or "efficiency" was the ultimate goal. If the instinct for workmanship was fulfilled in the design and production of an object, the result would be beautiful. The instinct for workmanship was part of human nature, but in the advanced stages of barbarism people had to manifest it through machines, which could make a "more perfect product" than could the hand. Nevertheless, these goods were not appreciated. They were despised precisely because they were perfect and did not exhibit the flaws that gave evidence of conspicuous waste. The rules of conspicuous waste demanded "novelty." Objects, therefore, did not conform to generic types but instead were a "congeries of idiosyncracies." Instead of "aesthetic beauty," which was based on the instinct for workmanship, people preferred another type of beauty, "pecuniary beauty," a taste that was bolstered by a set of specious laws and principles.

For Veblen the reason that the tradition of crafts initiated by Ruskin and Morris was attractive was precisely because, in the guise of producing something useful, it justified the imperfect and wasteful. "The honorific marks of hand labor," he claimed,

are certain imperfections and irregularities in the lines of the hand-wrought article, showing where the workman has fallen short in the execution of the design. The ground of the superiority of hand-wrought goods, therefore, is a certain margin of crudeness. The margin must never be so wide as to show bungling workmanship, since that would be evidence of low cost, nor so narrow as to suggest the ideal precision attained only by the machine, for that would be evidence of low cost.

Housewives most clearly demonstrated this "exaltation of the defective." In denying the instinct for workmanship and indulging in handwork, they demonstrated that they were essentially without real function except as objects of conspicuous leisure and consumption.[99]

Veblen was probably the first person to praise the machine-made quality of machine-made goods. He agreed with critics who claimed that the machine was not just a more advanced tool, that it had a mind of its own, but, unlike Ruskin, Morris, Triggs, and Price, Veblen welcomed this quality. He implied that in a more advanced stage of civilization people would agree with him and that through the machine they would reattain their instinct for workmanship. Designers and critics would test the implications of this proposition, especially as it bore upon the goods for the household, only after the First World War. In the meantime, housewives were left to grapple with the difficult conditions that Veblen so trenchantly outlined.

# 7

## THE HEART OF THE HOME

MANY OF THE MACHINES that found their way into American homes at the end of the nineteenth century were attached to power and service lines. Water pipes, electrical cables, sewage systems, telephone lines, hot-air ducts, and gas mains were manifestations of progress — the products of the Day of Roads. By connecting a house to the surrounding community and eventually to the world at large, they did their part in destroying an isolation that had always shackled man's capacities. But like the machines they drove and the fixtures that marked the points of their outlet, these power and service lines were also objects of suspicion. They disrupted age-old relationships and brought people into contact with one another in ways that they were not accustomed to or did not understand. The result often was not mutual enlightenment but consternation and even conflict.

The same combination of enthusiasm and distrust operated at another level. If power and service lines changed the relationship between the household and the world at large, they also did their part to alter the functions and positions of the members of the family. Once mother and daughter power was replaced by water and steam power, the roles and relationships of each member of the household had to be redefined. To many this change created opportunities, but to others the destruction of this familiar structure was disquieting.

The very nature of water pipes, electrical cables, sewage systems, telephone lines, hot-air ducts, gas mains, and other systems intensified the ambivalence that Americans felt toward them. Unlike a sewing machine, a stove, or a washbasin, an electrical cable, a gas main, or a sewage pipe was not finite. Each disappeared into a wall or the ground and then was connected to an invisible network that spread beyond the home. Because they were invisible and indeterminate, it was easier to take these wires, ducts, pipes, conduits, cables, and mains for granted and to accept them as part of the fabric of the home than the more obtrusive household machines. On the other hand, the same qualities made these power lines and service systems all the more suspicious. Once they were embedded in the walls or the ground, it was difficult to exercise any surveillance over them. The more inaccessible they were, the more anxiety there was that something would go wrong.

Americans were so committed to progress that it was difficult for them to express this ambivalence. Rather than address it directly, they often did so through humor. Misgivings about progress were a major theme of Mark Twain's work. He probably was one of the first people to comment on what now seems commonplace — a telephone conversation experienced by a third party who simply sits by and takes no part. This was one of the "solemnest curiosities of modern life." Twain noted that "you hear invitations given; you hear no thanks in return. You have listening pauses of dead silence, followed by irrelevant and unjustifiable exclamations of glad surprise, or sorrow, or dismay." To illustrate this new phenomenon, Twain interrupted the writing of "a deep article on a sublime philosophical subject" and took down this conversation:

Yes? Why, how did *that* happen?
Pause.
What did you say?
Pause.
Oh, no, I don't think it was.
Pause.
*No!* Oh, no, I don't mean *that*. I meant, put it in while it is still boiling, — or just before it *comes* to boil.
Pause.
WHAT?
Pause.
I turned it over with a back stitch on the selvage edge.
Pause.
Yes, I like that way, too; but I think it's better to baste it on the valenciennes or bombazine, or something of that sort. It gives such aroma, — and attracts so much notice.
Pause.
It's forty-ninth Deuteronomy, sixty-fourth to ninety-seventh inclusive. I think we ought to all read it often.

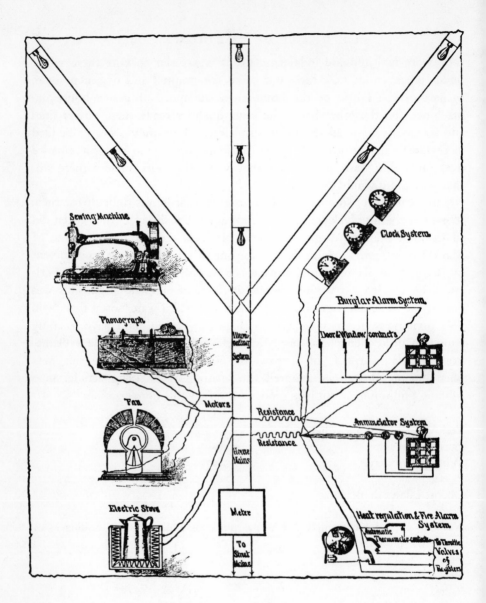

*180. A plan for wiring the electrical appliances of a house, 1890. This rudimentary diagram expresses the new manner in which different parts of the home were drawn together as electrical wires spread throughout the house.*

This was all good fun, but, as always, Twain's motives were complex. Although he might have welcomed the opportunity to interrupt writing his deep article, these peculiar conversations disrupted the habitual pattern of sounds in the household and therefore were annoying. Twain also noted that the telephone had a strange effect on women. Since it was not yet possible to dial directly, calls had to be placed through a central exchange. But women, who already were reputed to be the most avid users of the telephone, always shrank from calling the central exchange themselves. They felt there was something irregular or perhaps even illicit about this method of connecting two places. Husbands, therefore, had to place the calls; that made the telephone all the more irritating.[1]

Twain's remarks illuminate a significant fact about the history of utilities, especially as they were brought to the home. The development of water, electrical, sewage, telephone, steam, gas, and other services depended on technological and administrative innovations, but these accomplishments never took place in a vacuum. At one level or another, they were all shaped by what the public anticipated from them. These expectations were never one-sided; they always contained a mixture of enthusiasm and doubt.

✦✦✦

Every utility that entered or was part of the home at some time was thought to be a source of danger. Americans frequently were wary of gas and electric lines not only because they feared that these utilities could cause fires but also because they suspected that they emitted noxious fumes or rays. Every case of malfunction helped to stimulate this deep-seated uneasiness.

Of all utilities, sewage systems caused the most concern. They were dangerous because they carried filth, which was associated with disease, and because they were connected to or allied with sources of water used for washing, drinking, or cooking. The fear of sewage has probably always existed, but in the 1870s, the very time when plumbing services were first being widely installed in American homes, it was expressed more frequently than ever before. What to do about sewer gas, a substance all the more dangerous because it was virtually undetectable, occupied the efforts of many prominent doctors and sanitarians. How they dealt with this question is significant not only because it had a direct bearing on the design and organization of kitchen and bathroom facilities, but also because it illustrates how uneasy Americans were about the services that were connected to their homes.

Then !

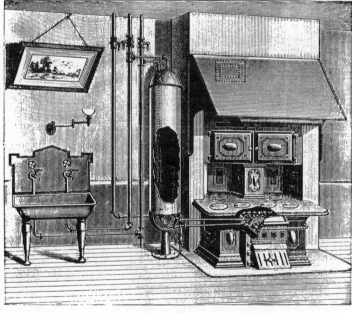

Now !

181. *"Then! Now!"* This contrast encapsulated an idea of
progress that not everyone could sustain. The illustrations
were the frontispiece of Women, Plumbers, and Doctors,
a book that tried to show that "if women and plumbers do
their whole sanitary duty, there will be comparatively little
occasion for the services of the doctors."

explained, "civilization should make some concessions." He recommended that plumbing be excluded from the part of the house normally in use. It was best somehow to annex the spaces that contained these facilities onto the back of the house, where they would not pollute the rest of the building.[5]

To make sense of these suspicions and to avoid the pessimism that they sometimes led to, it was necessary to have a strong belief in progress. George Waring, the sanitarian who also wrote about rural subjects and the organization of farm villages, never wavered in his belief that the human condition could be improved. To those who criticized plumbing and who claimed that the world had survived well enough without such improvements, Waring retorted that the world had not and still was not surviving well enough. The primary object of a well-regulated life was to secure happiness, and that aim was "crushed to the earth with every death of a wife or child or friend." Waring believed that the average age was not one half of what it could be "under perfect sanitary conditions." Once man learned to live as long as he could, happiness would therefore at least double.

Waring thought that the recent tendency to live in towns and cities had brought with it deplorable sanitary conditions. But he did not call for a return to an agrarian way of life. Man had always suffered from bad sanitation, no matter where he lived. Although Waring was always interested in rural problems, he also believed in the importance of cities. They were a manifestation of progress. Both contexts, therefore, needed improvement. Because of this conviction Waring tried to work out a suitable plumbing system. His approach is worth examining, not because he was more perceptive than his contemporaries, but because his views illustrate the range of solutions proposed for this complex problem.[6]

In 1870 Waring estimated that for half of the families in rural parts of the United States "the corn-field and the thicket [were] the only retreat provided." Many houses, especially those in cities, had commodes for liquid waste, but even in the best homes it was still necesssary to go to an outdoor toilet. The inconvenience of this system was self-evident. The privy was often at the bottom of the back yard, sometimes over a hundred feet away. The path was customarily bordered by wet grass and overhanging vines. In winter snowdrifts blocked the way, and there was no shelter from rain.

Everyone had to overcome these conditions, but Waring found that the burden fell especially hard on women. During stormy weather they often postponed the trip for days. If the pathway was exposed to a neighbor's view, they put off the trip till dusk. No amount of reasoning would convince a woman that it was "her duty, for the sake of preventing troubles of which she is yet ignorant to expose herself to the danger, the discomfort, and the annoyance that regularity under such circumstances implies."

Although people had always suffered from this dangerous and embarrassing trek, it was not until they began to believe in the possibility of improvement that there was a sustained attempt to do anything about it. But science itself did not indicate how to solve the problem. Doctors, sanitarians, and plumbers often disagreed about the best way of disposing of human wastes. By the 1860s the device that appealed to most experts and also to the public was the water closet, which flushed wastes through pipes either to a public sewer or to a cesspool.

Waring, however, thought that the water system had serious defects. One was that because it depended on a network of pipes that were hard to inspect and clean, it was the breeding ground for the already much-feared sewer gas. In the late 1860s, when Waring first wrote about the sewage problem, he admitted that he was not certain how sewer gas originated or moved; nevertheless, he suspected that the network of plumbing — usually installed by ignorant and careless tradesmen — was at fault. Another defect of the water system was that, particularly in country and suburban areas, it emptied into a cesspool. The wastes then seeped into the ground and often eventually contaminated the well of the household or that of a neighbor. This "subterranean communication" was extremely pernicious, and Waring ascribed many diseases to it. Also, the water system did not take advantage of human wastes as a source of fertilizer. Whether destined for a private cesspool or a public sewer, it did not, in short, convert "excrement into increment." To Waring, using wastes as fertilizer seemed natural; this cycle was inherently economical and it mirrored the reciprocal relationship of city and country that had become so pronounced during the nineteenth century.

In the late 1860s George Waring became an advocate of a system of waste disposal that he thought was healthy, efficient, and productive of useful fertilizer. Waring's method was originally proposed by Henry Moule, an English clergyman. In 1858 Moule had shown that when a small portion of dry earth covered a deposit of human waste, the fermentation of the substance and the consequent generation of noxious gases were prevented. When the mass formed by the repeated layers of waste

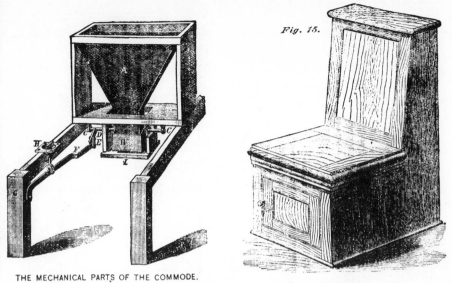

THE MECHANICAL PARTS OF THE COMMODE.
The same Fixtures are used in Closets.

THE COMMODE.

*183. George E. Waring: A dry earth commode. By pulling the lever (H),
a fixed amount of earth from the hopper (A) would be deposited on the
wastes.*

and earth was mixed with a rake, it did not smell, and it could be used as
enriched fertilizer or as dry earth to carry on the process.

One of the great advantages of the dry earth closet was the flexibility
with which it could be installed in the home. The simplest form of earth
closet was a commode, which contained in its wide back a hopper that
held the dry earth. Underneath, it had a box for receiving the deposits.
After each use, a lever was pulled and a fixed amount of earth dropped
on top of the waste. The dry earth commode needed only a trifling
amount of care: it was necessary once in four or five days to fill the
hopper and to empty the box from under the seat. An alternate box could
be put into service while the recently used one was "hung out in the open
air, to be freshened by sun or rain." The labor involved was no greater
than stoking a fire with coal or wood and carrying out a hod of ashes.
Unlike a water system, the dry earth commode was not fixed to one place
and did not entail a tangle of pipes running through the home. Waring
recommended that the best place for the commode was in a small closet or
hallway that connected two major rooms. He had one in such a location
in his house, and he had found that the sight and smell of it never prevented the members of his family from keeping the doors of the rooms
open when it was not in use.

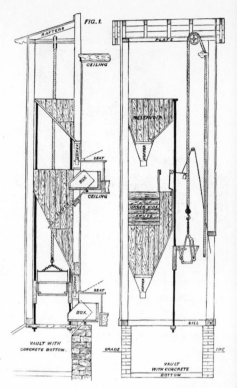

184. *George E. Waring: An earth
closet. This shaft was built on an
external wall of a house so that it
could be reached at the bottom
without entering the house.
Frederick Law Olmsted intended
that a similar system be used at
Riverside, Illinois. A Dry Earth
Company to service houses with
these earth closets was founded in
New Haven, Connecticut.*

In the country the earth would be carried by hand up to the hoppers,
but for suburban houses Waring recommended a more elaborate system,
one like that which was proposed for use at Riverside in Chicago. Waring
designed a system in which the closets on each level were placed directly
over each other. They were joined by a vertical shaft outside the house.
Through this channel, dry earth was hoisted up by a system of pulleys
and deposits were discharged. The shaft had a shallow vault at the bottom
for receiving the deposits and to house the hoisting apparatus. There was
no opening from any part of the house into the channel. The only access
to it was through a locked door in the back yard. The one person with
a key was the public dustman, who came around periodically to fill the
hoist system with dry earth and to remove the deposits. Waring thought
that this person's duties would be similar to those of other rubbish
removers. He would be efficient and unobtrusive. He did not have to
contact any member of the household to carry out his chores. Since the
deposit he removed was no more offensive than coal ashes, he did not
have to work stealthily at night, and his cart would not offend the public.

To deal with "house-slops" Waring proposed another system that was healthful and economical. For country or suburban houses with extensive grounds, Waring suggested that near the earth closet a funnel or sink be placed into which the waste water of the house would be poured. This inlet would be connected not to a public sewer, but instead to a cistern buried in the ground. When the liquid reached about a foot from the top of the cistern, with the aid of a siphon it was led out through a network of percolating land drains under the lawn or garden. The wastes thus were used as fertilizer, and there was no need for an offensive cesspool.

In houses with not enough land for this system Waring proposed that the house-slops be disposed of by filtering them through earth in a large barrel. The liquid wastes would be discharged through a funnel and pipe into this barrel, and as the water gradually percolated through, it would turn the earth into fertilizer. In 1868 Waring tried this method and then used the contents of the barrel to fertilize a lettuce patch that in the previous year had received $20 worth of horse manure. Waring was convinced that farmers or gardeners would find it profitable to contract with residents of suburbs and towns to remove their converted house-slops.

Waring's system of waste disposal did not depend on fancy gadgetry, and it was rooted in an idea about the cycle of nature. When he asked Horace Greeley what he thought about the dry earth system, Greeley characteristically answered: "I think that America will be worth 25 per cent more a hundred years hence than it would have been without it." But Waring's system was not widely adopted.[7]

One liability of Waring's approach was its inapplicability to large cities. His system required enough land per family to absorb twenty-five gallons of water a day through the percolating drain system. Once the pattern of settlement became more dense, Waring's absorbing barrels of earth were necessary. The fertilizer produced in principle was useful to farmers, but the barrels were heavy, and since most of them would be located at the center of a city where the population tended to cluster, the farmers would have to transport them for great distances. This method of disposal perhaps was no more objectionable than that used for other types of refuse, but the chance to get rid of human wastes through an invisible network of pipes was too attractive for most people to resist.

Waring never fully gave up his belief in the earth system, but by the mid-1870s he recognized that the water system would be generally adopted. Waring then began to work out the best arrangement of plumbing on that basis. The object of most of his suggestions was to nullify the effects of sewer gas. His early pamphlet *Earth-Closets and Earth Sewage* contained a long section of excerpts from medical reports that attested to the dangers of sewer gas, and throughout the 1870s and 1880s Waring continued to quote the reports of doctors, sanitarians, and public health officials to establish sewer gas as the primary issue of plumbing.

The evidence that made the most impact on Waring was a report by the Massachusetts State Board of Health on the propagation of typhoid. In identifying how that disease spread, the board relied heavily on the case of the Maplewood School for girls in Pittsfield, where fifty-three of seventy-four resident pupils had fallen victim to typhoid. An investigation revealed that the school building was located near a barnyard covered with water in which pigs wallowed, decaying vegetables often were stored in the cellar, the toilets were filthy, and the kitchen drain emptied only about ninety feet from the school.

These conditions pointed, as far as the investigators and Waring were concerned, directly to the causes of the disease. They thought typhoid was spread by drinking water that contained decomposed organic matter and by breathing air that was contaminated by any form of filth. From this evidence, Waring suspected that other diseases were also either generated "by fouled air or foul water or [were] made worse because of unhealthy surroundings."[8]

The principle Waring drew from this evidence was as old as Hippocrates: "Pure air, pure water, and pure soil." It was the task of the sanitarian to find out how each element was polluted and, therefore, how each could be preserved in or returned to its pure state. Waring always thought that supplying good drinking water to the home was a relatively simple matter. Since the 1840s that task had generally been assumed by public authorities in towns.[9] In the country, however, where each household provided water for itself, more caution had to be taken. Waring argued that earth acted as a purifying filter for water that seeped through the ground. But too often the earth became impregnated, and thereafter it was possible for water to flow laterally through a fissure to a well that in effect acted as a drain. To ensure a safe source of drinking water, Waring recommended several ways to protect the sides of wells to a depth at which seeping water would have shed its impurities.

Securing a dry cellar uncontaminated by foul substances was also an easy task. Since Waring, like other sanitarians, emphasized the connection between wet soil and tuberculosis, he advised his readers about what kind of materials could best be used to keep dampness from penetrating foundation walls and the cellar floors, and he also gave directions about how to lay a drain around the foundations to carry moisture beyond the house when the surrounding soil was especially wet.

The more difficult problem was how to prevent sewer gas from being generated in and escaping from plumbing into the home. Waring first thought that it was best to separate the house as much as possible from the sewer. The difficulty was that the conventional device, a water trap, did not create the proper separation. A sudden filling of the sewer by a rise of the tide or by a heavy rain would break even a large trap. Waring's alternative solution was a kind of intermediate barrier. Where severe frosts were not a problem, he recommended that the wastes of a house first be discharged into an outdoor tank and from there pass to a sewer. If gas was created in the sewer, it would thus pass to the outer air. In places where such a receptacle could only be close to a house, the tank would be completely enclosed and would be supplied with a ventilating pipe that went to the top of the house to draw the foul gases off above the building.[10]

Four years later, in 1879, Waring acknowledged that his advice had been misdirected. But he did not despair of finding the proper arrangement of plumbing, nor did he question whether sewer gas actually existed. Instead, Waring thought that the need for a new approach was gratifying because it was an indication of the rapid growth of knowledge about the subject. New information indicated that soil pipes were not to be separated from the main drain at all. The goal was a complete ventilation of the soil pipe, so that any sewer gas in the public line would rush straight up the house's pipe and out through the roof. To achieve this end, it was necessary to do away with the trap, however constructed, between the main sewer and the soil pipe and to ventilate the bottom of the soil pipe to permit air to rush through the whole system.[11]

Throughout the 1880s sanitarians disagreed about many aspects of this approach. Those who were convinced that it was correct focused on how to make the best soil pipe. They debated about what kind of cowl to have at the top of the stack and whether the pipe, once it penetrated the roof, should be tapered outward to facilitate the ventilation. Waring always maintained that no "complete scientific result" had been achieved about these matters, but he also held that no cowl was necessary and that an increase in diameter was useful. He relied heavily on tests made by English sanitarians showing that cowls, especially those that were created primarily for decorative purposes, all produced a restraining force on the air of the soil pipes and impeded the natural flow.

Another important problem was how to fit drainpipes together. The theory of the free ventilating of the soil pipe presupposed that if the pipe was completely without leaks, the slime on the inside would be neutralized as a breeder of sewer gas by the rush of air. In his earlier writings Waring had focused much of his attention on how to produce a leakproof soil pipe. At that time he tried to explain the baffling fact that horizontal pipes tended to corrode at the top — evidence, he assumed, that the corroding agent was not the water or the slime on the bottom side of the pipe, but, instead, the sewer gas, which rose to the top. This deduction gave Waring all the more reason to insist that the proper materials and joints be used to secure his "section of out-of-doors brought for convenience within the walls of the house." Since Waring found that lead pipes corroded easily, he advised the use of iron pipes and told how they should be joined. But in 1884 he tested a number of lead-caulked, cast-iron pipes and concluded that plumbers were not skilled and careful enough to make joints. He could then only suggest that each pipe be tested under heavy water pressure. It was up to each home owner to exercise extreme caution.[12]

For Waring's method to work it was important to have not only a tight-fitting pipe but also one with the proper internal surface. A good finish would prevent corrosion, but, more important, if it was smooth, it would discourage the accumulation of slime that engendered sewer gas. Through ventilation would nullify some of the potency of this slime, but it was also important to prevent the dangerous substance from sticking to the sides of the soil pipes in the first place. To find the right surface, Waring tested many materials and concluded that an enamel coating was the most effective.

Waring's system of ventilated soil pipes was often criticized because if sewer gas was allowed to run through the house, then the only line of defense against it was the traps that separated the fixtures from the main drain. From the mid-1870s to the mid-1880s no issue perplexed sanitarians and plumbers more than the invention of a foolproof trap. Waring was an active participant in the discussion of this issue. He always distrusted the simple S-trap and frequently quoted the experiments of a British physician who had conclusively shown that gas could seep through a trap and escape into a room. Other experimenters found that a strong flow through the soil pipe created a partial vacuum that caused atmospheric pressure to force the contents of the trap toward the drain. Traps could also be siphoned out simply when water passed through them. To deal with these problems, by 1880 it had become customary to ventilate S-traps by extending pipes from them to the open air. Waring and other sanitarians, however, found this "back ventilation" deficient because the contact with fresh air soon evaporated the water in the traps.

Because of this impasse manufacturers began to produce mechanical traps. One type supposedly retained its water through the use of a rubber ball; another depended on a hinged valve; a third used mercury to prevent siphoning. Waring invented a number of these traps, but shortly thereafter he acknowledged that they were fallible. The trap he eventually relied upon was invented by J. Pickering Putnam, the architect who later became an advocate of Edward Bellamy's Nationalism. Putnam carried out tests that showed how untrustworthy back ventilation was. The success of that method depended on variables that were extremely complex and that often changed after the installation of the system. Putnam's alternative approach was to examine how water emptied from an unventilated trap. He acknowledged that air rushing through the trap to fill a vacuum caused by a flow in the piping beyond carried the water with it, but he also noticed that some of the water struck against the walls of the trap and was thrown back to its original position. His conclusion was that the nature of the walls of the trap determined how much water was drained out. He therefore designed a trap that had enough obstacles to prevent the complete unsealing of the trap. George Waring felt that not only this invention but also the logical way Putnam arrived at it was a great breakthrough.[13] However, a sanitarian who advocated the back ventilation of traps accused Putnam of conducting misleading experiments to promote his own invention.[14]

Because there were so many conflicting claims about such issues, Waring was a strong supporter of the National Board of Health, an organization formed in 1879 to obtain information about all matters that related to public health. At a time when there was little reliable information about even such basic matters as the behavior of materials and the pattern of water circulation through a pipe, Waring hoped that the National Board of Health would not only resolve the many disputes about plumbing, but would also prevent the wasteful duplication of effort by cities and states that carried out their own tests to formulate building codes.[15] Waring soon found that even the studies carried out by the National Board of Health were not beyond dispute.

In 1881 Waring applied to the National Board of Health to carry out

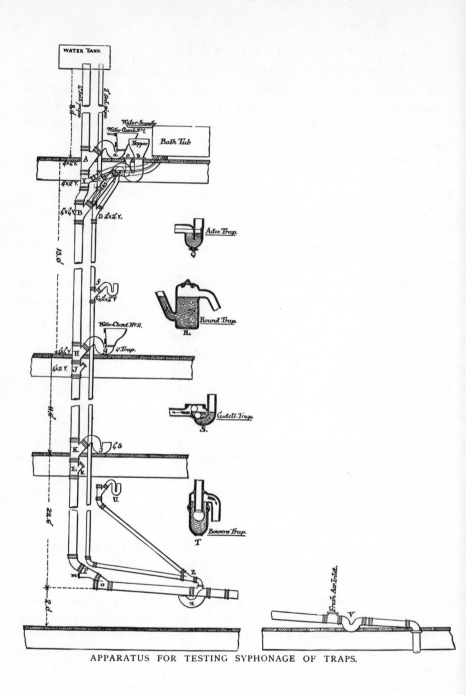

APPARATUS FOR TESTING SYPHONAGE OF TRAPS.

185. E. W. Bowditch and E. S. Philbrick: "Apparatus for Testing Syphonage of Traps," 1882. This apparatus was built to test the effectiveness of a
variety of traps, including J. P. Putnam's.

experiments on the siphonage of traps. Shortly thereafter, the board asked another sanitarian, Edward Philbrick, to verify Waring's results. The conclusions of the two experimenters disagreed, and Waring and Philbrick then carried on an acrimonious debate about each other's experimental techniques.[16] Waring's most publicized dispute, however, was about the nature of the sewage system that connected home with home. To prevent the accumulation of sewer gas, it was as important to have the right configuration of pipes under the streets as it was within houses, but there was no consensus about what the best system was. Waring designed or was a consultant for the sewage systems for Norfolk, Virginia; Keene, New Hampshire; San Diego, California; Omaha, Nebraska; and Buffalo, New York. His most famous project was in Memphis, Tennessee, a city that had frequently been struck by epidemics, the worst of which occurred in 1878 when 5,150 people died from yellow fever. In all of his projects Waring insisted on having a separate system for house wastes and for storm water. A combined system was economical, but Waring argued that, among other liabilities, it was dangerous because the diameter of its pipes had to be very large to accommodate the great rush of water in heavy storms. Between rains, the stream of water that would have been sufficient to keep a smaller drain clean was too thinly spread out and therefore lost its power to purify the drain. This argument was logical up to a point, but since there was no certainty about what caused sewer gas or how liquids moved through a sewage system, it was open to many criticisms and counterproposals.[17]

Because of such muddles, Waring could only conclude that sanitary science was in its infancy. Uncertain of the right answers, he decided to follow a rule of simplicity. Provided the soil stack was ventilated, Waring believed that a reasonably satisfactory system could be fashioned by avoiding needless complications. The first step toward this end was to reduce the number of fixtures — a point that criticized manufacturers and plumbers who tended to emphasize the need for as many appliances as possible.

The fixtures themselves also had to be simple. By 1880 there was, as Waring put it, an "embarrassing variety" of appliances available. Some were improvements over their predecessors; most, however, used new names and complications to duplicate old products. The type of toilet Waring favored was that which could easily be inspected and cleaned and which did not have an inaccessible "chamber of horrors" somewhere beneath the trap. Waring patented one of these toilets, the Dececo, which was based on a simple siphoning device.[18]

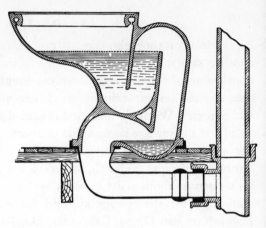

*186.   George E. Waring: The Dececo Water Closet. Waring's fixture was characterized by a deep water-seal trap at the bottom of the bowl and a second trap beneath the floor. One objection to it was that, because of the shape of the upper trap, the bowl had to be filled almost to the top. However, the Dececo avoided much of the gadgetry characteristic of other toilets.*

Simplicity was also necessary in the location of fixtures. Waring wanted to place the bathrooms on different floors of a house as nearly as possible over one another so that they could all be connected by short waste pipes into one vertical stack. Long horizontal runs were not only expensive but also more likely to cause siphonage. The pipes themselves ideally had to be visible and accessible. Waring thought that the "out of sight, out of mind" attitude was dangerous. It was better to have some frank decoration of the pipes than to conceal them.[19]

Although this approach made sense to sanitarians, it was not generally popular. Most people who could afford to do so had their fixtures and pipes encased in cabinetwork. In their New York mansions, built in the early 1880s when the fear of sewer gas was at its height, the Vanderbilts set a standard for built-in plumbing. They brought the most advanced services to their houses, but they did so primarily for the effect. The grand hall and picture galleries of W. H. Vanderbilt's house had spectacular lighting systems.[20] But the dressing rooms that contained toilet and washing facilities must have struck guests as especially lavish. One of these areas was annexed to each principal bedroom. The floor of the dressing room was carpeted; the ceiling was covered with glass decorated to imitate white lace, through which cupids seemed "to be struggling and about to fall." Full- and half-length mirrors covered the walls except where there were doors and windows. One wall was made up of sliding, mirror-covered panels that shielded a toilet, sink, and bath area. All the woodwork in the room was maple with gilt-lined carvings. The washbasin was hand-decorated, imported china, set into an onyx or marble slab that had gold- and silver-plated ornamental faucets. The toilet and bath were encased in decorative cabinetwork. Although the surrounding panels were demountable, no pipework met the eye.[21]

Ironically, it became acceptable to have exposed pipes and fittings only after it was generally understood that diseases did not come from these sources. A concern for cleanliness, therefore, was one of the lasting, if belated, results of the campaign against sewer gas. Other evidence of the fear of sewer gas remained for many years in building codes. Although by the turn of the century doctors and sanitarians understood that diseases were caused by specific microorganisms or bacteria, it often took city authorities many decades to update their codes so that, for instance, it was not mandatory to have back-ventilated traps in all instances. In this respect George Waring was right, if only for the wrong reasons. The plumbing specifications he derived from his rule of simplicity and his advocacy of the separate system are generally in accord with current practice.

✦✦✦

When the home was first being connected to the world at large by servicing systems, it was unclear how many and what kind of utilities there would eventually be. If the sound of a voice could be transmitted to and

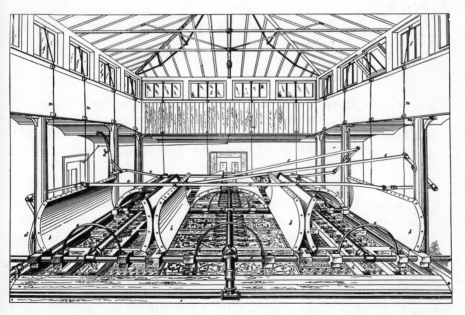

*187.   Richard M. Hunt: The lighting dome of the grand hall in the residence of W. H. Vanderbilt, 1882. Concealed in the dome were dozens of gas fixtures that illuminated the works of art in the Grand Hall below.*

*188.   Richard M. Hunt: Dressing room and bathroom in the residence of*
*W. H. Vanderbilt, 1882. Members of the second generation of Vanderbilts*
*were fascinated by the mechanical inventions of the period and celebrated*
*them in their homes with a previously unheard-of lavishness.*

from the home, then it did not seem far-fetched to expect that someday packages or other goods would also be mechanically transported. The mailman and delivery boy would thus be rendered obsolete, and it might even no longer be necessary to carry bundles home from the store.

Many people expected that the pneumatic tube would be the mechanism that would eventually perform this service. By the end of the nineteenth century this device was a part of the communication systems of most major cities in Europe and the United States. The first pneumatic tube was installed in London in 1853. It traveled only two hundred twenty yards, but year by year this system for carrying messages was extended until it covered London's entire business district. Beginning in the 1860s similar systems were installed in Paris, Berlin, Vienna, and other European cities.

The first pneumatic tube system in the United States was not installed until 1876, when the Western Union Telegraph Company laid one out in New York to transmit telegrams from one office to another. In the following fifteen years similar networks of pneumatic tubes were adopted for the same purpose in other cities, and they were also installed in large department stores, office buildings, institutions, and apartment houses.

By the early 1890s the pneumatic tube still was used only to carry at most a few pieces of paper, but innovations made in 1893 promised that this method of communication might fulfill the expectations that some people had for it. Before that date the diameter of pneumatic tubes was limited to two or three inches. Since the tubes did not weigh much, they could be stopped simply by striking a solid object at their destination. A heavier tube had to be brought to rest more gently. When an air cushion with an automatic receiving apparatus was devised for the Philadelphia post office's pneumatic tube system, the diameter was increased to six inches. Large quantities of mail could then be sent from one point to another.

In 1897 it became possible to transport bigger packages when an eight-inch-diameter system was installed in New York. Since further increases in carrying capacity seemed likely, it was not unreasonable to envisage a network of pneumatic tubes stretching out to a receiving station at the front door of every home. Such a system would have radically changed the relationship of one house to another and to the public domain. Because of the nature of the equipment involved, it would also have significantly altered the area of the home where its receiving station was located. But these issues never had to be confronted. Despite the claims made for it, the pneumatic tube never transcended its limited use for carrying messages or mail, and it was always restricted to local destinations.[22]

Other servicing systems promised great innovations for the home but never were put into use. Because of their potential, these systems had to be reckoned with in any speculation about the future of the home, but a more immediate problem was how to choose between already existing and competing servicing systems: to decide, for example, how to light the home. Americans who no longer wanted to rely on candles for illumination first had to choose between oil and gas lighting. One basis for a decision was economy. It was easy to determine the initial and ongoing costs of each system, but when convenience was also taken into consideration, the calculation became more complicated. Thus, oil lamps cost little to purchase, and there was no expense for installation, whereas extending gas lines to and throughout a house was a major undertaking. On the other hand, gas lights could be turned on almost automatically, but oil lamps demanded continual care.

Each system had more elusive, but perhaps more important, qualities that further clouded the choice. Oil and gas placed the home in different relationships to the surrounding community. Oil was usually bought at a store or delivered periodically to the home. Gas involved no direct personal transaction, except perhaps with a man who came every month to read the meter. The two systems also had different implications for the use of the spaces in the home. The oil lamp was movable. It could be placed on a table or in a wall bracket. Because of this flexibility the lighting tended to adjust to an arrangement of furniture. The opposite was true with gas. Lamps lit by gas were fixed at specific places in a room and furniture had to adapt to these positions.

After the invention of the incandescent light bulb a similar choice had to be made between gas and electricity. Electricity seemed to have many advantages. It gave a more even light than gas, it did not produce soot, and its fixtures did not have to be ventilated. But electric lighting did not immediately usurp gas. While some people were intrigued by this marvelous invention, others feared that it was dangerous. Thus, in 1881 Mrs. Cornelius Vanderbilt went to a ball dressed as an electric light, but shortly thereafter, when a newly installed electrical system caused a small fire in her Fifth Avenue home, she became hysterical and demanded that the whole installation be removed.[23]

Even those who acknowledged the benefits of electricity often shunned it simply because it was costly to convert a house already lit by gas, especially considering that gas was used for purposes other than lighting. When electricity became competitive in price with gas and long after it was a novelty, many home owners deferred the decision to install it because they were so committed to gas. Electricity also could do more than illuminate, but its supporters were slow to exploit its full capacities. Houses had been heated and domestic machines had been run by electricity for several decades before the first all-electric home was built.[24]

In deciding how to service the home, it was also important to determine the benefits of linking each house to its neighbors. The evolution of services usually had two stages. Devices were first installed within the confines

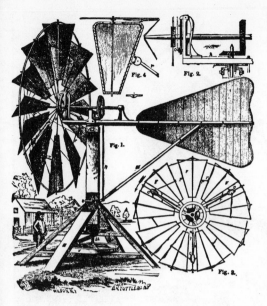

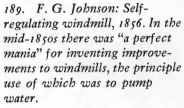

*189. F. G. Johnson: Self-regulating windmill, 1856. In the mid-1850s there was "a perfect mania" for inventing improvements to windmills, the principle use of which was to pump water.*

of the home grounds and in many cases merely updated long-established practices. These innovations extended the autonomy of the home for a while, but usually, especially when the density of settlement increased, the linking of the home to a general servicing network soon followed. Thus, improvements in the construction of cesspools prolonged the disposal of sewage within the home grounds. Yet no matter how efficient cesspools became, in populated areas they were eventually replaced by municipal sewage systems. The same pattern was true of water. There was a long history of improvements to windmills that helped farmers and residents of small towns pump water from their wells. Local systems were further improved by electrically powered pumps, and in 1903 a man in California even used the heat of the sun to pump water. Some of these methods are still used in sparsely settled areas, but when it was feasible to do so, the windmill, pump, and well were replaced by a network of pipes from a central source.[25] Even electricity was first generated locally. In the early 1880s several millionaires who lived on Fifth Avenue installed machinery to produce their own electricity; soon the construction of a central distributing plant made these small systems obsolete.[26]

The vast servicing networks that joined the parts of large cities and even of the entire nation were often considered signs of progress. Visionaries like Edward Tuckerman Potter dreamed that someday these systems

*190. "Sunshine as Power." Using the sun as a source of power was often discussed at the end of the nineteenth century. One successful attempt to put the idea into practice was made in 1903 at Pasadena, California, where the sun was used to drive an engine that pumped water to irrigate a field.*

would unite all mankind.[27] That thought occurred to other people, but many Americans also wondered whether these developments had gone too far. To give substance to these doubts, they looked for ways, perhaps as a third stage in the evolution of services, to reassert the autonomy of the home and the traditional values it represented.

The development of refrigeration techniques was one example of how an old pattern of servicing could be recast in a new guise. In the traditional home, food had been preserved in cold-storage areas, usually in the cellar. The delivery of ice to the home and the construction of airtight chambers improved a practice that had long been recognized as unreliable. But ice delivery had liabilities. It required not only a team of horses, a wagon, and two men, but also a plant where the ice could be made and stored. Some people argued that it would be far more efficient to supply refrigeration mechanically to the home from a central source. Companies that tried to do so actually did not furnish anything to their customers. Instead, they tried to extract heat and humidity from the areas that were to be refrigerated by pumping ammonia through a network of underground pipes from a central plant. At first these companies catered primarily to large businesses such as breweries, meat-packing plants, and dairies. Then in 1889 a system was installed in Denver to serve the small as well as the large customer. The inventors of this process thought that there would be tremendous savings in increasing the scale of the refrigerating plant. But their scheme was rendered impractical, at least for domestic use, by the manufacture of self-contained, electrically powered refrigerators, which, although still tied to a network of wires that extended beyond the home, seemed at least to reestablish the refrigeration process in the home.[28]

Although important to the home, different methods of refrigeration were not nearly so controversial as ways of heating a house. In the course of the nineteenth century the functions of the domestic fireplace gradually were undermined. In 1800 the American-born Count Rumford argued that if the fireplace's two functions — heating and cooking — were separated, each could be more efficient. As an alternative to the large open oven, he proposed a small cast-iron stove with a fire in a suspended grate beneath a pot that was surrounded by an air space. By suspending the fire, he confined the heat and permitted ready access to the air that fed the flames that in turn brought the pot to boil.[29]

*191. A refrigeration pipeline being laid under a street, St. Louis, Missouri, 1891. In the early 1890s there were several attempts to deliver refrigeration throughout a city from a central source.*

Elaborations in cast iron of the Pennsylvania Dutch oven also concentrated the fire. By the 1830s dozens of patents for cast-iron stoves had been granted. Many of these patents proposed genuine improvements; others were simply gimmicks. In 1839 one commentator already doubted whether most housewives knew how to take full advantage of their cast-iron stoves.[30] But the variety of cooking devices increased yearly, especially in the 1880s when the use of gas made possible even further concentration of the flame.[31]

The control of the flame of a fire also became important to those who wanted to increase the efficiency of fuel for heating. In an open fireplace often only 10 percent of the heat produced found its way into the room. Most of the rest went up the chimney. In 1763 Benjamin Franklin suggested that if the fire was confined to a small enclosed stove in which only enough air entered to feed the flame, the heat efficiency would be greatly increased. Franklin's ideas were not exploited until after 1800, but by 1830 stoves that followed his description were being produced in many parts of the United States.[32]

One problem with the Franklin stove was that its small flue did not allow much change in the air of a room. In their desire to heat a space efficiently, the owners of Franklin stoves made their houses as airtight as possible and thus created stuffy rooms. The solution was to place the stove in the basement where it would serve not as a radiator but as a convector. Fresh air was drawn from the outdoors into a furnace, heated, and then directed to each room of the house through ducts. By the middle of the nineteenth century, many wood- and coal-fired furnaces of this sort were on the market.

Through the concentration of the flame in a cast-iron enclosure, cooking and heating gained in efficiency but lost on other accounts. These modern inventions were often criticized on scientific grounds, but the most telling objection was subjective. With the cast-iron stove or furnace it was impossible to see the fire. This was almost tantamount to doing away with a member of the family. Harriet Beecher Stowe summarized that common reaction. Writing during the Civil War, she asked her readers:

Would our Revolutionary fathers have gone barefooted and bleeding over snows to defend air-tight stoves and cooking-ranges? It was the memory of the great open kitchen fire with its back-log and fore-stick of cord wood, its roaring, hilarious voice of invitation, its dancing tongue of flames, that called to them through the snows of that dreadful winter to keep up their courage, that made their hearts warm and bright with a thousand reflected memories.[33]

If some Americans reacted this way when the fire was put in a stove and relegated to the cellar, they were even more perplexed when so familiar a part of home was removed from the premises altogether. This was the goal of companies that offered to heat individual homes from a central plant. In 1877 Birdsill Holly devised a method of heating buildings by conveying steam from a main boiler through underground pipes. He first installed this system in his home town, Lockport, New York, and when it proved a success there, he formed a company to market the idea elsewhere. Holly's American District Steam Company soon had many competitors and by the early 1880s it seemed that steam-heating plants would soon become one of the major sources of heat in American cities. As one report on these developments noted, an era of "Communism in Hot-Air" seemed to be dawning.[34]

In heating their homes, as in other matters, Americans wanted to partake of the inventions that represented progress, but they also felt the need to hold onto the open fireplace. In the course of the nineteenth century, several ways of reconciling old and new in heating were devised. Many stoves in which the flame was not visible were decorated to suggest burning coals and logs.[35] Such artifice was hardly satisfactory. The more appealing way to mediate between progress and tradition was simply to have both a central heating system and an open fireplace. The furnace and its related equipment provided the bulk of the heating; the fireplace was used on special occasions to create a homelike atmosphere.

Once the fireplace no longer had to heat the home, architects were free to design it as they wanted. Those who leaned toward progress generally favored a subdued decorative scheme for the mantelpiece. They often used classical detailing, which had origins in Europe and connoted the best of good taste. But since this language of ornament was associated with the houses of wealthy colonial merchants and planters, it was also equally within a tradition of old American homes. Architects who wanted to cultivate an image of a humbler home of the past took a different approach. They used materials like stained wood, brick, terra-cotta, and rough stone to create a warm home scene around the fireplace. They often enhanced this effect by combining the mantelpiece with extensive shelves and cupboards that made a suitable context for bric-a-brac and other family mementos.

192. "The Hearth Stone." An engraving from a painting by W. H. Wilcox, supposedly of the hearthstone in the childhood home of John Howard Payne.

193. Charles F. McKim: A redesigned fireplace in an old house in Newport, Rhode Island, 1875. McKim tried to find out "what there is left in an old house to build upon for modern comfort and convenience."

Similar distinctions were also drawn in locating the fireplace. Some architects played down the fireplace in the design of a room and did not try to orient either the furniture or the anticipated pattern of activities around it. The fireplace was just another incident in the scheme of interior decoration. Others placed a fireplace in a spacious hall to welcome whoever came through the front door and also designed the living room around a huge open hearth that sometimes took the shape of an inglenook. In such rooms the crackling fire was an active participant in family life.

When the fireplace was important in the design of the interior of the house, it was usually also celebrated on the exterior. Following John C. Loudon's arguments about the need to express a building's use, Andrew Jackson Downing wrote that chimneys were characteristic of domestic architecture and suggested a number of ways to use these elements to enliven the appearance of a house. Without acknowledging Downing as a source, many architects accepted this line of reasoning and designed chimneys so elaborate that their true function seemed more for expression than for removal of smoke.

Having both a central heating system and an open fireplace may have suited most Americans who wanted to combine progress and tradition, but it did not satisfy J. Pickering Putnam. He believed that the open fireplace should be the center of attraction in a room; it was a "living and sympathetic companion." His interest in the open fireplace, however, went beyond sentiment. He thought that the open fireplace best approximated nature's method of heating, radiation from the sun. Radiation warmed the body, but it allowed the surrounding air, that which was used for respiration, to be cool and refreshing. The opposite was true with hot-air heating. The huge furnaces in American homes gave no direct radiation, and too often they made rooms stuffy and suffocating.

Putnam therefore wanted to redesign the open fireplace so that it would be both an efficient radiator and a convector. The task he set himself was, first of all, to find out how to shape the fireplace so that it could radiate the maximum amount of heat into a room, and then to devise a way to take advantage of the air that the fire had heated. In effect, Putnam wanted to produce a ventilating fireplace that would retain the values of the open fireplace, but that would be just as rational as any other heating device made according to the most advanced scientific principles.

When Putnam embarked on this project in the late 1870s, little was then understood about how to build fireplaces. He found that fireplaces had been built with so little knowledge that 85 to 95 percent of the heat

194. *Harry Fenn: "Suggestions for Chimneys," 1872. Fenn hoped that the use of such varied forms would help create a picturesque city.*

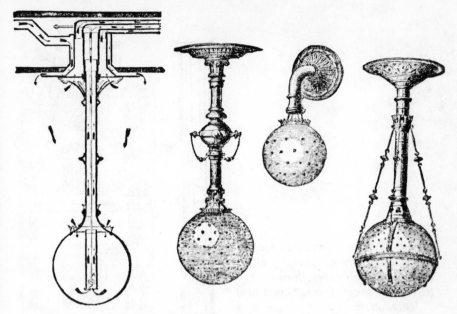

*195.   J. P. Putnam: "Ventilating Gasoliers," 1881.*

generated went up a chimney and was lost. The few ventilating fireplaces in use were almost as inefficient: only 30 to 40 percent of the heat was used.

The more Putnam looked into this subject, the more intrigued he became by the work of experimenters in the eighteenth century and the first decades of the nineteenth. In 1713 Gauger, a French doctor, had redesigned the shape of the fireplace to increase its efficiency as a radiator; Count Rumford later extended this work. Benjamin Franklin and David Arnott, an English doctor, had tried to make fireplaces that consumed the smoke given off from the fuel. These innovations marginally increased the efficiency of the fireplace, but the most important one was the ventilating fireplace, which Putnam attributed to Louis Savot, a French doctor of the early seventeenth century. In the following two hundred years numerous improvements had been made in Savot's fireplace, but by the 1870s, because of the popularity of other methods of heating or simply through a lack of concern for efficiency, most of them had been forgotten.

Putnam wanted to revive and refine the results that came from this tradition of experimentation so that he could make the ideal open fireplace. He found that shaping the sides of the fireplace and the chimney throat to produce an efficient radiator was much more straightforward than making use of the air heated by the fire. To accomplish that task,

Fig. 183. Front Elevation of House on Dartmouth Street.

*196. J. P. Putnam: Elevation and section through chimney of the architect's house, Boston, 1881. Although Putnam favored apartment buildings, he lived in a corner row house, presumably because no suitable cooperative accommodation was available. In designing his house, Putnam celebrated the chimneys, but the fresh-air registers were discreetly concealed.*

he first had to estimate how much air was needed in a room of a given size, but he found no information about how to determine this figure. Putnam realized that air seeped through the cracks of windows and even through the walls. To assess how much air was lost, he had to conduct his own experiments on the effect of cracks and the porosity of materials. Determining the best location of fresh-air inlets also was a difficult task, because gas lights needed to be ventilated. Putnam devised special gas fixtures so that the ventilation of the room could be coordinated.

The basic difficulty that Putnam found with most ventilating fireplaces then available was that they did not have a large enough air-heating surface. He designed the fireplaces in his own house to overcome this problem. Each was equipped with a valve that admitted air from the outdoors. The air was first moderately warmed as it passed the heated back and sides of the fireplace. It then rose into a large chamber above the mantelpiece and behind the chimney breast. There the air struck the walls of a specially designed smoke flue and then entered the room through an ornamented brass register at the top of the chimney breast. Excess air could be directed to the second story by a valve. Having entered the room at the ceiling, the warmed fresh air descended as it cooled until it reached the level of the fireplace, through which it escaped. The draft of the fireplace was thus supplied entirely with fresh air, and the amount of air change was determined by how much cold air was let into the fireplace. When the room was filled with people, the cold-air valve was closed, a damper at the top of the heating chamber was opened, and the warm-air supply register became a foul-air exhaust.

Usually Putnam concealed the convector in the chimney breast behind a decorative panel, but he suggested that if the convector was exposed, it could also be used as a radiator, sending additional heat into the room. The only obstacle to doing so was an inhibition about exposing what was behind the chimney breast to the eye. Putnam thought that in attempting to treat this equipment decoratively a new field might be opened to the architect. In his account of his experiments, he offered several designs for the fully exposed apparatus of the ventilating fireplace. All of them were

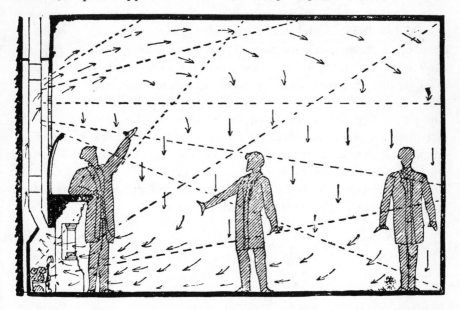

*197.  J. P. Putnam: "Diagram showing the Direction of Heat Rays and Air Currents." The arrows show the paths of fresh air coming from the distribution chamber. The dotted lines show how rays of heat emanate from the fire and the radiator above.*

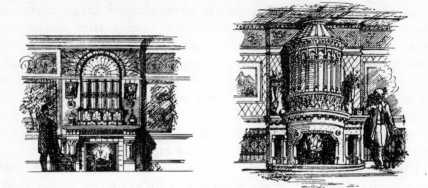

*198. J. P. Putnam: "The Open Fire-
Place." The sun, "the great radiator," is
used as a motif for the design of the open
fireplace.*

based on imagery derived from the sun. No other theme was more
appropriate for this attempt to approximate nature's method of heating.[36]

Although Putnam understood that the interior of a house could be
treated as a complete environmental system, he did not have the requisite
knowledge, and many of his arguments now seem either naive or falla-
cious. Other architects and engineers have made the same point since
1880, when his *Open Fire-Place in All Ages* was published, but Putnam's
importance does not come from the accuracy of his arguments or the
fact that he was a precursor. His work is significant because it was about
much more than an attempt to update the open fireplace. Using scientific
knowledge to re-create the natural environment he thought had existed in
old houses, Putnam touched upon and epitomized a theme that was central
to every aspect of the nineteenth-century home.

# THE HOME OF THE FUTURE

FOR MANY WHO LIVED THROUGH IT, the First World War was as momentous as the Civil War had been for those whose lives were enveloped by that conflict. But as different as the world of 1918 was from that which had existed only a few years before, the events of the following decades often seemed to separate Americans even more decisively from the past. The years after the First World War included a decade in which the automobile, airplane, radio, and movies became commonplace, a period in which neither big business nor an increasingly active federal government could do much about the longest and most severe economic depression in the nation's history, four years of a war that ended with the dropping of an atomic bomb, and an era in which, while the United States struggled to define its role in an ever-shrinking world, a man landed on the moon.

Americans had different reactions to these phenomena and events. Some believed that their problems were unique, and they tried to find new solutions to them. Others felt that in view of these changes it was all the more important to retain or regain aspects of the past. Both often demeaned the achievements of the nineteenth century. Those who believed that they were beginning a completely new phase of civilization considered the nineteenth century at best to be transitional; those who felt the need for a secure past most often drew upon images of what life had been like in a period that preceded the nineteenth century. From either perspective the home was often criticized, and in trying to define an alternative to this most prominent of all nineteenth-century institutions, American architects frequently attempted to produce an architecture that was distinctly different from that which had evolved in the century before the First World War.

These efforts have had, at best, only limited results, because no matter how pronounced change in this century has been, no upheaval has compared to that transformation of everyday life which occurred at the beginning of the nineteenth century. The forces that were then set in motion have continued to shape the way Americans live, and thus, although it has had to adjust to many new circumstances, the home has survived, as have the essential attributes of the architecture that by the First World War had come to be associated with it.

These characteristics extend from the home's setting to interior details. Throughout this century Americans have continued to be concerned about what makes an area a community or neighborhood. As the automobile has helped to extend the city and to redefine its internal structure, this question has increasingly become intertwined with other issues, especially those of schooling and race. But the idea of the village — whether rural, suburban, urban, or global — is no less important today than it was in 1915.

The automobile has also helped to reshape the spaces around the home. But just as the suburbs of the 1920s had to be annexed to and, therefore, were in part shaped by already existing settlements, so the nature and functions of the home grounds grew out of earlier ways of dividing up and using property. The spaces around new types of multifamily housing, whether for low-income groups or for those who want the convenience of an apartment, have developed along similar lines. Since they most often were built on center city lots that had been laid out in the nineteenth century, multifamily structures have had to respond to that context, even if only by adopting new designs to escape from old constraints.

How to finance the home has been and still remains a matter of great concern. In the 1920s and 1930s those who urged the federal government to build housing frequently contrasted their views with the laissez-faire attitudes of the nineteenth century. But in making their case they often cited as precedents the work of limited-dividend companies. When public housing programs were finally begun, they were considered a major breakthrough, but they were rarely seen as an alternative to home ownership. In fact, the most consequential housing legislation since the First World War has tried to subsidize and regulate the purchase of private houses and thus to help realize goals established long ago by building and loan associations.

Many architects who designed houses financed in this way thought they could define a new aesthetic, one that avoided the troublesome problem of historical associations, by focusing only on functional requirements to arrive at pure form. These were challenging propositions, but houses built according to them have always had difficulty in gaining popular acceptance. Even the architects who ostensibly favored a modern style had a deep-rooted interest in history that they found difficult to suppress, especially when they were far enough from the first phase of modern architecture to see the development of that approach to design as a historical phenomenon.

The interiors of houses built in this century at first glance would seem peculiar to Americans who lived before the First World War. But many of the issues that underlay features like the open plan, the picture window, and the family room arose long before the 1920s. Similarly, how many and what kind of spaces constitute a basic home are questions that have received many answers since the First World War, but most definitions have had to come to terms with versions of the provisions that were specified by Lawrence Veiller in 1910.

In many ways the countless machines and improvements that have found their way into the home in the last sixty years have made the modern housewife's job easier than ever before. But this condition has increasingly forced her to realize, as some of her counterparts in the nineteenth century began to do, that the critical issue in housework is not so much saving time but how and where to spend it. Resolving this dilemma has often resulted in the housewife's leaving the home and, in effect, ceasing to be exclusively a housewife.

Caring for the home has been facilitated by its many service lines, most of which already existed in 1915. The twentieth-century task has been to extend these services to as many people as possible. Of course, radio and television now play a crucial role in delivering information to the home. But the fact that in the 1930s a President decided to call a radio program a "Fireside Chat" was only one of many indications that these new methods of joining the home to the world at large raised searching questions about the past and the future that were similar to those posed earlier.

That the homes of the twentieth century have been conceived within a framework of ideas and issues that was defined in the nineteenth century does not diminish their significance or their quality. They are as rich and as fascinating as those built before the First World War, and they have a vital history of their own. Outlining the characteristics of American domestic architecture since the First World War, describing the processes that shaped it, and drawing out the implications this history may have for the American homes of the future will be subjects for another volume.

THE WIGWAM.

199. "The Wigwam" and "Modern Improvements." Nineteenth-century Americans made such contrasts to demonstrate how much progress there had been. But by 1883, when this illustration was published, the mansard roof of the house representing Modern Improvements was already out of date. When progress was so quick, many Americans could not help but think that something important had been lost in the process. So it has been ever since.

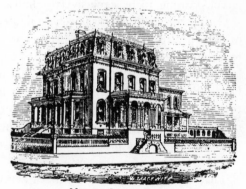

MODERN IMPROVEMENTS.

# NOTES

## CHAPTER 1

1. Fredrika Bremer, *The Homes of the New World* (New York, 1853), I, 53; see also Carl Carmer, *The Hudson* (New York, 1939), pp. 243–248.

2. For the significance of this period see Robert G. Albion, *The Rise of New York Port: 1815–1860* (New York, 1939); Philip D. Jordan, *The National Road* (Indianapolis, 1948); George Rogers Taylor, *The Transportation Revolution* (New York, 1951); Allan R. Pred, *The Spatial Dynamics of U.S. Urban-Industrial Growth, 1800–1914* (Cambridge, Mass., 1966).

3. The reforms of this period have not been adequately treated in one volume, but see Alice F. Tyler, *Freedom's Ferment* (Minneapolis, 1944); David Rothman, *The Discovery of the Asylum* (Boston, 1971).

4. For this discussion of the early history of American religion I have relied on Sidney E. Mead, *The Lively Experiment* (New York, 1963), pp. 16–54; Perry Miller, *The New England Mind: From Colony to Province* (Cambridge, Mass., 1953).

5. On Bushnell, see Barbara M. Cross, *Horace Bushnell: Minister to a Changing America* (Chicago, 1958); Horace Bushnell, *Christian Nurture*, intro. Luther A. Weigle and Williston Walker (New Haven, 1947), pp. xxiii–xl.

6. Bushnell, *Christian Nurture*, pp. xxiv–xxv. For the background at Yale see Sidney E. Mead, *Nathaniel William Taylor* (Chicago, 1942), pp. 25–30, 147–157.

7. Horace Bushnell, *Work and Play* (London, 1864), pp. 39–76.

8. Bushnell, *Work and Play*, pp. 78–115.

9. Bushnell, *Work and Play*, pp. 48–52, 82–89.

10. Horace Bushnell, "Barbarism, the First Danger," *American National Preacher* 21 (1847): 197–219; Horace Bushnell, *Prosperity Our Duty* (Hartford, 1847), p. 11.

11. Bushnell, "Barbarism," pp. 199–208; Horace Bushnell, *Society and Religion: A Sermon for California* (San Francisco, 1856), pp. 22–23.

12. Bushnell, *Prosperity*, p. 17; Mary B. Cheney, ed., *Life and Letters of Horace Bushnell* (New York, 1880), pp. 365–405.

13. Perry Miller, *Jonathan Edwards* (New York, 1949); Perry Miller, "From Edwards to Emerson," *Errand into the Wilderness* (Cambridge, Mass., 1956), pp. 184–203.

14. Bushnell, *Christian Nurture*, p. 6.

15. Bushnell, *Christian Nurture*, pp. 53, 54. Bushnell was probably referring to educators like Bronson Alcott.

16. Bushnell, *Christian Nurture*, pp. 1–23, 54, 74–101, 194–216, 291–314.

17. Horace Bushnell defended an interest in beautiful surroundings in "Taste and Fashion," *New Englander* 1 (1843): 153–168.

18. Colin B. Goodykoontz, *Home Missions on the American Frontier* (Caldwell, Idaho, 1939).

19. Frank L. Mott, *A History of American Magazines* (Cambridge, Mass., 1930–1968), I, 343–355, 369–374.

20. *Dictionary of American Biography.*

21. Catharine Sedgwick, *Home* (Boston, 1835).

22. The influx of immigrants to New York in this period is discussed in Robert Ernst, *Immigrant Life in New York City, 1825–1863* (New York, 1949).

23. Sedgwick, *Home*, pp. 135–144.

24. *Dictionary of American Biography.*

25. T. T. P. Luquer, "When Payne Wrote 'Home! Sweet Home!,'" *Scribner's Magazine* 58 (1915): 742–754.

26. Henry Harbaugh, "The Home Feeling," *Hours at Home* 1 (1865): 409.

27. "Beauties of Nature," *Western Farmer* 1 (1839): 60; J. L. Dwight, "The Religion of Beauty," *Dial* 1 (1840): 17–22; J. N. Danforth, "A Family Picture," *Mother's Magazine* 14 (1846): 161–166; "Theology of the Beautiful," *Hours at Home* 1 (1865): 112; Neil Harris, *The Artist in American Society* (New York, 1966), pp. 134–136.

28. "Rooms and Their Ornaments," *Mother's Magazine and Family Monitor* 21 (1853): 209–211; Samuel Philips, *The Christian Home* (Springfield, Mass., 1859), p. 360; Ik Marvel (Donald G. Mitchell), *Reveries of a Bachelor* (New York, 1852), pp. 15–16, 288–291.

29. William M. Thayer, *Hints for the Household* (Cleveland, 1853), p. 160; Anna Bache, *Scenes at Home: Or, The Adventures of a Fire Screen* (Philadelphia, 1852); T. S. Arthur, "The Two Homes," in Frances E. Percival, ed., *Sweet Home* (Boston, 1856), pp. 13–29.

30. Daniel P. Noyes, "Aim to Make Home Permanent and Attractive," *Mother's Magazine* 19 (1851): 101–103; Philips, *The Christian Home*, pp. 256–260.

31. "Mother and Home," *Mother's Magazine* 19 (1851): 23–25.

32. *Homes of American Authors* (New York, 1852).

33. *Homes of American Statesmen* (New York, 1854).

34. *Dictionary of American Biography.*

35. James A. Harrison, ed., *The Complete Works of Edgar Allan Poe* (New York, 1902), I, 360–361.

36. In writing about Poe, I am indebted to Richard Wilbur, "The House of Poe," in Robert Regan, ed., *Poe* (Englewood Cliffs, N.J., 1967), pp. 98–120.

37. The basic issues of architectural theory are briefly discussed in Wolfgang Herrmann, *Laugier and Eighteenth Century French Theory* (London, 1962), pp. 43–47.

38. On Renaissance architectural theory see Rudolf Wittkower, *Architectural Principles in the Age of Humanism* (London, 1952).

39. The classical language is succinctly but eloquently described in John Summerson, *The Classical Language of Architecture* (London, 1964).

40. The English background is dealt with in Christopher Hussey, *The Picturesque*

(London, 1927), pp. 186–230; and Walter Jackson Bate, *From Classic to Romantic* (New York, 1961), pp. 93–128. The distinction between forms and associations has frequently been discussed, but it is most brilliantly drawn out in Geoffrey Scott, *The Architecture of Humanism* (London, 1914).

41. On nationalism in architecture see Joseph Rykwert, *On Adam's House in Paradise* (New York, 1972), pp. 80–87.

42. On nationalism in American architecture see Oliver Larkin, *Art and Life in America* (New York, 1949), pp. 77–83, 91–97.

43. Criticism of the American achievement in the fine arts and the resulting response are discussed in Durand Echeverria, *Mirage in the West* (Princeton, 1957), pp. 55, 157–159; Roger Stein, *John Ruskin and Aesthetic Thought in America, 1840–1900* (Cambridge, Mass., 1967), pp. 9–11.

44. Horatio Greenough, *Form and Function*, ed. Harold A. Small, intro. Earl Loran (Berkeley, 1947), pp. 51–86; Theodore M. Brown, "Greenough, Paine, Emerson and the Organic Aesthetic," *Journal of Aesthetics and Art Criticism* 14 (1956): 304–317; Stein, *John Ruskin*, pp. 40–41.

45. William L. Lassiter, *Shaker Architecture* (New York, 1966); Julia Neal, *The Shaker Image* (Boston, 1974).

46. The posturing of the "best society" in this period is amusingly satirized in George William Curtis, *The Potiphar Papers* (New York, 1854).

47. William A. Alcott, *The Young Woman's Guide to Excellence* (Boston, 1847), p. 289.

48. For discussion of this point see David P. Handlin, "Yankees in Babylon: New England Architects in New York: 1820–1860" (unpublished B.A. thesis, Harvard College, 1965), pp. 54–58; M. Field, *Rural Architecture* (New York, 1857), p. 51; William Ranlett, *The Architect* (New York, 1851), II, 6.

49. George William Curtis, "Memoir of the Author," in Andrew Jackson Downing, *Rural Essays*, ed. Curtis (New York, 1853), pp. xi–lviii; Carmer, *The Hudson*, pp. 230–250; George B. Tatum, "Andrew Jackson Downing, Arbiter of American Taste" (unpublished Ph.D. dissertation, Princeton University, 1950).

50. John Gloag, *Mr. Loudon's England* (Newcastle upon Tyne, 1970), pp. 116, 220–221.

51. Interest in Loudon has recently been revived by C. L. Hersey, "Loudon and Architectural Associationism," *Architectural Review* 144 (1968): 89–92. Hersey emphasized Loudon's associationism but did not consider the function of "permanent" beauty in Loudon's theory; see Sutherland Lyall, "Loudon and Associationism," *Architectural Review* 144 (1968): 308. Vincent Scully, following on from Hersey, related Loudon's theory of architecture to Downing's: *The Shingle Style and the Stick Style* (rev. ed., New Haven, 1971), p. xxviii. Every student of American architecture owes a deep debt to Scully, but his discussion of Downing can be questioned on two points. In considering the source of Downing's interest in the connection between architecture and morality, Scully singled out the English architect, A. W. N. Pugin. Since Downing does not mention Pugin, this source seems unlikely. Ruskin as an influence is more probable (Stein, *John Ruskin*, pp. 36–46). But architects do not learn only from architects. Other influences, closer to home, and not specifically architectural, were at work. Also, Scully was primarily concerned with *Cottage Residences*; the ideas in *The Architecture of Country Houses* were only a "reiteration" of the earlier theories. The formulation of a theory of architecture in *Cottage Residences* may be clearer. Nevertheless, the changes in *The Architecture of Country Houses* are important.

52. John Claudius Loudon, *An Encyclopaedia of Cottage, Farm and Villa Architecture* (London, 1839), pp. 1105–1124.

53. Loudon, *An Encyclopaedia*, pp. 78–79.

54. John Summerson has characterized the style of the work represented in Loudon's *Encyclopaedia* as "cranky." See *Victorian Architecture* (New York, 1970), pp. 24, 71–72.

55. Andrew Jackson Downing, *A Treatise on the Theory and Practice of Landscape Gardening* (New York, 1841), pp. 9–27, 297–347.

56. Andrew Jackson Downing, *Cottage Residences* (New York, 1842), pp. 9–33, 61.

57. Andrew Jackson Downing, *The Architecture of Country Houses* (New York, 1850), pp. 1–38.

58. Downing, *The Architecture of Country Houses*, pp. 78–81.

59. Stein, *John Ruskin*, pp. 33–41, 46–56.

60. Downing, *The Architecture of Country Houses*, p. 2. Positive opinions of Downing: "Landscape Architecture and Rural Architecture," *United States Magazine and Democratic Review* 9 (1841): 554–560; "Landscape Architecture and Rural Architecture in America," *United States Magazine and Democratic Review* 16 (1845): 348–363. Negative opinions: "Our New Houses," *United States Magazine and Democratic Review* 21 (1847): 342–344.

61. Curtis, "Memoir," pp. xviii–xx; Carmer, *The Hudson*, pp. 230–234.

62. Curtis, "Memoir," pp. xxix–xxxi; Carmer, *The Hudson*, pp. 241, 247; Harris, *The Artist in American Society*, pp. 212, 213.

63. Downing, *The Architecture of Country Houses*, iv.

64. Solon Robinson, "Editor's Table," *American Agriculturalist* 11 (1850): 381; Harris, *The Artist in American Society*, p. 210.

65. Herbert A. Kellar, *Solon Robinson, Pioneer and Agriculturalist* (New York, 1968), I, 112–115, 533, 553–557.

66. Sigfried Giedion, *Space, Time and Architecture* (Cambridge, Mass., 1952), pp. 281–289; Walker Field, "A Reexamination of the Invention of the Balloon Frame" (unpublished B.A. thesis, Harvard College, 1942).

67. Gervase Wheeler, *Homes for the People* (New York, 1855), pp. 409–414.

68. Downing, *The Architecture of Country Houses*, pp. 50–52.

69. Downing, *The Architecture of Country Houses*, pp. iii, 3–4, 135–173.

70. Albert L. Demaree, *The American Agricultural Press, 1819–1860* (New York, 1914), pp. 69–70; Kellar, *Solon Robinson*, II, 499–502, 508–510.

71. Kellar, *Solon Robinson*, I, 308, 332.

72. Demaree, *The American Agricultural Press*, p. 74.

73. Downing, *The Architecture of Country Houses*, pp. 461–484.

74. Bushnell, *Christian Nurture*, pp. 15, 82.

75. Richard M. Shryock, *Medicine and Society in America* (New York, 1960), pp. 117–166.

76. "Dr. William A. Alcott," *American Journal of Education* 4 (1858): 629–656. Some of this research on Alcott was originally done with Robert H. Abzug.

77. William A. Alcott, "July and Independence," *Moral Reformer* 1 (1835): 198.

78. [William A. Alcott], *Forty Years in the Wilderness of Pills and Powders* (Boston, 1859), pp. 72–75.

79. William A. Alcott, *The Laws of Health* (Boston, 1859), p. 10.

80. William A. Alcott, *The Young Mother* (Boston, 1849), p. 276; Alcott, *The Laws of Health*, pp. 234–235.

81. William A. Alcott, *Essay on the Construction of School Houses* (Boston, 1832), pp. 5–6, 14, 16, 20.

82. William A. Alcott, *The Moral Philosophy of Courtship and Marriage* (Boston, 1859), p. 15.

83. William A. Alcott, *The House I Live In; Or, The Human Body* (Boston, 1839).

84. William A. Alcott, *The Young House-Keeper* (Boston, 1838), p. 21.

85. Alcott, *The Young Mother*, pp. 33–38.

86. William A. Alcott, *The Young Husband* (New York, 1839), pp. 349–350.

87. Alcott, *The Young Husband*, pp. 339–352; Alcott, *The Young Woman's Guide*, pp. 181–186.

88. Alcott, *The Young Husband*, pp. 84–97.

89. William A. Alcott, *City and Country* (Boston, 1839), pp. 2, 3, 6, 18–19.

90. Works on domestic economy (housewifery) were related to an allied subject (husbandry) and go back to Greek and Roman writers on agriculture and beyond; see M. I. Finley, *The World of Odysseus* (London, 1954), pp. 53–54; G. E. Fussell, *The Old English Farming Books* (London, 1947). For an American example of such books see *Mackenzies's Five Thousand Receipts* (Philadelphia, 1829).

91. Catharine E. Beecher, *A Treatise on Domestic Economy* (New York, 1847), pp. 302–324.

92. Morrill Wyman, *A Practical Treatise on Ventilation* (Boston, 1846).

93. See, for example, Luther V. Bell, *The Practical Methods of Ventilating Buildings* (Boston, 1848).

94. Wyman, *A Practical Treatise*, pp. 314–317.

95. For background about the history of public health reform see Richard Shryock, "The Origins and Significance of the Public Health Movement in the United States," *Annals of Medical History* 1 (1929): 644–665; John H. Powell, *Bring Out Your Dead* (Philadelphia, 1949); John L. Thomas, "Romantic Reform in America, 1815–1865," *American Quarterly* 17 (1965): 656–681; Charles E. and Carroll S. Rosenberg, "Pietism and the Origins of the American Public Health Movement," *Journal of the History of Medicine and Allied Science* 23 (1968): 16–35; John Duffy, *History of Public Health in New York City, 1625–1866* (New York, 1968); Barbara Rosenkrantz, *Public Health and the State* (Cambridge, Mass., 1972).

96. *Dictionary of American Biography*; Rosenkrantz, *Public Health*, pp. 14–17.

97. The condition of Irish immigrants is dealt with in Oscar Handlin, *Boston's Immigrants* (Cambridge, Mass., 1959), pp. 89–129; Rosenkrantz, *Public Health*, pp. 30–31.

98. Rosenkrantz, *Public Health*, p. 22.

99. Rosenkrantz, *Public Health*, pp. 23–36.

100. Bushnell, *Prosperity*, p. 23.

101. J. Hector St. John Crèvecoeur, *Letters from an American Farmer*, preface W. P. Trent; intro. Ludwig Lewisohn (New York, 1908), pp. 50, 72.

102. Gilbert Chinard, intro., *The Correspondence of Jefferson and Du Pont de Nemours* (Baltimore, 1931), pp. lxxii–lxxiii, 256–258; Yehoshua Arieli, *Individualism and Nationalism in American Ideology* (Cambridge, Mass., 1964), pp. 115–120, 137–138.

103. Charles H. Wiltse, *The Jeffersonian Tradition in American Democracy* (Chapel Hill, N.C., 1935), pp. 136–139; Gilbert Chinard, *Thomas Jefferson, The Apostle of Americanism* (Boston, 1939), pp. 232–234.

104. Thomas Jefferson, *Writings*, ed. P. L. Ford (New York, 1904), II, 178.

105. John Adams, "Discourse on Davila," *Works of John Adams*, ed. Charles F. Adams (Boston, 1851), VI, 232; Adams, "Defense of the Constitutions of Government of the United States of America," *Works*, IV, 489–490.

106. James Fenimore Cooper, *Home As Found*, intro. Lewis Leary (New York, 1961), pp. 13–15, 23–24.

107. Cooper, *Home As Found*, pp. 162–165; Henry Nash Smith, *Virgin Land* (Cambridge, Mass., 1970), pp. 220–224.

108. Cooper, *Home As Found*, pp. 106–109; James Fenimore Cooper, *The Crater* (New York, 1848).

109. Nathaniel Hawthorne, *The House of The Seven Gables*, intro. David Levin (New York, 1960), pp. 25, 192, 262–265, 314.

110. Anthony B. Norton, *Tippecanoe Songs of the Log Cabin Boys and Girls* (Mount Vernon, Ohio, 1888), p. 28.

111. B. H. Hibbard, *A History of the Public Land Policies* (New York, 1939); Helene S. Zahler, *Eastern Workingmen and National Land Policies, 1829–1862* (New York, 1941); Fred A. Shannon, "The Homestead Act and Labor Surplus," *American Historical Review* 41 (1936): 637–651; Smith, *Virgin Land*, pp. 165–173.

112. Zahler, *Eastern Workingmen*, p. 147.

113. Walt Whitman, *Franklin Evans; Or the Inebriate*, in Emory Holloway, ed., *Uncollected Poetry and Prose of Walt Whitman* (Garden City, N.Y.), I, 103–221.

114. Walt Whitman, *Leaves of Grass*, ed. Harold W. Blodgett and Sculley Bradley (New York, 1965), pp. 189, 194.

115. Walt Whitman, *New York Dissected*, ed. Emory Holloway and Ralph Adimari (New York, 1936), pp. 92–102.

116. Whitman, *New York Dissected*, p. 218. The picturesque qualities of the boardinghouse were described in Thomas Butler Gunn, *The Physiology of the New York Boarding House* (New York, 1857).

117. Whitman, *Leaves of Grass*, p. 723.

118. John Coolidge, *Mill and Mansion* (New York, 1942), pp. 32–43, 183–187.

119. Whitman, *New York Dissected*, pp. 101–102. The "model lodging houses" to which Whitman referred in fact were not successful; see Robert Bremner, "The Big Flat: History of a New York Tenement House," *American Historical Review* 64 (1958): 54–62.

120. Roy Lubove, *The Progressives and the Slums* (Pittsburgh, 1962), pp. 1–23.

121. Henry David Thoreau, *Walden*, intro. Basil Willey (New York, 1951), pp. 24–26, 43, 45, 48–49, 54, 58–66, 225, 262–265.

122. Francis Wayland, *The Elements of Political Economy* (Boston, 1837), pp. 111–117.

123. Charles Nordhoff, *The Communistic Societies of the United States* (New York, 1875); Mark Holloway, *Heavens on Earth* (New York, 1966). The best treatment of Owen in the United States is Arthur E. Bestor, *Backwoods Utopias* (Philadelphia, 1950).

124. A synopsis of Fourier's ideas, especially as Americans perceived them, is in Edith R. Curtis, *A Season in Utopia* (New York, 1961), pp. 164–168; see also Alexander Gray, *The Socialist Tradition* (New York, 1946), pp. 169–196.

125. Curtis, *A Season in Utopia*, pp. 13–161.

126. Amelia Russell, *Home Life of the Brook Farm Association* (Boston, 1900), pp. 40–41.

127. Russell, *Home Life*, pp. 92, 125; Curtis, *A Season in Utopia*, pp. 162–288.

128. This theme is touched upon in William R. Taylor, *Cavalier and Yankee* (New York, 1961), pp. 156–167.

129. Harriet Beecher Stowe, *Uncle Tom's Cabin*, ed. Kenneth Lynn (Cambridge, Mass., 1962), pp. 162, 451.

130. Mary T. Eastman, *Aunt Phillis's Cabin* (Philadelphia, 1852), pp. 29, 117; Martha Haines Butt, *Antifanaticism: A Tale of the South* (Philadelphia, 1853), pp. 25, 166.

131. Eastman, *Aunt Phillis's Cabin*, p. 267.

132. Robert Criswell, *Uncle Tom's Cabin Contrasted with Buckingham Hall* (New York, 1852), p. 55.

133. Lucien B. Chase, *English Serfdom and American Slavery* (New York, 1854), pp. 22, 45, 50.

134. Caroline Rush, *The North and the South: Or, Slavery and Its Contrasts* (Philadelphia, 1852), pp. 28, 77, 332.

135. W. L. G. Smith, *Life at the South: Or, Uncle Tom's Cabin As It Is* (Buffalo, 1852), pp. 42, 379.

136. William J. Grayson, *The Hireling and the Slave* (Charleston, 1856), pp. 23, 49–50.

137. George Fitzhugh, *Cannibals All!*, ed. C. Vann Woodward (Cambridge, Mass., 1960), pp. 222–223.

138. The history of the Mount Vernon Association is recounted in Elswyth Thane, *Mount Vernon is Ours* (New York, 1966); see also Susan Fenimore Cooper, *Mount Vernon: A Letter to the Children of America* (New York, 1859).

139. Thane, *Mount Vernon*, pp. 29–36.

140. Roy P. Basler, ed., *The Collected Works of Abraham Lincoln* (New Brunswick, N.J., 1953), II, 461–469; Allan Nevins, *A House Dividing* (New York, 1947), p. 78; Allan Nevins, *The Emergence of Lincoln* (New York, 1950), I, 359–367.

141. The history of the Sanitary Commission is dealt with in George M. Frederickson, *The Inner Civil War* (New York, 1968); there is no parallel history of the Christian Commission, but see A. S. Billingsley, *From the Flag to the Cross* (Philadelphia, 1871).

142. Walt Whitman, *The Wound Dresser*, ed. Richard M. Bucke (Boston, 1898), p. 45.

143. Louisa May Alcott, *Hospital Sketches* (Boston, 1863); Marjory Greenbie, *Lincoln's Daughters of Mercy* (New York, 1944); for a different view of what the Civil War meant to nurses, see Ann Douglas Wood, "The War within a War," *Civil War History* 18 (1972): 197–212.

144. United States Christian Commission, *Facts, Principles and Progress* (Philadelphia, 1864), p. 8; *A Memorial of the New York Branch of the United States Christian Commission* (New York, 1866).

145. John F. W. Ware, *Home to the Camp* (Boston, 1863), p. 4; John F. W. Ware, *Home to the Hospital* (Boston, 1864), p. 3.

146. David Q. Voight, *American Baseball* (Norman, Okla., 1966), p. 11.

147. United States Christian Commission, *Facts*, p. 35; "Telegraph Scene," *First Annual Report of the United States Christian Commission* (Philadelphia, 1863), p. 10.

148. For example, "The Great Northwestern Sanitary Fair," *Sanitary Commission Bulletin* 1 (1863): 65–71; *History of the Brooklyn and Long Island Fair* (Brooklyn, 1864); Charles J. Stillé, *Memorial of the Great Central Fair for the United States Sanitary Commission* (Philadelphia, 1864).

149. John F. W. Ware, "Home, The Residence," *Monthly Religious Magazine* 27 (1862): 93. This and other articles were published in John F. W. Ware, *Home Life* (Boston, 1864).

150. Harriet Beecher Stowe, "House and Home Papers," *Atlantic Monthly* 14 (1864): 567. "House and Home Papers" was serialized in the *Atlantic Monthly* from January to December 1864 and was published as a book in 1865. "The Chimney Corner" appeared in the same magazine from January to September 1866 and was issued as a volume in 1868.

151. Samuel Osgood, "The Home and the Flag," *Harper's New Monthly Magazine* 26 (1863): 664–670.

152. Austin Flint, ed., *Sanitary Memoirs of the War of the Rebellion* (New York, 1867), I, 20–23.

## CHAPTER 2

1. The statistics have been taken from Sam B. Warner, Jr., *The Urban Wilderness* (New York, 1972), p. 70.

2. Edward C. Kirkland, *Industry Comes of Age* (New York, 1962), pp. 163–180; Allan R. Pred, *The Spatial Dynamics of U.S. Urban-Industrial Growth, 1800–1914* (Cambridge, Mass., 1966), pp. 16–19, 143–177.

3. Information on Howells from Kenneth Lynn, *William Dean Howells: An American Life* (New York, 1971).

4. For the treatment of the small town in literature see Page Smith, *As a City upon a Hill* (New York, 1966), pp. 258–283. An undercurrent of discontent with the small town always existed, but criticism did not begin in earnest until the publication of Edgar Lee Masters's *Spoon River Anthology* in 1914.

5. John Fiske, "The Races of the Danube," *Atlantic Monthly* 39 (1877): 401–411; Herbert Baxter Adams, "The Germanic Origins of the New England Town," *Johns Hopkins University Studies* 1 (1883): 5–38. See also Barbara M. Solomon, *Ancestors and Immigrants* (Chicago, 1972), pp. 59–66.

6. The town in this context is discussed in John L. Thomas, "Utopia for an Urban Age: Henry George, Henry Demarest Lloyd, Edward Bellamy," *Perspectives in American History* 6 (1972): 135–163.

7. Nathaniel H. Egleston, *The Home and Its Surroundings* (New York, 1884), pp. 13, 22–23. The book was first published in 1878 with the title *Villages and Village Life*.

8. Most accounts of the small town, for instance, Lewis Atherton, *Main Street on the Middle Border* (Bloomington, Ind., 1954), have assumed that the community was unchanging. The one notable exception is Robert R. Dykstra, *The Cattle Towns* (New York, 1968). Dykstra primarily discusses the economic and political life of Kansas cattle towns, but for improvement work in Wichita, see Parris T. Farwell, *Village Improvement* (New York, 1913), pp. 332–333.

9. Farwell, *Village Improvement*, pp. 3–12; Egleston, *The Home*, p. 16.

10. Bushnell's most emphatic statement of this point was in "City Plans," in *Work and Play* (London, 1864), pp. 167–197.

11. Nathaniel H. Egleston's book on village improvement was dedicated to Downing. Andrew Jackson Downing, *Rural Essays*, ed. George William Curtis (New York, 1853), pp. 229–243.

12. William H. Burnham, "Old Home Week in New Hampshire," *New England Magazine* 22 (1900): 647–652; Helen Thoburn, "Pageantry in Country Places," *Rural Manhood* 4 (1913): 323–326.

13. Egleston, *The Home*, pp. 60–70; there has been no extended history of village improvement, but see Warren Manning, "The History of Village Improvement in the United States," *Craftsman* 5 (1904): 5–14.

14. Ellen Brainerd Peck, "The Founder of Arbor Day," *New England Magazine* 22 (1900): 269–275; *Dictionary of American Biography*.

15. Mary Caroline Robbins, "Village Improvement Societies," *Atlantic Monthly* 79 (1897): 214; for some of those who were benefactors to towns, see B. C. Northrop, *Village Improvement: Why American Villages Differ in Prosperity* (New York, 1891), pp. 12–14.

16. Melville Egleston, "The Land System of the New England Colonies," *Johns Hopkins University Studies* 4 (1886): 545–600; Glenn T. Trewartha, "Types of Rural Settlement in Colonial America," *Geographical Review* 36 (1946): 568–576; Sumner C. Powell, *Puritan Village: The Formation of a New England Town* (New York, 1965), pp. 107–108.

17. Trewartha, "Types of Rural Settlement," pp. 577–580; Richard L. Bushman, *From Puritan to Yankee* (Cambridge, Mass., 1967), pp. 54–82.

18. Marquis de Chastellux, *Travels in North-America* (London, 1787), I, 20.

19. Trewartha, "Types of Rural Settlement," pp. 580–596.

20. A short description of the American system of land subdivision is in Charles Mulford Robinson, *City Planning* (New York, 1916), p. 20. The history of the implementation of this system is admirably described in William D. Pattison, *Beginnings of the American Rectangular Land Survey System, 1784–1800* (Chicago, 1957).

21. The pattern of farm settlement is discussed throughout Gilbert C. Fite, *The Farmer's Frontier, 1865–1900* (New York, 1966): see also John Brinckerhoff Jackson, *American Space* (New York, 1972), pp. 39–56, 64–71, 171–180.

22. The problem of diagonal streets has long been understood. See Lewis M. Haupt, "On the Best Arrangement of City Streets," *Journal of the Franklin Institute* 103 (1877): 252–257.

23. One town that combined diagonal streets with public parks was Jeffersonville, Indiana. But soon after the plan was adopted, it was changed to a conventional grid. See John W. Reps, *The Making of Urban America* (Princeton, 1965), pp. 317–321.

24. Bushnell, "City Plans," pp. 171–172.

25. B. G. Northrop, *Village Improvement* (Boston, 1893), pp. 14–15. The building of small libraries has received little attention, but see F. N. Crunden, "The Public Library and Civic Improvement," *Chautauquan* 43 (1906): 335–344; George S. Bobinski, *Carnegie Libraries* (Chicago, 1969), pp. 34–75.

26. Northrop, *Village Improvement*, p. 14.

27. Horace Bushnell early saw the need not just for historical societies, but also for districts that in their buildings reflected the history of the city; see "City Plans," pp. 172–176.

28. Donald G. Cathcart, "Ulina Where the Residents Cooperate," *Rural Manhood* 5 (1914): 343–345.

29. Mitchell quoted in B. G. Northrop, *Rural Improvement* (New Haven, 1880), p. 44.

30. On fences and lawns see N. Egleston, *The Home*, pp. 134–154.

31. Northrop, *Rural Improvement*, pp. 11–13; Northrop, *Village Improvement*, p. 11; Horace Bushnell, "Hartford Park," *Hearth and Home* 1 (1869): 101–102; Stanley French, "The Cemetery as Cultural Institution: The Establishment of Mount Auburn and the Rural Cemetery Movement," *American Quarterly* 26 (1974): 37–59.

32. N. Egleston, *The Home*, pp. 217–240.

33. There is some dispute about who actually founded Arbor Day; see *Dictionary of American Biography* under Morton.

34. J. Sterling Morton, "Arbor Day: Its Origin and Growth," in Nathaniel H. Egleston, *Arbor Day — Its History and Observance* (Washington, D.C., 1896), p. 26; B. G. Northrop, "Observance of Arbor Day by Schools," in N. Egleston, *Arbor Day*, pp. 27–28.

35. *Dictionary of American Biography*; George E. Waring, "Farm-Villages," *Scribner's Monthly* 13 (1877): 756–767.

36. C. H. Forbes-Lindsay, "The Rural Settlement: Its Social, Economic and Aesthetic Advantages," *Craftsman* 14 (1908): 407–416.

37. Daniel A. Clarke, "The Functions and Charms of the Village," *Rural Manhood* 3 (1912): 288. St. Johnsbury, Vermont, was often cited as a successful factory town. The Fairbanks family not only ran a prosperous scale manufacturing business there but also acted as benefactor to the town, donating numerous parks, statues, and educational institutions. This example was not frequently followed. See Edwin A. Start, "A Model New England Village," *New England Magazine* 3 (1891): 702–718.

38. Frank L. McVey, *The Making of a Town* (Chicago, 1913), p. 4; Harlan Paul Douglass, *The Little Town* (New York, 1919), pp. 90–91.

39. Thorstein Veblen, *Absentee Ownership and Business Enterprise in Recent Times: The Case of America* (New York, 1923), p. 142.

40. Carl Carmer, *The Hudson* (New York, 1939), p. 147.

41. On school consolidation, see Farwell, *Village Improvement*, pp. 250–275; Paul L. Vogt, *An Introduction to Rural Sociology* (New York, 1917), pp. 281–284, 341–346. Trolley-car lines could be seen as aiding either centralization or decentralization; see Sylvester Baxter, "The Trolley Car in Rural Parts," *Harper's New Monthly Magazine* 97 (1898): 60–69. To encompass outlying districts, some associations preferred "Rural Improvement" to "Village Improvement"; see Northrop, *Rural Improvement*, p. 45.

42. Quoted in Frederick Law Olmsted, (Jr.), "Village Improvement," *Massachusetts Civic Association Leaflets* 5 (1905): 3–5.

43. French Strother, "Our Town Life — What Is It Worth?," *The World's Work* 14 (1907): 9452–9457.

44. Douglass, *The Little Town*, pp. 18–20, 244.

45. The common bond of such communities varied. It could be ideological. As many utopian communities were founded in this period as in the previous fifty years. They encompassed the updated Fourierism of the Greeley Colony, founded in Colorado in 1870, and the anarchism of Home, established in Washington in 1896. Religious, ethnic, and racial ties were also important. Obscure sects like the House of David continued to found communities, but broader affiliations were also important. Jews started settlements in Woodbine, New Jersey, and Arpin, Wisconsin; blacks founded towns in Mound Bayou, Mississippi, and Boley, Oklahoma; Italians began a farming community in Tontitown, Arkansas.

46. Northrop, *Village Improvement*, p. 5; for his ideas about "home," see Northrop, *Rural Improvement*, pp. 17–30.

47. The city was often referred to as a desert or jungle. "Wilderness" was used by Robert A. Woods in *The City Wilderness*, a book about settlement houses that he edited in 1898. Huckleberry Finn has frequently been depicted as the archetypical rebel against American domesticity and all it represents. But for a convincing counter-interpretation, see Kenneth S. Lynn, "Welcome Back to the Raft, Huck Honey!," *American Scholar* 46 (1977): 338–347.

48. They often noted tellingly that "God made the country, man made the town."

Antiurban literature is reviewed in Morton and Lucia White, *The Intellectual versus The City* (Cambridge, Mass., 1962).

49. There have been no systematic treatments of the picturesque view of the city. Some figures like the photographer Alfred Stieglitz and the painters of the Ashcan School have been studied because they were important in their fields. But others, for instance the journalist William Rideing and the illustrator Harry Fenn, have gone unnoticed. Mrs. Schuyler van Rensselaer, "Picturesque New York," *Century Magazine* 45 (1892): 164–175.

50. Adna Ferrin Weber, *The Growth of Cities in the Nineteenth Century* (New York, 1899), pp. 439, 442–445.

51. O. B. Bunce, "The City of the Future," *Appleton's Journal* 7 (1872): 158.

52. Chicago has been the subject of many useful histories. The best are: Everett Chamberlin, *Chicago and Its Suburbs* (Chicago, 1874); A. T. Andreas, *History of Chicago* (Chicago, 1884); Moses Kirkland, *History of Chicago* (Chicago, 1895); Homer Hoyt, *A Hundred Years of Land Values in Chicago* (Chicago, 1933); Bessie Pierce, *A History of Chicago* (New York, 1937–1957); Harold M. Mayer and Richard C. Wade, *Chicago: Growth of a Metropolis* (Chicago, 1969).

53. Andreas, *History of Chicago*, I, 33–110; Pierce, *A History of Chicago*, 3–42.

54. Andreas, *History of Chicago*, I, 244–263; Kirkland, *History of Chicago*, pp. 119–130; Hoyt, *A Hundred Years*, pp. 23–67.

55. Andreas, *History of Chicago*, II, 118–158, 673–700; Hoyt, *A Hundred Years*, pp. 74–88.

56. Hoyt, *A Hundred Years*, pp. 65–67; Mayer and Wade, *Chicago*, pp. 3–34.

57. Hoyt, *A Hundred Years*, pp. 88–101; Mayer and Wade, *Chicago*, pp. 35–66.

58. Chamberlin, *Chicago*, pp. 344–458; Mayer and Wade, *Chicago*, pp. 67–93.

59. Chamberlin, *Chicago*, pp. 385–390.

60. Chamberlin, *Chicago*, pp. 415–416; Frederick Law Olmsted, Jr., "Riverside, Illinois: A Residential Neighborhood Designed over Sixty Years Ago," *Landscape Architecture* 21 (1931): 256–291; Howard K. Menhinick, "Riverside Sixty Years Later," *Landscape Architecture* 22 (1932): 109–117; S. S. Fuller and others, *Riverside Then and Now* (Riverside, Ill., 1936).

61. Andreas, *History of Chicago*, II, 549–556; Hoyt, *A Hundred Years*, pp. 64, 86; Mayer and Wade, *Chicago*, pp. 94–97.

62. Daniel Burnham and Edward H. Bennett, *Plan of Chicago* (Chicago, 1909), p. 43.

63. Although the call for public parks was heard throughout the United States, Frederick Law Olmsted's voice was often the most articulate. See Frederick Law Olmsted, "Public Parks and the Enlargement of Towns," *Journal of Social Science* 3 (1871): 1–36; Frederick Law Olmsted, "The Justifying Value of a Public Park," *Journal of Social Science* 12 (1881): 147–164. On Central Park see Frederick Law Olmsted, Jr., and Theodora Kimball, *Frederick Law Olmsted, Landscape Architect* (New York, 1928), II.

64. Andreas, *History of Chicago*, II, 67–188; Chamberlin, *Chicago*, pp. 313–340; Burnham and Bennett, *Plan*, pp. 43–51. For a vision of what a park could be see Horace W. S. Cleveland, *Landscape Architecture as Applied to the Wants of the West*, ed. Roy Lubove (Pittsburgh, 1963).

65. Andreas, *History of Chicago*, III, 365–389, 471–507, 714–763; Hoyt, *A Hundred Years*, pp. 481–483.

66. On population see Pierce, *A History of Chicago*, III, 20–50. On the business district see Hoyt, *A Hundred Years*, pp. 135–136; Mayer and Wade, *Chicago*, pp. 132–133. On the development of the skyscrapers see Sigfried Giedion, *Space, Time and*

*Architecture* (Cambridge, Mass., 1952), pp. 315–327; William Jordy, *Progressive and Academic Ideals at the Turn of the Century* (Garden City, N.Y., 1972), pp. 1–179. On urban design implications of skyscrapers see Donald Hoffmann, "The Setback Skyscraper City of 1891," *Journal of the Society of Architectural Historians* 29 (1970): 181–187.

67. Stanley Buder, *Pullman, an Experiment in Industrial Order and Community Planning* (New York, 1967).

68. Mayer and Wade, *Chicago*, pp. 150–151.

69. Life in this housing is described in several articles in the *American Journal of Sociology*: Milton B. Hunt, "The Housing of Non-Family Groups of Men in Chicago," 16 (1910): 145–170; Sophonisba P. Breckinridge and Edith Abbott, "Chicago's Housing Problem: Families in Furnished Rooms," 16 (1910): 289–308; Breckinridge and Abbott, "Housing Conditions in Chicago, III: Back of the Yards," 16 (1911): 413–468; Abbott and Breckinridge, "Chicago Housing Conditions, IV: The West Side Revisited," 17 (1911): 1–34.

70. Andreas, *History of Chicago*, III, 164–167; Hoyt, *A Hundred Years*, pp. 144–149, 163–174, 208–211.

71. The fair is most fully described in Rossiter Johnson, ed., *A History of the World's Columbian Exposition* (New York, 1897–1898).

72. W. D. Howells, *The Altrurian Romances*, intro. Clara and Rudolf Kirk (Bloomington, Ind., 1968), pp. 159–161, 198–219, 227–236.

73. William T. Stead, *If Christ Came to Chicago*, ed. Harvey Wish (New York, 1964), pp. 400–428.

74. Lincoln Steffens, *The Shame of the Cities* (New York, 1904), pp. 233–276; Hoyt King, "The Reform Movement in Chicago," *Annals of the American Academy of Political and Social Science* 25 (1905): 33–45; Burnham and Bennett, *Plan*, pp. 43–51.

75. Chicago spirit was raised in 1906 when both the Cubs and the White Sox won pennants. That fact had as much to do with Burnham's finally being commissioned as anything else. The work was originally sponsored by the Merchants' Club, which merged with the Commercial Club in 1907.

76. Daniel Burnham, "The Commercial Value of Beauty," in Charles Moore, *Daniel Hudson Burnham: Architect, Planner of Cities* (Boston, 1921), II, 101–107.

77. Burnham and Bennett, *Plan*, pp. 61–118.

78. Burnham and Bennett, *Plan*, pp. 8, 82; on reform and nonpartisanship see Edward C. Banfield and James Q. Wilson, *City Politics* (Cambridge, Mass., 1967), pp. 138–167.

79. For reception of the plan see Mel Scott, *American City Planning since 1890* (Berkeley, 1969), pp. 138–141. On social distance see Harvey W. Zorbaugh, *The Gold Coast and the Slum* (Chicago, 1930); W. S. Bogardus, "Social Distance in the City," in Ernest W. Burgess, ed., *The Urban Community* (Chicago, 1926).

80. Hamlin Garland, "The New Chicago," *Craftsman* 24 (1913): 565.

81. Burnham, "The Commercial Value of Beauty," p. 102. Burnham lived in suburban Evanston.

82. Philadelphia was most often referred to as "The City of Homes"; see, for example, Charles Belmont Davis, "The City of Homes," *Harpers New Monthly Magazine* 89 (1894): 3–19. Other cities, however, were similarly described. See John Dennis, "Rochester: The City of Homes," *Chautauquan* 13 (1891): 40–43.

83. Clinton R. Woodruff, "The Nationalization of Municipal Movements," *Annals of the American Academy of Political and Social Science* 21 (1903): 100–108; "The Activities of Civic Organizations for Municipal Improvement in the United States," 25 (1905): 359–401.

84. This background is discussed in Scott, *American City Planning*, pp. 82–90, 95–101.

85. *The American City* began in 1909; *City Plan* in 1915. On the teaching of city planning and the background at Harvard see "James Sturgis Pray," *American Landscape Architect* 1 (1929): 16–17.

86. "Charles Mulford Robinson," *Transactions of the American Society of Landscape Architects* 2 (1909–1921): 93–99.

87. Robinson, "The Fair as a Spectacle," in Johnson, ed., *A History*, I, 493–512.

88. Charles Mulford Robinson, *The Improvement of Towns and Cities* (New York, 1901).

89. Charles Mulford Robinson, *Modern Civic Art* (New York, 1903); Charles Mulford Robinson, *The Call of the City* (New York, 1908), pp. 11 ,15.

90. On Howard see Walter L. Creese, *The Search for Environment* (New Haven, 1966), pp. 144–157. On Unwin see Creese, *The Search*, pp. 158–190; Walter L. Creese, ed., *The Legacy of Raymond Unwin* (Cambridge, Mass., 1967), pp. 1–41; Paul Evans, "Raymond Unwin and the Municipalization of the Garden City," *Transactions of the Martin Centre* 1 (1976): 251–274.

91. John Nolen, "Street Widths and Their Subdivision," *Proceedings of the National Conference on City Planning* 2 (1910): 147.

92. Robinson, *City Planning*, pp. 13–64.

93. Robinson, *City Planning*, pp. 69–70, 82.

94. Robinson, *Modern Civic Art*, p. 246.

95. For an early theoretical discussion of housing and rapid transit, see Lewis M. Haupt, "Rapid Transit in Cities," *Journal of the Franklin Institute* 125 (1888): 1–21; Lewis M. Haupt, "Feasibility of Underground Railroads in Philadelphia," *Journal of the Franklin Institute* 126 (1888): 448–464. Awareness of the complex issues is reflected in Henry C. Wright, "Transit and Housing," *Proceedings of the National Conference on Housing* 3 (1913): 68–74, 173–183.

96. Herbert Ladd Towle, "The Automobile and Its Mission," *Scribner's Magazine* 53 (1913): 149.

97. Robinson, *City Planning*, pp. 25–51; Frederick Law Olmsted, Jr., "Land Subdivision from the Point of View of a Development Company," *Proceedings of the National Conference on Housing* 4 (1915): 158–174.

98. Robinson, *City Planning*, pp. 52–64; an evocative account of the alley syndrome is Albion Fellows Bacon, "Alleys," *Proceedings of the National Conference on Housing* 1 (1911): 39–46.

99. Thomas Atkinson, *The Orientation of Buildings* (New York, 1912).

100. Robinson, *City Planning*, pp. 84–89, 127–181.

101. Robinson, *City Planning*, pp. 156–157. For a more sympathetic view of this issue, but one that arrives at the same conclusion, see Jane Addams, *The Spirit of Youth and the City Streets* (New York, 1909).

102. "Garden Cities Association of America," *Charities and the Commons* 17 (1907): 286; Scott, *American City Planning*, p. 90.

103. Budgett Meakin, *Model Factories and Villages* (London, 1905), pp. 382–416; Grosvenor Atterbury, "Model Towns in America," *Scribner's Magazine* 52 (1912): 20–35; Graham Romeyn Taylor, *Satellite Cities* (New York, 1915); James Ford, "Residential and Industrial Decentralization," in John Nolen, ed., *City Planning* (New York, 1916), pp. 332–352.

104. Robinson, *City Planning*, pp. 238–246; George B. Ford and Ralph F. Warner, *City Planning Progress in the United States* (Washington, D.C., 1917).

105. Henry George, *Our Land and Land Policy* (San Francisco, 1871); *Progress and Poverty* (San Francisco, 1879). The argument for the single tax is explained in Louis F. Post, *Taxation and Land Values* (Indianapolis, 1915).

106. Charles B. Fullerton, "Taxation and Housing," *Proceedings of the National Conference on Housing* 4 (1915): 92–101.

107. E. R. A. Seligman, "Housing and the Untaxing of Buildings," *Proceedings of the National Conference on Housing* 4 (1915): 102–108.

108. Robinson, *City Planning*, pp. 75–76, 151.

109. Gordon Whitnall, "History of Zoning," *Annals of the American Academy of Political and Social Science* 155 (1931): 1–14; W. L. Poland, "Outline of the Law of Zoning in the United States," *Annals of the American Academy of Political and Social Science* 155 (1931): 15–33.

110. Robinson, *City Planning*, pp. 79, 161–162.

111. Charles Mulford Robinson, *Third Ward Traits* (Rochester, 1899), p. 5.

112. John Dewey, "The School as a Social Center," *Proceedings of the National Education Association* 41 (1902), pp. 373–383; G. Stanley Hall, "Some Social Aspects of Education," *Educational Review* 23 (1902): 435–455; Clarence A. Perry, *The Wider Use of the School Plant* (New York, 1910); Arthur C. Comey, "Neighborhood Centers," in Nolen, ed., *City Planning*, pp. 117–138.

113. Edward J. Ward, *The Social Center* (New York, 1913), pp. 1–18, 96–122, 174–206. *Friendship Village* (New York, 1908), a novel by Zona Gale, contains a telling statement of these ideas.

114. George B. Ford, "Planning the City for Community Life," paper read at the National Conference on Community Centers, April 21, 1916.

115. Henry V. Hubbard, "The Size and Distribution of Playgrounds . . .," *Proceedings of the National Conference on City Planning* 6 (1914): 265–287; George B. Ford, "Discussion," *Proceedings of the National Conference on City Planning* 6 (1914): 95–96; Arthur C. Comey, *Detroit Suburban Planning* (Detroit, 1915), pp. 21–27.

116. Sage Foundation Homes Company, *Forest Hills Gardens* (New York, 1912); Clarence A. Perry, "The Neighborhood Unit," in *Regional Survey of New York and Its Environs* (New York, 1929), VII, 90–100, 132–140.

117. The activities of the City Club were described in *City Club Bulletin*, which began publication in February 1907.

118. Biographical information on Hooker is from a speech by Adena Miller Rich at a memorial service for him at Hull-House, Chicago, March 23, 1939; see also George R. and Cristiane Crasemann Collins, *Camillo Sitte and the Birth of Modern City Planning* (New York, 1965), p. 134.

119. George E. Hooker, "Congestion and its Causes in Chicago," *Proceedings of the National Conference on City Planning* 2 (1910): 42–57; George E. Hooker, *Through Routes for Chicago's Steam Railroads* (Chicago, 1914).

120. Collins and Collins, *Camillo Sitte*, pp. 47, 56, 72.

121. Quoted in Ward, *The Social Center*, p. 155.

122. "Annual Reports of Civic Committees," *City Club Bulletin* 5 (1912): 255–256, 260–262.

123. Alfred B. Yeomans, ed., *City Residential Land Development* (Chicago, 1916), pp. 1–5, 10–19, 48–49, 84–86.

124. William Drummond, "Discussion," *Proceedings of the National Conference on Housing* 3 (1913): 99.

125. Yeomans, ed., *City Residential Land Development*, pp. 37–44. For further city

planning projects by Drummond see the City Club of Chicago, *The Railway Terminal Problem of Chicago* (Chicago, 1913), pp. 55–76.

126. Yeomans, ed., *City Residential Land Development*, pp. 96–99.

## CHAPTER 3

1. Wright formulated these ideas early in his career. They first appeared in print in Frank Lloyd Wright, "A Home in a Prairie Town," *Ladies' Home Journal* 18 (1901): 17. Frank Lloyd Wright, "Non-Competitive Plan," in Alfred B. Yeomans, ed., *City Residential Land Development* (Chicago, 1916), pp. 96–102.

2. V. L. Parrington, "On the Lack of Privacy in American Village Homes," *House Beautiful* 13 (1903): 109–112.

3. Frank L. Mott, *A History of American Magazines* (Cambridge, Mass., 1930–1968), III, 161–162; IV, 338, 341–342; V, 36–48.

4. Frank J. Scott dedicated his book to Downing, and a Downingesque cottage appears in Scott, "Design for a Cottage," *New England Farmer* 2 (1850): 256–257. Scott's career is difficult to trace. He was born in 1828 and lived till 1919. Although he wrote *The Art of Beautifying the Home Grounds* in 1870, there is no evidence that he published anything on this subject afterward.

5. For biographical information on Jesup Scott see Henry Nash Smith, *Virgin Land* (Cambridge, Mass., 1970), pp. 159–162; Charles Glaab, "Jesup W. Scott and a West of Cities," *Ohio History* 73 (1964): 3–12.

6. Frank J. Scott, *National Works* (Toledo, Ohio, 1878).

7. Frank J. Scott, *The Art of Beautifying the Home Grounds* (New York, 1870), pp. 12, 14, 19, 24, 25, 27, 34, 51–52, 60, 61–62, 109–111.

8. Milton Bradley, "Social Relaxation," *Good Housekeeping* 1 (1885): 11.

9. Bradley, "Social Relaxation," p. 11; Maurice Thompson, *The Witchery of Archery* (New York, 1879).

10. Scott, *The Art of Beautifying*, p. 49.

11. See, for example, Edward Sprague Rand, *Flowers for the Parlor and Garden* (Boston, 1863); Ella Rodman Church, *The Home Garden* (New York, 1881); Frank H. Nutter and Walter J. Keith, *Quarter Acre Possibilities* (Minneapolis, 1898); Liberty H. Bailey, *Garden-Making* (New York, 1901); Samuel Parsons, Jr., *How to Plan the Home Grounds* (New York, 1901); Frank A. Waugh, *Landscape Gardening* (New York, 1901); Helena Ely, *A Woman's Handy Home* (New York, 1903); Kate V. Saint Maur, *A Self-Supporting Home* (New York, 1905); Grace Tabor, *Suburban Gardens* (New York, 1913).

12. A. J. Downing, *A Treatise on the Theory and Practice of Landscape Gardening*, supp. Henry Winthrop Sargent (New York, 1859), pp. 569–572; Samuel Swift, "Llewellyn Park," *House and Garden* 3 (1903): 327–335; John W. Reps, *The Making of Urban America* (Princeton, 1965), p. 339.

13. Alwyn T. Covell, "Co-operative Group Planning," *Architectural Record* 34 (1913): 467–475.

14. Swift, "Llewellyn Park," pp. 330–332.

15. E. Otis Williams, "The Homebuilders' Suburb of New Baltimore: Roland Park," *Indoors and Out* 3 (1907): 259–267; 4 (1907): 23–31; Edward Henry Bouton, "Local and Minor Streets," in John Nolen, ed., *City Planning* (New York, 1916), pp. 88–102; Norman T. Newton, *Design on the Land* (Cambridge Mass., 1971), pp. 468–471.

16. Nolen, ed., *City Planning*, p. ix; Yeomans, ed., *City Residential Land Develop-*

*ment*, pp. 6–8; E. H. Bouton, "Discussion," *Proceedings of the National Conference on Housing* 2 (1912): 234–236.

17. Charles Mulford Robinson, *The Improvement of Towns and Cities* (New York, 1901), pp. 113–118.

18. William Solotaroff, *Shade-Trees in Towns and Cities* (New York, 1911), pp. 65–81; Charles Mulford Robinson, *City Planning* (New York, 1916), pp. 109–181, 209–228.

19. A. Prescott Folwell, *Municipal Engineering Practice* (New York, 1916), pp. 75–80.

20. Frederick L. Ford, "The Removal of Overhead Wires," *American Civic Association Leaflets* 13 (1907).

21. The building of roads is dealt with in Charles E. Morrison, *Highway Engineering* (New York, 1908); Ira Osborne Baker, *A Treatise on Roads and Pavements* (New York, 1914).

22. Cable's Northampton years are well discussed in Philip Butcher, *George W. Cable: The Northampton Years* (New York, 1959).

23. Butcher, *Cable*, pp. 75–80; George W. Cable, "Home Culture Clubs," *Century Magazine* 36 (1888): 497–507.

24. Butcher, *Cable*, pp. 146–149.

25. George Washington Cable, *The Amateur Garden* (New York, 1914), pp. 3–39; William Haynes, "George Cable Talks of Gardens," *House and Garden* 32 (1917): 28–29.

26. Cable, *The Amateur Garden*, pp. 43–46, 109–127; George Washington Cable, "Neighborly Gardens," *Good Housekeeping* 38 (1904): 332–342, 419–421, 467–470; Frank P. Stewart, "Neighborhood Garden Clubs," *Suburban Life* 3 (1906), pp. 123–124.

27. Cable, *The Amateur Garden*, pp. 113–115; H. D. Hemenway, "Prize Garden Competition," *Art and Progress* 1 (1909): 38.

28. Samuel Crowther, *John H. Patterson* (Garden City, N.Y., 1923), pp. 190–207; National Cash Register Company, *A New Era in Manufacturing* (Dayton, Ohio, 1899), n.p.

29. N.C.R.C., *A New Era*, n.p.; National Cash Register Company, *Art, Nature and The Factory* (Dayton, Ohio, 1904), n.p.

30. National Cash Register Company, *Nature, The Factory and the Home* (Dayton, Ohio, 1903), n.p.

31. "Outdoor Art and Beautiful Homes Edition," *N.C.R.* 12 (1899): n.p.

32. N.C.R.C., *Art, Nature and the Factory*, n.p.

33. Robinson, *The Improvement of Towns and Cities*, pp. 147–148.

34. O. R. Geyer, "Cleaning and Beautifying the City," *American City* 16 (1917): 365–368.

35. Wilhelm Miller, *The Prairie Spirit in Landscape Gardening* (Urbana, Ill., 1915), pp. 2–4. See also Leonard K. Eaton, *Landscape Artist in America: The Life and Work of Jens Jensen* (Chicago, 1964). For Simonds's ideas on landscape gardening, see the articles he wrote in *House Beautiful* from 1898 to 1900.

36. Miller, *The Prairie Spirit*, p. 33. In addition to *The Prairie Spirit*, Miller also wrote a related pamphlet, *"The Illinois Way" of Beautifying the Farm* (Urbana, Ill., 1914).

37. Playground Association of America, *A Normal Course in Play for Professional Directors* (New York, 1910); Everett B. Mero, ed., *American Playgrounds* (Boston,

1908); Amalie Hofer Jerome, "The Playground as Social Center," *Annals of the American Academy of Political and Social Science* 35 (1910): 129–133; Jane Addams, *The Spirit of Youth and the City Streets* (New York, 1909).

38. H. D. Hemenway, *How to Make School Gardens* (New York, 1903); M. Louise Greene, *Among School Gardens* (New York, 1910); "Gardens in the Air," *Craftsman* 24 (1913): 386–394.

39. Frederick W. Speirs, Samuel McCune Lindsay, and Franklin B. Kirkbride, "Vacant-Lot Cultivation," *Charities Review* 8 (1898): 74–104; Harlean James, "Civic Gardening Which Develops the City People," *Craftsman* 25 (1914): 574–584; Melvin G. Holli, *Reform in Detroit* (New York, 1969), pp. 70–72.

40. Florence L. Cross, "The National Plant, Flower and Fruit Guild," *Charities and the Commons* 16 (1906): 611–614; Albion Fellows Bacon, *Beauty for Ashes* (New York, 1914), pp. 84–95.

41. Charles Dickens, *American Notes and Pictures from Italy* (London, 1857), p. 89.

42. For Jacob Riis's role in the use of photography, see Beaumont Newhall, *The History of Photography from 1839 to the Present Day* (New York, 1964), pp. 137–146; Jacob A. Riis, *How the Other Half Lives*, ed. Sam B. Warner, Jr. (Cambridge, Mass., 1970), pp. xii–xiv, 207–208.

43. For example, James Ford, "Housing and Disease," *Proceedings of the National Conference on Housing* 5 (1916): 190–197; James Ford, "Some Fundamentals of Housing Reform," *American City* 8 (1913): 473–481.

44. Historians of this legislation have focused on New York; see Lawrence Veiller, "Tenement House Reform in New York City, 1834–1900," in Robert W. DeForest and Lawrence Veiller, eds., *The Tenement House Problem* (New York, 1903), pp. 69–118; Roy Lubove, *The Progressives and the Slums* (Pittsburgh, 1962).

45. For examples of the struggle see Albion Fellows Bacon, *The Awakening of a State* (New York, 1910); Bacon, *Beauty for Ashes*, pp. 191–375; Lubove, *The Progressives and the Slums*.

46. Frederick Law Olmsted and J. J. R. Cross, "The 'Block' Building System of New York," *Plumber and Sanitary Engineer* 2 (1879): 134 (condensed from a report made in 1876).

47. "Improved Homes for Workingmen," *Plumber and Sanitary Engineer* 2 (1878): 1, 32.

48. "Report of the Committee," *Plumber and Sanitary Engineer* 2 (1879): 90–92.

49. Lubove, *The Progressives and the Slums*, pp. 30–31.

50. George E. Waring, Jr., "The Sanitary Conditions of Tenement Houses," *Plumber and Sanitary Engineer* 2 (1878): 13; "Plumbing Work in Tenement Houses," *Plumber and Sanitary Engineer* 2 (1879): 123.

51. Ernest Flagg, "The Ecole des Beaux Arts," *Architectural Record* 3 (1894): 302–313, 419–428; 4 (1894): 38–43.

52. Ernest Flagg, "The New York Tenement House Evil and Its Cure," *Scribner's Magazine* 16 (1894): 109–116.

53. A synopsis of the 1896 competition and an account of subsequent competitions is contained in James Ford, *Slums and Housing* (Cambridge, Mass., 1936), II, 883–890, 911–918.

54. Henry Atterbury Smith, "Exterior Stairs," *American Architect* 97 (1910): 93–94; "The Shively Sanitary Tenements," *American Architect* 97 (1910): 95–96; Henry C. Shively, *Hygienic and Economic Features of the East River Homes*, a pamphlet reprinted from *New York Architect* 5 (1911).

55. Biographical information from A. J. Bloor, "The Late Edward T. Potter,"

*American Architect and Building News* 87 (1905): 21–22; Richard Chaffee, "Edward Tuckerman Potter and Samuel L. Clemens: An Architect and His Client" (unpublished dissertation in the Avery Library, Columbia University, 1966); miscellaneous papers of Potter's on file at the Avery Library.

56. Potter first described these ideas in the New York *Tribune*, vol. 26, no. 8004 (Dec. 3, 1866). Charles Loring Brace, "Model Tenement Houses," *Plumber and Sanitary Engineer* 1 (1878): 47–48; E. T. Potter, "A Study of Some New York Tenement House Problems," *Charities Review* 1 (1892): 129–140.

57. Lewis W. Leeds, *A Treatise on Ventilation* (New York, 1871), pp. 81–82, 164–165.

58. E. T. Potter, "Urban Housing in New York," *American Architect and Building News* 3 (1878): 90–92, 137–138, 171–173; E. T. Potter, "New York Yards," *American Architect and Building News* 5 (1879): 163–164, 173–174; E. T. Potter, "Urban Housing," *American Architect and Building News* 6 (1879): 98–99.

59. Lawrence Veiller, "Buildings in Relation to Street and Site," *Proceedings of the National Conference on City Planning* 3 (1911): 80–96.

60. In preparing the 1901 law, the Tenement House Commission, perhaps out of respect, solicited Potter's opinions. His response was "Tenement-Houses," *American Architect and Building News* 70 (1900): 59–62; "Graded Factors of Good Housing," *American Architect and Building News* 74 (1901): 100–101.

61. Lawrence Veiller, *A Model Tenement House Law* (New York, 1910). This book was expanded to *A Model Housing Law* in 1914.

62. Veiller, "Buildings in Relation to Street and Site," pp. 85–89; Albion Fellows Bacon, "Alleys," *Proceedings of the National Conference on Housing* 1 (1911): 39–46; Charles B. Ball, "The Alley Problem," *Proceedings of the National Conference on Housing* 4 (1915): 132–140.

63. Thomas Jordan and Frederick Law Olmsted, Jr., "Discussion," *Proceedings of the National Conference on Housing* 1 (1911): 138, 140.

64. Ball, "The Alley Problem," pp. 136–137.

65. Veiller, "Buildings in Relation to Street and Site," p. 86.

66. Veiller, "Buildings in Relation to Street and Site," p. 87.

67. Raymond Unwin, "Discussion," *Proceedings of the National Conference on City Planning* 3 (1911): 97–107.

68. Grosvenor Atterbury, "Discussion," *Proceedings of the National Conference on City Planning* 3 (1911): 110–111.

69. Veiller, "Buildings in Relation to Street and Site," p. 81.

70. Duhring, Okie and Ziegler, Architects, "A Practical Housing Development," *Architectural Record* 34 (1913): 46–55.

71. George B. Ford, "Discussion," *Proceedings of the National Conference on Housing* 2 (1912): 264–268; Prescott F. Hall, "The Menace of the Three-Decker," *Proceedings of the National Conference on Housing* 5 (1916): 133–152.

72. George E. Hooker, "Discussion," *Proceedings of the National Conference on Housing* 2 (1912): 268–271.

73. O. B. Bunce, "The City of the Future," *Appleton's Journal* 7 (1872): 156–158; O. B. Bunce, "The City of the Future Once More," *Appleton's Journal* 7 (1872): 495–496.

74. Edward Bellamy, *Looking Backward*, intro. Robert L. Shurter (New York, 1951), p. 122; J. P. Putnam, *Architecture under Nationalism* (Boston, 1890), p. 90.

75. J. P. Putnam, "The Apartment-House," *American Architect and Building News* 27 (1890): 3–5; Putnam, *Architecture*, pp. 10–14.

76. Bunce, "The City of the Future," p. 157.

77. "The Apthorp Apartments — The Largest in the World," *Architecture* 18 (1908): 129–131; "The Apthorp Apartments," *American Architect* 97 (1910): illus. following p. 44.

78. G. C. Hesselgen Publishing Company, *Apartment Houses of the Metropolis* (New York, 1908), pp. 18–27.

79. Lewis W. Leeds, "A Modern Paris House," *Plumber and Sanitary Engineer* 2 1879): 268–269; see also "Parisian Flats," *Appleton's Journal* 6 (1871): 561–562.

80. William T. Stead, *If Christ Came to Chicago*, ed. Harvey Wish (New York, 1964), pp. 422–423; W. D. Howells, *The Altrurian Romances*, intro. Clara and Rudolf Kirk (Bloomington, Ind., 1968), pp. 159–161.

81. S. G. Young, *European Modes of Living* (New York, 1881).

82. "The Dakota Apartment House," *Sanitary Engineer* 11 (1885): 271. For a Chicago example of the same period, see "Correspondence," *American Architect and Building News* 2 (1877): 126.

83. G. Matlack Price, "A Pioneer in Apartment House Construction," *Architectural Record* 36 (1914): 74–76.

84. Hubert, Pirsson and Hoddick, Architects, "New York Flats and French Flats," *Architectural Record* 2 (1892): 57–60.

85. Hubert, Pirsson and Company, *Where and How to Build* (New York, 1892), pp. 78–79; Andrew Alpern, *Apartments for the Affluent* (New York, 1975), pp. 16–17.

86. Hubert, "New York Flats," pp. 61–64.

87. Irving K. Pond, "The Architecture of Apartment Houses," *Brickbuilder* 7 (1898): 116–119; Walter Kilham, "The Planning of Apartment Houses, III" *Brickbuilder* 12 (1903): 248–249.

88. Pond, "The Architecture of Apartment Houses," p. 139.

89. Walter B. Chambers, "The Duplex Apartment House," *Architectural Record* 29 (1911): 327.

90. E. T. Potter, "The Mechanical Problem in Concentrated Residence" (unpublished pamphlet in the Avery Library, Columbia University), p. 3.

91. E. T. Potter, "Diagram" *American Architect and Building News* 22 (1887): 187; E. T. Potter, "Plans for Apartment Houses," *American Architect and Building News* 23 (1888): n.p.; E. T. Potter, "Comparative Table," *American Architect and Building News* 26 (1889): 65; E. T. Potter, "The Problem of Concentrated Residence," *American Architect and Building News* 26 (1889): 156–158; E. T. Potter, "A System of Concentrated Residence," *American Architect and Building News* 26 (1889): 266–267.

92. Potter, "A Study," p. 136.

93. Hubert, "New York Flats," pp. 54–57.

94. Price, "A Pioneer in Apartment House Construction," p. 76.

# CHAPTER 4

1. The phrase may first have been used in John Bunyan's *Pilgrim's Progress*. Andrew Jackson Downing used it in *The Architecture of Country Houses*. The founder of the magazine *House Beautiful* was inspired by Robert Louis Stevenson's poem of the same title. See Frank L. Mott, *A History of American Magazines* (Cambridge, Mass., 1930–1968), V, 154–165.

2. Mark Twain, *Life on the Mississippi* (reprint, New York, 1963), pp. 186–190.

3. Kenneth R. Andrews, *Nook Farm* (Cambridge, Mass., 1950), pp. 16–24.

4. Andrews, *Nook Farm*, pp. 81–83; Richard Chaffee, "Edward Tuckerman Potter and Samuel L. Clemens: An Architect and His Client" (unpublished dissertation in the Avery Library, Columbia University, 1966).

5. Andrews, *Nook Farm*, pp. 83–84, 96–99, 231–240.

6. Fredrika Bremer, *The Homes of the New World* (New York, 1853), I, 49.

7. Frances E. Percival, *Sweet Home: Or, Friendship's Golden Altar* (Boston, 1856), p. 4.

8. Andrew Jackson Downing, *The Architecture of Country Houses* (New York, 1850), p. v.

9. No systematic studies of housing, land, and transportation costs were made in the United States in the nineteenth century. But see Lewis M. Haupt, "Rapid Transit in Cities," *Journal of the Franklin Institute* 125 (1888): 1–21; Grosvenor Atterbury, "Garden Cities," *Proceedings of the National Conference on Housing* 2 (1912): 106–113. For a recent historical study of some of these issues see Sam B. Warner, Jr., *Streetcar Suburbs* (Cambridge, Mass., 1962).

10. Beyond brief discussions about the balloon frame and the manufacture of nails (Sigfried Giedion, *Space, Time and Architecture*, Cambridge, Mass., 1953, pp. 345–353), little has been written about the mechanization of building materials and techniques. Giedion is surprisingly brief on the subject in *Mechanization Takes Command*. But see Dorothy S. Brady, "The Effect of Mechanization on Product Design in the Course of Industrial Development," *Third International Conference on Economic History* (1965), pp. 7–15.

11. William Franklin Willoughby, *Building and Loan Associations* (Boston, 1900), pp. 23–31; H. Morton Bodfish, *History of Building and Loan Associations in the United States* (Chicago, 1931), pp. 80–83; Alan Teck, *Mutual Savings Banks and Savings and Loan Associations* (New York, 1967), pp. 4–26.

12. Bodfish, *History of Building and Loan Associations*, pp. 187–196.

13. Willoughby, *Building and Loan Associations*, pp. 5–18; Teck, *Mutual Savings Banks*, pp. 24–29.

14. Teck, *Mutual Savings Banks*, pp. 29–42.

15. Willoughby, *Building and Loan Associations*, pp. 13–17.

16. Robert Treat Paine, *Co-operative Banks* (Boston, 1880), pp. 3–4.

17. Edmund Wrigley, *The Workingman's Way to Wealth* (Philadelphia, 1869), p. 1.

18. Paine, *Co-operative Banks*, pp. 8–12; Robert Treat Paine, *Homes for the People* (Boston, 1882), pp. 12–14.

19. W. D. P. Bliss, *The New Encyclopedia of Social Reform* (New York, 1908), pp. 303, 308–311; James Ford, *Co-operation in New England* (New York, 1913).

20. The early history of factory housing is discussed in John Coolidge, *Mill and Mansion* (New York, 1942), pp. 9–18. See also Budgett Meakin, *Model Factories and Villages* (Philadelphia, 1905); Graham Romeyn Taylor, *Satellite Cities* (New York, 1915). Information on the Howland Mill was obtained from E. R. L. Gould, *Eighth Special Report of the Commissioner of Labor: Housing of the Working People* (Washington, 1895), pp. 324–327, and from conversations with Llewellyn Howland.

21. Richard T. Ely, "Pullman: A Social Study," *Harper's New Monthly Magazine* 70 (1885): 452–466.

22. Ely, "Pullman," p. 464. Stanley Buder, *Pullman, an Experiment in Industrial Order and Community Planning* (New York, 1967), pp. 147–204.

23. Jane Addams, "A Modern Lear." This essay was written in 1894 but was not published until 1915, in Taylor, *Satellite Cities*, pp. 68–90.

24. Paine, *Co-operative Banks*, p. 12.

25. Edward Everett Hale, *Workingmen's Homes* (Boston, 1874), pp. 1–4, 155–157.

26. "Record of Progress," *Old and New* 1 (1870): 420–421.

27. "Record of Progress," *Old and New* 1 (1870): 416–419.

28. Hale, *Workingmen's Homes*, pp. 122–154. Charles K. Landis, *The Founder's Own Story of the Founding of Vineland, New Jersey* (Vineland, N.J., 1903).

29. Hale, *Workingmen's Homes*, pp. 88–121.

30. Hale, *Workingmen's Homes*, pp. 28–36.

31. Hale, *Workingmen's Homes*, pp. 37–54. Some of the information about Oakdale I gathered from conversations with residents who are descendants of the first settlers.

32. Friedrich Engels, *The Housing Question* (New York, 1938), p. 35.

33. *Dictionary of American Biography*; Vincent Yardley Bowditch, *Life and Correspondence of Henry Ingersoll Bowditch* (Boston, 1902); Barbara Rosenkrantz, *Public Health and the State* (Cambridge, Mass., 1972), pp. 56–73; Stephen H. Perkins and others, *Report of the Committee on the Expediency of Providing Better Tenements for the Poor* (Boston, 1846).

34. Henry Ingersoll Bowditch, *Consumption in New England* (Boston, 1862).

35. Bowditch, *Life and Correspondence*, I, 153–178. Robert H. Bremner, "An Iron Scepter Twined with Roses: The Octavia Hill System of Housing Management," *Social Science Review* 39 (1965): 222–231.

36. Massachusetts State Board of Health, *Annual Reports* 2 (1871): 47.

37. All references to the history of the Boston Cooperative Building Company come from annual reports published by the company (a set of these reports is on deposit at the Baker Library, Harvard Business School). An account of the Crystal Palace is in Henry I. Bowditch, *Centennial Discourse on Public Hygiene in America* (Boston, 1877), pp. 82–89; and *Memorials of the Lincoln Building, "Crystal Palace,"* published in the BCBC's report of 1889.

38. The chief precedents were a model tenement built in New York City by the Association for the Improvement of the Condition of the Poor: Robert H. Bremner, "The Big Flat: History of a New York Tenement House," *American Historical Review* 64 (1958): 54–62; a model lodging house erected in Boston in 1855: "Model Lodging-Houses in Boston," *Atlantic Monthly* 5 (1860): 673–680; J. L. E., "Boston Model Houses," *Plumber and Sanitary Engineer* 2 (1879): 95; English examples, most notably the work of Octavia Hill: John Nelson Tarn, *Five Per Cent Philanthropy* (Cambridge, Eng., 1973), pp. 100–101, 111–114; Bremner, "An Iron Scepter Twined with Roses," pp. 222–231.

39. Massachusetts State Board of Health, *Annual Reports* 4 (1873): 410–413.

40. Perkins and others, *Report of the Committee*, pp. 13–15.

41. Given that the average annual wage in the 1870s was about $400, these houses could only have been purchased by those with incomes well above that figure.

42. The background of other building development in Dorchester is described in Warner, *Streetcar Suburbs*.

43. Lawrence Veiller, *Housing Reform: A Hand-book for Practical Use in American Cities* (New York, 1910), pp. 71–72.

44. Lee K. Frankel, "Financing the Small House," *Proceedings of the National Conference on Housing* 2 (1912): 95–105.

45. Roy Lubove, *Community Planning in the 1920's* (Pittsburgh, 1963), pp. 5–15.

46. Lubove, *Community Planning*, p. 15; Frankel, "Financing the Small House," p. 100.

47. See, for example, Lee K. Frankel and Miles M. Dawson, *Workingmen's Insurance in Europe* (New York, 1910); Henry R. Seager, *Social Insurance* (New York, 1910).

48. George E. Hooker, "Discussion: Cooperative Housing," *Proceedings of the National Conference on Housing* 3 (1913): 109–110.

49. Elisha Harris Janes, "The Development and Financing of Apartment Houses in New York," *Brickbuilder* 18 (1909): 10–13. Nathanael West's father built apartment houses in New York. His difficulties are well described in Jay Martin, *Nathanael West: The Art of His Life* (New York, 1970), pp. 19–20, 76–78, 226–227.

50. Janes, "The Development and Financing of Apartment Houses," pp. 10–13; Charles Barnard, *Cooperation as a Business* (New York, 1881), pp. 59–63.

51. Barnard, *Cooperation*, p. 62.

52. Hubert is reported to have left New York City in 1893 and to have settled in California, where he spent his time patenting devices for making housekeeping easier. The change from New York to California may have been mirrored in the fact that Hubert's son, out of disillusionment with city life, tried to achieve a self-sufficient existence on a small plot of land — an environment quite the opposite of the cooperative apartment house. G. Matlack Price, "A Pioneer in Apartment House Construction," *Architectural Record* 36 (1914): 74–76; Philip G. Hubert, Jr., *Liberty and a Living* (New York, 1890).

53. A. C. David, "A Cooperative Studio Building," *Architectural Record* 14 (1903): 248.

54. "Architectural Aberrations: The Dorilton," *Architectural Record* 12 (1902): 221–226; "An Apartment House Aberration," *Architectural Record* 25 (1909): 434–437; H. W. Frohne, "Contemporary Apartment House Building in New York City," *Architectural Record* 28 (1910): 70.

55. The need to coordinate urban buildings was recognized as soon as cities began their great period of growth; see Thomas U. Walter, "Street Architecture," *Journal of the Franklin Institute* 27 (1841): 90–91.

56. E. C. Gardner, *The House That Jill Built, after Jack's Had Proved a Failure* (New York, 1882), p. 114.

57. John W. Root, "Style," *Inland Architect and Builder* 8 (1887): 99.

58. On Japanese architecture see Edward S. Morse, *Japanese Homes and Their Surroundings* (Boston, 1886); Clay Lancaster, *The Japanese Influence in America* (New York, 1963); Vincent Scully, Jr., *The Shingle Style and the Stick Style* (rev. ed., New Haven, 1971), pp. 135–139.

59. For a survey of the "styles" of domestic architecture see Marcus Whiffen, *American Architecture Since 1780* (Cambridge, Mass., 1969). On Richardson see Mrs. Schuyler van Rensselaer, *Henry Hobson Richardson and His Works* (Boston, 1888); Henry-Russell Hitchcock, *The Architecture of H. H. Richardson and His Times* (Hamden, Conn., 1961). On McKim, Mead and White see Scully, *The Shingle Style*, pp. 130–134; Leland Roth, "McKim, Mead and White Reappraised," in *A Monograph of the Works of McKim, Mead and White* (New York, 1973), pp. 7–57. On Maybeck see Esther McCoy, *Five California Architects* (New York, 1960), pp. 1–57; Kenneth H. Cardwell, *Bernard Maybeck: Artisan, Architect, Artist* (Santa Barbara, 1977). On the Greene brothers see McCoy, *Five California Architects*, pp. 103–147; Janann Strand, *A Greene and Greene Guide* (Pasadena, 1974).

60. Charles Keeler, *The Natural House* (San Francisco, 1904), pp. 19–23. In titling his book *The Shingle Style and the Stick Style*, Vincent Scully seems to be trying to maintain this argument, but the effects that he discusses could have been and, in fact, were achieved in other materials.

61. An example of the argument for masonry because of the depletion of forests is

Orson Squire Fowler, *A Home for All* (New York, 1857), pp. 16–17. The fireproof argument is made in Frank Lloyd Wright, "A Fireproof House for $5,000," *Ladies' Home Journal* 24 (1907): 24; Frank Chouteau Brown, "The Fireproof House," *House Beautiful* 27 (1910): 114–122. For concrete construction as a response to the Chicago fire see "Concrete from the Ruins," *American Builder* 6 (1872): 214.

62. Downing, *The Architecture of Country Houses*, p. 49.

63. Background to the "Theory of Transformation" is outlined in Wolfgang Herrmann, *Laugier and Eighteenth Century French Theory* (London, 1962), p. 46.

64. Arthur D. Gilman, "Lectures on Architecture," *American Architect and Building News* 14 (1883): 87–89, 111–114, 174–177, 209–210, 235–236, 245–246; Montgomery Schuyler, "A History of Old Colonial Architecture," *Architectural Record* 4 (1895): 312–366; Aymar Embury, *The Dutch Colonial House* (New York, 1913).

65. The early history of concrete is outlined in Peter Collins, *Concrete: The Vision of a New Architecture* (New York, 1959), pp. 19–96. See also Thaddeus Hyatt, *An Account of Some Experiments with Portland Cement* (London, 1877).

66. David W. King, ed., *Homes for Home-Builders* (New York, 1886), pp. 100–107; Louise W. Mears, "The Sod House," *Journal of Geography* 15 (1916): 385–389.

67. King, ed., *Homes*, pp. 107–114; George W. Hendry, "The Adobe Brick as a Historical Source," *Agricultural History* 5 (1931): 110–127.

68. Collins, *Concrete*, pp. 20–21.

69. H. H. Rice and W. M. Torrance, *The Manufacture of Concrete Blocks* (New York, 1906), pp. 11–21, 27–31.

70. "Small Garages Built of Cement," *Suburban Life* 13 (1911): 20; Charles E. White, "Housing the Automobile," *House Beautiful* 30 (1911): 84–86.

71. Rice and Torrance, *Concrete Blocks*, pp. 31–49.

72. Charles E. Pellew, "Experiments in Coloring Concrete," *Craftsman* 17 (1909): 331–333; Gardner Teall, "The Cement House and Its Place in Our Architecture," *Craftsman* 19 (1911): 571–577; Oswald C. Hering, *Concrete and Stucco Houses* (New York, 1912), pp. 11–49.

73. The advantages of concrete and stucco for the workman are emphasized in Samuel Howe, "A Square Deal for an Old Material," *House Beautiful* 34 (1913): 98–101.

74. Charles E. White, "When Cement is Used on the Exterior," *House Beautiful* 31 (1911): 12–15; Allen W. Jackson, *The Half-Timber House* (New York, 1913).

75. "Dwelling Constructed of 'Metal Lumber' and Concrete," *Cement Age* 6 (1909): 484–487.

76. M. J. Morehouse, "A Concrete House, a New Process," *House Beautiful* 26 (1909): 115–117.

77. Hering, *Concrete and Stucco*, pp. 50–55. Hewlett later became Buckminster Fuller's father-in-law. In the 1920s, the two collaborated on the production of a new fibrous building block.

78. Atterbury, "Garden Cities," pp. 106–113.

79. Grosvenor Atterbury, "How to Get Low-Cost Houses," *Proceedings of the National Conference on Housing* 5 (1916): 91–101; Grosvenor Atterbury, *The Economic Production of Workingmen's Homes* (New York, 1930), pp. 5–28.

80. Madeleine Stern, *Heads and Headlines: The Phrenological Fowlers* (Norman, Okla., 1971).

81. Fowler, *A Home for All* (New York, 1857), pp. 16–55; Walter Creese, "Fowler and the Domestic Octagon," *Art Bulletin* 28 (1946): 89–102.

82. The *Craftsman* frequently published designs for concrete bungalows. See, for

example, Gustave Stickley, "Craftsman Concrete Bungalows, Showing Economy of Construction," *Craftsman* 21 (1912): 662–675.

83. Milton Dana Morrill, *The Morrill Moulded Concrete Houses* (New York, 1917), pp. 8–10, 15–23; Milton Dana Morrill, "Inexpensive Homes of Reinforced Concrete," *Western Architect* 16 (1910): 103–106.

84. Winthrop A. Hamlin, *Low-Cost Cottage Construction in America* (Cambridge, Mass., 1917), pp. 16–24.

85. Morrill, *The Morrill Moulded Concrete Houses*, pp. 6–7.

86. Matthew Josephson, *Edison* (New York, 1961), pp. 424–425; Collins, *Concrete*, p. 90.

87. E. S. Larned, "The Edison Concrete House," *Cement Age* 6 (1908): 268–281; Collins, *Concrete*, p. 90.

88. *Cement Age* 3 (1907): 208; Charles de Kay, "Villas All Concrete," *Architectural Record* 17 (1905): 85–100; Collins, *Concrete*, pp. 56–60.

89. Hering, *Concrete and Stucco Houses*, pp. 100–105.

90. McCoy, *Five California Architects*, pp. 59–61.

91. "A New Architecture in a New Land," *Craftsman* 22 (1912): 467–475; E. M. Roorbach, "The Garden Apartments of California," *Architectural Record* 34 (1913): 518–530; E. M. Roorbach, "Outdoor Life in California Houses, as Expressed in the New Architecture of Irving J. Gill," *Craftsman* 24 (1913): 435–439; E. M. Roorbach, "Celebrating Simplicity in Architecture," *Western Architect* 19 (1913): 35–38; "The Bishop's School for Girls: A Progressive Departure from Traditional Architecture," *Craftsman* 26 (1914): 653–656; Irving J. Gill, "The Home of the Future: The New Architecture of the West: Small Homes for a Great Country," *Craftsman* 30 (1916): 140–151; McCoy, *Five California Architects*, pp. 63–98.

92. McCoy, *Five California Architects*, pp. 99–100.

93. The exact number depends on the definition of "house," "apartment house," "renovation," etc. The most complete list of Wright's work is in William A. Storrer, *A Complete Catalogue of Architecture by Frank Lloyd Wright* (Cambridge, Mass., 1974).

94. Wright, "A Fireproof House"; Frank Lloyd Wright, *An Autobiography* (New York, 1943), pp. 153–162. The date of Unity Temple is problematical. Drawings of the building were published as early as 1906, but in Frank Lloyd Wright, *Ausgeführte Bauten und Entwurfe* (Berlin, 1910), the date given is 1908. Frank Lloyd Wright, "In the Cause of Architecture," *Architectural Record* 23 (1908): 212, 215, shows the building "in process of construction."

95. Examples of Wright's use of stucco and cement are mentioned in Robert C. Spencer, Jr., "Decorative Use of Stucco and Cement," *House Beautiful* 23 (1907): 133–137; Sanford E. Thompson, "The Coming of the Concrete Age," *Suburban Life* 7 (1908): 116; Charles E. White, "Insurgent Architecture in the Middle West," *Country Life in America* 22, no. 10 (1912): 15–18; Charles E. White, "The Best Way to Use Cement," *House Beautiful* 34 (1913): 130–134.

96. "The American System of House Building," *Western Architect* 24 (1916): 121–123.

97. Root, "Style," pp. 99–101.

98. W. L. B. Jenney, "Architecture," *Inland Architect and Builder* 1 (1883): 63.

99. W. L. B. Jenney, "Building Stone," *Inland Architect and Builder* 2 (1883): 146.

100. N. Clifford Ricker, "Architectural Grammar," *Inland Architect and Builder* 8 (1886): 66–67.

101. A series of Ricker's articles on architectural history appeared in the *Scientific American Architects and Builders Edition* and in *Building* between 1886 and 1889. Ricker, "Architectural Grammar," p. 67.

102. Louis H. Sullivan, "Style," *Inland Architect and News Record* 11 (1888): 59–60.

103. Louis H. Sullivan, "Essay on Inspiration," *Inland Architect and Builder* 8 (1886): 61–64.

104. Frank Lloyd Wright, "In the Cause of Architecture," p. 158.

105. Wright's *Autobiography* should be read against the most recent biography: Robert C. Twombly, *Frank Lloyd Wright* (New York, 1973), pp. 3–17.

106. Thomas S. Hines, "Frank Lloyd Wright — The Madison Years," *Wisconsin Magazine of History* 50 (1967): 109–119; Twombly, *Frank Lloyd Wright*, pp. 17–25.

107. Wright, *An Autobiography*, pp. 184–190; Twombly, *Frank Lloyd Wright*, pp. 112–137.

108. A small but telling example of how unreliable information easily creeps into accounts about the early years: in *Frank Lloyd Wright* (p. 93) Twombly tells how on his trip to Europe in 1909, Wright not only met Johannes Brahms but also found him a dull conversationalist. Twombly received this information from a transcript of an interview with Lloyd Wright, Wright's son, in 1966. The anecdote enhances the self-image of Frank Lloyd Wright; Brahms, however, died in 1897. For other problems about the early years see Hines, "The Madison Years"; Eileen Michaels, "The Early Drawings of Frank Lloyd Wright Reconsidered," *Journal of the Society of Architectural Historians* 30 (1971): 294–303, in which Wright's reputation as a draftsman is questioned.

109. Wright, "In the Cause of Architecture," p. 158.

110. William Channing Gannett, *The House Beautiful* (River Forest, Ill., 1897), n.p.

111. Wright, "In the Cause of Architecture," pp. 160–161.

112. Grant C. Manson, *Frank Lloyd Wright to 1910* (New York, 1958), p. 6. Manson traces the connection between Froebel and Wright on pages 5–10. See also Richard MacCormac, "Froebel's Kindergarten Gifts and the Early Work of Frank Lloyd Wright," *Environment and Planning B* 6 (1974): 30–50.

113. Wright, "In the Cause of Architecture," p. 149; Wright, *An Autobiography*, p. 103.

114. Wright, "In the Cause of Architecture," pp. 149–150.

115. Frank Lloyd Wright, *Ausgeführte Bauten und Entwurfe* (Berlin, 1910), n.p. The primacy of the Winslow House was established by the fact that it was the first design in this important monograph. The Charnley House has some of the basic horizontal organization of the Winslow House and has often been credited to Wright. The Wainwright Building and the Getty Tomb follow somewhat less explicitly the same pattern. Wright's hand in these works may have been more prominent than either he or architectural historians have supposed. In effect, the student may have been teaching the Master. For the impact of the Getty Tomb and the Wainwright Building on Wright see Wright, *An Autobiography*, p. 70.

116. Wright, "In the Cause of Architecture," p. 149.

117. Wright's early interest in classical architecture has been described in Henry-Russell Hitchcock, "Frank Lloyd Wright and the Academic Tradition of the Early Eighteen-Nineties," *Journal of the Warburg and Courtauld Institutes* 7 (1944): 46–63. Hitchcock concludes that Wright gave up this interest in 1893, but only then did he begin to produce buildings that were truly classical.

118. Wright, *An Autobiography*, pp. 125–128.

119. Wright, "In the Cause of Architecture," p. 160.

121. Wright's mother put engravings of English cathedrals on the walls of the room that was to be his even before he was born. Wright, *An Autobiography*, p. 11.

122. Herrmann, *Laugier*, pp. 19–67; Eugène E. Viollet-le-Duc, *Discourses on Architecture*, trans. Henry Van Brunt (Boston, 1875), I, 64.

123. Horatio Greenough, *Form and Function*, ed. Harold A. Small, intro. Earl Loran (Berkeley, 1947), p. 22. Talbot Hamlin's *Greek Revival Architecture in America* (New York, 1944) is a valuable book, but he marks the end of the "revival" with the disappearance of the style, not the spirit. In the same period Thomas U. Walter wrote: "If architects would oftener aim to *think* as the Greeks thought, than to *do* as the Greeks did, our columnar architecture would possess a higher degree of originality, and its character and expression would gradually become conformed to the local circumstances of the country, and the republican spirit of its institutions." "Architecture," *Journal of the Franklin Institute* 27 (1841): 12.

124. For a contemporary Chicago comment on this distinction see Ricker, "Architectural Grammar," p. 67.

125. Louis Sullivan was the preeminent American dropout from the Ecole des Beaux Arts. William Le Baron Jenney attended the Ecole Centrale. N. Clifford Ricker was educated in Berlin.

126. Sullivan's interest in German culture is mentioned throughout his *Autobiography of an Idea*. N. Clifford Ricker, "The Grecian Architectural Style," *Scientific American Architects and Builders Edition* 3 (1887): 9–10.

127. W. L. B. Jenney, "Architecture," *Inland Architect and Builder* 3 (1884): 34.

128. Frederick Baumann, "Thoughts on Architecture," *Inland Architect and News Record* 16 (1890): 60–61.

129. For connections between Viollet-le-Duc and Wright (although Greek architecture is not mentioned) see Donald Hoffmann, "Frank Lloyd Wright and Viollet-le-Duc," *Journal of the Society of Architectural Historians* 28 (1969): 173–183.

130. Frederick Gutheim, ed., *Frank Lloyd Wright on Architecture* (New York, 1940), p. 4; for example, Wright, *Ausgeführte Bauten* (Berlin, 1911), pp. 104, 132.

131. Wright, "In the Cause of Architecture," pp. 159–160; Russell Sturgis, "The Larkin Building in Buffalo," *Architectural Record* 23 (1908): 320.

132. Wright, *Ausgeführte Bauten und Entwurfe*, n.p.; "The 'Village Bank' Series V," *Brickbuilder* 10 (1901): 160–161.

133. Frank Lloyd Wright, "In the Cause of Architecture, Second Paper," *Architectural Record* 35 (1914): 407.

134. Wright, *An Autobiography*, pp. 108–109.

135. Wright, "In the Cause of Architecture," p. 160.

136. One index to how traditional the Winslow House was and how much Wright developed in the following twenty years is the fact that the Winslow House was seen as just a "charming" variation on a standard type of American house: William H. Symonds, "Rectangular Houses Beautiful and Practicable," *Suburban Life* 15 (1912): 118–119. On Wright in Europe see N. Pevsner, "Frank Lloyd Wright's Peaceful Penetration of Europe," *Architect's Journal* 89 (1939): 731–734; Reyner Banham, *Theory and Design in the First Machine Age* (London, 1960), pp. 139–147.

137. Frank Lloyd Wright, "Ethics of Ornament," *Prairie School Review* 4 (1967): 16–17. Wright gave the lecture in 1909. His statement, "Construction should be decorated. Decoration never should be purposely constructed," is taken directly from "Proposition 5" in Owen Jones's *The Grammar of Ornament*.

138. Wright, "In the Cause of Architecture," p. 161.

139. Dimitri Tselos, "Exotic Influences in the Architecture of Frank Lloyd Wright,"

*Magazine of Art* 47 (1953): 160–169; Dimitri Tselos, "Frank Lloyd Wright and World Architecture," *Journal of the Society of Architectural Historians* 28 (1969): 58–72.

140. Wright, *An Autobiography*, pp. 194–201; Lancaster, *The Japanese Influence in America*, pp. 84–96; Robert Kostka, "Frank Lloyd Wright in Japan," *Prairie School Review* 3 (1966): 5–23.

141. The English influences are echoes of half-timbering (which can also be read as reminiscent of Japanese architecture), diamond panes of leaded glass in windows, and casement windows for which he had to send to England for hardware. Wright, "In the Cause of Architecture," p. 160; Robert C. Spencer, Jr., "Half-Timber and Casements," *House Beautiful* 11 (1901): 12–19; Robert C. Spencer, Jr., "The Window Problem," *House Beautiful* 11 (1902): 367–372.

142. Frank Lloyd Wright, "The Art and Craft of the Machine," in Edgar Kaufmann and Ben Raeburn, eds., *Frank Lloyd Wright: Writings and Buildings* (Cleveland, 1960), pp. 55–73. Wright reiterated the point about the machine's being a tool in Frank Lloyd Wright, "In the Cause of Architecture I — The Architect and the Machine," *Architectural Record* 61 (1927): 394–396. See chapter 6, note 85.

143. Wright, "In the Cause of Architecture, Second Paper," pp. 405–413.

144. The work of the Chicago, or Prairie, School has been treated in Mark L. Peisch, *The Chicago School of Architecture* (New York, 1965); H. Allen Brooks, *The Prairie School* (New York, 1972).

# CHAPTER 5

1. "Successful Houses," *House Beautiful* 1 (1897): 64–69; Robert C. Twombly, *Frank Lloyd Wright* (New York, 1973), pp. 40–43.

2. Henry James, *The American Scene*, intro. Leon Edel (Bloomington, Ind., 1968), pp. 166, 168–169, 177.

3. Andrew Jackson Downing, *The Architecture of Country Houses* (New York, 1850), pp. 73–75, 272–273, 276–278.

4. Robert Kerr, *The Gentleman's House* (London, 1864); John James Stevenson, *House Architecture* (London, 1880). As an index of the significance of these books, both volumes are in the Henry Hobson Richardson collection in the Loeb Library, Graduate School of Design, Harvard University.

5. Barry Parker contributed a series of twenty-eight articles, "Modern Country Homes of England," to the *Craftsman* from April 1910 to October 1912.

6. Charles Francis Osborne, *Notes on the Art of House Planning* (New York, 1888), pp. 7–21.

7. Gardner's obituary is in the Boston *Evening Transcript*, Feb. 8, 1915. Gardner illustrated Mitchell's (Ik Marvel's) *Rural Studies* (reissued as *Out-of-Town Places*).

8. E. C. Gardner, *Homes and How to Make Them* (Boston, 1874), p. 25.

9. Orson Squire Fowler, *A Home for All* (New York, 1857), pp. 7–12, 56–108, 116–123. Walter Creese, "Fowler and the Domestic Octagon," *Art Bulletin* 28 (1946): 89–102; Madeleine B. Stern, *Heads and Headlines* (Norman, Okla., 1971), pp. 87–98.

10. E. C. Gardner, *The House That Jill Built, after Jack's Had Proved a Failure* (New York, 1882), pp. 112–114.

11. E. C. Gardner, *Illustrated Homes: A Series of Papers Describing Real Homes and Real People* (Boston, 1875).

12. E. C. Gardner, "Model Homes for Model Housekeeping," *Good Housekeeping* 1, no. 1 (1885): 2–4.

13. Gardner, *Homes and How to Make Them*, pp. 57, 142–143.

14. Gardner, *Illustrated Homes*, pp. 91–126, 183–198, 202–203, 218–224, 227–228.

15. In analyzing house plans of this period, few historians have gone beyond an attempt to find the origins of the "open plan." See Richard MacCormac, "Froebel's Kindergarten Gifts and the Early Work of Frank Lloyd Wright," *Environment and Planning B* 6 (1974): 30–50.

16. E. C. Gardner, *Home Interiors* (Boston, 1878), pp. 103–128.

17. Gardner, *Homes and How to Make Them*, pp. 148–157; Gardner, *The House That Jill Built*, pp. 203–220; H. Hudson Holly, *Modern Dwellings* (New York, 1878), pp. 116–117; Vincent J. Scully, Jr., *The Shingle Style and the Stick Style* (rev. ed., New Haven, 1971), pp. 3–9.

18. Gardner, *Home Interiors*, pp. 78–102; Clarence Cook, *What Shall We Do With Our Walls* (New York, 1880); Candace Wheeler, "The Decoration of Walls," *Outlook* 52 (1895): 705–706; Candace Wheeler, "The Decoration and Use of Wild Flowers," *Atlantic Monthly* 95 (1905): 630–634.

19. Gardner, *Homes and How to Make Them*, pp. 137–145; Osborne, *Notes*, pp. 53–58.

20. Gardner, *Homes and How to Make Them*, pp. 162–169.

21. The origin of the piazza, porch, or veranda, and especially its relationship to the classical portico, is obscure; see Mrs. Schuyler van Rensselaer, *Art Out of Doors* (New York, 1893), pp. 123–135. Robert C. Spencer, Jr., "Planning the Home, A Chapter on Porches," *House Beautiful* 17 (1905): 26–27; Thomas Woodward, "When Furnishing the Summer Home," *Suburban Life* 6 (1908): 354–356; "Outdoor Living East and West," *Craftsman* 26 (1914): 406–417.

22. "Craftsman Summer Log Houses: The Entire Upper Story Arranged for 'Outdoor Sleeping,'" *Craftsman* 20 (1911): 506–511; "Out-of-Door Sleeping Rooms," *Suburban Life* 8 (1909): 328; Charles E. White, "The Sleeping-Porch as It Should Be," *Suburban Life* 18 (1914): 303–304.

23. This architecture is best seen in the pages of *Craftsman*, *Suburban Life*, *House Beautiful*, and *Country Life in America*. See, for example, George E. Walsh, "New 'Open-Air' Architecture," *House Beautiful* 24 (1908): 118–119.

24. The literature of etiquette is discussed in Arthur M. Schlesinger, *Learning How to Behave* (New York, 1946).

25. "All About the House," *Good Housekeeping* 1, no. 1 (1885): 21. See also Emma C. Hewitt, *Queen of Home: Her Reign from Infancy to Age, from Attic to Cellar* (Philadelphia, 1892).

26. For example, Harriet Beecher Stowe, "House and Home Papers," *Atlantic Monthly* 13 (1864): 40–47; Laura C. Holloway, *The Hearthstone* (Chicago, 1888), pp. 25–35.

27. Milton Bradley, "Home Amusement and Relaxation, Bending the Twig and Inclining the Tree of Life," *Good Housekeeping* 1, no. 1 (1885): 7–8; Milton Bradley, "Common Sense in Home Amusements," *Good Housekeeping* 1, no. 11 (1885): 6–7; Mrs. Hamilton Mott, ed., *Home Games and Parties* (Philadelphia, 1891).

28. Samuel B. Reed, *House-Plans for Everybody* (New York, 1878), p. 10.

29. Reed, *House-Plans*, pp. 9–12.

30. E. C. Gardner strongly criticized the additive approach.

31. Wayne Andrew, *The Vanderbilt Legend* (New York, 1941), pp. 331–335.

32. Edward C. Kirkland, *Dream and Thought in the Business Community* (Ithaca, 1956), p. 35.

33. Croly's background is discussed in Charles Forcey, *The Crossroads of Liberalism* (New York, 1961), pp. 4–25; Herbert Croly, *The Promise of American Life*, intro. Arthur M. Schlesinger, Jr. (Cambridge, Mass., 1956), p. v–viii.

34. Henry W. Desmond and Herbert Croly, *Stately Homes in America* (New York, 1903), pp. 3–92, 211–348.

35. Franz K. Winkler, "Architecture in the Billionaire District of New York City," *Architectural Record* 11 (1901): 679–699; Herbert Croly, "Rich Men and Their Homes," *Architectural Record* 12 (1902): 27–32; Kirkland, *Dream and Thought*, pp. 29–49.

36. The small house could be either for families of modest means or for those who wanted an inexpensive vacation home. Plans that suited both purposes were often published in the *Craftsman* and *House Beautiful*. See N. M. Woods, "Planning the Small House," *House Beautiful* 35 (1914): 148–150.

37. Council of Hygiene and Public Health of the Citizens' Association of New York, *Report upon the Sanitary Condition of the City* (New York, 1865), p. 258.

38. Robert Coit Chapin, *The Standard of Living among Workingmen's Families in New York City* (New York, 1909), pp. 18–19.

39. Emily W. Dinwiddie, *Housing Conditions in Philadelphia* (Philadelphia, 1904), pp. 20–21.

40. Lawrence Veiller, *A Model Tenement House Law* (New York, 1910), pp. 29–32.

41. For the development of housing standards see David P. Handlin, "Housing and City Planning in the United States, 1910–1945," *Transactions of the Martin Centre* 1 (1976): 317–334.

42. John R. Richards, "The Problem of the Old House," *Proceedings of the National Conference on Housing* 3 (1913): 48–50.

43. This kind of housing frequently figured in the picturesque view of cities; see H. C. Bunner, "Shantytown," *Scribner's Monthly* 20 (1880): 855–869; Mrs. Schuyler van Rensselaer, "Picturesque New York," *Century Magazine* 45 (1892): 174. For a reformer's view see Charles F. Weller, *Neglected Neighbors* (Philadelphia, 1909), pp. 201–249.

44. This theme was often treated in fiction. See H. C. Bunner, *The Story of a New York House* (New York, 1887).

45. Sophonisba P. Breckinridge and Edith Abbott, "Chicago's Housing Problem: Families in Furnished Rooms," *American Journal of Sociology* 16 (1910): 289–308. See also Franklin Kline Fritz, *The Furnished Room Problem in Philadelphia* (Philadelphia, 1910), pp. 60–66.

46. Lawrence Veiller, "Room Overcrowding and the Lodger Evil," *Proceedings of the National Conference on Housing* 2 (1912): 58–78, 171–184.

47. Albert Benedict Wolfe, *The Lodging House Problem in Boston* (Boston, 1906), pp. 5, 11–43.

48. Milton B. Hunt, "The Housing of Non-Family Groups of Men in Chicago," *American Journal of Sociology* 16 (1910): 145–170.

49. Hunt, "The Housing of Non-Family Groups," pp. 160–166.

50. What accounted for these preferences is unclear.

51. One of the rare sympathetic accounts of boarding with a family is in Emily Greene Balch, *Our Slavic Fellow Citizens* (New York, 1910), pp. 349–350.

52. Chapin, *The Standard of Living*, pp. 75–110, 229–250.

53. For biographical information on this remarkable woman, see Barbara M. Soloman, *Ancestors and Immigrants* (Chicago, 1972), pp. 188–191.

54. Balch, *Our Slavic Fellow Citizens*, p. 164; Eugène Viollet-le-Duc, *The Habitations of Man in All Ages*, trans. Benjamin Bucknall (Boston, 1876), pp. 11–12; J. P. Putnam, *The Open Fire-place in All Ages* (1st ed., 1881; Boston, 1886), pp. 12–17.

55. Balch, *Our Slavic Fellow Citizens*, pp. 335–360. Elizabeth Beardsley Butler, *Women and the Trades* (New York, 1909).

56. Balch, *Our Slavic Fellow Citizens*, pp. 349–362.

57. Margaret Byington, *Homestead, The Households of a Mill Town* (New York, 1910), pp. 46–62.

58. Elisha Harris Janes, "The Development of Duplex Apartments," *Brickbuilder* 21 (1912): 159–161.

59. Janes, "The Development," pp. 160–161; "The Tiffany House," *Architectural Record* 10 (1900): 191–202.

60. A. C. David, "A Co-operative Studio Building," *Architectural Record* 14 (1903): 233–254; Janes, "The Development," pp. 183–184.

61. Janes, "The Development," pp. 185–186.

62. Janes, "The Development," p. 204; "Duplex Apartment Houses," *Architectural Record* 29 (1911): 327–334.

63. Janes, "The Development," pp. 204–205.

64. David, "A Co-operative Studio Building," pp. 248–250.

65. B. Russell Herts, *The Decoration and Furnishing of Apartments* (New York, 1915), p. 137.

66. Martha Cutler, "Individuality in City Apartments," *House Beautiful* (1913), pp. 166–169; Costen Fitz Gibbon, "Apartment House Possibilities," *Architectural Record* 35 (1914): 59–68. Louis C. Tiffany was certainly one of the earliest to seek this effect; see "The Tiffany House," pp. 191–202; Donald G. Mitchell, "From Lobby to Peak," *Our Continent* 1 (1882): 15, 21, 37, 69, 85, 101, 117, 132, 148, 185, 217; *Artistic Houses* (New York, 1883) pp. 1–6.

67. The first flats in New York were sponsored in the mid-1850s by the famous doctor Valentine Mott, who had then just returned from Europe. This building, known as the Stuyvesant House, has often been confused with the Stuyvesant, a block of flats designed by Richard M. Hunt in the late 1860s; see "Parisian 'Flats,' " *Appleton's Journal* 6 (1871): 561–562; Charles H. Israels, "New York Apartment Houses," *Architectural Record* 11 (1901): 477–509.

68. Israels, "New York Apartment Houses," pp. 477–507; Irving K. Pond, "Architecture of Apartment Houses," *Brickbuilder* 7 (1898): 116–118, 139–141, 249–252.

69. Frank R. Stockton, *Rudder Grange* (New York, 1885), p. 77. This novel has revealing comments about living in "flats."

70. Israels, "New York Apartment Houses," pp. 495–497.

71. Herts, *The Decoration and Furnishing of Apartments*, pp. 53–83, 145–149.

# CHAPTER 6

1. Albion Fellows Bacon, *Beauty for Ashes* (New York, 1914), pp. 9, 11, 13–14, 18; Roy Lubove, "Albion Fellows Bacon and the Awakening of a State," *Midwest Review* 4 (1962): 63–72.

2. Melusina Fay Peirce, "Cooperative Housekeeping," *Atlantic Monthly* 22 (1868): 513–524, 682–697.

3. Cambridge Co-operative Housekeeping Society, *Prospectus* (Cambridge, Mass., 1869), n.p.; Mrs. Horace Mann, "Co-operative Housekeeping," *Hearth and Home* 1 (1869): 716.

4. Melusina Fay Peirce, *Cooperative Housekeeping* (Boston, 1884), pp. 75–84.

5. Aunt Miriam, "A Screw Loose in the Household Machinery," *Good Housekeeping* 10 (1890): 97–99.

6. Edward Bellamy, "A Vital Domestic Problem," *Good Housekeeping* 10 (1889): 74.

7. Mary Alice Matthews, "Cooperative Living" (unpublished Bachelor of Library Science thesis, State Library School, University of Illinois, 1903), p. 58.

8. Bellamy, "A Vital Domestic Problem," p. 75; Ellen Battelle Dietrick, "Cooperative Housekeeping Experiments," *Good Housekeeping* 18 (1894): 65–66.

9. Matthews, "Cooperative Living," pp. 56–57.

10. Mary Hinman Abel, *The Story of the New England Kitchen* (Boston, 1890); "Count Rumford and the New England Kitchen," *New England Kitchen* 1 (1894): 7–11.

11. Matthews, "Cooperative Living," p. 62.

12. "Co-operative Housekeeping at Last," *Good Housekeeping* 32 (1901): 490–492.

13. Mrs. Arthur Stanley, "Co-operation in Housekeeping," *Good Housekeeping* 12 (1891): 145; Christine Terhune Herrick, "Cooperative Housekeeping in America," *Munsey's Magazine* 31 (1904): 186.

14. Matthews, "Cooperative Living," pp. 66–67; for a successful experiment in Palo Alto, California, see Sarah T. Rorer, "Cooperation in Housekeeping," *Ladies' Home Journal* 12 (1895): 14.

15. Edward Bellamy, *Looking Backward*, intro. Edward L. Shurter (New York, 1951), pp. 121–128.

16. J. V. Sears, "Housekeeping Hereafter," *Atlantic Monthly* 48 (1881): 332, 335–336.

17. George F. Duysters, "Our Block — A Cooperative Possibility," *Nationalist* 2 (1890): 27–29; Matthews, "Cooperative Living," pp. 37–39.

18. H. C. Walsh, "Co-operative Housekeeping," *Lippincott's Magazine* 53 (1894): 549–552.

19. Charles Carroll, "Apartment-Houses," *Appleton's Journal* 5 (new series; 1878): 529–535.

20. "A Modern Apartment House," *Carpentry and Building* 3 (1881): 165.

21. J. P. Putnam, "The Apartment House," *American Architect and Building News* 27 (1890): 3–5; J. P. Putnam, *Architecture under Nationalism* (Boston, 1890), p. 13; J. P. Putnam, "The Charlesgate Apartment House," *American Architect and Building News* 32 (1891): 14, pl. 797.

22. J. P. Putnam, "The Commonwealth Hotel, J. P. Putnam, Architect," *Brickbuilder* 4 (1895): 80.

23. Charlotte Perkins Gilman, *Women and Economics* (Boston, 1900), pp. 248–260, 297–299.

24. "The New York Family Hotel," *Architectural Record* 11 (1901): 700–704; "Apartment Hotels in New York City," *Architectural Record* 13 (1903): 85–91.

25. Walter Kilham, "The Planning of Apartment Houses, III," *Brickbuilder* 12 (1903): 245.

26. "Apartment Hotels," pp. 89–91.

27. Patten's ideas are most accessible in Simon Patten, *The New Basis of Civilization*

(New York, 1905); see also Daniel M. Fox, *The Discovery of Abundance* (Ithaca, N. Y., 1967).

28. Martha B. and Robert W. Bruère, *Increasing Home Efficiency* (New York, 1914), pp. 3, 9–10, 35–42.

29. John Lloyd Thomas, "Workingmen's Hotels," *Municipal Affairs* 3 (1899): 73–93; Harriet Fayes, "Housing of Single Women," *Municipal Affairs* 3 (1899): 94–107; Matthews, "Cooperative Living," pp. 21–31.

30. W. D. P. Bliss, *The New Encyclopedia of Social Reform* (New York, 1908), p. 588.

31. Elizabeth Brown Graham, "Personal Experiences," *Ladies' Home Journal* 19 (1902): 24; Eulalie Andreas, "Apartments for Bachelor Girls," *House Beautiful* 32 (1912): 168–170.

32. Harriet Beecher Stowe, "Hartford," *Hearth and Home* 1 (1869): 712.

33. Sigfried Giedion in *Mechanization Takes Command* (New York, 1948), pp. 514–519; Reyner Banham in *The Architecture of the Well-Tempered Environment* (Chicago, 1969), pp. 95–100; and James Marston Fitch, *American Building: The Forces That Shaped It* (rev. ed., New York, 1970), pp. 118–121, have written about *The American Woman's Home*. For different reasons all have found that the Beecher sisters' house was a precursor of modern architecture. This interpretation ignores the essentially conservative message of the book.

34. Catharine E. Beecher and Harriet Beecher Stowe, *The American Woman's Home* (New York, 1869), pp. 23–83.

35. Joseph B. and Laura Lyman, *The Philosophy of Housekeeping* (Hartford, 1867), pp. 441–442, 447–455.

36. Ellen H. Richards, "The Social Significance of the Home Economics Movement," *Journal of Home Economics* 3 (1911): 117–125; "The Home Economics Movement in the United States," *Journal of Home Economics* 3 (1911): 323–341; Isabel Bevier, *Home Economics in Education* (Philadelphia, 1924), pp. 119–123.

37. *Training Schools of Cookery* (Washington, D.C., 1879), pp. 17–27.

38. Frederick A. Fernald, "Household Arts at the World's Fair," *Popular Science Monthly* 43 (1893): 803–812; "The Rumford Kitchen at the World's Fair," *New England Kitchen Magazine* 1 (1894): 11–12.

39. "Lake Placid Conference on Home Economics," *Journal of Home Economics* 1 (1909): 3–6; Linda Hull Larned, "National Household Economic Association," *Journal of Home Economics* 1 (1909): 185–187.

40. Emma Seifrit Weigley, "It Might Have Been Euthenics: The Lake Placid Conferences and the Home Economics Movement," *American Quarterly* 26 (1974): 79–96.

41. James Cassedy, *Charles V. Chapin* (Cambridge, Mass., 1962), pp. 94, 110–111.

42. Ellen H. Richards, *The Cost of Cleanness* (New York, 1908), p. 17.

43. Richards, *The Cost of Cleanness*, pp. 1–29; Helen Campbell, "Household Art and the Microbe," *House Beautiful* 6 (1899): 218–221. On closets see Nina Kinney, "A Housekeeper's House Plan," *House Beautiful* 5 (1899): 106–108; Ethel Bartholomew, "Women's Idea of Convenient Closets," *House Beautiful* 23 (March 1908): 31–32.

44. Sarah J. Hale, *Manners: Or, Happy Homes and Good Society All the Year Round* (Boston, 1868); Julia McNair Wright, *The Complete Home* (Philadelphia, 1879).

45. Edward T. James, ed., *Notable American Women, 1607–1950* (Cambridge, Mass., 1971), II, 188–189; III, 439–441.

46. Weigley, "It Might Have Been Euthenics," pp. 90–91.

47. Maria Parloa, *Home Economics* (New York, 1906), p. 61.

48. Richards, *The Cost of Cleanness*, pp. 8–10.

49. Lucy Salmon, *Domestic Service* (New York, 1901); see also Bellamy, "A Vital Domestic Problem," pp. 74–77. For a sympathetic account of the servant's position, see Jane Addams, *Democracy and Social Ethics* (New York, 1902), pp. 102–136.

50. The range of these inventions has never adequately been described or analyzed. Sigfried Giedion in *Mechanization Takes Command* touched on the subject, but it is much richer than he indicated.

51. To this extent, because they advocated the use of some machines, the Lymans' book on housekeeping was more advanced than that of Catharine Beecher and Harriet Beecher Stowe. See notes 34, 35.

52. Mary Pattison, *Principles of Domestic Engineering* (New York, 1915), title page and 147. Pattison's ideas can be compared with those of Charlotte Perkins Gilman in Mrs. Frank A. Pattison, "Scientific Management in Home-Making," *Annals of the American Academy of Arts and Science* 157 (1913): 96–103; Charlotte Perkins Gilman, "The Waste of Private Housekeeping," *Annals of the American Academy of Arts and Science* 157 (1913): 91–95.

53. Pattison, *Principles*, pp. 17, 148. On Taylor see Samuel Haber, *Efficiency and Uplift* (Chicago, 1964).

54. Pattison, *Principles*, pp. 59, 104, 149–150.

55. Christine Frederick, *The New Housekeeping* (Garden City, N.Y., 1913), pp. 153–168; Christine Frederick, *Household Engineering* (Chicago, 1920), pp. 377–392.

56. A. E. Kennelly, "Electricity in the Household," *Scribner's Magazine* 7 (1890): 102–115.

57. Rossiter Johnson, ed., *A History of the World's Columbian Exposition* (New York, 1897–1898), III, 368–395.

58. C. D. Wood, "The Use of Electricity in the Home," *House and Garden* 11 (1907): 102–105; Thomas C. Martin and Stephen L. Coles, *The Story of Electricity* (New York, 1919), I, 466–471; II, 88–100, 169–209.

59. Pattison, *Principles*, pp. 56, 65; Frederick, *The New Housekeeping*, p. 103.

60. Frank B. Gilbreth, *Bricklaying System* (New York, 1909).

61. Frederick, *The New Housekeeping*, frontispiece, pp. 248–257; Frederick, *Household Engineering*, p. 74.

62. Edward Bok, "The American Woman's Chance," *Ladies' Home Journal* 32 (November 1914): 3; Mrs. Percy V. Pennybacker, "The Club Woman's Answer," *Ladies' Home Journal* 33 (January 1915): 3; Edward Bok, "What Is Coming out of the War That Is Touching the American Woman?" *Ladies' Home Journal* 33 (January 1915): 35.

63. Catharine E. Beecher, *Educational Reminiscences* (New York, 1874), pp. 11–12.

64. Harriet Beecher Stowe, "House and Home Papers," *Atlantic Monthly* 13 (1864): 40–47.

65. Harriet Beecher Stowe, "The Cheapness of Beauty," *Hearth and Home* 1 (1869): 200.

66. Beecher, *Educational Reminiscences*, p. 11.

67. Arthur Cole, *The American Carpet Manufacture* (Cambridge, Mass., 1941), pp. 3–16.

68. Stowe, "House and Home Papers," p. 40.

69. Andrew Jackson Downing, *The Architecture of Country Houses* (New York, 1850), pp. 364–460.

70. Clarence Cook, "Beds and Tables, Stools and Candlesticks," *Scribner's Monthly* 10 (1875): 354, 499–500.

71. A selection of the furniture and goods produced by the movement is described in Robert Judson Clark, ed., *The Arts and Crafts Movement in America 1876–1916* (Princeton, 1972). Some of the broader aspects of the movement are treated in Mark Girouard, *Sweetness and Light* (Oxford, 1977), pp. 208–223.

72. Cook, "Beds and Tables, Stools and Candlesticks," *Scribner's Monthly* 10 (1875): 175–177; 11 (1875–76): 344–345, 346, 809–810. The first of Cook's articles appeared in *Scribner's Monthly* in June 1875; the last in May 1877. On Eastlake see Charles L. Eastlake, *Hints on Household Taste*, intro. J. Gloag (London, 1869).

73. Cook, "Beds and Tables," 11 (1875–76): 813–814. "An Architectural Masquerade," *American Architect and Building News* 12 (1882): 120. A history of the phenomenon of antique-collecting in the United States would be most fascinating, but no such work exists.

74. For an excellent account of Wheeler's life see Madeleine Stern, *We the Women* (New York, 1963), pp. 273–303. Candace Wheeler, *Yesterdays in a Busy Life* (New York, 1918); Candace Wheeler, *The Development of Embroidery in America* (New York, 1921).

75. Stern, *We the Women*, p. 275; "The Society of Decorative Art," *Scribner's Monthly* 22 (1881): 697–709; Candace Wheeler, "Art Education for Women," *Outlook* 55 (1897): 85; Wheeler, *The Development*, pp. 102–118.

76. Wheeler, *Yesterdays*, pp. 224–226; Lucy M. Salmon, "The Woman's Exchange: Charity or Business?," *Forum* 13 (1892): 394–406.

77. Candace Wheeler, "The New Woman and Her Home Needs," *Christian Union* 43 (1895): 895.

78. Wheeler, "Art Education for Women," p. 86. Candace Wheeler, "Interior Decoration as a Profession for Women," *Outlook* 51 (1895): 559.

79. Candace Wheeler, "Interior Decoration as a Profession for Women," pp. 559–560, 649.

80. Mrs. Burton Harrison, "Some Work of the 'Associated Artists,'" *Harper's New Monthly Magazine* 69 (1884): 343; "The New Decorations at the White House," *Harper's Weekly* 27 (1883): 11. The Associated Artists' work at the White House was removed in the McKim, Mead and White remodeling of 1904.

81. Harrison, "Some Work of the 'Associated Artists,'" pp. 344–351; Stern, *We the Women*, pp. 287–293.

82. Stern, *We the Women*, pp. 293–296.

83. Candace Wheeler, "The Decoration of Walls," *Outlook* 52 (1895): 705–706; Candace Wheeler, "Decorative Art," *Architectural Record* 4 (1895): 409–413; Candace Wheeler, "The Principles of Decoration," *Outlook* 53 (1896): 284–285; Candace Wheeler, "The Decorative Use of Wild Flowers," *Atlantic Monthly* 95 (1905): 630–634.

84. Her sense of progress, especially as applied to the household, is expressed in Candace Wheeler, "What the Century Has Done for the Household," *Outlook* 57 (1897): 225–229.

85. Frank Lloyd Wright, "The Art and Craft of the Machine," in Edgar Kaufmann and Ben Raeburn, eds., *Frank Lloyd Wright: Writings and Buildings* (Cleveland, 1960), pp. 57–73; Frank Lloyd Wright, "In the Nature of Materials," in H. Th. Wijdeveld, *The Life-Work of the American Architect Frank Lloyd Wright* (Santpoort, Holland, 1925), pp. 48–49. The date of "The Art and Craft of the Machine" is problematical. Most sources give it as 1901, and it was published for the first time in that year in the *Catalogue of the Fourteenth Annual Exhibition of the Chicago Architectural Club*. However, it is possible that Wright gave a version of the speech at Hull-House a few years earlier. In Wijdeveld, *The Life-Work*, published in 1925, Wright indicated that he had given the talk twenty-seven years previously, on the oc-

casion of the founding of a society of arts and crafts. This organization must have been the Chicago Arts and Crafts Society. See Mabel Key, "A Review of the Recent Exhibition of the Chicago Arts and Crafts Society," *House Beautiful* 6 (1899): 1–12. It is clear from Wright's comments in Wijdeveld that he was reacting as much against this society as against Oscar Lovell Triggs's Industrial Art League. See note 93.

86. The extent of this change in point of view varied. Some, like Will Price and the founders of Rose Valley (see note 89), felt it was necessary to create an immediate model of what the ideal society would be like; others, like Oscar Lovell Triggs and the Industrial Art League in Chicago, equivocated about the relationship to the existing order. For attitudes toward art, see Oscar Lovell Triggs, "Democratic Art," *Forum* 26 (1898): 66–79.

87. Of course Ruskin and Morris in the latter parts of their lives were also changing their focus from design to society. See Philip Henderson, *William Morris* (New York, 1967), pp. 173–324.

88. The most vivid picture of this life was presented in William Morris's *News from Nowhere*. The key issue that divided most people who believed, at whatever level, in this idea was how and when to get from the present to this felicitous state.

89. Clark, ed., *The Arts and Crafts Movement*, p. 27; Will Price, "Is Rose Valley Worth While," *Artsman* 1 (1903): 5–11.

90. Ziba Adrangi, "C. R. Ashbee: The Guild and the School of Handicraft," (unpublished dissertation for Part II of the Architecture Tripos, University of Cambridge, 1977). Adrangi had access to Alan Crawford's dissertation on Ashbee, which when published will be the definitive work on the subject.

91. The fact that Elbert Hubbard, one of the main advocates of the arts and crafts, chose to call a magazine he edited *The Philistine* epitomized this attitude.

92. Will Price, "The Building of a Chair," *Artsman* 1 (1903): 277–284.

93. Triggs's ideas are most accessible in Oscar Lovell Triggs, *Chapters in the History of the Arts and Crafts Movement* (Chicago, 1902). Mabel T. Priestman, "History of the Arts and Crafts Movement in America," *House Beautiful* 20 (October 1906): 15–16; 20 (November 1906): 14–15. I do not believe that Triggs was as content with the existing order as H. Allen Brooks makes out in "Chicago Architecture: Its Debt to the Arts and Crafts," *Journal of the Society of Architectural Historians* 30 (1971): 312–313.

94. The influence of the arts and crafts movement can be seen in John Dewey's *The School and Society* (Chicago, 1899) and *The Child and the Curriculum* (Chicago, 1902).

95. Priestman, "History of the Arts and Crafts Movement," pp. 15–16, 14–15.

96. Some of this work is included in Clark, ed., *The Arts and Crafts Movement*.

97. Horace Traubel, "The Problem of Cheap and Dear," *Artsman* 2 (1904): 21.

98. Thorstein Veblen, "Arts and Crafts," *Journal of Political Economy* 11 (1902): 108–111.

99. Thorstein Veblen, *The Theory of the Leisure Class* (reprint, New York, 1962), pp. 21–118.

# CHAPTER 7

1. Mark Twain, "A Telephonic Conversation," *Atlantic Monthly* 45 (1880): 841–843.

2. *Plumber and Sanitary Engineer* 1 (1879): 93; *Sanitary Engineer* 5 (1881): 59; "The Alleged Explosion of Sewer Gas," *Sanitary Engineer* 7 (1883): 265.

3. G. P. Brown, *Sewer Gas and Its Dangers* (Chicago, 1881), pp. 17, 18, 24, 27–28, 69–70, 100.

4. The Manhattan Anti Sewer Gas Company, *A Plain Exposition of the Only Practical and Sure System for the Prevention of Disease* (New York, 1883), pp. 2, 13.

5. Frank Hastings Hamilton, "Sewer-Gas," *Popular Science Monthly* 22 (1882): 2, 19.

6. Hamilton, "Sewer-Gas," p. 17.

7. George E. Waring, *Earth-Closets and Earth Sewage* (New York, 1870), pp. 13, 17, 20, 27, 39–48, 55. Greeley's remark is quoted by Waring.

8. George E. Waring, "The Sanitary Drainage of Houses and Towns," *Atlantic Monthly* 36 (1875): 345–346.

9. Nelson M. Blake, *Water for the Cities* (Syracuse, N.Y., 1956).

10. Waring, "The Sanitary Drainage," pp. 427–442, 535–553.

11. George E. Waring, "Recent Modifications in Sanitary Drainage," *Atlantic Monthly* 44 (1879): 56–62.

12. George E. Waring, "Notes on House-Drainage," *American Architect and Building News* 12 (1882): 29–30, 37, 71–72, 119–120; George E. Waring, "The Principles and Practices of House Drainage," *Century Magazine* 29 (1884): 45–51, 255–267.

13. J. P. Putnam and L. Frederick Rice, "The Siphonage and Evaporation of Traps," *American Architect and Building News* 15 (1884): 267–271; Waring, "The Principles," pp. 260–261.

14. "The Syphonage and Ventilation of Traps," *Sanitary Engineer* 10 (1884): 215–216; J. P. Putnam, "The Syphonage and Ventilation of Traps," *Sanitary Engineer* 10 (1884): 270–271.

15. George E. Waring, "The National Board of Health," *Atlantic Monthly* 44 (1879): 732–738.

16. Waring, "Notes," pp. 119–120; E. W. Bowditch and E. S. Philbrick, "The Siphonage and Ventilation of Traps," *American Architect and Building News* 12 (1882): 123–124, 131–132; George E. Waring, "The Siphonage of Traps," *American Architect and Building News* 12 (1882): 179–181.

17. The argument for the separate system is best outlined in George E. Waring, *Sewerage and Land Drainage* (New York, 1889), pp. 28–53.

18. Glenn Brown, "Water-Closets, XVII," *American Architect and Building News* 14 (1883): 76; George E. Waring, "The Dececo Water-Closet — A Correction," *American Architect and Building News* 14 (1883): 118; Waring, *Sewerage*, pp. 275–276.

19. George E. Waring, "Out of Sight, Out of Mind: Methods of Sewage Disposal," *Century Magazine* 47 (1894): 939–948.

20. "Arrangements for Lighting Residence of W. H. Vanderbilt, Esq.," *Sanitary Engineer* 6 (1882): 380.

21. "Sanitary Appliances in the Residence of W. H. Vanderbilt, Esq.," *Sanitary Engineer* 6 (1882): 428–429.

22. B. C. Batcheller, "Recent Progress in the Development of Pneumatic Dispatch Tubes," *Journal of the Franklin Institute* 146 (1898): 81–104.

23. Wayne Andrews, *The Vanderbilt Legend* (New York, 1941), p. 254; Matthew Josephson, *Edison* (New York, 1959), p. 261.

24. "Cost of Gas and Electric Lighting," *Bradstreet's Weekly* 5 (1882): 322–323; Sidney James, "Electricity as House-Maid," *House Beautiful* 20 (September 1906): 21–23.

25. H. Howson, "Mechanical Engineering Applied to Farm Implements," *Journal of*

*the Franklin Institute* 62 (1856): 46–47; Alfred R. Wolfe, "Note on the Economy of the Windmill as a Prime Mover," *Journal of the Franklin Institute* 114 (1882): 22–28; Arthur Inkersley, "Sunshine as Power," *Sunset Magazine* 10 (1903): 513–515.

26. Josephson, *Edison*, pp. 261–262.

27. Potter's speculations on this subject appear in his papers, now at the Avery Library, Columbia University. But see also E. T. Potter, "Ideal Transit," *Atlantic Monthly* 72 (1893): 809–814.

28. David Branson, "Artificial Refrigeration through Street Pipe Lines from Central Strations," *Journal of the Franklin Institute* 137 (1894): 81–93.

29. Sanborn C. Brown, ed., *Collected Works of Count Rumford* (Cambridge, Mass., 1969), III, 55–384; Sigfried Giedion, *Mechanization Takes Command* (New York, 1948), pp. 527–533.

30. "Description of a Kitchen Range and Fire Place," *Journal of the Franklin Institute* 23 (1839): 145; William J. Keep, "Early American Cooking Stoves," *Old-Time New England* 22 (1931): 70–87.

31. Giedion, *Mechanization*, pp. 537–541.

32. Jared Sparks, ed., *The Works of Benjamin Franklin* (London, 1882), VI, 34–64.

33. Harriet Beecher Stowe, "House and Home Papers," *Atlantic Monthly* 13 (1864): 42.

34. Charles E. Emery, "Heating Cities by Steam," *Journal of the Franklin Institute* 125 (1888): 199–222; Clarence O. Lewis, "Central Steam Heating Only One Holly Invention," Lockport, New York, *Union-Sun and Journal* (Oct. 21, 1964), p. 22; "Communism in Hot-Air," *American Architect and Building News* 2 (1877): 258.

35. Clarence Cook, "Beds and Tables, Stools and Candlesticks, II," *Scribner's Monthly* 11 (1876): 348.

36. J. P. Putnam, *The Open Fire-Place in All Ages* (1st ed., 1881; Boston, 1886), pp. 1, 2–11, 35–46, 89–169.

# ILLUSTRATION CREDITS

1. *Ladies' Repository* 23 (October 1863), frontispiece.

2. *The Happy Home and Parlor Magazine* 5 (February 1857), cover.

3. *Appleton's Journal* 8 (1872): 714.

4, 5. Various authors, *Homes of American Statesmen* (Hartford, 1885), p. 473, frontispiece.

6. William M. Thayer, *From Log-Cabin to White-House: The Life of James A. Garfield* (Boston, 1881), title page.

7. *Rural Manhood* 3 (1912): 293.

8. Grace Aguilar, *Home Influence* (New York, 1873), title page. Courtesy of the Schlesinger Library, Radcliffe College.

9. Andrew Jackson Downing, *Cottage Residences* (New York, 1842), p. 61.

10, 11. Andrew Jackson Downing, *The Architecture of Country Houses* (New York, 1850), pp. 79, 80.

12. G. F. and F. W. Woodward, *Woodward's Country Houses* (New York, 1866), p. 153.

13. Andrew Jackson Downing, *The Architecture of Country Houses*, p. 51.

14, 15. *The Plow* 1 (1852): 120, 121.

16. William A. Alcott, *The House I Live In* (New York, 1855), frontispiece.

17, 18. Lewis Leeds, *Lectures on Ventilation* (New York, 1868), pp. 86, 89.

19. Courtesy of the Cincinnati Historical Society.

20. Mary J. Eastman, *Aunt Phillis's Cabin: Or, Southern Life As It Is* (Philadelphia, 1852), frontispiece.

21. Robert Criswell, *Uncle Tom's Cabin Contrasted with Buckingham Hall* (New York, 1852), frontispiece.

22. Benson J. Lossing, *The Home of Washington* (New York, 1871), frontispiece.

23. *History of the Brooklyn and Long Island Fair* (Brooklyn, 1864), p. 76.

24. Charles Mulford Robinson, *City Planning* (New York: G. P. Putnam's Sons, 1916), p. 20.

25, 26, 27. Parris T. Farwell, *Village Improvement* (New York: Sturgis & Walton Co., 1913), pp. 240, 177, 30.

28. *House Beautiful* 27 (1910): 128–129.

29–32. George E. Waring, "Farm Villages," *Scribner's Monthly* 13 (1877): pp. 758, 759, 761, 762.

33. *Rural Manhood* 4 (1913): 246.

34. *Portrait and Biographical Album of Sedgwick County, Kansas* (Chicago, 1888), p. 1012.

35. *Hearth and Home* 2 (1869): 172.

36. Henry B. Schoolcraft, *Information Respecting the History, Condition and Prospects of the Indian Tribes of the United States* (Philadelphia, 1854), IV, 193.

37. Courtesy of the Chicago Historical Society.

38. Everett Chamberlin, *Chicago and Its Suburbs* (Chicago, 1874), p. 254.

39. Sophonisba P. Breckinridge and Edith Abbott, "Housing Conditions in Chicago, III: Back of the Yards," *American Journal of Sociology* 16 (1911): 434.

40. Everett Chamberlin, *Chicago and Its Suburbs*, p. 446.

41. Courtesy of the Chicago Historical Society.

42. Courtesy of the Oak Park Public Library.

43. Courtesy of Olmsted Associates, Brookline, Massachusetts.

44. Rossiter Johnson, ed., *A History of the World's Columbian Exposition* (New York, 1897–1898), I, 486.

45. Daniel H. Burnham and Edward H. Bennett, *Plan of Chicago* (Chicago, 1909), p. 101; courtesy of the Commercial Club of Chicago.

46. Charles M. Robinson, *City Planning*, p. 4.

47. The Russell Sage Foundation Homes Company, *Forest Hills Gardens* (New York, 1911; published by the company), p. 6.

48. Courtesy of the University of California, Santa Barbara Art Museum.

49–52. Alfred B. Yeomans, *City Residential Land Development* (Chicago: University of Chicago Press, 1916), pp. 17, 38, 37, 98.

53. Frank Lloyd Wright, *Ausgeführte Bauten und Entwurfe* (Berlin, 1910), pl. 13.

54. *House Beautiful* 13 (1903): 110.

55. Richard Nelson, *Suburban Homes for Business Men* (Cincinnati, 1874), p. 53.

56–59. Frank J. Scott, *The Art of Beautifying the Home Grounds* (New York, 1870), frontispiece, pp. 74, 55, 217.

60. Robert W. Shoppell, *How to Build, Furnish and Decorate* (New York, 1883), p. 32.

61. Richard Nelson, *Suburban Homes for Business Men*, p. 151.

62. Laura C. Holloway, *The Hearthstone: Or, Life at Home* (Chicago, 1888), p. 97.

63. Andrew Jackson Downing, *A Treatise on the Theory and Practice of Landscape Gardening* (New York, 1865), p. 568.

64. William Solotaroff, *Shade-Trees in Towns and Cities* (New York: John J. Wiley & Sons, 1911), p. 14.

65. A. Prescott Folwell, *Practical Street Construction* (New York: John J. Wiley & Sons, 1916), p. 138.

66. Wilhelm Miller, *The Prairie Spirit in Landscape Gardening* (Urbana, Ill.: University of Illinois College of Agriculture, 1915), p. 29.

67. "Gardens in the Air," *Craftsman* 24 (1913): 387.

68. Charles Weller, *Neglected Neighbors* (Philadelphia, 1909), p. 12.

69, 70. Ernest Flagg, "The New York Tenement House Evil and Its Cure," *Scribner's Magazine* 16 (1894): 108, 112.

71, 72. Henry C. Shiveley, *Hygienic and Economic Features of the East River Homes*, a pamphlet reprinted from *New York Architect* 5 (1911), n.p.

73. E. T. Potter, "Urban Housing," *American Architect and Building News* 6 (1879): 98.

74. Duhring, Okie and Ziegler, Architects, "A Practical Housing Development," *Architectural Record* 34 (1913): 53.

75, 76, 77. J. P. Putnam, "The Apartment-House," *American Architect and Building News* 27 (1890): 3, 4, 5.

78. O. B. Bunce, "The City of the Future," *Appleton's Journal* 7 (1872): 156.

79. Charles H. Israels, "New York Apartment Houses," *Architectural Record* 11 (1901): 493.

80. "The Dakota Apartment House," *Sanitary Engineer* 11 (1885): 271.

81. Hubert, Pirsson and Co., *Where and How to Build* (New York, 1892), p. 79.

82. Hubert, Pirsson and Hoddick, Architects, "New York Flats and French Flats," *Architectural Record* 2 (1892): 62.

83. *American Architect and Building News* 22 (1887): 187.

84. Charles H. Clark, "The Charter Oak City," *Scribner's Monthly* 13 (1876): 16.

85. Charles Barnard, "A Hundred Thousand Homes," *Scribner's Monthly* 11 (1876): 477.

86. Robert Treat Paine, *Co-operative Banks* (Boston, 1880), frontispiece.

87. Edward Everett Hale, *Workingmen's Homes* (Boston, 1874), frontispiece.

88. H. Morton Bodfish, *History of Building and Loan Associations in the United States* (Chicago: United States Building and Loan League, 1931), p. 183.

89. Henry I. Bowditch, *Consumption in New England* (Boston, 1862), p. 42.

90, 91. E. R. L. Gould, *Eighth Special Report of the Commissioner of Labor: Housing of the Working People* (Washington, D.C., 1895), pp. 202, 203.

92. Alfred T. White, *Improved Dwellings for the Laboring Classes* (New York, 1879), frontispiece.

93. G. W. Sheldon, *Artistic Country Seats* (New York, 1886), I, 9.

94, 95. *A Monograph of the Work of McKim, Mead and White* (New York: The Architectural Book Publishing Co., 1915), pls. 16, 84.

96. *American Architect and Building News* 17 (1885): illus. 480.

97. Marc Antoine Laugier, *Essai sur L'Architecture* (Paris, 1755), frontispiece.

98. Eugène E. Viollet-le-Duc, *Discourses on Architecture*, trans. Henry Van Brunt (Boston, 1875), I, 24.

99. David W. King, *Homes for Home-Builders* (New York, 1886), p. 102.

100. Courtesy of the University of California, Santa Barbara Art Museum.

101. H. H. Rice, *The Manufacturing of Concrete Blocks and Their Use in Building Construction* (New York: Engineering News Publishing Co., 1906), p. 32.

102. *Suburban Life* 13 (April 1911): 20.

103. M. J. Morehouse, "A Concrete House, A New Process," *House Beautiful* 26 (1909): 115.

104. Oswald C. Hering, *Concrete and Stucco Houses* (New York: McBride Nast & Co., 1912), p. 54.

105, 106. Grosvenor Atterbury, *The Economic Production of Workingmen's Homes* (New York, 1930), pp. 34, 35.

107, 108. O. S. Fowler, *A Home for All* (New York, 1857), frontispiece, p. 92.

109. Gustave Stickley, "Craftsman Concrete Bungalows Showing Economy of Construction," *Craftsman* 21 (1912): 664.

110, 111. Milton Dana Morrill, *The Morrill Moulded Concrete Houses* (New York, 1917), pp. 8, 6.

112. Irving Gill, "The Home of the Future: The New Architecture of the West," *Craftsman* 30 (1916): 140.

113. E. M. Roorbach, "The Garden Apartments of California," *Architectural Record* 34 (1913): 520.

114, 115. *Craftsman* 25 (1913): 287; 26 (1914): 440.

116, 117. Frank Lloyd Wright, *Ausgeführte Bauten und Entwurfe*, pls. 67, 36.

118. Grant C. Manson, *Frank Lloyd Wright to 1910* (New York: Reinhold Publishing Co., 1958), p. 53.

119. Frank Lloyd Wright, "In the Cause of Architecture," *Architectural Record* 23 (1908): 184.

120. Frank Lloyd Wright, *Ausgeführte Bauten* (Berlin, 1911), p. 13.

121. David P. Handlin.

122, 123. Frank Lloyd Wright, *Ausgeführte Bauten und Entwurfe*, pls. 91, 112.

124. William C. Gannett (Frank Lloyd Wright, designer), *The House Beautiful* (River Forest, Ill, 1897), n.p.

125. David P. Handlin.

126. Frank Lloyd Wright, *Ausgeführte Bauten* (1911), p. 104.

127. "Successful Houses III," *House Beautiful* 1 (1897): 68.

128, 129. Charles Francis Osborn, *Notes on the Art of House Planning* (New York, 1888), pp. 15, 19.

130–134. E. C. Gardner, *Illustrated Homes* (Boston, 1875), pp. 220, 229, 175, 171, 109.

135. "Hints for Home Decoration and Furnishing," *Art Amateur* 18 (1888): 119.

136. H. Hudson Holly, *Modern Dwellings* (New York, 1878), p. 117.

137. "Fifteen Good Halls and Stairways," *Ladies' Home Journal* 16 (1899): 18. Courtesy of the Schlesinger Library, Radcliffe College.

138. E. C. Gardner, *Homes and How to Make Them* (Boston, 1874), p. 154.

139. Catharine E. Beecher and Harriet Beecher Stowe, *The American Woman's Home* (New York, 1869), p. 97.

140. *Suburban Life* 8 (1909): 328.

141. Thomas R. Thorndyke, "The Western Home of a Musician," *American Homes and Gardens* 9 (1912): 179.

142-145. Samuel B. Reed, *House-Plans for Everybody* (New York, 1878), pp. 11, 9, 222, 220.

146. L. V. LeMoyne, *Country Residences in Europe and America* (New York: Doubleday Page & Co., 1908), p. 420.

147. Council of Hygiene and Public Health of the Citizens' Association of New York, *Report upon the Sanitary Condition of the City* (New York, 1865), p. 258.

148. Mrs. Schuyler van Rensselaer, "Picturesque New York," *Century Magazine* 45 (1892): 174.

149. Margaret F. Byington, *Homestead, The Households of a Mill Town* (New York, 1910), p. 53.

150. Milton B. Hunt, "The Housing of Non-Family Groups of Men in Chicago," *American Journal of Sociology* 16 (1910): 151.

151. Margaret F. Byington, *Homestead*, p. 28.

152. "The Tiffany House," *Architectural Record* 10 (1900): 200.

153. Elisha Harris Janes, "The Development of Duplex Apartments," *Brickbuilder* 21 (1912): 183.

154. A. C. David, "A Co-operative Studio Building," *Architectural Record* 14 (1903): 233.

155. "Stuyvesant Apartment House," *Architectural Record* 11 (1901): 429.

156. "Improved Dwelling Houses," *Scientific American* 63 (1890): 66.

157. A. E. Kennelly, "Electricity in the Household," *Scribner's Magazine* 7 (1890): 102.

158. *Brickbuilder* 4 (1895): pls. 26, 27.

159, 160, 161. Catharine E. Beecher and Harriet Beecher Stowe, *The American Woman's Home*, pp. 26, 28, 34.

162. Ethel Bartholomew, "Women's Idea of Convenient Closets," *House Beautiful* 23 (March 1908): 31.

163, 164. Christine Frederick, *The New Housekeeping* (Garden City, N.Y., Doubleday & Co., 1913), pp. 138, 80.

165. A. E. Kennelly, "Electricity in the Household," p. 105.

166, 167. Thomas C. Martin and Stephen L. Coles, *The Story of Electricity* (New York: M. M. Marcy, 1919), II, 180, 200.

168, 169, 170. Christine Frederick, *Household Engineering* (Chicago: American School of Home Economics, 1920), pp. 23, 22, 74.

171. Clarence Cook, "Beds and Tables, Stools and Candlesticks, I," *Scribner's Monthly* 10 (1875): 175.

172. Clarence Cook, "Beds and Tables, Stools and Candlesticks, IV," *Scribner's Monthly* 11 (1876): 812.

173. Charles Wyllys Elliott, *The Book of American Interiors* (Boston, 1876), p. 97.

174. Charles Eastlake, *Hints on Household Taste* (London, 1869), p. 74.

175. Candace Wheeler, "Art Education for Women," *Outlook* 55 (1897): 81.

176. Will Price, "Is Rose Valley Worth While," *Artsman* 1 (1903): 4.

177. "Three Craftsman Chairs," *Craftsman* 17 (1909): 328.

178. Louise Brigham, "How I Furnished My Entire Flat from Boxes," *Ladies' Home Journal* 25 (Sept. 1, 1910): 72. Courtesy of the Schlesinger Library, Radcliffe College.

179. *Ladies' Home Journal* 22 (1903): 34. Courtesy of the Schlesinger Library, Radcliffe College.

180. A. E. Kennelly, "Electricity in the Household," p. 114.

181, 182. Mrs. H. M. Plunkett, *Women, Plumbers, and Doctors* (New York, 1885), frontispiece, p. 123. Courtesy of the Schlesinger Library, Radcliffe College.

183, 184. George E. Waring, *Earth-Closets and Earth Sewage* (New York, 1870), pp. 37, 10.

185. "The Syphonage and Ventilation of Traps," *Sanitary Engineer* 6 (1882): 265.

186. George E. Waring, *Sewerage and Land Drainage* (New York, 1889), p. 276.

187, 188. *Sanitary Engineer* 6 (1882): 380, 429.

189. H. Howson, "Mechanical Engineering Applied to Farm Implements," *Journal of the Franklin Institute* 62 (1856): 46.

190. Arthur Inkersley, "Sunshine as Power," *Sunset Magazine* 10 (1903): 513.

191. David Branson, "Artificial Refrigeration through Street Pipe Lines from Central Stations," *Journal of the Franklin Institute* 137 (1894): 91.

192. Laura C. Holloway, *The Hearthstone*, frontispiece.

193. Clarence Cook, "Beds and Tables, Stools and Candlesticks, VII," *Scribner's Monthly* 13 (1876): 88.

194. O. B. Bunce, "The City of the Future," p. 157.

195-198. J. P. Putnam, *The Open Fire-Place in All Ages* (Boston, 1886), pp. 132, 140, 159, 161.

199. Chilion B. Allen, *The Man Wonderful in the House Beautiful* (New York, 1883), frontispiece.

# INDEX

Abbot, Edith, study of furnished rooms, with Breckinridge, 366–371
Adams, Herbert Baxter, 92
Adams, John, 62–63, 76
Addams, Jane, 245–246, 404
Adobe, 297
Aguilar, Grace, *Home Influence*, 25
*Aids to Reflection* (Coleridge), 6, 29
Alcott, Louisa May, *Little Women*, 86
Alcott, William Andrus, 48–55; on city and country, 54; *Essay on the Construction of School Houses*, 50; on family, 51–52, 53–54; on the garden, 53–54; on housekeeping, 53–54; *The House I Live In*, 52; on house siting, 54; on nursery, 52–53; on school architecture, 50–51; on school and the home, 51; theory of physiology of, 49–50
Alleys, 211–212
Allotment garden, 198
*Amateur Garden, The* (Cable), 190
American Federation of Women's Clubs, 410, 425
American Garden City Association, 152
American Home Economics Association, 410, 411
*American Kitchen Magazine*, 409
*American Notes* (Dickens), 198–199
*American Woman's Home, The* (Beecher and Stowe), 405–408
Ansonia, the, 402
*Antifanaticism: A Tale of the South* (Butt), 78
Antiques, 435–436
Apartment hotels, 402–403

Apartment houses, 214–231; appearance of, 268–269; Bruère and Bruère on, 403–404; cooperative, 267–269; cooperative housekeeping and, 398–401; courtyards of, 221, 223–224, 227; duplex, 377–379; entrances to, 221, 223, 224, 227; financing of, 266–269; first in New York, 520; "flat," 384–385; Hubert on, 223–226, 230–231, 267–268; landscaping, 219–221; Leeds on, 222; in New York, 220–231; lobby in, 220–221; Potter on, 227, 229–230; Parisian, 221–224; Putnam on, 216–219, 400–401; studio, 379–383. *See also* Tenements
Apthorp, the, 220, 227
Arbor Day, 103
Arcade, the, in Pullman, 131
Archery, 181
Architecture: American colonial, 28, 273, 275, 361–362; classical, 27, 28; concrete in history of, 275–277; Gothic, 27, 28, 270, 315–316; Greek, 316–318, 324, 327; as imitation of nature, 26; Japanese, 273, 326; and nationalism, 27–28, 270; Renaissance, 315–316, 324; rural, 45–47; theory of, after Civil War, 269–270; theory of transformation of, 274; wood in European, 273, 275. *See also* Beauty; Downing; Gill; Greenough; Jenney; Loudon; Ricker; Root; Shakers; Style; Sullivan; Wright, F. L.
*Architecture of Country Houses, The*, (Downing), 30, 37–38, 40, 41, 42, 45, 274, 429
*Architecture under Nationalism* (Putnam), 218

Arnott, David, 483
*Art of Beautifying the Home Grounds,
The* (Scott), 171, 172–173, 176, 179, 182
Arts and crafts, 442–448, 450, 525;
Wheeler on, 436–441: Wright on, 326–
327, 441, 524
*Artsman, The,* 442, 448
Ashbee, C. R., 444
Asheville, North Carolina, 360
Associated Artists, 439–441
Atterbury, Grosvenor, 152, 157, 213; on
use of concrete, 285–288
Atwater, W. O., 364
*Aunt Phillis's Cabin: Or, Southern Life
As It Is* (Eastman), 78
*Autobiography* (Wright), 321
Automobile, the, 138, 149, 188–189, 212,
285

Bache, Anna, *Scenes at Home: Or the
Adventures of a Fire Screen,* 17
Bacon, Albion Fellows, 386–388, 441;
*Beauty for Ashes,* 386
Bailey, Liberty Hyde, 141, 194
Balch, Emily, 374–375
Balloon frame system, 44
Baseball, 86, 181
Baumann, Frederick, 317
Beauty: in architecture, 27, 28, 269;
builders on, 30; Burnham on, 139;
Downing on, 36, 37–38, 42, 44–46, 235–
236, 269; and economy, 15, 30; Green-
ough on, 29; and "home feeling," 15–
16; Loudon on, 32–34; moral value of,
93–94; in Shaker architecture, 29; Stowe
on, 427; in towns and villages, 93–99.
*See also* Style
*Beauty for Ashes* (Bacon), 386
Beecher, Catharine: *The American
Woman's Home* (with Stowe), 405–
408; on domestic economy, 55–56, 58;
*Domestic Receipt Book,* 55; *Educa-
tional Reminiscences,* 425; on home
decoration, 425–426; *Treatise on Do-
mestic Economy,* 55–56
Beecher, Lyman, 86
Bellamy, Edward, 216, 392, 395–397, 400;
*Looking Backward,* 216, 395–396, 397.
*See also* Nationalism
Berkeley, California, 8
Biltmore, G. W. Vanderbilt's house, 193,
360, 361
Boardinghouses, 69–70, 371
Bok, Edward, 423–425
Boston, 83, 90; Dorchester section, 258–

259, 260; North End, 260; population
and public health, 59, 60; South End,
260–262, 371–372. *See also* Boston Co-
operative Building Company
Boston Cooking School, 394; *Magazine,*
409
Boston Cooperative Building Company,
253, 255–264
Bouton, Edward H., 186
Bowditch, Henry Ingersoll, 253–255, 256–
258; *Consumption in New England,* 254
*Boy's Town, A* (Howells), 91–92
Breckinridge, Sophonisba P., study of
furnished rooms, with Abbott, 366–371
Bremer, Fredrika, 3, 235–236; *Homes of
the New World,* 3
Brentmoor Park, St. Louis, 185
Brigham, Louise, 445
Brisbane, Albert, 74
Brook Farm, 74–76
Brookline, Massachusetts, 398
Brooklyn, New York, 71, 264
Brown, G. P., *Sewer Gas and Its
Dangers,* 457
Browne's Bookstore, Wright's, 328
Bruère, Martha and Robert, 403–404
Builders, 30, 43
Building and loan associations, 237–243,
246, 252. *See also* Ownership, home
Bunce, O. B., 220
Burke, Michael, 192
Burnham, Daniel, 132, 135–139, 315; on
"The Commercial Value of Beauty,"
139–140; *Plan of Chicago* (with E. H.
Bennett), 136–139
Bushnell, Horace, 60; "The Age of
Homespun," 6–8; background and
education of, 6; on "barbarism" and
"civilization," 7–8; on childhood, 8–11;
on city plans, 99; "Christian Nurture,"
8–11; "The Day of Roads," 7; "Ostrich
Nurture," 9; on village improvement,
94, 99, 102
Butt, Martha Haines, *Antifanaticism: A
Tale of the South,* 78
Byington, Margaret, 375

Cable, George Washington, 189–192; on
landscaping, 190–192; *The Amateur
Garden,* 190; *The Silent South,* 189
Calhoun, Georgia, 102
*Call of the City, The* (C. M. Robinson),
144, 145
Cambridge, Massachusetts, 91, 102, 391

Cambridge Cooperative Housekeeping
Society, 391–392
*Cannibals All!* (Fitzhugh), 81
Carpets, 52, 426–427, 433–434
Cemeteries, 102
Central heating systems, 57, 479, 481
Central Park, 130, 173
Chapin, Charles V., 410–411
Chapin, Robert Coit, 372–374; *The
Standard of Living among Working-
men's Families in New York City*, 372
*Chapters in the History of the Arts and
Crafts Movement* (Triggs), 448
Charity Organization Society, 205
Charlotte, North Carolina, 100
Chase, Lucien B., *English Serfdom and
American Slavery*, 80
Chastellux, Marquis de, 97
Cheney, Mamah, 306
Chicago, 119–140, 356; architects of, 317;
building code of, 368–369; City Club
of, 158, 160; City Club competition of
1913, 160–166, 167; districts and suburbs of, 122, 124–128, 131–132; early
history of, 120; fire, 130–131; furnished
rooms in, 368–371; Garland on, 139;
Haymarket riot, 133; Hull-House, 134,
135, 327, 441; improvement efforts in,
119, 129, 132, 135, 139; lodging houses
in, 372; old houses in, 367–371; parks in,
129–130, 135–137; population of, 120,
122, 131; prairie landscape of, 163;
railroads in, 121–122; skyscrapers in,
131, 139; Stead on, 134–135; transportation in, 125, 132. *See also* Burnham, D.;
World's Columbian Exposition
Chicago Avenue houses, Wright's, 310–
312
Chimney, the, 481, 482
*Chimney Corner, The* (Stowe), 86, 412–
413
Christianity, state of American, 4–6
City, the: compared with country, 54;
compared with town, 140–141; critics
of, 116; defenders of, 116–118; growth
of, 89–90, 116–117, 119; Howells on,
133–134; improvement efforts in, 118–
119, 141–143; picturesque, 116. *See also*
Boston; Chicago; City planning;
Garden cities; New York
City Club of Chicago, 158, 160; Competition of 1913, 160–166, 167
City planning, 43–157; growth of, 143,
152, 157–158, 160; Hooker on, 160; and

housing, 146–148; National Conferences
on, 143, 145; and neighborhood unit,
155–157; and transportation, 148–149;
Unwin on, 144–145; and zoning, 153–
154. *See also* City; Garden cities;
Robinson, C. M.
*City Planning* (Robinson), 145–146
Civil War, 84–88; soldiers' aid organiza-
tions in, 85–86; memorials, 101
Cleveland, Ohio, 147
Coleridge, Samuel Taylor, *Aids to
Reflection*, 6, 29
Colman, Samuel, 439–440
Commercial Club of Chicago, 137
Committee on Congestion of Population,
143
Communistic societies, 73–76
Communities, planned: communistic
societies as, 73–76; E. E. Hale on, 246–
247; Rose Valley Association as, 442–
443; suburbs as, 183–186; towns as, 247–
250, 500
*Complete Home, The* (J. M. Wright),
413
Concrete: Atterbury on, 285, 287–288; as
a block, 279–280, 284–285; *The Crafts-
man* on, 290–291; Edison on, 293–294;
Fowler on, 288–290; Gill on, 296;
history of, 275–277; Hering on, 294–
295; Morrill on, 291, 293; in F. L.
Wright's work, 299–302
Congregationalism, 8–9, 10–11
*Consumption in New England* (Bowditch), 254
Cook, Clarence, *The House Beautiful*,
430–435
Coonley, Avery, House, Wright's, 301
Cooper, James Fenimore, 63–65; *The
Crater*, 65; *Home as Found*, 63–65
Cooperation, 243–244
Cooperative housekeeping: and apartment hotels, 402–403; and apartment
houses, 398–401; in Brookline, Mass.,
398; Bruère and Bruère on, 403–404;
"central depot" for, 396–398; cleaning
and, 393; food preparation and, 393–
396, 402; Gilman on, 401–402; Peirce
on, 388–392; in Philadelphia, 397; sewing and, 392–393; societies for, 391–392,
393; for women, 404–405
Cooperative housing: Boston Cooperative
Building Company and, 253, 255–263;
Bowditch on, 253–255, 257; Hubert
Home Club and, 267–268

Cooperative stores, 243–244
Corson, Juliet, 409
*Cottage Residences* (Downing), 30, 34, 37, 45–46; critics of, 43
*Craftsman, The,* 290–291
*Crater, The* (Cooper), 65
Crèvecoeur, J. Hector St. John de, 61–62
Criswell, Robert, *Uncle Tom's Cabin Contrasted with Buckingham Hall,* 80
Croatians, 374
Croly, Herbert, 360–362; *The Promise of American Life,* 360–361
Croquet, 181
"Crystal Palace" (Lincoln Building), Boston, 254–257, 259
Curtis, George William, 203
Cunningham, Ann Pamela, 82–83
Cunningham, Louisa, 82

Dakota, the, 223, 224
Daniell, Maria, 410
Davenport, Iowa, 194–195
Davis, Alexander Jackson, 183
Dayton, Ohio, 193–194
Dearborn, Michigan, 363
Decorative arts, 436–441; and machines, 441–451
Dedham, Massachusetts, 249–250
de Forest, Lockwood, 439, 440
Denver, Colorado, 474
Department of Landscape Architecture, Harvard, 144
Desks, 50–51
Detroit, 83, 198
Dexter, Seymour, 241, 251
Dickens, Charles, *American Notes,* 198–199
Doctors, early nineteenth-century, 48
Dodge House, Gill's, 298
Domestic economy, 55–56. *See also* Home industries
*Domestic Receipt Book* (Beecher), 55
Douglass, Harlan Paul, 113–114
Downing, Andrew Jackson, 34–46, 171, 235–236, 269, 481; *The Architecture of Country Houses,* 30, 37–38, 40, 41, 42, 45, 274, 429; on beauty, 36, 37–38, 42, 44–46, 235–236; *Cottage Residences,* 30, 34, 37, 43, 45–46; *The Fruits and Fruit Trees of America,* 30; on health, 46, 48; on house planning, 332; life of, 30–31, 41–42, 46; on nature, 38, 40; Solon Robinson on, 43–44; on style, 36, 38–39; *A Treatise on . . . Landscape Garden-*

*ing,* 30, 34, 37; on "truth," 40, 44; on utility, 34, 36, 37; on village improvement, 94, 109
Drummond, William, 162–164
Dry earth closet, 460–462, 463
Duplex apartments, 377–379
Dust, 52, 189, 405, 411–412, 415

Earth construction, 277, 279, 291
*Earth Closets and Earth Sewage* (Waring), 464
East River Homes, 206
Eastlake, Charles, 434–435; *Hints on Household Taste,* 434
Eastman, Mary, *Aunt Phillis's Cabin: Or, Southern Life As It Is,* 78
Ecole des Beaux Arts, 203, 308, 317
Economy: and beauty, 15, 30; as a value, 424–425, 426, 427–429
Edison, Thomas, 293–294
Education, 8, 103; Alcott on, 51–53; Bushnell on, 8–11. *See also* Kindergarten; School
*Educational Reminiscences* (Beecher), 425
Edwards, Jonathan, 8
Egleston, Nathaniel H., 115, 116; *Village Improvement (The Home and Its Surroundings),* 116
Electricity, 419–422, 454, 475; for lighting, 474
*Elements of Political Economy, The* (Wayland), 73
Ely, Richard, 244–245
Emerson, Harrington, 417
Emerson, Ralph Waldo, 75, 417
*Encyclopaedia of Cottage, Farm and Villa Architecture* (Loudon), 31, 32–33, 34
Engels, Friedrich, 250–252; *The Housing Question,* 250
England, 28, 80, 81
*English Serfdom and American Slavery* (Chase), 80
*Essay on the Construction of School Houses* (W. A. Alcott), 50
Etiquette, 350–352
Everett, Edward, 83, 260

Factory, the: housing for, 70, 244–246; in villages, 108
Family, the: W. A. Alcott on, 51–52, 53–54; and interior space, 15–16, 351–354; expectations of, 21, 23; lodgers and,

371, 372–375; F. L. Wright on, 307–308;
unity of, 10
Faribault, Minnesota, 102
Fences, 101, 176–177
Fenn, Harry, 219, 482
Fireplace, the, 17, 19, 42, 53, 478–481;
Putnam on, 481, 483–486; Stowe on,
426, 478–479; Wyman on, 58
Fireproof House, F. L. Wright's, 299–300
Fiske, John, 92
Fitzhugh, George, *Cannibals All!* and
*Sociology for the South*, 81
Flagg, Ernest, 203–205, 206; on tenements,
207–210
Flower missions, 198
Food preparation systems, 393–396
Ford, George, 157, 214
Forest Hills Gardens, Long Island, 157,
161, 285–287
Fort Dearborn, 120
Fourier, Charles, 74, 75, 76, 81
Fourneau Economique, 393
Fowler, Orson Squire, 288–290, 336, 356;
*A Home for All*, 288, 356
Frankford, Pennsylvania, 237
Franklin, Benjamin, 12, 49, 243, 478, 483
*Franklin Evans: Or, The Inebriate*
(Whitman), 68
Franklin stove, 56, 478
Frederick, Christine, 419, 420, 422–423
Froebel, Friedrich, 308, 310, 515
*Fruits and Fruit Trees of America, The*
(Downing), 30
Furnished rooms, 366–371
Furniture design, 430–435

Games: indoor, 354; lawn, 181–182
Gannett, William Channing, *The House
Beautiful* (Wright, illus.), 308
Garage, the, 212, 280, 281
Garden, the, 171, 183, 213, 214; allotment,
198; and health, 53–54; roof, 198, 220.
See also Home grounds; Landscaping
Garden cities, 144–145, 152, 160, 285
Gardner, Eugene C., 334–349; *Homes and
How to Make Them*, 335; house
planning, 335–349; *The House That
Jill Built, after Jack's Had Proved a
Failure*, 336; *Illustrated Homes*, 336,
338, 341; on interiors, 336–338, 343–345,
348–349; on utility, 335
Garland, Hamlin, 139
Gary, Indiana, 152
Gas lighting, 473–474, 483

*Gentleman's House, The* (Kerr), 332–
333
George, Henry, 152–153, 268; *Our Land
and Land Policy*, 152
Gilbreth, Frank, 423
Gill, Irving, 295–299
Gilman, Charlotte Perkins, 401–402
Godwin, Edwin, 430
*Good Housekeeping*, 336, 364
Goodyear Tire and Rubber Company,
152
Government, housing financed by, 264–
265
Grant, Robert, *Unleavened Bread*, 361
Grayson, William, *The Hireling and the
Slave*, 81
Greene and Greene, 273
Greenough, Horatio, 29, 316
Grid system: land subdivision, 97–98;
New York's, 200–201; in Reclamation
Services' plan, 107; C. M. Robinson's
criticism of, 146; streets, 98–99, 146,
166, 209–210; Waring's transformation
of, 105–106; F. L. Wright's, 165–166
Griffin, Walter Burley, 195
Grimes, Bertha, 395
Guérin, Jules, 139
Guild of Handcraft, 444

*Habitation of Man in All Ages, The*
(Viollet-le-Duc), 317, 516
Haddam, Connecticut, 102
Hale, Edward Everett, 246–247; "How
They Lived at Naguadavick," 249;
"How They Live in Boston, and How
They Die There," 246–247; *Old and
New*, 247
Hale, Sarah J., *Happy Homes or Good
Society All the Year Round*, 413
Hall, the, 346, 347, 348
Hamilton, Ohio, 90, 91
*Happy Homes or Good Society All the
Year Round* (S. J. Hale), 413
Hardenbergh, Henry J., 223
Hartford, Connecticut, 8, 102, 152, 232–
235, 405
Haskell, Llewellyn S., 183–184, 185
Hawthorne, Nathaniel, 65–66; *The
House of the Seven Gables*, 65, 66
Health: W. A. Alcott on, 48–55; C. V.
Chapin on, 410–411; Downing on, 46,
48; garden and, 53–54; ministers on, 48;
playground and, 197–198; and sewer
gas, 455, 457–458; Shattuck on, 59–60;

Health (*Continued*)
in small town, 92; and street width,
150; and tenements, 199, 207, 210. *See
also* Public health; Tuberculosis;
Ventilation; Waring
Hearth. *See* Fireplace
Heating systems: cast-iron stoves, 477–
479; central, 57, 479, 481; Putnam on,
481–483, 486; ventilation and, 56–58
Hering, Oswald, 294–295
Herrick, Christine Terhune, 413
Hill, Octavia, 254, 255, 256
*Hints on Household Taste* (Eastlake),
434
*Hireling and the Slave, The* (Grayson),
81
Holly, Birdsill, 479
*Home* (Sedgwick), 12–13, 15, 24
*Home and Its Surroundings, The* (Egleston), 116
*Home as Found* (Cooper), 63–65
Home economics, 401–415
*Home Economics* (Parloa), 414
"Home feeling," 15–16, 26
*Home for All, A* (Fowler), 288, 356
Home grounds, suburban: Cable on, 190–
192; Miller on, 195–197; Parrington on,
167, 170; Patterson on, 193; F. J. Scott
on, 170–183; F. L. Wright on, 167, 323.
*See also* Landscaping; Parks; Trees;
Yard improvement contests
Home industries, 6–7, 55–56, 425–427; vs.
ready-made goods, 427–429
*Home Influence* (Aguilar), 25
*Home Life* (J. F. W. Ware), 86
Home religion, 4, 5–6, 10–11, 18, 61; in
popular literature, 11–14
"Home, Sweet Home" (Payne), 14–15
*Home to the Camp* and *Home to the
Hospital* (J. F. W. Ware), 85
*Homes and How to Make Them* (Gardner), 335
*Homes of American Authors*, 21, 23
*Homes of American Statesmen*, 21
*Homes of the New World* (Bremer), 3
Homespun, 6–7
Homestead, Pennsylvania, 375–377
Homestead Act, 68
Hooker, George E., 158, 160, 214, 265
*House and Home Papers* (Stowe), 86,
412–413, 426–427, 428
*House Architecture* (Stevenson), 332–
333
*House Beautiful, The* (Cook), 430–435

*House Beautiful, The* (Gannett, illus.
F. L. Wright), 308
"House Beautiful, The," Twain on,
232–233
"House Divided, The," 84
*House I Live In, The* (W. A. Alcott), 52
*House of the Seven Gables, The* (Hawthorne), 65, 66
*House-Plans for Everybody* (Reed), 356,
357, 360, 363
*House That Jill Built, after Jack's Had
Proved a Failure, The* (Gardner), 336
Housekeeping: W. A. Alcott on, 53–54;
electricity for, 419–422; Frederick on,
419, 420, 422, 423; literature on, 412–
413; machines for, 415–423; Parloa on,
414; Pattison on, 416–419; Richards on,
411, 415; scientific vs. traditional, 411–
413; Stowe and Beecher on, 405–408;
Terhune on, 413. *See also* Cooperative
housekeeping
*Houses and Home Life of the American
Aborigine* (Morgan), 333
*Housing Question, The* (Engels), 250
Howard, Ebenezer, 144, 152; *Tomorrow*,
144
Howells, William Dean, 90–92, 133–134,
222; *A Boy's Town*, 91–92; *Letters
from an Altrurian Traveler* and *A
Traveler from Altruria*, 133
Howland Mill, 244
Hoyle, Raphael, 41
Hubert, Philip, 223–224, 226, 230–231,
267–268, 377, 512
Hubert Home Club, 267, 268, 399, 400
Hull-House, 134, 135, 327, 441
Hunt, Jarvis, 104–105
Hunt, Richard M., 361, 471, 472
Hurley, Neil C., 421

*If Christ Came to Chicago* (Stead), 134,
135
*Illustrated Homes* (Gardner), 336, 338,
341
Immigrants, 59, 60, 371, 372, 374, 375
Improved Dwelling Council, 204
Improvement: criticism of, 141; emphasis
on beauty, 145; national coordination
of, 142. *See also* Chicago; City; City
planning; Robinson, C. M.; Town;
Village improvement; Yard improvement contests
*Improvement of Towns and Cities, The*
(Robinson), 144, 145

Indians, American, 71, 73
Insurance companies, housing financed by, 264–265
Interior decoration, 429–435; of apartments, 382–385; profession of, 439; of studio apartments, 381–382; Wheeler on, 440–441
Interior space, 330–332, 355–356; in Chicago houses, 356; climate and, 355; in colonial architecture, 352–353; etiquette and, 350–351, 352; family and, 15–16, 351–354; Gardner on, 336–338, 343–345, 348–349; at Homestead, Pa., 375–377; and income, 372–375; James on, 330–332, 355; in old houses, 366–371; Osborne on, 333–334; in shanty housing, 336; in tenements, 364–366; Wheeler on, 440–441; F. L. Wright on, 330. See also Apartment houses
Irish, 13, 59, 71

James, Henry, 330–332, 355
Jamestown, North Dakota, 100
Jane Club, the, 404
Jefferson, Thomas; on architecture, 28; on ordinance grid, 97; on property, 62–63; on slavery, 76
Jenney, William Le Baron, 303, 317

Kampffmeyer, Bernard, 151
Kansas City, Missouri, 194
Kensington School, 436–437
Kerr, Robert, 332; The Gentleman's House, 332–333
Kindergarten, 198, 310
King Lear, 245–246
Kitchen, the, 53, 408–409, 422, 423

Ladies' Home Journal, 299, 306, 423–425
Lake Forest, Illinois, 125, 127
Land, free, 68
Landis, Charles K., 247–249
Landscaping: of apartment houses, 219–221; of roof gardens, 220; of schools, 197–198; of streets, 186–189. See also Home grounds; Nature; Parks
Larkin Building, Wright's, 318
Laugier, Marc Antoine, Abbé, 275, 316
Laurel Hill Association, 94
Lawn, the, 179–180
Lawn games, 181–182
Lawn mowing, 42, 180, 181
Leaves of Grass (Whitman), 69
Leeds, Lewis, 222

Letters from an Altrurian Traveler (Howells), 133
Liderer, Baron de, 41
Life at the Fireside (Thayer), 21
Life at the South: Or, Uncle Tom's Cabin As It Is (W. L. G. Smith), 80–81
Life on the Mississippi (Twain), 232
Lighting systems, 473–474, 483
Limited dividend housing companies, 253, 263–264. See also Boston Cooperative Building Company
Lincoln, Abraham, 84
Lincoln Building. See "Crystal Palace"
Lindsay, Vachel, 110
Litchfield, Connecticut, 426, 427
Little Women (L. M. Alcott), 86
Llewellyn Park, New Jersey, 51, 183, 184–185
Lloyd-Jones, Jenkin, 306
Lodger, the, 372–375
Lodging houses, 372
Log cabin, 13, 61, 77; and hard cider, 67
Looking Backward (Bellamy), 216, 395–396, 397
Lord and Hewlett, 284–285
Loudon, John Claudius, 31, 32–34; on beauty, 32–34; Encyclopaedia of Cottage, Farm and Villa Architecture, 31, 32–33, 34; on style, 32–33; on utility, 32
Lowell, Massachusetts, 70, 265
Lyman, Joseph B. The Philosophy of Housekeeping (with Laura Lyman), 408
Lyman, Laura, 408, 413; The Philosophy of Housekeeping (with Joseph Lyman), 408

McCutchanville, Indiana, 386
Machines, 326–327, 452–455; and decorative arts, 441–451; for housekeeping, 415–423
McKim, Charles Follen, 480
McKim, Mead and White, 271, 273, 377–379
Madison, Wisconsin, 305
Manhattan Anti-Sewer Gas Company, 458
Manning, Warren, 152
Martin, D. D., House, Wright's, 309
Masonry, 273–275, 299
Massachusetts State Board of Health, 254, 464
Maybeck, Bernard, 273

Metal frames, 282–283
Metropolitan Life Insurance Company, 264, 265
Midway Plaisance, Chicago, 130
Mill, John Stuart, 389
Miller, Wilhelm, 195–197; *The Prairie Spirit in Landscape Gardening*, 195, 196
Mitchell, Donald G., 101, 335
Milwaukee Public Library competition, 315
*Model Tenement House Law, A* (Veiller), 211, 365
*Modern Civic Art* (Robinson), 144, 145, 148
*Modern Painters* (Ruskin), 41
Morgan, Lewis Henry, 333; *Houses and Home Life of the American Aborigine*, 333
Morrill, Milton Dana, 291–293
Morris, William, 282, 326, 430, 441–442, 450
Morton, J. Sterling, 103, 115
Mother, the: W. A. Alcott on, 53; and home, 17, 19; as homemaker, 21. *See also* Women
Moule, Henry, 460
Mount Auburn Cemetery, 102
Mount Vernon, 82–84
Mount Vernon Ladies' Association, 82–84
Mowatt, Anna Cora, 82
Municipal Art Society, New York, 143
"Municipal housekeeping," 60, 141
Murray, Charles Augustus, 41

Nanticoke, Pennsylvania, 292, 293
National Board of Health, 467
National Cash Register Company, 193–194
National Conference on City Planning, 143, 145, 210
National Education Association, 103
National Home Economics Association, 410
Nationalism, Bellamy's, 216, 218, 395–397, 400–401
Nature: architecture as imitation of, 26; and beauty, 15–16; in Chicago, 129–130; Downing on, 38, 40; Gill on, 295–296; in the home, 16, 17, 348–351; Miller on, 195–197; Ruskin on, 41; study, 198; Sullivan on, 305, 313; Wright on, 313–314, 323. *See also* Flower missions; Home grounds; Landscaping; Parks; Trees; Yard improvement contests

Navarro, the, 224, 225, 226, 377
Neighborhood center, 155, 159, 161, 162–163
Neighborhood unit, 155–157, 160, 165; Forest Hills Gardens as, 157–158
New Bedford, Massachusetts, 244
New Century Guild of Working Women, 393
New England, 8, 12, 77–78, 95, 355
New England Kitchen, 394
New England town, 92, 96–97
*New-England Tale, A* (Sedgwick), 12
New Haven, Connecticut, 394
New York (city), 12–13, 90, 117, 119: apartment hotels in, 402; apartment houses in, 220–231, 266–269; Central Park, 130, 173; Dickens on, 198–199; improvement in, 117, 142–143; pneumatic tubes in, 473; streets of, 200–201; tenements in, 70, 200–212, 263–264
Newark, New Jersey, 214
Newburgh, New York, 109
Newport, Rhode Island, 106–107, 127, 480
Nolen, John, 145
*North and South: Or, Slavery and Its Contrasts, The* (Rush), 80
Northampton, Massachusetts, 189–192
Northrop, Birdsey Grant, 94–95, 103, 115
Norton Grinding Company, 152
Nostalgia, 88–89
*Notes on the Art of House Planning* (Osborne), 333–335
Nursery, the, 52–53
Nurses, 85

Oak Park, Illinois, 125–126, 306; Wright's Chicago Avenue houses in, 310–312
Ohio, 13, 90–91
Oil lighting, 473–474
*Old and New* (E. E. Hale), 247
Old Home Day, 94
Olmsted, Frederick Law, 102; on New York's street grid, 200; on Riverside, 128, 462; on Roland Park, 186; on village improvement, 111–112
Olmsted, Frederick Law, Jr., 150, 157, 287
Olmsted, John C., 193
Omaha, Nebraska, 147
Oneida Perfectionists, 73
Open-air stairways, 205–206
*Open Fire-Place in All Ages, The* (Putnam), 486

Ornament in architecture, 270, 303–304;
F. L. Wright on, 323–326
Osborne, Charles Francis, *Notes on the Art of House Planning*, 333–335
Osgood, Samuel, 86–87; "The Home and the Flag," 86
*Our Land and Land Policy* (George), 152
Outdoor rooms. *See* Porch
Overcrowding, 364
Ownership, home, 236, 252; building and loan associations and, 237–243; and construction costs, 237; Engels on, 250–252; E. E. Hale on, 246–247; limited dividend and philanthropic housing companies and, 253, 255–263; insurance companies and, 264–265; Paine on, 242–243; statistics of, 237–238; tax benefits of, 238; and transportation, 236–237; Whitman on, 68–69, 70–71. *See also* Cooperative housing
Oxford Provident, 237

Paine, Robert Treat, 242–243, 246
Palmer, Potter, 124, 131
Parks, 102, 105, 129, 173, 175; in Chicago, 129–130, 135; in New York, 130, 173; in *Plan of Chicago* (Burnham and Bennett), 137–138
Parloa, Maria, 409, 414; *Home Economics*, 414
Parlor, the, 18–19, 354
Parrington, Vernon L., 167, 170
Pasadena, California, 99
Patten, Simon, 403
Patterson, John H., 193
Pattison, Mary, 416–419, 420, 422; *Principles of Domestic Engineering*, 416, 417, 419
Payne, John Howard, 14–15, 480; "Home, Sweet Home," 14–15
Peirce, Melusina Fay, 388–392, 436
Pennybacker, Mrs. Percy, 425
Perry, Clarence, 157
Philadelphia: building and loan in, 238; carpet manufacturing in, 427; cooperative housekeeping in, 397; "elastic street" of, 187–188; Potter on, 209; quadruple block of, 214–215; row houses of, 214
Philbrick, Edward, 469
*Philosophy of Housekeeping, The* (Lyman and Lyman), 408
Piazza. *See* Porch

Pingree, Hazen, 198
Pisé construction. *See* Earth construction
*Plan of Chicago* (Burnham and Bennett), 136–139
Playgrounds, 50, 197–198
*Plumber and Sanitary Engineer*, 201, 457
Plumbing, 456, 466–471. *See also* Putnam; Sewage systems; Sewer gas; Waring
Pneumatic tube, 397, 472–473
Poe, Edgar Allan, 23–24
Pond, Irving, 227
Popular literature, 11–12
Porch, the, 341, 349–350
Potter, Edward Tuckerman, 207–210, 227–230, 233, 475
*Practical Treatise on Ventilation, A* (Wyman), 56–57
*Prairie Spirit in Landscape Gardening, The* (Miller), 195, 196
Price, William L., 442–443, 445, 448
*Principles of Domestic Engineering* (Pattison), 416, 417, 419
*Principles of Scientific Management, The* (Taylor), 417
*Promise of American Life, The* (Croly), 360–361
Property, 61; Adams on, 62–63; communal, 72–76; Cooper on, 63–65; Hawthorne on, 65–66; Jefferson on, 62–63; Thoreau on, 71–72; Wayland on, 73
Public health, 58–60, 129, 253–255. *See also* Alcott, W. A.; Health; Richards; Shattuck; Waring; Wyman
Pullman, George, 131, 244, 245, 246
Pullman, Illinois, 131, 152, 244–246
Putnam, John Pickering, 216–219; *Architecture under Nationalism*, 218; on the fireplace, 481, 483–486; on Nationalism and the apartment house, 216, 218–219, 400–401; *The Open Fire-Place in All Ages*, 486; plumbing trap of, 467

Quincy, Josiah, 249–250

Railroad station, 101, 108
Railroads, growth of, 121–122
Ranger, Henry W., 379
Rapp, George, 73
Real estate speculation, 109
Reclamation Service, 107
Reed, Samuel B., 356–360; *House-Plans for Everybody*, 356, 357, 360, 363
Refrigeration, 476–477

Religion. *See* Home religion
Richards, Ellen, 410, 411, 415
Richardson, Henry H., 273
Ricker, N. Clifford, 304, 317
Ripley, George, 74–75
Riverside, Illinois, 127–128, 151, 186, 247, 462
Roads. *See* Bushnell; Robinson, C. M.; Streets
Robinson, Charles Mulford, 143–151, 185; *The Call of the City*, 144, 145; *City Planning*, 145–146; on housing, 146–148; on improvement, 144–145; *The Improvement of Towns and Cities*, 144, 145; *Modern Civic Art*, 144, 145, 148; on streets, 145–147, 150–151; on tenements, 149; *Third Ward Traits*, 154–155; on transportation, 148–149; on World's Columbian Exposition, 143–144; on zoning, 153–154
Robinson, Solon, 43–44, 46
Rochester, New York, 143, 154–155
Roland Park, Maryland, 151, 186
Roof garden, 198, 220
Rooming houses, 371–372
Root, John W., 271, 299, 303
Rorer, Sarah Y., 409
Rose Valley Association, 442–443, 448
Rumford, Count (Benjamin Thompson), 447, 483
Rumford Kitchen, 410
Rural architecture, 43–44, 45–46
Rush, Caroline, *The North and South: Or, Slavery and Its Contrasts*, 80
Ruskin, John, 41, 282, 315–316, 326, 441–442, 450; *Modern Painters*, 41

Salt, Titus, 247
Saltaire, 247
Sanitary fairs, 86, 87
St. Louis, Missouri, 33, 477
Sanitation. *See* Alcott, W. A.; Health; Plumbing; Public health; Sewer gas; Shattuck; Tenements; Waring
Savot, Louis, 423
Saxonville, Massachusetts, 95
*Scenes at Home: Or the Adventures of a Fire Screen* (Bache), 17
Schindler, Rudolf, 159, 278
School, the: W. A. Alcott on architecture of, 50–51; and Arbor Day, 103; landscaping, 197–198; location of, in towns, 111; Northrop on, 95; wider-use movement, 155–157. *See also* Education; Kindergarten
Schuyler, Montgomery, 306
Scott, Frank J., 171–183; *The Art of Beautifying the Home Grounds*, 171, 172–173, 176, 179, 182; on fences, 176–177; on the lawn, 179–180; influence of Downing on, 171; influence of Jesup Scott on, 172; on suburbs, 173–176; theory of landscaping of, 178–179
Scott, Jesup W., 172
Seattle, Washington, 167
Sedgwick, Catharine, 12–13; *Home*, 12–13, 15, 24; *A New-England Tale*, 12
Servants, 415, 418
Services, to the home, 455, 471–486. *See also* Electricity; Lighting systems; Pneumatic tube; Telegraph; Telephone
Sewage systems, 455–471. *See also* Putnam; Sewer gas; Trap, plumbing; Waring
Sewer gas, 455, 457–459, 471; Brown on, 457–458; Manhattan Anti-Sewer Gas Company on, 458; Waring on, 464, 465, 469
*Sewer Gas and Its Dangers* (Brown), 457
Settlement houses, 134–135
Sewing, 392–393
Shakers, 29, 73
Shantytowns, 366, 367
Shattuck, Lemuel, 59–60, 253
Sidewalk, the, 186–188
*Silent South, The* (Cable), 189
Silsbee, Joseph Lyman, 305, 310
Simonds, O. C., 195
Sitte, Camillo, 158; *Der Stadtebau*, 158
Slavery, 76, 77, 78, 80–81, 84
Smith, Henry Atterbury, 205–207, 210
Smith, W. L. G., *Life at the South: Or, Uncle Tom's Cabin As It Is*, 80–81
Smith College, 190
Society of Decorative Art, 437, 438, 439
*Sociology for the South* (Fitzhugh), 81
Sod, 277
Soil pipes, 465, 466
Spencer, Robert C., 306
*Stadtebau, Der* (Sitte), 158
*Standard of Living among Workingmen's Families in New York City* (R. C. Chapin), 372
Stead, William T., on apartment houses, 222; on Chicago, 134–135; *If Christ Came to Chicago*, 134, 135

Stevenson, J. J., *House Architecture*, 332–333
Stickley, Gustave, 444. *See also Crafts-man, The*
Stockbridge, Massachusetts, 94
Stone. *See* Masonry
Storage, 411–412
Stove, the, 477–479
Stowe, Harriet Beecher, 86, 412; *The American Woman's Home* (with C. Beecher), 405–408; "The Cheapness of Beauty," 427; *The Chimney Corner*, 86, 412–413; on the fireplace, 426, 478–479; on Hartford, 405; on home decoration, 405–408, 425, 426–427, 428; *House and Home Papers*, 86, 412–413, 426–427, 428; *Uncle Tom's Cabin*, 12, 77, 78
Streets: diagonal, 98; "elastic," 187–188; grid system of, 98–99, 146, 165–166, 200–201, 209–210; and housing, 149–151; landscaping of, 186–189; Nolen on, 145; planning of, 161; in Reclamation Service's plan, 107; C. M. Robinson on, 145–146, 149–151; surfaces of, 188–189; in village improvement work, 103; in Waring's farm villages, 105–107
Strother, French, 112–113
Stucco, 279, 282–283, 300–302
Studio apartments, 379–383
Sturgis, Russell, 318
Style: definitions of, 303–305; Downing on, 36, 38–39; Jenney on, 303; Loudon on, 32–33; Ricker on, 304; Root on, 303; Sullivan on, 305; F. L. Wright on, 302, 305. *See also* Architecture; Beauty
Suburban Homes Company, 204
Suburbs: in Chicago, 125, 127–128, 132; landscaping of, 173–180, 186–187; as planned communities, 183–186; and transportation, 157, 236–237
Sullivan, Louis H., 295, 299, 306, 307, 310, 321; "Essay on Inspiration," 305, 313

Taliesin, Wright's, 307–308
Taste, 429–435; Cook on, 430–431, 433–434, 435; Eastlake on, 434
Taxes on land, 152–153
Taylor, Frederick W., 417; *The Principles of Scientific Management*, 417
Taylor, Nathaniel W., 6
Telegraph, 86
Telephone, 454
Tenement House Commission, New York, 70

Tenement House Law: of 1879, 201; of 1901, 211
Tenements: and alleys, 211–212; in Boston, 59; competitions for improvement of, 201, 203–205; Dickens on, 198–199; "dumbbell" plan for, 201, 202, 204; Flagg's plan, 203–205; and health, 199; houses converted to, 366–370; in New York, 70, 200–212; Potter on, 207–210; C. M. Robinson on, 148; Smith's plans, 205–207; and social problems, 199; space standards in, 364–365, 375–376; Veiller on, 210–211, 212–213, 263, 365–366; ventilation of, 201, 203, 206, 207, 212, 365; Whitman on, 70. *See also* Apartment houses
Tennis, 181
Terhune, Albert Payson, 413
Terhune, Mary Virginia ("Marion Harland"), 413
Thayer, William Makepeace, 21, 22; *Life at the Fireside*, 21
*Theory of the Leisure Class, The* (Veblen), 448–451
*Third Ward Traits* (Robinson), 154–155
Thomas House, Wright's, 325, 326
Thoreau, Henry David, *Walden*, 71–73
Tiffany, Louis C., 377–378, 439, 440
*Tomorrow* (Howard), 144
Topographical Survey Commission of Baltimore, 149–150
Town, the: center of, 99, 101; decline of, 92–93; doctors and sanitarians on, 92; Douglass on, 113–114; historians on, 92; home, 116; ministers on, 92; and the neighborhood, 155; New England, 92, 96–97; real estate speculation in, 109; Reclamation Service plan for, 107; statistics, 89; Veblen on, 109; Waring on, 104–107; western, 97–99. *See also* City; City planning; Garden cities; Suburbs; Village improvement
Town planning. *See* City planning
*Town Planning in Practice* (Unwin), 145
Transformation, theory of, 274
Transportation, 7; automobile, 149; in Chicago, 125, 132, 146; railroad, 121–122; system, and housing, 148–149; and suburban growth, 157, 236–237
Trap, plumbing, 466–467, 469
Traubel, Horace, 448
*Traveler from Altruria, A* (Howells), 133
*Treatise on Domestic Economy* (Beecher), 55–56

*Treatise on the Theory and Practice of Landscape Gardening* (Downing), 30, 34, 37

Trees, 103; on streets, 186–188; wires and, 188. *See also* Arbor Day; Morton; Northrop

Triggs, Oscar Lovell, 446, 448; *Chapters in the History of the Arts and Crafts Movement*, 448

Tuberculosis, 205–206, 253–254

Twain, Mark, 232–235, 440, 453, 455; *Life on the Mississippi*, 232; "A Telephonic Conversation," 453, 455

Twentieth Century Food Company, 394, 395

Uncle Tom's Cabin (Stowe), 12, 77, 78
*Uncle Tom's Cabin Contrasted with Buckingham Hall* (Criswell), 80

United States, economic development of, 3–4

United States Christian Commission, 85–86

United States League, 238

United States Sanitary Commission, 85

United States Steel Corporation, 152

Unity Temple, Wright's, 318, 319, 514

*Unleavened Bread* (Grant), 361

Unwin, Raymond, 144–145, 149, 151, 213; *Town Planning in Practice*, 145

Utility in architecture: Downing on, 34, 36, 37; Gardner on, 335; Greenough on, 29; Loudon on, 32; and materials, 271; S. Robinson on, 43. *See also* Architecture; Beauty; Style

Vacation resorts, 95

Vanderbilt, Mrs. Cornelius, 474

Vanderbilt, George W., 193, 360, 361

Vanderbilt, William H., 360, 422, 471

Vanderbilt, Mrs. William K., 206

Van der Water, Christine Terhune, 413

Veblen, Thorstein, 109; *The Theory of the Leisure Class*, 448–451

Veiller, Lawrence: "Buildings in Relation to Street and Site," 210–211; on housing classification, 210–213; on limited dividend housing, 263–264; *A Model Tenement House Law*, 211, 365, 489; on tenement space requirements, 365–366, 387, 489

Ventilation: and "breathing space," 363–364; and climate, 355; and fireplaces, 481, 483–486; in schools, 50; in tene-

ments, 201, 203, 206, 207, 212, 365; Wyman on, 56–58

Village, the. *See* Town

Village Bank, Wright's, 318

Village improvement: Bushnell on, 94, 99, 102; and vacationers, 95, 139, 140; cemeteries in, 102; Civil War memorials in, 101; critics of, 108–109, 111; Douglass on, 114; Downing on, 94, 109; factories in, 108; housing in, 108; Laurel Hill Association, 94; libraries in, 99; Northrop on, 95; Olmsted on, 111–112; parks in, 102; railroad stations in, 101; societies, 94–96, 99–101, 109, 111–116, 186, 188; streets and roads in, 103; Strother on, 112–113; trees in, 103; village green in, 94; Waring on, 104–107. *See also* City; City planning; Garden cities; Town

*Village Improvement* (Egleston), 116

Vineland, New Jersey, 247–249

Viollet-le-Duc, Eugène, 276, 303, 316, 333, 434; *The Habitation of Man in All Ages*, influence on Frank Lloyd Wright, 317, 516

Virginia Constitution, 62

Volks Küche, 393

Wage problem, housing as, 265–266

Walker, Willard R., and Forrest A., 421

Waller, Edward C., Houses, Wright's, 321, 512

Walter, Thomas U., 512, 516

Ward, Edward J., 155

Ware, John F. W., 85, 86; *Home to the Camp* and *Home to the Hospital*, 85; *Home Life*, 86

Ware, Henry, 86

Waring, George E., 191, 471; dry earth closet of, 459–462, 463; *Earth Closets and Earth Sewage*, 464; on health, 459; on ideal farm village, 104–107; on municipal sewage systems, 469; on National Board of Health, 467–468; on plumbing fixtures, 469–470; on plumbing traps, 466–467, 469; on sewer gas, 464, 465, 469; on soil pipes, 465, 466; on tenements, 201, 203; on water closets, 460

Washington, George, 82–83

Water closets, 460

Waterlow, Sidney, 254

Wayland, Francis, *The Elements of Political Economy*, 73

Weber, Adna Ferrin, 116, 117
Webster, Daniel, 20, 83
Wheaton, Illinois, 104–105
Wheeler, Candace; and Associated
    Artists, 439–441; early life of, 436; on
    home decoration, 440–441; on interior
    decoration as a profession, 439; on
    machines, 441; and Society of Decora-
    tive Art, 437, 438, 439; and women,
    438–439; and Women's Exchange, 438
Whigs, 63, 67–68
Whipple, Henry B., 102
White House, 21, 22, 441
Whitman, Walt, 85; on boardinghouses,
    70; *Franklin Evans: Or, The Inebriate*,
    68; on home ownership, 68–69, 70–71;
    *Leaves of Grass*, 69
Williamsburg, Virginia, 363
Willis, Nathaniel Parker, 23
Wilmette, Illinois, 127
Wilson Tariff Act, 238
Windmill, the, 475
Wingate, Charles F., 201
Winslow House, Wright's, 301, 313–314,
    321, 515, 516
Women: W. A. Alcott on, 53–54; in arts
    and crafts, 446, 448, 450; Beecher and
    Stowe on, 405; in decorative arts, 436–
    441; Peirce on, 388–391; in works of
    Poe, 24. *See also* Bacon; Cooperative
    housekeeping; Home economics;
    Housekeeping; Mother
Women's Exchange, 437–438
Wood, 17, 271–273; vs. masonry, 273–275,
    299. *See also* Balloon frame system
Worcester, Massachusetts, 152
Workingman's Model Home, 409
World's Columbian Exposition of 1893,
    132, 135, 326, 409; home economics at,
    409–410; Howells on, 133, 134; C. M.
    Robinson on, 143–144
Wright, Frank Lloyd: on arts and crafts,
    326–327, 441, 524; *Autobiography*, 321;

Browne's Bookstore, 328; in City Club
    competition of 1913, 164–166, 167; Chi-
    cago Avenue Houses, 310–312; concrete
    in work of, 299–302; on contemporaries,
    327; Coonley House, 301; on democ-
    racy, 307–308, 327–328; English influ-
    ence on, 326; on family, 307–308;
    Fireproof House, 299–300; on Gothic,
    315–316; on Greek, 317–318, 324, 327;
    on home grounds, 167, 323; *The House
    Beautiful* (Gannett), 308; on house
    planning, 308–310; influence of Froebel
    on, 308, 310, 515; influence of Viollet-
    le-Duc on, 317, 516; interior space of,
    330; Japanese influence on, 326; Larkin
    Building, 318; life of, 305–307, 328–329;
    Martin House, 309; materials of, 323–
    324; Mayan influence on, 326; Mil-
    waukee Public Library competition,
    315; on nature, 313–314, 323; on orna-
    ment in architecture, 323–326; pre-
    Columbian influence on, 326; on
    Renaissance architecture, 315, 324;
    street grids in work of, 165–166; on
    style, 302, 305; Thomas House, 325, 326;
    Unity Temple, 318, 319, 514; Village
    Bank, 318; Waller Houses, 321, 512;
    Winslow House, 301, 313–314, 321, 515,
    516
Wright, Julia McNair, *The Complete
    Home*, 413
Wyman, Morrill, 56–58; *A Practical
    Treatise on Ventilation*, 56–57

Yard improvement contests; in Daven-
    port, Iowa, 194; in Dayton, Ohio, 192–
    194; in Kansas City, Mo., 194; in
    Northampton, Mass., 189–192. *See also*
    Cable; Home grounds; Landscaping;
    Miller, W.; Village improvement
Young, Sarah Gilman, 222–223

Zoning, 153–154